SCOTT®

2023 Specialized Catalogue of United Nations Stamps

FIRST EDITION

OFFICES IN NEW YORK • GENEVA • VIENNA
Souvenir cards • Proofs • Temporary Executive Authority of West New Guinea • Transitional Authority in East Timor • Interim Administration in Kosovo

Published May 2022

AMOS MEDIA

1660 Campbell Road, Suite A, Sidney, OH 45365
Publishers of *Linn's Stamp News, Linn's Stamp News Monthly, Coin World* and *Coin World Monthly.*

HENRY GITNER

IS YOUR

UNITED NATIONS HEADQUARTERS

Newly Revised United Nations Price List!

Many Lower Prices!

Mint sets & Mi4's • Year sets • Miniature sheets
Souvenir cards, Postal stationery • U.N. Related
Event & Personalized Sheets • UNTEA • Kosovo

1951-2021 Complete NH United Nations Available

New York, Geneva & Vienna singles, se-tenants with booklet singles, all personalized singles or strips with label including the non-Scott Vienna strips, unless Scott # is for full Sheet.

ALL PERSONALIZED & EVENT SHEETS, SINGLES & STRIPS OF 5 WITH LABELS AVAILABLE IN OUR WEB STORE

http://bit.ly/HGPI-UN-Pers

Henry Gitner Philatelists, Inc. HGPI

P.O. Box 3077-S, Middletown, NY 10940
Tel: 845-343-5151 Fax: 845-343-0068 Toll Free: 1-800-947-8267
E-mail: hgitner@hgitner.com http://www.hgitner.com

PayPal *PHILATELY - THE QUIET EXCITEMENT!*

Copyright Notice

Trademark Notice

Please Note

ISBN 0-89487-670-8

Scott Catalogue Mission Statement

The Scott Catalogue Team exists to serve the recreational, educational and commercial hobby needs of stamp collectors and dealers.

We strive to set the industry standard for philatelic information and products by developing and providing goods that help collectors identify, value, organize and present their collections.

Quality customer service is, and will continue to be, our highest priority.
We aspire toward achieving total customer satisfaction.

ADVERTISING INDEX

Introducing the 2023 Scott Specialized Catalogue of United Nations Stamps

The new 2023 Scott *Specialized Catalogue of United Nations Stamps* is the essential reference work for collectors of United Nations postage stamps and postal history. The catalog also includes listings and values for first-day covers, inscription blocks, panes and more.

Separate sections are included for the offices in New York, Geneva and Vienna; and U.N. souvenir cards, U.N. Proofs, U.N. Temporary Executive Authority of West New Guinea, U.N. Transitional Authority in East Timor and U.N. Interim Administration in Kosovo.

The United Nations section will no longer appear in the Scott *Specialized Catalogue of United States Stamps and Covers*, but simplified listings will continue to be included in the Scott *Standard Postage Stamp Catalogue*, Vol. 1.

In this first edition, new stamp listings for the three U.N. offices are included up through the Endangered Species stamps issued March 18, 2022.

A definite schedule for the next edition of the U.N. Specialized catalog is still in process. However, Scott editors are eyeing publication of the second edition in October 2023.

Best wishes in your stamp collecting pursuits!

Jay Bigalke,
Scott catalog editor-in-chief

TABLE OF CONTENTS

Understanding the listings

On the opposite page is an enlarged "typical" listing from this catalogue. Following are detailed explanations of each of the highlighted parts of the listing.

1 Scott number — Stamp collectors use Scott numbers to identify specific stamps when buying, selling, or trading stamps, and for ease in organizing their collections. Each stamp issued by a country has a unique number. Therefore, U.S. Scott 219 can only refer to a single stamp. Although the Scott Catalogue usually lists stamps in chronological order by date of issue, when a country issues a set of stamps over a period of time the stamps within that set are kept together without regard to date of issue. This follows the normal collecting approach of keeping stamps in their natural sets.

When a country is known to be issuing a set of stamps over a period of time, a group of consecutive catalogue numbers is reserved for the stamps in that set, as issued. If that group of numbers proves to be too few, capital-letter suffixes are added to numbers to create enough catalogue numbers to cover all items in the set. Scott uses a suffix letter, e.g., "A," "b," etc., only once. If there is a Scott 296B in a set, there will not be a Scott 296b also.

There are times when the block of numbers is too large for the set, leaving some numbers unused. Such gaps in the sequence also occur when the editors move an item elsewhere in the catalogue or remove it from the listings entirely. Scott does not attempt to account for every possible number, but rather it does attempt to assure that each stamp is assigned its own number.

Scott numbers designating regular postage normally are only numerals. Scott numbers for other types of stamps, e.g., air post, special delivery, and so on, will have a prefix of either a capital letter or a combination of numerals and capital letters.

2 Illustration number — used to identify each illustration. Where more than one stamp in a set uses the same illustration number, that number needs to be used with the description line (noted below) to be certain of the exact variety of the stamp within the set. Illustrations normally are 75, 100, or 150 percent of the original size of the stamp. An effort has been made to note all illustrations not at those percentages. Overprints are shown at 100 percent of the original, unless otherwise noted. Letters *in parentheses* which follow an illustration number refer to illustrations of overprints or surcharges.

3 Listing styles — there are two principal types of catalogue listings: major and minor.

Majors may be distinguished by having as their catalogue number a numeral with or without a capital-letter suffix and with or without a prefix.

Minors have a small-letter suffix (or, only have the small letter itself shown if the listing is immediately beneath its major listing). These listings show a variety of the "normal," or major item. Examples include color variation or a different watermark used for that stamp only.

Examples of major numbers are 9X1, 16, 28A, 6LB1, C13, RW1, and TS1. Examples of minor numbers are 22b, 279Bc and C3a.

4 Denomination — normally value printed on the stamp (generally known as the *face value*), which is — unless otherwise stated — the cost of the stamp at the time of issue.

5 Basic information on stamp or set — introducing each stamp issue, this section normally includes the date of issue, method of printing, perforation, watermark, and sometimes additional information. New information on method of printing, watermark or perforation measurement will appear when that information changes. Dates of issue are as precise as Scott is able to confirm, either year only, month and year, or month, day and year.

In stamp sets issued over more than one date, the year or span of years will be in bold type above the first catalogue number. Individual stamps in the set will have a date-of-issue appearing in italics. Stamps without a year listed appeared during the first year of the span. Dates are not always given for minor varieties.

6 Color or other description — this line provides information to solidify identification of the stamp. Historically, when stamps normally were printed in a single color, only the color appeared here. With modern printing techniques, which include multicolor presses which mix inks on the paper, earlier methods of color identification are no longer applicable. When space permits, a description of the stamp design will replace the terms "multi" or "multicolored." The color of the paper is noted in italic type when the paper used is not white.

7 Date of issue — As precisely as Scott is able to confirm, either year only; month and year, or month, day and year. In some cases, the earliest documented use (edu) is given. All dates, especially where no official date of issue has been given, are subject to change as new information is obtained. Many cases are known of inadvertent sale and use of stamps prior to dates of issue announced by postal officials. These are not listed here.

8 Value unused and Value used — the catalogue values are in U. S. dollars and are based on stamps that are in a grade of Very Fine unless stated otherwise. Unused values refer to items that have not seen postal or other duty for which they were intended. For pre-1890 issues, unused stamps must have at least most of their original gum; for later issues, complete gum is expected. Stamps issued without gum are noted. Unused values are for never-hinged stamps beginning at the point immediately following a prominent notice in the actual listing. Scott values for used self-adhesive stamps are for examples either on piece or off piece.

HARDING MEMORIAL ISSUE

Tribute to the memory of President Warren G. Harding, who died in San Francisco, Aug. 2, 1923

Warren Gamaliel Harding – A177

Plates of 400 subjects in four panes of 100 each.

FLAT PLATE PRINTINGS

Stamp designs: 19¼x22¼ mm

1923				*Perf. 11*
610	A177	2¢ **black**, *Sept. 1, 1923*	.50	.25
		intense black	.50	.25
		grayish black	.50	.25
		Never hinged	1.00	
		On cover		.30
		P# block of 6	30.00	—
		Never hinged	47.50	
		Double transfer	2.40	1.00
a.		Horiz. pair, imperf. vert	*2,000.*	
b.		Imperf, P#14870 block of 6	*25,000.*	
		Never hinged	25,000.	

No. 610a is valued in the grade of fine.

No. 610b comes from left side error panes found in a normal pad of No. 610 stamps before No. 611 was issued. Two left side plate blocks and one top position plate block are recorded. Plate #14870 was not used to print No. 611. Loose stamps separated from the top and left plate blocks are indistinguishable from No. 611.

Imperf

611	A177	2¢ **black**, *Nov. 15, 1923*	4.50	4.00
		Never hinged	9.00	
		On philatelic cover		8.00
		On commercial cover		15.00
		Pair	10.00	10.00
		Never hinged	20.00	
		Corner margin block of 4	22.00	22.50
		Margin block of 4, arrow	22.00	22.50
		Center line block	75.00	40.00
		Never hinged	130.00	
		P# block of 6	70.00	—
		Never hinged	90.00	

ROTARY PRESS PRINTINGS

Stamp designs 19¼mm by 22½mm

Perf. 10

612	A177	2¢ **black**, *Sept. 12, 1923*	15.00	1.75
		gray black	15.00	1.75
		Never hinged	32.50	
		On cover		3.25
		P# block of 4	300.00	
		Never hinged	500.00	
		Pair with full vertical gutter between	*350.00*	

Perf. 11

613	A177	2¢ **black**		*35,000.*
		Pair		*80,000.*

No. 613 was produced from rotary press sheet waste. It is valued in the grade of fine.

1 SCOTT NUMBER

2 ILLUS. NUMBER

3 LISTING STYLES — MINORS — MAJORS

4 DENOMINATION

5 BASIC INFORMATION ON STAMP OR SET

6 COLOR OR OTHER DESCRIPTION

7 DATE OF ISSUE

8 CATALOGUE VALUES — USED — UNUSED

9 CHANGES IN BASIC SET INFORMATION

10 OTHER VARIETIES

11 FOOTNOTE

Some sections in this book have more than two columns for values. Check section introductions and watch for value column headers. See the sections "Catalogue Values" and "Understanding Valuing Notations" for an explanation of the meaning of these values.

9 Changes in basic set information — bold or other type is used to show any change in the basic data between stamps within a set of stamps, e.g., perforation from one stamp to the next or a different paper or printing method or watermark.

10 Other varieties — these include additional shades, plate varieties, multiples, used on cover, plate number blocks. coil line pairs, coil plate number strips of three or five, ZIP blocks, etc.

On early issues, there may be a "Cancellation" section. Values in this section refer to single stamps off cover, unless otherwise noted. Values with a "+" are added to the basic used value. See "Basic Stamp Information" for more details on stamp and cancellation varieties.

11 Footnote — Where other important details about the stamps can be found.

Information on catalogue values and condition

Catalogue value

The Scott Catalogue value is a retail value; that is, an amount you could expect to pay for a stamp in the grade of Very Fine with no faults. Any exceptions to the grade valued will be noted in the text. The value listed for any given stamp is a reference that reflects recent actual dealer selling prices for that item.

Dealer retail price lists, public auction results, published prices in advertising and individual solicitation of retail prices from dealers, collectors and specialty organizations have been used in establishing the values found in this catalogue. Amos Media Co. values stamps, but Amos Media is not a company engaged in the business of buying and selling stamps as a dealer.

Use this catalogue as a guide for buying and selling. The actual price you pay for a stamp may be higher or lower than the catalogue value because of many different factors, including the amount of personal service a dealer offers, or increased or decreased interest in the country or topic represented by a stamp or set. An item may occasionally be offered at a lower price as a "loss leader," or as part of a special sale. You also may obtain an item inexpensively at public auction because of little interest at that time or as part of a large lot.

Stamps that are of a lesser grade than Very Fine, or those with condition problems, generally trade at prices lower than the values shown in this catalogue. Stamps of exceptional quality in both grade and condition often command higher prices than the values listed.

Catalogue values for all unused stamps in this catalog are for Never Hinged items. Values for used U.N. stamps are for postally used stamps with contemporaneous cancels. Used stamps soaked off of first-day covers sell for less.

Catalogue listing policy

It is the intent of Amos Media Co. to list all postage stamps of the world in the *Scott Standard Postage Stamp Catalogue.* The only strict criteria for listing is that stamps be decreed legal for postage by the issuing country and that the issuing country actually have an operating postal system. Whether the primary intent of issuing a given stamp or set was for sale to postal patrons or to stamp collectors is not part of our listing criteria. Scott's role is to provide basic comprehensive postage stamp information. It is up to each stamp collector to choose which items to include in a collection.

It is Scott's objective to seek reasons why a stamp should be listed, rather than why it should not. Nevertheless, there are certain types of items that will not be listed. These include the following:

1. Unissued items that are not officially distributed or released by the issuing postal authority. If such items are officially issued at a later date by the country, they will be listed. Unissued items consist of those that have been printed and then held from sale for reasons such as change in government, errors found on stamps or something deemed objectionable about a stamp subject or design.

2. Stamps "issued" by non-existent postal entities or fantasy countries, such as Nagaland, Occusi-Ambeno, Staffa, Sedang, Torres Straits and others. Also, stamps "issued" in the names of legitimate, stamp-issuing countries that are not authorized by those countries.

3. Semi-official or unofficial items not required for postage. Examples include items issued by private agencies for their own express services. When such items are required for delivery, or are valid as prepayment of postage, they are listed.

4. Local stamps issued for local use only. Postage stamps issued by governments specifically for "domestic" use, such as Haiti Scott 219-228, or the United States non-denominated stamps, are not considered to be locals, since they are valid for postage throughout the country of origin.

5. Items not valid for postal use. For example, a few countries have issued souvenir sheets that are not valid for postage. This area also includes a number of worldwide charity labels (some denominated) that do not pay postage.

6. Egregiously exploitative issues such as stamps sold for far more than face value, stamps purposefully issued in artificially small quantities or only against advance orders, stamps awarded only to a selected audience such as a philatelic bureau's standing order customers, or stamps sold only in conjunction with other products. All of these kinds of items are usually controlled issues and/or are intended for speculation. These items normally will be included in a footnote.

7. Items distributed by the issuing government only to a limited group, such as a stamp club, philatelic exhibition or a single stamp dealer, or other private company. These items normally will be included in a footnote.

8. Stamps not available to collectors. These generally are rare items, all of which are held by public institutions such as museums. The existence of such items often will be cited in footnotes.

The fact that a stamp has been used successfully as postage, even on international mail, is not in itself sufficient proof that it was legitimately issued. Numerous examples of so-called stamps from non-existent countries are known to have been used to post letters that have successfully passed through the international mail system.

There are certain items that are subject to interpretation. When a stamp falls outside our specifications, it may be listed along with a cautionary footnote.

A number of factors are considered in our approach to analyzing how a stamp is listed. The following list of factors is presented to share with you, the catalogue user, the complexity of the listing process.

Additional printings — "Additional printings" of a previously issued stamp may range from an item that is totally different to cases where it is impossible to differentiate from the original. At least a minor number (a small-letter suffix) is assigned if there is a distinct change in stamp shade, noticeably redrawn design, or a significantly different perforation measurement. A major number (numeral or numeral and capital-letter combination) is assigned if the editors feel the "additional printing" is sufficiently different from the original that it constitutes a different issue.

Commemoratives — Where practical, commemoratives with the same theme are placed in a set. For example, the U.S. Civil War Centennial set of 1961-65 and the Constitution Bicentennial series of 1989-90 appear as sets. Countries such as Japan and Korea issue such material on a regular basis, with an announced, or at least predictable, number of stamps known in advance. Occasionally, however, stamp sets that were released over a period of years have been separated. Appropriately placed footnotes will guide you to each set's continuation.

Definitive sets – Blocks of numbers generally have been reserved for definitive sets, based on previous experience with any given country. If a few more stamps were issued in a set than originally expected, they often have been inserted into the original set with a capital-letter suffix, such as U.S. Scott 1059A. If it appears that many more stamps than the originally allotted block will be released before the set is completed, a new block of numbers will be reserved, with the original one being closed off. In some cases, such as the U.S. Transportation and Great Americans series, several blocks of numbers exist. Appropriately placed footnotes will guide you to each set's continuation.

New country – Membership in the Universal Postal Union is not a consideration for listing status or order of placement within the catalogue. The index will tell you in what volume or page number the listings begin.

"No release date" items – The amount of information available for any given stamp issue varies greatly from country to country and even from time to time. Extremely comprehensive information about new stamps is available from some countries well before the stamps are released. By contrast some countries do not provide information about stamps or release dates. Most countries, however, fall between these extremes. A country may provide denominations or subjects of stamps from upcoming issues that are not issued as planned. Sometimes, philatelic agencies, those private firms hired to represent countries, add these later-issued items to sets well after the formal release date. This time period can range from weeks to years. If these items were officially released by the country, they will be added to the appropriate spot in the set. In many cases, the specific release date of a stamp or set of stamps may never be known.

Overprints – The color of an overprint is always noted if it is other than black. Where more than one color of ink has been used on overprints of a single set, the color used is noted. Early overprint and surcharge illustrations were altered to prevent their use by forgers.

Se-tenants – Connected stamps of differing features (se-tenants) will be listed in the format most commonly collected. This includes pairs, blocks or larger multiples. Se-tenant units are not always symmetrical. An example is Australia Scott 508, which is a block of seven stamps. If the stamps are primarily collected as a unit, the major number may be assigned to the multiple, with minors going to each component stamp. In cases where continuous-design or other unit se-tenants will receive significant postal use, each stamp is given a major Scott number listing. This includes issues from the United States, Canada, Germany and Great Britain, for example.

Scott numbering practices and special notices

Classification of stamps

The Scott *Specialized Catalogue of United Nations Stamps* lists the stamps of the United Nations and its offices. The next level is a listing by section on the basis of the function of the stamps or postal stationery. In each case, the items are listed in specialized detail. The principal sections cover regular postage stamps; semi postal stamps; air post stamps; and so on. Except for regular postage, catalogue numbers for most sections include a prefix letter (or number-letter combination) denoting the class to which the stamp belongs.

The Table of Contents notes each section and, where pertinent, the prefix used. Some, such as souvenir cards, do not have prefixes.

New issue listings

Updates to this catalogue appear each month in the *Linn's Stamp News Monthly* magazine. Included are corrections and updates to the current edition of this catalogue.

From time to time there will be changes in the listings from the *Linn's Stamp News Monthly* to the next edition of the catalogue, as additional information becomes available.

The catalogue update section of the *Linn's Stamp News Monthly* is the most timely presentation of this material available. For current subscription rates, see advertisements in this catalogue or write Linn's Stamp News, Box 4129, Sidney, OH 45365-4129.

Additions, deletions & number changes

A list of catalogue additions, deletions, and number changes from the previous edition of the catalogue appears in each volume. See Catalogue Additions, Deletions & Number Changes in the Table of Contents for the location of this list.

Understanding valuing notations

The *absence of a value* does not necessarily suggest that a stamp is scarce or rare. In the U.N. listings, a dash in the value column means that the stamp is known in a stated form or variety, but information is lacking or insufficient for purposes of establishing a usable catalogue value. These could include rarities or items that have a limited market.

Stamp values in *italics* generally refer to items which are difficult to value accurately. For expensive items, e.g., value at $1,000 or more, a value in italics represents an item which trades very seldom, such as a unique item. For inexpensive items, a value in italics represents a warning.

The Scott Catalogue values for used stamps reflect canceled-to-order material when such are found to predominate in the marketplace for the issue involved.

Scott values for used stamps are not for precanceled examples, unless so stated. Precanceled copies must not have additional postal cancellations.

An example of a warning to collectors is a stamp that used has a value considerably higher than the unused version. Here, the collector is cautioned to be certain the used version has a readable, contemporaneous cancellation.

The *minimum catalogue value* of a stamp is 25 cents, to cover a dealer's costs of purchase and preparation for resale. The minimum catalogue value of a first day cover is one dollar. As noted, the sum of these values does not properly represent the "value" of a packet of unsorted or unmounted stamps sold in bulk. Such large collections, mixtures or packets generally consist of the lower-valued stamps. There are examples where the catalogue value of a block of stamps is less than the sum of the values of the individual stamps. This situation is caused by the overhead involved in handling single stamps, and should not be considered a suggestion that all blocks be separated into individual stamps to achieve a higher market value.

Values in the "unused" column are for stamps with original gum, if issued with gum. The stamp is valued as hinged if the listing appears *before* the point at which stamps are valued as never hinged. This point is marked by prominent notes in many sections. A similar note will appear at the beginning of the section's listing, noting exactly where the dividing point between hinged and never hinged is for each section of the listings. Where a value for a used stamp is considerably higher than for the unused stamp, the value applies to a stamp showing a distinct contemporaneous cancellation.

Examination

Amos Media Co. will not pass upon the genuineness, grade or condition of stamps, because of the time and responsibility involved. Rather, there are several expertizing groups which undertake this work for both collectors and dealers. Neither will Amos Media Co. appraise or identify philatelic material. The Company cannot take responsibility for unsolicited stamps or covers sent by individuals.

All letters, E-mails, etc. are read attentively, but they are not always answered due to time considerations

How to order from your dealer

It is not necessary to write the full description of a stamp as listed in this catalogue. All that you need is the name of the country or U.N. Specialized section, the Scott Catalogue number and whether the item is unused or used. For example, "U.N. Scott 61" is sufficient to identify the stamp of the United Nations listed as the 3¢ Westminster value of a set of stamps issued in 1958. This stamp was issued April 14, 1958. It is violet blue in color and has a perforation of gauge 12. Sections without a prefix or suffix must be mentioned by name.

UNITED NATIONS

United Nations stamps are used on UN official mail sent from UN Headquarters in New York City, the UN European Office in Geneva, Switzerland, or from the Donaupark Vienna International Center or Atomic Energy Agency in Vienna, Austria to points throughout the world. They may be used on private correspondence sent through the UN post offices and are valid only at the individual UN post offices.

The UN stamps issued for use in Geneva and Vienna are listed in separate sections. Geneva issues were denominated in centimes and francs and Vienna issues in schillings (now cents and euros) and are valid only in Geneva or Vienna. The UN stamps issued for use in New York, denominated in cents and dollars, are valid only in New York.

Letters bearing Nos. 170-174 provide an exception as they were carried by the Canadian postal system.

See Switzerland Nos. 7O1-7O39 in Volume 6 of the Scott *Standard Postage Stamp Catalogue* for stamps issued by the Swiss Government for official use of the UN European Office and other UN affiliated organizations. See France official stamp listings for stamps issued by the French Government for official use of UNESCO.

+: When following the quantity, this indicates the total printed to date. Unless otherwise noted, these are the initial printing order. Final quantities frequently are not given for definitives and air post stamps. The total printed is shown here.

Blocks of four generally sell for four times the single stamp value.

Values for first day covers are for cacheted and unaddressed covers. Addressed covers sell for much less, and addressed and uncacheted first day covers sell for very little.

For imperforate stamps, see the Proofs section following U.N. Souvenir Cards.

Catalogue values for all unused stamps in this section are for Never Hinged items. Values for used UN stamps are for postally used stamps with contemporaneous cancels. Used stamps soaked off of first day covers sell for less.

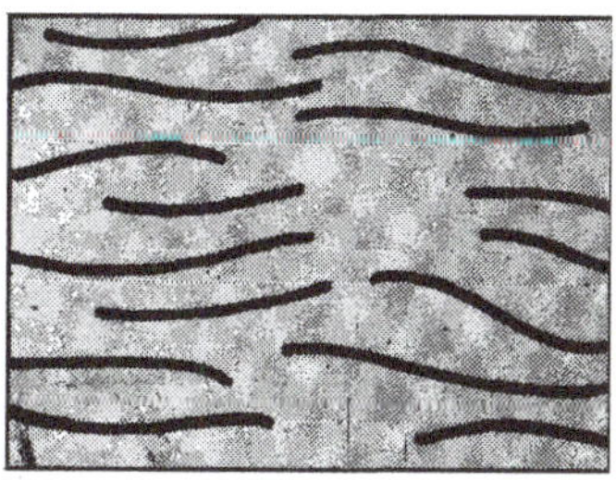

Wmk. 309 — Wavy Lines

Peoples of the World — A1

UN Headquarters Building — A2

"Peace, Justice, Security" — A3

UN Flag — A4

UN International Children's Emergency Fund — A5

World Unity — A6

Printed by Thomas De La Rue & Co., Ltd., London (1c, 3c, 10c, 15c, 20c, 25c), and Joh. Enschedé and Sons, Haarlem, Netherlands (1½c, 2c, 5c, 50c, $1). The 3c, 15c and 25c have frame engraved, center photogravure; other denominations are engraved. Panes of 50. Designed by O. C. Meronti (A1), Leon Helguera (A2), J. F. Doeve (A3), Ole Hamann (A4), S. L. Hartz (5c) and Hubert Woyty-Wimmer (20c).

Perf. 13x12½, 12½x13

1951 Engr. and Photo. Unwmk.

1	A1 1c **magenta,** *Oct. 24 (8,000,000)*	.25	.25
	First day cover		1.00
	Margin block of 4, UN seal	.25	—
2	A2 1½c **blue green,** *Oct. 24 (7,450,000)*	.25	.25
	First day cover		1.00
	Margin block of 4, UN seal	.25	—
	Precanceled *(361,700)*		*55.00*
3	A3 2c **purple,** *Nov. 16 (8,470,000)*	.25	.25
	First day cover		1.00
	Margin block of 4, UN seal	.25	—
4	A4 3c **magenta & blue,** *Oct. 24 (8,250,000)*	.25	.25
	First day cover		1.00
	Margin block of 4, UN seal	.25	—
5	A5 5c **blue,** *Oct. 24 (6,000,000)*	.25	.25
	First day cover		1.75
	Margin block of 4, UN seal	.40	—
6	A1 10c **chocolate,** *Nov. 16 (2,600,000)*	.25	.25
	First day cover		2.00
	Margin block of 4, UN seal	1.30	—
7	A4 15c **violet & blue,** *Nov. 16 (2,300,000)*	.25	.25
	First day cover		2.00
	Margin block of 4, UN seal	1.30	—
8	A6 20c **dark brown,** *Nov. 16 (2,100,000)*	.30	.25
	First day cover		2.00
	Margin block of 4, UN seal	2.00	—
9	A4 25c **olive gray & blue,** *Oct. 24 (2,100,000)*	.35	.25
	First day cover		2.00
	Margin block of 4, UN seal	2.00	—
10	A2 50c **indigo,** *Nov. 16 (1,785,000)*	3.00	1.50
	First day cover		8.00
	Margin block of 4, UN seal	14.00	—
11	A3 $1 **red,** *Oct. 24 (2,252,500)*	1.25	.90
	First day cover		8.00
	Margin block of 4, UN seal	8.00	—
	Nos. 1-11 (11)	6.65	4.65

First day covers of Nos. 1-11 and C1-C4 total 1,113,216.

The various printings of Nos. 1-11 vary in sheet marginal perforation. Some were perforated through left or right margins, or both; some through all margins.

Sheets of this issue carry a marginal inscription consisting of the UN seal and "First UN/Issue 1951." This inscription appears four times on each sheet. The listing "Margin block of 4, UN seal" or "Inscription block of 4" in this and following issues refers to a corner block.

Sheets of the 1½c, 2c, 50c and $1 have a cut-out of different shape in one margin. The printer trimmed this off entirely on most of the 1½c third printing, and partially on the 1½c fourth printing and $1 fifth and sixth printings.

See UN Offices in Geneva Nos. 4, 14.

Forgeries of the 1½c precancel abound. Examination by a competent authority is necessary.

Veterans' War Memorial Building, San Francisco — A7

Issued to mark the 7th anniversary of the signing of the United Nations Charter.

Engraved and printed by the American Bank Note Co., New York. Panes of 50. Designed by Jean Van Noten.

1952, Oct. 24 ***Perf. 12***

12	A7 5c **blue** *(1,274,670)*	.50	.35
	First day cover *(160,117)*		1.00
	Inscription block of 4	2.50	—

Globe and Encircled Flame — A8

4th anniversary of the adoption of the Universal Declaration of Human Rights.

Engraved and printed by Thomas De La Rue & Co., Ltd., London. Panes of 50. Designed by Hubert Woyty-Wimmer.

1952, Dec. 10 ***Perf. 13½x14***

13	A8 3c **deep green** *(1,554,312)*	.45	.35
	First day cover		2.00
	Inscription block of 4	3.00	—
14	A8 5c **blue** *(1,126,371)*	.55	.40
	First day cover		2.50
	First day cover, #13-14		10.00
	Inscription block of 4	4.00	—

First day covers of Nos. 13 and 14 total 299,309.

Refugee Family — A9

Issued to publicize "Protection for Refugees."

Engraved and printed by Thomas De La Rue & Co., Ltd., London. Panes of 50. Designed by Olav Mathiesen.

1953, Apr. 24 ***Perf. 12½x13***

15	A9 3c **dark red brown & rose brown** *(1,299,793)*	.25	.25
	First day cover		2.50
	Inscription block of 4	1.50	—
16	A9 5c **indigo & blue** *(969,224)*	.45	.40
	First day cover		3.75
	First day cover, #15-16		10.00
	Inscription block of 4	3.75	—

First day covers of Nos. 15 and 16 total 234,082.

Envelope, UN Emblem and Map — A10

Issued to honor the Universal Postal Union.

Engraved and printed by Thomas De La Rue & Co., Ltd., London. Panes of 50. Designed by Hubert Woyty-Wimmer.

1953, June 12 ***Perf. 13***

17	A10 3c **black brown** *(1,259,689)*	.40	.40
	First day cover		5.00
	Inscription block of 4	2.50	—
18	A10 5c **dark blue** *(907,312)*	1.25	1.00
	First day cover		5.00
	First day cover, #17-18		12.50
	Inscription block of 4	7.50	—

First day covers of Nos. 17 and 18 total 231,627.

Plate number ("1A" or "1B") in color of stamp appears below 47th stamp of sheet.

Gearwheels and UN Emblem — A11

Issued to publicize United Nations activities in the field of technical assistance.

Engraved and printed by Thomas De La Rue & Co. Ltd. London. Panes of 50. Designed by Olav Mathiesen.

1953, Oct. 24 ***Perf. 13x12½***

19 A11 3c **dark gray** *(1,184,348)*	.25	.25
First day cover		2.00
Inscription block of 4	2.00	—
20 A11 5c **dark green** *(968,182)*	.40	.45
First day cover		5.00
First day cover, #19-20		9.00
Inscription block of 4	5.00	—

First day covers of Nos. 19 and 20 total 229,211.

Hands Reaching Toward Flame — A12

Issued to publicize Human Rights Day.

Engraved and printed by Thomas De La Rue & Co., Ltd., London. Panes of 50. Designed by León Helguera.

1953, Dec. 10 ***Perf. 12½x13***

21 A12 3c **bright blue** *(1,456,928)*	.30	.30
First day cover		2.00
Inscription block of 4	1.50	—
22 A12 5c **rose red** *(983,831)*	1.00	1.00
First day cover		4.00
First day cover, #21-22		12.50
Inscription block of 4	5.75	—

First day covers of Nos. 21 and 22 total 265,186.

Ear of Wheat — A13

Issued to honor the Food and Agriculture Organization and printed by Thomas De La Rue & Co., Ltd., London. Panes of 50. Designed by Dirk Van Gelder.

1954, Feb. 11 ***Perf. 12½x13***

23 A13 3c **dark green & yellow** *(1,250,000)*	.30	.25
First day cover		2.00
Inscription block of 4	2.25	—
24 A13 8c **indigo & yellow** *(949,718)*	.75	.50
First day cover		4.00
First day cover, #23-24		6.00
Inscription block of 4	5.00	—

First day covers of Nos. 23 and 24 total 272,312.

UN Emblem and Anvil Inscribed "ILO" — A14

Design: 8c, inscribed "OIT."

Issued to honor the International Labor Organization.

Engraved and printed by Thomas De La Rue & Co., Ltd., London. Panes of 50. Designed by José Renau.

1954, May 10 ***Perf. 12½x13***

25 A14 3c **brown** *(1,085,651)*	.25	.25
First day cover		2.00
Inscription block of 4	1.50	—
26 A14 8c **magenta** *(903,561)*	1.00	.85
First day cover		4.00
First day cover, #25-26		7.50
Inscription block of 4	5.50	—

First day covers of Nos. 25 and 26 total 252,796.

UN European Office, Geneva — A15

Issued on the occasion of United Nations Day.

Engraved and printed by Thomas De La Rue & Co., Ltd., London. Panes of 50. Designed by Earl W. Purdy.

1954, Oct. 25 ***Perf. 14***

27 A15 3c **dark blue violet** *(1,000,000)*	1.25	1.00
First day cover		2.00
Inscription block of 4	6.50	—
28 A15 8c **red** *(1,000,000)*	.35	.30
First day cover		3.00
First day cover, #27-28		9.00
Inscription block of 4	1.75	—

First day covers of Nos. 27 and 28 total 233,544.

Mother and Child — A16

Issued to publicize Human Rights Day.

Engraved and printed by Thomas De La Rue & Co., Ltd. London. Panes of 50. Designed by Leonard C. Mitchell.

1954, Dec. 10 ***Perf. 14***

29 A16 3c **red orange** *(1,000,000)*	3.50	2.50
First day cover		3.00
Inscription block of 4	35.00	—

30 A16 8c **olive green** *(1,000,000)*	.75	.35
First day cover		3.75
First day cover, #29-30		12.50
Inscription block of 4	5.00	—

First day covers of Nos. 29 and 30 total 276,333.

Symbol of Flight — A17

Design: 8c, inscribed "OACI."
Issued to honor the International Civil Aviation Organization.
Engraved and printed by Waterlow & Sons, Ltd., London. Panes of 50. Designed by Angel Medina Medina.

1955, Feb. 9 ***Perf. 13½x14***

31 A17 3c **blue** *(1,000,000)*	1.00	.75
First day cover		2.00
Inscription block of 4	6.50	—
32 A17 8c **rose carmine** *(1,000,000)*	.60	.50
First day cover		3.00
First day cover, #31-32		9.00
Inscription block of 4	3.25	—

First day covers of Nos. 31 and 32 total 237,131.

UNESCO Emblem — A18

Issued to honor the UN Educational, Scientific and Cultural Organization.
Engraved and printed by Waterlow & Sons, Ltd., London. Panes of 50. Designed by George Hamori.

1955, May 11 ***Perf. 13½x14***

33 A18 3c **lilac rose** *(1,000,000)*	.35	.30
First day cover		2.00
Inscription block of 4	3.25	—
34 A18 8c **light blue** *(1,000,000)*	.30	.30
First day cover		3.00
First day cover, #33-34		7.50
Inscription block of 4	3.00	—

First day covers of Nos. 33 and 34 total 255,326.

United Nations Charter — A19

Design: 4c, Spanish inscription. 8c, French inscription.
10th anniversary of the United Nations.
Engraved and printed by Waterlow & Sons, Ltd., London. Panes of 50. Designed by Claude Bottiau.

1955, Oct. 24 ***Perf. 13½x14***

35 A19 3c **deep plum** *(1,000,000)*	.90	.55
First day cover		3.00
Inscription block of 4	4.25	—
36 A19 4c **dull green** *(1,000,000)*	.50	.35
First day cover		3.00
Inscription block of 4	2.75	—
37 A19 8c **bluish black** *(1,000,000)*	.35	.25
First day cover		4.00
First day cover, #35-37		11.00
Inscription block of 4	2.50	—
Nos. 35-37 (3)	1.75	1.15

Souvenir Sheet

1955, Oct. 24 **Wmk. 309** ***Imperf.***

38 A19 Sheet of 3 *(250,000)*	50.00	18.00
Hinged	35.00	
a. 3c **deep plum**	7.00	3.00
b. 4c **dull green**	7.00	3.00
c. 8c **bluish black**	7.00	3.00
First day cover		18.00
d. As No. 38, corrected plates (see footnote)	55.00	27.50

No. 38 measures 108x83mm and has marginal inscriptions in deep plum.
Two printings were made of the sheet: No. 38 (200,000) and No. 38d (50,000). No. 38 may be distinguished by the broken lines in the background shading on the 8c. It leaves a small white spot below the left leg of the "n" of "Unies." On No. 38d, the broken line was retouched, eliminating the white spot. The 4c was also retouched.
Nos. 38 and 38d used are valued with first day of issue cancels. Value, postally used example, $70.
First day covers of Nos. 35-38 total 455,791.
Examples of No. 38 are known with the 4c and 8c stamps misaligned.

Hand Holding Torch — A20

Issued in honor of Human Rights Day.
Engraved and printed by Waterlow & Sons, Ltd., London. Panes of 50. Designed by Hubert Woyty-Wimmer.

1955, Dec. 9 **Unwmk.** ***Perf. 14x13½***

39 A20 3c **ultramarine** *(1,250,000)*	.30	.30
First day cover		1.25
Inscription block of 4	1.80	—
40 A20 8c **green** *(1,000,000)*	.40	.30
First day cover		1.25
First day cover, #39-40		2.50
Inscription block of 4	3.00	—

First day covers of Nos. 39 and 40 total 298,038.

Symbols of Telecommunication — A21

Design: 8c, inscribed "UIT."
Issued in honor of the International Telecommunication Union.
Engraved and printed by Thomas De La Rue & Co., Ltd., London. Panes of 50. Designed by Hubert Woyty-Wimmer.

1956, Feb. 17 ***Perf. 14***

41 A21 3c **turquoise blue** *(1,000,000)* .25 .25
First day cover 1.25
Inscription block of 4 2.00 —
42 A21 8c **deep carmine** *(1,000,000)* .30 .30
First day cover 1.75
First day cover, #41-42 3.50
Inscription block of 4 3.50 —

Plate number ("1A" or "1B") in color of stamp appears below 47th stamp of sheet.

Globe and Caduceus — A22

Design: 8c, inscribed "OMS."
Issued in honor of the World Health Organization.
Engraved and printed by Thomas De La Rue & Co., Ltd., London. Panes of 50. Designed by Olav Mathiesen.

1956, Apr. 6 ***Perf. 14***

43 A22 3c **bright greenish blue** *(1,250,000)* .25 .25
First day cover 1.00
Inscription block of 4 2.00 —
44 A22 8c **golden brown** *(1,000,000)* .25 .25
First day cover 1.50
First day cover, #43-44 10.00
Inscription block of 4 3.00 —

First day covers of Nos. 43 and 44 total 260,853.

General Assembly — A23

Design: 8c, French inscription.
Issued to commemorate United Nations Day.
Engraved and printed by Thomas De La Rue & Co., Ltd., London. Panes of 50. Designed by Kurt Plowitz.

1956, Oct. 24 ***Perf. 14***

45 A23 3c **dark blue** *(2,000,000)* .25 .25
First day cover 1.00
Inscription block of 4 .75 —
46 A23 8c **gray olive** *(1,500,000)* .25 .25
First day cover 1.00
First day cover, #45-46 5.50
Inscription block of 4 1.30 —

First day covers of Nos. 45 and 46 total 303,560.

Flame and Globe — A24

Issued to publicize Human Rights Day
Engraved and printed by Thomas De La Rue & Co., Ltd., London. Panes of 50. Designed by Rashid-ud Din.

1956, Dec. 10 ***Perf. 14***

47 A24 3c **plum** *(5,000,000)* .25 .25
First day cover 1.00
Inscription block of 4 .60 —
48 A24 8c **dark blue** *(4,000,000)* .25 .25
First day cover 1.00
First day cover, #47-48 2.50
Inscription block of 4 1.00 —

First day covers of Nos. 47 and 48 total 416,120.

Weather Balloon — A25

Design: 8c, Agency name in French.
Issued to honor the World Meterological Organization.
Engraved and printed by Thomas De La Rue & Co., Ltd., London. Panes of 50. Designed by A. L. Pollock.

1957, Jan. 28 ***Perf. 14***

49 A25 3c **violet blue** *(5,000,000)* .25 .25
First day cover 1.00
Inscription block of 4 .50 —
50 A25 8c **dark carmine rose** *(3,448,985)* .25 .25
First day cover 1.00
First day cover, #49-50 1.75
Inscription block of 4 .65 —

First day covers of Nos. 49 and 50 total 376,110.

Badge of UN Emergency Force — A26

Issued in honor of the UN Emergency Force.
Engraved and printed by Thomas De La Rue & Co., Ltd., London. Panes of 50. Designed by Ole Hamann.

1957, Apr. 8 ***Perf. 14x12½***

51 A26 3c **light blue** *(4,000,000)* .25 .25
First day cover 1.00
Inscription block of 4 .50 —
52 A26 8c **rose carmine** *(3,000,000)* .25 .25
First day cover 1.00
First day cover, #51-52 1.50
Inscription block of 4 .70 —

First day covers of Nos. 51 and 52 total 461,772.

Nos. 51-52 Re-engraved

1957, Apr.-May ***Perf. 14x12½***

53 A26 3c **blue** *(2,736,206)* .25 .25
Inscription block of 4 .75 —
54 A26 8c **rose carmine** *(1,000,000)* .35 .25
Inscription block of 4 2.00 —

On Nos. 53-54 the background within and around the circles is shaded lightly, giving a halo effect. The lettering is more distinct with a line around each letter.

UN Emblem and Globe — A27

Design: 8c, French inscription.
Issued to honor the Security Council.
Engraved and printed by Thomas De La Rue & Co., Ltd., London. Panes of 50. Designed by Rashid-ud Din.

1957, Oct. 24 ***Perf. 12½x13***

55 A27 3c **orange brown** *(3,674,968)* .25 .25
First day cover 1.00
Inscription block of 4 .40 —
56 A27 8c **dark blue green** *(2,885,938)* .25 .25
First day cover 1.00
First day cover, #55-56 1.75
Inscription block of 4 .70 —

First day covers of Nos. 55 and 56 total 460,627.

Flaming Torch — A28

Issued in honor of Human Rights Day.
Engraved and printed by Thomas De La Rue & Co., Ltd., London. Panes of 50. Designed by Olav Mathiesen.

1957, Dec. 10 ***Perf. 14***

57 A28 3c **red brown** *(3,368,405)* .25 .25
First day cover 1.00
Inscription block of 4 .40 —
58 A28 8c **black** *(2,717,310)* .25 .25
First day cover 1.00
First day cover, #57-58 1.25
Inscription block of 4 .65 —

First day covers of Nos. 57 and 58 total 553,669.

UN Emblem Shedding Light on Atom — A29

Design: 8c, French inscription.
Issued in honor of the International Atomic Energy Agency.
Engraved and printed by the American Bank Note Co., New York. Panes of 50. Designed by Robert Perrot.

1958, Feb. 10 ***Perf. 12***

59 A29 3c **olive** *(3,663,305)* .25 .25
First day cover 1.00
Inscription block of 4 .40 —
60 A29 8c **blue** *(3,043,622)* .25 .25
First day cover 1.00
First day cover, #59-60 1.00
Inscription block of 4 .85 —

First day covers of Nos. 59 and 60 total 504,832.

Central Hall, Westminster — A30

Design: 8c, French inscription.
Central Hall, Westminster, London, was the site of the first session of the United Nations General Assembly, 1946.
Engraved and printed by the American Bank Note Co., New York. Panes of 50. Designed by Olav Mathiesen.

1958, Apr. 14 ***Perf. 12***

61 A30 3c **violet blue** *(3,353,716)* .25 .25
First day cover 1.00
Inscription block of 4 .40 —
62 A30 8c **rose claret** *(2,836,747)* .25 .25
First day cover 1.00
First day cover, #61-62 1.50
Inscription block of 4 .60 —

First day covers of Nos. 61 and 62 total 449,401.

UN Seal — A31

Engraved and printed by Bradbury, Wilkinson & Co., Ltd., England. Panes of 50. Designed by Herbert M. Sanborn.

1958, Oct. 24 ***Perf. 13½x14***

63 A31 4c **red orange** *(9,000,000)* .25 .25
First day cover 1.00
First day cover of #63 also bearing #64 *85.00*
Inscription block of 4 .50 —

1958, June 2 ***Perf. 13x14***

64 A31 8c **bright blue** *(5,000,000)* .25 .25
First day cover *(219,422)* 1.00
Inscription block of 4 .55 —
Margin block of 4, Bradbury, Wilkinson imprint 3.00 —

Gearwheels — A32

Design: 8c, French inscription.
Issued to honor the Economic and Social Council.
Engraved and printed by the American Bank Note Co., New York. Panes of 50. Designed by Ole Hamann.

1958, Oct. 24 **Unwmk.** ***Perf. 12***

65 A32 4c **dark blue green** *(2,556,784)* .25 .25
First day cover 1.00
Inscription block of 4 .40 —
66 A32 8c **vermilion** *(2,175,117)* .25 .25
First day cover 1.00
First day cover, #65-66 1.00
Inscription block of 4 .70 —

First day covers of Nos. 63, 65 and 66 total 626,236.

Hands Upholding Globe — A33

Issued for Human Rights Day and to commemorate the 10th anniversary of the signing of the Universal Declaration of Human Rights.
Engraved and printed by the American Bank Note Co., New York. Panes of 50. Designed by Leonard C. Mitchell.

1958, Dec. 10 **Unwmk.** ***Perf. 12***

67 A33 4c **yellow green** *(2,644,340)* .25 .25
First day cover 1.00
Inscription block of 4 .40 —
68 A33 8c **red brown** *(2,216,838)* .25 .25
First day cover 1.00
First day cover, #67-68 1.00
Inscription block of 4 .65 —

First day covers of Nos. 67 and 68 total 618,124.

New York City Building, Flushing Meadows — A34

Design: 8c, French inscription.
New York City Building at Flushing Meadows, New York, was the site of many General Assembly meetings, 1946-50.
Engraved and printed by Canadian Bank Note Company, Ltd., Ottawa. Panes of 50. Designed by Robert Perrot.

1959, Mar. 30 **Unwmk.** ***Perf. 12***

69 A34 4c **light lilac rose** *(2,035,011)* .25 .25
First day cover 1.00
Inscription block of 4 .40 —
70 A34 8c **aquamarine** *(1,627,281)* .25 .25
First day cover 1.00
First day cover, #69-70 1.25
Inscription block of 4 .60 —

First day covers of Nos. 69 and 70 total 440,955.

A35

Design: UN emblem and symbols of agriculture, industry and trade.
Issued to honor the Economic Commission for Europe.
Engraved and printed by Canadian Bank Note Company, Ltd., Ottawa. Panes of 50. Designed by Ole Hamann.

1959, May 18 **Unwmk.** ***Perf. 12***

71 A35 4c **blue** *(1,743,502)* .25 .25
First day cover 1.00
Inscription block of 4 .60 —
72 A35 8c **red orange** *(1,482,898)* .25 .25
First day cover 1.00
First day cover, #71-72 1.25
Inscription block of 4 .85 —

First day covers of Nos. 71 and 72 total 433,549.

A36

Designs: 4c, Figure Adapted from Rodin's "Age of Bronze." 8c, same, French inscription.
Issued to honor the Trusteeship Council.
Engraved and printed by Canadian Bank Note Co., Ltd., Ottawa. Panes of 50. Designed by León Helguera; lettering by Ole Hamann.

1959, Oct. 23 **Unwmk.** ***Perf. 12***

73 A36 4c **bright red** *(1,929,677)* .25 .25
First day cover 1.00
Inscription block of 4 .60 —
74 A36 8c **dark olive green** *(1,587,647)* .25 .25
First day cover 1.00
First day cover, #73-74 1.25
Inscription block of 4 1.25 —

First day covers of Nos. 73 and 74 total 466,053.

World Refugee Year Emblem — A37

Design: 8c, French inscription.
Issued to publicize World Refugee Year, July 1, 1959-June 30, 1960.
Engraved and printed by Canadian Bank Note Co., Ltd., Ottawa. Panes of 50. Designed by Olav Mathiesen.

1959, Dec. 10 **Unwmk.** ***Perf. 12***

75 A37 4c **olive & red** *(2,168,963)* .25 .25
First day cover 1.00
Inscription block of 4 .50 —
76 A37 8c **olive & bright greenish blue** *(1,843,886)* .25 .25
First day cover 1.00
First day cover, #75-76 1.50
Inscription block of 4 .75 —

First day covers of Nos. 75 and 76 total 502,262.

Chaillot Palace, Paris — A38

Design: 8c, French inscription.
Chaillot Palace in Paris was the site of General Assembly meetings in 1948 and 1951.
Engraved and printed by Thomas De La Rue & Co., Ltd., London. Panes of 50. Designed by Hubert Woyty-Wimmer.

1960, Feb. 29 Unwmk. *Perf. 14*

77 A38 4c **rose lilac & blue** *(2,276,678)* .25 .25
First day cover 1.00
Inscription block of 4 .40 —
78 A38 8c **dull green & brown** *(1,930,869)* .25 .25
First day cover 1.00
First day cover, #77-78 1.75
Inscription block of 4 .70 —

First day covers of Nos. 77 and 78 total 446,815.

Map of Far East and Steel Beam — A39

Design: 8c, French inscription.
Issued to honor the Economic Commission for Asia and the Far East (ECAFE).
Printed by the Government Printing Bureau, Tokyo. Panes of 50. Designed by Hubert Woyty-Wimmer.

1960, Apr. 11 Photo. Unwmk. *Perf. 13x13½*

79 A39 4c **deep claret, blue green & dull yellow** *(2,195,945)* .25 .25
First day cover 1.00
Inscription block of 4 .40 —
80 A39 8c **olive green, blue & rose** *(1,897,902)* .25 .25
First day cover 1.00
First day cover, #79-80 1.50
Inscription block of 4 .75 —

First day covers of Nos. 79 and 80 total 415,127.

Tree, FAO and UN Emblems — A40

Design: 8c, French inscription.
Issued to commemorate the Fifth World Forestry Congress, Seattle, Washington, Aug. 29-Sept. 10.
Printed by the Government Printing Bureau, Tokyo. Panes of 50. Designed by Ole Hamann.

1960, Aug. 29 Photo. Unwmk. *Perf. 13½*

81 A40 4c **dark blue, green & orange** *(2,188,293)* .25 .25
First day cover 1.00
Inscription block of 4 .40 —
82 A40 8c **yellow green, black & orange** *(1,837,778)* .25 .25
First day cover 1.00
First day cover, #81-82 1.50
Inscription block of 4 .75 —

First day covers of Nos. 81 and 82 total 434,129.

UN Headquarters and Preamble to UN Charter — A41

Design: 8c, French inscription.
Issued to commemorate the 15th anniversary of the United Nations.
Engraved and printed by the British American Bank Note Co., Ltd., Ottawa, Canada. Panes of 50. Designed by Robert Perrot.

1960, Oct. 24 Unwmk. *Perf. 11*

83 A41 4c **blue** *(2,631,593)* .25 .25
First day cover 1.00
Inscription block of 4 .40 —
84 A41 8c **gray** *(2,278,022)* .25 .25
First day cover 1.00
First day cover, #83-84 1.25
Inscription block of 4 .65 —

Souvenir Sheet

Imperf

85 Sheet of 2 *(1,000,000)* 1.25 1.25
a. A41 4c **blue** .55 .55
b. A41 8c **gray** .55 .55
First day cover *(256,699)* 1.00

No. 85 has dark gray marginal inscription. Size: 92x71mm. Broken "I" and "V" flaws occur in "ANNIVERSARY" in marginal inscription. Value $40. Examples are known with the two stamps misaligned.

Block and Tackle — A42

Design: 8c, French inscription.
Issued to honor the International Bank for Reconstruction and Development.
Printed by the Government Printing Bureau, Tokyo. Panes of 50. Designed by Angel Medina Medina.

1960, Dec. 9 Photo. Unwmk. *Perf. 13½x13*

86 A42 4c **multicolored** *(2,286,117)* .25 .25
First day cover 1.00
Inscription block of 4 .40 —
87 A42 8c **multicolored** *(1,882,019)* .25 .25
First day cover 1.00
First day cover, #86-87 1.00
Inscription block of 4 .60 —

First day covers of Nos. 86 and 87 total 559,708.

Scales of Justice from Raphael's Stanze — A43

Design: 8c, French inscription.
Issued to honor the International Court of Justice.
Printed by the Government Printing Bureau, Tokyo, Japan. Panes of 50. Designed by Kurt Plowitz.

1961, Feb. 13 Photo. Unwmk. *Perf. 13½x13*

88 A43 4c **yellow, orange brown & black** *(2,234,588)*	.25	.25
First day cover		1.00
Inscription block of 4	.40	—
89 A43 8c **yellow, green & black** *(2,023,968)*	.25	.25
First day cover		1.00
First day cover, #88-89		1.00
Inscription block of 4	.60	—

First day covers of Nos. 88 and 89 total 447,467.

Seal of International Monetary Fund — A44

Design: 7c, French inscription.
Issued to honor the International Monetary Fund.
Printed by the Government Printing Bureau, Tokyo, Japan. Panes of 50. Designed by Roy E. Carlson and Hordur Karlsson, Iceland.

1961, Apr. 17 Photo. Unwmk. *Perf. 13x13½*

90 A44 4c **bright bluish green** *(2,305,010)*	.25	.25
First day cover		1.00
Inscription block of 4	.40	—
91 A44 7c **terra cotta & yellow** *(2,147,201)*	.25	.25
First day cover		1.00
First day cover, #90-91		1.00
Inscription block of 4	.60	—

First day covers of Nos. 90 and 91 total 448,729.

Abstract Group of Flags — A45

Printed by Courvoisier S.A., La Chaux-de-Fonds, Switzerland. Panes of 50. Designed by Herbert M. Sanborn.

1961, June 5 Photo. Unwmk. *Perf. 11½*

92 A45 30c **multicolored** *(3,370,000)*	.45	.30
First day cover *(182,949)*		1.00
Inscription block of 4	2.00	—

See UN Offices in Geneva No. 10.

Cogwheel and Map of Latin America — A46

Design: 11c, Spanish inscription.
Issued to honor the Economic Commission for Latin America.
Printed by the Government Printing Bureau, Tokyo. Panes of 50. Designed by Robert Perrot.

1961, Sept. 18 Photo. Unwmk. *Perf. 13½*

93 A46 4c **blue, red & citron** *(2,037,912)*	.25	.25
First day cover		1.00
Inscription block of 4	.75	—
94 A46 11c **green, lilac & orange vermilion** *(1,835,097)*	.25	.25
First day cover		1.00
First day cover, #93-94		1.00
Inscription block of 4	1.50	—

First day covers of Nos. 93 and 94 total 435,820.

Africa House, Addis Ababa, and Map — A47

Design: 11c, English inscription.
Issued to honor the Economic Commission for Africa.
Printed by Courvoisier S.A., La Chaux-de-Fonds, Switzerland. Panes of 50. Designed by Robert Perrot.

1961, Oct. 24 Photo. Unwmk. *Perf. 11½*

95 A47 4c **ultramarine, orange, yellow & brown** *(2,044,842)*	.25	.25
First day cover		1.00
Inscription block of 4	.30	—
96 A47 11c **emerald, orange, yellow & brown** *(1,790,894)*	.25	.25
First day cover		1.00
First day cover, #95-96		1.00
Inscription block of 4	1.00	—

First day covers of Nos. 95 and 96 total 435,131.

Mother Bird Feeding Young and UNICEF Seal — A48

Designs: 3c, Spanish inscription. 13c, French inscription.
15th anniversary of the United Nations Children's Fund.
Printed by Courvoisier S.A., La Chaux-de-Fonds, Switzerland. Panes of 50. Designed by Minoru Hisano.

1961, Dec. 4 Photo. Unwmk. *Perf. 11½*

97 A48 3c **brown, gold, orange & yellow** *(2,867,456)*	.25	.25
First day cover		1.00
Inscription block of 4	.20	—
98 A48 4c **brown, gold, blue & emerald** *(2,735,899)*	.25	.25
First day cover		1.00
Inscription block of 4	.30	—
99 A48 13c **deep green, gold, purple & pink** *(1,951,715)*	.25	.25
First day cover		1.00
First day cover, #97-99		1.25
Inscription block of 4	1.00	—
Nos. 97-99 (3)	.75	.75

First day covers of Nos. 97-99 total 752,979.

Family and Symbolic Buildings — A49

Design: 7c, inscribed "Services Collectifs".

Issued to publicize the UN program for housing and urban development, and in connection with the expert committee meeting at UN headquarters, Feb. 7-21.

Printed by Harrison and Sons, Ltd., London, England. Panes of 50. Designed by Olav Mathiesen.

1962, Feb. 28 Photo. Unwmk. *Perf. 14½x14*

Central design multicolored

100 A49 4c **bright blue** *(2,204,190)*	.25	.25
First day cover		1.00
Inscription block of 4	.35	—
a. Black omitted	*200.00*	
b. Yellow omitted	—	
c. Brown omitted	—	
101 A49 7c **orange brown** *(1,845,821)*	.25	.25
First day cover		1.00
First day cover, #100-101		1.25
Inscription block of 4	.65	—
a. Red omitted	—	
b. Black omitted	—	
c. Gold omitted	—	

First day covers of Nos. 100-101 total 466,178.

"The World Against Malaria" — A50

Issued in honor of the World Health Organization and to call attention to the international campaign to eradicate malaria from the world.

Printed by Harrison and Sons, Ltd., London, England. Panes of 50. Designed by Rashid-ud Din.

1962, Mar. 30 Photo. Unwmk. *Perf. 14x14½*

Word frame in gray

102 A50 4c **orange, yellow, brown, green & black** *(2,047,000)*	.25	.25
First day cover		1.00
Inscription block of 4	.50	—
103 A50 11c **green, yellow, brown & indigo** *(1,683,766)*	.25	.25
First day cover		1.00
First day cover, #102-103		1.25
Inscription block of 4	1.00	—

First day covers of Nos. 102-103 total 522,450.

"Peace" — A51

UN Flag — A52

Hands Combining "UN" and Globe — A53

UN Emblem over Globe — A54

Printed by Harrison & Sons, Ltd. London, England (1c, 3c and 11c), and by Canadian Bank Note Co., Ltd., Ottawa (5c). Panes of 50. Designed by Kurt Plowitz (1c), Ole Hamann (3c), Renato Ferrini (5c) and Olav Mathiesen (11c).

Photo.; Engr. (5c)

1962, May 25 Unwmk. *Perf. 14x14½*

104 A51 1c **vermilion, blue, black & gray** *(5,000,000)*	.25	.25
First day cover		1.00
Inscription block of 4	.40	—
105 A52 3c **light green, Prussian blue, yellow & gray** *(5,000,000)*	.25	.25
First day cover		1.00
Inscription block of 4	.40	—
Perf. 12		
106 A53 5c **dark carmine rose** *(4,000,000)*	.25	.25
First day cover		1.00

Inscription block of 4 .75 —

Perf. 12½

107 A54 11c **dark & light blue & gold** *(4,400,000)* .25 .25
First day cover 1.00
First day cover, #104-107 4.50
Inscription block of 4 1.10 —
Nos. 104-107 (4) 1.00 1.00

First day covers of Nos. 104-107 total 738,985.
Size of 5c, No. 106: 36½x23½mm.
See No. 167. See UN Offices in Geneva Nos. 2 and 6.

Flag at Half-mast and UN Headquarters — A55

Issued on the 1st anniversary of the death of Dag Hammarskjold, Secretary General of the United Nations 1953-61, in memory of those who died in the service of the United Nations.
Printed by Courvoisier S. A., La Chaux-de-Fonds, Switzerland. Panes of 50. Designed by Ole Hamann.

1962, Sept. 17 Photo. Unwmk. *Perf. 11½*

108 A55 5c **black, light blue & blue** *(2,195,707)* .25 .25
First day cover 1.00
Inscription block of 4 .75 —
109 A55 15c **black, gray olive & blue** *(1,155,047)* .25 .25
First day cover 1.00
First day cover, #108-109 1.50
Inscription block of 4 1.10 —

First day covers of Nos. 108-109 total 513,963.

World Map Showing Congo — A56

Design: 11c inscribed "Operation des Nations Unies au Congo."
Issued to commemorate the United Nations Operation in the Congo.
Printed by Courvoisier S. A., La Chaux-de-Fonds, Switzerland. Panes of 50. Designed by George Hamori.

1962, Oct. 24 Photo. Unwmk. *Perf. 11½*

110 A56 4c **olive, orange, black & yellow** *(1,477,958)* .25 .25
First day cover 1.00
Inscription block of 4 .75 —
111 A56 11c **blue green, orange, black & yellow** *(1,171,255)* .25 .25
First day cover 1.00
First day cover, #110-111 1.25
Inscription block of 4 1.10 —

First day covers of Nos. 110-111 total 460,675.

Globe in Universe and Palm Frond — A57

Design: 4c, English inscription.

Issued to honor the Committee on Peaceful Uses of Outer Space.
Printed by Bradbury, Wilkinson and Co., Ltd., England. Panes of 50. Designed by Kurt Plowitz.

1962, Dec. 3 Engr. Unwmk. *Perf. 14x13½*

112 A57 4c **violet blue** *(2,263,876)* .25 .25
First day cover 1.00
Inscription block of 4 .35 —
113 A57 11c **rose claret** *(1,681,584)* .25 .25
First day cover 1.00
First day cover, #112-113 1.50
Inscription block of 4 1.10 —

First day covers of Nos. 112-113 total 529,780.

Development Decade Emblem — A58

Design: 11c, French inscription.
UN Development Decade and UN Conference on the Application of Science and Technology for the Benefit of the Less Developed Areas, Geneva, Feb. 4-20.
Printed by Courvoisier S. A., La Chaux-de-Fonds, Switzerland. Panes of 50. Designed by Rashid-ud Din.

1963, Feb. 4 Photo. Unwmk. *Perf. 11½*

114 A58 5c **pale green, maroon, dark blue & Prussian blue** *(1,802,406)* .25 .25
First day cover 1.00
Inscription block of 4 .50 —
115 A58 11c **yellow, maroon, dark blue & Prussian blue** *(1,530,190)* .25 .25
First day cover 1.00
First day cover, #114-115 1.25
Inscription block of 4 .90 —

First day covers of Nos. 114-115 total 460,877.

Stalks of Wheat — A59

Design: 11c, French inscription.
Issued for the "Freedom from Hunger" campaign of the Food and Agriculture Organization.
Printed by Courvoisier S. A., La Chaux-de-Fonds, Switzerland. Panes of 50. Designed by Ole Hamann.

1963, Mar. 22 Photo. Unwmk. *Perf. 11½*

116 A59 5c **vermilion, green & yellow** *(1,666,178)* .25 .25
First day cover 1.00
Inscription block of 4 .50 —
117 A59 11c **vermilion, deep claret & yellow** *(1,563,023)* .25 .25
First day cover 1.00
First day cover, #116-117 1.25
Inscription block of 4 .90 —

First day covers of Nos. 116-117 total 461,868.

Bridge over Map of New Guinea — A60

1st anniversary of the United Nations Temporary Executive Authority (UNTEA) in West New Guinea (West Irian).

Printed by Courvoisier S.A., La Chaux-de-Fonds, Switzerland. Panes of 50. Designed by Henry Bencsath.

1963, Oct. 1 Photo. Unwmk. *Perf. 11½*

118 A60 25c **blue, green & gray** *(1,427,747)* .50 .40
First day cover *(222,280)* 1.00
Inscription block of 4 2.50 —

General Assembly Building, New York — A61

Design: 11c, French inscription.

Since October 1955 all sessions of the General Assembly have been held in the General Assembly Hall, UN Headquarters, NY.

Printed by the Government Printing Bureau, Tokyo. Panes of 50. Designed by Kurt Plowitz.

1963, Nov. 4 Photo. Unwmk. *Perf. 13*

119 A61 5c **violet blue, blue, yellow green & red** *(1,892,539)* .25 .25
First day cover 1.00
Inscription block of 4 .50 —
120 A61 11c **green, yellow green, blue, yellow & red** *(1,435,079)* .25 .25
First day cover 1.00
First day cover, #119-120 1.00
Inscription block of 4 .80 —

First day covers of Nos. 119-120 total 410,306.

Flame — A62

Design: 11c inscribed "15e Anniversaire."

15th anniversary of the signing of the Universal Declaration of Human Rights.

Printed by the Government Printing Bureau, Tokyo. Panes of 50. Designed by Rashid-ud Din.

1963, Dec. 10 Photo. Unwmk. *Perf. 13*

121 A62 5c **green, gold, red & yellow** *(2,208,008)* .25 .25
First day cover 1.00
Inscription block of 4 .60 —
122 A62 11c **carmine, gold, blue & yellow** *(1,501,125)* .25 .25
First day cover 1.00
First day cover, #121-122 1.00
Inscription block of 4 .80 —

First day covers of Nos. 121-122 total 567,907.

Ships at Sea and IMCO Emblem — A63

Design: 11c, inscribed "OMCI."

Issued to honor the Intergovernmental Maritime Consultative Organization.

Printed by Courvoisier S.A., La Chaux-de-Fonds, Switzerland. Panes of 50. Designed by Henry Bencsath; emblem by Olav Mathiesen.

1964, Jan. 13 Photo. Unwmk. *Perf. 11½*

123 A63 5c **blue, olive, ocher & yellow** *(1,805,750)* .25 .25
First day cover 1.00
Inscription block of 4 .60 —
124 A63 11c **dark blue, dark green, emerald & yellow** *(1,583,848)* .25 .25
First day cover 1.00
First day cover, #123-124 1.00
Inscription block of 4 .80 —

First day covers of Nos. 123-124 total 442,696.

World Map, Sinusoidal Projection — A64

UN Emblem — A65

Three Men United Before Globe — A66

Stylized Globe and Weather Vane — A67

Printed by Thomas De La Rue & Co. Ltd., London (2c) and Courvoisier S.A., La Chaux-de-Fonds, Switzerland (7c, 10c and 50c). Panes of 50.

Designed by Ole Hamann (2c), George Hamori (7c, 10c) and Hatim El Mekki (50c).

1964-71 Photo. Unwmk. *Perf. 14*

125 A64 2c **light & dark blue, orange & yellow green** *(3,800,000)* .25 .25
First day cover 1.00
Inscription block of 4 .60 —

a. Perf. 13x13½, *Feb. 24, 1971 (1,500,000)* .25 .25

Perf. 11½

126 A65 7c **dark blue, orange brown & black** *(2,700,000)* .25 .25
First day cover 1.00
Inscription block of 4 .75 —

127 A66 10c **blue green, olive green & black** *(3,200,000)* .25 .25
First day cover 1.00
First day cover, #125-127 4.00
Inscription block of 4 1.00 —

128 A67 50c **multicolored** *(2,520,000)* .55 .45
First day cover *(210,713)* 1.00
Inscription block of 4 3.25 —
Nos. 125-128 (4) 1.30 1.20

Issue dates: 50c, Mar. 6; 2c, 7c, 10c, May 29, 1964.
First day covers of 2c, 7c and 10c total 524,073.
See UN Offices in Geneva Nos. 3 and 12.

Arrows Showing Global Flow of Trade — A68

Design: 5c, English inscription.
Issued to commemorate the UN Conference on Trade and Development, Geneva, Mar. 23-June 15.
Printed by Thomas De La Rue & Co., Ltd., London. Panes of 50. Designed by Herbert M. Sanborn and Ole Hamann.

1964, June 15 Photo. Unwmk. *Perf. 13*

129 A68 5c **black, red & yellow** *(1,791,211)* .25 .25
First day cover 1.00
Inscription block of 4 .50 —

130 A68 11c **black, olive & yellow** *(1,529,526)* .25 .25
First day cover 1.00
First day cover, #129-130 1.25
Inscription block of 4 .80 —

First day covers of Nos. 129-130 total 422,358.

Poppy Capsule and Reaching Hands — A69

Design: 11c, Inscribed "Echec au Stupéfiants."
Issued to honor international efforts and achievements in the control of narcotics.
Printed by the Canadian Bank Note Co., Ottawa. Panes of 50. Designed by Kurt Plowitz.

1964, Sept. 21 Engr. Unwmk. *Perf. 12*

131 A69 5c **rose red & black** *(1,508,999)* .25 .25
First day cover 1.00
Inscription block of 4 .50 —

132 A69 11c **emerald & black** *(1,340,691)* .25 .25
First day cover 1.00
First day cover, #131-132 1.50
Inscription block of 4 1.00 —

First day covers of Nos. 131-132 total 445,274.

Padlocked Atomic Blast — A70

Signing of the nuclear test ban treaty pledging an end to nuclear explosions in the atmosphere, outer space and under water.
Printed by Artia, Prague, Czechoslovakia. Panes of 50. Designed by Ole Hamann.

Litho. and Engr.

1964, Oct. 23 Unwmk. *Perf. 11x11½*

133 A70 5c **dark red & dark brown** *(2,422,789)* .25 .25
First day cover *(298,652)* 1.00
Inscription block of 4 .50 —

Education for Progress — A71

Design: 11c, French inscription.
Issued to publicize the UNESCO world campaign for universal literacy and for free compulsory primary education.
Printed by Courvoisier, S. A., La Chaux-de-Fonds, Switzerland. Panes of 50. Designed by Kurt Plowitz.

1964, Dec. 7 Photo. Unwmk. *Perf. 12½*

134 A71 4c **orange, red, bister, green & blue** *(2,375,181)* .25 .25
First day cover 1.00
Inscription block of 4 .50 —

135 A71 5c **bister, red, dark & light blue** *(2,406,877)* .25 .25
First day cover 1.00
Inscription block of 4 .55 —

136 A71 11c **green, light blue, black & rose** *(1,773,645)* .25 .25
First day cover 1.00
First day cover, #134-136 1.25
Inscription block of 4 1.25 —
Nos. 134-136 (3) .75 .75

First day covers of Nos. 134-136 total 727,875.

Progress Chart of Special Fund, Key and Globe — A72

Design: 11c, French inscription.
Issued to publicize the Special Fund program to speed economic growth and social advancement in low-income countries.
Printed by the Government Printing Bureau, Tokyo. Panes of 50. Designed by Rashid-ud Din, Pakistan.

1965, Jan. 25 Photo. Unwmk. *Perf. 13½x13*

137 A72 5c **dull blue, dark blue, yellow & red** *(1,949,274)* .25 .25
First day cover 1.00
Inscription block of 4 .50 —

138 A72 11c **yellow green, dark blue, yellow & red** *(1,690,908)* .25 .25
First day cover 1.00
First day cover, #137-138 1.00
Inscription block of 4 .75 —
a. Black omitted (UN emblem on key) —

First day covers of Nos. 137-138 total 490,608.

UN Emblem, Stylized Leaves and View of Cyprus — A73

Design: 11c, French inscription.
Issued to honor the United Nations Peace-keeping Force on Cyprus.
Printed by Courvoisier S.A., Switzerland. Panes of 50. Designed by George Hamori, Australia.

1965, Mar. 4 Photo. Unwmk. *Perf. 11½*

139 A73 5c **orange, olive & black** *(1,887,042)* .25 .25
First day cover 1.00
Inscription block of 4 .50 —
140 A73 11c **yellow green, blue green & black** *(1,691,767)* .25 .25
First day cover 1.00
First day cover, #139-140 1.00
Inscription block of 4 .75 —

First day covers of Nos. 139-140 total 438,059.

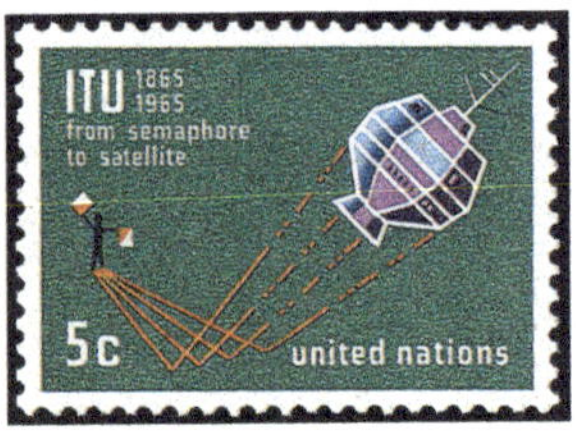

"From Semaphore to Satellite" — A74

Design: 11c, French inscription.
Centenary of the International Telecommunication Union.
Printed by Courvoisier S.A., Switzerland. Panes of 50. Designed by Kurt Plowitz, United States.

1965, May 17 Photo. Unwmk. *Perf. 11½*

141 A74 5c **aquamarine, orange, blue & purple** *(2,432,407)* .25 .25
First day cover 1.00
Inscription block of 4 .50 —
142 A74 11c **light violet, red orange, bister & bright green** *(1,731,070)* .25 .25
First day cover 1.00
First day cover, #141-142 1.00
Inscription block of 4 .75 —

First day covers of Nos. 141-142 total 434,393.

ICY Emblem — A75

Design: 15c, French inscription.

20th anniversary of the United Nations and International Cooperation Year.
Printed by Bradbury, Wilkinson and Co., Ltd., England. Panes of 50. Designed by Olav Mathiesen, Denmark.

1965, June 26 Engr. Unwmk. *Perf. 14x13½*

143 A75 5c **dark blue** *(2,282,452)* .25 .25
First day cover 1.00
Inscription block of 4 .50 —
144 A75 15c **lilac rose** *(1,993,562)* .25 .25
First day cover 1.00
First day cover, #143-144 1.00
Inscription block of 4 .95 —

Souvenir Sheet

145 A75 Sheet of two *(1,928,366)* .35 .35
First day cover 1.00

No. 145 contains one each of Nos. 143-144 with dark blue and ocher marginal inscription, ocher edging. Size: 92x70mm.
First day covers of Nos. 143-145 total: New York, 748,876; San Francisco, 301,435.

"Peace" — A76

Opening Words, UN Charter — A77

UN Headquarters and Emblem — A78

UN Emblem — A79

UN Emblem Encircled — A80

Printed by Government Printing Bureau, Tokyo (1c); Government Printing Office, Austria (15c, 20c); Government Printing Office (Bundesdruckerei), Berlin (25c), and Courvoisier S.A., Switzerland ($1). Panes of 50.
Designed by Kurt Plowitz US (1c); Olav S. Mathiesen, Denmark (15c); Vergniaud Pierre-Noel, US (20c); Rashid-ud Din, Pakistan (25c), and Ole Hamann, Denmark ($1).

1965-66 Photo. Unwmk. *Perf. 13½x13*

146 A76 1c **vermilion, blue, black & gray** *(7,000,000)* .25 .25
First day cover 1.00
Inscription block of 4 .40 —

Perf. 14

147 A77 15c **olive bister, dull yellow, black & deep claret** *(2,500,000)* .25 .25
First day cover 1.00

Inscription block of 4 — 1.00 —

Perf. 12

148 A78 20c **dark blue, blue, red & yellow** *(3,000,000)* .25 .25
First day cover 1.00
First day cover, #147-148 1.00
Inscription block of 4 1.10 —
a. Yellow omitted —

Litho. and Embossed

Perf. 14

149 A79 25c **light & dark blue** *(3,200,000)* .30 .25
First day cover 1.00
First day cover, #146, 149 1.25
Inscription block of 4 1.40 —
Inscription block of 6, "Bundesdruckerei Berlin" imprint 20.00
First day cover, "Bundesdruckerei," margin block of 6 32.50
a. 25c **light & dark blue,** new dk blue plate/cylinder (see footnote) .30 .25
Inscription block of 4 1.40 —
b. As "a," tagged *('76)* 10.00 10.00
Inscription block of 4 45.00 —

Photo.

Perf. 11½

150 A80 $1 **aquamarine & sapphire** *(2,570,000)* 1.60 1.60
First day cover *(181,510)* 2.00
Inscription block of 4 7.50 —
Nos. 146-150 (5) 2.65 2.60

Issued: 1c, No. 149, 9/20/65; No. 149a, 11/5/65; 15c, 20c, 10/25/65; $1, 3/25/66.

First day covers of Nos. 146 and 149 total 443,964. Those of Nos. 147-148 total 457,596.

On No. 149, the dark blue "halo" of the U.N. emblem is large, overlapping the "25c." Marginal inscriptions (U.N. emblem and "1965") are 6mm in diameter, and imprint "Bundesdruckerei Berlin" is present.

On No. 149a, a new dark blue plate/cylinder was used, making the "halo" of the U.N. emblem smaller. Marginal inscriptions are 8mm in diameter and the "Bundesdruckerei" imprint is not present. No. 149b was printed from the new dark blue plate/cylinder.

See UN Offices in Geneva Nos. 5, 9 and 11.

Fields and People — A81

Design: 11c, French inscription.

Issued to emphasize the importance of the world's population growth and its problems and to call attention to population trends and development.

Printed by Government Printing Office, Austria. Panes of 50. Designed by Olav S. Mathiesen, Denmark.

1965, Nov. 29 Photo. Unwmk. *Perf. 12*

151 A81 4c **multicolored** *(1,966,033)* .25 .25
First day cover 1.00
Inscription block of 4 .40 —
152 A81 5c **multicolored** *(2,298,731)* .25 .25
First day cover 1.00
Inscription block of 4 .40 —
153 A81 11c **multicolored** *(1,557,589)* .25 .25
First day cover 1.00
First day cover, #151-153 1.50
Inscription block of 4 1.00 —
Nos. 151-153 (3) .75 .75

First day covers of Nos. 151-153 total 710,507.

Globe and Flags of UN Members — A82

Design: 15c, French inscription.

Issued to honor the World Federation of United Nations Associations.

Printed by Courvoisier S.A., Switzerland. Panes of 50. Designed by Olav S. Mathiesen, Denmark.

1966, Jan. 31 Photo. Unwmk. *Perf. 11½*

154 A82 5c **multicolored** *(2,462,215)* .25 .25
First day cover 1.00
Inscription block of 4 .40 —
155 A82 15c **multicolored** *(1,643,661)* .25 .25
First day cover 1.00
First day cover, #154-155 1.25
Inscription block of 4 1.00 —

First day covers of Nos. 154-155 total 474,154.

WHO Headquarters, Geneva — A83

Design: 11c, French inscription.

Issued to commemorate the opening of the World Health Organization Headquarters, Geneva.

Printed by Courvoisier, S.A., Switzerland. Panes of 50. Designed by Rashid-ud Din.

1966, May 26 Photo. *Perf. 12½x12*

Granite Paper

156 A83 5c **lt & dk blue, orange, green & bister** *(2,079,893)* .25 .25
First day cover 1.00
Inscription block of 4 .50 —
157 A83 11c **orange, lt & dark blue, green & bister** *(1,879,879)* .25 .25
First day cover 1.00
First day cover, #156-157 1.00
Inscription block of 4 1.00 —

First day covers of Nos. 156-157 total 466,171.

Coffee — A84

Design: 11c, Spanish inscription.

Issued to commemorate the International Coffee Agreement of 1962.

Printed by the Government Printing Bureau, Tokyo. Panes of 50. Designed by Rashid-ud Din, Pakistan.

1966, Sept. 19 Photo. *Perf. 13½x13*

158 A84 5c **orange, lt blue, green, red & dk brown** *(2,020,308)* .25 .25
First day cover 1.00
Inscription block of 4 .50 —
159 A84 11c **lt blue, yellow, green, red & dk brown** *(1,888,682)* .25 .25
First day cover 1.00
First day cover, #158-159 1.00
Inscription block of 4 1.00 —

First day covers of Nos. 158-159 total 435,886.

UN Observer — A85

Issued to honor the Peace Keeping United Nation Observers.
Printed by Courvoisier, S.A. Panes of 50. Designed by Ole S. Hamann.

1966, Oct. 24 Photo. *Perf. 11½*
Granite Paper

160 A85 15c **steel blue, orange, black & green** *(1,889,809)* .25 .25
First day cover *(255,326)* 1.00
Inscription block of 4 1.10 —

Children of Various Races — A86

Designs: 5c, Children riding in locomotive and tender. 11c, Children in open railroad car playing medical team (French inscription).
20th anniversary of the United Nations Children's Fund (UNICEF).
Printed by Thomas De La Rue & Co., Ltd. Panes of 50. Designed by Kurt Plowitz.

1966, Nov. 28 Litho. *Perf. 13x13½*

161 A86 4c **pink & multi** *(2,334,989)* .25 .25
First day cover 1.00
Inscription block of 4 .40 —
162 A86 5c **pale green & multi** *(2,746,941)* .25 .25
First day cover 1.00
Inscription block of 4 .40 —
a. Yellow omitted — —
163 A86 11c **light ultramarine & multi** *(2,123,841)* .25 .25
First day cover 1.00
First day cover, #161-163 1.00
Inscription block of 4 .90 —
b. Dark blue omitted —
Nos. 161-163 (3) .75 .75

First day covers of Nos. 161-163 total 987,271.

Hand Rolling up Sleeve and Chart Showing Progress — A87

Design: 11c, French inscription.
United Nations Development Program.
Printed by Courvoisier, S.A. Panes of 50. Designed by Olav S. Mathiesen.

1967, Jan. 23 Photo. *Perf. 12½*

164 A87 5c **green, yellow, purple & orange** *(2,204,679)* .25 .25
First day cover 1.00
Inscription block of 4 .40 —
165 A87 11c **blue, chocolate, light green & orange** *(1,946,159)* .25 .25
First day cover 1.00
First day cover, #164-165 1.00
Inscription block of 4 1.00 —

First day covers of Nos. 164-165 total 406,011.

Type of 1962 and

UN Headquarters, NY, and World Map — A88

Printed by Courvoisier, S.A. Panes of 50. Designed by Jozsef Vertel, Hungary (1½c); Renato Ferrini, Italy (5c).

1967 Photo. *Perf. 11½*

166 A88 1½c **ultramarine, black, orange & ocher** *(4,000,000)* .25 .25
First day cover *(199,751)* 1.00
Inscription block of 4 .40 —

Size: 33x23mm

167 A53 5c **red brown, brown & orange yellow** *(5,500,000)* .25 .25
First day cover *(212,544)* 1.00
Inscription block of 4 .50 —

Issue dates: 1½c, Mar. 17; 5c, Jan. 23.
For 5c of type A88, see UN Offices in Geneva No. 1.

Fireworks — A89

Design: 11c, French inscription.

Issued to honor all nations which gained independence since 1945.

Printed by Harrison & Sons, Ltd. Panes of 50. Designed by Rashid-ud Din.

1967, Mar. 17 Photo. *Perf. 14x14½*

168 A89 5c **dark blue & multi** *(2,445,955)*	.25	.25
First day cover		1.00
Inscription block of 4	.40	—
169 A89 11c **brown lake & multi** *(2,011,004)*	.25	.25
First day cover		1.00
First day cover, #168-169		1.00
Inscription block of 4	.90	—

First day covers of Nos. 168-169 total 390,499.

"Peace" — A90

UN Pavilion, EXPO '67 — A91

Designs: 5c, Justice. 10c, Fraternity. 15c, Truth.

EXPO '67, International Exhibition, Montreal, Apr. 28-Oct. 27, 1967.

Under special agreement with the Canadian Government Nos. 170-174 were valid for postage only on mail posted at the UN pavilion during the Fair. The denominations are expressed in Canadian currency.

Printed by British American Bank Note Co., Ltd., Ottawa. The 8c was designed by Olav S. Mathiesen after a photograph by Michael Drummond. The others were adapted by Ole S. Hamann from reliefs by Ernest Cormier on doors of General Assembly Hall, presented to UN by Canada.

1967, Apr. 28 Engr. & Litho. *Perf. 11*

170 A90 4c **red & red brown** *(2,464,813)*	.25	.25
First day cover		1.00
Inscription block of 4	.40	—
171 A90 5c **blue & red brown** *(2,177,073)*	.25	.25
First day cover		1.00
Inscription block of 4	.40	—
Litho.		
172 A91 8c **multicolored** *(2,285,440)*	.25	.25
First day cover		1.00
Inscription block of 4	.50	—
Engr. and Litho.		
173 A90 10c **green & red brown** *(1,955,352)*	.25	.25
First day cover		1.00
Inscription block of 4	.80	—
174 A90 15c **dark brown & red brown** *(1,899,185)*	.25	.25
First day cover		1.00
First day cover, #170-174		1.00
Inscription block of 4	.85	
Nos. 170-174 (5)	1.25	1.25

First day covers of Nos. 170-174 total 901,625.

Luggage Tags and UN Emblem — A92

Issued to publicize International Tourist Year, 1967.

Printed by Government Printing Office, Berlin. Panes of 50. Designed by David Dewhurst.

1967, June 19 Litho. *Perf. 14*

175 A92 5c **reddish brown & multi** *(2,593,782)*	.25	.25
First day cover		1.00
Inscription block of 4	.40	—
176 A92 15c **ultramarine & multi** *(1,940,457)*	.25	.25
First day cover		1.00
First day cover, #175-176		1.00
Inscription block of 4	1.00	—

First day covers of Nos. 175-176 total 382,886.

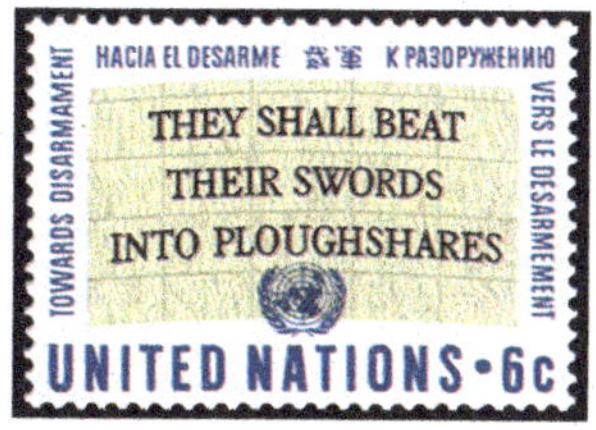

Quotation from Isaiah 2:4 — A93

Design: 13c, French inscription.

Issued to publicize the UN General Assembly's resolutions on general and complete disarmament and for suspension of nuclear and thermonuclear tests.

Printed by Heraclio Fournier S.A., Spain. Panes of 50. Designed by Ole Hamann.

1967, Oct. 24 Photo. *Perf. 14*

177 A93 6c **ultramarine, yellow, gray & brown** *(2,462,277)*	.25	.25
First day cover		1.00
Inscription block of 4	.50	—
178 A93 13c **magenta, yellow, gray & brown** *(2,055,541)*	.25	.25
First day cover		1.00
First day cover, #177-178		1.00
Inscription block of 4	1.00	—

First day covers of Nos. 177-178 total 403,414.

Art at UN Issue

Miniature Sheet

Stained Glass Memorial Window by Marc Chagall, at UN Headquarters — A94

"The Kiss of Peace" by Marc Chagall — A95

Printed by Joh. Enschede and Sons, Netherlands. No. 180 issued in panes of 50. Design adapted by Ole Hamann from photograph by Hans Lippmann.

Sizes: a, 41x46mm. b, 24x46mm. c, 41x33½mm. d, 36x33½mm. e, 29x33½mm. f, 41½x47mm.

1967, Nov. 17 **Litho.** ***Rouletted 9***

179 A94 6c Sheet of 6, #a.-f. *(3,178,656)* .40 .40
First day cover 1.00

Perf. 13x13½

180 A95 6c **multicolored** *(3,438,497)* .25 .25
First day cover 1.00
Inscription block of 4 .50 —

No. 179 contains six 6c stamps, each rouletted on 3 sides, imperf. on fourth side. Size: 124x80mm. On Nos. 179a-179c, "United Nations 6c" appears at top; on Nos. 179d-179f, at bottom. No. 179f includes name "Marc Chagall."

First day covers of Nos. 179-180 total 617,225.

Globe and Major UN Organs — A96

Design: 13c, French inscriptions.
Issued to honor the United Nations Secretariat.
Printed by Courvoisier, S. A., Switzerland. Panes of 50. Designed by Rashid-ud Din.

1968, Jan. 16 **Photo.** ***Perf. 11½***

181 A96 6c **multicolored** *(2,772,965)* .25 .25
First day cover 1.00
Inscription block of 4 .50 —
182 A96 13c **multicolored** *(2,461,992)* .25 .25
First day cover 1.00
First day cover, #181-182 1.00
Inscription block of 4 1.00 —

First day covers of Nos. 181-182 total 411,119.

Art at UN Issue

Statue by Henrik Starcke — A97

The 6c is part of the "Art at the UN" series. The 75c belongs to the regular definitive series. The teakwood Starcke statue, which stands in the Trusteeship Council Chamber, represents mankind's search for freedom and happiness.
Printed by Courvoisier, S.A., Switzerland. Panes of 50.

1968, Mar. 1 **Photo.** ***Perf. 11½***

183 A97 6c **blue & multi** *(2,537,320)* .25 .25
First day cover 1.00
Inscription block of 4 .50 —
184 A97 75c **rose lake & multi** *(2,300,000)* 1.10 .90
First day cover 1.25
First day cover, #183-184 5.00
Inscription block of 4 5.00 —

First day covers of Nos. 183-184 total 413,286.
See UN Offices in Geneva No. 13.

Factories and Chart — A98

Design: 13c, French inscription ("ONUDI," etc.).
Issued to publicize the UN Industrial Development Organization.
Printed by Canadian Bank Note Co., Ltd., Ottawa. Panes of 50. Designed by Ole Hamann.

1968, Apr. 18 **Litho.** ***Perf. 12***

185 A98 6c **greenish blue, lt greenish blue, black & dull claret** *(2,439,656)* .25 .25
First day cover 1.00
Inscription block of 4 .50 —
186 A98 13c **dull red brown, light red brown, black & ultra** *(2,192,453)* .25 .25
First day cover 1.00
First day cover, #185-186 1.00
Inscription block of 4 .80 —

First day covers of Nos. 185-186 total 396,447.

UN Headquarters — A99

Printed by Aspioti Elka-Chrome Mines, Ltd., Athens. Panes of 50. Designed by Olav S. Mathiesen.

1968, May 31 **Litho.** ***Perf. 12x13½***

187 A99 6c **green, blue, black & gray** *(4,000,000)* .25 .25
First day cover *(241,179)* 1.00
Inscription block of 4 .50 —

Radarscope and Globe — A100

Design: 20c, French inscription.
Issued to publicize World Weather Watch, a new weather system directed by the World Meteorological Organization.
Printed by the Government Printing Bureau, Tokyo. Designed by George A. Gundersen and George Fanais, Canada.

1968, Sept. 19 **Photo.** ***Perf. 13x13½***

188 A100 6c **green, black, ocher, red & blue** *(2,245,078)* .25 .25
First day cover 1.00
Inscription block of 4 .50 —
189 A100 20c **lilac, black, ocher, red & blue** *(2,069,966)* .30 .25
First day cover 1.00
First day cover, #188-189 1.00
Inscription block of 4 1.40 —

First day covers of Nos. 188-189 total 620,510.

Human Rights Flame — A101

Design: 13c, French inscription.
Issued for International Human Rights Year, 1968.
Printed by Harrison & Sons, Ltd., England. Designed by Robert Perrot, France.

1968, Nov. 22 Photo.; Foil Embossed *Perf. 12½*

190 A101 6c **bright blue, deep ultra & gold** *(2,394,235)* .25 .25
First day cover 1.00
Inscription block of 4 .50 —
191 A101 13c **rose red, dark red & gold** *(2,284,838)* .25 .25
First day cover 1.00
First day cover, #190-191 1.00
Inscription block of 4 .90 —

First day covers of Nos. 190-191 total 519,012.

Books and UN Emblem — A102

Design: 13c, French inscription in center, denomination panel at bottom.
United Nations Institute for Training and Research (UNITAR).
Printed by the Government Printing Bureau, Tokyo. Panes of 50. Designed by Olav S. Mathiesen.

1969, Feb. 10 Litho. *Perf. 13½*

192 A102 6c **yellow green & multi** *(2,436,559)* .25 .25
First day cover 1.00
Inscription block of 4 .40 —
193 A102 13c **bluish lilac & multi** *(1,035,151)* .25 .25
First day cover 1.00
First day cover, #192-193 1.00
Inscription block of 4 1.00 —

First day covers of Nos. 192-193 total 439,608.

UN Building, Santiago, Chile — A103

Design: 15c, Spanish inscription.
The UN Building in Santiago, Chile, is the seat of the UN Economic Commission for Latin America and of the Latin American Institute for Economic and Social Planning.
Printed by Government Printing Office, Berlin. Panes of 50. Design by Ole Hamann, adapted from a photograph.

1969, Mar. 14 Litho. *Perf. 14*

194 A103 6c **light blue, violet blue & light green** *(2,543,992)* .25 .25
First day cover 1.00
Inscription block of 4 .40 —
195 A103 15c **pink, cream & red brown** *(2,030,733)* .25 .25
First day cover 1.00
First day cover, #194-195 1.00
Inscription block of 4 1.00 —

First day covers of Nos. 194-195 total 398,227.

"UN" and UN Emblem — A104

Printed by Government Printing Bureau, Tokyo. Panes of 50. Designed by Leszek Holdanowicz and Marek Freudenreich, Poland.

1969, Mar. 14 Photo. *Perf. 13½*

196 A104 13c **bright blue, black & gold** *(4,000,000)* .25 .25
First day cover *(177,793)* 1.00
Inscription block of 4 1.00 —

See UN Offices in Geneva No. 7.

UN Emblem and Scales of — A105

Design: 13c, French inscription.
20th anniversary session of the UN International Law Commission.
Printed by Courvoisier S.A., Switzerland. Panes of 50. Designed by Robert Perrot, France.

Granite Paper

1969, Apr. 21 Photo. *Perf. 11½*

197 A105 6c **bright green, ultra & gold** *(2,501,492)* .25 .25
First day cover 1.00
Inscription block of 4 .50 —
198 A105 13c **crimson, lilac & gold** *(1,966,004)* .25 .25
First day cover 1.00
First day cover, #197-198 1.00
Inscription block of 4 .90 —

First day covers of Nos. 197-198 total 439,324.

Allegory of Labor, Emblems of UN and ILO — A106

Design: 20c, French inscription.
Printed by Government Printing Bureau, Tokyo. Panes of 50. Designed by Nejat M. Gur, Turkey.
Issued to publicize "Labor and Development" and to commemorate the 50th anniversary of the International Labor Organization.

1969, June 5 **Photo.** ***Perf. 13***

199 A106 6c **blue, deep blue, yellow & gold** *(2,078,381)* .25 .25
First day cover 1.00
Inscription block of 4 .50 —
200 A106 20c **orange vermilion, magenta, yellow & gold** *(1,751,100)* .25 .25
First day cover 1.00
First day cover, #199-200 1.00
Inscription block of 4 1.40 —

First day covers of Nos. 199-200 total 514,155.

Art at UN Issue

Ostrich, Tunisian Mosaic, 3rd Century — A107

Design: 13c, Pheasant; French inscription.
The mosaic "The Four Seasons and the Genius of the Year" was found at Haidra, Tunisia. It is now at the Delegates' North Lounge, UN Headquarters, New York.
Printed by Heraclio Fournier, S. A., Spain. Panes of 50. Designed by Olav S. Mathiesen.

1969, Nov. 21 **Photo.** ***Perf. 14***

201 A107 6c **blue & multi** *(2,280,702)* .25 .25
First day cover 1.00
Inscription block of 4 .40 —
202 A107 13c **red & multi** *(1,918,554)* .25 .25
First day cover 1.00
First day cover, #201-202 1.00
Inscription block of 4 1.00 —

First day covers of Nos. 201-202 total 612,981.

Art at UN Issue

Peace Bell, Gift of Japanese — A108

Design: 25c, French inscription.
The Peace Bell was a gift of the people of Japan in 1954, cast from donated coins and metals. It is housed in a Japanese cypress structure at UN Headquarters, New York.
Printed by Government Printing Bureau, Tokyo. Panes of 50. Designed by Ole Hamann.

1970, Mar. 13 **Photo.** ***Perf. 13½x13***

203 A108 6c **violet blue & multi** *(2,604,253)* .25 .25
First day cover 1.00
Inscription block of 4 .50 —
204 A108 25c **claret & multi** *(2,090,185)* .30 .25
First day cover 1.00
First day cover, #203-204 1.00
Inscription block of 4 1.50 —

First day covers of Nos. 203-204 total 502,384.

Mekong River, Power Lines and Map of Mekong Delta — A109

Design: 13c, French inscription.
Issued to publicize the Lower Mekong Basin Development project under UN auspices.
Printed by Heraclio Fournier, S.A., Spain. Panes of 50. Designed by Ole Hamann.

1970, Mar. 13 ***Perf. 14***

205 A109 6c **dark blue & multi** *(2,207,309)* .25 .25
First day cover 1.00
Inscription block of 4 .40 —
206 A109 13c **deep plum & multi** *(1,889,023)* .25 .25
First day cover 1.00
First day cover, #205-206 1.00
Inscription block of 4 1.00 —

First day covers of Nos. 205-206 total 522,218.

"Fight Cancer" — A110

Design: 13c, French inscription.
Issued to publicize the fight against cancer in connection with the 10th International Cancer Congress of the International Union Against Cancer, Houston, Texas, May 22-29.
Printed by Government Printing Office, Berlin. Panes of 50. Designed by Leonard Mitchell.

1970, May 22 **Litho.** ***Perf. 14***

207 A110 6c **blue & black** *(2,157,742)* .25 .25
First day cover 1.00
Inscription block of 4 .40 —
208 A110 13c **olive & black** *(1,824,714)* .25 .25
First day cover 1.00
First day cover, #207-208 1.00
Inscription block of 4 .90 —

First day covers of Nos. 207-208 total 444,449.

UN Emblem and Olive Branch — A111

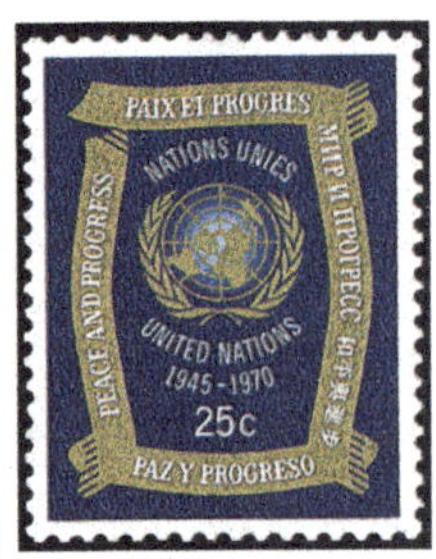

UN Emblem — A112

Design: 13c, French inscription.

25th anniv. of the UN. First day covers were postmarked at UN Headquarters, NY, and at San Francisco.

Printed by Courvoisier, S.A., Switzerland. Designed by Ole Hamann and Olav S. Mathiesen (souvenir sheet).

1970, June 26 Photo. *Perf. 11½*

209 A111 6c **red, gold, dark & light blue** *(2,365,229)* .25 .25
First day cover 1.00
Inscription block of 4 .40 —

210 A111 13c **dark blue, gold, green & red** *(1,861,613)* .25 .25
First day cover 1.00
Inscription block of 4 .90 —

Perf. 12½

211 A112 25c **dark blue, gold & light blue** *(1,844,669)* .35 .25
First day cover 1.00
First day cover, #209-211 1.25
Inscription block of 4 1.50 —
Nos. 209-211 (3) .85 .75

Souvenir Sheet

Imperf

212 Sheet of 3 *(1,923,639)* .80 .80
a. A111 6c **red, gold & multicolored** .25 .25
b. A111 13c **violet blue, gold & multi** .25 .25
c. A112 25c **violet blue, gold & light blue** .30 .30
First day cover 1.00

No. 212 contains 3 imperf. stamps, gold border and violet blue marginal inscription. Size: 94½x78mm.

First day covers of Nos. 209-212 total: New York, 846,389; San Francisco, 471,100.

Scales, Olive Branch and Symbol of Progress — A113

Design: 13c, French inscription.

Issued to publicize "Peace, Justice and Progress" in connection with the 25th anniversary of the United Nations.

Printed by Government Printing Bureau, Tokyo. Panes of 50. Designed by Ole Hamann.

1970, Nov. 20 Photo. *Perf. 13½*

213 A113 6c **gold & multi** *(1,921,441)* .25 .25
First day cover 1.00
Inscription block of 4 .50 —

214 A113 13c **silver & multi** *(1,663,669)* .25 .25
First day cover 1.00
First day cover, #213-214 1.00
Inscription block of 4 1.00 —

First day covers of Nos. 213-214 total 521,419.

Sea Bed, School of Fish and Underwater Research — A114

Issued to publicize peaceful uses of the sea bed.

Printed by Setelipaino, Finland. Panes of 50. Designed by Pentti Rahikainen, Finland.

1971, Jan. 25 Photo. & Engr. *Perf. 13*

215 A114 6c **blue & multi** *(2,354,179)* .25 .25
First day cover *(405,554)* 1.00
Inscription block of 4 .50 —

See UN Offices in Geneva No. 15.

Refugees, Sculpture by Kaare K. Nygaard — A115

International support for refugees.

Printed by Joh. Enschede and Sons, Netherlands. Panes of 50. Designed by Dr. Kaare K. Nygaard and Martin J. Weber.

1971, Mar. 2 Litho. *Perf. 13x12½*

216 A115 6c **brown, ocher & black** *(2,247,232)* .25 .25
First day cover 1.00
Inscription block of 4 .40 —

217 A115 13c **ultramarine, greenish blue & black** *(1,890,048)* .25 .25
First day cover 1.00
First day cover, #216-217 1.00
Inscription block of 4 1.00 —

First day covers of Nos. 216-217 total 564,785.

See UN Offices in Geneva No. 16.

Wheat and Globe — A116

Publicizing the UN World Food Program.

Printed by Heraclio Fournier, S.A., Spain. Panes of 50. Designed by Olav S. Mathiesen.

1971, Apr. 13 Photo. *Perf. 14*

218 A116 13c **red & multicolored** *(1,968,542)* .25 .25
First day cover *(409,404)* 1.00
Inscription block of 4 1.00 —

See UN Offices in Geneva No. 17.

UPU Headquarters, Bern — A117

Opening of new Universal Postal Union Headquarters, Bern.

Printed by Courvoisier, S.A. Panes of 50. Designed by Olav S. Mathiesen.

1971, May 28 **Photo.** ***Perf. 11½***

219 A117 20c **brown orange & multi** *(1,857,841)* .30 .25
First day cover *(375,119)* 1.00
Inscription block of 4 1.30 —

See UN Offices in Geneva No. 18.

A118

"Eliminate Racial Discrimination" A119

International Year Against Racial Discrimination.
Printed by Government Printing Bureau, Tokyo. Panes of 50. Designers: Daniel Gonzague (8c); Ole Hamann (13c).

1971, Sept. 21 **Photo.** ***Perf. 13½***

220 A118 8c **yellow green & multi** *(2,324,349)* .25 .25
First day cover 1.00
Inscription block of 4 .40 —
221 A119 13c **blue & multi** *(1,852,093)* .25 .25
First day cover 1.00
First day cover, #220-221 1.00
Inscription block of 4 1.00 —

First day covers of Nos. 220-221 total 461,103.
See UN Offices in Geneva Nos. 19-20.

UN Headquarters, New York — A120

UN Emblem and Symbolic Flags — A121

No. 222 printed by Heraclio Fournier, S.A., Spain. No. 223 printed by Government Printing Bureau, Tokyo. Panes of 50. Designers: O. S. Mathiesen (8c); Robert Perrot (60c).

1971, Oct. 22 **Photo.** ***Perf. 13½***

222 A120 8c **violet blue & multi** *(5,600,000)* .25 .25
First day cover 1.00
Inscription block of 4 .60 —

Perf. 13

223 A121 60c **ultra & multi** *(3,500,000)+* .80 .80
First day cover 1.25
First day cover, #222-223 2.50
Inscription block of 4 3.75 —

First day covers of Nos. 222-223 total 336,013.

Maia, by Pablo Picasso — A122

To publicize the UN International School.
Printed by Courvoisier, S.A. Panes of 50. Designed by Ole Hamann.

1971, Nov. 19 **Photo.** ***Perf. 11½***

224 A122 8c **olive & multi** *(2,668,214)* .25 .25
First day cover 1.00
Inscription block of 4 .50 —
225 A122 21c **ultra & multi** *(2,040,754)* .25 .25
First day cover 1.00
First day cover, #224-225 1.50
Inscription block of 4 1.50 —

First day covers of Nos. 224-225 total 579,594.
See UN Offices in Geneva No. 21.

Letter Changing Hands — A123

Printed by Bundesdruckerei, Berlin. Panes of 50. Designed by Olav S. Mathiesen.

1972, Jan. 5 **Litho.** ***Perf. 14***

226 A123 95c **carmine & multi** *(2,000,000)* 1.30 1.10
First day cover *(188,193)* 1.25
Inscription block of 4 5.75 —

"No More Nuclear Weapons" A124

To promote non-proliferation of nuclear weapons.
Printed by Heraclio Fournier, S. A., Spain. Panes of 50. Designed by Arne Johnson, Norway.

1972, Feb. 14 **Photo.** ***Perf. 13½x14***

227 A124 8c **dull rose, black, blue & gray** *(2,311,515)* .25 .25
First day cover *(268,789)* 1.00
Inscription block of 4 .60 —

See UN Offices in Geneva No. 23.

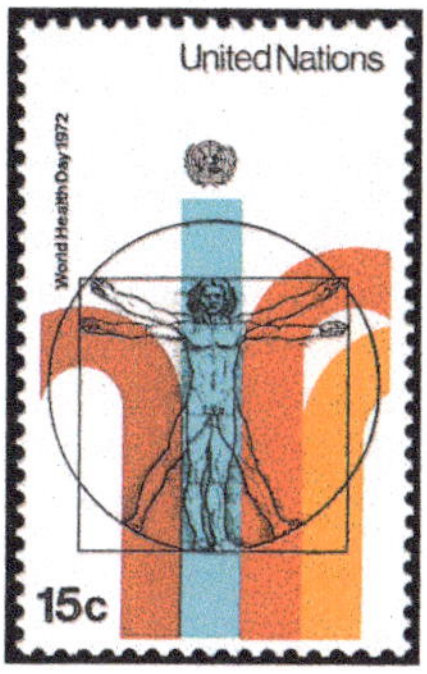

Proportions of Man, by Leonardo da Vinci — A125

World Health Day, Apr. 7.
Printed by Setelipaino, Finland. Panes of 50. Designed by George Hamori.

1972, Apr. 7 Litho. & Engr. *Perf. 13x13½*

228 A125 15c **black & multi** *(1,788,962)* .25 .25
First day cover *(322,724)* 1.00
Inscription block of 4 1.00 —

See UN Offices in Geneva No. 24.

"Human Environment" — A126

UN Conf. on Human Environment, Stockholm, June 5-16, 1972.
Printed by Joh. Enschede and Sons, Netherlands. Panes of 50. Designed by Robert Perrot.

1972, June 5 Litho. & Embossed *Perf. 12½x14*

229 A126 8c **red, buff, green & blue** *(2,124,604)* .25 .25
First day cover 1.00
Inscription block of 4 .50 —
230 A126 15c **blue green, buff, green & blue** *(1,589,943)* .25 .25
First day cover 1.00
First day cover, #229-230 1.00
Inscription block of 4 1.10 —

First day covers of Nos. 229-230 total 437,222.
See UN Offices in Geneva Nos. 25-26.

"Europe" and UN Emblem — A127

Economic Commission for Europe, 25th anniversary.
Printed by Government Printing Bureau, Tokyo. Panes of 50. Designed by Angel Medina Medina.

1972, Sept. 11 Litho. *Perf. 13x13½*

231 A127 21c **yellow brown & multi** *(1,748,675)* .30 .30
First day cover *(271,128)* 1.00
Inscription block of 4 1.50 —

See UN Offices in Geneva No. 27.

Art at UN Issue

The Five Continents by José Maria Sert — A128

Design shows part of ceiling mural of the Council Hall, Palais des Nations, Geneva. It depicts the five continents joining in space.
Printed by Courvoisier, S. A. Panes of 50. Designed by Ole Hamann.

1972, Nov. 17 Photo. *Perf. 12x12½*

232 A128 8c **gold, brown & golden brown** *(2,573,478)* .25 .25
First day cover 1.00
Inscription block of 4 .50 —
233 A128 15c **gold, blue green & brown** *(1,768,432)* .25 .25
First day cover 1.00
First day cover, #232-233 1.00
Inscription block of 4 1.10 —

First day covers of Nos. 232-233 total 589,817.
See UN Offices in Geneva Nos. 28-29.

Olive Branch and Broken Sword — A129

Disarmament Decade, 1970-79.
Printed by Ajans-Turk, Turkey. Panes of 50. Designed by Kurt Plowitz.

1973, Mar. 9 Litho. *Perf. 13½x13*

234 A129 8c **blue & multi** *(2,272,716)* .25 .25
First day cover 1.00
Inscription block of 4 .50 —
235 A129 15c **lilac rose & multi** *(1,643,712)* .25 .25
First day cover 1.00
First day cover, #234-235 1.00
Inscription block of 4 1.40 —

First day covers of Nos. 234-235 total 548,336.
See UN Offices in Geneva Nos. 30-31.

Poppy Capsule and Skull — A130

Fight against drug abuse.
Printed by Heraclio Fournier, S.A., Spain. Panes of 50. Designed by George Hamori.

1973, Apr. 13	**Photo.**	***Perf. 13½***	
236 A130 8c **deep orange & multi** *(1,846,780)*		.25	.25
First day cover			1.00
Inscription block of 4		.50	—
237 A130 15c **pink & multi** *(1,466,806)*		.25	.25
First day cover			1.00
First day cover, #236-237			1.00
Inscription block of 4		1.40	—

First day covers of Nos. 236-237 total 394,468.
See UN Offices in Geneva No. 32.

Honeycomb — A131

5th anniversary of the United Nations Volunteer Program.
Printed by Heraclio Fournier, S.A., Spain. Panes of 50. Designed by Courvoisier, S.A.

1973, May 25	**Photo.**	***Perf. 14***	
238 A131 8c **olive bister & multi** *(1,868,176)*		.25	.25
First day cover			1.00
Inscription block of 4		.50	—
239 A131 21c **gray blue & multi** *(1,530,114)*		.30	.30
First day cover			1.00
First day cover, #238-239			1.00
Inscription block of 4		1.50	—

First day covers of Nos. 238-239 total 396,517.
See UN Offices in Geneva No. 33.

Map of Africa with Namibia — A132

To publicize Namibia (South-West Africa) for which the UN General Assembly ended the mandate of South Africa and established the UN Council for Namibia to administer the territory until independence.
Printed by Heraclio Fournier, S.A., Spain. Panes of 50. Designed by George Hamori.

1973, Oct. 1	**Photo.**	***Perf. 14***	
240 A132 8c **emerald & multi** *(1,775,260)*		.25	.25
First day cover			1.00
Inscription block of 4		.60	—
241 A132 15c **bright rose & multi** *(1,687,782)*		.25	.25
First day cover			1.00
First day cover, #240-241			1.00
Inscription block of 4		1.40	—

First day covers of Nos. 240-241 total 385,292.
See UN Offices in Geneva No. 34.

UN Emblem and Human Rights Flame — A133

25th anniversary of the adoption and proclamation of the Universal Declaration of Human Rights.
Printed by Government Printing Bureau, Tokyo. Panes of 50. Designed by Alfred Guerra.

1973, Nov. 16	**Photo.**	***Perf. 13½***	
242 A133 8c **deep carmine & multi** *(2,026,245)*		.25	.25
First day cover			1.00
Inscription block of 4		.60	—
243 A133 21c **blue green & multi** *(1,558,201)*		.25	.25
First day cover			1.00
First day cover, #242-243			1.00
Inscription block of 4		1.40	—

First day covers of Nos. 242-243 total 398,511.
See UN Offices in Geneva Nos. 35-36.

ILO Headquarters, Geneva — A134

New Headquarters of International Labor Organization.
Printed by Heraclio Fournier, S.A., Spain. Panes of 50. Designed by Henry Bencsath.

1974, Jan. 11	**Photo.**	***Perf. 14***	
244 A134 10c **ultra & multi** *(1,734,423)*		.25	.25
First day cover			1.00
Inscription block of 4		.75	—
245 A134 21c **blue green & multi** *(1,264,447)*		.30	.25
First day cover			1.00
First day cover, #244-245			1.00
Inscription block of 4		1.50	—

First day covers of Nos. 244-245 total 282,284.
See UN Offices in Geneva Nos. 37-38.

UPU Emblem and Post Horn Encircling Globe — A135

Centenary of Universal Postal Union.
Printed by Ashton-Potter Ltd., Canada. Panes of 50. Designed by Arne Johnson.

1974, Mar. 22	**Litho.**	***Perf. 12½***	
246 A135 10c **gold & multi** *(2,104,919)*		.25	.25
First day cover *(342,774)*			1.00
Inscription block of 4		1.00	—

See UN Offices in Geneva Nos. 39-40.

Art at UN Issue

Peace Mural, by Candido Portinari — A136

The mural, a gift of Brazil, is in the Delegates' Lobby, General Assembly Building.
Printed by Heraclio Fournier, S.A., Spain. Panes of 50. Design adapted by Ole Hamann.

1974, May 6 **Photo.** ***Perf. 14***

247 A136 10c **gold & multi** *(1,769,342)*	.25	.25
First day cover		1.00
Inscription block of 4	.75	—
248 A136 18c **ultra & multi** *(1,477,500)*	.35	.30
First day cover		1.00
First day cover, #247-248		1.00
Inscription block of 4	1.40	—

First day covers of Nos. 247-248 total 271,440.
See UN Offices in Geneva Nos. 41-42.

Dove and UN Emblem — A137

UN Headquarters — A138

Globe, UN Emblem, Flags — A139

Printed by Heraclio Fournier, S.A., Spain. Panes of 50.
Designed by Nejat M. Gur (2c); Olav S. Mathiesen (10c); Henry Bencsath (18c).

1974, June 10 **Photo.** ***Perf. 14***

249 A137 2c **dark & light blue** *(6,900,000)*	.25	.25
First day cover		1.00
Inscription block of 4	.25	—
250 A138 10c **multicolored** *(4,000,000)*	.25	.25
First day cover		1.00
Inscription block of 4	.60	—
251 A139 18c **multicolored** *(2,300,000)*	.25	.25
First day cover		1.00
First day cover, #249-251		1.00
Inscription block of 4	1.40	—
Nos. 249-251 (3)	.75	.75

First day covers of Nos. 249-251 total 307,402.
+ Printing orders to Feb. 1990.

Children of the World — A140

World Population Year
Printed by Heraclio Fournier, S.A., Spain. Panes of 50. Designed by Henry Bencsath.

1974, Oct. 18 **Photo.** ***Perf. 14***

252 A140 10c **light blue & multi** *(1,762,595)*	.25	.25
First day cover		1.00
Inscription block of 4	1.00	—
253 A140 18c **lilac & multi** *(1,321,574)*	.35	.25
First day cover		1.00
First day cover, #252-253		1.00
Inscription block of 4	1.50	—

First day covers of Nos. 253-254 total 354,306.
See UN Offices in Geneva Nos. 43-44.

Law of the Sea — A141

Declaration of UN General Assembly that the sea bed is common heritage of mankind, reserved for peaceful purposes.
Printed by Heraclio Fournier, S.A., Spain. Panes of 50. Designed by Asher Kalderon.

1974, Nov. 22 **Photo.** ***Perf. 14***

254 A141 10c **green & multi** *(1,621,328)*	.25	.25
First day cover		1.00
Inscription block of 4	.75	—
255 A141 26c **orange red & multi** *(1,293,084)*	.35	.30
First day cover		1.00
First day cover, #254-255		1.00
Inscription block of 4	1.60	—

First day covers of Nos. 254-255 total 280,686.
See UN Offices in Geneva No. 45.

Satellite and Globe — A142

Peaceful uses (meteorology, industry, fishing, communications) of outer space.
Printed by Setelipaino, Finland. Panes of 50. Designed by Henry Bencsath.

1975, Mar. 14 **Litho.** ***Perf. 13***

256 A142 10c **multicolored** *(1,681,115)*	.25	.25
First day cover		1.00
Inscription block of 4	.75	—

257 A142 26c **multicolored** *(1,463,130)* .35 .30
First day cover 1.00
First day cover, #256-257 1.00
Inscription block of 4 1.50 —

First day covers of Nos. 256-257 total 330,316.
See UN Offices in Geneva Nos. 46-47.

Equality Between Men and Women — A143

International Women's Year
Printed by Questa Colour Security Printers, Ltd., England. Panes of 50. Designed by Asher Kalderon and Esther Kurti.

1975, May 9 **Litho.** ***Perf. 15***

258 A143 10c **multicolored** *(1,402,542)* .25 .25
First day cover 1.00
Inscription block of 4 .75 —
259 A143 18c **multicolored** *(1,182,321)* .35 .30
First day cover 1.00
First day cover, #258-259 1.00
Inscription block of 4 1.50 —

First day covers of Nos. 258-259 total 285,466.
See UN Offices in Geneva Nos. 48-49.

UN Flag and "XXX" — A144

30th anniversary of the United Nations.
Printed by Ashton-Potter, Ltd., Canada. Nos. 260-261 panes of 50. Stamps designed by Asher Calderon, sheets by Olav S. Mathiesen.

1975, June 26 **Litho.** ***Perf. 13***

260 A144 10c **olive bister & multi** *(1,904,545)* .25 .25
First day cover 1.00
Inscription block of 4 .75 —
261 A144 26c **purple & multi** *(1,547,766)* .40 .35
First day cover 1.00
First day cover, #260-261 1.00
Inscription block of 4 1.90 —

Souvenir Sheet

Imperf

262 Sheet of 2 *(1,196,578)* .60 .50
a. A144 10c **olive bister & multicolored** .25 .25
b. A144 26c **purple & multicolored** .35 .25
First day cover 1.00

No. 262 has blue and bister margin with inscription and UN emblem.
First day covers of Nos. 260-262 total: New York 477,912; San Francisco, 237,159.
See Offices in Geneva Nos. 50-52.

Hand Reaching up over Map of Africa and Namibia — A145

"Namibia-United Nations direct responsibility." See note after No. 241.
Printed by Heraclio Fournier S.A., Spain. Panes of 50. Designed by Henry Bencsath.

1975, Sept. 22 **Photo.** ***Perf. 13½***

263 A145 10c **multicolored** *(1,354,374)* .25 .25
First day cover 1.00
Inscription block of 4 .75 —
264 A145 18c **multicolored** *(1,243,157)* .30 .30
First day cover 1.00
First day cover, #263-264 1.00
Inscription block of 4 1.50 —

First day covers of Nos. 263-264 total 281,631.
See UN Offices in Geneva Nos. 53-54.

Wild Rose Growing from Barbed Wire — A146

United Nations Peace-keeping Operations
Printed by Setelipaino, Finland. Panes of 50. Designed by Mrs. Eeva Oivo.

1975, Nov. 21 **Engr.** ***Perf. 12½***

265 A146 13c **ultramarine** *(1,628,039)* .25 .25
First day cover 1.00
Inscription block of 4 1.00 —
266 A146 26c **rose carmine** *(1,195,580)* .40 .40
First day cover 1.00
First day cover, #265-266 1.00
Inscription block of 4 1.90 —

First day covers of Nos. 265-266 total 303,711.
See UN Offices in Geneva Nos. 55-56.

Symbolic Flags Forming Dove — A147

UN Emblem — A149

People of All Races — A148

United Nations Flag — A150

Dove and Rainbow — A151

Printed by Ashton-Potter, Ltd., Canada (3c, 4c, 30c, 50c), and Questa Colour Security Printers, Ltd., England (9c). Panes of 50.
Designed by Waldemar Andrzesewski (3c); Arne Johnson (4c); George Hamori (9c, 30c); Arthur Congdon (50c).

1976 Litho. *Perf. 13x13½, 13½x13*

267	A147	3c **multicolored** *(4,000,000)*	.25	.25
		First day cover		1.00
		Inscription block of 4	.40	—
268	A148	4c **multicolored** *(4,000,000)*	.25	.25
		First day cover		1.00
		Inscription block of 4	.50	—

Photo.

Perf. 14

269	A149	9c **multicolored** *(3,270,000)+*	.25	.25
		First day cover		1.00
		Inscription block of 4	.70	—

Litho.

Perf. 13x13½

270	A150	30c **blue, emerald & black** *(2,500,000)*	.35	.35
		First day cover		2.00
		Inscription block of 4	1.90	—
271	A151	50c **yellow green & multi** *(2,000,000)*	.65	.65
		First day cover		1.00
		First day cover, #267-268, 270-271		1.50
		Inscription block of 4	3.50	—
		Nos. 267-271 (5)	1.75	1.75

Issue dates: 3c, 4c, 30c, 50c, Jan. 6; 9c, Nov. 19.
First day covers of Nos. 267-268, 270-271 total 355,165; of Nos. 269 and 280 total 366,556.
See UN Offices in Vienna No. 8.

Interlocking Bands and UN Emblem — A152

World Federation of United Nations Associations.
Printed by Heraclio Fournier, S.A., Spain. Panes of 50. Designed by George Hamori.

1976, Mar. 12 Photo. *Perf. 14*

272	A152	13c **blue, green & black** *(1,331,556)*	.25	.25
		First day cover		1.00
		Inscription block of 4	.80	—
273	A152	26c **green & multi** *(1,050,145)*	.35	.30
		First day cover		1.00
		First day cover, #272-273		1.00
		Inscription block of 4	1.60	—

First day covers of Nos. 272-273 total 300,775.
See UN Offices in Geneva No. 57.

Cargo, Globe and Graph — A153

UN Conference on Trade and Development (UNCTAD), Nairobi, Kenya, May 1976.
Printed by Courvoisier, S.A. Panes of 50. Designed by Henry Bencsath.

1976, Apr. 23 Photo. *Perf. 11½*

274	A153	13c **deep magenta & multi** *(1,317,900)*	.25	.25
		First day cover		1.00
		Inscription block of 4	.80	—
275	A153	31c **dull blue & multi** *(1,216,959)*	.40	.30
		First day cover		1.00
		First day cover, #274-275		1.00
		Inscription block of 4	1.90	—

First day covers of Nos. 274-275 total 234,657.
See UN Offices in Geneva No. 58.

Houses Around Globe — A154

Habitat, UN Conference on Human Settlements, Vancouver, Canada, May 31-June 11.
Printed by Heraclio Fournier, S.A., Spain. Panes of 50. Designed by Eliezer Weishoff.

1976, May 28 **Photo.** ***Perf. 14***

276 A154 13c **red brown & multi** *(1,346,589)* .25 .25
First day cover 1.00
Inscription block of 4 .75 —
277 A154 25c **green & multi** *(1,057,924)* .40 .30
First day cover 1.00
First day cover, #276-277 1.00
Inscription block of 4 1.75 —

First day covers of Nos. 276-277 total 232,754.
See UN Offices in Geneva Nos. 59-60.

Magnifying Glass, Sheet of Stamps, UN Emblem — A155

United Nations Postal Administration, 25th anniversary.
Printed by Courvoisier, S.A. Designed by Henry Bencsath.

1976, Oct. 8 **Photo.** ***Perf. 11½***

278 A155 13c **blue & multi** *(1,996,309)* .25 .25
First day cover 1.00
Inscription block of 4 .90 —
279 A155 31c **green & multi** *(1,767,465)* 1.00 1.00
First day cover 1.50
First day cover, #278-279 2.00
Inscription block of 4 6.25 —
Panes of 20, #278-279 26.00 —

First day covers of Nos. 278-279 total 366,784.
Upper margin blocks are inscribed "XXV ANNIVERSARY"; lower margin blocks "UNITED NATIONS POSTAL ADMINISTRATIONS."
See UN Offices in Geneva Nos. 61-62.

Grain — A156

World Food Council.
Printed by Questa Colour Security Printers, Ltd., England. Panes of 50. Designed by Eliezer Weishoff.

1976, Nov. 19 **Litho.** ***Perf. 14½***

280 A156 13c **multicolored** *(1,515,573)* .25 .25
First day cover 1.00
Inscription block of 4 1.10 —

See UN Offices in Geneva No. 63.

WIPO Headquarters, Geneva — A157

World Intellectual Property Organization (WIPO).
Printed by Heraclio Fournier, S. A., Spain. Panes of 50. Designed by Eliezer Weishoff.

1977, Mar. 11 **Photo.** ***Perf. 14***

281 A157 13c **citron & multi** *(1,330,272)* .25 .25
First day cover 1.00
Inscription block of 4 .75 —
282 A157 31c **bright green & multi** *(1,115,406)* .45 .35
First day cover 1.00
First day cover, #281-282 1.00
Inscription block of 4 2.00 —

First day covers of Nos. 281-282 total 364,184.
See UN Offices in Geneva No. 64.

Drops of Water Falling into Funnel — A158

UN Water Conference, Mar del Plata, Argentina, Mar. 14-25.
Printed by Government Printing Bureau, Tokyo. Panes of 50. Designed by Elio Tomei.

1977, Apr. 22 **Photo.** ***Perf. 13½x13***

283 A158 13c **yellow & multi** *(1,317,536)* .25 .25
First day cover 1.00
Inscription block of 4 .75 —
284 A158 25c **salmon & multi** *(1,077,424)* .40 .35
First day cover 1.00
First day cover, #283-284 1.00
Inscription block of 4 2.00 —

First day covers of Nos. 283-284 total 321,585.
See UN Offices in Geneva Nos. 65-66.

Burning Fuse Severed — A159

UN Security Council.
Printed by Heraclio Fournier, S.A., Spain. Panes of 50. Designed by Witold Janowski and Marek Freudenreich.

1977, May 27 **Photo.** ***Perf. 14***

285 A159 13c **purple & multi** *(1,321,527)* .25 .25
First day cover 1.00
Inscription block of 4 .75 —
286 A159 31c **dark blue & multi** *(1,137,195)* .45 .30
First day cover 1.00
First day cover, #285-286 1.00
Inscription block of 4 2.00 —

First day covers of Nos. 285-286 total 309,610.
See UN Offices in Geneva Nos. 67-68.

"Combat Racism" — A160

Fight against racial discrimination.

Printed by Setelipaino, Finland. Panes of 50. Designed by Bruno K. Wiese.

1977, Sept. 19 **Litho.** ***Perf. 13½x13***

287 A160 13c **black & yellow** *(1,195,739)* .25 .25
First day cover 1.00
Inscription block of 4 .75 —
288 A160 25c **black & vermilion** *(1,074,639)* .40 .30
First day cover 1.00
First day cover, #287-288 1.00
Inscription block of 4 1.75 —

First day covers of Nos. 287-288 total 356,193.
See UN Offices in Geneva Nos. 60-70.

Atom, Grain, Fruit and Factory — A161

Peaceful uses of atomic energy.
Printed by Heraclio Fournier, S.A., Spain. Panes of 50. Designed by Henry Bencsath.

1977, Nov. 18 **Photo.** ***Perf. 14***

289 A161 13c **yellow bister & multi** *(1,316,473)* .25 .25
First day cover 1.00
Inscription block of 4 .75 —
290 A161 18c **dull green & multi** *(1,072,246)* .30 .25
First day cover 1.00
First day cover, #289-290 1.00
Inscription block of 4 1.40 —

First day covers of Nos. 289-290 total 325,348.
See UN Offices in Geneva Nos. 71-72.

Opening Words of UN Charter — A162

"Live Together in Peace" — A163

People of the World — A164

Printed by Questa Colour Security Printers, United Kingdom. Panes of 50. Designed by Salahattin Kanidinc (1c); Elio Tomei (25c); Paula Schmidt ($1).

1978, Jan. 27 **Litho.** ***Perf. 14½***

291 A162 1c **gold, brown & red** *(4,800,000)+* .25 .25
First day cover 1.00
Inscription block of 4 .20 —
292 A163 25c **multicolored** *(3,000,000)+* .35 .30
First day cover 1.00
Inscription block of 4 1.40 —
293 A164 $1 **multicolored** *(3,400,000)+* 1.25 1.25
First day cover 1.00
First day cover, #291-293 1.75
Inscription block of 4 5.25 —
Nos. 291-293 (3) 1.85 1.80

\+ Printing orders to Sept. 1989.
First day covers of Nos. 291-293 total 264,782.
See UN Offices in Geneva No. 73.

Smallpox Virus — A165

Global eradication of smallpox.
Printed by Courvoisier, S.A. Panes of 50. Designed by Herbert Auchli.

1978, Mar. 31 **Photo.** ***Perf. 12x11½***

294 A165 13c **rose & black** *(1,188,239)* .25 .25
First day cover 1.00
Inscription block of 4 .75 —
295 A165 31c **blue & black** *(1,058,688)* .40 .40
First day cover 1.00
First day cover, #294-295 1.25
Inscription block of 4 1.75 —

First day covers of Nos. 294-295 total 306,626.
See UN Offices in Geneva Nos. 74-75.

Open Handcuff — A166

Liberation, justice and cooperation for Namibia.
Printed by Government Printing Office, Austria. Panes of 50. Designed by Cafiro Tomei.

1978, May 5 **Photo.** ***Perf. 12***

296 A166 13c **multicolored** *(1,203,079)* .25 .25
First day cover 1.00
Inscription block of 4 .75 —
297 A166 18c **multicolored** *(1,066,738)* .30 .25
First day cover 1.00
First day cover, #296-297 1.00
Inscription block of 4 1.40 —

First day covers of Nos. 296-297 total 324,471.
See UN Offices in Geneva No. 76.

Multicolored Bands and Clouds — A167

International Civil Aviation Organization for "Safety in the Air."
Printed by Heraclio Fournier, S.A., Spain. Panes of 50. Designed by Cemalettin Mutver.

1978, June 12	**Photo.**	***Perf. 14***	
298 A167 13c **multicolored** *(1,295,617)*		.25	.25
First day cover			1.00
Inscription block of 4		.75	—
299 A167 25c **multicolored** *(1,101,256)*		.35	.30
First day cover			1.00
First day cover, #298-299			1.00
Inscription block of 4		1.50	—

First day covers of Nos. 298-299 total 329,995.
See UN Offices in Geneva Nos. 77-78.

General Assembly — A168

Printed by Government Printing Bureau, Tokyo. Panes of 50. Designed by Jozsef Vertel.

1978, Sept. 15	**Photo.**	***Perf. 13½***	
300 A168 13c **multicolored** *(1,093,005)*		.25	.25
First day cover			1.00
Inscription block of 4		.75	—
301 A168 18c **multicolored** *(1,065,934)*		.35	.30
First day cover			1.00
First day cover, #300-301			1.00
Inscription block of 4		1.50	—

First day covers of Nos. 300-301 total 283,220.
See UN Offices in Geneva Nos. 79-80.

Hemispheres as Cogwheels — A169

Technical Cooperation Among Developing Countries Conference, Buenos Aires, Argentina, Sept. 1978.
Printed by Heraclio Fournier, S.A., Spain. Panes of 50. Designed by Simon Keter and David Pesach.

1978, Nov. 17	**Photo.**	***Perf. 14***	
302 A169 13c **multicolored** *(1,251,272)*		.25	.25
First day cover			1.00
Inscription block of 4		1.00	—
303 A169 31c **multicolored** *(1,185,213)*		.50	.40
First day cover			1.00
First day cover, #302-303			1.25
Inscription block of 4		2.25	—

First day covers of Nos. 302-303 total 272,556.
See UN Offices in Geneva No. 81.

Hand Holding Olive Branch — A170

Various Races Tree — A171

Globe, Dove with Olive Branch — A172

Birds and Globe — A173

Printed by Heraclio Fournier, S.A., Spain. Panes of 50.
Designed by Raymon Müller (5c); Alrun Fricke (14c); Eliezer Weishoff (15c); Young Sun Hahn (20c).

1979, Jan. 19	**Photo.**	***Perf. 14***	
304 A170 5c **multicolored** *(3,000,000)*		.25	.25
First day cover			1.00
Inscription block of 4		.40	—
305 A171 14c **multicolored** *(3,000,000)*+		.25	.25
First day cover			1.00
Inscription block of 4		.80	—
306 A172 15c **multicolored** *(3,000,000)*+		.25	.25
First day cover			1.00
Inscription block of 4		1.25	—
307 A173 20c **multicolored** *(3,400,000)*+		.30	.25
First day cover			1.00
First day cover, #304-307			2.25
Inscription block of 4		1.40	—
Nos. 304-307 (4)		1.05	1.00

First day covers of Nos. 304-307 total 295,927.
+ Printing orders to June 1990.

UNDRO Against Fire and Water — A174

Office of the UN Disaster Relief Coordinator (UNDRO).
Printed by Heraclio Fournier, S.A., Spain. Panes of 50. Designed by Gidon Sagi.

1979, Mar. 9	**Photo.**	***Perf. 14***	
308 A174 15c **multicolored** *(1,448,600)*		.25	.25
First day cover			1.00
Inscription block of 4		.85	—
309 A174 20c **multicolored** *(1,126,295)*		.35	.30
First day cover			1.00
First day cover, #308-309			1.25
Inscription block of 4		1.50	—

First day covers of Nos. 308-309 total 266,694.
See UN Offices in Geneva Nos. 82-83.

Child and IYC Emblem — A175

International Year of the Child.
Printed by Heraclio Fournier, S.A., Spain. Panes of 20 (5x4). Designed by Helena Matuszewska (15c) and Krystyna Tarkowska-Gruszecka (31c).

1979, May 4 **Photo.** ***Perf. 14***

310 A175 15c **multicolored** *(2,290,329)* .25 .25
First day cover 1.00
Inscription block of 4 1.00 —
311 A175 31c **multicolored** *(2,192,136)* .35 .35
First day cover 1.00
First day cover, #310-311 2.25
Inscription block of 4 1.50 —
Panes of 20, #310-311 12.00

First day covers of Nos. 310-311 total 380,022.
See UN Offices in Geneva Nos. 84-85.

Map of Namibia, Olive Branch — A176

For a free and independent Namibia.
Printed by Ashton-Potter Ltd., Canada. Panes of 50. Designed by Eliezer Weishoff.

1979, Oct. 5 **Litho.** ***Perf. 13½***

312 A176 15c **multicolored** *(1,470,231)* .25 .25
First day cover 1.00
Inscription block of 4 .75 —
313 A176 31c **multicolored** *(1,355,323)* .30 .35
First day cover 1.00
First day cover, #312-313 1.25
Inscription block of 4 1.50 —

First day covers of Nos. 312-313 total 250,371.
See UN Offices in Geneva No. 86.

Scales and Sword of Justice — A177

International Court of Justice, The Hague, Netherlands.
Printed by Setelipaino, Finland. Panes of 50. Designed by Henning Simon.

1979, Nov. 9 **Litho.** ***Perf. 13x13½***

314 A177 15c **multicolored** *(1,244,972)* .25 .25
First day cover 1.00
Inscription block of 4 .75 —
315 A177 20c **multicolored** *(1,084,483)* .30 .35
First day cover 1.00
First day cover, #314-315 1.25
Inscription block of 4 1.50 —

First day covers of Nos. 314-315 total 322,901.
See UN Offices in Geneva Nos. 87-88.

Graph of Economic Trends — A178

Key — A179

New International Economic Order.
Printed by Questa Colour Security Printers, United Kingdom. Panes of 50. Designed by Cemalettin Mutver (15c), George Hamori (31c)

1980, Jan. 11 **Litho.** ***Perf. 15x14½***

316 A178 15c **multicolored** *(1,163,801)* .25 .25
First day cover 1.00
Inscription block of 4 .85 —
317 A179 31c **multicolored** *(1,103,560)* .45 .35
First day cover 1.00
First day cover, #316-317 1.00
Inscription block of 4 2.00 —

First day covers of Nos. 316-317 total 211,945.
See UN Offices in Geneva No. 89; Vienna No. 7.

Women's Year Emblem — A180

United Nations Decade for Women.
Printed by Questa Colour Security Printers, United Kingdom. Panes of 50. Designed by Susanne Rottenfusser.

1980, Mar. 7 **Litho.** ***Perf. 14½x15***

318 A180 15c **multicolored** *(1,409,350)* .25 .25
First day cover 1.00
Inscription block of 4 .75 —
319 A180 20c **multicolored** *(1,182,016)* .30 .25
First day cover 1.00
First day cover, #318-319 1.00
Inscription block of 4 1.50 —

First day covers of Nos. 318-319 total 289,314.
See UN Offices in Geneva Nos. 90-91; Vienna Nos. 9-10.

UN Emblem and "UN" on Helmet — A181

Arrows and UN Emblem — A182

United Nations Peace-keeping Operations.
Printed by Joh. Enschede en Zonen, Netherlands. Panes of 50. Designed by Bruno K. Wiese (15c), James Gardiner (31c)

1980, May 16 **Litho.** ***Perf. 14x13***

320 A181 15c **blue & black** *(1,245,521)* .25 .25
First day cover 1.00
Inscription block of 4 .90 —
321 A182 31c **multicolored** *(1,191,009)* .40 .40
First day cover 1.00
First day cover, #320-321 1.00
Inscription block of 4 2.10 —

First day covers of Nos. 320-321 total 208,442.
See UN Offices in Geneva No. 92; Vienna No. 11.

"35" and Flags — A183

Globe and Laurel — A184

35th Anniversary of the United Nations.
Printed by Ashton-Potter Ltd, Canada. Nos. 322-323, panes of 50. Designed by Cemalettin Matver (15c), Mian Mohammad Saeed (31c).

1980, June 26 **Litho.** ***Perf. 13x13½***

322 A183 15c **multicolored** *(1,554,514)* .25 .25
First day cover 1.00
Inscription block of 4 .85 —
323 A184 31c **multicolored** *(1,389,606)* .40 .35
First day cover 1.00
First day cover, #322-323 1.00
Inscription block of 4 1.90 —

Souvenir Sheet

Imperf

324 Sheet of 2 *(1,215,505)* .65 .65
a. A183 15c **multicolored** .25 .25
b. A184 31c **multicolored** .40 .40
First day cover 1.00

First day covers of Nos. 322-324 total: New York, 369,345; San Francisco, 203,701.
See UN Offices in Geneva Nos. 93-95; Vienna Nos. 12-14.

Flag of Turkey — A185

Printed by Courvoisier, S.A., Switzerland. Panes of 16. Designed by Ole Hamann.

Each pane contains 4 blocks of 4 (Nos. 325-328, 329-332, 333-336, 337-340). A se-tenant block of 4 designs centers each pane.

1980, Sept. 26 **Litho.** ***Perf. 12***

Granite Paper

325 A185 15c shown *(3,490,725)* .25 .25
326 A185 15c Luxembourg *(3,490,725)* .25 .25
327 A185 15c Fiji *(3,490,725)* .25 .25
328 A185 15c Viet Nam *(3,490,725)* .25 .25
a. Se-tenant block of 4, #325-328 1.00 1.00
329 A185 15c Guinea *(3,442,633)* .25 .25
330 A185 15c Surinam *(3,442,633)* .25 .25
331 A185 15c Bangladesh *(3,442,633)* .25 .25
332 A185 15c Mali *(3,442,633)* .25 .25
a. Se-tenant block of 4, #329-332 1.00 1.00
333 A185 15c Yugoslavia *(3,416,292)* .25 .25
334 A185 15c France *(3,416,292)* .25 .25
335 A185 15c Venezuela *(3,416,292)* .25 .25
336 A185 15c El Salvador *(3,416,292)* .25 .25
a. Se-tenant block of 4, #333-336 1.00 1.00
337 A185 15c Madagascar *(3,442,497)* .25 .25
338 A185 15c Cameroon *(3,442,497)* .25 .25
339 A185 15c Rwanda *(3,442,497)* .25 .25
340 A185 15c Hungary *(3,442,497)* .25 .25
a. Se-tenant block of 4, #337-340 1.00 1.00
First day covers of Nos. 325-340, each .35
Set of 4 diff. panes of 16 7.00
Nos. 325-340 (16) 4.00 4.00

First day covers of Nos. 325-340 total 6,145,595.
See Nos. 350-365, 374-389, 399-414, 425-440, 450-465, 477-492, 499-514, 528-543, 554-569, 690-697, 719-726, 744-751, 795-802, 921-924, 1063-1066, 1083-1086, 1150-1157, 1179-1186, 1245-1252.

Symbolic Flowers — A186

Symbols of Progress — A187

Printed by Ashton-Potter Ltd., Canada. Panes of 50. Designed by Eliezer Weishoff (15c), Dietman Kowall (20c).

1980, Nov. 21 **Litho.** ***Perf. 13½x13***

341 A186 15c **multicolored** *(1,192,165)* .25 .25
First day cover 1.00
Inscription block of 4 1.00 —
342 A187 20c **multicolored** *(1,011,382)* .40 .35
First day cover 1.00
First day cover, #341-342 1.00
Inscription block of 4 1.75 —

First day covers of Nos. 341-342 total 232,149.
See UN Offices in Geneva, Nos. 96-97; Vienna Nos. 15-16.

Inalienable Rights of the Palestinian People — A188

Printed by Courvoisier S.A., Switzerland. Panes of 50. Designed by David Dewhurst.

1981, Jan. 30 **Photo.** ***Perf. 12x11½***

343 A188 15c **multicolored** *(993,489)* .30 .25
First day cover *(127,187)* 1.00
Inscription block of 4 1.25 —

See UN Offices in Geneva No. 98; Vienna No. 17.

Interlocking Puzzle Pieces — A189

Stylized Person — A190

International Year of the Disabled.
Printed by Heraclio Fournier S.A., Spain. Panes of 50. Designed by Sophia Van Heeswijk (20c) and G.P. Van der Hyde (35c).

1981, Mar. 6 **Photo.** ***Perf. 14***

344 A189 20c **multicolored** *(1,218,371)* .25 .25
First day cover 1.00
Inscription block of 4 1.10 —
345 A190 35c **black & orange** *(1,107,298)* .40 .45
First day cover 1.00
First day cover, #344-345 1.25
Inscription block of 4 2.00 —

First day covers of Nos. 344-345 total 204,891.
See UN Offices in Geneva Nos. 99-100; Vienna Nos. 18-19.

Art at UN Issue

Desislava and Sebastocrator Kaloyan, Bulgarian Mural, 1259, Boyana Church, Sofia — A191

Printed by Courvoisier. Panes of 50. Designed by Ole Hamann.

1981, Apr. 15 **Photo.** ***Perf. 11½***
Granite Paper

346 A191 20c **multicolored** *(1,252,648)* .25 .25
First day cover 1.00
Inscription block of 4 1.40 —
347 A191 31c **multicolored** *(1,061,056)* .40 .45
First day cover 1.00
First day cover, #346-347 1.00
Inscription block of 4 1.90 —

First day covers of Nos. 346-347 total 210,978.
See UN Offices in Geneva No. 101; Vienna No. 20.

Solar Energy — A192

Conference Emblem — A193

Conference on New and Renewable Sources of Energy, Nairobi, Aug. 10-21.
Printed by Setelipaino, Finland. Panes of 50. Designed by Ulrike Dreyer (20c); Robert Perrot (40c).

1981, May 29 **Litho.** ***Perf. 13***

348 A192 20c **multicolored** *(1,132,877)* .25 .25
First day cover 1.00
Inscription block of 4 1.00 —
349 A193 40c **multicolored** *(1,158,319)* .50 .50
First day cover 1.00
First day cover, #348-349 1.25
Inscription block of 4 2.25 —

First day covers of Nos. 348-349 total 240,205.
See UN Offices in Geneva No. 102; Vienna No. 21.

Flag Type of 1980

Printed by Courvoisier, S.A., Switzerland. Panes of 16. Designed by Ole Hamann.
Each pane contains 4 blocks of 4 (Nos. 350-353, 354-357, 358-361, 362-365). A se-tenant block of 4 designs centers each pane.

1981, Sept. 25 **Granite Paper** **Litho.**

350 A185 20c Djibouti *(2,342,224)* .25 .25
351 A185 20c Sri Lanka *(2,342,224)* .25 .25
352 A185 20c Bolivia *(2,342,224)* .25 .25
353 A185 20c Equatorial Guinea *(2,342,224)* .25 .25
a. Se-tenant block of 4, #350-353 1.00 1.00
354 A185 20c Malta *(2,360,297)* .25 .25
355 A185 20c Czechoslovakia *(2,360,297)* .25 .25
356 A185 20c Thailand *(2,360,297)* .25 .25
357 A185 20c Trinidad & Tobago *(2,360,297)* .25 .25
a. Se-tenant block of 4, #354-357 1.00 1.00
358 A185 20c Ukrainian SSR *(2,344,755)* .25 .25
359 A185 20c Kuwait *(2,344,755)* .25 .25
360 A185 20c Sudan *(2,344,755)* .25 .25
361 A185 20c Egypt *(2,344,755)* .25 .25
a. Se-tenant block of 4, #358-361 1.00 1.00
362 A185 20c US *(2,450,537)* .25 .25
363 A185 20c Singapore *(2,450,537)* .25 .25
364 A185 20c Panama *(2,450,537)* .25 .25
365 A185 20c Costa Rica *(2,450,537)* .25 .25
a. Se-tenant block of 4, #362-365 1.00 1.00
First day covers, #350-365, each .40
Set of 4 diff. panes of 16 10.00
Nos. 350-365 (16) 4.00 4.00

First day covers of Nos. 350-365 total 3,961,237.

Seedling and Tree Cross-section A194

"10" and Symbols of Progress — A195

United Nations Volunteers Program, 10th anniv.

Printed by Walsall Security Printers, Ltd., United Kingdom. Pane of 50. Designed by Gabriele Nussgen (18c), Angel Medina Medina (28c).

1981, Nov. 13 **Litho.**

366 A194 18c **multicolored** *(1,246,833)*	.25	.25
First day cover		1.00
Inscription block of 4	1.25	—
367 A195 28c **multicolored** *(1,282,868)*	.55	.55
First day cover		1.00
First day cover, #366-367		1.00
Inscription block of 4	2.50	—

First day covers of Nos. 366-367 total 221,106.

See UN Offices in Geneva Nos. 103-104; Vienna Nos. 22-23.

A196

A197

A198

Respect for Human Rights (17c), Independence of Colonial Countries and People (28c), Second Disarmament Decade (40c).

Printed by Courvoisier, S.A., Switzerland. Panes of 50. Designed by Rolf Christianson (17c); George Hamori (28c); Marek Kwiatkowski (40c).

1982, Jan. 22 ***Perf. 11½x12***

368 A196 17c **multicolored** *(3,000,000)+*	.25	.25
First day cover		1.00
Inscription block of 4	1.10	—
369 A197 28c **multicolored** *(3,000,000)+*	.45	.40
First day cover		1.00
Inscription block of 4	2.00	—
370 A198 40c **multicolored** *(3,000,000)*	.75	.70
First day cover		1.00
First day cover, #368-370		1.25
Inscription block of 4	3.25	—
Nos. 368-370 (3)	1.45	1.35

First day covers of Nos. 368-370 total 243,073.

Sun and Hand Holding Seedling — A199

Sun, Plant Land and Water — A200

10th Anniversary of United Nations Environment Program.

Printed by Joh. Enschede En Zonen, Netherlands. Panes of 50. Designed by Philine Hartert (20c); Peer-Ulrich Bremer (40c).

1982, Mar. 19 **Litho.** ***Perf. 13½x13***

371 A199 20c **multicolored** *(1,017,117)*	.25	.25
First day cover		1.00
Inscription block of 4	1.10	—
372 A200 40c **multicolored** *(884,798)*	.65	.65
First day cover		1.00
First day cover, #371-372		1.25
Inscription block of 4	3.00	—

First day covers of Nos. 371-372 total 288,721.

See UN Offices in Geneva Nos. 107-108; Vienna Nos. 25-26.

UN Emblem and Olive Branch in Outer Space — A201

Exploration and Peaceful Uses of Outer Space.

Printed By Enschede. Panes of 50. Designed by Wiktor C. Nerwinski.

1982, June 11 **Litho.** ***Perf. 13x13½***

373 A201 20c **multicolored** *(1,083,426)*	.45	.45
First day cover *(156,965)*		1.00
Inscription block of 4	2.00	—

See UN Offices in Geneva Nos. 109-110; Vienna No. 27.

Flag Type of 1980

Printed by Courvoisier. Panes of 16. Designed by Ole Hamann.

Issued in 4 panes of 16. Each pane contains 4 blocks of four (Nos. 374-377, 378-381, 383-385, 386-389). A se-tenant block of 4 designs centers each pane.

1982, Sept. 24 **Litho.** ***Perf. 12***

Granite Paper

374 A185 20c Austria *(2,314,006)*	.25	.25
375 A185 20c Malaysia *(2,314,006)*	.25	.25
376 A185 20c Seychelles *(2,314,006)*	.25	.25
377 A185 20c Ireland *(2,314,006)*	.25	.25
a. Se-tenant block of 4, #374-377	1.50	1.50
378 A185 20c Mozambique *(2,300,958)*	.25	.25
379 A185 20c Albania *(2,300,958)*	.25	.25
380 A185 20c Dominica *(2,300,958)*	.25	.25
381 A185 20c Solomon Islnads *(2,300,958)*	.25	.25
a. Se-tenant block of 4, #378-381	1.50	1.50
382 A185 20c Philippines *(2,288,589)*	.25	.25
383 A185 20c Swaziland *(2,288,589)*	.25	.25
384 A185 20c Nicaragua *(2,288,589)*	.25	.25
385 A185 20c Burma *(2,288,589)*	.25	.25
a. Se-tenant block of 4, #382-385	1.50	1.50
386 A185 20c Cape Verde *(2,285,848)*	.25	.25
387 A185 20c Guyana *(2,285,848)*	.25	.25
388 A185 20c Belgium *(2,285,848)*	.25	.25

389 A185 20c Nigeria *(2,285,848)* .25 .25
a. Se-tenant block of 4, #386-389 1.50 1.50
First day cover, #374-389, each .40
Set of 4 diff. panes of 16 9.00
Nos. 374-389 (16) 4.00 4.00

First day covers of Nos. 374-389 total 3,202,744.

Conservation and Protection of Nature — A202

Printed by Fournier. Panes of 50. Designed by Hamori.

1982, Nov. 19 Photo. *Perf. 14*

390 A202 20c Leaf *(1,110,027)* .30 .30
First day cover 1.00
margin block of 4, inscription 1.60 —
391 A202 28c Butterfly *(848,772)* .55 .50
First day cover 1.00
First day cover, #390-391 1.00
Inscription block of 4 2.25 —

First day covers of Nos. 390-391 total 214,148.
See UN Offices in Geneva Nos. 111-112; Vienna Nos. 28-29.

A203

A204

World Communications Year
Printed by Walsall. Panes of 50. Designed by Hanns Lohrer (A203) and Lorena Berengo (A204).

1983, Jan. 28 Litho. *Perf. 13*

392 A203 20c **multicolored** *(1,282,079)* .25 .25
First day cover 1.00
Inscription block of 4 1.00 —
393 A204 40c **multicolored** *(931,903)* .65 .65
First day cover 1.00
First day cover, #392-393 1.00
Inscription block of 4 3.25 —

First day covers of Nos. 392-393 total 183,499.
See UN Offices in Geneva No. 113; Vienna No. 30.

A205

A206

Safety at Sea.
Printed by Questa. Panes of 50. Designed by Jean-Marie Lenfant (A205), Ari Ron (A206).

1983, Mar. 18 Litho. *Perf. 14½*

394 A205 20c **multicolored** *(1,252,456)* .25 .25
First day cover 1.00
Inscription block of 4 1.25 —
395 A206 37c **multicolored** *(939,910)* .60 .55
First day cover 1.00
First day cover, #394-395 1.00
Inscription block of 4 2.50 —

First day covers of Nos. 394-395 total 199,962.
See UN Offices in Geneva Nos. 114-115; Vienna Nos. 31-32.

World Food Program — A207

Printed by Government Printers Bureau, Japan. Designed by Marek Kwiatkowski.

1983, Apr. 22 Engr. *Perf. 13½*

396 A207 20c **rose lake** *(1,238,997)* .35 .35
First day cover *(180,704)* 1.00
Inscription block of 4 1.50 —

See UN Offices in Geneva No. 116; Vienna Nos. 33-34.

A208

A209

UN Conference on Trade and Development.
Printed by Carl Uberreuter Druck and Verlag M. Salzer, Austria. Panes of 50. Designed by Dietmar Braklow (A208), Gabriel Genz (A209).

1983, June 6 Litho. *Perf. 14*

397 A208 20c **multicolored** *(1,060,053)* .25 .35
First day cover 1.00
Inscription block of 4 1.25 —

398 A209 28c **multicolored** *(948,981)* .70 .65
First day cover 1.25
First day cover, #397-398 1.40
Inscription block of 4 2.75 —

First day covers of Nos. 397-398 total 200,131.
See UN Offices in Geneva Nos. 117-118; Vienna Nos. 35-36.

Flag Type of 1980

Printed by Courvoisier. Panes of 16. Designed by Ole Hamann.
Issued in 4 panes of 16. Each pane contains 4 blocks of four (Nos. 399-402, 403-406, 407-410, 411-414). A se-tenant block of 4 designs centers each pane.

1983, Sept. 23 **Photo.** ***Perf. 12***
Granite Paper

399 A185 20c Great Britain *(2,490,599)* .25 .25
400 A185 20c Barbados *(2,490,599)* .25 .25
401 A185 20c Nepal *(2,490,599)* .25 .25
402 A185 20c Israel *(2,490,599)* .25 .25
a. Se-tenant block of 4, #399-402 1.50 1.50
403 A185 20c Malawi *(2,483,010)* .25 .25
404 A185 20c Byelorussian SSR *(2,483,010)* .25 .25
405 A185 20c Jamaica *(2,483,010)* .25 .25
406 A185 20c Kenya *(2,483,010)* .25 .25
a. Se-tenant block of 4, #403-406 1.50 1.80
407 A185 20c People's Republic of China *(2,474,140)* .25 .25
408 A185 20c Peru *(2,474,140)* .25 .25
409 A185 20c Bulgaria *(2,474,140)* .25 .25
410 A185 20c Canada *(2,474,140)* .25 .25
a. Se-tenant block of 4, #407-410 1.50 1.80
411 A185 20c Somalia *(2,482,070)* .25 .25
412 A185 20c Senegal *(2,482,070)* .25 .25
413 A185 20c Brazil *(2,482,070)* .25 .25
414 A185 20c Sweden *(2,482,070)* .25 .25
a. Se-tenant block of 4, #411-414 1.50 1.80
First day cover, #399-414, each .40
Set of 4 diff. panes of 16 10.00
Nos. 399-414 (16) 4.00 4.00

First day covers of Nos. 399-414 total 2,214,134.

Window Right — A210

Peace Treaty with Nature — A211

35th Anniversary of the Universal Declaration of Human Rights.
Printed by Government Printing Office, Austria. Panes of 16 (4x4). Designed by Friedensreich Hundertwasser, Austria.

1983, Dec. 9 **Photo. & Engr.** ***Perf. 13½***

415 A210 20c **multicolored** *(1,591,102)* .30 .25
First day cover 1.00
Inscription block of 4 1.25 —
416 A211 40c **multicolored** *(1,566,789)* .70 .65
First day cover 1.25
First day cover, #415-416 1.40
Inscription block of 4 3.00 —
Panes of 16, #415-416 16.00

First day covers of Nos. 415-416 total 176,269.
See UN Offices in Geneva Nos. 119-120; Vienna Nos. 37-38.

International Conference on Population — A212

Printed by Bundesdruckerei, Federal Republic of Germany. Panes of 50. Designed by Marina Langer-Rosa and Helmut Langer, Federal Republic of Germany.

1984, Feb. 3 **Litho.** ***Perf. 14***

417 A212 20c **multicolored** *(905,320)* .25 .25
First day cover 1.00
Inscription block of 4 1.40 —
418 A212 40c **multicolored** *(717,084)* .65 .65
First day cover 1.00
First day cover, #417-418 1.00
Inscription block of 4 2.50 —

First day covers of Nos. 417-418 total 118,068.
See UN Offices in Geneva No. 121; Vienna No. 39.

Tractor Plowing — A213

Rice Paddy — A214

World Food Day, Oct. 16
Printed by Walsall Security Printers, Ltd., United Kingdom. Panes of 50. Designed by Adth Vanooijen, Netherlands.

1984, Mar. 15 **Litho.** ***Perf. 14½***

419 A213 20c **multicolored** *(853,641)* .30 .30
First day cover 1.00
Inscription block of 4 1.50 —
420 A214 40c **multicolored** *(727,165)* .60 .60
First day cover 1.00
First day cover, #419-420 1.40
Inscription block of 4 2.50 —

First day covers of Nos. 419-420 total 116,009.
See UN Offices in Geneva Nos. 122-123; Vienna Nos. 40-41.

Grand Canyon — A215

Ancient City of Polonnaruwa, Sri Lanka — A216

World Heritage

Printed by Harrison and Sons, United Kingdom. Panes of 50. Designs adapted by Rocco J. Callari, U.S., and Thomas Lee, China.

1984, Apr. 18 **Litho.** ***Perf. 14***

421 A215 20c **multicolored** *(814,316)* .25 .25
First day cover 1.00
Inscription block of 4 1.00 —
422 A216 50c **multicolored** *(579,136)* .75 .75
First day cover 1.00
First day cover, #421-422 1.10
Inscription block of 4 3.50 —

First day covers of Nos. 421-422 total 112,036.

See Nos. 601-602, UN Offices in Geneva Nos. 124-125, 211-212; Vienna Nos. 42-43, 125-126.

A217

A218

Future for Refugees

Printed by Courvoisier. Panes of 50. Designed by Hans Erni, Switzerland.

1984, May 29 **Photo.** ***Perf. 11½***

423 A217 20c **multicolored** *(956,743)* .30 .30
First day cover 1.00
Inscription block of 4 1.25 —
424 A218 50c **multicolored** *(729,036)* .90 .90
First day cover 1.00
First day cover, #423-424 1.25
Inscription block of 4 4.00 —

First day covers of Nos. 423-424 total 115,789.

See UN Offices in Geneva Nos. 126-127; Vienna Nos. 44-45.

Flag Type of 1980

Printed by Courvoisier. Panes of 16. Designed by Ole Hamann.

Issued in 4 panes of 16. Each pane contains 4 blocks of four (Nos. 425-428, 429-432, 433-436, 437-440). A se-tenant block of 4 designs centers each pane.

1984, Sept. 21 **Photo.** ***Perf. 12***
Granite Paper

425 A185 20c Burundi *(1,941,471)* .25 .25
426 A185 20c Pakistan *(1,941,471)* .25 .25
427 A185 20c Benin *(1,941,471)* .25 .25
428 A185 20c Italy *(1,941,471)* .25 .25
a. Se-tenant block of 4, #425-428 1.80 1.80
429 A185 20c Tanzania *(1,969,051)* .25 .25
430 A185 20c United Arab Emirates *(1,969,051)* .25 .25
431 A185 20c Ecuador *(1,969,051)* .25 .25
432 A185 20c Bahamas *(1,969,051)* .25 .25
a. Se-tenant block of 4, #429-432 1.80 1.80
433 A185 20c Poland *(2,001,091)* .25 .25
434 A185 20c Papua New Guinea *(2,001,091)* .25 .25
435 A185 20c Uruguay *(2,001,091)* .25 .25
436 A185 20c Chile *(2,001,091)* .25 .25
a. Se-tenant block of 4, #433-436 1.80 1.80
437 A185 20c Paraguay *(1,969,875)* .25 .25
438 A185 20c Bhutan *(1,969,875)* .25 .25
439 A185 20c Central African Republic *(1,969,875)* .25 .25
440 A185 20c Australia *(1,969,875)* .25 .25
a. Se-tenant block of 4, #437-440 1.80 1.80
First day cover, #425-440, each .50
Set of 4 diff. panes of 16 15.00
Nos. 425-440 (16) 4.00 4.00

First day covers of Nos. 425-440 total 1,914,972.

International Youth Year — A219

Printed by Waddingtons Ltd., United Kingdom. Panes of 50. Designed by Ramon Mueller, Federal Republic of Germany.

1984, Nov. 15 **Litho.** ***Perf. 13½***

441 A219 20c **multicolored** *(884,962)* .35 .35
First day cover 1.00
Inscription block of 4 1.25 —
442 A219 35c **multicolored** *(740,023)* .85 .85
First day cover 1.00
First day cover, #441-442 1.25
Inscription block of 4 4.25 —

First day covers of Nos. 441-442 total 125,315.

See UN Offices in Geneva No. 128; Vienna Nos. 46-47.

ILO Turin Center — A220

Printed by the Government Printing Bureau, Japan. Panes of 50. Engraved by Mamoru Iwakuni and Hiroshi Ozaki, Japan.

1985, Feb. 1 **Engr.** ***Perf. 13½***

443 A220 23c **blue** *(612,942)* .45 .45
First day cover *(76,541)* 1.00
Inscription block of 4 2.00 —

See UN Offices in Geneva Nos. 129-130; Vienna No. 48.

UN University
A221

Printed by Helio Courvoiser, Switzerland. Panes of 50. Designed by Moshe Pereg, Israel, and Hinedi Geluda, Brazil.

50c, Farmer plowing, discussion group.

1985, Mar. 15 Photo. *Perf. 11½*

444 A221 50c multi *(625,043)*	.95	.95
First day cover *(77,271)*		1.25
Inscription block of 4	4.25	—

See UN Offices in Geneva Nos. 131-132; Vienna No. 49.

Peoples of the World United — A222

Painting UN Emblem — A223

Printed by Carl Ueberreuter Druck and Verlag M. Salzer, Austria. Panes of 50. Designed by Fritz Henry Oerter, Federal Republic of Germany (22c), and Rimondi Rino, Italy ($3).

1985, May 10 Litho. *Perf. 14*

445 A222 22c **multicolored** *(2,000,000)+*	.30	.30
First day cover		1.00
Inscription block of 4	1.25	—
446 A223 $3 **multicolored** *(2,000,000)+*	3.75	1.50
First day cover		3.50
First day cover, #445-446		5.75
Inscription block of 4	16.50	—

First day covers of Nos. 445-446 total 88,613.
See UN Offices in Geneva Nos. 133-134; Vienna Nos. 50-51.

The Corner, 1947 — A224

Alvaro Raking Hay, 1953 — A225

UN 40th anniversary. Oil paintings (details) by American artist Andrew Wyeth (b. 1917). Printed by Helio Courvoisier, Switzerland. Nos. 447-448 panes of 50. Designed by Rocco J. Callari, U.S., and Thomas Lee, China (#449).

1985, June 26 Photo. *Perf. 12 x 11½*

447 A224 22c **multicolored** *(944,960)*	.35	.35
First day cover		1.00
Inscription block of 4	1.25	—
448 A225 45c **multicolored** *(680,079)*	1.00	1.00
First day cover		1.00
First day cover, #447-448		1.50
Inscription block of 4	4.00	—

Souvenir Sheet

Imperf

449 Sheet of 2 *(506,004)*	1.10	1.30
a. A224 22c **multicolored**	.40	.50
b. A225 45c **multicolored**	.70	.80
First day cover		1.00

First day covers of Nos. 447-449 total; New York, 210,189; San Francisco, 92,804.
See UN Offices in Geneva Nos. 135-137; Vienna Nos. 52-54.

Flag Type of 1980

Printed by Helio Courvoisier, Switzerland. Designed by Ole Hamann.

Issued in panes of 16; each contains 4 blocks of four (Nos. 450-453, 454-457, 458-461, 462-465). A se-tenant block of 4 designs is at the center of each pane.

1985, Sept. 20 Photo. *Perf. 12*
Granite Paper

450 A185 22c Grenada *(1,270,755)*	.30	.30
451 A185 22c Federal Republic of Germany *(1,270,755)*	.30	.30
452 A185 22c Saudi Arabia *(1,270,755)*	.30	.30
453 A185 22c Mexico *(1,270,755)*	.30	.30
a. Se-tenant block of 4, #450-453	2.75	3.00
454 A185 22c Uganda *(1,216,878)*	.30	.30
455 A185 22c St. Thomas & Prince *(1,216,878)*	.30	.30
456 A185 22c USSR *(1,216,878)*	.30	.30
457 A185 22c India *(1,216,878)*	.30	.30
a. Se-tenant block of 4, #454-457	2.75	3.00
458 A185 22c Liberia *(1,213,231)*	.30	.30
459 A185 22c Mauritius *(1,213,231)*	.30	.30
460 A185 22c Chad *(1,213,231)*	.30	.30
461 A185 22c Dominican Republic *(1,213,231)*	.30	.30
a. Se-tenant block of 4, #458-461	2.75	3.00
462 A185 22c Sultanate of Oman *(1,215,533)*	.30	.30
463 A185 22c Ghana *(1,215,533)*	.30	.30
464 A185 22c Sierra Leone *(1,215,533)*	.30	.30
465 A185 22c Finland *(1,215,533)*	.30	.30
a. Se-tenant block of 4, #462-465	2.75	3.00
First day covers, #460-465, each		.50
Set of 4 diff. panes of 16	16.00	
Nos. 450-465 (16)	4.80	4.80

First day covers of Nos. 450-465 total 1,774,193.

UNICEF Child Survival Campaign — A226

Printed by the Government Printing Bureau, Japan. Panes of 50. Designed by Mel Harris, United Kingdom (#466) and Dipok Deyi, India (#467).

1985, Nov. 22 Photo. & Engr. *Perf. 13½*

466 A226 22c Asian Toddler *(823,724)* .30 .30
First day cover 1.00
Inscription block of 4 1.40 —
467 A226 33c Breastfeeding *(632,753)* .65 .65
First day cover 1.00
First day cover, #466-467 1.75
Inscription block of 4 2.75 —

First day covers of Nos. 466-467 total 206,923.
See UN Offices in Geneva Nos. 138-139; Vienna Nos. 55-56.

Africa in Crisis — A227

Printed by Helio Courvoisier, Switzerland. Pane of 50. Designed by Wosene Kosrof, Ethiopia.

1986, Jan. 31 Photo. *Perf. 11½x12*

468 A227 22c **multicolored** *(708,169)* .40 .40
First day cover *(80,588)* 1.25
Inscription block of 4 1.90 —

Campaign against hunger. See UN Offices in Geneva No. 140; Vienna No. 57.

Water Resources — A228

Printed by the Government Printing Bureau, Japan. Pane of 40, 2 blocks of 4 horizontal by 5 blocks of 4 vertical. Designed by Thomas Lee, China.

1986, Mar. 14 Photo. *Perf. 13½*

469 A228 22c Dam *(525,839)* .50 .50
470 A228 22c Irrigation *(525,839)* .50 .50
471 A228 22c Hygiene *(525,839)* .50 .50
472 A228 22c Well *(525,839)* .50 .50
a. Block of 4, #469-472 2.00 2.00
First day cover, #472a 4.50
First day cover, #469-472, each 1.50
Inscription block of 4, #469-472 3.25 —
Pane of 40, #469-472 35.00

UN Development Program. No. 472a has continuous design.
First day covers of Nos. 469-472 total 199,347.
See UN Offices in Geneva Nos. 141-144; Vienna Nos. 58-61.

Human Rights Stamp of 1954 — A229

Stamp collecting: 44c, Engraver. Printed by the Swedish Post Office, Sweden. Panes of 50. Designed by Czeslaw Slania and Ingalill Axelsson, Sweden.

1986, May 22 Engr. *Perf. 12½*

473 A229 22c **dark violet & bright blue** *(825,782)* .25 .25
First day cover 1.00
Inscription block of 4 1.40 —
474 A229 44c **brown & emerald green** *(738,552)* .75 .75
First day cover 1.00
First day cover, #473-474 1.25
Inscription block of 4 2.75 —

First day covers of Nos. 473-474 total: New York, 121,143; Chicago, 89,557.
See UN Offices in Geneva Nos. 146-147; Vienna Nos. 62-63.

Bird's Nest in Tree — A230

Peace in Seven Languages — A231

Printed by the Government Printing Bureau, Japan. Panes of 50. Designed by Akira Iriguchi, Japan (#475), and Henryk Chylinski, Poland (#476).

1986, June 20 Photo. & Embossed *Perf. 13½*

475 A230 22c **multicolored** *(836,160)* .50 .50
First day cover 1.00
Inscription block of 4 2.25 —
476 A231 33c **multicolored** *(663,882)* 1.25 1.25
First day cover 2.00
First day cover, #475-476 4.50
Inscription block of 4 6.00 —

International Peace Year.
First day covers of Nos. 475-476 total 149,976.
See UN Offices in Geneva Nos. 148-149; Vienna Nos. 64-65.

Flag Type of 1980

Printed by Helio Courvoisier, Switzerland. Designed by Ole Hamann. Issued in panes of 16; each contains 4 blocks of four (Nos. 477-480, 481-484, 485-488, 489-492). A se-tenant block of 4 designs centers each pane.

1986, Sept. 19 Photo. *Perf. 12*
Granite Paper

477 A185 22c New Zealand *(1,150,584)* .30 .30
478 A185 22c Lao PDR *(1,150,584)* .30 .30
479 A185 22c Burkina Faso *(1,150,584)* .30 .30
480 A185 22c Gambia *(1,150,584)* .30 .30
a. Se-tenant block of 4, #477-480 2.75 3.00
481 A185 22c Maldives *(1,154,870)* .30 .30
482 A185 22c Ethiopia *(1,154,870)* .30 .30
483 A185 22c Jordan *(1,154,870)* .30 .30
484 A185 22c Zambia *(1,154,870)* .30 .30
a. Se-tenant block of 4, #481-484 2.75 3.00
485 A185 22c Iceland *(1,152,740)* .30 .30
486 A185 22c Antigua & Barbuda *(1,152,740)* .30 .30
487 A185 22c Angola *(1,152,740)* .30 .30
488 A185 22c Botswana *(1,152,740)* .30 .30
a. Se-tenant block of 4, #485-488 2.75 3.00
489 A185 22c Romania *(1,150,412)* .30 .30
490 A185 22c Togo *(1,150,412)* .30 .30
491 A185 22c Mauritania *(1,150,412)* .30 .30
492 A185 22c Colombia *(1,150,412)* .30 .30
a. Se-tenant block of 4, #489-492 2.75 3.00
First day covers, #477-492, each .50
Set of 4 diff. panes of 16 16.00
Nos. 477-492 (16) 4.80 4.80

First day covers of Nos. 477-492 total 1,442,284.

Souvenir Sheet

World Federation of UN Associations, 40th anniv. — A232

Printed by Johann Enschede and Sons, Netherlands. Designed by Rocco J. Callari, U.S.

Designs: 22c, Mother Earth, by Edna Hibel, U.S. 33c, Watercolor by Salvador Dali (b. 1904), Spain. 39c, New Dawn, by Dong Kingman, U.S. 44c, Watercolor by Chaim Gross, U.S.

1986, Nov. 14 **Litho.** ***Perf. 13x13½***

493	A232 Sheet of 4 *(433,888)*	2.50	2.50
a.	22c **multicolored**	.30	.40
b.	33c **multicolored**	.40	.40
c.	39c **multicolored**	.60	.50
d.	44c **multicolored**	.90	.75
	First day cover *(106,194)*		2.00

No. 493 has inscribed margin picturing UN and WFUNA emblems.

See UN Offices in Geneva No. 150; Vienna No. 66.

Trygve Halvdan Lie (1896-1968), first Secretary-General — A233

Printed by the Government Printing Office, Austria. Panes of 50. Designed by Rocco J. Callari, U.S., from a portrait by Harald Dal, Norway.

1987, Jan. 30 **Photo. & Engr.** ***Perf. 13½***

494	A233 22c **multicolored** *(596,440)*	.75	.75
	First day cover *(84,819)*		1.25
	Inscription block of 4	3.25	—

See Offices in Geneva No. 151; Vienna No. 67.

International Year of Shelter for the Homeless A234

Printed by Johann Enschede and Sons, Netherlands. Panes of 50. Designed by Wladyslaw Brykczynski, Poland.

Designs: 22c, Surveying and blueprinting. 44c, Cutting lumber.

1987, Mar. 13 **Litho.** ***Perf. 13½x12½***

495	A234 22c **multicolored** *(620,627)*	.35	.35
	First day cover		1.25
	Inscription block of 4	1.60	—
496	A234 44c **multicolored** *(538,096)*	.90	.90
	First day cover		1.75
	First day cover, #495-496		2.50
	Inscription block of 4	4.25	—

First day covers of Nos. 495-496 total 94,090.

See Offices in Geneva Nos. 154-155; Vienna Nos. 68-69.

Fight Drug Abuse — A235

Printed by the House of Questa, United Kingdom. Panes of 50. Designed by Susan Borgen and Noel Werrett, U.S.

Designs: 22c, Construction. 33c, Education.

1987, June 12 **Litho.** ***Perf. 14½x15***

497	A235 22c **multicolored** *(674,563)*	.45	.45
	First day cover		1.00
	Inscription block of 4	2.25	—
498	A235 33c **multicolored** *(643,153)*	.90	.90
	First day cover		1.00
	First day cover, #497-498		1.75
	Inscription block of 4	4.50	—

First day covers of Nos. 497-498 total 106,941.

See Offices in Geneva Nos. 156-157; Vienna Nos. 70-71.

Flag Type of 1980

Printed by Courvoisier. Designed by Ole Hamann.

Issued in panes of 16; each contains 4 block of four (Nos. 499-502, 503-506, 507-510, 511-514). A se-tenant block of 4 designs centers each pane.

1987, Sept. 18 **Photo.** ***Perf. 12***

Granite Paper

499	A185 22c Comoros *(1,235,828)*	.30	.35
500	A185 22c Yemen PDR *(1,235,828)*	.30	.35
501	A185 22c Mongolia *(1,235,828)*	.30	.35
502	A185 22c Vanuatu *(1,235,828)*	.30	.35
a.	Se-tenant block of 4, #499-502	3.25	3.25
503	A185 22c Japan *(1,244,534)*	.30	.35
504	A185 22c Gabon *(1,244,534)*	.30	.35
505	A185 22c Zimbabwe *(1,244,534)*	.30	.35
506	A185 22c Iraq *(1,244,534)*	.30	.35
a.	Se-tenant block of 4, #503-506	3.25	3.25
507	A185 22c Argentina *(1,238,065)*	.30	.35
508	A185 22c Congo *(1,238,065)*	.30	.35
509	A185 22c Niger *(1,238,065)*	.30	.35
510	A185 22c St. Lucia *(1,238,065)*	.30	.35
a.	Se-tenant block of 4, #507-510	3.25	3.25
511	A185 22c Bahrain *(1,239,323)*	.30	.35
512	A185 22c Haiti *(1,239,323)*	.30	.35
513	A185 22c Afghanistan *(1,239,323)*	.30	.35
514	A185 22c Greece *(1,239,323)*	.30	.35
a.	Se-tenant block of 4, #511-514	3.25	3.25
	First day covers, #499-514, each		1.00
	Set of 4 diff. panes of 16	17.50	
	Nos. 499-514 (16)	4.80	5.60

United Nations Day — A236

Printed by The House of Questa, United Kingdom. Panes of 12. Designed by Elisabeth von Janota Bzowski (#515) and Fritz Henry Oerter (#516), Federal Republic of Germany.

Designs: Multinational people in various occupations.

1987, Oct. 23 **Litho.** ***Perf. 14½x15***

515	A236 22c **multicolored** *(1,119,286)*	.35	.35
	First day cover		1.00
	Inscription block of 4	1.75	—

516 A236 39c **multicolored** *(1,065,468)*	.55	.55
First day cover		1.25
First day cover, #515-516		1.60
Inscription block of 4	2.25	—
Panes of 12, #515-516	12.00	

See Offices in Geneva Nos. 158-159; Vienna Nos. 74-75.

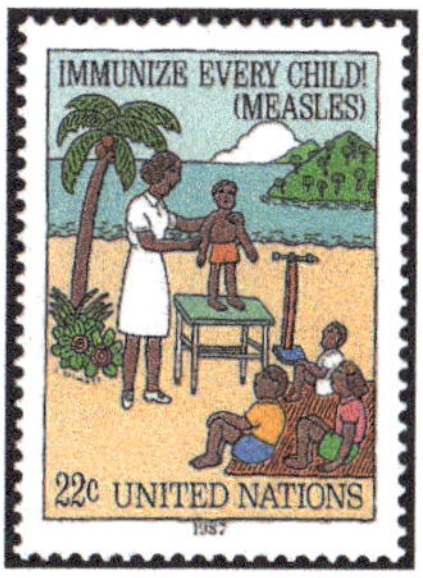

Immunize Every Child — A237

Printed by The House of Questa, United Kingdom. Panes of 50. Designed by Seymour Chwast, U.S.
Designs: 22c, Measles. 44c, Tetanus.

1987, Nov. 20 **Litho.** ***Perf. 15x14½***

517 A237 22c **multicolored** *(660,495)*	.75	.75
First day cover		1.50
Inscription block of 4	2.75	—
518 A237 44c **multicolored** *(606,049)*	1.50	1.50
First day cover		1.50
First day cover, #517-518		2.00
Inscription block of 4	7.50	—

See Offices in Geneva Nos. 160-161; Vienna Nos. 76-77.

Intl. Fund for Agricultural Development (IFAD) — A238

Printed by CPE Australia Ltd., Australia. Panes of 50. Designed by Santiago Arolas, Switzerland.
Designs: 22c, Fishing. 33c, Farming.

1988, Jan. 29 **Litho.** ***Perf. 13½***

519 A238 22c **multicolored** *(392,649)*	.35	.35
First day cover		1.00
Inscription block of 4	1.50	—
520 A238 33c **multicolored** *(475,185)*	.75	.75
First day cover		1.25
First day cover, #519-520		2.50
Inscription block of 4	3.50	—

See Offices in Geneva Nos. 162-163; Vienna Nos. 78-79.

A239

Printed by Heraclio Fournier, S.A., Spain. Panes of 50. Designed by David Ben-Hador, Israel.

1988, Jan. 29 **Photo.** ***Perf. 13½x14***

521 A239 3c **multicolored** *(3,000,000)+*	.25	.25
First day cover		1.00
Inscription block of 4	.75	—

Survival of the Forests — A240

Printed by The House of Questa, United Kingdom. Panes of six se-tenant pairs. Designed by Braldt Bralds, the Netherlands.
Tropical rain forest: 25c, Treetops. 44c, Ground vegetation and tree trunks. Printed se-tenant in a continuous design.

1988, Mar. 18 **Litho.** ***Perf. 14x15***

522 A240 25c **multicolored** *(647,360)*	.75	.75
First day cover		2.00
523 A240 44c **multicolored** *(647,360)*	1.00	1.00
First day cover		4.50
a. Pair, #522-523	2.00	*3.00*
First day cover, #523a		6.50
Inscription block of 4	6.00	
Pane of 12, #522-523	14.00	

See Offices in Geneva Nos. 165-166; Vienna Nos. 80-81.

Intl. Volunteer Day — A241

Printed by Johann Enschede and Sons, the Netherlands. Panes of 50. Designed by James E. Tennison, U.S.
Designs: 25c, Edurahon. 50c, Vocational training, horiz.

1988, May 6 **Litho.** ***Perf. 13x14, 14x13***

524 A241 25c **multicolored** *(000,444)*	.45	.45
First day cover		1.00
Inscription block of 4	2.00	—
525 A241 50c **multicolored** *(447,784)*	.95	.95
First day cover		1.50
First day cover, #524-525		1.75
Inscription block of 4	4.25	—

See Offices in Geneva Nos. 167-168; Vienna Nos. 82-83.

Health in Sports — A242

Printed by the Government Printing Bureau, Japan. Panes of 50. Paintings by LeRoy Neiman, American sports artist.
Designs: 25c, Cycling, vert. 35c, Marathon.

1988, June 17 Litho. *Perf. 13½x13, 13x13½*

526 A242 25c **multicolored** *(658,991)*	.45	.45
First day cover		1.75
Inscription block of 4	2.25	—
527 A242 38c **multicolored** *(420,421)*	1.00	1.00
First day cover		2.00
First day cover, #526-527		3.50
Inscription block of 4	6.00	—

See Offices in Geneva Nos. 169-170; Vienna Nos. 84-85.

Flag Type of 1980

Printed by Helio Courvoisier, Switzerland. Designed by Ole Hamann, Denmark. Issued in panes of 16; each contains 4 blocks of four (Nos. 528-531, 532-535, 536-539 and 540-543). A se-tenant block of 4 centers each pane.

1988, Sept. 15 Photo. *Perf. 12*

Granite Paper

528 A185 25c Spain *(1,029,443)*	.45	.45
529 A185 25c St. Vincent & Grenadines *(1,029,443)*	.45	.45
530 A185 25c Ivory Coast *(1,029,443)*	.45	.45
531 A185 25c Lebanon *(1,029,443)*	.45	.45
a. Se-tenant block of 4, #528-531	3.00	3.00
532 A185 25c Yemen (Arab Republic) *(1,010,774)*	.45	.45
533 A185 25c Cuba *(1,010,774)*	.45	.45
534 A185 25c Denmark *(1,010,774)*	.45	.45
535 A185 25c Libya *(1,010,774)*	.45	.45
a. Se-tenant block of 4, #532-535	3.00	3.00
536 A185 25c Qatar *(1,016,941)*	.45	.45
537 A185 25c Zaire *(1,016,941)*	.45	.45
538 A185 25c Norway *(1,016,941)*	.45	.45
539 A185 25c German Democratic Republic *(1,016,941)*	.45	.45
a. Se-tenant block of 4, #536-539	3.00	3.00
540 A185 25c Iran *(1,009,234)*	.45	.45
541 A185 25c Tunisia *(1,009,234)*	.45	.45
542 A185 25c Samoa *(1,009,234)*	.45	.45
543 A185 25c Belize *(1,009,234)*	.45	.45
a. Se-tenant block of 4, #540-543	3.00	3.00
First day covers, #528-543, each		1.00
Set of 4 diff. panes of 16	21.00	
Nos. 528-543 (16)	7.20	7.20

See note after No. 340.

Universal Declaration of Human Rights, 40th. Anniv. — A243

Printed by Helio Couvoisier, Switzerland. Panes of 50. Designed by Rocco J. Callari, U.S.

1988, Dec. 9 Photo. & Engr. *Perf. 11x11½*

544 A243 25c **multicolored** *(893,706)*	.45	.45
First day cover		1.75
Inscription block of 4	2.25	—

Souvenir Sheet

545 A243 $1 **multicolored** *(411,863)*	1.00	1.00
First day cover		1.75

No. 545 has multicolored decorative margin inscribed with the preamble to the human rights declaration in English.
See Offices in Geneva Nos. 171-172; Vienna Nos. 86-87.

World Bank — A244

Printed by Johann Enschede and Sons, the Netherlands. Panes of 50. Designed by Saturnino Lumboy, Philippines.

1989, Jan. 27 Litho. *Perf. 13x14*

546 A244 25c Energy and nature *(612,114)*	.60	.60
First day cover		1.25
Inscription block of 4	2.50	—
547 A244 45c Agriculture *(528,184)*	1.10	1.10
First day cover		1.50
First day cover, #546-547		1.75
Inscription block of 4	5.50	—

First day covers of Nos. 546-547 total 103,087 (NYC), 56,501 (Washington).
See Offices in Geneva Nos. 173-174; Vienna Nos. 88-89.

A245

UN Peace-Keeping Force, awarded 1988 Nobel Peace Prize.
Printed by CPE Australia, Ltd., Australia. Panes of 50. Designed by Tom Bland, Australia.

1989, Mar. 17 Litho. *Perf. 14x13½*

548 A245 25c **multicolored** *(808,842)*	.45	.45
First day cover *(52,115)*		1.25
Inscription block of 4	2.00	—

See Offices in Geneva No. 175; Vienna No. 90.

Aerial Photograph of New York Headquarters — A246

Printed by Johann Enschede and Sons, the Netherlands. Panes of 25. Designed by Rocco J. Callari, United States, from a photograph by Simon Nathan.

1989, Mar. 17 Litho. *Perf. 14½x14*

549	A246 45c **multicolored** *(2,000,000)+*	.65	.65
	First day cover *(41,610)*		1.50
	Inscription block of 4	2.75	—

World Weather Watch, 25th Anniv. (in 1988) — A247

Printed by Johann Enschede and Sons, the Netherlands. Panes of 50.

Satellite photographs: 25c, Storm system off the U.S. east coast. 36c, Typhoon Abby in the north-west Pacific.

1989, Apr. 21 Litho. *Perf. 13x14*

550	A247 25c **multicolored** *(849,819)*	.50	.50
	First day cover		1.25
	Inscription block of 4	2.25	—
551	A247 36c **multicolored** *(826,547)*	1.10	1.10
	First day cover		1.75
	First day cover, #550-551		2.00
	Inscription block of 4	6.50	—

First day covers of Nos. 550-551 total 92,013.

See Offices in Geneva Nos. 176-177; Vienna Nos. 91-92.

Offices in Vienna, 10th Anniv.
A248 A249

Printed by the Government Printing Office, Austria. Panes of 25. Designed by Paul Flora (25c) and Rudolf Hausner (90c), Austria.

1989, Aug. 23 Photo. & Engr., Photo. (90c) *Perf. 14*

552	A248 25c **multicolored** *(580,663)*	1.25	1.25
	First day cover		2.25
	Inscription block of 4	5.00	—
553	A249 90c **multicolored** *(505,776)*	2.50	2.50
	First day cover		3.00
	First day cover, #552-553		5.00
	Inscription block of 4	7.00	—
	Panes of 25, #552-553	70.00	

First day covers of Nos. 552-553 total 89,068.

See Offices in Geneva Nos. 178-179; Vienna Nos. 93-94.

Flag Type of 1980

Printed by Helio Courvoisier, Switzerland. Designed by Ole Hamann, Denmark. Issued in panes of 16; each contains 4 blocks of 4 (Nos. 554-557, 558-561, 562-565, 566-569). A se-tenant block of 4 designs centers each pane.

1989, Sept. 22 Photo. *Perf. 12*
Granite Paper

554	A185 25c Indonesia *(959,076)*	.60	.55
555	A185 25c Lesotho *(959,076)*	.60	.55
556	A185 25c Guatemala *(959,076)*	.60	.55
557	A185 25c Netherlands *(959,076)*	.60	.55
a.	Se-tenant block of 4, #554-557	4.00	4.00
558	A185 25c South Africa *(960,502)*	.60	.55
559	A185 25c Portugal *(960,502)*	.60	.55
560	A185 25c Morocco *(960,502)*	.60	.55
561	A185 25c Syrian Arab Republic *(960,502)*	.60	.55
a.	Se-tenant block of 4, #558-561	4.00	4.00
562	A185 25c Honduras *(959,814)*	.60	.55
563	A185 25c Kampuchea *(959,814)*	.60	.55
564	A185 25c Guinea-Bissau *(959,814)*	.60	.55
565	A185 25c Cyprus *(959,814)*	.60	.55
a.	Se-tenant block of 4, #562-565	4.00	4.00
566	A185 25c Algeria *(959,805)*	.60	.55
567	A185 25c Brunei *(959,805)*	.60	.55
568	A185 25c St. Kitts and Nevis *(959,805)*	.60	.55
569	A185 25c United Nations *(959,805)*	.60	.55
a.	Se-tenant block of 4, #566-569	4.00	4.00
	First day covers, #554-569, each		1.25
	Set of 4 diff. panes of 16	30.00	
	Nos. 554-569 (16)	9.60	8.80

First day covers of Nos. 554-569 total 794,934.

Declaration of Human Rights, 10th Anniv. (in 1988) — A250

Printed by Johann Enschede and Sons, the Netherlands. Panes of 12+12 se-tenant labels containing Articles 1 (25c) or 2 (45c) inscribed in English, French or German. Designed by Rocco J. Callari and Robert Stein, US.

Paintings: 25c, The Table of Universal Brotherhood, by Jose Clemente Orozco. 45c, Study for Composition II, by Vassily Kandinsky.

1989, Nov. 17 Litho. *Perf. 13½*

570	A250 25c **multicolored** *(1,934,135)*	.35	.35
	First day cover		1.00
	Inscription block of 3 + 3 labels	1.10	—
571	A250 45c **multicolored** *(1,922,171)*	.80	.80
	First day cover		1.50
	First day cover, #570-571		1.50
	Inscription block of 3 + 3 labels	2.50	—
	Panes of 12, #570-571	12.00	

First day covers of Nos. 570-571 total 146,489 (NYC), 46,774 (Washington).

See Nos. 582-583, 599-600, 616-617, 627-628; Offices in Geneva Nos. 180-181, 193-194, 209-210, 224-225, 234-235; Vienna Nos. 95-96, 108-109, 123-124, 139-140, 150-151.

Intl. Trade Center — A251

Printed by House of Questa, United Kingdom. Panes of 50. Designed by Richard Bernstein, US.

1990, Feb. 2 **Litho.** ***Perf. 14½x15***

572 A251 25c **multicolored** *(429,081)* 1.00 1.00
First day cover *(52,614)* 1.00
Inscription block of 4 4.00 —

See Offices in Geneva No. 182; Vienna No. 97.

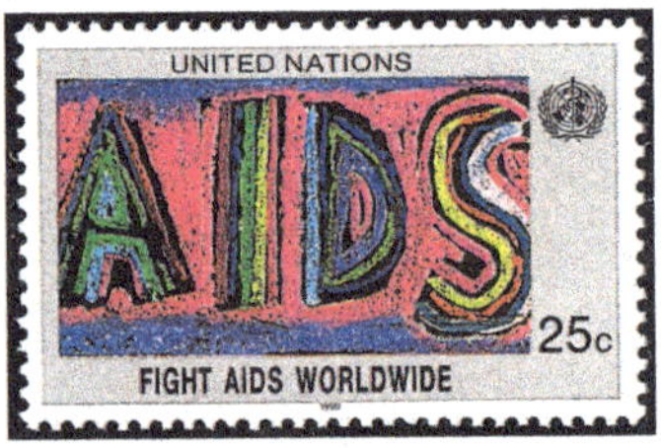

Fight AIDS Worldwide A252

Printed by Johann Enschede and Sons, the Netherlands. Panes of 50. Designed by Jacek Tofil, Poland (25c) and Fritz Henry Oerter, Federal Republic of Germany (40c).

Design: 40c, Shadow over crowd.

1990, Mar. 16 **Litho.** ***Perf. 13½x12½***

573 A252 25c **multicolored** *(492,078)* .35 .35
First day cover 1.00
Inscription block of 4 1.50 —
574 A252 40c **multicolored** *(394,149)* 1.15 1.15
First day cover 1.25
First day cover, #573-574 3.50
Inscription block of 4 5.00 —

First day covers of Nos. 573-574 total 95,854.
See Offices in Geneva Nos. 184-185, Vienna Nos. 99-100.

Medicinal Plants — A253

Printed by Helio Courvoisier, Switzerland. Panes of 50. Designed by Rocco J. Callari & Robert Stein, US from illustrations from "Curtis's Botanical Magazine".

25c, Catharanthus roseus. 90c, Panax quinquefolium.

1990, May 4 **Photo.** **Granite Paper** ***Perf. 11½***

575 A253 25c multi *(796,792)* .45 .45
First day cover 1.00
Inscription block of 4 1.75 —
576 A253 90c multi *(605,617)* 1.40 1.40
First day cover 1.25
First day cover, #575-576 2.50
Inscription block of 4 5.50 —

First day covers of Nos. 575-576 total 100,548.
See Offices in Geneva Nos. 186-187, Vienna Nos. 101-102.

United Nations, 45th Anniv. — A254

Printed by Johann Enschede and Sons, the Netherlands. Panes of 50. Designed by Kris Geysen, Belgium (25c), Nejat M. Gur, Turkey (45c), Robert Stein, US (No. 579).

Design: 45c, "45," emblem.

1990, June 26 **Litho.** ***Perf. 14½x13***

577 A254 25c **multicolored** *(581,718)* .50 .50
First day cover 1.00
Inscription block of 4 2.25 —
578 A254 45c **multicolored** *(582,769)* 1.90 1.90
First day cover 1.00
First day cover, #577-578 2.00
Inscription block of 4 8.00 —

Souvenir Sheet

579 Sheet of 2, #577-578 *(315,946)* 3.50 3.50
First day cover 3.50

First day covers of Nos. 577-579 total 129,011.
See Offices in Geneva Nos. 188-190; Vienna Nos. 103-105.

Crime Prevention — A255

Printed by Heraclio Fournier, S.A. Spain. Panes of 50. Designed by Josef Ryzec, Czechoslovakia.

1990, Sept. 13 **Photo.** ***Perf. 14***

580 A255 25c Crimes of youth *(533,089)* .65 .65
First day cover 1.00
Inscription block of 4 3.00 —
581 A255 36c Organized crime *(427,215)* 1.25 1.25
First day cover 1.75
First day cover, #580-581 2.50
Inscription block of 4 5.75 —

First day covers of Nos. 580-581 total 68,660.
See Offices in Geneva Nos. 191-192; Vienna Nos. 106-107.

Human Rights Type of 1989

Printed by Johann Enschede and Sons, the Netherlands. Panes of 12+12 se-tenant labels containing Articles 7 (25c) or 8 (45c) inscribed in English, French or German. Designed by Rocco J. Callari and Robert Stein, US.

Artwork: 25c, Fragment from the sarcophagus of Plotinus, c. 270 A.D. 45c, Combined Chambers of the High Court of Appeal by Charles Paul Renouard.

1990, Nov. 16 **Litho.** ***Perf. 13½***

582 A250 25c **black, gray & tan** *(1,492,950)* .35 .35
First day cover 1.00
Inscription block of 3 + 3 labels 1.10 —
583 A250 45c **black & brown** *(1,490,934)* .65 .65
First day cover 1.00
First day cover, #582-583 1.50
Inscription block of 3 + 3 labels 2.75 —
Panes of 12, #582-583 14.00

First day covers of Nos. 582-583 total 108,560.
See Offices in Geneva Nos. 193-194; Vienna Nos. 108-109.

Economic Commission for Europe — A256

Printed by Heraclio Fournier, S.A., Spain. Panes of 40. Designed by Carlos Ochagavia, Argentina.

1991, Mar. 15	**Litho.**	***Perf. 14***	
584	A256 30c Two storks *(590,102)*	.85	.85
585	A256 30c Woodpecker, ibex *(590,102)*	.85	.85
586	A256 30c Capercaille, plover *(590,102)*	.85	.85
587	A256 30c Falcon, marmot *(590,102)*	.85	.85
a.	Block of 4, #584-587	3.75	3.75
	First day cover, #587a		4.00
	First day cover, #584-587, any single		4.50
	Inscription block of 4, #587a	5.00	—
	Pane of 40, #584-587	35.00	

First day covers of Nos. 584-587 total 53,502.

See Offices in Geneva Nos. 195-198; Vienna Nos. 110-113.

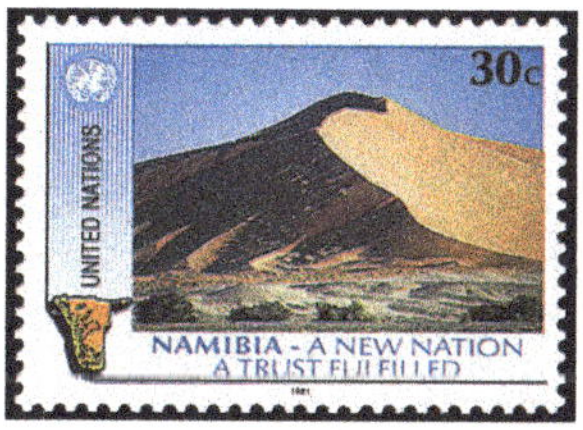

Namibian Independence A257

Printed by Heraclio Fournier, S.A., Spain. Designed by Rocco J. Callari, US, from photographs by John Isaac, India.

1991, May 10	**Litho.**	***Perf. 14***	
588	A257 30c Dunes, Namib Desert *(360,825)*	.50	.50
	First day cover		1.00
	Inscription block of 4	2.25	—
589	A257 50c Savanna *(415,648)*	1.10	1.00
	First day cover		1.25
	First day cover, #588-589		2.50
	Inscription block of 4	4.75	—

First day covers of Nos. 588-589 total 114,258.

See Offices in Geneva Nos. 199-200; Vienna Nos. 114-115.

A258

The Golden Rule by Norman Rockwell — A259

UN Headquarters, New York — A260

Printed by Johann Enschede and Sons, the Netherlands (30c), Helio Courvoisier, S.A., Switzerland (50c), and by Government Printing Bureau, Japan ($2). Panes of 50. Designed by Rocco J. Callari (30c), Norman Rockwell, US (50c), Rocco J. Callari and Robert Stein, US ($2).

1991	**Litho.**	***Perf. 13½***	
590	A258 30c **multi,** *Sept. 11, (2,000,000)+*	.60	.60
	First day cover		1.00
	Inscription block of 4	2.50	—
	Photo.		
	Perf. 12x11½		
591	A259 50c **multi,** *Sept. 11, (2,000,000)+*	1.00	1.00
	First day cover		1.00
	Inscription block of 4	5.00	
	Engr.		
592	A260 $2 **dark blue,** *May 10, (2,000,000)+*	2.75	2.75
	First day cover		2.75
	Inscription block of 4	11.00	—

First day covers of Nos. 590-591 total 66,016, No. 592, 36,022.

See Offices in Geneva Nos. 199-200; Vienna Nos. 114-115.

Rights of the Child — A261

Printed by The House of Questa, United Kingdom. Panes of 50. Designed by Nicole Delia Legnani, US (30c) and Alissa Duffy, US (70c).

1991, June 14	**Litho.**	***Perf. 14½***	
593	A261 30c Children, globe *(440,151)*	1.00	1.00
	First day cover		1.00
	Inscription block of 4	4.50	—
594	A261 70c House, rainbow *(447,803)*	2.00	2.00
	First day cover		1.50
	First day cover, #593-594		2.00
	Inscription block of 4	9.00	—

First day covers of Nos. 593-594 total 96,324.

See Offices in Geneva Nos. 203-204; Vienna Nos. 117-118.

Banning of Chemical Weapons A262

Printed by Heraclio Fournier, S.A., Spain. Panes of 50. Designed by Oscar Asboth, Austria (30c), Michael Granger, France (90c).

Design: 90c, Hand holding back chemical drums.

1991, Sept. 11 **Litho.** ***Perf. 13½***

595	A262 30c **multicolored** *(367,548)*	.75	.75
	First day cover		1.25
	Inscription block of 4	3.75	—
596	A262 90c **multicolored** *(346,161)*	2.25	2.25
	First day cover		1.50
	First day cover, #595-596		2.50
	Inscription block of 4	11.00	—

First day covers of Nos. 595-596 total 91,552.

See Offices in Geneva Nos. 205-206; Vienna Nos. 119-120.

UN Postal Administration, 40th Anniv. — A263

Printed by The House of Questa, United Kingdom. Panes of 25. Designed by Rocco J. Callari, US.

1991, Oct. 24 **Litho.** ***Perf. 14x15***

597	A263 30c No. 1 *(442,548)*	.65	.65
	First day cover		1.00
	Inscription block of 4	2.75	—
598	A263 40c No. 3 *(419,127)*	.85	.85
	First day cover		1.00
	First day cover, #597-598		1.50
	Inscription block of 4	4.00	—
	Panes of 25, #597-598	45.00	

First day covers of Nos. 597-598 total 81,177 (New York), 58,501 (State College, PA).

See Offices in Geneva Nos. 207-208; Vienna Nos. 121-122.

Human Rights Type of 1989

Printed by Johann Enschede and Sons, the Netherlands. Panes of 12+12 se-tenant labels containing Articles 13 (30c) or 14 (50c) inscribed in English, French or German. Designed by Robert Stein, US.

Artwork: 30c, The Last of England, by Ford Madox Brown. 40c, The Emigration to the East, by Tito Salas.

1991, Nov. 20 **Litho.** ***Perf. 13½***

599	A250 30c **multicolored** *(1,261,198)*	.35	.35
	First day cover		1.00
	Inscription block of 3 + 3 labels	1.75	—
600	A250 50c **multicolored** *(1,255,077)*	.80	1.00
	First day cover		1.00
	First day cover, #599-600		2.25
	Inscription block of 3 + 3 labels	3.50	—
	Panes of 12, #599-600	14.00	

First day covers of Nos. 599-600 total 136,605.

See Offices in Geneva Nos. 209-210; Vienna Nos. 123-124.

World Heritage Type of 1984

Printed by Cartor S.A., France. Panes of 50. Designed by Robert Stein, U.S.

Designs: 30c, Uluru Natl. Park, Australia. 50c, The Great Wall of China.

1992, Jan. 24 **Litho.** ***Perf. 13***

Size: 35x28mm

601	A215 30c **multicolored** *(337,717)*	.55	.55
	First day cover		1.00
	Inscription block of 4	2.50	—
602	A215 50c **multicolored** *(358,000)*	.90	.90
	First day cover		1.25
	First day cover, #601-602		1.75
	Inscription block of 4	4.25	—

First day covers of Nos. 601-602 total 62,733.

See Offices in Geneva Nos. 211-212; Vienna Nos. 125-126.

Clean Oceans — A264

Printed by The House of Questa, United Kingdom. Panes of 12. Designed by Braldt Bralds, Netherlands.

1992, Mar. 13 **Litho.** ***Perf. 14***

603	A264 29c Ocean surface *(983,126)*	.45	.50
604	A264 29c Ocean bottom *(983,126)*	.45	.50
a.	Pair, #603-604	.90	1.10
	First day cover, #604a		2.00
	First day cover, #603-604, any single		1.00
	Inscription block of 4, #603-604	3.25	—
	Pane of 12, #603-604	9.00	

First day covers of Nos. 603-604 total 75,511.

See Offices in Geneva Nos. 214-215, Vienna Nos. 127-128.

Earth Summit — A265

Printed by Helio Courvoisier S.A., Switzerland. Panes of 40. Designed by Peter Max, US.

Designs: No. 605, Globe at LR. No. 606, Globe at LL. No. 607, Globe at UR. No. 608, Globe at UL.

1992, May 22 **Photo.** ***Perf. 11½***

605	A265 29c **multicolored** *(806,268)*	.65	.65
606	A265 29c **multicolored** *(806,268)*	.65	.65
607	A265 29c **multicolored** *(806,268)*	.65	.65
608	A265 29c **multicolored** *(806,268)*	.65	.65
a.	Block of 4, #605-608	4.00	3.50
	First day cover, #608a		3.50
	First day cover, #605-608, each		7.50
	Inscription block of 4, #608a	5.00	—
	Pane of 40, #605-608	27.50	

First day covers of Nos. 605-608a total 110,577.

See Offices in Geneva Nos. 216-219, Vienna Nos. 129-132.

Mission to Planet Earth — A266

Printed by Helio Courvoisier, S.A., Switzerland. Designed by Attilla Hejja, US.

Designs: No. 609, Satellites over city, sailboats, fishing boat. No. 610, Satellite over coast, passenger liner, dolphins, whale, volcano.

1992, Sept. 4 **Photo.** ***Rouletted 8***

Granite Paper

609 A266 29c **multicolored** *(643,647)* 1.50 1.50
610 A266 29c **multicolored** *(643,647)* 1.50 1.50
a. Pair, #609-610 3.00 3.00
First day cover, #610a 5.00
First day cover, #609-610, each 11.00
Inscription block of 4 9.00 —
Pane of 10, #609-610 21.00

First day covers of Nos. 609-610a total 69,343.
See Offices in Geneva Nos. 220-221, Vienna Nos. 133-134.

Science and Technology for Development A267

Printed by Unicover Corp., US. Designed by Saul Mandel, US.
Design: 50c, Animal, man drinking.

1992, Oct. 2 **Litho.** ***Perf. 14***

611 A267 29c **multicolored** *(453,365)* .40 .40
First day cover 1.00
Inscription block of 4 1.75 —
612 A267 50c **multicolored** *(377,377)* .70 .70
First day cover 1.00
First day cover, #611-612 4.25
Inscription block of 4 3.25

First day covers of Nos. 611-612 total 69,195.
See Offices in Geneva Nos. 222-223, Vienna Nos. 135-136.

UN University Building, Tokyo — A268

UN Headquarters, New York — A269

Printed by Cartor SA, France (4c, 40c), Walsall Security Printers, Ltd., UK (29c). Designed by Banks and Miles, UK (4c, 40c), Robert Stein, US (29c).
Design: 40c, UN University Building, Tokyo, diff.

1992, Oct. 2 **Litho.** ***Perf. 14, 13½x13 (29c)***

613 A268 4c **multicolored** *(1,500,000)+* .25 .25
First day cover 1.00
Inscription block of 4 .70 —
614 A269 29c **multicolored** *(1,750,000)+* .50 .50
First day cover 1.00
Inscription block of 4 2.25 —
615 A268 40c **multicolored** *(1,500,000)+* .65 .65
First day cover 1.00
First day cover, #613-615 2.00
Inscription block of 4 3.75 —
Nos. 613-615 (3) 1.40 1.40

First day covers of Nos. 613-615 total 62,697.

Human Rights Type of 1989

Printed by Johann Enschede and Sons, the Netherlands. Panes of 12+12 se-tenant labels containing Articles 19 (29c) and 20 (50c) inscribed in English, French or German. Designed by Robert Stein, US.
Artwork: 29c, Lady Writing a Letter with her Maid, by Vermeer. 50c, The Meeting, by Ester Almqvist.

1992, Nov. 20 **Litho.** ***Perf. 13½***

616 A250 29c **multicolored,** *(1,184,531)* .40 .40
First day cover 1.50
Inscription block of 3 + 3 labels 1.75 —
617 A250 50c **multicolored,** *(1,107,044)* .60 .60
First day cover 1.50
First day cover, #616-617 2.25
Inscription block of 3 + 3 labels 2.75 —
Panes of 12, #616-617 14.00

First day covers of Nos. 616-617 total 104,470.
See Offices in Geneva Nos. 224-225; Vienna Nos. 139-140.

Aging With Dignity — A270

Printed by Cartor SA, France. Designed by C.M. Dudash, US.
Designs: 29c, Elderly couple, family. 52c, Old man, physician, woman holding fruit basket.

1993, Feb. 5 **Litho.** ***Perf. 13***

618 A270 29c **multicolored** *(336,933)* .45 .45
First day cover 1.00
Inscription block of 4 2.25 —
619 A270 52c **multicolored** *(308,080)* 1.00 1.00
First day cover 1.00
First day cover, #618-619 1.25
Inscription block of 4 4.75

First day covers of Nos. 618-619 total 52,932.
See Offices in Geneva Nos. 226-227; Vienna Nos. 141-142.

Endangered Species — A271

Printed by Johann Enschede and Sons, the Netherlands. Designed by Rocco J. Callari and Norman Adams, US.
Designs: No. 620, Hairy-nosed wombat. No. 621, Whooping crane. No. 622, Giant clam. No. 623, Giant sable antelope.

1993, Mar. 2 **Litho.** ***Perf. 13x12½***

620 A271 29c **multicolored** *(1,200,000)+* .45 .45
621 A271 29c **multicolored** *(1,200,000)+* .45 .45
622 A271 29c **multicolored** *(1,200,000)+* .45 .45
623 A271 29c **multicolored** *(1,200,000)+* .45 .45
a. Block of 4, #620-623 2.00 2.00
First day cover, #623a 3.75
First day cover, #620-623, each 2.00
Inscription block of 4, #623a 2.50 —
Pane of 16, #620-623 9.00

First day covers of Nos. 620-623a total 64,794.
See Nos. 639-642, 657-660, 674-677, 700-703, 730-733, 757-760, 773-776, 789-792, 818-821, 842-845, 858-861, 876-879, 908-911, 925-928, 949-952, 975-978, 999-1002, 1031-1034, 1042-1045, 1074-1077; Offices in Geneva Nos. 228-231, 246-249, 264-267, 280-283, 298-301, 318-321, 336-339, 352-355, 367-370, 386-389, 407-410, 418-421, 436-439, 453-456, 465-468, 480-483, 496-

499, 513-516, 540-543, 549-552, 572-575; Vienna Nos. 143-146, 162-165, 180-183, 196-199, 214-217, 235-238, 253-256, 269-272, 284-287, 308-311, 329-332, 342-345, 360-363, 376-379, 388-391, 417-420, 438-441, 465-468, 501-504, 511-514, 534-537.

Healthy Environment — A272

Printed by Leigh-Mardon Pty. Limited, Australia. Designed by Milton Glaser, US.
Designs: 29c, Personal. 50c, Family.

1993, May 7 **Litho.** ***Perf. 15x14½***

624 A272 29c Man *(430,463)*	.50	.50
First day cover		1.00
Inscription block of 4	2.25	—
625 A272 50c Family *(326,692)*	.90	.90
First day cover		1.00
First day cover, #624-625		2.00
Inscription block of 4	3.75	—

WHO, 45th anniv. First day covers of Nos. 624-625 total 55,139.
See Offices in Geneva Nos. 232-233; Vienna Nos. 147-148.

A273

Printed by House of Questa, Ltd., United Kingdom. Designed by Salahattin Kanidinc, US.

1993, May 7 **Litho.** ***Perf. 15x14***

626 A273 5c **multicolored** *(1,500,000)*+	.25	.25
First day cover *(23,452)*		1.00
Inscription block of 4	.65	—

Human Rights Type of 1989

Printed by Johann Enschede and Sons, the Netherlands. Panes of 12 + 12 se-tenant labels containing Articles 25 (29c) and 26 (35c) inscribed in English, French or German. Designed by Robert Stein, US.
Artwork: 29c, Shucking Corn, by Thomas Hart Benton. 35c, The Library, by Jacob Lawrence.

1993, June 11 **Litho.** ***Perf. 13½***

627 A250 29c **multicolored** *(1,049,134)*	.40	.40
First day cover		1.00
Inscription block of 3 + 3 labels	1.75	—
628 A250 35c **multicolored** *(1,045,346)*	.45	.45
First day cover		1.00
First day cover, #627-628		1.25
Inscription block of 3 + 3 labels	2.50	—
Panes of 12, #627-628	16.00	

First day covers of Nos. 627-628 total 77,719.
See Offices in Geneva Nos. 234-235; Vienna Nos. 150-151.

Intl. Peace Day — A274

Printed by the PTT, Switzerland. Designed by Hans Erni, Switzerland.
Denomination at: #629, UL. #630, UR. #631, LL. #632, LR.

1993, Sept. 21 **Litho. & Engr.** ***Rouletted 12½***

629 A274 29c **blue & multi** *(298,367)*	.75	.75
630 A274 29c **blue & multi** *(298,367)*	.75	.75
631 A274 29c **blue & multi** *(298,367)*	.75	.75
632 A274 29c **blue & multi** *(298,367)*	.75	.75
a. Block of 4, #629-632	4.00	4.00
First day cover, #629-632, each		5.00
First day cover, #632a		6.00
Inscription block of 4, #632a	7.50	—
Pane of 40, #629-632	65.00	

First day covers of Nos. 629-632a total 41,743.
See Offices in Geneva Nos. 236-239; Vienna Nos. 152-155.

Environment-Climate A275

Printed by House of Questa, Ltd., United Kingdom. Designed by Braldt Bralds, Netherlands.
Designs: No. 633, Chameleon. No. 634, Palm trees, top of funnel cloud. No. 635, Bottom of funnel cloud, deer, antelope. No. 636, Bird of paradise.

1993, Oct. 29 **Litho.** ***Perf. 14½***

633 A275 29c **multicolored** *(383,434)*	.75	.75
634 A275 29c **multicolored** *(383,434)*	.75	.75
635 A275 29c **multicolored** *(383,434)*	.75	.75
636 A275 29c **multicolored** *(383,434)*	.75	.75
a. Strip of 4, #633-636	4.00	4.00
First day cover, #636a		2.75
First day cover, #633-636, each		3.75
Inscription block, 2 #636a	10.00	—
Pane of 24, #633-636	30.00	

First day covers of Nos. 633-636a total 38,182.
See Offices in Geneva Nos. 240-243; Vienna Nos. 156-159.

Intl. Year of the Family — A276

Printed by Cartor S.A., France. Designed by Rocco J. Callari, US.
Designs: 29c, Mother holding child, two children, woman. 45c, People tending crops.

1994, Feb. 4 **Litho.** ***Perf. 13.1***

637 A276 29c **green & multi** *(590,000)*+	.70	.70
First day cover		1.00
Inscription block of 4	3.25	—
638 A276 45c **blue & multi** *(540,000)*+	.90	.90
First day cover		1.00
First day cover, #637-638		1.25
Inscription block of 4	4.00	—

First day covers of Nos. 637-638 total 47,982. See Offices in Geneva Nos. 244-245; Vienna Nos. 160-161.

Endangered Species Type of 1993

Printed by Johann Enschede and Sons, the Netherlands. Designed by Rocco J. Callari, US (frame), and Kerrie Maddeford, Australia (stamps).

Designs: No. 639, Chimpanzee. No. 640, St. Lucia Amazon. No. 641, American crocodile. No. 642, Dama gazelle.

1994, Mar. 18 **Litho.** ***Perf. 12.7***

639 A271 29c **multicolored** *(1,200,000)+*	.45	.45
640 A271 29c **multicolored** *(1,200,000)+*	.45	.45
641 A271 29c **multicolored** *(1,200,000)+*	.45	.45
642 A271 29c **multicolored** *(1,200,000)+*	.45	.45
a. Block of 4, #639-642	2.00	2.00
First day cover, #642a		3.50
First day cover, #639-642, each		1.50
Inscription block of 4, #642a	2.50	—
Pane of 16, #639-642	8.50	

First day covers of Nos. 639-642 total 79,599. See Offices in Geneva Nos. 246-249; Vienna Nos. 162-165.

Protection for Refugees — A277

Printed by Leigh-Mardon Pty. Limited, Australia. Designed by Francoise Peyroux, France.

1994, Apr. 29 **Litho.** ***Perf. 14.3x14.8***

643 A277 50c **multicolored** *(600,000)+*	.90	.90
First day cover *(33,558)*		1.25
Inscription block of 4	4.50	—

See Offices in Geneva No. 250; Vienna No. 166.

Dove of Peace — A278

Sleeping Child, by Stanislaw Wyspianski — A279

Mourning Owl, by Vanessa Isitt — A280

Printed by Cartor S.A., France, and Norges Banks Seddeltrykkeri, Norway (#646).

1994, Apr. 29 **Litho.** ***Perf. 12.9***

644 A278 10c **multicolored** *(1,000,000)+*	.25	.25
First day cover		1.00
Inscription block of 4	.75	—
645 A279 19c **multicolored** *(1,000,000)+*	.30	.30
First day cover		1.25
Inscription block of 4	1.50	—

Engr.

Perf. 13.1

646 A280 $1 **red brown** *(1,000,000)+*	1.50	1.50
First day cover		3.00
Inscription block of 4	7.00	—
Nos. 644-646 (3)	2.05	2.05

First day covers of Nos. 644-646 total 48,946.

Intl. Decade for Natural Disaster Reduction — A281

Printed by The House of Questa, UK. Designed by Kenji Koga, Japan.

Earth seen from space, outline map of: #647, North America. #648, Eurasia. #649, South America, #650, Australia and South Asia.

1994, May 27 **Litho.** ***Perf. 13.9x14.2***

647 A281 29c **multicolored** *(630,000)+*	1.75	1.75
648 A281 29c **multicolored** *(630,000)+*	1.75	1.75
649 A281 29c **multicolored** *(630,000)+*	1.75	1.75
650 A281 29c **multicolored** *(630,000)+*	1.75	1.75
a. Block of 4, #647-650	7.50	7.50
First day cover, #650a		7.50
First day cover, #647-650, each		6.00
Inscription block of 4, #650a	8.00	—
Pane of 40, #647-650	75.00	

First day covers of Nos. 647-650 total 37,135. See Offices in Geneva Nos. 251-254; Vienna Nos. 170-173.

Population and Development A282

Printed by Johann Enschede and Sons, the Netherlands. Designed by Jerry Smath, US.

Designs: 29c, Children playing. 52c, Family with house, car, other possessions.

1994, Sept. 1 Litho. *Perf. 13.2x13.6*

651 A282 29c **multicolored** *(590,000)+* .40 .40
First day cover 1.00
Inscription block of 4 2.00 —
652 A282 52c **multicolored** *(540,000)+* .80 .80
First day cover 1.00
First day cover, #651-652 2.25
Inscription block of 4 3.75 —

First day covers of Nos. 651-652 total 45,256.
See Offices in Geneva Nos. 258-259; Vienna Nos. 174-175.

UNCTAD, 30th Anniv. — A283

Printed by Johann Enschede and Sons, the Netherlands. Designed by Luis Sarda, Spain.

1994, Oct. 28

653 A283 29c **multicolored** *(590,000)+* .40 .40
First day cover 1.00
Inscription block of 4 1.75 —
654 A283 50c **multi, diff.** *(540,000)+* .80 .80
First day cover 1.00
First day cover, #653-654 1.50
Inscription block of 4 3.00

First day covers of Nos. 653-654 total 42,763. See Offices in Geneva Nos. 260-261; Vienna Nos. 176-177.

UN, 50th Anniv. — A284

Printed by Swiss Postal Service. Designed by Rocco J. Callari, US.

1995, Jan. 1 Litho. & Engr. *Perf. 13.4*

655 A284 32c **multicolored** *(938,644)* .90 .90
First day cover *(39,817)* 1.25
Inscription block of 4 4.00 —

See Offices in Geneva No. 262; Vienna No. 178.

Social Summit, Copenhagen — A285

Printed by Austrian Government Printing Office. Designed by Friedensreich Hundertwasser.

1995, Feb. 3 Photo. & Engr. *Perf. 13.6x13.9*

656 A285 50c **multicolored** *(495,388)* 1.00 1.00
First day cover *(31,797)* 2.00
Inscription block of 4 4.00 —

See Offices in Geneva No. 263; Vienna No. 179.

Endangered Species Type of 1993

Printed by Johann Enschede and Sons, the Netherlands. Designed by Chris Calle, US.

Designs: No. 657, Giant armadillo. No. 658, American bald eagle. No. 659, Fijian/Tongan banded iguana. No. 660, Giant panda.

1995, Mar. 24 Litho. *Perf. 13x12½*

657 A271 32c **multicolored** *(756,000)+* .40 .40
658 A271 32c **multicolored** *(756,000)+* .40 .40
659 A271 32c **multicolored** *(756,000)+* .40 .40
660 A271 32c **multicolored** *(756,000)+* .40 .40
a. Block of 4, 657-660 2.25 2.25
First day cover, #660a 5.00
First day cover, #657-660, each 1.75
Inscription block of 4, #660a 2.50 —
Pane of 16, #657-660 9.00

First day covers of Nos. 657-660 total 67,311. See Offices in Geneva Nos. 264-267; Vienna Nos. 180-183.

Intl. Youth Year, 10th Anniv. — A286

Printed by The House of Questa (UK). Designed by Gottfried Kumpf, Austria.

Designs: 32c, Seated child. 55c, Children cycling.

1995, May 26 Litho. *Perf. 14.4x14.7*

661 A286 32c **multicolored** *(358,695)* .55 .55
First day cover 1.00
Inscription block of 4 2.50 —
662 A286 55c **multicolored** *(288,424)* .95 .95
First day cover 1.00
First day cover, #661-662 1.50
Inscription block of 4 4.25 —

First day covers of Nos. 661-662 total 42,846. See Offices in Geneva Nos. 268-269; Vienna Nos. 184-185.

UN, 50th Anniv. — A287

Printed by Johann Enschede Security Printing, the Netherlands. Designed by Paul and Chris Calle, US.

Designs: 32c, Hand with pen signing UN Charter, flags. 50c, Veterans' War Memorial, Opera House, San Francisco.

1995, June 26 Engr. *Perf. 13.3x13.6*

663 A287 32c **black** *(501,961)* .55 .55
First day cover 1.00
Inscription block of 4 2.25 —
664 A287 50c **maroon** *(419,932)* 1.00 1.00
First day cover 1.00
First day cover, #663-664 1.50
Inscription block of 4 4.25 —

Souvenir Sheet
Litho. & Engr.
Imperf

665	Sheet of 2, #663-664 *(347,963)*+	3.00	3.00
a.	A287 32c **black**	1.25	1.25
b.	A287 50c **maroon**	1.50	1.50
	First day cover		2.75

First day covers of Nos. 663-665 total: New York, 69,263; San Francisco, 53,354.

No. 665 exists with gold China 1996 overprint. Value $20.

See Offices in Geneva Nos. 270-272; Vienna Nos. 186-188.

4th World Conference on Women, Beijing — A288

Printed by Postage Stamp Printing House, MPT, People's Republic of China. Designed by Ting Shao Kuang, People's Republic of China.

Designs: 32c, Mother and child. 40c, Seated woman, cranes flying above.

1995, Sept. 5 **Photo.** ***Perf. 12***

666	A288 32c **multicolored** *(561,847)*	.50	.50
	First day cover		1.25
	Inscription block of 4	2.25	—

Size: 28x50mm

667	A288 40c **multicolored** *(499,850)*	.85	.85
	First day cover		1.25
	First day cover, #666-667		2.50
	Inscription block of 4	3.75	—

First day covers of Nos. 666-667 total 103,963. See Offices in Geneva Nos. 273-274; Vienna Nos. 189-190.

UN Headquarters A289

Designed by John B. De Santis, Jr. US.

1995, Sept. 5 **Litho.** ***Perf. 15***

668	A289 20c **multicolored**	.35	.35
	First day cover *(18,326)*		1.50
	Inscription block of 4	2.00	—

Miniature Sheet

United Nations, 50th Anniv. — A290

Designed by Ben Verkaaik, Netherlands.

Printed by House of Questa, UK.

Designs: #669a-669 l, Various people in continuous design (2 blocks of six stamps with gutter between).

1995, Oct. 24 **Litho.** ***Perf. 14***

669	A290 Sheet of 12 *(214,639 sheets)*	5.00	5.00
	First day cover		12.00
a.-l.	32c any single	.40	.40
	First day cover, #669a-669l, each		7.00
670	Souvenir booklet *(85,256 booklets)*	5.50	
a.	A290 32c Booklet pane of 3, vert. strip of 3 from UL of sheet	1.35	1.35
b.	A290 32c Booklet pane of 3, vert. strip of 3 from UR of sheet	1.35	1.35
c.	A290 32c Booklet pane of 3, vert. strip of 3 from LL of sheet	1.35	1.35
d.	A290 32c Booklet pane of 3, vert. strip of 3 from LR of sheet	1.35	1.35
	First day covers, #670a-670d, set booklet tab singles		100.00

First day covers of Nos. 669-670 total 47,632. See Offices in Geneva Nos. 275-276; Vienna Nos. 191-192.

WFUNA, 50th Anniv. — A291

Designed by Rudolf Mirer, Switzerland.

Printed by Johann Enschede and Sons, the Netherlands.

1996, Feb. 2 **Litho.** ***Perf. 13x13½***

671	A291 32c **multicolored** *(580,000)*+	.50	.50
	First day cover		1.00
	Inscription block of 4	2.25	—

See Offices in Geneva No. 277; Vienna No. 193.

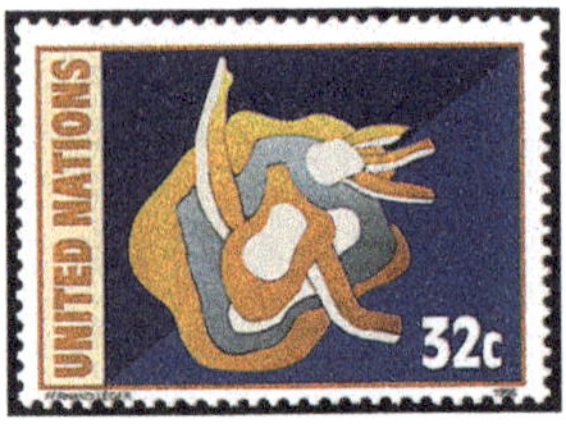

Mural, by Fernand Leger — A292

Designed by Fernand Leger, France.
Printed by House of Questa, UK.

1996, Feb. 2 **Litho.** ***Perf. 14½x15***

672 A292 32c **multicolored** *(780,000)+*	.45	.45
First day cover		1.25
Inscription block of 4	2.00	—
673 A292 60c **multi, diff.** *(680,000)+*	.95	.95
First day cover		1.75
First day cover, #672-673		2.25
Inscription block of 4	4.00	—

Endangered Species Type of 1993

Printed by Johann Enschede and Sons, the Netherlands. Designed by Diane Bruyninckx, Belgium.

Designs: No. 674, Masdevallia veitchiana. No. 675, Saguaro cactus. No. 676, West Australian pitcher plant. No. 677, Encephalartos horridus.

1996, Mar. 14 **Litho.** ***Perf. 12½***

674 A271 32c **multicolored** *(640,000)+*	.45	.45
675 A271 32c **multicolored** *(640,000)+*	.45	.45
676 A271 32c **multicolored** *(640,000)+*	.45	.45
677 A271 32c **multicolored** *(640,000)+*	.45	.45
a. Block of 4, #674-677	2.25	2.25
First day cover, #677a		5.00
First day cover, #674-677, each		1.75
Inscription block of 4, #677a	2.75	—
Pane of 16, #674-677	10.00	

See Offices in Geneva Nos. 280-283; Vienna Nos. 196-199.

City Summit (Habitat II) — A293

Printed by Johann Enschede and Sons, the Netherlands. Designed by Teresa Fasolino, US.

Designs: No. 678, Deer. No. 679, Man, child, dog sitting on hill, overlooking town. No. 680, People walking in park, city skyline. No. 681, Tropical park, Polynesian woman, boy. No. 682, Polynesian village, orchids, bird.

1996, June 3 **Litho.** ***Perf. 14x13½***

678 A293 32c **multicolored** *(475,000)+*	.80	.80
679 A293 32c **multicolored** *(475,000)+*	.80	.80
680 A293 32c **multicolored** *(475,000)+*	.80	.80
681 A293 32c **multicolored** *(475,000)+*	.80	.80
682 A293 32c **multicolored** *(475,000)+*	.80	.80
a. Strip of 5, #678-682	7.00	7.00
First day cover, #682a		6.00
First day cover, #678-682, each		7.00
Inscription block of 10, 2 #682a	14.50	
Sheet of 25	35.00	

See Offices in Geneva Nos. 284-288; Vienna Nos. 200-204.

Sport and the Environment — A294

Printed by The House of Questa, UK. Designed by LeRoy Neiman, US.

Designs: 32c, Men's basketball. 50c, Women's volleyball, horiz.

1996, July 19 **Litho.** ***Perf. 14x14½, 14½x14***

683 A294 32c **multicolored** *(680,000)+*	.65	.65
First day cover		1.25
Inscription block of 4	3.00	—
684 A294 50c **multicolored** *(680,000)+*	1.40	1.40
First day cover		1.50
First day cover, #683-684		1.75
Inscription block of 4	6.25	—

Souvenir Sheet

685 A294 Sheet of 2, #683-684 *(370,000)+*	2.50	2.50
First day cover		2.50

See Offices in Geneva Nos. 289-291; Vienna Nos. 205-207.
1996 Summer Olympic Games, Atlanta, GA.

Plea for Peace — A295

Printed by House of Questa, UK.
Designed by: 32c, Peng Yue, China. 60c, Cao Chenyu, China.

Designs: 32c, Doves. 60c, Stylized dove.

1996, Sept. 17 **Litho.** ***Perf. 14½x15***

686 A295 32c **multicolored** *(580,000)+*	.50	.50
First day cover		1.00
Inscription block of 4	2.25	—
687 A295 60c **multicolored** *(580,000)+*	.90	.90
First day cover		1.00
First day cover, #686-687		1.75
Inscription block of 4	4.25	—

See Offices in Geneva Nos. 292-293; Vienna Nos. 208-209.

UNICEF, 50th Anniv. — A296

Printed by The House of Questa, UK. Designed by The Walt Disney Co.

Fairy Tales: 32c, Yeh-Shen, China. 60c, The Ugly Duckling, by Hans Christian Andersen.

1996, Nov. 20 **Litho.** ***Perf. 14½x15***

688 A296 32c **multicolored** *(1,000,000)*+ .45 .45
First day cover 1.00
Pane of 8 + label 4.00
689 A296 60c **multicolored** *(1,000,000)*+ 1.10 1.10
First day cover 1.00
First day cover, #688-689 2.00
Pane of 8 + label 12.00

See Offices in Geneva Nos. 294-295; Vienna Nos. 210-211.

Flag Type of 1980

Printed by Helio Courvoisier, S.A., Switzerland. Designed by Oliver Corwin,US, and Robert Stein, UN. Each pane contains 4 blocks of 4 (Nos. 690-693, 694-697). A se-tenant block of 4 designs centers each pane.

1997, Feb. 12 **Photo.** ***Perf. 12***

Granite Paper

690 A185 32c Tajikistan *(940,000)*+ .75 1.00
691 A185 32c Georgia *(940,000)*+ .75 1.00
692 A185 32c Armenia *(940,000)*+ .75 1.00
693 A185 32c Namibia *(940,000)*+ .75 1.00
a. Block of 4, #690-693 10.00 13.00
694 A185 32c Liechtenstein *(940,000)*+ .75 1.00
695 A185 32c Republic of Korea *(940,000)*+ .75 1.00
696 A185 32c Kazakhstan *(940,000)*+ .75 1.00
697 A185 32c Latvia *(940,000)*+ .75 1.00
a. Block of 4, #694-697 10.00 13.00
First day cover, #690-697, each 3.00
Set of 2 panes of 16 34.00

First day covers of Nos. 690-697 total 136,114.

Cherry Blossoms, UN Headquarters — A297

Peace Rose — A298

Printed by The House of Questa, Ltd., UK.

1997, Feb. 12 **Litho.** ***Perf. 14½***

698 A297 8c **multicolored** *(700,000)*+ .25 .25
First day cover 1.00
Inscription block of 4 .70 —
699 A298 55c **multicolored** *(700,000)*+ .90 .90
First day cover 1.25
First day cover, #698-699 2.50
Inscription block of 4 3.75 —

First day covers of Nos. 698-699 total 34,794.

Endangered Species Type of 1993

Printed by Johann Enschedé and Sons, the Netherlands. Designed by Rocco J. Callari, US.

Designs: No. 700, African elephant. No. 701, Major Mitchell's cockatoo. No. 702, Black-footed ferret. No. 703, Cougar.

1997, Mar. 13 **Litho.** ***Perf. 12½***

700 A271 32c **multicolored** *(532,000)*+ .40 .40
701 A271 32c **multicolored** *(532,000)*+ .40 .40
702 A271 32c **multicolored** *(532,000)*+ .40 .40
703 A271 32c **multicolored** *(532,000)*+ .40 .40
a. Block of 4, #700-703 2.25 2.25
First day cover, #703a 3.00
First day cover, #700-703, each 2.50
Inscription block of 4, #703a 2.50
Pane of 16 9.00

First day covers of Nos. 700-703 total 66,863.
See Offices in Geneva Nos. 298-301; Vienna Nos. 214-217.

Earth Summit, 5th Anniv. — A299

Printed by Helio Courvoisier SA, Switzerland. Designed by Peter Max, US.

Designs: No. 704, Sailboat. No. 705, Three sailboats. No. 706, Two people watching sailboat, sun. No. 707, Person, sailboat.
$1, Combined design similar to Nos. 704-707.

1997, May 30 **Photo.** ***Perf. 11.5***

Granite Paper

704 A299 32c **multicolored** *(328,566)* .90 .90
705 A299 32c **multicolored** *(328,566)* .90 .90
706 A299 32c **multicolored** *(328,566)* .90 .90
707 A299 32c **multicolored** *(328,566)* .90 .90
a. Block of 4, #704-707 5.00 5.00
First day cover, #707a 3.00
First day cover, #704-707, each 6.00
Inscription block of 4, #707a 6.00

Souvenir Sheet

708 A299 $1 **multicolored** *(181,667)* 3.25 3.25
First day cover 2.75
a. Ovptd. in sheet margin *(154,435)* *17.50 17.50*
First day cover, #708a 16.50

First day covers of Nos. 704-708 total: New York, 52,528; San Francisco, 49,197.

See Offices in Geneva Nos. 302-306; Vienna Nos. 218-222.

No. 708 contains one 60x43mm stamp. Overprint in sheet margin of No. 708a reads "PACIFIC 97 / World Philatelic Exhibition / San Francisco, California / 29 May - 8 June 1997".

Transportation — A300

Printed by The House of Questa, UK. Panes of 20.
Designed by Michael Cockcroft, UK.

Ships: No. 709, Clipper ship. No. 710, Paddle steamer. No. 711, Ocean liner. No. 712, Hovercraft. No. 713, Hydrofoil.

1997, Aug. 29 **Litho.** ***Perf. 14x14½***

709 A300 32c **multicolored** *(303,767)* .65 .65
710 A300 32c **multicolored** *(303,767)* .65 .65
711 A300 32c **multicolored** *(303,767)* .65 .65
712 A300 32c **multicolored** *(303,767)* .65 .65
713 A300 32c **multicolored** *(303,767)* .65 .65
a. Strip of 5, #709-713 4.25 4.25
First day cover, #713a 4.00
First day cover, #709-713, each 5.75
Inscription block of 10, 2#713a 10.00
Sheet of 20 20.00

First day covers of Nos. 709-713 total 29,287.
See Offices in Geneva Nos. 307-311; Vienna Nos. 223-227.

No. 713a has continuous design.

Philately — A301

Printed by Joh. Enschedé and Sons, the Netherlands. Panes of 20. Designed by Robert Stein, US.
Designs: 32c, No. 473. 50c, No. 474.

1997, Oct. 14 **Litho.** ***Perf. 13½x14***

No.	Description	Unused	Used
714	A301 32c **multicolored** *(363,237)*	.60	.60
	First day cover		1.25
	Inscription block of 4	3.00	—
715	A301 50c **multicolored** *(294,967)*	1.50	1.50
	First day cover		1.50
	First day cover, #714-715		4.00
	Inscription block of 4	6.75	—

First day covers of Nos. 714-715 total 43,684.
See Offices in Geneva Nos. 312-313; Vienna Nos. 228-229.

World Heritage Convention, 25th Anniv. — A302

Printed by Government Printing Office, Austria. Panes of 20. Designed by Robert Stein, US, based on photographs by Guo Youmin, People's Republic of China.
Terracotta warriors of Xian: 32c, Single warrior. 60c, Massed warriors. No. 718a, like #716. No. 718b, like #717. No. 718c, like Geneva #314. No. 718d, like Geneva #315. No. 718e, like Vienna #230. No. 718f, like Vienna #231.

1997, Nov. 19 **Litho.** ***Perf. 13½***

No.	Description	Unused	Used
716	A302 32c **multicolored** *(549,095)*	.75	.75
	First day cover		1.25
	Inscription block of 4	3.25	—
717	A302 60c **multicolored** *(505,265)*	1.25	1.25
	First day cover		1.75
	First day cover, #716-717		3.50
	Inscription block of 4	5.25	—
718	Souvenir booklet *(304,406 booklets)*	8.50	
a.-f.	A302 8c any single	.35	.35
g.	Booklet pane of 4 #718a	1.40	1.40
h.	Booklet pane of 4 #718b	1.40	1.40
i.	Booklet pane of 4 #718c	1.40	1.40
j.	Booklet pane of 4 #718d	1.40	1.40
k.	Booklet pane of 4 #718e	1.40	1.40
l.	Booklet pane of 4 #718f	1.40	1.40

First day covers of Nos. 716-718 total 33,386.
See Offices in Geneva Nos. 314-316; Vienna Nos. 230-232.

Flag Type of 1980

Printed by Helio Courvoisier, S.A., Switzerland. Designed by Oliver Corwin, and Robert Stein, US. Each pane contains 4 blocks of 4 (Nos. 719-722, 723-726). A se-tenant block of 4 designs centers each pane.
No. 719, Micronesia. No. 720, Slovakia. No. 721, Democratic People's Republic of Korea. No. 722, Azerbaijan. No. 723, Uzbekistan. No. 724, Monaco. No. 725, Czech Republic. No. 726, Estonia.

1998, Feb. 13 **Photo.** ***Perf. 12***
Granite Paper

No.	Description	Unused	Used
719	A185 32c multi *(718,000)*+	.80	.80
720	A185 32c multi *(718,000)*+	.80	.80
721	A185 32c multi *(718,000)*+	.80	.80
722	A185 32c multi *(718,000)*+	.80	.80
a.	Block of 4, #719-722	12.50	12.50
723	A185 32c multi *(718,000)*+	.80	.80
724	A185 32c multi *(718,000)*+	.80	.80
725	A185 32c multi *(718,000)*+	.80	.80
726	A185 32c multi *(718,000)*+	.80	.80
a.	Block of 4, #723-726	12.50	12.50
	First day cover, #719-726, each		2.50
	Set of 2 panes of 16	40.00	
	Nos. 719-726 (8)	6.40	6.40

A303

A304

A305

Printed by The House of Questa, UK. Designed by Zhang Le Lu, China (1c), Robert Stein, US (2c), Gregory Halili, Philippines (21c). Panes of 20.

1998, Feb. 13 **Litho.** ***Perf. 14½x15, 15x14½***

No.	Description	Unused	Used
727	A303 1c **multicolored** *(1,000,000)*+	.25	.25
	First day cover		1.00
	Inscription block of 4	.20	—
728	A304 2c **multicolored** *(1,000,000)*+	.25	.25
	First day cover		1.00
	Inscription block of 4	.20	—
729	A305 21c **multicolored** *(1,000,000)*+	.40	.40
	First day cover		1.25
	First day cover, #727-729		4.00
	Inscription block of 4	1.75	—
	Nos. 727-729 (3)	.90	.90

Endangered Species Type of 1993

Printed by Johann Enschedé and Sons, the Netherlands. Designed by Rocco J. Callari, US and Pat Medearis-Altman, New Zealand.
Designs: No. 730, Lesser galago. No. 731, Hawaiian goose. No. 732, Golden birdwing. No. 733, Sun bear.

1998, Mar. 13 **Litho.** ***Perf. 12½***

No.	Description	Unused	Used
730	A271 32c **multicolored** *(502,000)*+	.45	.45
731	A271 32c **multicolored** *(502,000)*+	.45	.45
732	A271 32c **multicolored** *(502,000)*+	.45	.45
733	A271 32c **multicolored** *(502,000)*+	.45	.45
a.	Block of 4, #730-733	2.25	2.25
	First day cover, #733a		4.00

	First day cover, #730-733, each		3.50
	Inscription block of 4, #733a	2.50	—
	Pane of 16	10.00	

See Offices in Geneva Nos. 318-321; Vienna Nos. 235-238.

Intl. Year of the Ocean — A306

Printed by Johann Enschedé and Sons, the Netherlands. Designed by Larry Taugher, US.

1998, May 20 **Litho.** ***Perf. 13x13½***

734	A306 Sheet of 12 *(280,000)+*	12.50	12.50
	First day cover		9.00
a.-l.	32c any single	1.00	1.00
	First day cover, #734a-734l, each		3.50

See Offices in Geneva No. 322; Vienna No. 239.

Rain Forests — A307

Printed by Government Printing Bureau, Japan. Designed by Rick Garcia, US.

1998, June 19 **Litho.** ***Perf. 13x13½***

735	A307 32c Jaguar *(570,000)+*	.50	.50
	First day cover		2.50
	Inscription block of 4	2.25	—

Souvenir Sheet

736	A307 $2 like #735 *(280,000)+*	3.00	3.00
	First day cover		3.00

See Offices in Geneva Nos. 323-324; Vienna Nos. 240-241.

U.N. Peacekeeping Forces, 50th Anniv. — A308

Printed by Helio Courvoisier, S.A. (Switzerland). Designed by Andrew Davidson, UK.

Designs: 33c, Commander with binoculars. 40c, Two soldiers on vehicle.

1998, Sept. 15 **Photo.** ***Perf. 12***

737	A308 33c **multicolored** *(485,000)+*	.50	.50
	First day cover		1.50
	Inscription block of 4	2.25	—
738	A308 40c **multicolored** *(445,000)+*	.75	.75
	First day cover		1.50
	First day cover, #737-738		2.00
	Inscription block of 4	3.75	—

See Offices in Geneva Nos. 325-326; Vienna Nos. 242-243.

Universal Declaration of Human Rights, 50th Anniv. — A309

Printed by Cartor Security Printing (France). Designed by Jean-Michel Folon, France.

Stylized people: 32c, Carrying flag. 55c, Carrying pens.

1998, Oct. 27 **Litho. & Photo.** ***Perf. 13***

739	A309 32c **multicolored** *(485,000)+*	.45	.45
	First day cover		1.50
	Inscription block of 4	2.25	—
740	A309 55c **multicolored** *(445,000)+*	.90	.90
	First day cover		1.50
	First day cover, #739-740		7.00
	Inscription block of 4	4.00	—

See Offices in Geneva Nos. 327-328; Vienna Nos. 244-245.

Schönbrunn Palace, Vienna — A310

Printed by the House of Questa, UK. Panes of 20. Designed by Robert Stein, US.

Designs: 33c, #743f, The Gloriette. 60c, #743b, Wall painting on fabric (detail), by Johann Wenzl Bergl, vert. No. 743a, Blue porcelain vase, vert. No. 743c, Porcelain stove, vert. No. 743d, Palace. No. 743e, Great Palm House (conservatory).

1998, Dec. 4 Litho. *Perf. 14*
741 A310 33c **multicolored** *(485,000)+* .55 .55
First day cover 1.25
Inscription block of 4 2.00 —
742 A310 60c **multicolored** *(445,000)+* 1.25 1.00
First day cover 1.50
First day cover, #741-742 2.50
Inscription block of 4 4.50 —

Souvenir Booklet

743 Booklet *(110,000)+* 19.50
a.-c. A310 11c any single .35 .35
d.-f. A310 15c any single 1.40 1.40
g. Booklet pane of 4 #743d 5.50 5.50
h. Booklet pane of 3 #743a 1.00 1.00
i. Booklet pane of 3 #743b 1.00 1.00
j. Booklet pane of 3 #743c 1.00 1.00
k. Booklet pane of 4 #743e 5.50 5.50
l. Booklet pane of 4 #743f 5.50 5.50

See Offices in Geneva Nos. 329-331; Vienna Nos. 246-248.

Flag Type of 1980

Printed by Helio Courvoisier S.A., Switzerland. Designed by Oliver Corwin, Robert Stein and Blake Tarpley, US. Each pane contains 4 blocks of 4 (Nos. 744-747, 748-751). A se-tenant block of 4 designs centers each pane.

1999, Feb. 5 Photo. *Perf. 12*
744 A185 33c Lithuania *(524,000)+* .75 .75
745 A185 33c San Marino *(524,000)+* .75 .75
746 A185 33c Turkmenistan *(524,000)+* .75 .75
747 A185 33c Marshall Islands *(524,000)+* .75 .75
a. Block of 4, #744-747 8.00 8.00
748 A185 33c Moldova *(524,000)+* .75 .75
749 A185 33c Kyrgyzstan *(524,000)+* .75 .75
750 A185 33c Bosnia & Herzegovina *(524,000)+* .75 .75
751 A185 33c Eritrea *(524,000)+* .75 .75
a. Block of 4, #748-751 8.00 8.00
First day cover, #744-751, each 2.75
Set of 2 panes of 16 35.00
Nos. 744-751 (8) 6.00 6.00

First day covers of Nos. 744-751 total 102,040.

Flags and Globe — A311

Roses — A312

Designed by Blake Tarpley (#752), Rorie Katz, (#753), US.
Printed by Johann Enschedé and Sons, the Netherlands (#752), Helio Courvoisier SA, Switzerland (#753).

1999, Feb. 5 Litho. *Perf. 14x13½*
752 A311 33c **multicolored** *(960,000)+* .50 .50
First day cover 1.00
Inscription block of 4 2.25 —

Photo.
Granite Paper
Perf. 11½x12

753 A312 $5 **multicolored** *(420,000)+* 6.00 6.00
First day cover 5.50
First day cover, #752-753 6.50
Inscription block of 4 25.00 —

First day covers of Nos. 752-753 total 32,142.

World Heritage Sites, Australia — A313

Printed by House of Questa, UK. Panes of 20. Designed by Passmore Design, Australia.

Designs: 33c, #756f, Willandra Lakes region. 60c, #756b, Wet tropics of Queensland. No. 756a, Tasmanian wilderness. No. 756c, Great Barrier Reef. No. 756d, Uluru-Kata Tjuta Natl. Park. No. 756e, Kakadu Natl. Park.

1999, Mar. 19 Litho. *Perf. 13*
754 A313 33c **multicolored** *(480,000)+* .60 .60
First day cover 2.00
Inscription block of 4 3.00 —
755 A313 60c **multicolored** *(440,000)+* 1.25 1.25
First day cover 2.00
First day cover, #754-755 3.00
Inscription block of 4 6.00 —

Souvenir Booklet

756 Booklet *(97,000)+* 35.00
a.-c. A313 5c any single .70 .70
d.-f. A313 15c any single 1.50 1.50
g. Booklet pane of 4, #756a 2.80 2.80
h. Booklet pane of 4, #756d 6.00 6.00
i. Booklet pane of 4, #756b 2.80 2.80
j. Booklet pane of 4, #756e 6.00 6.00
k. Booklet pane of 4, #756c 2.80 2.80
l. Booklet pane of 4, #756f 6.00 6.00

First day covers of Nos. 754-756 total 42,385.

See Offices in Geneva Nos. 333-335; Vienna Nos. 250-252.

Endangered Species Type of 1993

Printed by Johann Enschedé and Sons, the Netherlands. Designed by Jimmy Wang, China.

Designs: No. 757, Tiger. No. 758, Secretary bird. No. 759, Green tree python. No. 760, Long-tailed chinchilla.

1999, Apr. 22 Litho. *Perf. 12½*
757 A271 33c **multicolored** *(494,000)+* .60 .60
758 A271 33c **multicolored** *(494,000)+* .60 .60
759 A271 33c **multicolored** *(494,000)+* .60 .60
760 A271 33c **multicolored** *(494,000)+* .60 .60
a. Block of 4, #757-760 3.00 3.00
First day cover, #760a 3.50
First day cover, #757-760, each 2.25
Inscription block of 4, #760a 2.75 —
Pane of 16 10.00

First day covers of Nos. 757-760 total 49,656.

See Offices in Geneva Nos. 336-339; Vienna Nos. 253-256.

UNISPACE III, Vienna — A314

Printed by Helio Courvoisier SA, Switzerland. Designed by Attila Hejja, US.

Designs: No. 761, Probe on planet's surface. No. 762, Planetary rover. No. 763, Composite of Nos. 761-762.

1999, July 7 Photo. *Rouletted 8*
761 A314 33c **multicolored** *(1,000,000)+* .50 .50
762 A314 33c **multicolored** *(1,000,000)+* .50 .50
a. Pair, #761-762 1.75 1.75
First day cover, #762a 2.00
First day cover, #761-762, each 8.00
Inscription block of 4 4.00 —
Pane of 10, #761-762 10.00 —

Souvenir Sheet

Perf. 14½

763 A314 $2 **multicolored** *(530,000)+* 4.00 4.00
First day cover 3.00
a. Ovptd. in sheet margin 15.00 15.00
First day cover 8.00

No. 763a was issued 7/7/00 and is overprinted in violet blue "WORLD STAMP EXPO 2000 / ANAHEIM, CALIFORNIA / U.S.A./ 7-16 JULY 2000."

First day covers of Nos. 761-763 total 48,190.

See Offices in Geneva Nos. 340-342; Vienna Nos. 257-259.

UPU, 125th Anniv. — A315

Printed by Helio Courvoisier S.A., Switzerland. Panes of 24. Designed by Mark Hess, US.

Various people, 19th century methods of mail transportation, denomination at: No. 764, UL. No. 765, UR. No. 766, LL. No. 767, LR.

1999, Aug. 23 Photo. *Perf. 11¾*

764 A315 33c **multicolored** *(378,000)+* .45 .45
765 A315 33c **multicolored** *(378,000)+* .45 .45
766 A315 33c **multicolored** *(378,000)+* .45 .45
767 A315 33c **multicolored** *(378,000)+* .45 .45
a. Block of 4, #764-767 2.50 2.50
Inscription block of 4 3.00 —
First day cover, #767a 2.00
First day covers, #764-767, set of 4 individual covers 25.00
Sheet of 20 17.00

First day covers of Nos. 764-767 total 25,294.

See Offices in Geneva Nos. 343-346; Vienna Nos. 260-263.

In Memoriam — A316

Printed by Walsall Security Printers, Ltd., United Kingdom. Panes of 20. Designed by Robert Stein, US.

Designs: 33c, $1, UN Headquarters. Size of $1 stamp: 34x63mm.

1999, Sept. 21 Litho. *Perf. 14½x14*

768 A316 33c **multicolored** *(550,000)+* .80 .80
Inscription block of 4 4.00 —
First day cover 1.25

Souvenir Sheet

Perf. 14

769 A316 $1 **multicolored** *(235,000)+* 2.00 2.00
First day cover 1.75

First day covers of Nos. 768-769 total 42,130.

See Offices in Geneva Nos. 347-348, Vienna Nos. 264-265.

Education, Keystone to the 21st Century — A317

Printed by Government Printing Office, Austria. Panes of 20. Designed by Romero Britto, Brazil.

1999, Nov. 18 Litho. *Perf. 13½x13¾*

770 A317 33c Two readers *(450,000)+* .50 .50
First day cover 1.25
Inscription block of 4 2.25 —
771 A317 60c Heart *(430,000)+* 1.00 1.00
First day cover 1.75
First day cover, #770-771 2.50
Inscription block of 4 4.50 —

First day covers of Nos. 770-771 total 34,679.

See Offices in Geneva Nos. 349-350, Vienna Nos. 266-267.

International Year of Thanksgiving — A318

Printed by Cartor Security Printing, France. Panes of 20. Designed by Rorie Katz, US.

2000, Jan. 1 Litho. *Perf. 13¼x13½*

772 A318 33c **multicolored** *(550,000)+* .50 .50
First day cover 1.25
Inscription block of 4 3.25 —

On No. 772 parts of the design were applied by a thermographic process producing a shiny, raised effect. See Offices in Geneva No. 351, Vienna No. 268.

Endangered Species Type of 1993

Printed by Johann Enschedé and Sons, the Netherlands. Designed by Suzanne Duranceau, Canada.

Designs: No. 773, Brown bear. No. 774, Black-bellied bustard. No. 775, Chinese crocodile lizard. No. 776, Pygmy chimpanzee.

2000, Apr. 6 Litho. *Perf. 12¾x12½*

773 A271 33c **multicolored** *(490,000)+* .50 .50
774 A271 33c **multicolored** *(490,000)+* .50 .50
775 A271 33c **multicolored** *(490,000)+* .50 .50
776 A271 33c **multicolored** *(490,000)+* .50 .50
a. Block of 4, #773-776 2.50 2.50
First day cover, #776a 2.75
First day cover, #773-776, each 1.50
Inscription block of 4, #776a 2.75 —
Pane of 16 10.00

See Offices in Geneva Nos. 352-355; Vienna Nos. 269-272.

Our World 2000 — A319

Printed by Cartor Security Printing, France. Panes of 20. Designed by Robert Stein, US.

Winning artwork in Millennium painting competition: 33c, Crawling Toward the Millennium, by Sam Yeates, US. 60c, Crossing, by Masakazu Takahata, Japan, vert.

2000, May 30 **Litho.** ***Perf. 13x13½, 13½x13***

777	A319 33c **multicolored** *(400,000)+*	.60	.60
	First day cover		1.00
	Inscription block of 4	2.50	—
778	A319 60c **multicolored** *(360,000)+*	1.00	1.00
	First day cover		1.00
	First day cover, #777-778		2.00
	Inscription block of 4	4.50	—

See Offices in Geneva No. 356-357, Vienna No. 273-274.

UN, 55th Anniv. — A320

Printed by Cartor Security Printing, France. Panes of 20. Designed by Rorie Katz, US.

Designs: 33c, Workmen removing decorative discs in General Assembly Hall, 1956. 55c, UN Building in 1951.

2000, July 7 **Litho.** ***Perf. 13¼x13***

779	A320 33c **multicolored** *(400,000)+*	.55	.55
	First day cover		1.00
	Inscription block of 4	2.50	—
780	A320 55c **multicolored** *(360,000)+*	.95	.95
	First day cover		1.00
	First day cover, #779-780		2.00
	Inscription block of 4	4.25	—

Souvenir Sheet

781	A320 Sheet of 2, #779-780 *(277,000)+*	3.00	3.00
	First day cover		2.50

See Offices in Geneva No. 358-360, Vienna No. 275-277.

International Flag of Peace — A321

Printed by House of Questa, UK. Panes of 20. Designed by Mateja Prunk, Slovenia.

2000, Sept. 15 **Litho.** ***Perf. 14½x14***

782	A321 33c **multicolored** *(400,000)+*	.65	.65
	First day cover		1.25
	Inscription block of 4	2.60	—

The UN in the 21st Century — A322

Printed by Government Printing Office, Austria. Designed by Wilson McLean, UK.

No. 783: a, Farmers, animals in rice paddy. b, Vehicle chassis being lifted. c, People voting. d, Baby receiving inoculation. e, Woman, man at pump. f, Mason, construction workers.

2000, Sept. 15 **Litho.** ***Perf. 14***

783	A322 Sheet of 6 *(274,000)+*	7.50	7.50
	First day cover		7.50
a.-f.	33c any single	1.25	1.25
	First day covers, each		6.00

See Offices in Geneva No. 361; Vienna No. 278.

World Heritage Sites, Spain A323

Printed by House of Questa, UK. Panes of 20. Designed by Robert Stein, US.

Designs: Nos. 784, 786a, Alhambra, Generalife and Albayzin, Granada. Nos. 785, 786d, Amphitheater of Mérida. #786b, Walled Town of Cuenca. #786c, Aqueduct of Segovia. #786e, Toledo. #786f, Güell Park, Barcelona.

2000, Oct. 6 **Litho.** ***Perf. 14¾x14½***

784	A323 33c **multicolored** *(400,000)+*	.55	.55
	First day cover		1.25
	Inscription block of 4	2.60	—
785	A323 60c **multicolored** *(360,000)+*	1.10	1.10
	First day cover		1.25
	First day cover, #784-785		2.00
	Inscription block of 4	5.00	—

Souvenir Booklet

786	Booklet *(63,000)+*	15.00	
a.-c.	A323 5c any single	.45	.45
d.-f.	A323 15c any single	.80	.80
g.	Booklet pane of 4, #786a	1.80	1.80
h.	Booklet pane of 4, #786d	3.20	3.20

i.	Booklet pane of 4, #786b	1.80	1.80
j.	Booklet pane of 4, #786e	3.20	3.20
k.	Booklet pane of 4, #786c	1.80	1.80
l.	Booklet pane of 4, #786f	3.20	3.20

See Offices in Geneva Nos. 362-364, Vienna Nos. 279-281.

Respect for Refugees — A324

Printed by Johann Enschedé and Sons, the Netherlands. Panes of 20. Designed by Yuri Gevorgian, Armenia.

2000, Nov. 9 **Litho.** ***Perf. 13¼x12¾***

787 A324 33c **multicolored** *(540,000)+*	.75	.75
First day cover		1.50
Inscription block of 4	3.25	—

Souvenir Sheet

788 A324 $1 **multicolored** *(225,000)+*	2.00	2.00
First day cover		2.00

See Offices in Geneva Nos. 365-366, Vienna Nos. 282-283.

Endangered Species Type of 1993

Printed by Johann Enschedé and Sons, the Netherlands. Designed by Grace DeVito, US.

Designs: No. 789, Common spotted cuscus. No. 790, Resplendent quetzal. No. 791, Gila monster. No. 792, Guereza.

2001, Feb. 1 **Litho.** ***Perf. 12¾x12½***

789 A271 34c **multicolored** *(430,000)+*	.60	.60
790 A271 34c **multicolored** *(430,000)+*	.60	.60
791 A271 34c **multicolored** *(430,000)+*	.60	.60
792 A271 34c **multicolored** *(430,000)+*	.60	.60
a. Block of 4, #789-792	3.00	3.00
First day cover, #792a		3.50
First day cover, #789-792 each		1.25
Inscription block of 4, #792a	2.75	—
Pane of 16	10.00	

See Offices in Geneva Nos. 367-370; Vienna Nos. 284-287.

Intl. Volunteers Year — A325

Printed by Johann Enschedé and Sons, the Netherlands. Panes of 20. Designed by Rorie Katz and Robert Stein, US.

Paintings by: 34c, Jose Zaragoza, Brazil. 80c, John Terry, Australia.

2001, Mar. 29 **Litho.** ***Perf. 13¼***

793 A325 34c **multicolored** *(390,000)+*	.65	.65
First day cover		1.25
Inscription block of 4	2.60	
794 A325 80c **multicolored** *(360,000)+*	1.60	1.60
First day cover		1.75
First day cover, #793-794		2.50
Inscription block of 4	6.50	

See Offices in Geneva Nos. 371-372; Vienna Nos. 288-289.

Flag Type of 1980

Printed by Helio Courvoisier, Switzerland. Designed by Ole Hamann. Issued in panes of 16; each contains 4 blocks of 4 (Nos. 795-798, 799-802). A se-tenant block of 4 designs centers each pane.

No. 795, Slovenia. No. 796, Palau. No. 797, Tonga. No. 798, Croatia. No. 799, Former Yugoslav Republic of Macedonia. No. 800, Kiribati. No. 801, Andorra. No. 802, Nauru.

2001, May 25 **Photo.** ***Perf. 12***

Granite Paper

795 A185 34c multi *(460,000)+*	1.25	1.25
796 A185 34c multi *(460,000)+*	1.25	1.25
797 A185 34c multi *(460,000)+*	1.25	1.25
798 A185 34c multi *(460,000)+*	1.25	1.25
a. Block of 4, #795-798	15.00	15.00
799 A185 34c multi *(460,000)+*	1.25	1.25
800 A185 34c multi *(460,000)+*	1.25	1.25
801 A185 34c multi *(460,000)+*	1.25	1.25
802 A185 34c multi *(460,000)+*	1.25	1.25
a. Block of 4, #799-802	15.00	15.00
First day cover, #795-802, each		1.25
Set of 2 panes of 16	40.00	
Nos. 795-802 (8)	10.00	10.00

Sunflower — A326

Rose — A327

Printed by Johann Enschedé and Sons, the Netherlands. Panes of 20. Designed by Rorie Katz, US.

2001, May 25 **Litho.** ***Perf. 13¼x13¾***

803 A326 7c **multicolored** *(550,000)+*	.25	.25
First day cover		1.00
Margin block of 4, inscription	.50	—
804 A327 34c **multicolored** *(650,000)+*	.60	.60
First day cover		1.00
First day cover, #803-804		1.40
Margin block of 4, inscription	3.00	—

World Heritage Sites, Japan
A328

Printed by Johann Enschedé and Sons, the Netherlands. Panes of 20. Designed by Rorie Katz, US.

Designs: 34c, #807a, Kyoto. 70c, #807d, Shirakawa-Go and Gokayama. #807b, Nara. #807c, Himeji-Jo. #807e, Itsukushima Shinto Shrine. #807f, Nikko.

2001, Aug. 1 **Litho.** ***Perf. 12¾x13¼***

805 A328 34c **multicolored** *(380,000)+* .60 .60
First day cover 1.25
Inscription block of 4 2.50 —
806 A328 70c **multicolored** *(360,000)+* 1.25 1.25
First day cover 1.25
First day cover, #805-806 2.00
Inscription block of 4 5.50 —

Souvenir Booklet

807 Booklet *(51,000)+* 14.00
a.-c. A328 5c any single .40 .40
d.-f. A328 20c any single .75 .75
g. Booklet pane of 4, #807a 1.60 1.60
h. Booklet pane of 4, #807d 3.00 3.00
i. Booklet pane of 4, #807b 1.60 1.60
j. Booklet pane of 4, #807e 3.00 3.00
k. Booklet pane of 4, #807c 1.60 1.60
l. Booklet pane of 4, #807f 3.00 3.00

See Offices in Geneva Nos. 373-375, Vienna Nos. 290-292.

Dag Hammarskjöld (1905-61), UN Secretary General — A329

Printed by Banknote Corporation of America, US. Panes of 20. Designed by Robert Stein, US.

2001, Sept. 18 **Engr.** ***Perf. 11x11¼***

808 A329 80c **blue** *(530,000)+* 1.50 1.50
First day cover 2.00
Inscription block of 4 6.00 —

See Offices in Geneva No. 376, Vienna No. 293.

A330

UN Postal Administration, 50th Anniv. — A331

Printed by Johann Enschedé and Sons, the Netherlands. Panes of 20. Designed by Rorie Katz, US.

2001, Oct. 18 **Litho.** ***Perf. 13½***

809 A330 34c Stamps, streamers *(350,000)+* .55 .55
First day cover 1.00
Inscription block of 4 2.75 —
810 A330 80c Stamps, gifts *(310,000)+* 1.50 1.50
First day cover 1.25
First day cover, #809-810 2.00
Inscription block of 4 6.50 —

Souvenir Sheet

811 A331 Sheet of 2 #811a *(180,000)+* 8.00 8.00
a. $1 **blue & light blue,** 38mm diameter 4.00 4.00
First day cover 10.00

See Offices in Geneva Nos. 377-379, Vienna Nos. 294-296.

Climate Change — A332

Printed by Walsall Security Printers Limited, UK. Panes of 24. Designed by Robert Giusti, US.

Designs: No. 812, Canada geese, greenhouses, butterfly, thistle. No. 813, Canada geese, iceberg, penguins, tomato plant. No. 814, Palm tree, solar collector. No. 815, Hand planting ginkgo cutting.

2001, Nov. 16 **Litho.** ***Perf. 13¼***

812 A332 34c **multicolored** *(70,500)+* 1.00 1.00
813 A332 34c **multicolored** *(70,500)+* 1.00 1.00
814 A332 34c **multicolored** *(70,500)+* 1.00 1.00
815 A332 34c **multicolored** *(70,500)+* 1.00 1.00
a. Horiz. strip, #812-815 4.50 4.50
Inscription block of 8 8.00 —
First day cover, #815a 2.75
First day cover, #812-815, each 9.00
Pane of 24 24.00 —

See Offices in Geneva Nos. 380-383, Vienna Nos. 297-300.

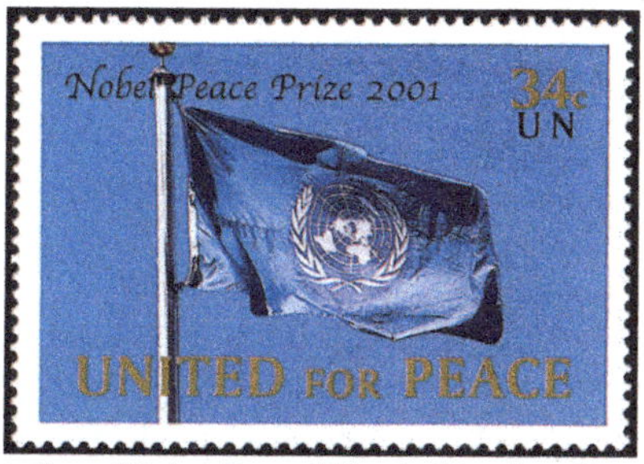

Awarding of Nobel Peace Prize to Secretary General Kofi Annan and UN — A333

Printed by Cartor S. A., France. Panes of 12. Designed by Robert Stein, US.

2001, Dec. 10 **Litho.** ***Perf. 13¼***

816	A333 34c **multicolored** *(840,000)+*	.70	.70
	Inscription block of 4	3.50	—
	First day cover		1.00
	Pane of 12	11.50	—

See Offices in Geneva Nos. 384, Vienna Nos. 301.

Children and Stamps — A334

Printed by Government Printing Office, Austria. Panes of 20. Designed by Jerry Smath, US.

2002, Mar. 1 **Litho.** ***Perf. 13¾***

817	A334 80c **multicolored** *(120,000)+*	1.40	1.40
	First day cover		1.50
	Inscription block of 4	6.00	—

Endangered Species Type of 1993

Printed by Johann Enschedé and Sons, the Netherlands. Designed by Teresa Fasolino, US.

Designs: No. 818, Hoffmann's two-toed sloth. No. 819, Bighorn sheep. No. 820, Cheetah. No. 821, San Esteban Island chuckwalla.

2002, Apr. 4 **Litho.** ***Perf. 12¾x12½***

818	A271 34c **multicolored** *(414,000)+*	.80	.80
819	A271 34c **multicolored** *(414,000)+*	.80	.80
820	A271 34c **multicolored** *(414,000)+*	.80	.80
821	A271 34c **multicolored** *(414,000)+*	.80	.80
a.	Block of 4, #818-821	3.25	3.25
	First day cover, #821a		3.50
	First day cover, #818-821 each		1.50
	Inscription block of 4, #821a	3.50	—
	Pane of 16	13.50	—

See Offices in Geneva Nos. 386-389; Vienna 308-311.

Independence of East Timor — A335

Printed by The House of Questa, UK. Designed by Karen Kelleher, US. Panes of 20

Designs: 34c, Wooden ritual mask. 57c, Decorative door panel.

2002, May 20 **Litho.** ***Perf. 14x14½***

822	A335 34c **multicolored** *(355,000)+*	.70	.70
	First day cover		1.25
	Inscription block of 4	3.00	—
823	A335 57c **multicolored** *(325,000)+*	1.20	1.20
	First day cover		1.50
	First day cover, #822-823		2.50
	Inscription block of 4	5.00	—

See Offices in Geneva Nos. 390-391; Vienna Nos. 312-313.

Intl. Year of Mountains — A336

Printed by Cartor Security Printing, France. Designed by Robert Stein and Rorie Katz, US.

Designs: No. 824, Khan Tengri, Kyrgyzstan. No. 825, Mt. Kilimanjaro, Tanzania. No. 826, Mt. Foraker, US. No. 827, Paine Grande, Chile.

2002, May 24 **Litho.** ***Perf. 13x13¼***

824	A336 34c **multicolored** *(1,362,000)+*	.75	.75
	First day cover		3.00
825	A336 34c **multicolored** *(1,362,000)+*	.75	.75
	First day cover		3.00
826	A336 80c **multicolored** *(1,362,000)+*	1.25	1.50
	First day cover		5.00
	First day cover, #824, 826		3.25
827	A336 80c **multicolored** *(1,362,000)+*	1.25	1.50
a.	Vert. strip or block of four, #824-827	8.00	10.00
	First day cover		5.00
	First day cover, #825, 827		3.25
	First day cover, #823-827		3.00
	Pane of 12, 3 each #824-827	20.00	—

See Offices in Geneva Nos. 392-395; Vienna Nos. 314-317.

World Summit on Sustainable Development, Johannesburg A337

Printed by The House of Questa, UK. Designed by Peter Max, US.

Designs: No. 828, Sun, Earth, planets, stars. No. 829, Three women. No. 830, Sailboat. No. 831, Three faceless people.

2002, June 27 Litho. ***Perf. 14½x14***

828	A337 37c **multicolored** *(1,350,000)+*	.75	.75
	First day cover		1.25
829	A337 37c **multicolored** *(1,350,000)+*	.75	.75
	First day cover		1.25
830	A337 60c **multicolored** *(1,350,000)+*	1.25	1.25
	First day cover		2.00
	First day cover, #828, 830		2.25
831	A337 60c **multicolored** *(1,350,000)+*	1.25	1.25
a.	Vert. strip or block of four, #828-831	8.00	10.00
	First day cover		2.00
	First day cover, #829, 831		2.25
	First day cover, #828-831		4.50
	Pane of 12, 3 each #828-831	20.00	—

See Offices in Geneva Nos. 396-399; Vienna Nos. 318-321.

World Heritage Sites, Italy
A338

Printed by Cartor Security Printing, France. Panes of 20. Designed by Rorie Katz, US.

Designs: 37c, #834d, Florence. 70c, #834a, Amalfi Coast. #834b, Aeolian Islands. #834c, Rome. #834e, Pisa. #834f, Pompeii.

2002, Aug. 30 Litho. ***Perf. 13½x13¼***

832	A338 37c **multicolored** *(365,000)+*	.70	.70
	First day cover		1.25
	Inscription block of 4	3.00	—
833	A338 70c **multicolored** *(345,000)+*	1.40	1.40
	First day cover		2.40
	First day cover, #832-833		3.00
	Inscription block of 4	6.00	—

Souvenir Booklet

834	Booklet *(52,000)+*	16.00	
a.-c.	A338 5c any single	.40	.40
d.-f.	A338 15c any single	.90	.90
g.	Booklet pane of 4, #834d	3.60	3.60
h.	Booklet pane of 4, #834a	1.60	1.60
i.	Booklet pane of 4, #834e	3.60	3.60
j.	Booklet pane of 4, #834b	1.60	1.60
k.	Booklet pane of 4, #834f	3.60	3.60
l.	Booklet pane of 4, #834c	1.60	1.60

See Offices in Geneva Nos. 400-402, Vienna Nos. 322-324.
See Italy Nos. 2506-2507.

AIDS Awareness — A339

Printed by Walsall Security Printers Limited, UK. Panes of 20. Designed by Rorie Katz, US.

2002, Oct. 24 Litho. ***Perf. 13½***

835	A339 70c **multicolored** *(365,000)+*	1.50	1.50
	Inscription block of 4	6.50	
	First day cover, #835		2.00
	Pane of 20	30.00	

See No. B1, Offices in Geneva Nos. 403, B1, Vienna Nos. 325, B1.

Indigenous Art — A340

Printed by House of Questa, UK.
Designed by Rorie Katz and Robert Stein, US.

No. 836: a, Detail of Paracas textile, Peru. b, Sinu culture anthropo-zoomorphic pendant, Colombia. c, Hicholi Indian embroidery, Mexico. d, Rigpaktsa back ornament, Brazil. e, Wool crafts, Chile. f, Huari feathered woven hat, Bolivia.

2003, Jan. 31 Litho. ***Perf. 14¼***

836	A340 Sheet of 6 *(165,000)+*	8.50	8.50
	First day cover		7.50
a.-f.	37c Any single	1.40	1.40

See Offies in Geneva No. 405; Vienna No. 326.

Clasped Hands — A341

UN Emblem — A342

UN Headquarters
A343

Printed by House of Questa, UK (23c, 37c); Walsall Security Printers Ltd., UK (70c). Designed by Rorie Katz, US (23c, 37c), Robert Stein and Rorie Katz (70c). Panes of 20.

2003, Mar. 28 **Litho.** *Perf. 14¼*

837 A341 23c **multicolored** *(870,000)*+	.40	.40
First day cover		1.00
Inscription block of 4	1.75	—

Litho. with Foil Application

838 A342 37c **gold & multicolored** *(870,000)*+	.60	.60
First day cover		1.00
Inscription block of 4	2.75	—

Litho. with Hologram

Perf. 13¼x12¾

839 A343 70c **multicolored** *(910,000)*+	1.40	1.40
First day cover		1.75
First day cover, #837-839		3.00
Inscription block of 4	5.75	—

Powered Flight, Cent.
A344

Printed by Government Printing Office, Austria. Designed by Robert Stein, US. Panes of 16 (eight pairs).

2003, Mar. 28 **Litho.** *Perf. 13½x13¾*

840 23c **multicolored** *(175,000)*+	1.00	1.00
841 70c **multicolored** *(175,000)*+	1.75	1.75
a. A344 Tete beche pair, #840-841	3.00	3.00
First day cover, #841a		2.75
Inscription block of 4	8.00	

Endangered Species Type of 1993

Printed by Johann Enschedé and Sons, the Netherlands. Designed by Joseph Hautman, US.

Designs: No. 842, Great hornbill. No. 843, Scarlet ibis. No. 844, Knob-billed goose. No. 845, White-faced whistling duck.

2003, Apr. 3 **Litho.** *Perf. 12¾x12½*

842 A271 37c **multicolored** *(364,000)*+	.80	.80
843 A271 37c **multicolored** *(364,000)*+	.80	.80
844 A271 37c **multicolored** *(364,000)*+	.80	.80
845 A271 37c **multicolored** *(364,000)*+	.80	.80
a. Block of 4, #842-845	3.25	3.25
First day cover, #845a		3.00
First day cover, #842-845 each		1.00
Inscription block of 4, #845a	3.75	—
Pane of 16	13.50	—

See Offices in Geneva Nos. 407-410; Vienna 329-332.

Intl. Year of Freshwater — A345

Printed by De La Rue Global Services, United Kingdom. Panes of 20. Designed by Rick Garcia, US.

2003, June 20 **Litho.** *Perf. 14¼x14½*

846 A345 23c Wildlife, garbage *(211,000)*+	1.50	1.50
847 A345 37c Trees, canoe *(211,000)*+	2.00	2.00
a. Horiz. pair, #846-847	7.50	7.50
First day cover, #847a		3.00
Inscription block of 4	15.00	—

See Offices in Geneva, Nos. 411-412; Vienna Nos. 333-334.

Ralph Bunche (1903-71), Diplomat — A346

Printed by Johann Enschedé and Sons, the Netherlands. Panes of 20. Designed by Rorie Katz, US.

Litho. With Foil Application

2003, Aug. 7 *Perf. 13½x14*

848 A346 37c **blue & multicolored** *(405,000)*+	.80	.80
First day cover		1.75
Inscription block of 4	3.50	—
Pane of 20	16.50	—

See Offices in Geneva No. 413; Vienna No. 336.

In Memoriam of Victims of Aug. 19 Bombing of UN Complex in Baghdad, Iraq — A347

Printed by Cartor Security Printing, France. Panes of 20. Designed by Jenny J. Karia and Robert Stein, US.

2003, Oct. 24 **Litho.** ***Perf. 13¼x13***

849	A347 60c **multicolored** *(850,000)*+	1.25	1.25
	First day cover		2.00
	Inscription block of 4	5.00	—
	Pane of 20	25.00	—

See Offices in Geneva No. 414, Vienna No. 337.

World Heritage Sites, United States A348

Printed by De La Rue Global Services, United Kingdom. Panes of 20. Designed by Rorie Katz, US.

Designs: 37c, #852a, Yosemite National Park. 60c, #852d, Hawaii Volcanoes National Park. #852b, Great Smoky Mountains National Park. #852c, Olympic National Park. #852e, Everglades National Park. #852f, Yellowstone National Park.

2003, Oct. 24 **Litho.** ***Perf. 14½x14¼***

850	A348 37c **multicolored** *(303,000)*+	.90	.90
	First day cover		1.25
	Inscription block of 4	3.75	—
851	A348 60c **multicolored** *(193,000)*+	1.50	1.50
	First day cover		2.10
	First day cover, #850-851		3.00
	Inscription block of 4	6.50	—

Souvenir Booklet

852	Booklet *(38,500)*+	15.00	
a.-c.	A348 10c any single	.35	.35
d.-f.	A348 20c any single	.70	.70
g.	Booklet pane of 4 #852a	1.40	1.40
h.	Booklet pane of 4 #852d	2.80	2.80
i.	Booklet pane of 4 #852b	1.40	1.40
j.	Booklet pane of 4 #852e	2.80	2.80
k.	Booklet pane of 4 #852c	1.40	1.40
l.	Booklet pane of 4 #852f	2.80	2.80

See Offices in Geneva Nos. 415-417, Vienna Nos. 338-340.

UN Security Council — A349

UN Emblem — A350

UN General Assembly — A351

Flags — A352

UN Headquarters — A353

2003, Nov. 26 **Litho.** ***Perf. 13¼***

853	A349 37c **multicolored** + label	12.50	12.50
854	A350 37c **multicolored** + label	12.50	12.50
855	A351 37c **multicolored** + label	12.50	12.50
856	A352 37c **multicolored** + label	12.50	12.50
857	A353 37c **multicolored** + label	12.50	12.50
a.	Vert. strip of 5, #853-857, + 5 labels	65.00	65.00
	Sheet, 4 #857a	260.00	—
	First day cover, #857a		—
	First day cover, #853-857, each		15.00

The full sheet sold for $14.95 with or without personalized labels. The personalization of labels was available only at UN Headquarters, and not through mail order.

One thousand full sheets with sheet margins inscribed "Hong Kong Stamp Expo" were sold only at that venue. Value $135. Also exists with sheet margins inscribed "Essen." Value $125.

A sheet containing two strips of five stamps similar to Nos. 853-857 but dated "2005" and ten labels sold for $4.95. These sheets were only available canceled. Value $100. An imperforate error of this sheet is known.

Endangered Species Type of 1993

Printed by Johann Enschedé and Sons, the Netherlands. Designed by Yuan Lee, U.S.

Designs: No. 858, American black bear. No. 859, Musk deer. No. 860, Golden snub-nosed monkey. No. 861, Wild yak.

2004, Jan. 29 Litho. *Perf. 12¾x12½*

858	A271 37c **multicolored** *(316,000)+*	.90	.90
859	A271 37c **multicolored** *(316,000)+*	.90	.90
860	A271 37c **multicolored** *(316,000)+*	.90	.90
861	A271 37c **multicolored** *(316,000)+*	.90	.90
a.	Block of 4, #858-861	4.00	4.00
	First day cover, #861a		4.00
	First day cover, #858-861, each		1.50
	Inscription block of 4, #861a	3.75	—
	Pane of 16	15.00	—

See Offices in Geneva Nos. 418-421; Vienna Nos. 342-345.

Indigenous Art Type of 2003

Printed by Johann Enschedé and Sons, the Netherlands. Designed by Rorie Katz and Robert Stein, US.

No. 862: a, Viking wood carving depicting Saga of Sigurd Favnesbane, Norway. b, Stele, Italy. c, Detail of matador's suit, Spain. d, Amphora, Greece. e, Bronze figurine of bull, Czech Republic. f, Detail of lacquer box illustration depicting scene from "On the Seashore," by Alexander Pushkin, Russia.

2004, Mar. 4 Litho. *Perf. 13¼*

862	A340 Sheet of 6 *(134,000)+*	6.00	6.00
	First day cover		8.50
a.-f.	37c Any single	1.00	1.00
	First day cover, a.-f., each		3.00

See Offices in Geneva No. 422; Vienna No. 346.

Road Safety — A354

Printed by Cartor Security Printing. Panes of 20. Designed by Michel Granger, France.

Road map art with: 37c, Automobile with road signs, city skyline. 70c, Automobile, hand, vert.

2004, Apr. 7 Litho. *Perf. 13x13¼, 13¼x13*

863	A354 37c **multicolored** *(266,000)+*	.85	.85
	First day cover		1.25
	Inscription block of 4	3.50	—
864	A354 70c **multicolored** *(196,000)+*	1.40	1.40
	First day cover		2.50
	First day cover, #863-864		3.75
	Inscription block of 4	6.50	—

See Offices in Geneva Nos. 423-424, Vienna Nos. 347-348.

Japanese Peace Bell, 50th Anniv. A355

Printed by Imprimerie des Timbres-Poste, France. Panes of 20. Designed by Martin Mörck, Norway.

2004, June 3 Litho. & Engr. *Perf. 13¼x13*

865	A355 80c **multicolored** *(376,000)+*	1.25	1.25
	First day cover		2.25
	Inscription block of 4	5.50	—
	Pane of 20	27.50	

See Offices in Geneva No. 425; Vienna No. 349.

World Heritage Sites, Greece A356

Printed by Johann Enschedé and Sons, the Netherlands. Panes of 20. Designed by Rorie Katz, US.

Designs: No. 866, Acropolis, Athens. Nos. 867, 868e, Delos. No. 868a, Delphi. No. 868b, Pythagoreion and Heraion of Samos. No. 868c, Olympia. No. 868d, Mycenae and Tiryns.

2004, Aug. 12 Litho. *Perf. 14x13¼*

866	A356 37c **multicolored** *(275,000)+*	.70	.70
	First day cover		1.25
	Inscription block of 4	2.75	—
a.	Booklet pane of 4	3.00	—
867	A356 60c **multicolored** *(195,000)+*	1.10	1.10
	First day cover		2.10
	First day cover, #866-867		2.75
	Inscription block of 4	4.75	—

Souvenir Booklet

868	Booklet, #866a, 868f-868j *(31,000)+*	15.00	
a.-d.	A356 23c any single	.55	.55
e.	A356 37c multi	.90	.90
f.	Booklet pane of 4 #868a	2.20	2.20
g.	Booklet pane of 4 #868b	2.20	2.20
h.	Booklet pane of 4 #868c	2.20	2.20
i.	Booklet pane of 4 #868d	2.20	2.20
j.	Booklet pane of 4 #868e	3.60	3.60

See Offices in Geneva Nos. 426-428, Vienna Nos. 350-352. No. 868 sold for $7.20.

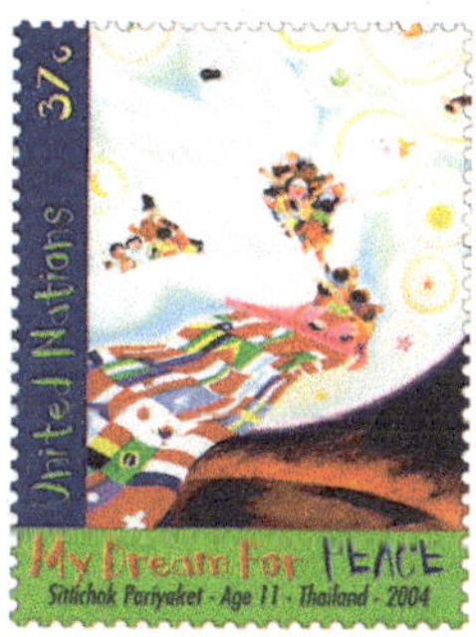

My Dream for Peace — A357

Printed by Government Printing Office, Austria. Panes of 20.

Winning designs of Lions Club International children's global peace poster contest by: 37c, Sittichok Pariyaket, Thailand. 80c, Bayan Fais Abu Bial, Israel.

2004, Sept. 21 Litho. *Perf. 14*

869	A357 37c **multicolored** *(276,000)+*	.60	.60
	First day cover		1.25
	Inscription block of 4	2.75	—
	Pane of 20	12.00	—
870	A357 80c **multicolored** *(206,000)+*	1.40	1.40
	First day cover		2.25
	First day cover, #869-870		3.00
	Inscription block of 4	6.00	—
	Pane of 20	28.00	—

See Offices in Geneva Nos. 429-430, Vienna Nos. 353-354.

A358

Human Rights — A359

Printed by Banknote Corportation of America, US. Designed by Yuri Gervorgian, Armenia.

2004, Oct. 14 **Litho.** ***Perf. 11¼***

871 A358 37c **multicolored** *(464,000)+*	.75	.75
First day cover		1.25
Pane of 8	6.00	—
872 A359 70c **multicolored** *(464,000)+*	1.40	1.40
First day cover		2.40
First day cover, #871-872		3.00
Pane of 8	11.50	—

See Offices in Geneva Nos. 431-432, Vienna Nos. 355-356.

Disarmament — A360

Printed by Government Printing Office, Austria. Designed by Michel Granger, France.

2004, Oct. 15 **Litho.** ***Perf. 13¾***

873 A360 37c **multicolored** *(270,000)+*	.80	.80
First day cover		2.00
Inscription block of 4	3.25	—
Pane of 20	16.50	—

The U.N. Postal Administration announced that it would begin offering canceled-to-order stamps at the same price as mint stamps, effective Feb. 4, 2005. It has been reliably reported that this did not happen.

United Nations, 60th Anniv. A361

Printed by Banknote Corporation of America, US. Designed by Czeslaw Slania, Sweden.

2005, Feb. 4 **Litho. & Engr.** ***Perf. 11x11¼***

874 A361 80c **multicolored** *(395,000)+*	1.50	1.50
First day cover		2.50
Inscription block of 4	6.25	—
Pane of 20	30.00	

Souvenir Sheet

Litho.

Imperf

875 A361 $1 **multicolored** *(135,000)+*	17.50	17.50
First day cover		12.00

See Offices in Geneva Nos. 434-435; Vienna Nos. 357-358.

Endangered Species Type of 1993

Printed by Johann Enschedé and Sons, the Netherlands. Designed by Boris Zlotsky, US.

Designs: No. 876, Blue orchid. No. 877, Swan orchid. No. 878, Christmas orchid. No. 879, Aerangis modesta.

2005, Mar. 3 **Litho.** ***Perf. 12¾x12½***

876 A271 37c **multicolored** *(248,000)+*	1.10	1.10
877 A271 37c **multicolored** *(248,000)+*	1.10	1.10
878 A271 37c **multicolored** *(248,000)+*	1.10	1.10
879 A271 37c **multicolored** *(248,000)+*	1.10	1.10
a. Block of 4, #876-879	4.50	4.50
First day cover, #879a		3.75
First day cover, #876-879, each		1.50
Inscription block of 4, #879a	4.75	—
Pane of 16	18.00	

See Offices in Geneva Nos. 436-439; Vienna Nos. 360-363.

Non-Violence, Sculpture by Carl Fredrik Reuterswärd, New York — A362

Armillary Sphere, Sculpture by Paul Manship, Geneva — A363

Terra Cotta Warriors, Vienna — A364

Single Form, Sculpture by Barbara Hepworth, New York — A365

Sphere Within a Sphere, Sculpture by Arnaldo Pomodoro, New York — A366

2005, Mar. 3 **Litho.** ***Perf. 13¼***

880	A362 80c **multicolored** + label	*35.00*	*35.00*
881	A363 80c **multicolored** + label	*35.00*	*35.00*
882	A364 80c **multicolored** + label	*35.00*	*35.00*
883	A365 80c **multicolored** + label	*35.00*	*35.00*
884	A366 80c **multicolored** + label	*35.00*	*35.00*
a.	Vert. strip of 5, #880-884, + 5 labels	*175.00*	*175.00*
	Sheet, 2 #884a	*350.00*	—
	First day cover, #884a		—
	First day cover, #880-884, each		15.00
b.	Sheet of 10, both #884 37c (error)	*3,250.*	
c.	Vert. strip of 5, #884 37c (error)	*1,450.*	

The full sheet sold for $14.95 with or without personalized labels. The personalization of labels was available only at UN Headquarters, and not through mail order.

The full sheet exists with sheet margins and labels commemorating the Riccione 2005 Philatelic Exhibition. This sheet went on sale 8/20/05 and was also sold for $14.95. Value $175.

Nature's Wisdom A367

Printed by Cartor Security Printing, France. Panes of 20. Designed by Robert Stein, US.

Designs: 37c, Ice climber, Norway. 80c, Egret, Japan.

2005, Apr. 21 **Litho.** ***Perf. 13½x13¼***

885	A367 37c **multicolored** *(280,000)*+	.65	.65
	First day cover		1.40
	Inscription block of 4	2.75	—
	Pane of 20	13.00	—
886	A367 80c **multicolored** *(200,000)*+	1.50	1.50
	First day cover		3.00
	First day cover, #885-886		3.50
	Inscription block of 4	6.00	—
	Pane of 20	30.00	—

See Offices in Geneva Nos. 440-441, Vienna Nos. 364-365.

Intl. Year of Sport — A368

Printed by Cartor Security Printing, France. Designed by Roland Hirter, Switzerland.

2005, June 3 **Litho.** ***Perf. 13x13¼***

887	A368 37c Sailing *(255,000)*+	.65	.65
	First day cover		1.25
	Inscription block of 4	2.75	—
	Pane of 20	13.00	—
888	A368 70c Running *(185,000)*+	1.25	1.25
	First day cover		2.50
	First day cover, #887-888		3.50
	Inscription block of 4	5.25	—
	Pane of 20	25.00	—

See Offices in Geneva Nos. 442-443; Vienna Nos. 366-367.

World Heritage Sites, Egypt A369

Printed by Johann Enschedé and Sons, the Netherlands. Panes of 20. Designed by Rorie Katz, US.

Designs: Nos. 889, 891a, Memphis and its Necropolis. Nos. 890, 891d, Ancient Thebes. No. 891b, Philae. No. 891c, Abu Mena. No. 891e, Islamic Cairo. No. 891f, St. Catherine area.

2005, Aug. 4 Litho. *Perf. 14x13¼*

889	A369 37c **multicolored** *(275,000)+*	.60	.60
	First day cover		1.40
	Inscription block of 4	2.75	—
890	A369 80c **multicolored** *(195,000)+*	1.40	1.40
	First day cover		3.00
	First day cover, #889-890		3.50
	Inscription block of 4	6.00	—

Souvenir Booklet

891	Booklet, #891g-891l *(29,000)+*	15.00	
a.-c.	A369 23c any single	.50	.50
d.-f.	A369 37c any single	.75	.75
g.	Booklet pane of 4 #891a	2.00	2.00
h.	Booklet pane of 4 #891b	2.00	2.00
i.	Booklet pane of 4 #891c	2.00	2.00
j.	Booklet pane of 4 #891d	3.00	3.00
k.	Booklet pane of 4 #891e	3.00	3.00
l.	Booklet pane of 4 #891f	3.00	3.00

See Offices in Geneva Nos. 444-446, Vienna Nos. 368-370.

My Dream for Peace Type of 2004

Printed by Government Printing Office, Austria. Panes of 20.

Winning designs of Lions Club International children's global peace poster contest by: 37c, Vittoria Sansebastiano, Italy. 80c, Jordan Harris, US.

2005, Sept. 21 Litho. *Perf. 14*

892	A357 37c **multicolored** *(270,000)+*	.60	.60
	First day cover		1.40
	Inscription block of 4	2.75	—
	Pane of 20	12.00	—
893	A357 80c **multicolored** *(200,000)+*	1.40	1.40
	First day cover		3.00
	First day cover, #892-893		3.50
	Inscription block of 4	5.75	—
	Pane of 20	28.00	—

See Offices in Geneva Nos. 447-448, Vienna Nos. 371-372.

Food for Life A370

Printed by Government Printing Office, Austria. Designed by Andrew Davidson, United Kingdom.

Designs: 37c, Oats, children and adults. 80c, Wheat, mothers breastfeeding babies.

2005, Oct. 20 Litho. *Perf. 13¾*

894	A370 37c **multicolored** *(245,000)+*	.60	.60
	First day cover		1.25
	Inscription block of 4	2.75	—
	Pane of 20	12.00	—
895	A370 80c **multicolored** *(185,000)+*	1.40	1.40
	First day cover		2.75
	First day cover, #894-895		3.25
	Inscription block of 4	5.75	—
	Pane of 20	28.00	—

See Offices in Geneva Nos. 449-450; Vienna Nos. 373-374.

Stylized Flags in Heart and Hands — A371

Printed by Cartor Security Printing, France. Panes of 20. Designed by Eliezer Weishoff, Israel.

2006, Feb. 3 Litho. *Perf. 13x13¼*

896	A371 25c **multicolored** *(670,000)+*	.75	.75
	First day cover		1.75
	Inscription block of 4	2.75	—
	Pane of 20	13.50	—

Indigenous Art Type of 2003

Printed by Johann Enschedé and Sons, the Netherlands. Designed by Robert Stein, US.

No. 897 — Musical instruments: a, Drum, Ivory Coast. b, Drum, Tunisia. c, Stringed instruments, Morocco. d, Drums, Sudan. e, Instruments, Cameroun. f, Harp, Congo.

2006, Feb. 3 Litho. *Perf. 13¼*

897	A340 Sheet of 6 *(88,000)+*	10.00	10.00
	First day cover		6.50
a.-f.	37c Any single	1.50	1.50

See Offices in Geneva No. 452; Vienna No. 375.

UN Symbols Type of 2003

2006, Mar. 6 Litho. *Perf. 13¼*

898	A349 39c **multicolored** + label	5.00	5.00
899	A350 39c **multicolored** + label	5.00	5.00
900	A351 39c **multicolored** + label	5.00	5.00
901	A352 39c **multicolored** + label	5.00	5.00
902	A353 39c **multicolored** + label	5.00	5.00
a.	Vert. strip of 5, #898-902, + 5 labels	25.00	25.00
	Sheet, 4 #902a	100.00	—

The full sheet sold for $14.95 with or without personalized labels. The personalization of labels was available only at UN Headquarters, and not through mail order.

Sculpture Type of 2005

2006, Mar. 6 Litho. *Perf. 13¼*

903	A362 84c **multicolored** + label	12.00	12.00
a.	Perf. 14½x14 + label	16.00	16.00
904	A363 84c **multicolored** + label	12.00	12.00
a.	Perf. 14½x14 + label	16.00	16.00
905	A364 84c **multicolored** + label	12.00	12.00
a.	Perf. 14½x14 + label	16.00	16.00
906	A365 84c **multicolored** + label	12.00	12.00
a.	Perf. 14½x14 + label	16.00	16.00
907	A366 84c **multicolored** + label	12.00	12.00
a.	Perf. 14½x14 + label	16.00	16.00
b.	Vert. strip of 5, #903-907, + 5 labels	*60.00*	*60.00*
	Sheet, 2 #907b	*120.00*	*120.00*
c.	Vert. strip of 5, #903a-907a, + 5 labels	*80.00*	*80.00*
	Sheet, 2 #907c	*160.00*	*160.00*

The full sheet sold for $14.95 with or without personalized labels. The personalization of labels was available only at UN Headquarters, and not through mail order.

Nos. 903a-907a issued 9/21/06. Nos. 903a-907a were from sheet for 2006 Berlin Stamp Show. The year "2006" is slightly smaller on Nos. 903a-907a than on Nos. 903-907.

Full sheets with different margins were sold at the Washington 2006 World Philatelic Exhibition, where the labels could be personalized. These are worth slightly more than the generic No. 907b sheet.

Endangered Species Type of 1993

Printed by Johann Enschedé and Sons, the Netherlands. Designed by John D. Dawson, US.

Designs: No. 908, Golden mantella. No. 909, Panther chameleon. No. 910, Peruvian rainbow boa. No. 911, Dyeing poison frog.

2006, Mar. 16 Litho. *Perf. 12¾x12½*

908	A271 39c **multicolored** *(212,000)+*	.90	.90
909	A271 39c **multicolored** *(212,000)+*	.90	.90
910	A271 39c **multicolored** *(212,000)+*	.90	.90
911	A271 39c **multicolored** *(212,000)+*	.90	.90
a.	Block of 4, #908-911	4.00	4.00
	First day cover, #911a		4.50
	First day cover, #908-911, each		1.75
	Inscription block of 4, #911a	3.75	—
	Pane of 16	14.50	—

See Offices in Geneva Nos. 453-456; Vienna Nos. 376-379.

Dove Between War and Peace — A372

Designed by Armando Milani, Italy.

2006, Apr. 10 **Litho.** ***Perf. 13¼***

912	A372 75c **multicolored** + label	3.75	3.75
	First day cover		10.00
	Sheet of 10 + 10 labels	55.00	—

The full sheet sold for $14.95 with or without personalized labels. The personalization of labels was available only at UN Headquarters, and not through mail order.

Intl. Day of Families — A373

Printed by Johann Enschedé and Sons, the Netherlands. Designed by Shelly Bartek, US.

Designs: 39c, Family harvesting grapes. 84c, Children playing with toy sailboats.

2006, May 27 **Litho.** ***Perf. 14x13½***

913	A373 39c **multicolored** *(226,000)+*	.70	.70
	First day cover		1.25
	Inscription block of 4	3.00	—
	Pane of 20	14.00	—
914	A373 84c **multicolored** *(186,000)+*	1.50	1.50
	First day cover		2.75
	First day cover, #913-914		3.25
	Inscription block of 4	6.25	—
	Pane of 20	30.00	—

See Offices in Geneva Nos. 457-458; Vienna Nos. 380-381.

World Heritage Sites, France A374

Printed by Cartor Security Printing, France. Panes of 20. Designed by Robert Stein, US.

Eiffel Tower and: Nos. 915, 917a, Banks of the Seine. Nos. 916, 917d, Roman Aqueduct. No. 917b, Provins. No. 917c, Carcasonne. No. 917e, Mont Saint-Michel. No. 917f, Chateau de Chambord.

Litho. & Embossed with Foil Application

2006, June 17 ***Perf. 13½x13¼***

915	A374 39c **multicolored** *(260,000)+*	.75	.75
	First day cover		2.25
	Inscription block of 4	3.25	—
916	A374 84c **multicolored** *(180,000)+*	1.75	1.75
	First day cover		4.25
	First day cover, #889-890		3.50
	Inscription block of 4	7.50	—

Souvenir Booklet

917	Booklet, #917g-917l *(28,000)+*	16.00	
a.-c.	A374 24c any single	.50	.50
d.-f.	A374 39c any single	.80	.80
g.	Booklet pane of 4 #917a	2.00	2.00
h.	Booklet pane of 4 #917b	2.00	2.00
i.	Booklet pane of 4 #917c	2.00	2.00
j.	Booklet pane of 4 #917d	3.25	3.25
k.	Booklet pane of 4 #917e	3.25	3.25
l.	Booklet pane of 4 #917f	3.25	3.25

See Offices in Geneva Nos. 459-461, Vienna Nos. 382-384.

My Dream for Peace Type of 2004

Printed by Cartor Security Printing, France. Panes of 20.

Winning designs of Lions Club International children's global peace poster contest by: 39c, Cheuk Tat Li, Hong Kong. 84c, Kosshapan Paitoon, Thailand.

2006, Sept. 21 **Litho.** ***Perf. 13½x13***

918	A357 39c **multicolored** *(246,000)+*	.80	.80
	First day cover		1.25
	Inscription block of 4	3.25	—
	Pane of 20	16.00	—
919	A357 84c **multicolored** *(186,000)+*	1.75	1.75
	First day cover		2.75
	First day cover, #918-919		3.00
	Inscription block of 4	7.00	—
	Pane of 20	35.00	—

See Offices in Geneva Nos. 462-463; Vienna Nos. 385-386.

Flags and Coins — A375

Printed by Cartor Security Printing, France. Designed by Rorie Katz, US.

No. 920 Flag of: a, People's Republic of China, 1 yuan coin. b, Australia, 1 dollar coin. c, Ghana, 50 cedi coin. d, Israel, 10 agorot coin. e, Russia, 1 ruble coin. f, Mexico, 10 peso coin. g, Japan, 10 yen coin. h, Cambodia, 200 riel coin.

2006, Oct. 5 **Litho.** ***Perf. 13¼x13***

920	Sheet of 8	7.00	7.00
a.-h.	A375 39c Any single	.75	.75
	First day cover		10.00

A column of rouletting in the middle of the sheet separates it into two parts. See Nos. 930, 953, 998, 1022, 1039, 1078, 1103; Offices in Geneva Nos. 464, 469, 484, 512, 532, 546, 576, 594; Vienna Nos. 387, 392, 421, 459, 483, 507, 539, 558.

Flag Type of 1980

Printed by Government Printing Office, Austria. Designed by Rorie Katz, US. Issued in panes of 16; each pane contains 4 blocks of 4. A se-tenant block of 4 designs centers each pane.

2007, Feb. 2 **Litho.** ***Perf. 14***

921	A185 39c Tuvalu *(275,000)+*	1.10	1.10
922	A185 39c Switzerland *(275,000)+*	1.10	1.10
923	A185 39c Timor-Leste *(275,000)+*	1.10	1.10
924	A185 39c Montenegro *(275,000)+*	1.10	1.10
a.	Block of 4, #921-924	12.50	12.50
	First day cover, #921-924, each		1.50
	Pane of 16	24.00	
	Nos. 921-924 (4)	4.40	4.40

Endangered Species Type of 1993

Printed by Johann Enschedé and Sons, the Netherlands. Designed by John Rowe, US.

Designs: No. 925, Drill. No. 926, Common squirrel monkey. No. 927, Ring-tailed lemur. No. 928, Collared mangabey.

2007, Mar. 15 **Litho.** ***Perf. 12¾x12½***

925	A271 39c **multicolored** *(212,000)+*	.85	.85
926	A271 39c **multicolored** *(212,000)+*	.85	.85
927	A271 39c **multicolored** *(212,000)+*	.85	.85
928	A271 39c **multicolored** *(212,000)+*	.85	.85
a.	Block of 4, #925-928	3.50	3.50
	First day cover, #928a		3.50
	First day cover, #925-928, each		1.75
	Inscription block of 4, #928a	4.00	—
	Pane of 16	14.00	—

See Offices in Geneva Nos. 465-468; Vienna Nos. 388-391.

UN Emblem — A376

Designed by Robert Stein.

2007, Feb. 5 **Litho.** ***Perf. 14½x14***

929	A376 84c **dark blue** + label	*17.50*	*10.00*
	First day cover, strip of 5 + 5 labels		*55.00*
	Sheet of 10 + 10 labels	*175.00*	—

The full sheet sold for $14.95. The sheet has two each of five different labels that could not be personalized. The sheet was distributed to members of the Japanese mission on Sept. 21, 2006, but it was not sold to the public until 2007. The sheet's availability to the public was not announced through press releases or on the UNPA website prior to the day of issue or afterward. It was sent to standing order customers in May 2007.

Compare with Type A377.

Flags and Coins Type of 2006

Printed by Cartor Security Printing, France. Designed by Rorie Katz, US.

No. 930 — Flag of: a, Brazil, 50 centavo coin. b, Thailand, 1 baht coin. c, Viet Nam, 5,000 dong coin. d, Ecuador, 10 centavo coin. e, India, 5 rupee coin. f, South Africa, 5 cent coin. g, Barbados, 25 cent coin. h, Republic of Korea, 500 won coin.

2007, May 3 **Litho.** ***Perf. 13¼x13***

930	Sheet of 8 *(125,000)+*	8.00	8.00
a.-h.	A375 39c Any single	.75	.75
	First day cover		12.50

A column of rouletting in the middle of the sheet separates it into two parts. See Offices in Geneva No. 469; Vienna No. 392.

UN Emblem — A377

2007, June 1 **Litho.** ***Perf. 13¼***

931	A377 84c **blue** + label	*4.50*	*4.50*
	First day cover, strip of 5 + 5 labels		—
	Sheet of 10 + 10 labels	*45.00*	—

The full sheet sold for $14.95. The sheet has two each of five different labels that could not be personalized.

Compare with Type A376.

Peaceful Visions — A378

Printed by Lowe-Martin Company, Canada. Designed by Slavka Kolesar, Canada. Panes of 20.

Designs: 39c, "Nest." 84c, "Sisters Weave the Olive Branch."

2007, June 1 **Litho.** ***Perf. 13x12½***

932	A378 39c **multicolored** *(264,000)+*	.90	.90
	First day cover		1.50
	Inscription block of 4	3.60	—
	Pane of 20	18.00	—
933	A378 84c **multicolored** *(214,000)+*	1.80	1.80
	First day cover		3.25
	First day cover, #932-933		3.75
	Inscription block of 4	7.25	—
	Pane of 20	36.00	—

See Offices in Geneva Nos. 470-471; Vienna Nos. 398-399.

UN Symbols Type of 2003

2007, May 14 **Litho.** ***Perf. 13¼***

934	A349 41c **multicolored** + label	3.25	3.25
935	A350 41c **multicolored** + label	3.25	3.25
936	A351 41c **multicolored** + label	3.25	3.25
937	A352 41c **multicolored** + label	3.25	3.25
938	A353 41c **multicolored** + label	3.25	3.25
a.	Vert. strip of 5, #934-938, + 5 labels	17.00	17.00
	First day cover, #938a		—
	Sheet, 4 #938a	67.50	—

The full sheet sold for $14.95 with or without personalized labels. The personalization of labels was available only at UN Headquarters, and not through mail order.

UN Flag — A379

2007, May 14 **Litho.** ***Perf. 13¼***

939	A379 90c **blue** + label	*5.00*	*6.00*
	First day cover		65.00
	Sheet of 10 + 10 labels	*60.00*	—

The full sheet sold for $14.95. The sheet has two each of five different labels that could not be personalized.

A second printing of No. 939 has the "U" and "N" more closely spaced, and it has different labels and different pane borders. Value about the same.

Helmet of UN Peacekeeper — A380

Printed by Lowe-Martin Group, Canada. Panes of 20.

2007, Aug. 9 **Litho.** ***Perf. 12½x13¼***

940 A380 90c **multicolored** *(550,000)+* 1.90 1.90
First day cover 3.00
Inscription block of 4 7.60 —
Pane of 20 38.00 —

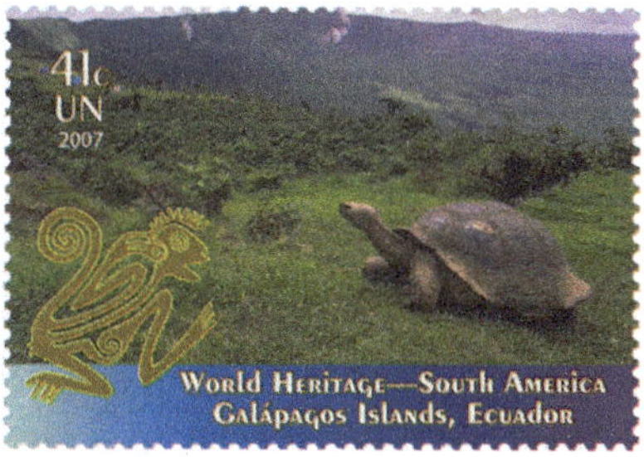

World Heritage Sites, South America
A381

Printed by Lowe-Martin Group, Canada. Panes of 20. Designed by Rorie Katz, US.

Designs: No. 941, Galapagos Islands, Ecuador. Nos. 942, 943a, Rapa Nui, Chile. No. 943b, Cueva de las Manos, Argentina. No. 943c, Machu Picchu, Peru. No. 943d, Tiwanaku, Bolivia. No. 943e, Iguaçu National Park, Brazil.

2007, Aug. 9 **Litho.** ***Perf. 13¼x13***

941 A381 41c **multicolored** *(254,000)+* .85 .85
First day cover 1.50
Inscription block of 4 3.40 —
a. Booklet pane of 4 3.40 —
942 A381 90c **multicolored** *(254,000)+* 1.90 1.90
First day cover 3.25
First day cover, #941-942 3.75
Inscription block of 4 7.60 —

Souvenir Booklet

943 Booklet, #941a, 943f-943j *(26,500)+* 17.00
a.-c. A381 26c Any single .60 .60
d.-e. A381 41c Either single 1.00 1.00
f. Booklet pane of 4 #943a 2.40 2.40
g. Booklet pane of 4 #943b 2.40 2.40
h. Booklet pane of 4 #943c 2.40 2.40
i. Booklet pane of 4 #943d 4.00 4.00
j. Booklet pane of 4 #943e 4.00 4.00

See Offices in Geneva Nos. 472-474, Vienna Nos. 400-402. No. 943 sold for $8.50.

Humanitarian Mail — A382

Printed by Lowe-Martin Group, Canada. Panes of 10.

2007, Sept. 6 **Litho.** ***Perf. 12½x13¼***

944 A382 90c **multicolored** *(288,000)+* 1.90 1.90
First day cover 3.50
Inscription block of 4 7.75 —
Pane of 10 19.00 —

See Offices in Geneva No. 475, Vienna No. 403, Switzerland No. 9021.

Space for Humanity
A383

Printed by Johann Enschedé and Sons, the Netherlands. Panes of 6. Designed by Donato Giancola, US.

Designs: 41c, Space Shuttle. 90c, Astronauts spacewalking. $1, International Space Station.

2007, Oct. 25 **Litho.** ***Perf. 13½x14***

945 A383 41c **multicolored** *(264,000)+* .85 .85
First day cover 1.50
Inscription block of 4 3.40 —
Sheet of 6 5.10 —
946 A383 90c **multicolored** *(264,000)+* 1.90 1.90
First day cover 3.25
First day cover, #945-946 4.00
Inscription block of 4 7.60 —
Sheet of 6 11.40 —

Souvenir Sheet

947 A383 $1 **multicolored** *(110,000)+* 2.50 2.50
First day cover 4.00
a. With World Space Week emblem in margin *(110,000)+* 3.00 3.00
First day cover 4.00

See Offices in Geneva Nos. 476-478, Vienna Nos. 409-411.

Intl. Holocaust Remembrance Day — A384

Printed by Lowe-Martin Company, Canada. Panes of 9. Designed by Matías Delfino, Argentina.

2008, Jan. 27 **Litho.** ***Perf. 13***

948 A384 41c **multicolored** *(495,000)+* .85 .85
First day cover 1.90
Sheet of 9 7.75 —

See Offices in Geneva No. 479, Vienna No. 412, Israel No. 1715.

Endangered Species Type of 1993

Printed by Johann Enschedé and Sons, the Netherlands. Designed by Suzanne Duranceau, Canada.

Designs: No. 949, South African fur seal. No. 950, Orange cup coral. No. 951, Longsnout seahorse. No. 952, Gray whale.

2008, Mar. 6 **Litho.** ***Perf. 12¾x12½***

949 A271 41c **multicolored** *(164,000)+* 1.00 1.00
950 A271 41c **multicolored** *(164,000)+* 1.00 1.00
941 A271 41c **multicolored** *(164,000)+* 1.00 1.00
952 A271 41c **multicolored** *(164,000)+* 1.00 1.00
a. Block of 4, #949-952 4.50 4.50
First day cover, #952a 4.50

First day cover, #949-952, each		1.75
Inscription block of 4, #952a	4.25	—
Pane of 16	16.00	—

See Offices in Geneva Nos. 480-483; Vienna Nos. 417-420.

Flags and Coins Type of 2006

Printed by Cartor Security Printing, France. Designed by Rorie Katz, US.

No. 953 — Flag of: a, United Kingdom, 2 pound coin. b, Singapore, 5 dollar coin. c, Colombia, 500 peso coin. d, Sri Lanka, 10 rupee coin. e, Philippines, 1 peso coin. f, Indonesia, 500 rupiah coin. g, United Arab Emirates, 1 dirham coin. h, Libya, 50 dinar coin.

2008, May 8 **Litho.** ***Perf. 13¼x13***

953	Sheet of 8 *(100,000)*+	7.00	7.00
a.-h.	A375 41c Any single	.85	.85
	First day cover		9.25

A column of rouletting in the middle of the sheet separates it into two parts. See Offices in Geneva No. 484; Vienna No. 421.

Sculpture and Flags — A385

UN Flag — A386

UN General Assembly — A387

Flags — A388

UN Headquarters — A389

Designed by Rorie Katz, US.

2008, May 12 **Litho.** ***Perf. 13¼***

954	A385 42c **multicolored** + label	*3.50*	*3.50*
955	A386 42c **multicolored** + label	*3.50*	*3.50*
956	A387 42c **multicolored** + label	*3.50*	*3.50*
957	A388 42c **multicolored** + label	*3.50*	*3.50*
958	A389 42c **multicolored** + label	*3.50*	*3.50*
a.	Vert. strip of 5, #954-958, + 5 labels	*17.50*	*17.50*
	First day cover, #958a		—
	Sheet, 4 #958a	*70.00*	—

The full sheet sold for $14.95 with or without personalized labels. The personalization of labels was available only at UN Headquarters, and not through mail order.

UN Emblem — A390

Designed by Rorie Katz, US.

2008, May 12 **Litho.** ***Perf. 13¼***

959	A390 94c **blue** + label	*4.50*	*4.50*
	First day cover		—
	Sheet of 10 + 10 labels	*45.00*	—

The full sheet sold for $14.95 with or without labels that could be personalized. There are five non-personalized labels. The personalization of labels was available only at UN Headquarters, and not through mail order.

Wheelchair Accessibility Symbol — A391

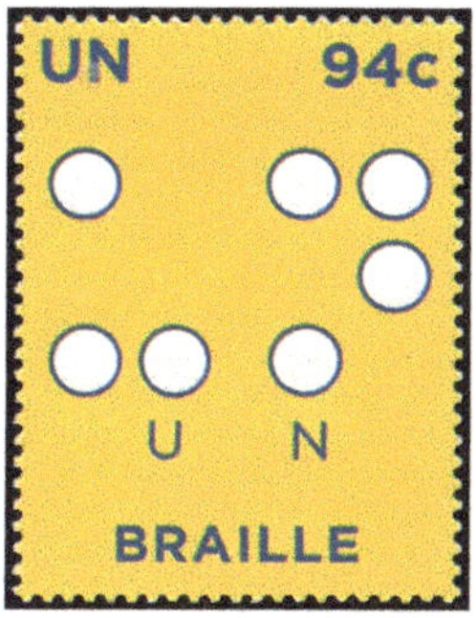

"UN" in Braille — A392

Printed by Johann Enschedé and Sons, the Netherlands. Panes of 20. Designed by Rorie Katz, US.

2008, June 6 Litho. & Embossed *Perf. 14x13¼*

960 A391 42c **blue & yellow** *(224,000)+*	.85	.85
First day cover		1.60
Inscription block of 4	3.40	—
Sheet of 20	17.00	—
961 A392 94c **yellow & blue** *(174,000)+*	1.90	1.90
First day cover		3.50
First day cover, #960-961		4.00
Inscription block of 4	7.60	—
Sheet of 20	38.00	—

Convention on the Rights of Persons with Disabilities. See Offices in Geneva Nos. 485-486, Vienna Nos. 427-428.

Sport for Peace A393

Printed by Johann Enschedé and Sons, the Netherlands. Panes of 9 (#962-963). Designed by Romero Britto, Brazil.
Designs: 42c, $1.25, Sprinter. 94c, Hurdler.

2008, Aug. 8 Litho. *Perf. 14½*

962 A393 42c **multicolored** *(389,700)+*	.85	.85
First day cover		1.60
Inscription block of 4	3.40	—
Pane of 9	7.75	—
963 A393 94c **multicolored** *(389,700)+*	1.90	1.90
First day cover		3.50
First day cover, #962-963		4.00
Inscription block of 4	7.60	—
Pane of 9	17.50	—

Souvenir Sheet

Perf. 12¾x13¼

964 A393 $1.25 **multicolored** *(150,000)+*	6.00	6.00
First day cover		5.00

2008 Summer Olympics, Beijing. See Offices in Geneva Nos. 487-489, Vienna Nos. 429-431.

Sport for Peace — A394

2008, Aug. 8 Litho. *Perf. 13¼*

965 A394 94c **multicolored** + label	*3.75*	*3.75*
First day cover		12.50
Pane of 10 + 10 labels	*37.50*	—

2008 Summer Olympics, Beijing. The full pane sold for $14.95 with or without personalized labels. There are two non-personalized labels. The personalization of labels was available only at UN Headquarters, and not through mail order.
No. 965 is often collected as a single stamp with the two different labels attached; value thus $6.50.

"We Can End Poverty" A395

Printed by Sweden Post, Sweden. Panes of 20.
Winning designs in children's art contest by: 42c, Grace Tsang, Hong Kong. 94c, Bryan Jevoncia, Indonesia, vert.

2008, Sept. 18 Litho. *Perf. 12¾x12½*

966 A395 42c **multicolored** *(225,000)+*	.85	.85
First day cover		1.25
Inscription block of 4	3.40	—
Sheet of 20	17.00	—

Perf. 12½x12¾

967 A395 94c **multicolored** *(165,000)+*	1.90	1.90
First day cover		3.25
First day cover, #966-967		4.00
Inscription block of 4	7.60	—
Sheet of 20	38.00	—

See Offices in Geneva Nos. 490-491, Vienna Nos. 432-433.

Climate Change Types of Geneva and Vienna and

A396

Climate Change A397

Printed by Lowe-Martin Group, Canada. Panes of 4. Designed by Rorie Katz, US.

No. 968 — Parched ground and snail shell with quarter of Earth in: a, LR. b, LL. c, UR. d, UL.

No. 969 — Coral reef with quarter of Earth in: a, LR. b, LL. c, UR. d, UL.

No. 970: a, Like #969a. b, Like #969b. c, Like #969c. d, Like #969d. e, Like Geneva #493a. f, Like Geneva #493b. g, Like Geneva #493c. h, Like Geneva #493d. i, Like Vienna #434a. j, Like Vienna #434b. k, Like Vienna #434c. l, Like Vienna #434d. m, Like Geneva #492a. n, Like Geneva #492b. o, Like Geneva #492c. p, Like Geneva #492d. q, Like Vienna #435a. r, Like Vienna #435b. s, Like Vienna #435c. t, Like Vienna #435d.

All stamps have blue panels inscribed "Climate Change."

2008, Oct. 23 — Litho. — *Perf. 13¼x13*

No.	Description	Unused	Used
968	Sheet of 4 *(100,000)*+	4.75	4.75
a.-d.	A396 42c Any single	1.10	1.10
	First day cover		4.50
e.	Booklet pane of 4, #968a-968d	6.00	6.00
969	Sheet of 4 *(100,000)*+	10.00	10.00
a.-d.	A397 94c Any single	2.50	2.50
	First day cover		9.75
	First day cover, #968-969		14.00

Souvenir Booklet

No.	Description	Unused	Used
970	Booklet, #968e, 970u-970y *(22,500)*+	20.00	
a.-d.	A397 27c Any single	.75	.75
e.-h.	G77 27c Any single	.75	.75
i.-l.	V72 27c Any single	.75	.75
m.-p.	G76 42c Any single	1.00	1.00
q.-t.	V73 42c Any single	1.00	1.00
u.	Booklet pane of 4, #970a-970d	3.00	3.00
v.	Booklet pane of 4, #970e-970h	3.00	3.00
w.	Booklet pane of 4, #970i-970l	3.00	3.00
x.	Booklet pane of 4, #970m-970p	4.00	4.00
y.	Booklet pane of 4, #970q-970t	4.00	4.00

No. 970 sold for $9. See Offices in Geneva Nos. 492-494, Vienna Nos. 434-436.

Paintings of Flowers by Jaime Arredondo — A398

Printed by Lowe-Martin Company, Inc., Canada. Panes of 20.

Designs: 1c, Cielo rosado. 9c, Rosa de sangre. 10c, Espíritu de mujer.

2009, Feb. 6 — Litho. — *Perf. 13¼*

No.	Description	Unused	Used
971	A398 1c **multicolored** *(570,000)*+	.30	.30
	First day cover		1.90
	Inscription block of 4	1.50	—
	Sheet of 20	3.00	—
972	A398 9c **multicolored** *(570,000)*+	.30	.30
	First day cover		1.90
	Inscription block of 4	1.50	—
	Sheet of 20	3.00	—
973	A398 10c **multicolored** *(570,000)*+	.30	.30
	First day cover		1.90
	First day cover, #971-973		3.75
	Inscription block of 4	1.50	—
	Sheet of 20	3.00	—
	Nos. 971-973 (3)	.90	.90

U Thant (1909-74), Secretary General — A399

Printed by Johann Enschedé and Sons, the Netherlands. Panes of 20.

Litho. With Foil Application

2009, Feb. 6 — *Perf. 14x13½*

No.	Description	Unused	Used
974	A399 94c **purple & multicolored** *(255,000)*+	2.00	2.00
	First day cover		3.00
	Inscription block of 4	8.00	—
	Sheet of 20	40.00	—

See Offices in Geneva No. 495, Vienna No. 437.

Endangered Species Type of 1993

Printed by Johann Enschedé and Sons, the Netherlands. Designed by Roger Kent, United Kingdom.

Designs: No. 975, Emperor dragonfly. No. 976, Southern wood ant. No. 977, Rosalia longicorn. No. 978, Apollo butterfly.

2009, Apr. 16 — Litho. — *Perf. 12¾x12½*

No.	Description	Unused	Used
975	A271 42c **multicolored** *(156,000)*+	1.25	1.25
976	A271 42c **multicolored** *(156,000)*+	1.25	1.25
977	A271 42c **multicolored** *(156,000)*+	1.25	1.25
978	A271 42c **multicolored** *(156,000)*+	1.25	1.25
a.	Block of 4, #975-978	5.50	5.50
	First day cover, #978a		5.00
	First day cover, #975-978, each		1.50
	Inscription block of 4, #978a	5.00	—
	Pane of 16	20.00	—
b.	Pane of 16, imperf.	*5,000.*	

See Offices in Geneva Nos. 496-499; Vienna Nos. 438-441.

World Heritage Sites, Germany A400

Printed by Johann Enschedé and Sons, the Netherlands. Panes of 20. Designed by Grit Fiedler, Germany.

Designs: Nos. 979, 981a, Town Hall and Roland on the Marketplace, Bremen. Nos. 980, 981d, Aachen Cathedral. No. 981b, Wartburg Castle. No. 981c, Palaces and Parks of Potsdam and Berlin. No. 981e, Luther Memorials in Eisleben and Wittenberg. No. 981f, Monastic Island of Reichenau.

2009, May 7 — Litho. — *Perf. 14x13½*

No.	Description	Unused	Used
979	A400 44c **multicolored** *(220,000)*+	.90	.90
	First day cover		1.25
	Inscription block of 4	3.60	—
980	A400 98c **multicolored** *(220,000)*+	2.00	2.00
	First day cover		3.00
	First day cover, #979-980		4.00
	Inscription block of 4	8.00	—

Souvenir Booklet

No.	Description	Unused	Used
981	Booklet, #981g-981l *(21,000)*+	20.00	
a.-c.	A400 27c any single	.60	.60
d.-f.	A400 42c any single	1.00	1.00
g.	Booklet pane of 4 #981a	2.40	2.40

h.	Booklet pane of 4 #981b	2.40	2.40
i.	Booklet pane of 4 #981c	2.40	2.40
j.	Booklet pane of 4 #981d	4.00	4.00
k.	Booklet pane of 4 #981e	4.00	4.00
l.	Booklet pane of 4 #981f	4.00	4.00

See Offices in Geneva Nos. 500-502, Vienna Nos. 442-444.

UN Flag — A401

Let Us Beat Swords Into Plowshares, Sculpture by Evgeny Vuchetich — A402

Single Form, Sculpture by Barbara Hepworth — A403

Window Cleaner — A404

UN Headquarters — A405

2009, June 5 **Litho.** ***Perf. 13¼***

982	A401 44c **multicolored** + label	*2.00*	*2.00*
a.	Perf. 11¼x11 + label	*10.00*	*10.00*
b.	Perf. 14¼x14½ + label	*1.80*	*1.80*
983	A402 44c **multicolored** + label	*2.00*	*2.00*
a.	Perf. 11¼x11 + label	*10.00*	*10.00*
b.	Perf. 14¼x14½ + label	*1.80*	*1.80*
984	A403 44c **multicolored** + label	*2.00*	*2.00*
a.	Perf. 11¼x11 + label	*10.00*	*10.00*
b.	Perf. 14¼x14½ + label	*1.80*	*1.80*
985	A404 44c **multicolored** + label	*2.00*	*2.00*
a.	Perf. 11¼x11 + label	*10.00*	*10.00*
b.	Perf. 14¼x14½ + label	*1.80*	*1.80*
986	A405 44c **multicolored** + label	*2.00*	*2.00*
a.	Perf. 11¼x11 + label	*10.00*	*10.00*
b.	Perf. 14¼x14½ + label	*1.80*	*1.80*
c.	Vert. strip of 5, #982-986, + 5 labels	*10.00*	*10.00*
	Sheet, 4 #986c	*40.00*	—
d.	Vert. strip of 5, #982a-986a, + 5 labels	*50.00*	*50.00*
	Sheet, 4 #986d	*200.00*	—
e.	Vert. strip of 5, #982b-986b, + 5 labels	*9.00*	*7.50*
	Sheet, 4 #986e	*37.50*	—

The full sheets sold for $14.95 with or without personalized labels. The personalization of labels was available only at UN Headquarters, and not through mail order. The sheet of No. 986d has "ver. 2" in the lower right selvage. The sheet of No. 986e has "Ver. 3" in the lower right selvage.

Flags and UN Headquarters — A406

Single Form, Sculpture by Barbara Hepworth — A407

UN Flag — A408

Sphere Within a Sphere, Sculpture by Arnaldo Pomodoro — A409

UN Headquarters and Chrysler Building — A410

2009, June 5 Litho. ***Perf. 13¼***

987	A406 98c **multicolored** + label	*4.00*	*4.00*
a.	Perf. 11¼x11 + label	*9.00*	*9.00*
b.	Perf. 14¼x14½ + label	*3.50*	*3.50*
988	A407 98c **multicolored** + label	*4.00*	*4.00*
a.	Perf. 11¼x11 + label	*9.00*	*9.00*
b.	Perf. 14¼x14½ + label	*3.50*	*3.50*
989	A408 98c **multicolored** + label	*4.00*	*4.00*
a.	Perf. 11¼x11 + label	*9.00*	*9.00*
b.	Perf. 14¼x14½ + label	*3.50*	*3.50*
990	A409 98c **multicolored** + label	*4.00*	*4.00*
a.	Perf. 11¼x11 + label	*9.00*	*9.00*
b.	Perf. 14¼x14½ + label	*3.50*	*3.50*
991	A410 98c **multicolored** + label	*4.00*	*4.00*
a.	Perf. 11¼x11 + label	*9.00*	*9.00*
b.	Perf. 14¼x14½ + label	*3.50*	*3.50*
c.	Vert. strip of 5, #987-991, + 5 labels	*20.00*	*20.00*
	Sheet, 2 #991c	*40.00*	—
d.	Vert. strip of 5, #987a-991a, + 5 labels	*45.00*	*45.00*
	Sheet, 2 #991d	*90.00*	—
e.	Vert. strip of 5, #987b-991b, + 5 labels	*17.50*	*17.50*
	Sheet, 2 #991e	*35.00*	—

The full sheets sold for $14.95 with or without personalized labels. The personalization of labels was available only at UN Headquarters, and not through mail order. The sheet of No. 991d has "ver. 2" in the lower right selvage. The sheet of No. 991e has "VER. 3" in the lower right selvage.

Economic and Social Council — A411

Printed by Sweden Post, Sweden. Panes of 20. Designed by Rorie Katz, US.

Designs: 44c, Water and sanitation. 98c, Traditional medicines.

2009, Aug. 6 Litho. ***Perf. 12¾x12½***

992	A411 44c **multicolored** *(220,000)+*	2.00	.90
	First day cover		1.60
	Inscription block of 4	6.00	—
	Sheet of 20	30.00	—
993	A411 98c **multicolored** *(170,000)+*	5.00	2.00
	First day cover		3.50
	First day cover, #992-993		4.25
	Inscription block of 4	16.00	—
	Sheet of 20	80.00	—

See Offices in Geneva Nos. 503-504, Vienna Nos. 450-451.

UN Emblem — A412

2009, Sept. 22 Litho. ***Perf. 13¼***

994	A412 98c **multicolored** + label	*5.50*	*5.50*
	Sheet of 10 + 10 labels	*55.00*	—
a.	Perf. 11¼x11 + label	*5.00*	*5.00*
	Sheet of 10 + 10 labels	*50.00*	—

The full sheets sold for $14.95 with or without personalized labels. There are five different non-personalized labels. The personalization of labels was available only at UN Headquarters, and not through mail order. The sheet of No. 994a has "ver. 2" in the lower right selvage.

Miniature Sheet

Millennium Development Goals — A413

Printed by Lowe Martin Group, Canada. Designed by Rorie Katz, US.

No. 995: a, Bowl of hot food. b, Pencil. c, Female symbol. d, Teddy bear. e, Pregnant woman, heart. f, Medicine bottle. g, Stylized tree. h, Conjoined people.

2009, Sept. 25 Litho. ***Perf. 13¼***

995	A413 Sheet of 8 *(60,000)+*	8.50	8.50
	First day cover		9.75
a.-h.	44c Any single	1.20	1.20

See Offies in Geneva No. 505; Vienna No. 457.

Mohandas K. Gandhi — A414

Printed by Lowe-Martin Group, Canada. Designed by Dr. Ferdie Pacheco, US. Panes of 20.

2009, Oct. 2 **Litho.** ***Perf. 13¼***

996 A414 $1 **multicolored** *(570,000)+*	2.25	2.25
First day cover		3.00
Inscription block of 4	10.00	—
Pane of 20	45.00	—

Miniature Sheet

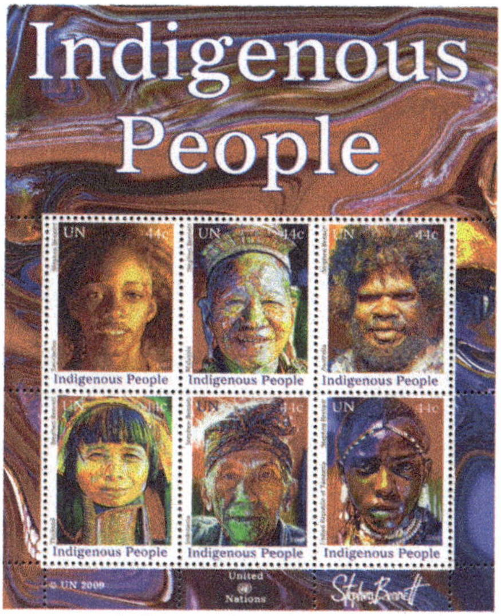

Indigenous People — A415

Printed by Lowe-Martin Group, Canada. Designed by Stephen Bennett, US.

No. 997 — Portraits of person from: a, Seychelles. b, Malaysia. c, Australia. d, Thailand. e, Indonesia. f, Tanzania.

2009, Oct. 8 **Litho.** ***Perf. 12½***

997 A415 Sheet of 6 *(65,000)+*	7.00	7.00
a.-f. 44c Any single	1.15	1.15
First day cover		10.00

See Offices in Geneva No. 511, Vienna No. 458.

Flags and Coins Type of 2006

Printed by Cartor Security Printing, France. Designed by Rorie Katz, US.

No. 998 — Flag of: a, Bahamas, 10 cent coin. b, Jamaica, 20 dollar coin. c, Honduras, 50 centavo coin. d, Kuwait, 100 fils coin. e, Panama, 1 cuarto de Balboa coin. f, Guatemala, 50 centavo coin. g, St. Lucia, 1 cent coin. h, Yemen, 20 rial coin.

2010, Feb. 5 **Litho.** ***Perf. 13¼x13***

998 Sheet of 8 *(66,000)+*	9.75	9.75
a.-h. A375 44c Any single	1.20	1.20
First day cover		10.00

A column of rouletting in the middle of the sheet separates it into two parts. See Offices in Geneva No. 512; Vienna No. 459.

Endangered Species Type of 1993

Printed by Johann Enschedé and Sons, the Netherlands. Designed by Rosie Sanders, United Kingdom.

Designs: No. 999, Monkey puzzle tree. No. 1000, Quiver tree. No. 1001, Bristlecone pine tree. No. 1002, Scarlet ball cactus.

2010, Apr. 15 **Litho.** ***Perf. 12¾x12½***

999 A271 44c **multicolored** *(140,000)+*	1.25	1.25
1000 A271 44c **multicolored** *(140,000)+*	1.25	1.25
1001 A271 44c **multicolored** *(140,000)+*	1.25	1.25
1002 A271 44c **multicolored** *(150,000)+*	1.25	1.25
a. Block of 4, #999-1002	5.50	5.50
First day cover, #1002a		5.00
First day cover, #999-1002, each		2.00
Inscription block of 4, #1002a	5.25	—
Pane of 16	20.00	—

See Offices in Geneva Nos. 513-516; Vienna Nos. 465-468.

The stamp pictured above was printed in limited quantities and sold for far more than face value. The label attached to the stamp could not be personalized. Value for stamp and label, $3. A similar stamp dated "2011" with a different label attached exists.

One Planet, One Ocean Types of Geneva and Vienna and

A416

One Planet, One Ocean — A417

Printed by Johann Enschedé and Sons, the Netherlands. Designed by Robert Wyland, US.

No. 1003: a, Turtle at top, eel at left, fish at LR. b, Fish at LL, turtle's flipper at bottom. c, Fish at left, yellow sponge at LR, Lobster at right. d, Lobster at left, turtle at right.

No. 1004: a, Octopus at left, fish at LR. b, Fish at left and right, turtle's head at bottom. c, Lobster at left. fish at LL and LR. d, Fish at LL and LR, turtle's body at UR.

No. 1005: a, Like #1003a. b, Like #1003b, c, Like #1003c, d, Like #1003d. e, Like Vienna #471a. f, Like Vienna #471b. g, Like Vienna #471c, h, Like Vienna #471d. i, Like Geneva #519a. j, Like Geneva #519b, k, Like Geneva #519c. l, Like Geneva #519d. m, Like #1004a. n, Like #1004b. o, Like #1004c, p, Like #1004d. q, Like Vienna #472a. r, Like Vienna #472b. s, Like Vienna #472c. t, Like Vienna #472d. u, Like Geneva #520a. v, Like Geneva #520b. w, Like Geneva #520c. x, Like Geneva #520d.

2010, May 6 **Litho.** ***Perf. 14x13¼***

1003 A416 Sheet of 4 *(65,000)+*	3.60	3.60
a.-d. 44c Any single	.90	.90
1004 A417 Sheet of 4 *(65,000)+*	8.00	8.00
a.-d. 98c Any single	2.00	2.00
First day cover, #1003-1004		16.50

Souvenir Booklet

Perf. 13¼x13

1005	Booklet, #1005y-1005z, 1005aa-1005ad *(21,000)+*	18.00	
a.-d.	A416 28c any single	.60	.60
e.-h.	V91 28c any single	.60	.60
i.-l.	G85 28c any single	.60	.60
m.-p.	A417 44c any single	.90	.90
q.-t.	V92 44c any single	.90	.90
u.-x.	G86 44c any single	.90	.90
y.	Booklet pane of 4 #1005a-1005d	2.40	2.40
z.	Booklet pane of 4 #1005e-1005h	2.40	2.40
aa.	Booklet pane of 4 #1005i-1005l	2.40	2.40
ab.	Booklet pane of 4 #1005m-1005p	3.60	3.60
ac.	Booklet pane of 4 #1005q-1005t	3.60	3.60
ad.	Booklet pane of 4 #1005u-1005x	3.60	3.60

Intl. Oceanographic Commission, 50th anniv. See Offices in Geneva Nos. 519-521, Vienna Nos. 471-473.

People of Different Cultures — A418

People of Different Cultures as New York Buildings — A419

Printed by Lowe-Martin Group, Canada. Designed by Christopher Corr, United Kingdom.

2010, June 4 **Litho.** ***Perf. 13***

1006	A418 3c **multicolored** *(400,000)+*	.25	.25
	First day cover		2.00
	Inscription block of 4	.25	—
	Pane of 20	1.25	—
1007	A419 4c **multicolored** *(400,000)+*	.25	.25
	First day cover		2.00
	First day cover, #1006-1007		2.00
	Inscription block of 4	.35	—
	Pane of 20	1.60	—

UN Headquarters and New York Skyline — A420

Shanghai Skyline A421

2010, June 4 **Litho.** ***Perf. 13¼***

1008	A420 98c **multicolored**	3.00	3.00
1009	A421 98c **multicolored**	3.00	3.00
a.	Horiz. pair, #1008-1009	6.00	6.00
	Pane, 5 #1009a	30.00	—

Expo 2010, Shanghai. Nos. 1008-1009 were sold only in full panes for $14.95.

United Nations, 65th Anniv. — A422

Printed by Lowe-Martin Group, Canada. Designed by Rorie Katz, United States.

Litho. With Foil Application

2010, June 28 ***Perf. 13¼***

1010	A422 98c **light blue & gold** *(150,000)+*	2.25	2.25
	First day cover		3.25
	Inscription block of 4	9.00	—
	Pane of 15	32.50	—

Souvenir Sheet

1011	Sheet of 2 #1011a *(36,000)+*	5.00	5.00
a.	A422 98c **dark blue & gold**	2.50	2.50
	First day cover		7.50

See Offices in Geneva No. 522, Vienna No. 474.

A423

A424

A425

A426

United Nations Sea Transport — A427

Printed by UAB Garsu Pasaulis, Lithuania. Designed by Simon Williams, United Kingdom.

2010, Sept. 2 **Litho.** ***Perf. 13¼x13***

1012 A423 44c **multicolored** *(128,000)+*	.90	.90
1013 A424 44c **multicolored** *(128,000)+*	.90	.90
1014 A425 44c **multicolored** *(128,000)+*	.90	.90
1015 A426 44c **multicolored** *(128,000)+*	.90	.90
1016 A427 44c **multicolored** *(128,000)+*	.90	.90
a. Horiz. strip of 5, #1012-1016	5.00	5.00
First day cover, #1016a		6.00
First day cover, #1012-1016, each		1.50
Inscription block of 10	9.00	—
Pane of 20	18.00	—

See Offices in Geneva Nos. 523-527, Vienna Nos. 475-479.

Intl. Year of Biodiversity — A428

Printed by Lowe-Martin Group, Canada. Panes of 20. Designed by Deborah Halperin, US.

Drawings from Art Forms from Nature, by Ernst Heinrich: 15c, Hummingbird. $1.50, Liverwort.

2010, Oct. 18 **Litho.** ***Perf. 13***

1017 A428 15c **multicolored** *(400,000)+*	.30	.30
First day cover		1.25
Inscription block of 4	1.20	—
Pane of 20	6.00	—
1018 A428 $1.50 **multicolored** *(400,000)+*	3.00	3.00
First day cover		5.75
First day cover, #1017-1018		4.75
Inscription block of 4	12.00	—
Pane of 20	60.00	—

See Offices in Geneva Nos. 517-518; Vienna Nos. 469-470.

Miniature Sheet

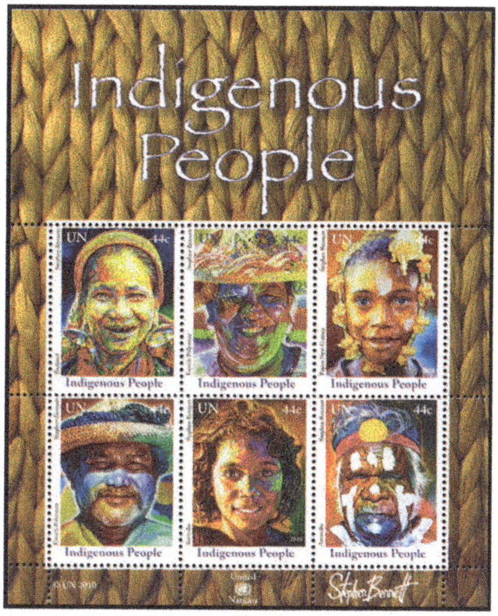

Indigenous People — A429

Printed by Lowe-Martin Group, Canada. Designed by Stephen Bennett, US.

No. 1019 — Portraits of person from: a, Thailand. b, French Polynesia (woman, denomination in black). c, Papua New Guinea. d, French Polynesia (man, denomination in white). e, Australia (child). f, Australia (old man with headband).

2010, Oct. 21 **Litho.** ***Perf. 13***

1019 A429 Sheet of 6 *(55,000)+*	6.00	6.00
a.-f. 44c Any single	1.00	1.00
First day cover		8.00

See Offices in Geneva No. 529; Vienna No. 480.

United Nations Headquarters, New York — A430

Printed by Cartor Security Printing, France. Panes of 20. Designed by Scott Solberg, US.

United Nations Headquarters: 11c, Aerial view. $5, Ground-level view.

2011, Feb. 4 **Litho.** ***Perf. 13***

1020 A430 11c **multicolored** *(400,000)+*	.25	.25
First day cover		1.25
Inscription block of 4	1.00	—
Pane of 20	5.00	—
1021 A430 $5 **multicolored** *(400,000)+*	9.00	9.00
First day cover		13.50
First day cover, #1020-1021		12.50
Inscription block of 4	37.50	—
Pane of 20	200.00	—

See Offices in Geneva Nos. 530-531; Vienna Nos. 481-482.

Flags and Coins Type of 2006

Printed by Cartor Security Printing, France. Designed by Rorie Katz, US.

No. 1022 — Flag of: a, Mauritius, 1 rupee coin. b, Guyana, 10 dollar coin. c, Timor, 5 cent coin. d, Iceland, 100 krónur coin. e, Chile, 1 peso coin. f, Norway, 20 kroner coin. g, Fiji, 50 cent coin. h, Comoro Islands, 100 franc coin.

2011, Mar. 3 **Litho.** ***Perf. 13¼x13***

1022	Sheet of 8 *(60,000)*+	8.75	8.75
a.-h.	A375 44c Any single	1.10	1.10
	First day cover		9.75

A column of rouletting in the middle of the sheet separates it into two parts. See Offices in Geneva No. 532; Vienna No. 483.

UN Emblem — A431

2011, Apr. 7 **Litho.** ***Perf. 14¾***

1023	A431 98c **blue** + label	*4.00*	*4.00*
	Sheet of 10 + 10 labels	*32.00*	—

The full sheets sold for $14.95. There are 10 different non-personalized labels.

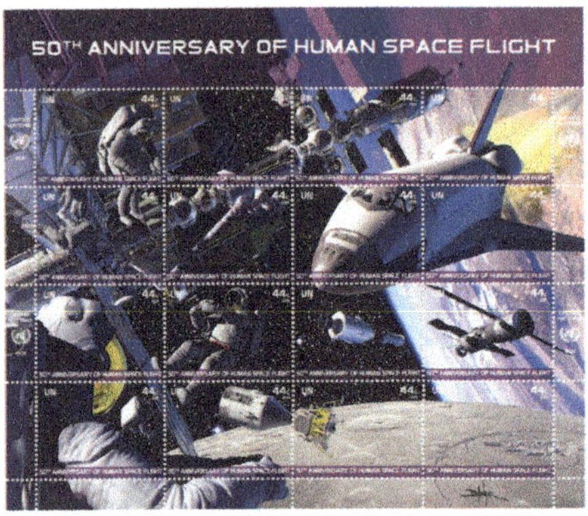

Human Space Flight, 50th Anniv. — A432

Printed by Lowe-Martin Group, Canada. Designed by Peter Bollinger, US.
No. 1024: Various parts of outer space scene.
No. 1025, vert.: a, Cosmonaut and rocket. b, Astronaut on ladder of Lunar Module.

2011, Apr. 12 **Litho.** ***Perf. 13x13¼***

1024	A432	Sheet of 16 *(52,000)*+	16.00	16.00
		First day cover		17.50
a.-p.		44c any single	1.00	1.00

Souvenir Sheet

1025	A432	Sheet of 2	15.00	15.00
		First day cover		4.25
a.		44c **multicolored**	4.50	4.50
b.		98c **multicolored**	11.50	11.50

See Offices in Geneva Nos. 533-534; Vienna Nos. 484-485. No. 1024 contains two 40x48mm stamps that were printed as part of a larger sheet of six stamps, Vienna No. 485c, which was broken up into its component two-stamp souvenir sheets, and also sold as one unit. Value $90, complete unit.

UNESCO World Heritage Sites in Nordic Countries — A433

Printed by Johann Enschedé and Sons, the Netherlands. Panes of 20. Designed by Rorie Katz, US.
Designs: 44c, Surtsey Volcanic Island, Iceland. 98c, Drottningholm Castle, Sweden.

2011, May 5 **Litho.** ***Perf. 14x13½***

1026	A433 44c **multicolored** *(190,000)*+	.90	.90
	First day cover		1.60
	Inscription block of 4	3.60	—
	Pane of 20	18.00	—
1027	A433 98c **multicolored** *(190,000)*+	2.00	2.00
	First day cover		3.50
	First day cover, #1025-1026		4.25
	Inscription block of 4	8.00	—
	Pane of 20	40.00	—

See Offices in Geneva Nos. 535-536; Vienna Nos. 496-497.

AIDS Ribbon — A434

Printed by Lowe-Martin Group, Canada. Panes of 4. Designed by Rorie Katz, US.

2011, June 3 **Litho.** ***Die Cut***

Self-Adhesive

1028	A434 44c **red & blue** *(200,000)*+	1.75	1.75
	Pane of 4	7.00	
	First day cover, pane of 4		5.25

See Offices in Geneva No. 537; Vienna No. 498.

Economic and Social Council (ECOSOC) — A435

Printed by Cartor Security Printing, France. Panes of 20. Designed by Rorie Katz, US.

Education: 44c, Child and teacher. 98c, Child writing on blackboard.

2011, July 1 Litho. *Perf. 14¼*

1029 A435 44c **multicolored** *(180,000)+*	1.50	1.50
First day cover		1.60
Inscription block of 4	6.00	—
Pane of 20	30.00	—
1030 A435 98c **multicolored** *(180,000)+*	3.50	3.50
First day cover		3.50
First day cover, #1029-1030		5.00
Inscription block of 4	14.00	—
Pane of 20	70.00	—

See Offices in Geneva Nos. 538-539; Vienna Nos. 499-500.

Endangered Species Type of 1993

Printed by Johann Enschedé and Sons, the Netherlands. Designed by Wendy Wray, U.S.

Designs: No. 1031, Bali starling. No. 1032, California condor. No. 1033, Japanese crane. No. 1034, Black-fronted piping-guan.

2011, Sept. 7 Litho. *Perf. 12¾x12½*

1031 A271 44c **multicolored** *(116,000)+*	1.10	1.10
1032 A271 44c **multicolored** *(116,000)+*	1.10	1.10
1033 A271 44c **multicolored** *(116,000)+*	1.10	1.10
1034 A271 44c **multicolored** *(116,000)+*	1.10	1.10
a. Block of 4, #1031-1034	5.00	5.00
First day cover, #1034a		5.00
First day cover, #1031-1034, each		2.00
Inscription block of 4, #1034a	4.50	—
Pane of 16	22.50	—

See Offices in Geneva Nos. 540-543; Vienna Nos. 501-504.

Intl. Year of Forests — A436

Printed by Lowe-Martin Group, Canada. Panes of 8. Designed by Sergio Baradat, U.S.

Designs: 44c, Tree with wildlife, man with mask. 98c, Tree roots.

2011, Oct. 13 Litho. With Foil Application *Perf. 12½*

1035 44c **multicolored** *(92,000)+*	1.25	1.25
1036 98c **multicolored** *(92,000)+*	2.50	2.50
a. A436 Vert. pair, #1035-1036	3.75	3.75
First day cover, #1036a		4.25
Pane of 8	15.00	—

See Offices in Geneva Nos. 544-545; Vienna Nos. 505-506.

UN Emblem — A437

2012, Jan. 23 Litho. *Perf. 14¾*

1037 A437 $1.05 **blue** + label	*2.75*	*2.75*
Sheet of 10 + 10 labels	*27.50*	—

The full sheet sold for $14.95. The generic label exists as shown, and with dragon in yellow against red background. Labels could be personalized. The personalization of labels was available only at UN Headquarters, and not through mail order.

A438

No. 1038: a, Desk in lobby. b, Sculpture of Jesus holding lamb. c, Stained-glass window. d, Meeting room. e, Guided tour. f, Flags in front of United Nations buildings. g, United Nations Peacekeepers helmet in showcase. h, Gift shop. i, View of curved floors above lobby. j, Street signs.

2012, Jan. 23 Litho. *Perf. 14¾*

1038 A438 Sheet of 10	*30.00*	*30.00*
a.-j. $1.05 Any single + label	*3.00*	*3.00*

The full sheet sold for $14.95. The generic labels are shown. Labels could be personalized. The personalization of labels was available only at UN Headquarters, and not through mail order.

Flags and Coins Type of 2006

Printed by Cartor Security Printing, France. Designed by Rorie Katz, US.

No. 1039 — Flag of: a, Nepal, 1 rupee coin. b, Bahrain, 100 fils coin. c, Paraguay, 1000 guarani coin. d, Ethiopia, 25 cent coin. e, Peru, 1 sol coin. f, Solomon Islands, 20 cent coin. g, Dominican Republic, 1 peso coin. h, Canada, 1 dollar coin.

2012, Feb. 3 Litho. *Perf. 13¼x13*

1039 Sheet of 8 *(43,000)+*	7.25	7.25
a.-h. A375 45c Any single	.90	.90
First day cover		10.00

A column of rouletting in the middle of the sheet separates it into two parts. See Offices in Geneva No. 546; Vienna No. 507.

A439

Autism Awareness — A440

Printed by Joh. Enschedé Stamps Security Printers, Netherlands. Panes of 20.

Drawings by autistic people: No. 1040, An Abstract Garden II, by Trent Altman, U.S. No. 1041, Crazy Love, by Hannah Kandel, U.S.

2012, Apr. 2 **Litho.** ***Perf. 14x13½***

1040 A439 $1.05 **multicolored** *(100,000)*+		2.10	2.10
1041 A440 $1.05 **multicolored** *(100,000)*+		2.10	2.10
a.	Pair, #1040-1041	4.20	4.20
	First day cover, #1040-1041		5.75
	Inscription block of 4	8.50	—
	Pane of 20	42.00	—

See Offices in Geneva Nos. 547-548; Vienna Nos. 508-509.

Endangered Species Type of 1993

Printed by Johann Enschedé and Sons, the Netherlands. Designed by Diana Marques, Portugal.

Designs: No. 1042, Giant panda. No. 1043, Short-horned chameleon. No. 1044, Oncilla. No. 1045, Cotton-headed tamarin.

2012, Apr. 19 **Litho.** ***Perf. 12¾x12½***

1042 A271 45c **multicolored** *(108,000)*+		1.10	1.10
1043 A271 45c **multicolored** *(108,000)*+		1.10	1.10
1044 A271 45c **multicolored** *(108,000)*+		1.10	1.10
1045 A271 45c **multicolored** *(108,000)*+		1.10	1.10
a.	Block of 4, #1042-1045	5.00	5.00
	First day cover, #1045a		5.00
	First day cover, #1042-1045, each		2.00
	Inscription block of 4, #1045a	4.50	—
	Pane of 16	22.50	—

See Offices in Geneva Nos. 549-552; Vienna Nos. 511-514.

Tinker Bell — A441

Tinker Bell — A442

2012, June 1 **Litho.** ***Perf. 14¾***

1046 A441 $1.05 **multicolored** + label		*3.00*	*3.00*
1047 A442 $1.05 **multicolored** + label		*3.00*	*3.00*
a.	Vert. pair, #1046-1047, + 2 labels	*6.00*	*6.00*
	Sheet of 10, 5 each #1046-1047, + 10 labels	*30.00*	*30.00*

The full sheet sold for $14.95. The generic labels are shown. Labels could be personalized. The personalization of labels was available only at UN Headquarters, and not through mail order.

Rio + 20 Conference on Sustainable Development, Rio de Janeiro — A443

Printed by Lowe-Martin Group, Canada. Panes of 20. Designed by Gail Armstrong, United Kingdom.

2012, June 1 **Litho.** ***Perf. 13x13¼***

1048 A443 $1.05 **multicolored** *(146,000)*+		2.10	2.10
	First day cover		3.50
	Inscription block of 4	8.40	—
	Pane of 20	42.50	—

See Offices in Geneva No. 553; Vienna No. 515.

Sport for Peace A444

Printed by Cartor Security Printing, France. Panes of 9. Designed by Daniel Stolle, Finland.

2012 Paralympics events: 45c, Goalball. $1.05, Sitting volleyball.

Litho. With Foil Application

2012, Aug. 17 ***Perf. 14½***

1049 A444 45c **multicolored** *(121,500)*+		.90	.90
	First day cover		1.60
	Inscription block of 4	3.60	—
	Pane of 9	8.25	—
1050 A444 $1.05 **multicolored** *(121,500)*+		2.10	2.10
	First day cover		3.75
	First day cover, #1049-1050		4.25

	Inscription block of 4	8.40	—
	Pane of 9	19.00	—
a.	Souvenir sheet of 1 *(34,000)*+	3.50	3.50
	First day cover		3.25

See Offices in Geneva Nos. 554-555; Vienna Nos. 516-517.

UNESCO World Heritage Sites in Africa A445

Printed by Lowe-Martin Group, Canada. Panes of 20. Designed by Rorie Katz, US.

Designs: 45c, Kilamanjaro National Park, Tanzania. $1.05, Old Towns of Djenné, Mali.

2012, Sept. 5 **Litho.** ***Perf. 13¼***

1051 A445	45c **multicolored** *(150,000)*+	.90	.90
	First day cover		1.60
	Inscription block of 4	3.60	—
	Pane of 20	18.00	—
1052 A445	$1.05 **multicolored** *(150,000)*+	2.10	2.10
	First day cover		3.75
	First day cover, #1051-1052		4.25
	Inscription block of 4	8.50	—
	Pane of 20	42.50	—

See Offices in Geneva Nos. 556-557; Vienna Nos. 518-519.

Miniature Sheet

Indigenous People — A446

Printed by Lowe-Martin Group, Canada. Designed by Stephen Bennett, US.

No. 1053 — Portrait of person from: a, Namibia. b, Japan. c, China. d, Ethiopia. e, Mongolia. f, Tanzania.

2012, Oct. 11 **Litho.** ***Perf. 13¼x13***

1053 A446	Sheet of 6 *(43,000)*+	5.50	5.50
a.-f.	45c Any single	.90	.90
	First day cover		8.00

See Offices in Geneva No. 558; Vienna No. 520.

UN Emblem — A447

2013, Jan. 28 **Litho.** ***Perf. 14¾***

1054 A447	$1.10 **multicolored** + label	*4.00*	*4.00*
	Sheet of 10 + 10 labels	*40.00*	—

The full sheet sold for $14.95. The generic label exists as shown, and with snake against red background. Labels could be personalized. The personalization of labels was available only at UN Headquarters, and not through mail order.

A448

No. 1055: a, Flags in front of Secretariat Building, brown panel at right. b, Aerial view of headquarters and East River, yellow orange panel at left. c, Secretariat Building and wall of General Assembly building, yellow orange panel at left. d, Headquarters and East River, brown panel at right. e, General Asembly and Secretariat Buildings, flags at right, brown panel at right. f, Sculpture and fountain at night, yellow orange panel at left. g, Secretariat Building and cherry blossoms, yellow orange panel at left. h, Secretariat Building, trees without leaves, flags at left, brown panel at right. i, Aerial view of headquarters at night, brown panel at right. j, Headquarters, yellow panel at left.

2013, Jan. 28 **Litho.** ***Perf. 14¾***

1055 A448	Sheet of 10	*30.00*	*30.00*
a.-j.	$1.10 Any single + label	*3.00*	*3.00*

The full sheet sold for $14.95. The generic labels are shown. Labels could be personalized. The personalization of labels was available only at UN Headquarters, and not through mail order.

World Radio Day — A449

Printed by Lowe-Martin Group, Canada. Panes of 20. Designed by Rorie Katz, US.

Designs: 46c, Radio antenna. $1.10, Audrey Hepburn at microphone.

2013, Feb. 13 — Litho. — *Perf. 13¼x13*

1056	A449	46c **multicolored** *(135,200)+*	.95	.95
		First day cover		1.60
		Inscription block of 4	3.80	—
		Pane of 20	19.00	—
1057	A449	$1.10 **multicolored** *(135,200)+*	2.25	2.25
		First day cover		3.75
		First day cover, #1056-1057		4.50
		Inscription block of 4	9.00	—
		Pane of 20	45.00	—

See Offices in Geneva Nos. 559-560; Vienna Nos. 521-522.

Circle of People — A450

United Nations Headquarters — A451

Printed by Johann Enschedé and Sons, the Netherlands. Panes of 20. Designed by Sergio Baradat, US.

2013, Mar. 5 — Litho. — *Perf. 14x13½*

1058	A450	$1.10 **multicolored** *(200,000)+*	2.25	2.25
		First day cover		3.00
		Inscription block of 4	9.00	—
		Pane of 20	45.00	—
		Perf. 13½x14		
1059	A451	$3 **multicolored** *(200,000)+*	6.00	6.00
		First day cover		8.00
		First day cover, #1058-1059		10.00
		Inscription block of 4	24.00	—
		Pane of 20	120.00	—

See Offices in Geneva Nos. 561-562; Vienna Nos. 523-524.

World Heritage Sites, China A452

Printed by Johann Enschedé and Sons, the Netherlands. Panes of 20. Designed by Sergio Baradat, U.S.

Designs: Nos. 1060, 1062a, Mogao Caves. Nos. 1061, 1062d, Imperial Palace, Beijing. No. 1062b, Potala Palace, Lhasa. No. 1062c, Great Wall of China. No. 1062e, Mount Huangshan. No. 1062f, Mausoleum of the First Qing Emperor.

2013, Apr. 11 — Litho. — *Perf. 14x13½*

1060	A452	46c **multicolored** *(150,000)+*	.95	.95
		First day cover		1.60
		Inscription block of 4	3.80	—
		Pane of 20	19.00	—
1061	A452	$1.10 **multicolored** *(150,000)+*	2.25	2.25
		First day cover		3.75
		First day cover, #1060-1061		4.50
		Inscription block of 4	9.00	—
		Pane of 20	45.00	—

Souvenir Booklet

1062	Booklet, #1062g-1062l *(18,000)+*	20.00	
a.-c.	A452 33c any single	.70	.70
d.-f.	A452 46c any single	.95	.95
g.	Booklet pane of 4 #1062a	2.80	—
h.	Booklet pane of 4 #1062b	2.80	—
i.	Booklet pane of 4 #1062c	2.80	—
j.	Booklet pane of 4 #1062d	3.80	—
k.	Booklet pane of 4 #1062e	3.80	—
l.	Booklet pane of 4 #1062f	3.80	—

See Offices in Geneva Nos. 563-565, Vienna Nos. 525-527.

Flag Type of 1980

Printed by Lowe Martin Group, Canada. Designed by Rorie Katz, US. Issued in panes of 16; each pane contains 4 blocks of 4. A se-tenant block of 4 designs centers each pane.

2013, May 2 — Litho. — *Perf. 13*

1063	A185	$1.10 Myanmar *(144,000)+*	2.25	2.25
1064	A185	$1.10 Russian Federation *(144,000)+*	2.25	2.25
1065	A185	$1.10 South Sudan *(144,000)+*	2.25	2.25
1066	A185	$1.10 Cape Verde *(144,000)+*	2.25	2.25
a.		Block of 4, #1063-1066	12.00	12.00
		First day cover, #1063-1066, each		3.50
		Pane of 16	36.00	
		Nos. 1063-1066 (4)	9.00	9.00

World Oceans Day — A453

Printed by Lowe-Martin Group, Canada. Designed by Rorie Katz, US.

No. 1067 — Fish from *One Fish, Two Fish, Red Fish, Blue Fish,* by Dr. Seuss: a, Green fish, red fish, sign. b, Red fish facing right. c, Green fish facing left, sign. d, Yellow fish, sign. e, Blue fish. f, Red fish facing left, sign. g, Red fish facing right, water droplets, tail of yellow and red fish, sign. h, Yellow and red fish, green fish, side of blue fish. i, Head of blue fish, sign post. j, Sign and wave. k, Sign, red fish, side and tail of blue fish, wave. l, Side of blue fish, green fish, wave.

2013, May 31 — Litho. — *Perf. 13*

1067	A453	Sheet of 12 *(47,000)+*	11.50	11.50
		First day cover		14.50
a.-l.		46c any single	.95	.95

See Offices in Geneva No. 500, Vienna No. 520.

Nebulae — A454

Printed by UAB Garsu Pasaulis, Lithuania. Panes of 8. Designed by Sergio Baradat, U.S.

Designs: No. 1068, V838 Mon. No. 1069, WR 25, Tr16-244. 46c, 30 Doradus.

2013, Aug. 9	**Litho.**	***Perf. 13¼***	
1068 A454 $1.10 **multicolored** *(116,000)+*		2.25	2.25
1069 A454 $1.10 **multicolored** *(116,000)+*		2.25	2.25
a. Pair, #1068-1069		4.50	4.50
First day cover, #1069a			6.00
Inscription block of 4		9.00	—
Pane of 8		18.00	—

Souvenir Sheet

1070 A454 46c **multicolored** *(29,000)+*		2.50	2.50
First day cover			2.00

No. 1070 contains one 44x44mm stamp. See Offices in Geneva Nos. 567-569; Vienna Nos. 529-531.

World Humanitarian Day — A455

No. 1071 — "The World Needs More" in speech balloon in: a, Somali (Uduunku. . .). b, Thai. c, Arabic (people in background). d, Portuguese (O Mundo. . .). e, Russian. f, Korean. g, Swahili (Mahitaji. . .). h, Chinese. i, Urdu (aerial view of village in background). j, English.

2013, Aug. 19	**Litho.**	***Perf. 14¾***	
1071 A455 Sheet of 10		*30.00*	*30.00*
a.-j. $1.10 Any single + label		*3.00*	*3.00*

The full sheet sold for $14.95. The generic labels are shown. Labels could be personalized. The personalization of labels was available only at UN Headquarters, and not through mail order.

Works of Disabled Artists — A456

Printed by UAB Garsu Pasaulis, Lithuania. Panes of 20. Designed by Rorie Katz, U.S.

Designs: 46c, Self-portrait II by Chuck Close, U.S. $1.10, Tears and Laughter, by Josephine King, United Kingdom.

2013, Sept. 20	**Litho.**	***Perf. 13¼x13***	
1072 A456 46c **multicolored** *(148,000)+*		.95	.95
First day cover			1.60
Inscription block of 4		3.80	—
Pane of 20		19.00	—
1073 A456 $1.10 **multicolored** *(148,000)+*		2.25	2.25
First day cover			3.75
First day cover, #1072-1073			4.50
Inscription block of 4		9.00	—
Pane of 20		45.00	—

See Offices in Geneva Nos. 570-571; Vienna Nos. 532-533.

Endangered Species Type of 1993

Printed by Johann Enschedé and Sons, the Netherlands. Designed by Fernando J. S. Correia, Portugal.

Designs: No. 1074, Asian tapir. No. 1075, Mongoose lemur. No. 1076, Flat-headed cat. No. 1077, Aye-aye.

2013, Oct. 10	**Litho.**	***Perf. 12¾x12½***	
1074 A271 $1.10 **multicolored** *(108,000)+*		2.50	2.50
1075 A271 $1.10 **multicolored** *(108,000)+*		2.50	2.50
1076 A271 $1.10 **multicolored** *(108,000)+*		2.50	2.50
1077 A271 $1.10 **multicolored** *(108,000)+*		2.50	2.50
a. Block of 4, #1074-1077		11.00	11.00
First day cover, #1077a			11.00
First day cover, #1074-1077, each			3.50
Inscription block of 4, #1077a		10.00	—
Pane of 16		40.00	—

See Offices in Geneva Nos. 572-575; Vienna Nos. 534-537.

Flags and Coins Type of 2006

Printed by Cartor Security Printing, France. Designed by Rorie Katz, US.

No. 1078 — Flag of: a, Montenegro, 20 cent coin. b, Grenada, 5 cent coin. c, United States, 25 cent coin. d, Gabon, 100 franc coin. e, Palau, 1 cent coin. f, Niger, 100 franc coin. g, Saint Kitts and Nevis, 5 cent coin. h, Venezuela, 1 bolivar coin.

2013, Nov. 6	**Litho.**	***Perf. 13¼x13***	
1078 Sheet of 8 *(41,000)+*		7.75	7.75
a.-h. A375 46c Any single		.95	.95
First day cover			10.50

A column of rouletting in the middle of the sheet separates it into two parts. See Offices in Geneva No. 576; Vienna No. 539.

UN Emblem — A457

2014, Jan. 28	**Litho.**	***Perf. 14¾***	
1079 A457 $1.15 **multicolored** + label		*3.00*	*3.00*
Sheet of 10 + 10 labels		*30.00*	—

The full sheet sold for $14.95. The generic label exists as shown, with horse on orange background. Labels could be personalized. The personalization of labels was available only at UN Headquarters, and not through mail order. See Nos. 1149, 1187, 1209.

A458

No. 1080: a, The Golden Rule, mosaic by Norman Rockwell, dark green panel at right. b, Renovated Delegate's Lounge, yellow green panel at left. c, Renovated ECOSOC Chamber, red brown panel at left. d, Dag Hammarskjold Library, dark blue panel at right. e, Helmet of United Nations Peacekeeper and United Nations Flag, dark blue panel at right. f, United Nations Headquarters, dark green panel at left. g, Renovated Security Council Chamber, yellow green panel at left. h, Flags of member nations, red brown panel at right. i, Mankind's Struggle for Lasting Peace, by José Vela-Zanetti, dark blue panel at right. j, Relational Painting No. 90, by Fritz Glarner, yellow green panel at left.

2014, Jan. 28 **Litho.** ***Perf. 14¾***

1080	A458	Sheet of 10	*30.00*	*30.00*
a.-j.		$1.15 Any single + label	3.00	3.00

The full sheet sold for $14.95. The generic labels are shown. Labels could be personalized. The personalization of labels was available only at UN Headquarters, and not through mail order.

International Day of Happiness — A459

Printed by Lowe-Martin Group, Canada. Panes of 20. Designed by Rorie Katz, U.S.

Designs: 47c, Woman smiling, photograph by Mario Castello, "Happy." $1.15, People kissing on beach, photograph by Henryk T. Kaiser, "Feliz."

2014, Mar. 17 **Litho.** ***Perf. 13¼x13***

1081	A459	47c **multicolored** *(130,000)+*	.95	.95
		First day cover		1.60
		Inscription block of 4	3.80	—
		Pane of 20	19.00	—
1082	A459	$1.15 **multicolored** *(130,000)+*	2.40	2.40
		First day cover		4.00
		First day cover, #1081-1082		4.75
		Inscription block of 4	9.60	—
		Pane of 20	48.00	—

See Offices in Geneva Nos. 577-578; Vienna Nos. 540-541.

Flag Type of 1980

Printed by Lowe Martin Group, Canada. Designed by Rorie Katz, U.S. Issued in panes of 16; each pane contains 4 blocks of 4. A se-tenant block of 4 designs centers each pane.

2014, Mar. 27 **Litho.** ***Perf. 13x13¼***

1083	A185	$1.15 Afghanistan *(100,000)+*	3.00	3.00
1084	A185	$1.15 Serbia *(100,000)+*	3.00	3.00
1085	A185	$1.15 Cambodia *(100,000)+*	3.00	3.00
1086	A185	$1.15 Democratic Republic of the Congo *(100,000)+*	3.00	3.00
a.		Block of 4, #1083-1086	15.00	15.00
		First day cover, #1083-1086, each		3.00
		Pane of 16	48.00	
		Nos. 1083-1086 (4)	12.00	12.00

Miniature Sheet

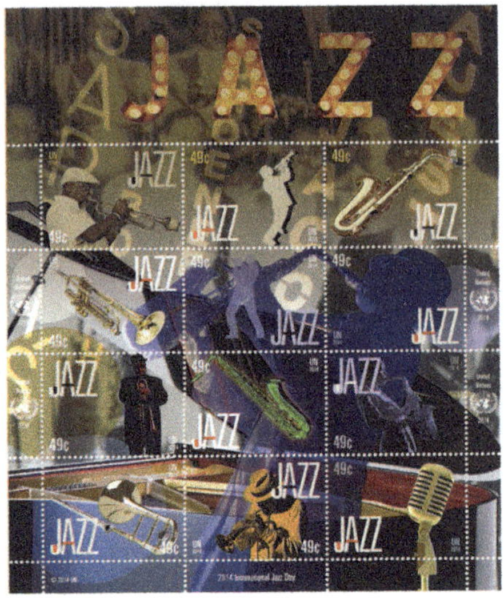

International Year of Jazz — A460

Printed by Cartor Security Printing, France. Designed by Sergio Baradat, U.S.

No. 1087: a, Trumpeter with cap and mute in trumpet. b, Silhouette of trumpeter in tan. c, Saxophone. d, Trumpet. e, Silhouette of trumpeter in lilac. f, Saxophonist wearing hat. g, Man with hat holding trombone. h, Green saxophone. i, Saxophonist without hat. j, Trombone. k, Trumpeter wearing hat. l, Microphone.

2014, Apr. 30 **Litho.** ***Perf. 13x13¼***

1087	A460	Sheet of 12 *(45,000)+*	12.00	12.00
		First day cover		15.00
a.-l.		49c Any single	1.00	1.00

See Offices in Geneva No. 579; Vienna No. 542.

A461

A462

Printed by Lowe-Martin Group, Canada. Panes of 20. Designed by Sergio Baradat, U.S.

2014, June 6 **Litho.** ***Perf. 13¼x13***

1088 A461 33c **multicolored** *(140,000)+*		.70	.70
	First day cover		1.00
	Inscription block of 4	2.80	—
	Pane of 20	14.00	—
1089 A462 $2 **multicolored** *(140,000)+*		4.00	4.00
	First day cover		6.00
	First day cover, #1088-1089		6.25
	Inscription block of 4	16.00	—
	Pane of 20	80.00	—

See Offices in Geneva Nos. 580-581; Vienna Nos. 544-545.

Taj Mahal and Tourists A463

Taj Mahal and Pink Sky A464

Taj Mahal and Sun A465

Taj Mahal and Reflecting Pool A466

Taj Mahal and Camel A467

Taj Mahal and Elephant A468

Printed by Lowe-Martin Group, Canada. Panes of 20. Designed by Rorie Katz, U.S.

2014, July 16 **Engr.** ***Perf. 13¼x13***

1090 A463 49c **multicolored** *(130,000)+*		1.00	1.00
	First day cover		1.75
	Inscription block of 4	4.00	—
	Pane of 20	20.00	—
1091 A464 $1.15 **multicolored** *(130,000)+*		2.40	2.40
	First day cover		4.00
	First day cover, #1090-1091		4.75
	Inscription block of 4	9.60	—
	Pane of 20	48.00	—

Souvenir Booklet

1092	Booklet, #1092g-1092l *(14,000)+*	20.50	
a.	A463 34c multi	.70	.70
b.	A465 34c multi	.70	.70
c.	A466 34c multi	.70	.70
d.	A464 49c multi	1.00	1.00
e.	A467 49c multi	1.00	1.00
f.	A468 49c multi	1.00	1.00
g.	Booklet pane of 4 #1092a	2.80	—
h.	Booklet pane of 4 #1092b	2.80	—
i.	Booklet pane of 4 #1092c	2.80	—
j.	Booklet pane of 4 #1092d	4.00	—
k.	Booklet pane of 4 #1092e	4.00	—
l.	Booklet pane of 4 #1092f	4.00	—

See Offices in Geneva Nos. 582-584, Vienna Nos. 546-548.

International Year of Family Farming — A469

Printed by Lowe-Martin Group, Canada. Panes of 20. Designed by Sergio Baradat, U.S.
Designs: 49c, People and fruits. $1.15, People fishing.

2014, Aug. 21 **Litho.** ***Perf. 13x13¼***

1093 A469 49c **multicolored** *(120,000)+*	1.00	1.00
First day cover		1.75
Inscription block of 4	4.00	—
Pane of 20	20.00	—
1094 A469 $1.15 **multicolored** *(120,000)+*	2.40	2.40
First day cover		4.00
First day cover, #1093-1094		4.75
Inscription block of 4	9.60	—
Pane of 20	48.00	—

See Offices in Geneva Nos. 585-586; Vienna Nos. 549-550.

Global Education First Initiative — A470

Printed by Lowe-Martin Group, Canada. Panes of 20. Designed by Oamul Lu, People's Republic of China.
Designs: $1.15, Teacher and students in forest. $1.50, Chemistry teacher and student.

2014, Sept. 18 **Litho.** ***Perf. 13x13¼***

1095 A470 $1.15 **multicolored** *(130,000)+*	2.40	2.40
First day cover		3.50
Inscription block of 4	9.75	—
Pane of 20	48.00	—

Souvenir Sheet

Perf. 12½

1096 A470 $1.50 **multicolored** *(35,000)+*	6.00	5.00
First day cover		5.00

No. 1096 contains one 32x32mm stamp. See Offices in Geneva Nos. 588-589; Vienna Nos. 551-552.

Endangered Species — A471

Printed by Johann Enschedé and Sons, the Netherlands. Designed by Amadeo Bachar, U.S.
Maps and: No. 1097, Denise's pygmy seahorses. No. 1098, Whale shark. No. 1099, Scalloped hammerhead shark. No. 1100, Asian arowana.

2014, Oct. 23 **Litho.** ***Perf. 12¾x12½***

1097 A471 $1.15 **multicolored** *(100,000)+*	2.40	2.40
1098 A471 $1.15 **multicolored** *(100,000)+*	2.40	2.40
1099 A471 $1.15 **multicolored** *(100,000)+*	2.40	2.40
1100 A471 $1.15 **multicolored** *(100,000)+*	2.40	2.40
a. Block of 4, #1097-1100	9.75	9.75
First day cover, #1100a		11.00
First day cover, #1097-1100, each		3.50
Inscription block of 4, #1100a	9.75	—
Pane of 16	39.00	—

See Offices in Geneva Nos. 590-593; Vienna Nos. 553-556.

A472

No. 1101: a, United Nations emblem in gray, bottom panel in blue. b, Aerial view of United Nations Headquarters, bottom panel in red, year date at left. c, View of United Nations Headquarters from across East River, bottom panel in red, year date at right. d, Interior balconies, bottom panel in blue. e, Crowd in lobby, bottom panel in blue. f, Sun reflecting off United Nations Building, street lights, bottom panel in red. g, United Nations emblem in brown, bottom panel in red. h, Woman and two men near General Assembly Building, bottom panel in blue. i, United Nations Building, flags, trees without leaves, bottom panel in blue. j, General Assembly and United Nations Buildings, bottom panel in red.

2014, Oct. 23 **Litho.** ***Perf. 14¾***

1101 A472 Sheet of 10	*32.50*	*32.50*
a.-j. $1.15 Any single + label	*3.00*	*3.00*

The full sheet sold for $14.95. The generic labels are shown. Labels could be personalized. The personalization of labels was available only at UN Headquarters, and not through mail order.

UN Emblem — A473

Designed by Rorie Katz, U.S.

2015, Jan. 23 **Litho.** ***Perf. 14¾***

1102 A473 $1.15 **multicolored** + label	*3.00*	*3.00*
Sheet of 10 + 10 labels	*30.00*	—

The full sheet sold for $14.95. The generic label exists as shown, with ram on deep bister background. Labels could be personalized. The personalization of labels was available only at UN Headquarters, and not through mail order.

Flags and Coins Type of 2006

Printed by Cartor Security Printing, France. Designed by Rorie Katz, U.S.
No. 1103 — Flag of: a, Kiribati, 10 cent coin. b, Tonga, 2 seniti coin. c, Costa Rica, 10 centimos coin. d, Bhutan, 25 chetrum coin. e, Zimbabwe, 5 dollar coin. f, Angola, 1 kwanza coin. g, Congo Democratic Republic, 1 franc coin. h, Liberia, 25 cent coin.

2015, Feb. 6 **Litho.** ***Perf. 13¼x13***

1103	Sheet of 8 *(38,000)*+	8.00	8.00
a.-h.	A375 49c Any single	1.00	1.00
	First day cover		11.00

A column of rouletting in the middle of the sheet separates it into two parts. See Offices in Geneva No. 594; Vienna No. 558.

Miniature Sheets

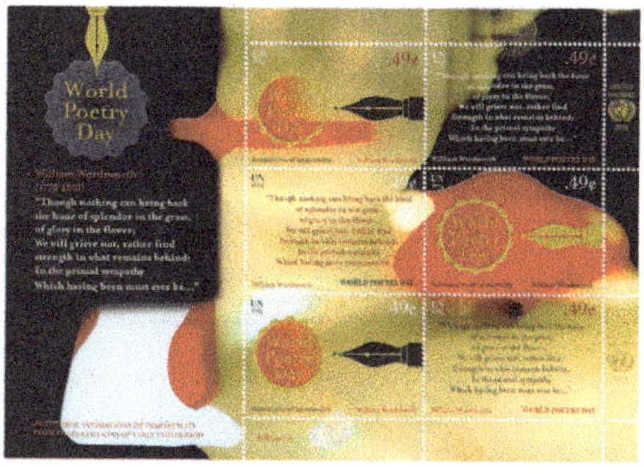

A474

World Poetry Day — A475

Printed by Cartor Security Printing. France. Designed by Sergio Baradat, U.S.

No. 1104: a, Black pen, denomination in red brown. b, William Wordsworth quotation in cream, denomination in red. c, Wordsworth quotation in red brown, denomination in white. d, Gold pen, denomination in white. e, Black pen, denomination in white. f, Wordsworth quotation in black, denomination in red brown.

No. 1105: a, Gold pen, denomination in white, tree top and rose in background. b, José Martí quotation, denomination in lilac, tree tops in background. c, Martí quotation, denomination in white, tree top and rose in background. d, Gold pen, denomination in lilac, tree trunks and tree top in background. e, Gold pen, denomination in lilac, tree trunks and rose in background. f, Martí quotation, denomination in lilac, tree trunks in background.

2015, Mar. 20 **Litho.** ***Perf. 14½x14¼***

1104	A474 Sheet of 6 *(35,000)*+	6.00	6.00
a.-f.	49c Any single	1.00	1.00
1105	A475 Sheet of 6 *(35,000)*+	14.50	14.50
a.-f.	$1.20 Any single	2.40	2.40
	First day cover, #1104-1105		26.00

See Offices in Geneva Nos. 595-596; Vienna Nos. 559-560.

Endangered Species — A476

Printed by Johann Enschedé and Sons, the Netherlands. Designed by John Keulemans and William Hart, United Kingdom.

Designs: No. 1106, King bird-of-paradise. No. 1107, Blue bird-of-paradise. No. 1108, Princess Stephanie's bird-of-paradise. No. 1109, Carola's parotia.

2015, Apr. 16 **Litho.** ***Perf. 12½x12¾***

1106	A476 $1.20 **multicolored** *(92,000)*+	2.40	2.40
1107	A476 $1.20 **multicolored** *(92,000)*+	2.40	2.40
1108	A476 $1.20 **multicolored** *(100,000)*+	2.40	2.40
1109	A476 $1.20 **multicolored** *(100,000)*+	2.40	2.40
a.	Block of 4, #1106-1109	9.75	9.75
	First day cover, #1109a		11.50
	First day cover, #11106-1109, each		3.75
	Inscription block of 4, #1109a	9.75	—
	Pane of 16	39.00	—
	Nos. 1106-1109 (4)	9.60	9.60

See Offices in Geneva Nos. 597-600; Vienna Nos. 561-564.

A477

A478

Printed by Lowe-Martin Group, Canada. Panes of 20. Designed by Sergio Baradat, U.S.

2015, May 7 **Litho.** ***Perf. 13¼x13***

1110	A477 35c **multicolored** *(130,000)*+	.70	.70
	First day cover		1.60
	Inscription block of 4	2.80	—
	Pane of 20	14.00	—

1111 A478 40c **multicolored** *(130,000)+* .80 .80
First day cover 1.90
First day cover, #1110-1111 2.60
Inscription block of 4 3.60 —
Pane of 20 16.00 —

See Offices in Vienna Nos. 565-566.

Miniature Sheet

A479

No. 1112: a, United Nations Headquarters and flags, panel at right. b, Flags, panel at left. c, Stairway and pillars, panel at left. d, Reflection of buildings in windows, panel at right. e, Circular meeting room, panel at right. f, United Nations Headquarters, panel at left. g, Trees and United Nations Building, panel at left. h, Let Us Beat Swords Into Plowshares statue, panel at right. i, General Assembly Building, flags and street, panel at right. j, Arrival sculpture, panel at left.

2015, May 7 **Litho.** ***Perf. 14¾***
1112 A479 Sheet of 10 *30.00 30.00*
a.-j. $1.20 Any single + label *3.00 3.00*

The full sheet sold for $14.95. The generic labels are shown. Labels could be personalized. The personalization of labels was available only at UN Headquarters, and not through mail order.

World Heritage Sites, Southeast Asia — A480

Printed by Johann Enschedé and Sons, the Netherlands. Panes of 20. Designed by Sergio Baradat, U.S.

Designs: Nos. 1113, 1115a, Luang Prabang, Laos. Nos. 1114, 1115d, Borobodur Temple, Indonesia. No. 1115b, Angkor Wat, Cambodia. No. 1115c, Ayutthaya, Thailand. No. 1115e, Cordillera, Philippines. No. 1115f, Hué Monuments, Viet Nam.

2015, June 5 **Litho.** ***Perf. 14x13½***
1113 A480 49c **multicolored** *(130,000)+* 1.00 1.00
First day cover 1.60
Inscription block of 4 4.00 —
Pane of 20 20.00 —
1114 A480 $1.20 **multicolored** *(130,000)+* 2.40 2.40
First day cover 4.00
First day cover, #1113-1114 4.75
Inscription block of 4 9.60 —
Pane of 20 48.00 —

Souvenir Booklet

1115 Booklet, #1115g-1115l *(13,000)+* 20.50
a.-c. A480 35c any single .70 .70
d.-f. A480 49c any single 1.00 1.00
g. Booklet pane of 4 #1115a 2.80 —
h. Booklet pane of 4 #1115b 2.80 —
i. Booklet pane of 4 #1115c 2.80 —
j. Booklet pane of 4 #1115d 4.00 —
k. Booklet pane of 4 #1115e 4.00 —
l. Booklet pane of 4 #1115f 4.00 —

See Offices in Geneva Nos. 601-603, Vienna Nos. 567-569.

End Violence Against Children A481

Printed by Cartor Security Printing, France. Panes of 20. Designed by Chris Sharp, U.S.

Designs: 49c, Armed violence reduction. $1.20, Sexual violence against children.

2015, Aug. 20 **Litho.** ***Perf. 14½x14¼***
1116 A481 49c **multicolored** *(120,000)+* 1.00 1.00
First day cover 1.60
Inscription block of 4 4.00 —
Pane of 20 20.00 —
1117 A481 $1.20 **multicolored** *(120,000)+* 2.40 2.40
First day cover 4.00
First day cover, #1116-1117 4.75
Inscription block of 4 9.60 —
Pane of 20 48.00 —

See Offices in Geneva Nos. 604-605; Vienna Nos. 570-571.

United Nations, 70th Anniv. — A482

Designed by Sergio Baradat, U.S.

2015, Sept. 25 **Litho.** ***Perf. 14¾***
1118 A482 $1.20 **multicolored** + label *3.00 3.00*
Sheet of 10 + 10 labels *30.00* —

The full sheet sold for $14.95. The generic label exists as shown, depicting Pope Francis. Labels could be personalized. The personalization of labels was available only at UN Headquarters, and not through mail order. On. Sept. 27, No. 1118 was issued in a sheet of 10 + 10 labels depicting Chinese characters.

See Vienna No. 577.

General Assembly Hall — A483

Visitors Lobby — A484

Security Council A485

Woodrow Wilson Reading Room of Dag Hammarskjöld Library A486

General Assembly Hall — A487

Printed by Cartor Security Printing, France. Panes of 6. Designed by Rorie Katz, U.S.

2015, Oct. 25 **Litho.** ***Perf. 13¾***

1119	A483 49c **multicolored** *(105,000)+*		1.00	1.00
1120	A484 49c **multicolored** *(105,000)+*		1.00	1.00
	a.	Pair, #1119-1120	2.00	2.00
		First day cover, #1119-1120		2.75
		Inscription block of 4	4.00	—
		Pane of 6	6.00	—
1121	A485 $1.20 **multicolored** *(105,000)+*		2.40	2.40
1122	A486 $1.20 **multicolored** *(105,000)+*		2.40	2.40
	a.	Pair, #1121-1122	4.80	4.80
		First day cover, #1119-1120		6.75
		Inscription block of 4	9.60	—
		Pane of 6	14.50	—
		Nos. 1119-1122 (4)	6.80	6.80

Souvenir Sheet

Perf. 13½

1123	A487 $1.20 **multicolored** *(35,000)+*		4.00	4.00
		First day cover		3.75

United Nations, 70th anniv. See Offices in Geneva Nos. 607-611; Vienna Nos. 572-576.

United Nations Educational, Scientific and Cultural Organization (UNESCO), 70th Anniv. — A488

2015, Nov. 5 **Litho.** ***Perf. 14¾***

1124	A488 $1.20 **multicolored** + label	*3.50*	*3.50*
	Sheet of 10 + 10 labels	*35.00*	—

The full sheet sold for $14.95. Ten different generic labels, one of which is shown, are on the sheet. Labels could be personalized. The personalization of labels was available only at UN Headquarters, and not through mail order.

21st United Nations Climate Change Conference, Paris — A489

Printed by La Poste, France. Panes of 30. Designed by Rorie Katz, U.S.

2015, Nov. 24 **Litho.** ***Perf. 13¼***

1125 A489 $1.20 **multicolored** *(120,000)+* 2.40 2.40
First day cover 3.75
Inscription block of 4 9.60 —
Pane of 30 72.00 —

Values are for stamps with surrounding selvage. See Offices in Geneva No. 612; Vienna No. 578.

UN Emblem — A490

2016, Jan. 8 **Litho.** ***Perf. 14¾***

1126 A490 $1.20 **multicolored** + label *3.00 3.00*
Sheet of 10 + 10 labels *30.00* —

The full sheet sold for $14.95. The generic label, with monkey on red background, is shown. A sheet of 10 No. 1126 + 10 labels depicting M. S. Subbulaskshmi was issued on Oct. 2, 2016. Labels could be personalized. The personalization of labels was available only at UN Headquarters, and not through mail order. See Nos. 1231, 1263.

Free and Equal — A491

Printed by Cartor Security Printing, France. Panes of 20. Designed by Sergio Baradat, U.S.

Designs: 49c, Group of stylized people. $1.20, Woman with butterfly wings.

2016, Feb. 5 **Litho.** ***Perf. 13½x13¼***

1127 A491 49c **multicolored** *(120,000)+* 1.00 1.00
First day cover 1.60
Inscription block of 4 4.00 —
Pane of 20 20.00 —

1128 A491 $1.20 **multicolored** *(120,000)+* 2.40 2.40
First day cover 4.00
First day cover, #1127-1128 4.75
Inscription block of 4 9.60 —
Pane of 20 48.00 —

See Offices in Geneva Nos. 613-614; Vienna Nos. 579-580.

HeForShe Movement — A492

Printed by Lowe-Martin Group, Canada. Panes of 20. Designed by Mirko Ilic, U.S.

Designs: 49c, Man, green background. $1.20, Woman, yellow background.

2016, Mar. 8 **Litho.** ***Perf. 12½x13***

1129 A492 49c **multicolored** *(120,000)+* 1.00 1.00
First day cover 1.60
Inscription block of 4 4.00 —
Pane of 20 20.00 —

1130 A492 $1.20 **multicolored** *(120,000)+* 2.40 2.40
First day cover 4.00
First day cover, #1129-1130 4.75
Inscription block of 4 9.60 —
Pane of 20 48.00 —

See Offices in Geneva Nos. 615-616; Vienna Nos. 581-582.

Miniature Sheet

Angry Birds — A493

No. 1131: a, Red, the Pigs, double-decker bus. b, Red with wing extended. c, Red and five Hatchlings. d, Red, New York City skyscrapers. e, Red, Eiffel Tower, recycling container. f, Red in jungle. g, Earth, Hatchlings, Chuck, Red, Bomb, Stella and Matilda. h, Red turning faucet, Pigs in tub. i, Red drinking from squirt bottle, Lower Manhattan skyline. j, Red with shovel, Pyramids.

2016, Apr. 22 **Litho.** ***Perf. 14¾***

1131 A493 Sheet of 10 *30.00 30.00*
a.-j. $1.15 Any single + label *3.00 3.00*

The full sheet sold for $14.95. The generic labels are shown. Labels could be personalized. The personalization of labels was available only at UN Headquarters, and not through mail order.

Miniature Sheets

A494

International Dance Day — A495

Printed by Cartor Security Printing, France. Designed by Sergio Baradat, U.S.

No. 1132 — Illustration of Chinese dancers by Marcos Chin: a, Woman with arm extended upward. b, Two women, denomination in magenta. c, Woman facing left with arm extended outward. d, Two women, denomination in white. e, Woman with closed eyes. f, Woman with closed eyes with two pale yellow lines touching flower.

No. 1133 — Illustration of Thai dancers by Chin: a, Back of dancer's head, hand of another dancer. b, Dancer wearing mask, leg and arm of other dancers. c, Dancer with costume with blue shoulders, dancer with arm extended. d, Dancer with arm extended, leg and arm of other dancers. e, Two dancers with green and yellow costumes. f, Dancer with hand and arm from other dancers.

2016, Apr. 29 **Litho.** ***Perf. 13¼x13***

1132	A494	Sheet of 6 *(32,500)+*	5.75	5.75
a.-f.		47c Any single	.95	.95
1133	A495	Sheet of 6 *(32,500)+*	14.50	14.50
a.-f.		$1.15 Any single	2.40	2.40
		First day cover, #1132-1133		26.00

g.		As #1133, with "Thailand 2018 / World Stamp Exhibition / 28 Nov. - 3 Dec." overprinted in sheet margin	*65.00*	*65.00*

Issued: No. 1133g, 11/28/18. See Offices in Geneva Nos. 617-618; Vienna Nos. 583-584.

International Day of United Nations Peacekeepers — A496

Printed by Lowe-Martin Group, Canada. Panes of 20. Designed by Sergio Baradat, U.S.

Designs: 47c, Peacekeeper saluting. $1.15, Man disabling landmine.

Litho. With Foil Application

2016, May 29 ***Perf. 13¼x13***

1134	A496	47c **multicolored** *(150,000)+*	.95	.95
		First day cover		1.60
		Inscription block of 4	3.80	—
		Pane of 20	19.00	—
1135	A496	$1.15 **multicolored** *(150,000)+*	2.40	2.40
		First day cover		4.00
		First day cover, #1134-1135		4.50
		Inscription block of 4	9.60	—
		Pane of 20	48.00	—

See Offices in Geneva Nos. 619-620; Vienna Nos. 586-587.

Miniature Sheet

United Nations Postal Administration, 65th Anniv. — A497

No. 1136 — Old United Nations stamps: a, New York #1. b, New York #127. c, Vienna #86. d, New York #415. e, New York #301. f, New York #548. g, New York #474. h, Vienna #100. i, New York #476. j, Vienna #122.

2016, May 30 **Litho.** ***Perf. 14¾***

1136	A497	Sheet of 10	*30.00*	*30.00*
a.-j.		$1.15 Any single + label	*3.00*	*3.00*

The full sheet sold for $14.95. The generic labels are shown. Labels could be personalized. The personalization of labels was available only at UN Headquarters, and not through mail order.

Sport for Peace
A498

Printed by Cartor Security Printing, France. Panes of 6. Designed by Sergio Baradat and Linsey Thoeng, U.S.
Olympic rings and: No. 1137, Shot put, high jump. No. 1138, Runner, javelin. No. 1139, Dove facing left. No. 1140, Dove facing right.

2016, July 22 **Litho.** ***Perf. 14¼***

1137	A498	47c **multicolored** *(84,000)+*	.95	.95
1138	A498	47c **multicolored** *(84,000)+*	.95	.95
a.		Pair, #1137-1138	1.90	1.90
		First day cover, #1137-1138		2.60
		Inscription block of 4	3.80	—
		Pane of 6	5.75	—
1139	A498	$1.15 **multicolored** *(84,000)+*	2.40	2.40
1140	A498	$1.15 **multicolored** *(84,000)+*	2.40	2.40
a.		Pair, #1139-1140	4.80	4.80
		First day cover, #1139-1140		6.50
		Inscription block of 4	9.60	—
		Pane of 6	14.50	—
		Nos. 1137-1140 (4)	6.70	6.70

See Offices in Geneva Nos. 621-624; Vienna Nos. 588-591.

Souvenir Sheet

United Nations Economic and Social Commission for Asia and the Pacific Building, Bangkok — A499

Printed by Beijing Postage Stamp Printing House, People's Republic of China.
No. 1141: a, Left third of building, b, Center third of building, c, Right third of building.

2016, Aug. 10 **Litho.** ***Perf. 13¼x13***

1141	A499	Sheet of 3	24.00	24.00
a.		$1.15 multi	5.00	5.00
b.		2fr multi	9.50	9.50
c.		€1.70 multi	8.50	8.50

32nd Asian International Stamp Exhibition. No. 1141 sold for $6.

World Heritage Sites, Czech Republic
A500

Printed by Cartor Security Printing, France. Panes of 20. Designed by Sergio Baradat, U.S.
Designs: Nos. 1142, 1144a, Historic Center of Prague. Nos. 1143, 1144d, Holy Trinity Column, Olomouc. No. 1144b, Gardens and Castle at Kromeríz. No. 1144c, Historic Town Center of Kutná Hora. No. 1144e, Lednice-Valtice Cultural Landscape. No. 1144f, Historic Center of Cesky Krumlov.

2016, Sept. 8 **Litho.** ***Perf. 14¼***

1142	A500	47c **multicolored** *(110,000)+*	.95	.95
		First day cover		1.60
		Inscription block of 4	3.80	—
		Pane of 20	19.00	—
1143	A500	$1.15 **multicolored** *(110,000)+*	2.40	2.40
		First day cover		4.00
		First day cover, #1142-1143		4.50
		Inscription block of 4	9.60	—
		Pane of 20	48.00	—

Souvenir Booklet

1144	Booklet, #1144g-1144l	20.00	
a.-c.	A500 34c any single	.70	.70
d.-f.	A500 47c any single	.95	.95
g.	Booklet pane of 4 #1144a	2.80	—
h.	Booklet pane of 4 #1144b	2.80	—
i.	Booklet pane of 4 #1144c	2.80	—
j.	Booklet pane of 4 #1144d	3.80	—
k.	Booklet pane of 4 #1144e	3.80	—
l.	Booklet pane of 4 #1144f	3.80	—

See Offices in Geneva Nos. 625-627; Vienna Nos. 592-594, Czech Republic Nos. 3683-3684.

Miniature Sheet

World Wildlife Conference, Johannesburg — A501

Printed by Cartor Security Printing, France. Designed by Sergio Baradat, U.S.
No. 1145 — Part of map of Africa and: a, Addax. b, White rhinoceros. c, African lion. d, Disa uniflora.

2016, Sept. 24 **Litho.** ***Perf. 13x13½***

1145	A501	Sheet of 4 *(30,000)+*	9.75	9.75
a.-d.		$1.15 Any single	2.40	2.40
		First day cover		11.00

See Offices in Geneva No. 628; Vienna No. 596.

Miniature Sheet

World Post Day — A502

No. 1146 — Mail box from: a, Japan. b, Spain. c, Germany. d, Brazil. e, China. f, Denmark. g, India. h, Austria. i, England. j, United States.

2016, Oct. 6 **Litho.** ***Perf. 14¾***

1146	A502	Sheet of 10	*30.00*	*30.00*
a.-j.		$1.15 Any single + label	*3.00*	*3.00*

The full sheet sold for $14.95. The generic labels are shown. Labels could be personalized. The personalization of labels was available only at UN Headquarters, and not through mail order.

Sustainable Development Goals — A503

Printed by Lowe-Martin, Canada. Designed by Lindsey Thoeng, U.S.

No. 1147 — Inscription: a, 1 No poverty. b, 2 Zero hunger. c, 3 Good health and well-being. d, 4 Quality education. e, 5 Gender equality. f, 6 Clean water and sanitation. g, 7 Affordable and clean energy. h, 8 Decent work and economic growth. i, 9 Industry, innovation and infrastructure. j, 10 Reduced inequalities. k, 11 Sustainable cities and communities. l, 12 Responsible consumption and production. m, 13 Climate action. n, 14 Life below water. o, 15 Life on land. p, 16 Peace, justice and strong institutions. q, 17 Partnerships for the goals.

2016, Oct. 24 **Litho.** ***Perf. 13¼***

1147	A503	Sheet of 17 + label *(28,000)*+	17.00	17.00
a.-q.		47c Any single	1.00	1.00
		First day cover		21.00

See Offices in Geneva No. 629; Vienna No. 597.

Souvenir Sheet

Monkey King From Chinese Novel *Journey to the West* — A504

No. 1148 — Various depictions of Monkey King with inscriptions in: a, English. b, French. c, German.

2016, Dec. 2 **Litho. With Foil Application** ***Perf. 12***

1148	A504	Sheet of 3	20.00	20.00
a.		$1.15 multi	4.00	4.00
b.		2fr multi	7.00	7.00
c.		€1.70 multi	6.75	6.75

33rd Asian International Stamp Exhibition, Nanning, People's Republic of China. No. 1148 sold for $6.

United Nations Emblem Type of 2014 Dated "2017" in Purple

2017, Jan. 13 **Litho.** ***Perf. 14¾***

1149	A457	$1.15 **multicolored** + label	*3.00*	*3.00*
		Sheet of 10 + 10 labels	*30.00*	—

The full sheet sold for $14.95. The generic label exists as shown, with rooster on red background. Labels could be personalized. The personalization of labels was available only at UN Headquarters, and not through mail order.

Flag Type of 1980

Printed by Lowe Martin Company, Inc., Canada. Designed by Sergio Baradat, U.S. Issued in panes of 16; each pane contains 4 blocks of 4. A se-tenant block of 4 designs centers each pane.

2017, Feb. 3 **Litho.** ***Perf. 13x13¼***

1150	A185	$1.15 Albania *(88,000)*+	2.40	2.40
1151	A185	$1.15 Benin *(88,000)*+	2.40	2.40
1152	A185	$1.15 Bulgaria *(88,000)*+	2.40	2.40
1153	A185	$1.15 Comoros *(88,000)*+	2.40	2.40
a.		Block of 4, #1150-1153	12.00	12.00
1154	A185	$1.15 Congo Republic *(88,000)*+	2.40	2.40
1155	A185	$1.15 Ethiopia *(88,000)*+	2.40	2.40
1156	A185	$1.15 Georgia *(88,000)*+	2.40	2.40
1157	A185	$1.15 Iraq *(88,000)*+	2.40	2.40
a.		Block of 4, #1154-1157	12.00	12.00
		First day cover, #1150-1157, each		4.00
		Set of 2 different panes of 16	96.00	
		Nos. 1150-1157 (8)	19.20	19.20

Miniature Sheet

A505

No. 1158: a, Three Smurfs. b, Smurf holding glass of water. c, Smurf holding fruit. d, Smurf with backpack with solar panels. e, Smurf lifting dumbbell. f, Smurf carrying mallet. g, Smurf holding book. h, Two Smurfs with ladder. i, Male and female Smurfs. j, Butterfly.

2017, Mar. 20	**Litho.**	***Perf. 14¾***	
1158 A505	Sheet of 10	*30.00*	*30.00*
a.-j.	$1.15 Any single + label	*3.00*	*3.00*

The full sheet sold for $14.95. The generic labels are shown. Labels could be personalized. The personalization of labels was available only at UN Headquarters, and not through mail order.

Miniature Sheets

A506

International Dance — A507

Printed by Cartor Security Printing, France. Designed by Sergio Baradat, U.S.

No. 1159 — Illustration of Polynesian dancers by Pascal Campion: a, Woman with arms raised, denomination at LR. b, Woman with arms raised, denomination at UL. c, Two women wearing head coverings, red necklace, denomination at UR. d, One woman wearing head covering and red necklace, denomination at UR. e, Woman with feathered headdress, green necklace, hair of another woman at right, denomination at UR. f, Woman wearing feathered headdress and green necklace, denomination at UR.

No. 1160 — Illustration of Native American tribal dancers by Campion: a, Dancer facing right, denomination in blue at UL. b, Dancer, denomination in orange at UL. c, Back of dancer, denomination in gray lilac at UR. d, Dancer looking downward, denomination in gray lilac at UL. e, Dancer with headband over eyebrows, denomination in orange red at UR, "International Dance" in white. f, Dancer, denomination in orange red at UR, "International Dance" in light blue.

2017, Mar. 23	**Litho.**	***Perf. 13¼x13***	
1159 A506	Sheet of 6 *(22,000)+*	6.00	6.00
a.-f.	49c Any single	1.00	1.00
1160 A507	Sheet of 6 *(22,000)+*	14.50	14.50
a.-f.	$1.15 Any single	2.40	2.40
	First day cover, #1159-1160		27.00

See Offices in Geneva Nos. 630-631; Vienna Nos. 599-600.

Souvenir Sheet

Australian Animals — A508

No. 1161: a, Koalas. b, Kangaroos. c, Emu.

Litho. With Foil Application

2017, Mar. 30		***Perf. 13¼x13***	
1161 A508	Sheet of 3	12.00	12.00
a.	$1.15 multi	4.00	4.00
b.	2fr multi	4.00	4.00
c.	€1.70 multi	4.00	4.00

2017 FIAP International Stamp Exhibition, Melbourne, Australia. No. 1161 sold for $6.

Endangered Species — A509

Printed by Johann Enschedé and Sons, the Netherlands. Designed by Rorie Katz, U.S.

Designs: No. 1162, Masobe gecko. No. 1163, Thresher shark. No. 1164, Clarion angelfish. No. 1165, Blaine's fishhook cactus.

2017, May 11	**Litho.**	***Perf. 12¾x12½***	
1162 A509	$1.15 **multicolored** *(64,000)+*	2.40	2.40
1163 A509	$1.15 **multicolored** *(64,000)+*	2.40	2.40
1164 A509	$1.15 **multicolored** *(64,000)+*	2.40	2.40
1165 A509	$1.15 **multicolored** *(64,000)+*	2.40	2.40
a.	Block of 4, #1162-1165	9.75	9.75
	First day cover, #1165a		12.00
	First day cover, #1162-1165, each		4.25
	Inscription block of 4, #1165a	9.75	—
	Pane of 16	39.00	—
	Nos. 1162-1165 (4)	9.60	9.60

See Offices in Geneva Nos. 632-635; Vienna Nos. 601-604.

World Environment Day — A510

Printed by Lowe-Martin Group, Canada. Panes of 20. Designed by Sergio Baradat, U.S.

Designs: 49c, Hopewell Rocks, New Brunswick, Canada. $1.15, Polar bear, Baffin Island, Nunavut, Canada.

2017, June 5 **Litho.** ***Perf. 13¼***

1166 A510 49c **multicolored** *(110,000)+*		1.00	1.00
	First day cover		2.10
	Inscription block of 4	4.00	—
	Pane of 20	20.00	—
1167 A510 $1.15 **multicolored** *(110,000)+*		2.40	2.40
	First day cover		5.00
	First day cover, #1166-1167		5.50
	Inscription block of 4	9.60	—
	Pane of 20	48.00	—

See Offices in Geneva Nos. 636-637; Vienna Nos. 605-606.

Miniature Sheet

International Day of Yoga — A511

No. 1168: a, Orange woman on stomach holding her legs. b, Dark blue man siting with legs raised. c, Blue woman with arms extended. d, Beige man sitting with legs crossed and arms raised. e, Purple man with arms extended leaning backward to touch toes. f, Light blue woman bent backward with feet and hands on ground. g, Blue violet woman bent backward to touch raised leg. h, Red woman on one knee. i, Pale blue woman with arms extended touching raised leg. j, Orange man bent over with hands on ground.

2017, June 21 **Litho.** ***Perf. 14¾***

1168 A511	Sheet of 10	*30.00*	*30.00*
a.-j.	$1.15 Any single + label	*3.00*	*3.00*

The full sheet sold for $14.95. The generic labels are shown. Labels could be personalized. The personalization of labels was available only at UN Headquarters, and not through mail order.

World Heritage Sites Along the Silk Roads A512

Printed by Cartor Security Printing, France. Panes of 20. Designed by Sergio Baradat, U.S.

Designs: Nos. 1169, 1171a, Longmen Grottoes, People's Republic of China. Nos. 1170, 1171d, Sulaiman-Too Sacred Mountain, Kyrgyzstan. No. 1171b, Historic Center of Bukhara, Uzbekistan. No. 1171c, Tabriz Historic Bazaar Complex, Iran. No. 1171e, Kunya-Urgench, Turkmenistan. No. 1171f, Safranbolu, Turkey.

2017, Aug. 3 **Litho.** ***Perf. 14¼***

1169 A512 49c **multicolored** *(110,000)+*		1.00	1.00
	First day cover		2.10
	Inscription block of 4	4.00	—
	Pane of 20	20.00	—
1170 A512 $1.15 **multicolored** *(110,000)+*		2.40	2.40
	First day cover		5.00
	First day cover, #1169-1170		5.50
	Inscription block of 4	9.60	—
	Pane of 20	48.00	—

Souvenir Booklet

1171	Booklet, #1171g-1171l *(8,500)+*	22.50	
a.-c.	A512 34c any single	.75	.75
d.-f.	A512 49c any single	1.10	1.10
g.	Booklet pane of 4 #1171a	3.00	—
h.	Booklet pane of 4 #1171b	3.00	—
i.	Booklet pane of 4 #1171c	3.00	—
j.	Booklet pane of 4 #1171d	4.50	—
k.	Booklet pane of 4 #1171e	4.50	—
l.	Booklet pane of 4 #1171f	4.50	—

Complete booklet sold for $11. See Offices in Geneva Nos. 638-640; Vienna Nos. 607-609.

Doves A513

Moths A514

Doves — A515

Printed by Johann Enschedé and Sons, the Netherlands. Panes of 20. Designed by Stranger and Stranger, U.S.

2017, Sept. 21 **Litho.** ***Perf. 14x14¼***

1172 A513 49c **multicolored** *(110,000)+*		1.00	1.00
First day cover			1.90
Inscription block of 4		4.00	—
Pane of 20		20.00	—
1173 A514 $1.15 **multicolored** *(110,000)+*		2.40	2.40
First day cover			4.50
First day cover, #1172-1173			5.00
Inscription block of 4		9.60	—
Pane of 20		48.00	—

Souvenir Sheet

Perf. 14¼x13¾

1174 A515 $1.15 **multicolored** *(27,000)+*	2.40	2.40
First day cover		4.00

International Day of Peace. See Offices in Geneva Nos. 641-643; Vienna Nos. 611-613.

World Food Day — A516

Printed by Royal Johann Enschedé. Panes of 20. Designed by Helen Dardik, Canada.

Designs: 49c, Vegetables. $1.15, Bowls of food, jar of oil.

2017, Oct. 16 **Litho.** ***Perf. 13¼x14***

1175 A516 49c **multicolored** *(110,000)+*	1.00	1.00
First day cover		2.10
Inscription block of 4	4.00	—
Pane of 20	20.00	—
1176 A516 $1.15 **multicolored** *(110,000)+*	2.40	2.40
First day cover		5.00
First day cover, #1175-1176		5.50
Inscription block of 4	9.60	—
Pane of 20	48.00	—

See Offices in Geneva Nos. 644-645; Vienna Nos. 614-615.

Souvenir Sheet

Universal Declaration of Human Rights — A517

Printed by Johann Enschedé Stamps Security Printers, B.V., the Netherlands. Designed by Rorie Katz, U.S. No. 1177 — Text of Universal Declaration of Human Rights in: a, English. b, French. c, German.

Litho. With Foil Application

2017, Oct. 27 ***Perf. 14x13¼***

1177 A517 Sheet of 3 *(30,000)+*	12.00	12.00
a. $1.15 multi	4.00	4.00
b. 2fr multi	4.00	4.00
c. €1.70 multi	4.00	4.00

United Nations Expo 2017, Bellefonte, Pennsylvania. No. 1177 sold for $6.

Souvenir Sheet

Landmarks in Paris — A518

Printed by Johann Enschedé Stamps Security Printers, B.V., the Netherlands. Designed by Sergio Baradat, U.S. No. 1178: a, Fame of Louis XVI, statue by Antoine Coysevox. b, Fontaines de la Concorde. c, Gargolye on Notre Dame Cathedral.

2017, Nov. 9 **Litho.** ***Perf. 13¼x14***

1178 A518 Sheet of 3 *(20,000)+*	12.00	12.00
a. $1.15 multi	4.00	4.00
b. 2fr multi	4.00	4.00
c. €1.70 multi	4.00	4.00

Autumn Philatelic Show, Paris. No. 1178 sold for $6.

Flag Type of 1980

Printed by Lowe Martin Group, Canada. Designed by Rorie Katz, U.S. Issued in panes of 16; each pane contains 4 blocks of 4. A se-tenant block of 4 designs centers each pane.

2018, Jan. 12 **Litho.** ***Perf. 13x13¼***

1179 A185 $1.15 Lesotho *(88,000)+*	2.40	2.40
1180 A185 $1.15 Libya *(88,000)+*	2.40	2.40
1181 A185 $1.15 Mozambique *(88,000)+*	2.40	2.40
1182 A185 $1.15 Romania *(88,000)+*	2.40	2.40
a. Block of 4, #1179-1182	12.00	12.00
1183 A185 $1.15 Rwanda *(88,000)+*	2.40	2.40
1184 A185 $1.15 Seychelles *(88,000)+*	2.40	2.40
1185 A185 $1.15 South Africa *(88,000)+*	2.40	2.40
1186 A185 $1.15 Ukraine *(88,000)+*	2.40	2.40
a. Block of 4, #1183-1186	12.00	12.00
First day cover, #1179-1186, each		4.25
Set of 2 different panes of 16	78.00	
Nos. 1179-1186 (8)	19.20	19.20

United Nations Emblem Type of 2014 Dated "2018" in Purple

2018, Feb. 2 **Litho.** ***Perf. 14¾***

1187 A457 $1.15 **multicolored** + label	*3.00*	*3.00*
Sheet of 10 + 10 labels	*30.00*	—

The full sheet sold for $14.95. The generic label depicts a dog. Labels could be personalized. The personalization of labels was available only at UN Headquarters, and not through mail order.

Endangered Species — A519

Printed by Johann Enschedé Stamps Security Printers, the Netherlands. Designed by Rorie Katz, U.S.

Designs: No. 1188, Red-crested turaco. No. 1189, Andean hairy armadillo. No. 1190, Lurestan newt. No. 1191, Goldenseal.

2018, Mar. 2 **Litho.** ***Perf. 12¾x12½***

1188 A519 $1.15 **multicolored** *(64,000)+*	2.40	2.40
1189 A519 $1.15 **multicolored** *(64,000)+*	2.40	2.40
1190 A519 $1.15 **multicolored** *(64,000)+*	2.40	2.40
1191 A519 $1.15 **multicolored** *(64,000)+*	2.40	2.40
a. Block of 4, #1188-1191	9.75	9.75
First day cover, #1191a		12.00
First day cover, #1188-1191, each		4.25
Inscription block of 4, #1191a	9.75	—
Pane of 16	39.00	—
Nos. 1188-1191 (4)	9.60	9.60

See Offices in Geneva Nos. 646-649; Vienna Nos. 616-619.

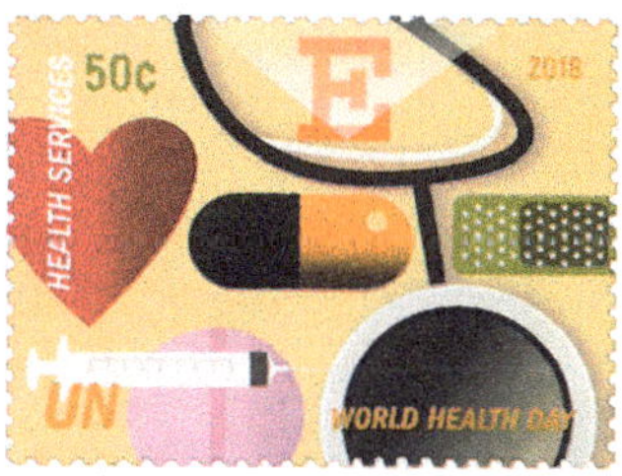

World Health Day — A520

Printed by Lowe-Martin Group, Canada. Panes of 20. Designed by Sergio Baradat, U.S.

Designs: 50c, Heart, pill, bandage, letter from eye chart, syringe and stethoscope. $1.15, Head with gears, heart, clock, stylized people, circle with arrows.

2018, Apr. 6 **Litho.** ***Perf. 13x13¼***

1192 A520 50c **multicolored** *(110,000)+*	1.00	1.00
First day cover		2.10
Inscription block of 4	4.00	—
Pane of 20	20.00	—
1193 A520 $1.15 **multicolored** *(110,000)+*	2.40	2.40
First day cover		5.00
First day cover, #1192-1193		5.50
Inscription block of 4	9.60	—
Pane of 20	48.00	—

See Offices in Geneva Nos. 650-651; Vienna Nos. 620-621.

Universal Declaration of Human Rights, 70th Anniv. — A521

Printed by Lowe-Martin Group, Canada. Panes of 20. Designed by Rorie Katz, U.S.

2018, May 3 **Litho.** ***Perf. 13¼***

1194 A521 $2.50 **multicolored** *(100,000)+*	5.00	5.00
First day cover		7.25
Inscription block of 4	20.00	—
Pane of 20	100.00	—

United Nations Headquarters — A522

Printed by Lowe-Martin Group, Canada. Panes of 20. Designed by Rorie Katz, U.S.

2018, May 29 **Litho.** ***Perf. 13¼***

1195 A522 65c **multicolored** *(270,000)+*	1.40	1.40
First day cover		2.75
Inscription block of 4	5.75	—
Pane of 20	28.00	—

UNISPACE + 50 Conferences — A523

Printed by Johann Enschedé Stamps BV, Netherlands. Panes of 20. Designed by Sergio Baradat, U.S. Designs: 50c, Milky Way Galaxy. No. 1197, International Space Station and Space Shuttle Endeavour.

No. 1198, Astronaut Scott Kelly during spacewalk.

2018, June 20 **Litho.** ***Perf. 14x14¼***

1196	A523 50c **multicolored** *(90,000)*+	1.00	1.00
	First day cover		2.10
	Inscription block of 4	4.00	—
	Pane of 20	20.00	—
1197	A523 $1.15 **multicolored** *(90,000)*+	2.40	2.40
	First day cover		5.00
	First day cover, #1196-1197		5.50
	Inscription block of 4	9.60	—
	Pane of 20	48.00	—

Souvenir Sheet

Perf. 13¾

1198	A523 $1.15 **multicolored** *(24,000)*+	3.00	3.00
	First day cover		4.25

No. 1198 contains one 45x45mm stamp. See Offices in Geneva Nos. 653-655; Vienna Nos. 623-625.

World Heritage Sites in the United Kingdom A524

Printed by Cartor Security Printing, France. Panes of 20. Designed by Rorie Katz, U.S.

Designs: Nos. 1199, 1201a, Giant's Causeway. Nos. 1200, 1201d, Palace of Westminster. No. 1201b, Stonehenge. No. 1201c, Conwy Castle. No. 1201e, Edinburgh. No. 1201f, Maritime Greenwich.

2018, Aug. 15 **Litho.** ***Perf. 14¼***

1199	A524 50c **multicolored** *(104,000)*+	1.00	1.00
	First day cover		2.10
	Inscription block of 4	4.00	—
	Pane of 20	20.00	—
1200	A524 $1.15 **multicolored** *(104,000)*+	2.40	2.40
	First day cover		5.00
	First day cover, #1199-1200		5.50
	Inscription block of 4	9.60	—
	Pane of 20	48.00	—

Souvenir Booklet

1201	Booklet, #1201g-1201l *(7,500)*+	22.50	
a.-c.	A524 35c any single	.75	.75
d.-f.	A524 50c any single	1.10	1.10
g.	Booklet pane of 4 #1201a	3.00	—
h.	Booklet pane of 4 #1201b	3.00	—
i.	Booklet pane of 4 #1201c	3.00	—
j.	Booklet pane of 4 #1201d	4.50	—
k.	Booklet pane of 4 #1201e	4.50	—
l.	Booklet pane of 4 #1201f	4.50	—

Complete booklet sold for $11. See Offices in Geneva Nos. 657-659; Vienna Nos. 626-628.

Miniature Sheet

Thomas the Tank Engine — A525

No. 1202: a, Thomas and four people. b, Reg lifting bicycle. c, Thomas, conductor holding potted plant. d, Ashima and Thomas. e, Thomas and Nia. f, Passenger car, children and tuba. g, Thomas and giraffe. h, Monkeys on Thomas. i, Water splashing on grimy Thomas. j, Nia, Thomas and ring of colors.

2018, Sept. 12 **Litho.** ***Perf. 14¾***

1202	A525 Sheet of 10	*30.00*	*30.00*
a.-j.	$1.15 Any single + label	*3.00*	*3.00*

The full sheet sold for $14.95. The generic labels are shown. Labels could be personalized. The personalization of labels was available only at UN Headquarters, and not through mail order.

Souvenir Sheet

Characters From Cantonese Opera *Hua Mulan* — A526

Printed by Cartor Security Printing, France. Designed by Ye Luying, China. No. 1203: a, Baozhen. b, Guanyu. c, Mulan.

2018, Sept. 21 **Litho.** ***Perf. 13¼x13***

1203	A526 Sheet of 3 *(18,000)*+	13.00	13.00
a.	$1.15 multi	4.25	4.25
b.	2fr multi	4.25	4.25
c.	€1.80 multi	4.25	4.25

Macao 2018 Asian International Stamp Exhibition. The vignettes are laser cut. No. 1203 sold for $6.30.

Miniature Sheet

International Music Day — A527

Printed by Johann Enschedé Stamps BV, the Netherlands. Designed by Sergio Baradat, U.S.

No. 1204: a, Trombone. b, Flute and clarinet. c, Cornet. d, Tuba, bell at right. e, Tuba, bell at left, red in background. f, French horn, red in background. g, Trumpet, bell at UR. h, Baritone horn. i, Saxophone. j, French horn, blue in background. k, Trumpet, bell at LR. l, Tuba, bell at left, blue in background.

2018, Oct. 1 **Litho.** ***Perf. 14x13¼***

1204 A527 Sheet of 12 *(18,000)*+ 12.00 12.00

First day cover 16.00

a.-l. 50c Any single 1.00 1.00

See Offices in Geneva No. 660; Vienna No. 629.

Non-Violence, Sculpture by Carl Fredrik Reuterswärd — A528

Printed by Johann Enschedé Stamps BV, the Netherlands. Panes of 50. Designed by Martin Mörck, Norway.

2018, Oct. 2 **Litho.** ***Perf. 13¼x14***

1205 A528 1c **multicolored** *(600,000)*+ .25 .25

First day cover 3.00

Inscription block of 4 .25 —

See Offices in Vienna Nos. 630-631.

Diwali Candles — A529

Diwali Candles — A530

2018, Oct. 19 **Litho.** ***Perf. 14¾***

1206 A529 $1.15 **multicolored** + label *3.00 3.00*

1207 A530 $1.15 **multicolored** + label *3.00 3.00*

a. Vert. pair, #1206-1207, + 2 labels *6.00 6.00*

Sheet of 10, 5 each #1206-1207, + 10 labels *30.00 30.00*

The full sheet sold for $14.95. The generic labels are shown. Labels could be personalized. The personalization of labels was available only at UN Headquarters, and not through mail order.

Souvenir Sheet

Arena di Verona — A531

Printed by La Poste, France. Designed by Chris Thornock, U.S.

No. 1208: a, Left side of Arena. b, Central portion of Arena with four upper-tier arches. c, Right side of Arena.

2018, Nov. 23 **Litho.** ***Perf. 13¼x13***

1208 A531 Sheet of 3 *(18,000)*+ 13.00 13.00

a. $1.15 multi 4.25 4.25

b. 2fr multi 4.25 4.25

c. €1.80 multi 4.25 4.25

Veronafil 2018 Stamp Exhibition, Verona, Italy. No. 1208 sold for $6.30.

United Nations Emblem Type of 2014 Dated "2019" in Purple

2019, Jan. 11 **Litho.** ***Perf. 14¾***

1209 A457 $1.15 **multicolored** + label *3.00 3.00*

Sheet of 10 + 10 labels *30.00* —

The full sheet sold for $14.95. The generic label depicts a pig. Labels could be personalized. The personalization of labels was available only at UN Headquarters, and not through mail order.

Miniature Sheet

World Languages — A532

Printed by Cartor Security Printing, France. Designed by Sergio Baradat, U.S.

No. 1210 — Word bubbles with word for "Hello" in: a, Chinese and Portuguese (Olá). b, Swahili (Habari) and Persian. c, Italian (Ciao). d, Bengali. e, English. f, Thai and Czech or Slovak (Ahoj).

2019, Feb. 21 **Litho.** ***Perf. 13¼x13***

1210 A532 Sheet of 6 *(22,000)*+ 6.75 6.75

a.-f. 55c Any single 1.10 1.10

First day cover, #1210 11.00

See Offices in Geneva No. 661; Vienna No. 632.

Stop Sexual Exploitation and Abuse — A533

Printed by Lowe-Martin Group, Canada. Panes of 20. Designed by Chris Gash, U.S.

2019, Mar.15 **Litho.** ***Perf. 13¼x13***

1211 A533 85c **multicolored** *(140,000)+* 1.75 1.75
First day cover 3.75
Inscription block of 4 7.00 —
Pane of 20 35.00 —

Endangered Species — A534

Printed by Johann Enschedé Stamps Security Printers, the Netherlands. Designed by Rongliang Wang, People's Republic of China.

Designs: No. 1212, Hawksbill turtle. No. 1213, Queen conch. No. 1214, Mushroom coral. No. 1215, Humpback whale.

2019, Apr. 26 **Litho.** ***Perf. 12¾x12½***

1212 A534 $1.15 **multicolored** *(60,000)+* 2.40 2.40
1213 A534 $1.15 **multicolored** *(60,000)+* 2.40 2.40
1214 A534 $1.15 **multicolored** *(60,000)+* 2.40 2.40
1215 A534 $1.15 **multicolored** *(60,000)+* 2.40 2.40
a. Block of 4, #1212-1215 9.75 9.75
First day cover, #1215a 12.00
First day cover, #1212-1215, each 4.50
Inscription block of 4, #1215a 9.75 —
Pane of 16 39.00 —

See Offices in Geneva Nos. 663-666; Vienna Nos. 634-637.

Souvenir Sheet

Diphaglossine Bee and Corydalis Flavula — A535

Printed by Lowe-Martin Group, Canada. Designed by Rorie Katz, U.S.

2019, May 20 **Litho. With Foil Application** ***Perf. 13***

1216 A535 $3 **multicolored** *(18,000)+* 7.50 7.50
First day cover 9.50

World Bee Day. See Offices in Geneva No. 667; Vienna No. 638.

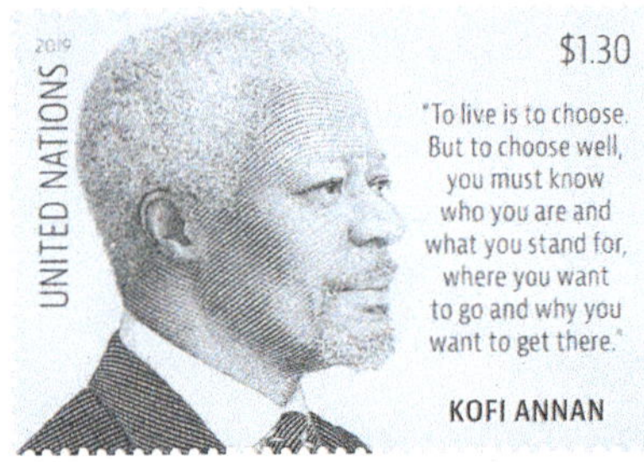

Kofi Annan (1938-2018), Seventh United Nations Secretary-General — A536

Printed by Johann Enschedé Stamps BV, the Netherlands. Panes of 20. Designed by Rorie Katz, U.S.

2019, May 31 **Litho.** ***Perf. 14x14¼***

1217 A536 $1.30 **gray blue & black** *(210,000)+* 2.60 2.60
First day cover 4.75
Inscription block of 4 10.40 —
Sheet of 20 52.00 —

Souvenir Sheet

Pandas — A537

Printed by Cartor Security Printing, France. Designed by Rorie Katz, U.S.

No. 1218: a, Qiqi. b,Qiqi and Diandian. c, Diandian.

2019, June 11 **Litho.** ***Perf. 13½x13***

1218 A537 Sheet of 3 *(23,000)+* 13.00 13.00
a. $1.15 multi 4.25 4.25
b. 2fr multi 4.25 4.25
c. €1.80 multi 4.25 4.25

China 2019 World Stamp Exhibition, Wuhan, People's Republic of China. On July 31, 2019, a sheet containing Nos. 1218a-1218c with a different sheet margin was issued for Singpex 2019 International Stamp Exhibition, with a printing quantity of 21,000 sheets. No. 1218 and the sheet issued in July each sold for $6.30.

A538

A539

A540

A541

International Labor Organization, Cent. — A542

Printed by Johann Enschedé Stamps BV, Netherlands. Sheets of 20. Designed by Owen Smith, U.S.

2019, June 28	**Litho.**	***Perf. 13½x14***	
1219 A538 55c **multicolored** *(80,000)*+		1.10	1.10
1220 A539 55c **multicolored** *(80,000)*+		1.10	1.10
1221 A540 55c **multicolored** *(80,000)*+		1.10	1.10
1222 A541 55c **multicolored** *(80,000)*+		1.10	1.10
1223 A542 55c **multicolored** *(80,000)*+		1.10	1.10
a. Horiz. strip of 5, #1219-1223		5.50	5.50
First day cover, #1223a			8.00
Inscription block of 10		11.00	—
Pane of 20		22.00	—
Nos. 1219-1223 (5)		5.50	5.50

See Offices in Geneva Nos. 668-672, Vienna Nos. 639-643.

Climate Change A543

Printed by Cartor Security Printing, France. Panes of 20. Designed by Sergio Baradat, U.S. Designs: 55c, Mountain. No. 1225, Fish.
No. 1226, Polar bear.

2019, Sept. 23	**Litho.**	***Perf. 14¼***	
1224 A543 55c **multicolored** *(90,000)*+		1.10	1.10
First day cover			2.40
Inscription block of 4		4.40	—
Pane of 20		22.00	—
1225 A543 $1.15 **multicolored** *(90,000)*+		2.40	2.40
First day cover			5.00
First day cover, #1224-1225			5.50
Inscription block of 4		9.60	—
Pane of 20		48.00	—

Souvenir Sheet

Perf.

1226 A543 $1.15 **multicolored** *(11,000)*+		2.40	2.40
First day cover			2.40

2019 United Nations Climate Change Conference, Madrid. No. 1226 contains one 47mm diameter stamp. See Offices in Geneva Nos. 673-675; Vienna Nos. 649-651.

Mohandas K. Gandhi (1869-1948), Indian Nationalist Leader — A544

Printed by Johann Enschedé Stamps BV, the Netherlands. Panes of 20. Designed by Rorie Katz, U.S.

2019, Oct. 2	**Litho.**	***Perf. 14¼***	
1227 A544 $2.75 **pink & black** *(210,000)*+		5.50	5.50
First day cover			8.00
Inscription block of 4		22.00	—
Sheet of 20		110.00	—

World Heritage Sites in Cuba A545

Printed by Cartor Security Printing, France. Panes of 20. Designed by Sergio Baradat, U.S.

Designs: Nos. 1228, 1230a, Morro Castle. Nos. 1229, 1230d, Vinales Valley. No. 1230b, Trinidad. No. 1230c, Camagüey. No. 1230e, Cienfuegos. No. 1230f, San Pedro de la Rosa Castle.

2019, Oct. 24 Litho. With Foil Application ***Perf. 14¼***

1228	A545 55c **multicolored** *(90,000)+*	1.10	1.10
	First day cover		2.40
	Inscription block of 4	4.40	—
	Pane of 20	22.00	—
1229	A545 $1.15 **multicolored** *(90,000)+*	2.40	2.40
	First day cover		5.00
	First day cover, #1228-1229		5.50
	Inscription block of 4	9.60	—
	Pane of 20	48.00	—

Souvenir Booklet

1230	Booklet, #1230g-1230l *(6,500)+*	24.00	
a.-c.	A545 35c Any single	.75	.75
d.-f.	A545 55c Any single	1.25	1.25
g.	Booklet pane of 4 #1230a	3.00	—
h.	Booklet pane of 4 #1230b	3.00	—
i.	Booklet pane of 4 #1230c	3.00	—
j.	Booklet pane of 4 #1230d	5.00	—
k.	Booklet pane of 4 #1230e	5.00	—
l.	Booklet pane of 4 #1230f	5.00	—

Complete booklet sold for $12. See Offices in Geneva Nos. 677-679; Vienna Nos. 652-654.

United Nations Emblem Type of 2016 Dated "2020" in Purple

2020, Jan. 10 Litho. ***Perf. 14¾***

1231	A490 $1.20 **multicolored** + label	*3.00*	*3.00*
	Sheet of 10 + 10 labels	*30.00*	—

The full sheet sold for $14.95. The generic label has a rat on red background. The personalization of labels was available only at UN Headquarters, and not through mail order.

Endangered Species — A546

Printed by Johann Enschedé Stamps Security Printers, the Netherlands. Designed by Rorie Katz, U.S.

Designs: No. 1232, Great hammerhead shark. No. 1233, Egyptian vulture. No. 1234, Andean flamingo. No. 1235, Argali sheep.

2020, Feb. 17 Litho. ***Perf. 12¾x12½***

1232	A546 $1.20 **multicolored** *(56,000)+*	2.40	2.40
1233	A546 $1.20 **multicolored** *(56,000)+*	2.40	2.40
1234	A546 $1.20 **multicolored** *(56,000)+*	2.40	2.40
1235	A546 $1.20 **multicolored** *(56,000)+*	2.40	2.40
a.	Block of 4, #1232-1235	9.75	9.75
	First day cover, #1235a		12.50
	First day cover, #1232-1235, each		4.50
	Inscription block of 4, #1235a	9.75	—
	Pane of 16	39.00	—

See Offices in Geneva Nos. 680-683; Vienna Nos. 655-658.

Blank Stamp On Which Stickers Can Be Applied — A547

Printed by Cartor Security Printing (No. 1236) and La Poste (Nos. 1236a, 1236b), France. Designed by Rorie Katz, U.S.

2020, Mar. 19 Litho. ***Die Cut***

Self-Adhesive

1236	A547 $1.20 **multicolored,** with rounded corners, *(40,000)+*	2.40	2.40
a.	With perpendicular corners and black frame line	2.40	2.40
b.	Booklet pane of 6 #1236a *(5,000)+*	14.50	
	First day cover, #1236		4.50

No. 1236 was issued as a souvenir sheet having two different sheet margins, each with different stickers. No. 1236a was issued in a booklet containing six panes of one stamp, with each pane having different margins and stickers. Each booklet pane contained one sticker depicting Hello Kitty, a color wheel with Hello Kitty at the center, one of six different Sustainable Development Goal emblems, along with a variety of other stickers. The two souvenir sheets had the same sheet margin and stickers found on two of the panes of No. 1236b. No. 1236b was sold folded, without any means of separation between the individual panes.

Miniature Sheet

Act Now Climate Action Campaign — A548

No. 1237: a, Man in shower. b, Hand on light switch. c, Bicyclist. d, Electric plug and socket. e, Knife, fork, vegetables. f, Hand, container and recycling arrow. g, Produce stand. h, Clothing on clothes hanger. i, Man placing bottle in recycling bin. j, Man carrying reusable shopping bag.

2020, Mar. 27 Litho. ***Perf. 14¾***

1237	A548 Sheet of 10 + 10 labels	*30.00*	*30.00*
a.-j.	$1.20 Any single + label	*3.00*	*3.00*

The full sheet sold for $14.95. The generic labels are shown. Labels could be personalized. The personalization of labels was available only at UN Headquarters, and not through mail order.

Linblad Cove, Antarctica, Drawing by Zaria Forman — A549

Our Changing Seas IV, Glazed Stoneware and Porcelain Item by Courtney Mattison — A550

Printed by La Poste, France. Panes of 10. Designed by Rorie Katz, U.S.

2020, Apr. 22 **Litho.** ***Perf. 13¼***

1238	A549	55c	**multicolored** *(120,000)+*	1.10	1.10
			First day cover		2.40
			Inscription block of 4	4.40	—
			Pane of 10	11.00	—
1239	A550	$1.20	**multicolored** *(120,000)+*	2.40	2.40
			First day cover		5.25
			First day cover, #1238-1239		5.75
			Inscription block of 4	9.60	—
			Pane of 10	24.00	—

Earth Day, 50th anniv. Because of the COVID-19 pandemic, Nos. 1238-1239 were not available for sale on day of issue stated on the first-day covers as they had not yet been printed and delivered. See Offices in Geneva Nos. 685-686; Vienna Nos. 660-661.

United Nations Peacekeeping Vehicles — A551

United Nations Peacekeepers — A552

Two Female United Nations Peacekeepers and Helicopter — A553

United Nations Peacekeeping Vehicles — A554

Helmet and Knapsacks of United Nations Peacekeepers — A555

2020, May 29 **Litho.** ***Perf. 14¾***

1240	A551	$1.20	**multicolored** + label	*3.00*	*3.00*
1241	A552	$1.20	**multicolored** + label	*3.00*	*3.00*
1242	A553	$1.20	**multicolored** + label	*3.00*	*3.00*
1243	A554	$1.20	**multicolored** + label	*3.00*	*3.00*
1244	A555	$1.20	**multicolored** + label	*3.00*	*3.00*
a.			Vert. strip of 5, #1240-1244, + 5 labels	*15.00*	*15.00*
			Sheet of 10, 2 each #1240-1244, + 10 labels	*30.00*	*30.00*
			Nos. 1240-1244 (5)	15.00	15.00

International Day of United Nations Peacekeepers. The full sheet sold for $14.95. The generic labels are shown. Labels could be personalized. The personalization of labels was available only at UN Headquarters, and not through mail order.

Flag Type of 1980

Printed by Royal Johann Enschedé, Netherlands. Designed by Rorie Katz, U.S. Issued in panes of 16; each pane contains 4 blocks of 4. A se-tenant block of 4 designs centers each pane.

2020, Aug. 20 **Litho.** ***Perf. 14x13¼***

1245	A185	$1.20	Bahrain *(64,000)+*	2.40	2.40
1246	A185	$1.20	Belarus *(64,000)+*	2.40	2.40
1247	A185	$1.20	Brazil *(64,000)+*	2.40	2.40
1248	A185	$1.20	Cyprus *(64,000)+*	2.40	2.40
a.			Block of 4, #1245-1248	9.60	9.60
1249	A185	$1.20	Dominica *(64,000)+*	2.40	2.40
1250	A185	$1.20	Mauritania *(64,000)+*	2.40	2.40
1251	A185	$1.20	Mongolia *(64,000)+*	2.40	2.40
1252	A185	$1.20	Paraguay *(64,000)+*	2.40	2.40
a.			Block of 4, #1249-1252	9.60	9.60
			First day cover, #1245-1252, each		4.50
			Set of 2 different panes of 16	78.00	
			Nos. 1245-1252 (8)	19.20	19.20

World Heritage Sites in Russia A556

Printed by Cartor Security Printing, France. Panes of 20. Designed by Sergio Baradat, U.S.

Designs: Nos. 1253, 1255a, Lake Baikal. Nos. 1254, 1255d, Kremlin and Red Square, Moscow. No. 1255b, Kazan Kremlin. No. 1255c, Novodevichy Convent. No. 1255e, Saint Petersburg. No. 1255f, Kizhi Pogost.

2020, Sept. 11 **Litho.** ***Perf. 14½x14¼***

1253 A556	55c **multicolored** *(90,000)+*	1.10	1.10
	First day cover		2.40
	Inscription block of 4	4.40	—
	Pane of 20	22.00	—
1254 A556	$1.20 **multicolored** *(90,000)+*	2.40	2.40
	First day cover		5.25
	First day cover, #1253-1254		5.75
	Inscription block of 4	9.60	—
	Pane of 20	48.00	—

Souvenir Booklet

1255	Booklet, #1255g-1255l *(6,500)+*	24.00	
a.-c.	A556 35c any single	.75	.75
d.-f.	A556 55c any single	1.25	1.25
g.	Booklet pane of 4 #1255a	3.00	—
h.	Booklet pane of 4 #1255b	3.00	—
i.	Booklet pane of 4 #1255c	3.00	—
j.	Booklet pane of 4 #1255d	5.00	—
k.	Booklet pane of 4 #1255e	5.00	—
l.	Booklet pane of 4 #1255f	5.00	—

Complete booklet sold for $12. See Offices in Geneva Nos. 688-690; Vienna Nos. 663-665.

Souvenir Sheet

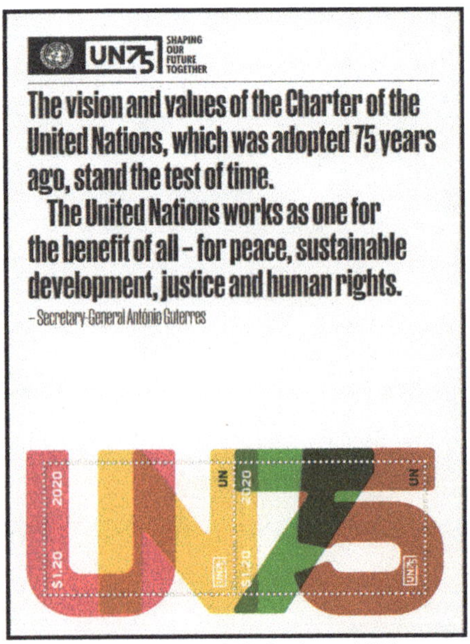

United Nations, 75th Anniv. — A557

Printed by La Poste, France. Designed by Matt Willey/Pentagram, U.S.

No. 1256: a, Pink "U," yellow "N." b, Green "7," red "5."

2020, Oct. 24 **Litho.** ***Perf. 13¼***

1256 A557	Sheet of 2 *(32,000)+*	4.80	4.80
a.-b.	$1.20 Either single	2.40	2.40
	First day cover, #1256		9.00

See Offices in Geneva No. 691; Vienna No. 667.

Souvenir Sheet

United Nations Building and Emblem — A558

Printed by Royal Johann Enschedé, Netherlands. Designed by Sergio Baradat, U.S.

Litho. With Foil Application

2020, Nov. 24 ***Die Cut Perf. 11½***

Self-Adhesive

1257 A558	$7.75 **multicolored** *(30,000)+*	15.50	15.50
	First day cover		19.00

Crypto stamp. Unused value is for sheets with unscratched panels at right. See Offices in Geneva No. 692; Vienna No. 668.

Fish A559

Grain Stalk A560

Butterfly — A561

Elephants — A562

Tree A563

2020, Dec. 5	**Litho.**	***Perf. 14¾***	
1258 A559 $1.20 **multicolored** + label		*3.00*	*3.00*
1259 A560 $1.20 **multicolored** + label		*3.00*	*3.00*
1260 A561 $1.20 **multicolored** + label		*3.00*	*3.00*
1261 A562 $1.20 **multicolored** + label		*3.00*	*3.00*
1262 A563 $1.20 **multicolored** + label		*3.00*	*3.00*
a. Vert. strip of 5, #1258-1262, + 5 labels		*15.00*	*15.00*
Sheet of 10, 2 each #1258-1262, + 10 labels		*30.00*	*30.00*
Nos. 1258-1262 (5)		*15.00*	*15.00*

World Soil Day. The full sheet sold for $14.95. The generic labels are shown. Labels could be personalized. The personalization of labels was available only at UN Headquarters, and not through mail order.

United Nations Emblem Type of 2016 Dated "2021" in Purple

2021, Jan. 22	**Litho.**	***Perf. 14¾***	
1263 A490 $1.20 **multicolored** + label		*3.00*	*3.00*
Sheet of 10 + 10 labels		*30.00*	—

The full sheet sold for $14.95. The generic label has an ox on red background. The personalization of labels was available only at UN Headquarters, and not through mail order.

International Day for the Elimination of Racial Discrimination — A564

Printed by Cartor Security Printing, France. Panes of 10. Designed by Rorie Katz, U.S.

2021, Mar. 19	**Litho.**	***Perf. 13¼x13***	
1264 A564 $1.20 **multicolored** *(110,000)*+		2.40	2.40
First day cover			4.50
Inscription block of 4		9.75	—
Sheet of 10		24.00	—

See Offices in Geneva No. 693; Vienna Nos. 669.

Endangered Species — A565

Printed by Johann Enschedé Stamps Security Printers, the Netherlands. Designed by Rorie Katz, U.S.

Designs: No. 1265, Waigeo cuscus. No. 1266, Helmeted honeyeater. No. 1267, Venus flytrap. No. 1268, American alligator.

2021, Apr. 7	**Litho.**	***Perf. 12¾x12½***	
1265 A565 $1.20 **multicolored** *(48,000)*+		2.40	2.40
1266 A565 $1.20 **multicolored** *(48,000)*+		2.40	2.40
1267 A565 $1.20 **multicolored** *(48,000)*+		2.40	2.40
1268 A565 $1.20 **multicolored** *(48,000)*+		2.40	2.40
a. Block of 4, #1265-1268		9.75	9.75
First day cover, #1268a			12.50
First day cover, #1265-1268, each			4.50
Inscription block of 4, #1268a		9.75	—
Pane of 16		39.00	—
Nos. 1265-1268 (4)		9.60	9.60

See Offices in Geneva Nos. 694-697; Vienna Nos. 670-673.

Miniature Sheet

United Nations Postal Administration, 70th Anniv. — A566

No. 1260 — United Nations stamps. a, #171. b, #548. c, #873. d, #5. e, #268. f, #1. g, #249. h, #310. i, #35. j, #160.

2021, Apr. 30	**Litho.**	***Perf. 14¾***	
1269 A566 Sheet of 10		*30.00*	*30.00*
a.-j. $1.20 Any single + label		*3.00*	*3.00*

The full sheet sold for $14.95. The generic labels are shown. Labels could be personalized. The personalization of labels was available only at UN Headquarters, and not through mail order.

Sailors in Sailboat and Bird — A567

Sailors in Sailboat — A568

Sailors in Sailboat and Bird — A569

Batter, Catcher and Umpire — A570

Batter and Baseball — A571

Pitcher and Baseball — A572

Olympic Gold Medalist and Dove — A573

Printed by Royal Johann Enschedé, Netherlands. Sheets of 8. Designed by Satoshi Hashimoto, Japan.

2021, July 23 **Litho.** ***Perf. 13½***

1270	A567 55c **multicolored** *(108,000)*+	1.10	1.10
1271	A568 55c **multicolored** *(54,000)*+	1.10	1.10
1272	A569 55c **multicolored** *(54,000)*+	1.10	1.10
a.	Horiz. strip of 3, #1270-1272	3.30	3.30
	First day cover, strip of 4, #1272a, 1270		6.00
	First day cover, pane of 8, 4 #1270, 2 each #1271-1272		17.00
	Pane of 8, 4 #1270, 2 each #1271-1272	8.80	—
1273	A570 $1.20 **multicolored** *(108,000)*+	2.40	2.40
1274	A571 $1.20 **multicolored** *(54,000)*+	2.40	2.40
1275	A572 $1.20 **multicolored** *(54,000)*+	2.40	2.40
a.	Horiz. strip of 3, #1273-1275	7.20	7.20
	First day cover, strip of 4, #1275a, 1273		13.00
	First day cover, pane of 8, 4 #1273, 2 each #1274-1275		22.00
	Pane of 8, 4 #1273, 2 each #1274-1275	14.40	—
	Nos. 1270-1275 (6)	10.50	10.50

Souvenir Sheet

1276	A573 $1.20 **multicolored** *(23,000)*+	2.40	2.40
	First day cover		4.50

Sports for Peace, 2020 Summer Olympics, Tokyo. The 2020 Summer Olympics were postponed until 2021 because of the COVID-19 pandemic. See Offices in Geneva Nos. 698-704, Vienna Nos. 674-680.

Mother Teresa (1910-97), Humanitarian — A574

Printed by Royal Johann Enschedé, the Netherlands. Panes of 20. Designed by Rorie Katz, U.S.

2021, Aug. 12 **Litho.** ***Perf. 14¼***

1277	A574 $1.80 **dark blue & black** *(160,000)*+	3.75	3.75
	First day cover		5.75
	Inscription block of 4	15.00	—
	Sheet of 20	75.00	—

Waterway, Railway and Bridges World Heritage Sites — A575

Printed by Cartor Security Printing, France. Panes of 20. Designed by Sergio Baradat, U.S.

Designs: Nos. 1278, 1280a, Rideau Canal, Canada. Nos. 1279, 1280d, Grand Canal, People's Republic of China. No. 1280b, Rhaetian Railway, Switzerland and Italy. No. 1280c, Forth Bridge, Scotland. No. 1280e, Darjeeling Himalayan Railway, India. No. 1280f, Old Bridge, Mostar, Bosnia and Herzegovina.

2021, Aug. 25 Litho. *Perf. 14¼*

1278 A575	55c **multicolored** *(90,000)*+	1.10	1.10
	First day cover		2.00
	Inscription block of 4	4.40	—
	Pane of 20	22.00	—
1279 A575	$1.20 **multicolored** *(90,000)*+	2.40	2.40
	First day cover		4.50
	First day cover, #1278-1279		5.75
	Inscription block of 4	9.60	—
	Pane of 20	48.00	—

Souvenir Booklet

1280	Booklet, #1280g-1280l *(5,700)*+	24.00	
a.-c.	A575 35c any single	.75	.75
d.-f.	A575 55c any single	1.25	1.25
g.	Booklet pane of 4 #1280a	3.00	—
h.	Booklet pane of 4 #1280b	3.00	—
i.	Booklet pane of 4 #1280c	3.00	—
j.	Booklet pane of 4 #1280d	5.00	—
k.	Booklet pane of 4 #1280e	5.00	—
l.	Booklet pane of 4 #1280f	5.00	—

Complete booklet sold for $12. See Offices in Geneva Nos. 705-707; Vienna Nos. 681-683.

Souvenir Sheet

Expo 2020, Dubai — A576

Printed by Cartor Security Printing, France. Designed by Sergio Baradat, U.S.

No. 1281: a, Mobility Pavilion. b, Opportunity Pavilion. c, Sustainability Pavilion.

2021, Oct. 1 Litho. *Perf. 13½x13*

1281 A576	Sheet of 3 *(15,000)*+	14.50	14.50
a.	$1.30 multi	4.75	4.75
b.	2fr multi	4.75	4.75
c.	€1.80 multi	4.75	4.75

Expo 2020 was postponed until 2021 because of the COVID-19 pandemic. No. 1281 sold for $7.04.

Souvenir Sheet

United Nations Biodiversity Conference, Kunming, People's Republic of China — A577

Printed by Cartor Security Printing, France. Designed by Sergio Baradat, U.S.

No. 1282: a, Flower. b, Insect. c, Bird.

2021, Oct. 11 Litho. *Perf. 13½x13*

1282 A577	Sheet of 3 *(48,000)*+	14.50	14.50
a.	$1.30 multi	4.75	4.75
b.	2fr multi	4.75	4.75
c.	€1.80 multi	4.75	4.75

No. 1282 sold for $7.04.

Miniature Sheet

Celebrations — A578

No. 1283: a, Birthday cake. b, Flower bouquet. c, Three balloons. d, Menorah. e, Heart and arrow. f, Christmas tree and ornament. g, "Thank you." h, Champagne flutes. i, Diamond ring. j, Mosque.

2021, Nov. 4 Litho. *Perf. 14½x14¼*

1283 A578	Sheet of 10	*32.50*	*32.50*
a.-j.	$1.30 Any single + label	*3.25*	*3.25*

The full sheet sold for $15.95. The generic labels are shown. Labels could be personalized. The personalization of labels was available only at UN Headquarters, and not through mail order.

World Toilet Day — A579

Printed by Cartor Security Printing, France. Panes of 20. Designed by Gail Armstrong, U.K.

2021, Nov. 19	**Litho.**	***Perf. 14¼***	
1284 A579 58c **multicolored** *(100,000)*+		1.25	1.25
First day cover			3.25
Inscription block of 4		5.00	—
Sheet of 20		25.00	—

Miniature Sheet

UNICEF, 75th Anniv. — A580

No. 1285 — Inscription: a, Health. b, Disability. c, Mental Health. d, Water Sanitation Hygiene. e, Gender. f, Vaccination. g, Climate. h, Humanitarian Response. i, Nutrition. j, Education.

2021, Dec. 11	**Litho.**	***Perf. 14½***	
1285 A580 Sheet of 10		*32.50*	*32.50*
a.-j. $1.30 Any single + label		*3.25*	*3.25*

The full sheet sold for $15.95. The generic labels are shown. Labels could be personalized. The personalization of labels was available only at UN Headquarters, and not through mail order.

Ice Hockey Player and Goaltender — A581

Three Ice Hockey Players and Puck A582

Snowboarder With Yellow Green Vest — A583

Snowboarder in Air With Orange Vest — A584

Printed by Cartor Security Printing, France. Panes of 6.

2022, Jan. 14	**Litho.**	***Perf. 14¼***	
1286 A581 58c **multicolored** *(145,550)*+		1.25	1.25
1287 A582 58c **multicolored** *(145,550)*+		1.25	1.25
a. Horiz. pair, #1286-1287		2.50	2.50
First day cover, #1286-1287			4.25
Inscription block of 4		5.00	—
Pane of 6		7.50	—
1288 A583 $1.30 **multicolored** *(145,550)*+		2.60	2.60
1289 A584 $1.30 **multicolored** *(145,550)*+		2.60	2.60
a. Horiz. pair, #1288-1289		5.20	5.20
First day cover, #1288-1289			9.50
Inscription block of 4		10.50	—
Pane of 6		16.00	—
Nos. 1286-1289 (4)		7.70	7.70

Sports for Peace, 2022 Winter Olympics, Beijing. See Offices in Geneva Nos. 710-713; Vienna Nos. 687-690.

Tiger Facing Right — A585

Tiger Facing Left — A586

Printed by Cartor Security Printing, France. Designed by Tiger Pan, People's Republic of China. Panes of 10 + 10 labels.

2022, Jan. 21	**Litho.**		***Perf. 14¼***
1290 A585 $1.30 **multicolored** + label		*3.25*	*3.25*
1291 A586 $1.30 **multicolored** + label		*3.25*	*3.25*
a. Horiz. pair, #1290-1291, + 2 labels		*6.50*	*6.50*
Sheet of 10, 5 each #1290-1291, + 10 labels		*32.50*	*32.50*

New Year 2022 (Year of the Tiger). The full sheet sold for $15.95. The generic labels are shown. Labels could be personalized. The personalization of labels was available only at UN Headquarters, and not through mail order.

Biggie, Mr. Dinkles, Fruits and Vegetables — A587

Guy Diamond, Tiny Diamond, Fruits and Vegetables — A588

Poppy and Vegetables — A589

Branch, Fruits and Vegetables — A590

Prince Darnell, Cooper, Fruits and Vegetables — A591

2022, Feb. 22	**Litho.**		***Perf. 14¾***
1292 A587 $1.30 **multicolored** + label		*3.25*	*3.25*
1293 A588 $1.30 **multicolored** + label		*3.25*	*3.25*
1294 A589 $1.30 **multicolored** + label		*3.25*	*3.25*
1295 A590 $1.30 **multicolored** + label		*3.25*	*3.25*
1296 A591 $1.30 **multicolored** + label		*3.25*	*3.25*
a. Vert. strip of 5, #1292-1296, + 5 labels		*16.25*	*16.25*
Sheet of 10, 2 each #1292-1296, + 10 labels		*32.50*	*32.50*
Nos. 1292-1296 (5)		*16.25*	*16.25*

Trolls Food Heroes Campaign. The full sheet sold for $15.95. The generic labels are shown. Labels could be personalized. The personalization of labels was available only at UN Headquarters, and not through mail order.

Endangered Species — A592

Printed by Johann Enschedé Stamps Security Printers, the Netherlands. Designed by Sergio Baradat, U.S.

Designs: No. 1297, Pygmy three-toed sloth. No. 1298, Andean condor. No. 1299, Keel-billed toucan. No. 1300, Jaguar.

2022, Mar. 18	**Litho.**		***Perf. 12¾x12½***
1297 A592 $1.30 **multicolored** *(44,000)*+		2.60	2.60
1298 A592 $1.30 **multicolored** *(44,000)*+		2.60	2.60
1299 A592 $1.30 **multicolored** *(44,000)*+		2.60	2.60
1300 A592 $1.30 **multicolored** *(44,000)*+		2.60	2.60
a. Block of 4, #1297-1300		10.50	10.50
First day cover, #1300a			14.50
First day cover, #1297-1300, each			5.75
Inscription block of 4, #1300a		10.50	—
Pane of 16		42.00	—
Nos. 1297-1300 (4)		10.40	10.40

See Offices in Geneva Nos. 714-717; Vienna Nos. 691-694.

SEMI-POSTAL STAMPS

Souvenir Sheet

AIDS Awareness — SP1

Printed by Walsall Security Printers Limited, UK. Designed by Rorie Katz, US.

2002, Oct. 24 **Litho.** ***Perf. 14½***

B1 SP1 37c + 6c **multicolored** *(175,000)+*	3.50	3.50
First day cover, #B1		3.50

See Offices in Geneva No. B1, Vienna No. B1.

Miniature Sheet

Campaign Against COVID-19 Pandemic — SP2

Printed by Schellenberg Druck AG, Switzerland. Designed by Rorie Katz, U.S.

No. B2: a, Hand washing. b, Question mark in speech bubble. c, Social distancing. d, Smiling face. e, Cross in broken circle. f, Hands making heart shape.

2020, Aug. 11 **Litho.** ***Perf. 13¼***

B2 SP2 Sheet of 6 *(128,000)+*	21.00	21.00
a. 55c+50c multi	2.10	2.10
b. $1.20+50c multi	3.50	3.50
c. 1fr+50c multi	3.50	3.50
d. 1.50fr+50c multi	4.50	4.50
e. 85c+50c multi	3.50	3.50
f. €1+50c multi	3.75	3.75
First day cover, #B2		25.00

Surtax for World Health Organization COVID Solidarity Response Fund.

SP3

Photograph of John Lennon (1940-80), by Bob Gruen — SP4

Printed by Cartor Security Printing, France. Panes of 20. Designed by Rorie Katz, U.S.

2021, Sept. 21 **Litho.** ***Perf. 14¼***

B3 SP3 $1.30 +50c **multicolored** *(150,000)+*	3.75	3.75
First day cover		5.75
Inscription block of 4	15.00	—
Sheet of 20	75.00	—

Souvenir Sheet

Litho. With Foil Application

B4 SP4 $2.60 +$1 **multicolored** *(20,000)+*	7.25	7.25
First day cover		9.75

International Day of Peace. Surtax for United Nations peacekeeping efforts.

AIR POST STAMPS

Plane and Gull — AP1

Swallows and UN Emblem — AP2

Engraved and printed by Thomas De La Rue & Co., Ltd., London. Panes of 50. Designed by Ole Hamann (AP1) and Olav Mathiesen (AP2).

1951, Dec. 14 **Unwmk.** ***Perf. 14***

C1	AP1	6c **henna brown** *(2,500,000)*	.25	.25
		First day cover		2.00
		Inscription block of 4	.25	—
C2	AP1	10c **bright blue green** *(2,750,000)*	.30	.30
		First day cover		2.00
		Inscription block of 4	1.10	—
C3	AP2	15c **deep ultramarine** *(3,250,000)*	.40	.40
		First day cover		3.00
		Inscription block of 4	1.60	—
a.		15c **Prussian blue**	65.00	
C4	AP2	25c **gray black** *(2,250,000)*	.85	.85
		First day cover		7.50
		First day cover, #C1-C4		30.00
		Inscription block of 4	4.75	—
		Nos. C1-C4 (4)	1.80	1.80

First day covers of Nos. 1-11 and C1-C4 total 1,113,216.

Early printings of Nos. C1-C4 have wide, imperforate sheet margins on three sides. Later printings were perforated through all margins.

Airplane Wing and Globe — AP3

Engraved and printed by Thomas De La Rue & Co., Ltd., London. Panes of 50. Designed by W. W. Wind.

1957, May 27 ***Perf. 12½x14***

C5	AP3	4c **maroon** *(5,000,000)*	.25	.25
		First day cover *(282,933)*		1.00
		Inscription block of 4	.30	—

For 5c see No. C6.

Type of 1957 and

UN Flag and Plane — AP4

Engraved and printed by Waterlow & Sons, Ltd., London. Panes of 50. Designed by W. W. Wind (5c) and Olav Mathiesen (7c).

1959, Feb. 9 **Unwmk.** ***Perf. 12½x13½***

C6	AP3	5c **rose red** *(4,000,000)*	.25	.25
		First day cover		1.00
		Inscription block of 4	.50	—

Perf. 13½x14

C7	AP4	7c **ultramarine** *(4,000,000)*	.25	.25
		First day cover		1.00
		First day cover, #C6-C7		17.50
		Inscription block of 4	.75	—

First day covers of Nos. C6 and C7 total 413,556.

Outer Space — AP5

UN Emblem — AP6

Bird of Laurel Leaves — AP7

Printed by Courvoisier S.A., La Chaux-de-Fonds, Switzerland. Panes of 50. Designed by Claude Bottiau (6c), George Hamori (8c) and Kurt Plowitz (13c).

1963, June 17 **Photo.** **Unwmk.** ***Perf. 11½***

C8	AP5	6c **black, blue & yellow green** *(4,000,000)*	.25	.25
		First day cover		1.00
		Inscription block of 4	.45	—
C9	AP6	8c **yellow, olive green & red** *(4,000,000)*	.25	.25
		First day cover		1.00
		Inscription block of 4	.60	—

Perf. 12½x12

C10	AP7	13c **ultra, aquamarine, gray & carmine** *(2,700,000)*	.25	.25
		First day cover		1.00
		First day cover, #C8-C10		8.50
		Inscription block of 4	.90	—

First day covers of Nos. C8-C10 total 536,824.

"Flight Across the Globe" — AP8

Jet Plane and Envelope — AP9

Printed by the Austrian Government Printing Office, Vienna, Austria. Panes of 50. Designed by Ole Hamann (15c) and George Hamori (25c).

1964, May 1 Photo. Unwmk. *Perf. 11½x12, 12x11½*

C11 AP8 15c **violet, buff, gray & pale green** *(3,000,000)*	.30	.30
First day cover		1.00
Inscription block of 4	1.40	—
a. Gray omitted	*225.00*	
C12 AP9 25c **yellow, orange, gray, blue & red** *(2,000,000)*	.50	.50
First day cover		1.00
First day cover, #C11-C12		8.00
Inscription block of 4	2.50	—
Nos. C8-C12 (5)	1.55	1.55

First day covers of Nos. C11-C12 total 353,696.
For 75c in type AP8, see UN Offices in Geneva No. 8.

Jet Plane and UN Emblem — AP10

Printed by Setelipaino, Finland. Panes of 50. Designed by Ole Hamann.

1968, Apr. 18 Litho. *Perf. 13*

C13 AP10 20c **multicolored** *(3,000,000)*	.35	.35
First day cover *(225,378)*		1.00
Inscription block of 4	1.60	—

Wings, Envelopes and UN Emblem — AP11

Printed by Setelipaino, Finland. Panes of 50. Designed by Olav S. Mathiesen.

1969, Apr. 21 Litho. *Perf. 13*

C14 AP11 10c **orange vermilion, orange, yellow & black** *(4,000,000)*	.25	.25
First day cover *(132,686)*		1.00
Inscription block of 4	.75	—

UN Emblem and Stylized Wing — AP12

Birds in Flight — AP13

Clouds — AP14

"UN" and Plane — AP15

Printed by Government Printing Bureau, Japan (9c); Heraclio Fournier, S. A., Spain (11c, 17c); Setelipaino, Finland (21c). Panes of 50. Designed by Lyell L. Dolan (9c), Arne Johnson (11c), British American Bank Note Co. (17c) and Asher Kalderon (21c).

1972, May 1 Litho. & Engr. *Perf. 13x13½*

C15 AP12 9c **light blue, dark red & violet blue** *(3,000,000)+*	.25	.25
First day cover		1.00
Inscription block of 4	.50	—

Photo.

Perf. 14x13½

C16 AP13 11c **blue & multicolored** *(3,000,000)+*	.25	.25
First day cover		1.00
Inscription block of 4	.75	—

Perf. 13½x14

C17 AP14 17c **yellow, red & orange** *(3,000,000)+*	.25	.25
First day cover		1.00
Inscription block of 4	1.10	—

Perf. 13

C18 AP15 21c **silver & multi** *(3,500,000)*	.25	.25
First day cover		1.00
First day cover, #C15-C18		3.50
Inscription block of 4	1.25	—
Nos. C15-C18 (4)	1.00	1.00

First day covers of Nos. C15-C18 total 553,535.

Globe and Jet — AP16

Pathways Radiating from UN Emblem — AP17

Bird in Flight, UN Headquarters AP18

Printed by Setelipaino, Finland. Panes of 50. Designed by George Hamori (13c), Shamir Bros. (18c) and Olav S. Mathiesen (26c).

1974, Sept. 16 Litho. *Perf. 13, 12½x13 (18c)*

C19 AP16 13c **multicolored** *(2,500,000)*+		.25	.25
First day cover			1.00
Inscription block of 4		.80	—
C20 AP17 18c **gray olive & multicolored** *(2,000,000)*		.25	.25
First day cover			1.00
Inscription block of 4		1.10	—
C21 AP18 26c **blue & multi** *(2,000,000)*		.35	.35
First day cover			1.25
First day cover, #C19-C21			2.50
Inscription block of 4		1.60	—
Nos. C19-C21 (3)		.85	.85

First day covers of Nos. C19-C21 total 309,610.

Winged Airmail Letter — AP19

Symbolic Globe and Plane — AP20

Printed by Heraclio Fournier, S.A. Panes of 50. Designed by Eliezer Weishoff (25c) and Alan L. Pollock (31c).

1977, June 27 Photo. *Perf. 14*

C22 AP19 25c **greenish blue & multi** *(2,000,000)*+		.35	.35
First day cover			1.25
Inscription block of 4		1.60	—
C23 AP20 31c **magenta** *(2,000,000)*		.45	.45
First day cover			1.25
First day cover, #C22-C23			1.50
Inscription block of 4		1.90	—

First day covers of Nos. C22-C23 total 209,060.

ENVELOPES

Used values for all postal stationery are for non-philatelic contemporaneous usages.

Emblem of United Nations — U1

Printed by the International Envelope Corp., Dayton, Ohio. Die engraved by the American Bank Note Co., New York.

1953, Sept. 15 Embossed

U1 U1 3c **blue,** entire *(555,000)*	.25	.25
Entire, first day cancel *(102,278)*		.50

Printed by International Envelope Corp., Dayton, Ohio.

1958, Sept. 22 Embossed

U2 U1 4c **ultramarine,** entire *(1,000,000)*	.25	.25
Entire, first day cancel *(213,621)*		.50

Stylized Globe and Weather Vane — U2

Printed by United States Envelope Co., Springfield, Mass. Designed by Hatim El Mekki.

1963, Apr. 26 Litho.

U3 U2 5c **multicolored,** entire *(1,115,888)*	.25	.25
Entire, first day cancel *(165,188)*		.75

Printed by Setelipaino, Finland.

1969, Jan. 8 Litho.

U4 U2 6c **black, blue, magenta & dull yellow,** entire *(850,000)*	.25	.25
Entire, first day cancel *(152,593)*		.75

Headquarters Type of Regular Issue, 1968

Printed by Eureka Co., a division of Litton Industries.

1973, Jan. 12 Litho.

U5 A99 8c **sepia, blue & olive,** entire *(700,000)*	.45	.50
Entire, first day cancel *(145,510)*		.75

Headquarters Type of Regular Issue, 1974

Printed by United States Envelope Co., Springfield, Mass.

1975, Jan. 10 Litho.

U6 A138 10c **blue, olive bister & multi,** entire *(547,500)*	.40	.40
Entire, first day cancel *(122,000)*		.90

Bouquet of Ribbons — U3

Printed by Carl Ueberreuter Druck and Verlag M. Salzer, Austria. Designed by George Hamori, Australia.

1985, May 10 **Litho.**

U7 U3 22c **multicolored,** entire *(250,000)* 3.25 1.75
Entire, first day cancel *(28,600)* 1.00

New York Headquarters U4

Printed by Mercury Walch, Australia. Designed by Rocco J. Callari, United States.

1989, Mar. 17 **Litho.**

U8 U4 25c **multicolored,** entire *(350,000)* 2.00 2.00
Entire, first day cancel *(28,567)* 3.00

For surcharge see No. U9A.

No. U8 Surcharged

1991, Apr. 15 **Litho.**

U9 U4 25c +4c **multicolored,** entire *(50,000)+* 3.00 *6.00*
Entire, first day cover 5.00

No. U8 Surcharged

1995 **Litho.**

U9A U4 25c +7c **multicolored,** entire 2.50 *6.00*
Entire, first day cover 6.00

Cripticandina, by Alfredo La Placa — U5

Illustration reduced.
Design sizes: No. U10, 79x38mm. No. U11, 89x44mm.

1997, Feb. 12 **Litho.**

U10 U5 32c **multicolored,** #6¾, entire *(65,000)+* 2.00 2.00
Entire, first day cancel 5.50
U11 U5 32c **multicolored,** #10, entire *(80,000)+* 2.00 2.00
Entire, first day cancel 3.50

Nos. U10-U11 Surcharged

1999, Jan. 10 **Litho.**

U12 U5 32c +1c **multicolored,** on #U10, entire 2.50 *3.00*
First day cancel, entire 2.50
U13 U5 32c +1c **multicolored,** on #U11, entire 2.50 *3.00*
First day cancel, entire 2.50

New York Headquarters — U6

Design sizes: No. U14, 34x34mm. No. U15, 36x36mm.

2001, May 25 **Litho.**

U14 U6 34c **multicolored,** #6¾, entire 2.00 .90
Entire, first day cancel 1.10
U15 U6 34c **multicolored,** #10, entire 2.00 .90
Entire, first day cancel 1.10

Nos. U14-U15 Surcharged

2002, June 30 **Litho.**

U16 U6 34c +3c **multicolored,** entire (#U14) 2.00 *3.00*
Entire, first day cancel 2.00
U17 U6 34c +3c **multicolored,** entire (#U15) 2.00 *3.00*
Entire, first day cancel 2.00

UN Headquarters — U7

Printed by Australia Post Spintpak, Australia.
Design sizes: No. U18, 37x47mm. No. U19, 40x52mm.

2003, Mar. 28 **Litho.**

U18 U7 37c **multicolored,** #6¾, entire *(62,000)+* 1.25 .50
Entire, first day cancel 1.50
U19 U7 37c **multicolored,** #10, entire *(72,000)+* 1.25 .50
Entire, first day cancel 1.50

Nos. U18-U19 Surcharged

2006, Jan. 8 **Litho.**

U20 U7 37c +2c **multicolored,** entire (#U18) 1.75 *2.50*
Entire, first day cancel 1.50
U21 U7 37c +2c **multicolored,** entire (#U19) 1.50 *2.50*
Entire, first day cancel 2.00

Nos. U18-U19 Surcharged Like No. U20

2007, May 14 **Litho.**

U22 U7 37c +4c **multicolored,** entire (#U18) 1.75 *2.50*
Entire, first day cancel 2.75
U23 U7 37c +4c **multicolored,** entire (#U19) 1.75 *2.50*
Entire, first day cancel 6.00

United Nations Emblem — U8

Printed by Lowe-Martin Group, Canada. Designed by Robert Stein, US.
Design sizes: No. U24, 22x28mm. No. U25, 29x38mm.

2007, Aug. 9 **Litho.**

U24 U8 41c **multicolored,** #6¾, entire *(35,000)+* 1.75 1.50
Entire, first day cancel 2.50
U25 U8 41c **multicolored,** #10, entire *(35,000)+* 1.50 1.10
Entire, first day cancel 2.50

Nos. U24-U25 Surcharged Like No. U20

2008, May 12 **Litho.**

U26 U8 41c +1c **multicolored,** entire (#U24) 2.50 *3.00*
Entire, first day cancel 3.00
U27 U8 41c +1c **multicolored,** entire (#U25) 2.50 *3.00*
Entire, first day cancel 3.00

Nos. U24-U25 Surcharged Like No. U20

2009, June 5 **Litho.**

U28 U8 41c +3c **multicolored,** entire (#U24) 3.00 *4.00*
Entire, first day cancel 4.00
U29 U8 41c +3c **multicolored,** entire (#U25) 3.00 *4.00*
Entire, first day cancel 4.00

UN Headquarters and Cherry Blossoms — U9

Printed by Johann Enschedé and Sons, the Netherlands. Designed by Rorie Katz, United States.
Design size: No. U30, 32x28mm. No. U31, 42x32mm.

2010, June 4 **Litho.**

U30 U9 44c **multicolored,** #6¾, entire *(24,000)+* 2.50 2.00
Entire, first day cancel 4.00
U31 U9 44c **multicolored,** #10, entire *(25,000)+* 2.50 2.00
Entire, first day cancel 4.00

Nos. U30-U31 Surcharged

2012, Jan. 23 **Litho.**

U32 U9 44c+1c **multicolored,** entire (#U30) 3.00 *4.00*
Entire, first day cancel 4.00
U33 U9 44c+1c **multicolored,** entire (#U31) 3.50 *4.00*
Entire, first day cancel 5.00

Circle and Dots — U10

Printed by Johann Enschedé and Sons, the Netherlands. Designed by Sergio Baradat, U.S.
Diameter of denomination circle: No. U34, 16mm. No. U35, 18mm.

2013, Mar. 5 **Litho.**

U34 U10 46c **orange,** #6¾, entire *(17,000)+* 2.50 1.25
Entire, first day cancel *4.75*
U35 U10 46c **orange,** #10, entire *(18,000)+* 3.00 1.50
Entire, first day cancel *4.75*

Nos. U34-U35 Surcharged Like No. U20

2014, June 6 **Litho.**

U36 U10 46c+3c **multicolored,** entire (#U34) 1.25 1.25
Entire, first day cancel 1.25
U37 U10 46c+3c **multicolored,** entire (#U35) 1.25 1.25
Entire, first day cancel 1.25

United Nations Headquarters, Emblem and *Single Form* Sculpture, by Barbara Hepworth — U11

Printed by Lowe-Martin Group, Canada. Designed by Sergio Baradat, U.S.
Design sizes: No. U38, 25x34mm. No. U39, 32x45mm.

2017, Apr. 13 **Litho.**

U38 U11 49c **multicolored,** #6¾, entire *(20,000)+* 1.50 1.50
Entire, first day cancel 2.50
U39 U11 49c **multicolored,** #10, entire *(23,000)+* 1.50 1.50
Entire, first day cancel 2.50

Nos. U38-U39 Surcharged Like No. U12

2018, May 25 **Litho.**

U40 U11 49c+1c **multicolored,** entire (#U38) 1.60 1.60
Entire, first day cancel 1.60
U41 U11 49c+1c **multicolored,** entire (#U39) 1.60 1.60
Entire, first day cancel 1.60

Nos. U38-U39 Surcharged Like No. U20

2019, Feb. 1 **Litho.**

U42 U11 49c+6c **multicolored,** entire (#U38) 1.75 1.75
Entire, first day cancel 1.75
U43 U11 49c+6c **multicolored,** entire (#U39) 1.75 1.75
Entire, first day cancel 1.75

AIR POST ENVELOPES AND AIR LETTER SHEETS

Used values for all postal stationery are for non-philatelic contemporaneous usages.

Letter Sheet
Type of Air Post Stamp of 1951
Inscribed "Air Letter" at Left

Printed by Dennison & Sons, Long Island City, NY.

1952, Aug. 29 **Litho.**

UC1 AP2 10c **blue,** *bluish,* entire *(187,000)* 17.50 17.50
Entire, 1st day cancel *(57,274)* 4.00

Designed by C. Mutver.

Letter Sheet
Inscribed "Air Letter" and "Aerogramme" at Left

1954, Sept. 14 **Litho.**

UC2 AP2 10c **royal blue,** *bluish,* entire, *(207,000)* 9.50 5.00
Entire, 1st day cancel *400.00*
a. No white border, *1958 (148,800)* 7.00 *8.00*

No. UC2 was printed with a narrow white border (½ to 1mm wide) surrounding the stamp. On No. UC2a, this border has been partly or entirely eliminated.

UN Flag and Plane — UC1

(UN Emblem Embossed)

Printed by International Envelope Corp., Dayton, O.
Die engraved by American Bank Note Co., New York.

1959, Sept. 21 **Embossed**

UC3 UC1 7c **blue,** entire *(550,000)* .90 *1.25*
Entire, 1st day cancel *(172,107)* .90

Letter Sheet
Type of Air Post Stamp of 1959

Printed by Thomas De La Rue & Co., Ltd., London.

1960, Jan. 18 **Litho.**

UC4 AP4 10c **ultramarine,** *bluish,* entire *(405,000)* .65 .65
Entire, 1st day cancel *(122,425)* .45

Printed on protective tinted paper containing colorless inscription "United Nations" in the five official languages of the UN.

Letter Sheet
Type of Air Post Stamp of 1951
Inscribed "Correo Aereo" instead of "Poste Aerienne"

Printed by Thomas De La Rue & Co., Ltd., London.

1961, June 26 **Litho.**

UC5 AP1 11c **ultramarine,** *bluish,* entire *(550,000)* .50 .50
Entire, 1st day cancel *(128,557)* .50
a. 11c **dark blue,** *green* entire, *July 16, 1965 (419,000)* 1.25 —

Printed on protective tinted paper containing colorless inscription "United Nations" in the five official languages of the UN.

UN Emblem — UC2

Printed by United States Envelope Co., Springfield, Mass. Designed by George Hamori.

1963, Apr. 26 **Litho.**

UC6 UC2 8c **multicolored,** entire *(880,000)* .30 .30
Entire, 1st day cancel *(165,208)* 1.00

Letter Sheet

UN Emblem and Stylized Plane — UC3

Printed by Setelipaino, Finland. Designed by Robert Perrot.

1968, May 31 **Litho.**

UC7 UC3 13c **violet blue & light blue,** entire *(750,000)* .30 .30
Entire, 1st day cancel *(106,700)* .50

Type of 1963

Printed by Setelipaino, Finland.

1969, Jan. 8 **Litho.**

UC8 UC2 10c **pink, Prussian blue, orange & sepia,** entire *(750,000)* .35 .35
Entire, 1st day cancel *(153,472)* .40

Letter Sheet

UN Emblem, "UN," Globe and Plane — UC4

Printed by Joh. Enschede and Sons. Designed by Edmondo Calivis, Egypt. Sheet surface printed in greenish blue.

1972, Oct. 16 **Litho.**

UC9 UC4 15c **violet blue & greenish blue,** entire *(500,000)* .60 .60
Entire, 1st day cancel *(85,500)* .80

Bird Type of Air Post Stamp, 1972

Printed by Eureka Co., a division of Litton Industries.

1973, Jan. 12 **Litho.**

UC10 AP13 11c **blue & multicolored,** entire *(700,000)* .40 .40
Entire, 1st day cancel *(134,500)* .80

Globe and Jet Air Post Type of 1974

Printed by United States Envelope Co., Springfield, Mass.

1975, Jan. 10 **Litho.**

UC11 AP16 13c **blue & multicolored,** entire *(555,539)* .60 .60
Entire, 1st day cancel *(122,000)* .80

Letter Sheet

Headquarters Type of Regular Issue, 1971

Printed by Joh. Enschede and Sons, Netherlands.

1975, Jan. 10 **Photo.**

UC12 A120 18c **blue & multicolored**, entire *(400,000)* .60 .60
Entire, 1st day cancel *(70,500)* .80

Letter Sheet

"UN" Emblem and Birds — UC5

Printed by Joh. Enschede and Sons. Designed by Angel Medina Medina.

1977, June 27 **Litho.**

UC13 UC5 22c **multicolored,** entire *(400,000)* .65 .60
Entire, 1st day cancel *(70,000)* .80

Letter Sheet

Paper Airplane UC6

Printed by Joh. Enschede and Sons.
Designed by Margaret-Ann Champion.

1982, Apr. 28 **Litho.**

UC14 UC6 30c **black,** *pale green,* entire *(400,000)* 1.50 1.50
Entire, 1st day cancel *(61,400)* 1.25

Letter Sheet No. UC14 Surcharged

1987, July 7 **Litho.**

UC15 UC6 30c + 6c **black,** *green,* entire *(43,000)* *52.50 50.00*
Entire, 1st day cancel 45.00

New York Headquarters UC7

Printed by Mercury Walch, Australia. Designed by Thomas Lee, China.

1989, Mar. 17 **Litho.**

UC16 UC7 39c **multicolored,** entire *(350,000)* 3.00 3.00
Entire, 1st day cancel *(14,798)* 5.00

No. UC16 Surcharged

1991, Feb. 12 **Litho.**

UC17 UC7 39c + 6c **multicolored,** entire *(35,563)* 18.50 27.50
Entire, first day cancel 7.50

UC8

Designed by Robert Stein. Printed by Mercury-Walch, Australia.

1992, Sept. 4 **Litho.**

UC18 UC8 45c **multicolored,** entire, *(185,000)+* 2.75 3.00
First day cancel 10.00

Letter Sheet No. UC18 Surcharged

1995, July 9 **Litho.**

UC19 UC8 45c +5c **multicolored,** entire 4.50 7.50
First day cover 9.00

Cherry Blossoms — UC9

1997, Mar. 13 **Litho.**

UC20 UC9 50c **multicolored,** entire *(115,000)+* 3.50 2.00
Entire, first day cancel 5.00

No. UC20 Surcharged

1999, Aug. 23 **Litho.**

UC21 UC9 50c +10c **multicolored,** entire 2.25 *4.00*
Entire, first day cancel 3.00

No. UC20 Surcharged

2001, Jan. 9 **Litho.**

UC22 UC9 50c +20c **multicolored,** entire 2.00 *4.00*
Entire, first day cancel 3.50

Cherry Blossoms at New York Headquarters — UC10

2001, May 25 **Litho.**

UC23 UC10 70c **multicolored,** entire 2.00 1.75
Entire, first day cancel 8.00

No. UC23 Surcharged

2006, Jan. 8 **Litho.**
UC24 UC10 70c +5c **multicolored,** entire 2.50 3.00
Entire, first day cancel 3.00

No. UC23 Surcharged Like No. UC24

2007, May 14 **Litho.**
UC25 UC10 70c +20c **multicolored,** entire 3.25 *4.00*
Entire, first day cancel 3.50

United Nations Emblem and Airplane — UC11

Printed by Sprintpak, Australia. Designed by Robert Stein, US.

2007, Aug. 9 **Litho.**
UC26 UC11 90c **multicolored,** entire *(40,000)+* 2.75 2.75
Entire, first day cancel 3.25

No. UC26 Surcharged Like No. UC24

2008, May 12 **Litho.**
UC27 UC11 90c +4c **multicolored,** entire 2.25 *4.00*
Entire, first day cancel 3.00

No. UC26 Surcharged Like No. UC24

2009, June 5 **Litho.**
UC28 UC11 90c +8c **multicolored,** entire 2.25 *4.00*
Entire, first day cancel 3.50

UN Emblem and Airplane Type of 2007

Printed by Johann Enschedé and Sons, the Netherlands. Designed by Rorie Katz, United States.

2010, June 4 **Litho.**
UC29 UC11 98c **multicolored,** entire *(25,000)+* 3.00 2.25
Entire, first day cancel 4.00

No. UC29 Surcharged Like No. UC24

2012, Jan. 23 **Litho.**
UC30 UC11 98c+7c **multicolored,** entire 2.40 *4.00*
Entire, first day cancel 2.75

Surcharge on No. UC30 is below the indicium.

Circle and Dots Envelope Type of 2013

Printed by Johann Enschedé and Sons, the Netherlands. Designed by Sergio Baradat, U.S.

2013, Mar. 5 **Litho.**
UC31 U10 $1.10 **orange,** entire *(17,000)+* 2.40 2.40
Entire, first day cancel 2.40

No. UC31 Surcharged Like No. UC24

2014, June 6 **Litho.**
UC32 U10 $1.10+5c **multicolored,** entire 2.50 2.50
Entire, first day cancel 2.50

POSTAL CARDS

Values are for entire cards.

Type of Postage Issue of 1951

Printed by Dennison & Sons, Long Island City, N.Y.

1952, July 18 **Litho.**
UX1 A2 2c **blue,** *buff (899,415)* .25 .25
First day cancel *(116,023)* .45

Printed by British American Bank Note Co., Ltd., Ottawa, Canada.

1958, Sept. 22 **Litho.**
UX2 A2 3c **gray olive,** *buff (575,000)* .25 .25
First day cancel *(145,557)* .45

World Map, Sinusoidal Projection — PC1

Printed by Eureka Specialty Printing Co., Scranton, Pa.

1963, Apr. 26 **Litho.**
UX3 PC1 4c **light blue, violet blue, orange & bright citron** *(784,000)* .25 .25
First day cancel *(112,280)* .45
a. Bright citron omitted —

UN Emblem and Post Horn — PC2

Printed by Canadian Bank Note Co., Ltd., Ottawa. Designed by John Mason.

1969, Jan. 8 **Litho.**
UX4 PC2 5c **blue & black** *(500,000)* .25 .25
First day cancel *(95,975)* .45

"UN" — PC3

Printed by Government Printing Bureau, Tokyo. Designed by Asher Kalderon.

1973, Jan. 12 **Litho.**
UX5 PC3 6c **gray & multicolored** *(500,000)* .25 .25
First day cancel *(84,500)* .50

Type of 1973

Printed by Setelipaino, Finland.

1975, Jan. 10 **Litho.**

UX6 PC3 8c **light green & multi** *(450,000)*	.60	.60
First day cancel *(72,500)*		.45

UN Emblem — PC4

Printed by Setelipaino, Finland. Designed by George Hamori.

1977, June 27 **Litho.**

UX7 PC4 9c **multicolored** *(350,000)*	.60	.60
First day cancel *(70,000)*		.45

PC5

Printed by Courvoisier. Designed by Salahattin Kanidinc.

1982, Apr. 28 **Photo.**

UX8 PC5 13c **multicolored** *(350,000)*	.60	.60
First day cancel *(59,200)*		.50

Views of New York Headquarters PC6

Designs: No. UX9, Spring at U.N. Headquarters, vert. No. UX10, Cherry Blossoms, U.N. Gardens, vert. No. UXC11, Row of Flags of member states. No. UX12, U.N. General Assembly. No. UX13, River view, U.N. Headquarters. No. UX14, U.N. Headquarters, vert. No. UX15, Row of flags of member states, vert. No. UX16, Night view, U.N. Headquarters, vert. No. UX17, U.N. Security Council. No. UX18, U.N. Gardens.

Printed by Johann Enschede and Sons, the Netherlands. Designed by Thomas Lee, China, from photographs.

1989, Mar. 17 **Litho.**

UX9 PC6 15c **multicolored** *(120,000)+*	.65	1.00
First day cancel		2.00
UX10 PC6 15c **multicolored** *(120,000)+*	.65	1.00
First day cancel		2.00
UX11 PC6 15c **multicolored** *(120,000)+*	.65	1.00
First day cancel		2.00
UX12 PC6 15c **multicolored** *(120,000)+*	.65	1.00
First day cancel		2.00
UX13 PC6 15c **multicolored** *(120,000)+*	.65	1.00
First day cancel		2.00
UX14 PC6 36c **multicolored** *(120,000)+*	.85	1.50
First day cancel		2.00
UX15 PC6 36c **multicolored** *(120,000)+*	.85	1.50
First day cancel		2.00
UX16 PC6 36c **multicolored** *(120,000)+*	.85	1.50
First day cancel		2.00
UX17 PC6 36c **multicolored** *(120,000)+*	.85	1.50
First day cancel		2.00
UX18 PC6 36c **multicolored** *(120,000)+*	.85	1.50
First day cancel		2.00
Nos. UX9-UX18 (10)	7.50	12.50

Nos. UX9-UX13 and UX14-UX18 sold only in sets. Nos. UX9-UX13 sold for $2 and Nos. UX14-UX18 sold for $3.

First day cancels of Nos. UX9-UX18 total 125,526.

New York Headquarters Type of 1991

Printed by Mercury-Walch, Australia.

1992, Sept. 4 **Litho.**

UX19 A260 40c **blue** *(150,000)+*	3.50	4.00
First day cancel *(9,603)*		10.00

Secretariat Building, Roses — PC7

UN Complex — PC8

Printed by Mercury-Walsh, Australia.

1998, May 20 **Litho.**

UX20 PC7 21c **multicolored** *(150,000)+*	1.25	1.25
First day cancel		1.50
UX21 PC8 50c **multicolored** *(150,000)+*	2.00	2.00
First day cancel		2.25

Illustrations of the buildings and other scenes are shown on the back of each card.

New York Headquarters — PC9

2001, May 25 **Litho.**

UX22 PC9 70c **multicolored**	1.75	1.75
Entire, first day cancel		1.75

No. UX20 Surcharged

2002, June 30 **Litho.**

UX23 PC7 21c +2c **multicolored**	1.10	*2.00*
First day cancel		7.50

PC10

PC11

PC12

PC13

PC14

PC15

PC16

PC17

PC18

Illustrations from *This is the United Nations,* by M. Sasek — PC19

Printed by Banknote Corporation of America, US.

2003, Mar. 28 **Litho.**

UX24 PC10 23c **multicolored** *(61,500)*+	.75	.75
Entire, first day cancel		.75
UX25 PC11 23c **multicolored** *(61,500)*+	.75	.75
Entire, first day cancel		.75
UX26 PC12 23c **multicolored** *(61,500)*+	.75	.75
Entire, first day cancel		.75
UX27 PC13 23c **multicolored** *(61,500)*+	.75	.75
Entire, first day cancel		.75
UX28 PC14 23c **multicolored** *(61,500)*+	.75	.75
Entire, first day cancel		.75
UX29 PC15 70c **multicolored** *(86,500)*+	1.40	1.40
Entire, first day cancel		1.25
UX30 PC16 70c **multicolored** *(86,500)*+	1.40	1.40
Entire, first day cancel		1.25
UX31 PC17 70c **multicolored** *(86,500)*+	1.40	1.40
Entire, first day cancel		1.25
UX32 PC18 70c **multicolored** *(86,500)*+	1.40	1.40
Entire, first day cancel		1.25

UXC33 PC19 70c **multicolored** *(86,500)*+ 1.40 1.40
Entire, first day cancel 1.25
Nos. UX24-UX33 (10) 10.75 10.75

Nos. UX24-UX28 and UX29-UX33 were sold only in shrink-wrapped sets.

AIR POST POSTAL CARDS

Values are for entire cards.

Type of Air Post Stamp of 1957

Printed by British American Bank Note Co., Ltd., Ottawa.

1957, May 27 **Litho.**
UXC1 AP3 4c **maroon,** *buff (631,000)* .25 .30
First day cancel *(260,005)* .50

No. UXC1 Srchd. in Maroon at Left of Stamp

1959, June 5 **Litho.**
UXC2 AP3 4c + 1c **maroon,** buff (1,119,000) .30 .50
Cancel first day of public use, June 8 300.00
a. Double Surcharge —
b. Inverted Surcharge —
c. Double surcharge, one inverted *200.00*

This surcharge also exists on a No. U1 envelope. Status uncertain.

Type of Air Post Stamp, 1957

Printed by Eureka Specialty Printing Co., Scranton, Pa.

1959, Sept. 21 **Litho.**
UXC3 AP3 5c **crimson,** *buff (500,000)* .65 .65
First day cancel *(119,479)* .45

Outer Space — APC1

Printed by Eureka Specialty Printing Co., Scranton, Pa.

1963, Apr. 26 **Litho.**
UXC4 APC1 6c **black & blue** *(350,000)* .55 .60
First day cancel *(109,236)* .40

APC2

Printed by Eureka-Carlisle Co., Scranton, Pa. Designed by Olav S. Mathiesen.

1966, June 9 **Litho.**
UXC5 APC2 11c **dark red, rose, yellow & brown** *(764,500)* .30 .30
First day cancel *(162,588)* .40

1968, May 31 **Litho.**
UXC6 APC2 13c **dark green, bright green & yellow** *(829,000)* .40 .40
First day cancel *(106,500)* .45

UN Emblem and Stylized Planes — APC3

Printed by Canadian Bank Note Co., Ltd., Ottawa. Designed by Lawrence Kurtz.

1969, Jan. 8 **Litho.**
UXC7 APC3 8c **gray, dull yellow, lt blue, indigo & red** *(500,000)* .65 .65
First day cancel *(94,037)* .40

Type of Air Post Stamp of 1972

Printed by Government Printing Bureau, Tokyo. Designed by L. L. Dolan.

1972, Oct. 16 **Litho.**
UXC8 AP12 9c **orange, red, gray & green** *(500,000)* .45 .45
First day cancel *(85,600)* .50

Type of 1969

Printed by Government Printing Bureau, Tokyo

1972, Oct. 16 **Litho.**
UXC9 APC3 15c **lilac, light blue, pink & carmine** *(500,000)* .50 .50
First day cancel *(84,800)* .45

Types of Air Post Stamps, 1972-74

Printed by Setelipaino, Finland.

1975, Jan. 10 **Litho.**
UXC10 AP14 11c **greenish blue, blue & dark blue** *(250,000)* .50 .50
First day cancel *(70,500)* .45
UXC11 AP17 18c **gray & multicolored** *(250,000)* .50 .50
First day cancel *(70,500)* .45

Flying Mailman — APC4

Printed by Courvoisier. Designed by Arieh Glaser.

1982, Apr. 28 **Photo.**
UXC12 APC4 28c **multicolored** *(350,000)* .45 .50
First day cancel *(58,700)* 1.40

OFFICES IN GENEVA, SWITZERLAND

For use only on mail posted at the Palais des Nations (UN European Office), Geneva. Inscribed in French unless otherwise stated.

100 Centimes = 1 Franc

Catalogue values for all unused stamps in this country are for Never Hinged items.

Types of United Nations Issues 1961-69 and

United Nations European Office, Geneva — G1

Printed by Setelipaino, Finland (5c, 70c, 80c, 90c, 2fr, 10fr), Courvoisier, S.A., Switzerland (10c, 20c, 30c, 50c, 60c, 3fr).
Government Printing Office, Austria (75c) and Government Printing Office, Federal Republic of Germany (1fr).
Panes of 50. 30c designed by Ole Hamann, others as before.

Designs: 5c, UN Headquarters, New York, and world map. 10c, UN flag. 20c, Three men united before globe. 50c, Opening words of UN Charter. 60c, UN emblem over globe. 70c, "un" and UN emblem. 75c, "Flight Across Globe." 80c, UN Headquarters and emblem. 90c, Abstract group of flags. 1fr, UN emblem. 2fr, Stylized globe and weather vane. 3fr, Statue by Henrik Starcke. 10fr, "Peace, Justice, Security."
The 20c, 80c and 90c are inscribed in French. The 75c and 10fr carry French inscription at top, English at bottom.

1969-70 Photo. Unwmk.

Perf. 13 (5c, 70c, 90c); 12½x12 (10c);

1 A88 5c **purple & multi,** *Oct. 4, 1969 (3,300,000)* .25 .30
First day cover 1.00
Inscription block of 4 .40
a. Green omitted —
2 A52 10c **salmon & multi,** *Oct. 4, 1969 (4,300,000)+* .25 .30
First day cover 1.00
Inscription block of 4 .40 —

Perf. 11½ (20c-60c, 3fr)

3 A66 20c **black & multi,** *Oct. 4, 1969 (4,500.000)* .25 .30
First day cover 1.00
Inscription block of 4 .50 —
4 G1 30c **dark blue & multi,** *Oct. 4, 1969 (3,000,000)* .25 .30
First day cover 1.00
Inscription block of 4 .60 —
5 A77 50c **ultra & multi,** *Oct. 4, 1969 (3,300,000)* .25 .30
First day cover 1.25
Inscription block of 4 .80 —
6 A54 60c **dark brown, salmon & gold,** *Apr. 17, 1970 (3,300,000)+* .25 .30
First day cover 1.00
Inscription block of 4 1.25 —
7 A104 70c **red, black & gold,** *Sept. 22, 1970 (3,300,000)+* .30 .35
First day cover 1.00
Inscription block of 4 1.50 —

Perf. 11½x12 (75c)

8 AP8 75c **carmine rose & multi,** *Oct. 4, 1969 (3,300,000)+* .35 .40
First day cover 1.00
Inscription block of 4 1.75 —

Perf. 13½x14 (80c)

9 A78 80c **blue green, red & yellow,** *Sept. 22, 1970 (3,300,000)* .35 .40
First day cover 1.00
Inscription block of 4 1.75 —
10 A45 90c **blue & multi,** *Sept. 22, 1970 (3,300,000)* .40 .45
First day cover 1.00
Inscription block of 4 1.75 —

Litho. & Embossed

Perf. 14 (1fr)

11 A79 1fr **light & dark green,** *Oct. 4, 1969 (3,000,000)* .40 .45
First day cover 1.00
Inscription block of 4 2.00 —

Photo.

Perf. 12x11½ (2fr)

12 A67 2fr **blue & multi,** *Sept. 22, 1970 (3,000,000)+* .75 .85
First day cover 2.00
Inscription block of 4 3.50 —
13 A97 3fr **olive & multi,** *Oct. 4, 1969 (3,000,000)+* 1.00 1.10
First day cover 2.25
Inscription block of 4 5.00 —

Engr.

Perf. 12 (10fr)

14 A3 10fr **dark blue,** *Apr. 17, 1970 (2,250,000)+* 3.50 3.75
First day cover 8.50
Inscription block of 4 16.00 —
Nos. 1-14 (14) 8.55 9.55

+ Printing orders to June 1984.
First day covers of Nos. 1-5, 8, 11, 13 total 607,578; of Nos. 6 and 14, 140,055; of Nos. 7, 9-10 and 12, 220,000.

Sea Bed Type of UN

1971, Jan. 25 Photo. & Engr. *Perf. 13*

15 A114 30c **green & multi** *(1,935,871)* .25 .30
First day cover *(152,590)* 1.00
Inscription block of 4 .65 —

Refugee Type of UN

1971, Mar. 12 Litho. *Perf. 13x12½*

16 A115 50c **deep carmine, deep orange & black** *(1,820,114)* .25 .30
First day cover *(148,220)* 1.00
Inscription block of 4 1.05 —

World Food Program Type of UN

1971, Apr. 13 Photo. *Perf. 14*

17 A116 50c **dark violet & multi** *(1,824,170)* .25 .30
First day cover *(151,580)* 1.00
Inscription block of 4 1.05 —

UPU Headquarters Type of UN

1971, May 28 Photo. *Perf. 11½*

18 A117 75c **green & multi** *(1,821,878)* .35 .40
First day cover *(140,679)* 1.00
Inscription block of 4 1.00 —

Eliminate Racial Discrimination Types of UN

Designed by Daniel Gonzague (30c) and Ole Hamann (50c).

1971, Sept. 21 Photo. *Perf. 13½*

19 A118 30c **blue & multi** *(1,838,474)* .25 .30
First day cover 1.00
Inscription block of 4 1.00 —
20 A119 50c **yellow green & multi** *(1,804,126)* .25 .30
First day cover 1.00
First day cover, #19-20 1.25
Inscription block of 4 1.10 —

First day covers of Nos. 19-20 total 308,420.

Picasso Type of UN

1971, Nov. 19 Photo. *Perf. 11½*

21 A122 1.10fr **multicolored** *(1,467,993)* .75 .80
First day cover *(195,215)* 1.25
Inscription block of 4 3.00 —

Palais des Nations, Geneva — G2

Printed by Courvoisier, S. A. Panes of 50. Designed by Ole Hamann.

1972, Jan. 5 **Photo.** ***Perf. 11½***

22 G2 40c **olive, blue, salmon & dark green** *(3,500,000)+* .25 .30
First day cover *(152,300)* 1.00
Inscription block of 4 1.05 —

+ Initial printing order.

Nuclear Weapons Type of UN

1972, Feb. 14 **Photo.** ***Perf. 13½x14***

23 A124 40c **yellow, green, black, rose & gray** *(1,567,305)* .25 .30
First day cover *(151,350)* 1.00
Inscription block of 4 1.25 —

World Health Day Type of UN

1972, Apr. 7 **Litho. & Engr.** ***Perf. 13x13½***

24 A125 80c **black & multi** *(1,543,368)* .45 .50
First day cover *(192,600)* 1.00
Inscription block of 4 2.00 —

Human Environment Type of UN

Lithographed & Embossed

1972, June 5 ***Perf. 12½x14***

25 A126 40c **olive, lemon, green & blue** *(1,594,089)* .25 .30
First day cover 1.00
Inscription block of 4 1.00 —
26 A126 80c **ultra, pink, green & blue** *(1,568,009)* .45 .50
First day cover 1.40
First day cover, #25-26 1.75
Inscription block of 4 1.80 —

First day covers of Nos. 25-26 total 296,700.

Economic Commission for Europe Type of UN

1972, Sept. 11 **Litho.** ***Perf. 13x13½***

27 A127 1.10fr **red & multi** *(1,604,082)* 1.00 1.10
First day cover *(149,630)* 1.75
Inscription block of 4 4.25 —

Art at UN (Sert) Type of UN

1972, Nov. 17 **Photo.** ***Perf. 12x12½***

28 A128 40c **gold, red & brown** *(1,932,428)* .30 .35
First day cover 1.00
Inscription block of 4 1.25 —
29 A128 80c **gold, brown & olive** *(1,759,600)* .60 .65
First day cover 1.25
First day cover, #28-29 1.75
Inscription block of 4 2.50 —

First day covers of Nos. 28-29 total 295,470.

Disarmament Decade Type of UN

1973, Mar. 9 **Litho.** ***Perf. 13½x13***

30 A129 60c **violet & multi** *(1,586,845)* .40 .45
First day cover 1.00
Inscription block of 4 1.60 —
31 A129 1.10fr **olive & multi** *(1,408,169)* .85 .90
First day cover 1.40
First day cover, #30-31 1.75
Inscription block of 4 3.50 —

First day covers of Nos. 30-31 total 260,680.

Drug Abuse Type of UN

1973, Apr. 13 **Photo.** ***Perf. 13½***

32 A130 60c **blue & multi** *(1,481,432)* .45 .50
First day cover *(144,760)* 1.00
Inscription block of 4 1.90 —

Volunteers Type of UN

1973, May 25 **Photo.** ***Perf. 14***

33 A131 80c **gray green & multi** *(1,443,519)* .35 .40
First day cover *(143,430)* 1.10
Inscription block of 4 1.50 —

Namibia Type of UN

1973, Oct. 1 **Photo.** ***Perf. 13½***

34 A132 60c **red & multi** *(1,673,898)* .35 .40
First day cover *(148,077)* 1.00
Inscription block of 4 1.50 —

Human Rights Type of UN

1973, Nov. 16 **Photo.** ***Perf. 13½***

35 A133 40c **ultramarine & multi** *(1,480,791)* .30 .35
First day cover 1.00
Inscription block of 4 1.25 —
36 A133 80c **olive & multi** *(1,343,349)* .50 .55
First day cover 1.25
First day cover, #35-36 1.75
Inscription block of 4 2.10 —

First day covers of Nos. 35-36 total 438,260.

ILO Headquarters Type of UN

1974, Jan. 11 **Photo.** ***Perf. 14***

37 A134 60c **violet & multi** *(1,212,703)* .45 .50
First day cover 1.00
Inscription block of 4 1.90 —
38 A134 80c **brown & multi** *(1,229,851)* .65 .70
First day cover 1.10
First day cover, #37-38 1.25
Inscription block of 4 2.75 —

First day covers of Nos. 37-38 total 240,660.

Centenary of UPU Type of UN

1974, Mar. 22 **Litho.** ***Perf. 12½***

39 A135 30c **gold & multi** *(1,567,517)* .25 .30
First day cover 1.00
Inscription block of 4 1.25 —
40 A135 60c **gold & multi** *(1,430,839)* .60 .65
First day cover 1.25
First day cover, #39-40 1.50
Inscription block of 4 2.50 —

First day covers of Nos. 39-40 total 231,840.

Art at UN (Portinari) Type of UN

1974, May 6 **Photo.** ***Perf. 14***

41 A136 60c **dark red & multi** *(1,202,357)* .40 .45
First day cover 1.00
Inscription block of 4 1.75 —
42 A136 1fr **green & multi** *(1,230,045)* .70 .75
First day cover 1.20
First day cover, #41-42 1.50
Inscription block of 4 3.00 —

First day covers of Nos. 41-42 total 249,130.

World Population Year Type of UN

1974, Oct. 18 **Photo.** ***Perf. 14***

43 A140 60c **bright green & multi** *(1,292,954)* .50 .55
First day cover 1.00
Inscription block of 4 2.25 —
44 A140 80c **brown & multi** *(1,221,288)* .70 .75
First day cover 1.00
First day cover, #43-44 1.25
Inscription block of 4 3.25 —

First day covers of Nos. 43-44 total 189,597.

Law of the Sea Type of UN

1974, Nov. 22 **Photo.** ***Perf. 14***

45 A141 1.30fr **blue & multicolored** *(1,266,270)* 1.00 1.10
First day cover *(181,000)* 1.25
Inscription block of 4 4.00 —

Outer Space Type of UN

1975, Mar. 14 **Litho.** ***Perf. 13***

46 A142 60c **multicolored** *(1,339,704)* .50 .55
First day cover 1.00
Inscription block of 4 2.00 —

47 A142 90c **multicolored** *(1,383,888)* .75 .80
First day cover 1.00
First day cover, #46-47 1.50
Inscription block of 4 3.25 —

First day covers of Nos. 46-47 total 250,400.

International Women's Year Type of UN

1975, May 9 Litho. *Perf. 15*

48 A143 60c **multicolored** *(1,176,080)* .40 .45
First day cover 1.00
Inscription block of 4 1.90 —
49 A143 90c **multicolored** *(1,167,863)* .70 .75
First day cover 1.00
First day cover, #48-49 1.50
Inscription block of 4 3.25 —

First day covers of Nos. 48-49 total 250,660.

30th Anniversary Type of UN

1975, June 26 Litho. *Perf. 13*

50 A144 60c **green & multi** *(1,442,075)* .40 .45
First day cover 1.00
Inscription block of 4 2.00 —
51 A144 90c **violet & multi** *(1,612,411)* .70 .75
First day cover 1.00
First day cover, #50-51 1.25
Inscription block of 4 3.25 —

Souvenir Sheet

Imperf

52 Sheet of 2 *(1,210,148)* 1.00 1.10
a. A144 60c **green & multicolored** .30 .35
b. A144 90c **violet & multicolored** .60 .65
First day cover 1.25

No. 52 has blue and bister margin with inscription and UN emblem. Size: 92x70mm.

First day covers of Nos. 50-52 total 402,500.

Namibia Type of UN

1975, Sept. 22 Photo. *Perf. 13½*

53 A145 50c **multicolored** *(1,261,019)* .30 .35
First day cover 1.00
Inscription block of 4 1.25 —
54 A145 1.30fr **multicolored** *(1,241,990)* .85 .90
First day cover 1.10
First day cover, #53-54 1.25
Inscription block of 4 4.00 —

First day covers of Nos. 53-54 total 226,260.

Peace-keeping Operations Type of UN

1975, Nov. 21 Engr. *Perf. 12½*

55 A146 60c **greenish blue** *(1,249,305)* .35 .40
First day cover 1.00
Inscription block of 4 1.50 —
56 A146 70c **bright violet** *(1,249,935)* .65 .65
First day cover 1.00
First day cover, #55-56 1.25
Inscription block of 4 2.75 —

First day covers of Nos. 55-56 total 229,245.

WFUNA Type of UN

1976, Mar. 12 Photo. *Perf. 14*

57 A152 90c **multicolored** *(1,186,563)* .90 .95
First day cover 1.00
Inscription block of 4 4.00 —

First day covers of No. 57 total 121,645.

UNCTAD Type of UN

1976, Apr. 23 Photo. *Perf. 11½*

58 A153 1.10fr **sepia & multi** *(1,167,284)* .90 .95
First day cover *(107,030)* 1.25
Inscription block of 4 4.00 —

Habitat Type of UN

1976, May 28 Photo. *Perf. 14*

59 A154 40c **dull blue & multi** *(1,258,986)* .25 .30
First day cover 1.00
Inscription block of 4 1.00 —
60 A154 1.50fr **violet & multi** *(1,110,507)* .75 .80
First day cover 1.25
First day cover, #59-60 1.60
Inscription block of 4 3.50 —

First day covers of Nos. 59-60 total 242,530.

UN Emblem, Post Horn and Rainbow — G3

UN Postal Administration, 25th anniversary.

Printed by Courvoisier, S.A. Panes of 20 (5x4). Designed by Hector Viola.

1976, Oct. 8 Photo. *Perf. 11½*

61 G3 80c **tan & multicolored** *(1,794,009)* .50 .55
First day cover 2.00
Inscription block of 4 2.50 —
62 A3 1.10fr **light green & multi** *(1,751,178)* 1.60 1.75
First day cover 2.00
Inscription block of 4 8.00 —
First day cover, #61-62 3.00
Panes of 20, #61-62 37.50

Upper margin blocks are inscribed "XXVe ANNIVERSAIRE"; lower margin blocks "ADMINISTRATION POSTALE DES NATIONS UNIES."

First day covers of Nos. 61-62 total 152,450.

World Food Council Type of UN

1976, Nov. 19 Litho. *Perf. 14½*

63 A156 70c **multicolored** *(1,507,630)* .50 .55
First day cover *(170,540)* 1.00
Inscription block of 4 2.25 —

WIPO Type of UN

1977, Mar. 11 Photo. *Perf. 14*

64 A157 80c **red & multi** *(1,232,664)* .60 .65
First day cover *(212,470)* 1.00
Inscription block of 4 2.75 —

Drop of Water and Globe — G4

UN Water Conference, Mar del Plata, Argentina, Mar. 14-25.

Printed by Government Printing Bureau, Tokyo. Panes of 50. Designed by Eliezer Weishoff.

1977, Apr. 22 Photo. *Perf. 13½x13*

65 G4 80c **ultramarine & multi** *(1,146,650)* .50 .55
First day cover 1.00
Inscription block of 4 2.25 —
66 G4 1.10fr **dark carmine & multi** *(1,138,236)* .80 .85
First day cover 1.25
First day cover, #65-66 1.75
Inscription block of 4 3.50 —

First day covers of Nos. 65-66 total 289,836.

Hands Protecting UN Emblem — G5

UN Security Council.
Printed by Heraclio Fournier, S.A., Spain. Panes of 50. Designed by George Hamori.

1977, May 27 **Photo.** ***Perf. 11***

67	G5 80c **blue & multi** *(1,096,030)*	.50	.55
	First day cover		1.00
	Inscription block of 4	2.25	—
68	G5 1.10fr **emerald & multi** *(1,075,925)*	.80	.85
	First day cover		1.25
	First day cover, #67-68		1.75
	Inscription block of 4	3.50	—

First day covers of Nos. 67-68 total 305,349.

Colors of Five Races Spun into One Firm Rope — G6

Fight against racial discrimination.
Printed by Setelipaino, Finland. Panes of 50. Designed by M. A. Munnawar.

1977, Sept. 19 **Litho.** ***Perf. 13½x13***

69	G6 40c **multicolored** *(1,218,834)*	.25	.30
	First day cover		1.00
	Inscription block of 4	1.10	—
70	G6 1.10fr **multicolored** *(1,138,250)*	.65	.70
	First day cover		1.25
	First day cover, #69-70		1.75
	Inscription block of 4	2.75	—

First day covers of Nos. 69-70 total 308,722.

Atomic Energy Turning Partly into Olive Branch — G7

Peaceful uses of atomic energy.
Printed by Heraclio Fournier, S.A., Spain. Panes of 50. Designed by Witold Janowski and Marek Freudenreich.

1977, Nov. 18 **Photo.** ***Perf. 14***

71	G7 80c **dark carmine & multi** *(1,147,787)*	.55	.60
	First day cover		1.00
	Inscription block of 4	2.50	—
72	G7 1.10fr **Prussian blue & multi** *(1,121,209)*	.75	.80
	First day cover		1.20
	First day cover, #71-72		1.50
	Inscription block of 4	3.50	—

First day covers of Nos. 71-72 total 298,075.

"Tree" of Doves — G8

Printed by Questa Colour Security Printers, United Kingdom. Panes of 50. Designed by M. Hioki.

1978, Jan. 27 **Litho.** ***Perf. 14½***

73	G8 35c **multicolored** *(3,000,000)+*	.25	.30
	First day cover *(259,735)*		1.00
	Inscription block of 4	.75	—

Globes with Smallpox Distribution — G9

Global eradication of smallpox.
Printed by Courvoisier, S.A. Panes of 50. Designed by Eliezer Weishoff.

1978, Mar. 31 **Photo.** ***Perf. 12x11½***

74	G9 80c **yellow & multi** *(1,116,044)*	.60	.65
	First day cover		1.00
	Inscription block of 4	2.50	—
75	G9 1.10fr **light green & multi** *(1,109,946)*	.90	.95
	First day cover		1.25
	First day cover, #74-75		2.00
	Inscription block of 4	3.75	—

First day covers of Nos. 74-75 total 254,700.

Namibia Type of UN

1978, May 5 **Photo.** ***Perf. 12***

76	A166 80c **multicolored** *(1,183,208)*	.85	.90
	First day cover *(316,610)*		1.00
	Inscription block of 4	3.50	—

Jets and Flight Patterns — G10

International Civil Aviation Organization for "Safety in the Air."
Printed by Heraclio Fournier, S.A., Spain. Panes of 50. Designed by Tomas Savrda.

1978, June 12 **Photo.** ***Perf. 14***

77	G10 70c **multicolored** *(1,275,106)*	.40	.45
	First day cover		1.00
	Inscription block of 4	1.75	—
78	G10 80c **multicolored** *(1,144,339)*	.70	.75
	First day cover		1.00
	First day cover, #77-78		1.60
	Inscription block of 4	3.00	—

First day covers of Nos. 77-78 total 255,700.

General Assembly, Flags and Globe — G11

Printed by Government Printing Bureau, Tokyo. Panes of 50. Designed by Henry Bencsath.

1978, Sept. 15 — Photo. — *Perf. 13½*

79	G11	70c **multicolored** *(1,204,441)*	.45	.50
		First day cover		1.00
		Inscription block of 4	2.25	—
80	G11	1.10fr **multicolored** *(1,183,889)*	.85	.90
		First day cover		1.25
		First day cover, #79-80		1.75
		Inscription block of 4	3.75	—

First day covers of Nos. 79-80 total 245,600.

Technical Cooperation Type of UN

1978, Nov. 17 — Photo. — *Perf. 14*

81	A169	80c **multicolored** *(1,173,220)*	.70	.75
		First day cover *(264,700)*		1.00
		Inscription block of 4	3.25	—

Seismograph Recording Earthquake — G12

Office of the UN Disaster Relief Coordinator (UNDRO).
Printed by Heraclio Fournier, S.A., Spain. Panes of 50. Designed by Michael Klutmann.

1979, Mar. 9 — Photo. — *Perf. 14*

82	G12	80c **multicolored** *(1,183,155)*	.50	.55
		First day cover		1.00
		Inscription block of 4	2.00	—
83	G12	1.50fr **multicolored** *(1,168,121)*	.80	.85
		First day cover		1.40
		First day cover, #82-83		1.90
		Inscription block of 4	3.50	—

First day covers of Nos. 82-83 total 162,070.

Children and Rainbow — G13

International Year of the Child.
Printed by Heraclio Fournier, S.A., Spain. Panes of 20 (5x4). Designed by Arieh Glaser.

1979, May 4 — Photo. — *Perf. 14*

84	G13	80c **multicolored** *(2,251,623)*	.35	.40
		First day cover		1.25
		Inscription block of 4	1.60	—
85	G13	1.10fr **multicolored** *(2,220,463)*	.65	.70
		First day cover		1.75
		Inscription block of 4	2.75	—
		First day cover, #84-85		1.25
		Panes of 20, #84-85	20.00	

First day covers of Nos. 84-85 total 176,120.

Namibia Type of UN

1979, Oct. 5 — Litho. — *Perf. 13½*

86	A176	1.10fr **multicolored** *(1,229,830)*	.60	.65
		First day cover *(134,160)*		1.25
		Inscription block of 4	2.25	—

International Court of Justice, Scales — G14

International Court of Justice, The Hague, Netherlands.
Printed by Setelipaino, Finland. Panes of 50. Designed by Kyohei Maeno.

1979, Nov. 9 — Litho. — *Perf. 13x13½*

87	G14	80c **multicolored** *(1,123,193)*	.40	.45
		First day cover		1.00
		Inscription block of 4	1.75	—
88	G14	1.10fr **multicolored** *(1,063,067)*	.60	.65
		First day cover		1.25
		First day cover, #87-88		1.75
		Inscription block of 4	2.75	—

First day covers of Nos. 87-88 total 158,170.

New Economic Order Type of UN

1980, Jan. 11 — Litho. — *Perf. 15x14½*

89	A179	80c **multicolored** *(1,315,918)*	.85	.90
		First day cover *(176,250)*		1.00
		Inscription block of 4	3.50	—

Women's Year Emblem — G15

United Nations Decade for Women.
Printed by Questa Colour Security Printers, United Kingdom. Panes of 50. Designed by M.A. Munnawar.

1980, Mar. 7 — Litho. — *Perf. 14½x15*

90	G15	40c **multicolored** *(1,265,221)*	.30	.35
		First day cover		1.00
		Inscription block of 4	1.40	—
91	G15	70c **multicolored** *(1,240,375)*	.70	.75
		First day cover		1.10
		First day cover, #90-91		1.25
		Inscription block of 4	3.50	—

First day covers of Nos. 90-91 total 204,350.

Peace-keeping Operations Type of UN

1980, May 16 — Litho. — *Perf. 14x13*

92	A181	1.10fr **blue & green** *(1,335,391)*	.85	.90
		First day cover *(184,700)*		1.00
		Inscription block of 4	3.50	—

35th Anniversary Type of UN and Dove and "35" — G16

35th Anniversary of the United Nations.

Printed by Ashton-Potter Ltd., Canada. Panes of 50. Designed by Gidon Sagi (40c), Cemalattin Mutver (70c).

1980, June 26 **Litho.** ***Perf. 13x13½***

93 G16 40c **blue green & black** *(1,462,005)*	.35	.35
First day cover		1.00
Inscription block of 4	1.40	—
94 A183 70c **multicolored** *(1,444,639)*	.65	.70
First day cover		1.00
First day cover, #93-94		1.50
Inscription block of 4	3.00	—

Souvenir Sheet

Imperf

95 Sheet of 2 *(1,235,200)*	1.10	1.20
a. G16 40c **blue green & black**	.30	.35
b. A183 70c **multicolored**	.80	.85
First day cover		1.00

First day covers of Nos. 93-95 total 379,800.

ECOSOC Type of UN and

Family Climbing Line Graph — G17

Printed by Ashton-Potter Ltd., Canada. Panes of 50. Designed by Eliezer Weishoff (40c), A. Medina Medina (70c).

1980, Nov. 21 **Litho.** ***Perf. 13½x13***

96 A186 40c **multicolored** *(986,435)*	.30	.35
First day cover		1.00
Inscription block of 4	1.25	—
97 G17 70c **multicolored** *(1,016,462)*	.60	.65
First day cover		1.00
First day cover #96-97		1.50
Inscription block of 4	2.50	—

Economic and Social Council.

First day covers of Nos. 96-97 total 210,460.

Palestinian Rights

Printed by Courvoisier S.A., Switzerland. Panes of 50. Designed by David Dewhurst.

1981, Jan. 30 **Photo.** ***Perf. 12x11½***

98 A188 80c **multicolored** *(1,031,737)*	.55	.60
First day cover *(117,480)*		1.00
Inscription block of 4	2.75	—

International Year of the Disabled.

Printed by Heraclio Fournier S.A., Spain. Panes of 50.

Designed by G.P. Van der Hyde (40c) and Sophia van Heeswijk (1.50fr).

1981, Mar. 6 **Photo.** ***Perf. 14***

99 A190 40c **black & blue** *(1,057,909)*	.25	.30
First day cover		1.00
Inscription block of 4	1.00	—
100 V4 1.50fr **black & red** *(994,748)*	1.00	1.10
First day cover		1.25
First day cover, #99-100		1.75
Inscription block of 4	4.00	—

First day covers of Nos. 99-100 total 202,853.

Art Type of UN

1981, Apr. 15 **Photo.** ***Perf. 11½***

Granite Paper

101 A191 80c **multicolored** *(1,128,782)*	.80	.85
First day cover *(121,383)*		1.00
Inscription block of 4	3.75	—

Energy Type of 1981

1981, May 29 **Litho.** ***Perf. 13***

102 A192 1.10fr **multicolored** *(1,096,806)*	.75	.80
First day cover *(113,700)*		1.25
Inscription block of 4	3.50	—

Volunteers Program Type and

Symbols of Science, Agriculture and Industry — G18

Printed by Walsall Security Printers, Ltd., United Kingdom. Panes of 50.

Designed by Gabriele Nussgen (40c), Bernd Mirbach (70c).

1981, Nov. 13 **Litho.**

103 A194 40c **multicolored** *(1,032,700)*	.45	.50
First day cover		1.00
Inscription block of 4	2.25	—
104 G18 70c **multicolored** *(1,123,672)*	.90	.95
First day cover		1.00
First day cover, #103-104		1.50
Inscription block of 4	4.25	—

First day covers of Nos. 103-104 total 190,667.

Fight against Apartheid — G19

Flower of Flags — G20

Printed by Courvoisier, S.A., Switzerland. Panes of 50. Designed by Tomas Savrda (30c); Dietmar Kowall (1fr).

1982, Jan. 22 ***Perf. 11½x12***

105 G19 30c **multicolored** *(3,000,000)+*	.25	.30
First day cover		1.00
Inscription block of 4	1.10	—
106 G20 1fr **multicolored** *(3,000,000)+*	.80	.85
First day cover		1.00
First day cover, #105-106		1.25
Inscription block of 4	3.25	—

First day covers of Nos. 105-106 total 199,347.

Human Environment Type of UN and

Sun and Leaves — G21

10th Anniversary of United Nations Environment Program.

Printed by Joh. Enschede en Zonen, Netherlands. Panes of 50. Designed by Sybille Brunner (40c); Philine Hartert (1.20fr).

1982, Mar. 19 **Litho.** ***Perf. 13½x13***

107 G21 40c **multicolored** *(948,743)*	.30	.35
First day cover		1.00
Inscription block of 4	1.50	—

108 A199 1.20fr **multicolored** *(901,096)* 1.10 1.40
First day cover 1.10
First day cover, #107-108 1.40
Inscription block of 4 5.25 —

First day covers of Nos. 107-108 total 190,155.

Outer Space Type of UN and

Satellite, Applications of Space Technology — G22

Exploration and Peaceful Uses of Outer Space.
Printed by Enschede. Panes of 50. Designed by Wiktor C. Nerwinski (80c) and George Hamori (1fr).

1982, June 11 **Litho.** ***Perf. 13x13½***
109 A201 80c **multicolored** *(964,593)* .60 .65
First day cover 1.00
Inscription block of 4 3.00 —
110 G22 1fr **multicolored** *(898,367)* .80 .85
First day cover 1.25
First day cover, #109-110 1.50
Inscription block of 4 3.75 —

First day covers of Nos. 109-110 total 205,815.

Conservation & Protection of Nature

1982, Nov. 19 **Photo.** ***Perf. 14***
111 A202 40c Bird *(928,143)* .45 .50
First day cover 1.00
Inscription block of 4 2.10 —
112 A202 1.50fr Reptile *(047,173)* 1.10 1.20
First day cover 1.25
First day cover, #111-112 1.75
Inscription block of 4 5.25 —

First day covers of Nos. 111-112 total 198,504.

World Communications Year

1983, Jan. 28 **Litho.** ***Perf. 13***
113 A204 1.20fr **multicolored** *(894,025)* 1.25 1.40
First day cover *(131,075)* 1.25
Inscription block of 4 5.25 —

Safety at Sea Type of UN and

G23

Designed by Valentin Wurnitsch (A22).

1983, Mar. 18 **Litho.** ***Perf. 14½***
114 A205 40c **multicolored** *(892,365)* .40 .45
First day cover 1.00
Inscription block of 4 1.75 —
115 G23 80c **multicolored** *(882,720)* .80 .85
First day cover 1.00
First day cover, #114-115 1.50
Inscription block of 4 3.50 —

First day covers of Nos. 114-115 total 219,592.

World Food Program

1983, Apr. 22 **Engr.** ***Perf. 13½***
116 A207 1.50fr **blue** *(876,591)* 1.25 1.40
First day cover 1.25
Inscription block of 4 5.25 —

Trade Type of UN and

G24

Designed by Wladyslaw Brykczynski (A23).

1983, June 6 **Litho.** ***Perf. 14***
117 A208 80c **multicolored** *(902,495)* .50 .55
First day cover 1.00
Inscription block of 4 2.50 —
118 G24 1.10fr **multicolored** *(921,424)* .90 .95
First day cover 1.00
First day cover, #117-118 1.40
Inscription block of 4 4.00 —

First day covers of Nos. 117-118 total 146,507.

Homo Humus Humanitas — G25

Right to Create — G26

35th Anniversary of the Universal Declaration of Human Rights.
Printed by Government Printing Office, Austria. Designed by Friedensreich Hundertwasser, Austria. Panes of 16 (4x4).

1983, Dec. 9 **Photo. & Engr.** ***Perf. 13½***
119 G25 40c **multicolored** *(1,770,921)* .45 .50
First day cover 1.00
Inscription block of 4 2.00 —

120 G26 1.20fr **multicolored** *(1,746,735)* .95 1.00
First day cover 1.10
Inscription block of 4 4.25 —
First day cover, #119-120 1.40
Panes of 16, #119-120 22.50

First day covers of Nos. 119-120 total 315,052.

International Conference on Population Type

1984, Feb. 3 **Litho.** ***Perf. 14***

121 A212 1.20fr **multicolored** *(776,879)* .90 .95
First day cover *(105,377)* 1.00
Inscription block of 4 4.00 —

Fishing — G27

Women Farm Workers, Africa — G28

World Food Day, Oct. 16
Printed by Walsall Security Printers, Ltd., United Kingdom. Panes of 50. Designed by Adth Vanooijen, Netherlands.

1984, Mar. 15 **Litho.** ***Perf. 14½***

122 G27 50c **multicolored** *(744,506)* .30 .35
First day cover 1.00
Inscription block of 4 1.60 —
123 G28 80c **multicolored** *(784,047)* .60 .65
First day cover 1.25
First day cover, #122-123 1.75
Inscription block of 4 2.75 —

First day covers of Nos. 122-123 total 155,234.

Valletta, Malta — G29

Los Glaciares National Park, Argentina — G30

World Heritage
Printed by Harrison and Sons, United Kingdom. Panes of 50. Designs adapted by Rocco J. Callari, US, and Thomas Lee, China.

1984, Apr. 18 **Litho.** ***Perf. 14***

124 G29 50c **multicolored** *(763,627)* .60 .65
First day cover 1.00
Inscription block of 4 2.50 —
125 G30 70c **multicolored** *(784,489)* .85 .90
First day cover 1.25
First day cover, #124-125 1.75
Inscription block of 4 4.50 —

First day covers of Nos. 124-125 total 164,498.

G31

G32

Future for Refugees
Printed by Courvoisier. Panes of 50. Designed by Hans Erni, Switzerland.

1984, May 29 **Photo.** ***Perf. 11½***

126 G31 35c **multicolored** *(880,762)* .30 .35
First day cover 1.00
Inscription block of 4 1.50 —
127 G32 1.50fr **multicolored** *(829,895)* 1.10 1.20
First day cover 1.25
First day cover, #126-127 1.75
Inscription block of 4 5.00 —

First day covers of Nos. 126-127 total 170,306.

International Youth Year — G33

Printed by Waddingtons Ltd., United Kingdom. Panes of 50. Designed by Eliezer Weishoff, Israel.

1984, Nov. 15 **Litho.** ***Perf. 13½***

128 G33 1.20fr **multicolored** *(755,622)* 1.25 1.40
First day cover *(96,680)* 1.00
Inscription block of 4 5.50 —

ILO Type of UN and

ILO Turin Center — G34

Printed by the Government Printing Bureau, Japan. Panes of 50. Engraved by Mamoru Iwakuni and Hiroshi Ozaki, Japan (No. 129) and adapted from photographs by Rocco J. Callari, US, and Thomas Lee, China (No. 130).

1985, Feb. 1 **Engr.** ***Perf. 13½***

129 A220 80c **dull red** *(654,431)* .70 .75
First day cover 1.00
Inscription block of 4 3.00 —
130 G34 1.20fr U Thant Pavilion *(609,493)* 1.10 1.20
First day cover 1.50
First day cover, #129-130 2.25
Inscription block of 4 4.75 —

First day covers of Nos. 129-130 total 118,467.

UN University Type

50c, Pastoral scene, advanced communications.

1985, Mar. 15 **Photo.** ***Perf. 11½***

131 A221 50c multi *(625,087)* .60 .65
First day cover 1.00
Inscription block of 4 2.75 —
132 A221 80c like No. 131 *(712,674)* 1.00 1.10
First day cover 1.25
First day cover, #131-132 1.75
Inscription block of 4 4.50 —

First day covers of Nos. 131-132 total 93,324.

Flying Postman — G35

Interlocked Peace Doves — G36

Printed by Carl Ueberreuter Druck and Verlag M. Salzer, Austria. Panes of 50. Designed by Arieh Glaser, Israel (No. 133), and Carol Sliwka, Poland (No. 134).

1985, May 10 **Litho.** ***Perf. 14***

133 G35 20c **multicolored** *(2,000,000)+* .25 .30
First day cover 1.00
Inscription block of 4 1.25 —
134 G36 1.20fr **multicolored** *(2,000,000)+* 1.25 1.40
First day cover 1.50
First day cover, #133-134 2.00
Inscription block of 4 6.00 —

First day covers of Nos. 133-134 total 103,165.

40th Anniversary Type

Designed by Rocco J. Callari, U.S., and Thomas Lee, China (No. 137).

1985, June 26 **Photo.** ***Perf. 12 x 11½***

135 A224 50c **multicolored** *(764,924)* .60 .65
First day cover 1.00
Inscription block of 4 2.50 —
136 A225 70c **multicolored** *(779,074)* .90 .95
First day cover 1.25
First day cover, #135-136 2.00
Inscription block of 4 4.00 —

Souvenir Sheet

Imperf

137 Sheet of 2 *(498,041)* 2.25 2.40
a. A224 50c **multicolored** .85 .90
b. A225 70c **multicolored** 1.10 1.20
First day cover 1.25

First day covers of Nos. 135-137 total 252,418.

UNICEF Child Survival Campaign Type

Printed by the Government Printing Bureau, Japan. Panes of 50. Designed by Mel Harris, United Kingdom (No. 138) and Adth Vanooijen, Netherlands (No. 139).

1985, Nov. 22 **Photo. & Engr.** ***Perf. 13½***

138 A226 50c Three girls *(657,409)* .40 .45
First day cover 1.00
Inscription block of 4 2.00 —
139 A226 1.20fr Infant drinking *(593,568)* 1.10 1.20
First day cover 1.25
First day cover, #138-139 1.75
Inscription block of 4 4.50 —

First day covers of Nos. 138-139 total 217,696.

Africa in Crisis Type

Printed by Helio Courvoisier, Switzerland. Panes of 50. Designed by Alemayehou Gabremedhiu, Ethiopia.

1986, Jan. 31 **Photo.** ***Perf. 11½x12***

140 A227 1.40fr Mother, hungry children *(590,576)* 1.25 1.40
First day cover *(80,159)* 2.00
Inscription block of 4 5.25 —

UN Development Program Type

Forestry. Printed by the Government Printing Bureau, Japan. Pane of 40, 2 blocks of 4 horizontal and 5 blocks of 4 vertical. Designed by Thomas Lee, China.

1986, Mar. 14 **Photo.** ***Perf. 13½***

141 A228 35c Erosion control *(547,567)* 1.60 1.75
142 A228 35c Logging *(547,567)* 1.60 1.75
143 A228 35c Lumber transport *(547,567)* 1.60 1.75
144 A228 35c Nursery *(547,567)* 1.60 1.75
a. Block of 4, #141-144 6.50 7.50
First day cover, #144a 8.50
First day cover, #141-144, each 2.50
Inscription block of 4, #144a 7.50 —
Pane of 40, #141-144 70.00

No. 144a has a continuous design.
First day covers of Nos. 141-144 total 200,212.

Dove and Sun — G37

Printed by Questa Color Security Printers, Ltd., United Kingdom. Panes of 50. Designed by Ramon Alcantara Rodriguez, Mexico.

1986, Mar. 14 **Litho.** ***Perf. 15x14½***

145 G37 5c **multicolored** *(2,000,000)+* .25 .30
First day cover *(58,908)* 1.00
Inscription block of 4 .60 —

Stamp Collecting Type

Designs: 50c, UN Human Rights stamp. 80c, UN stamps. Printed by the Swedish Post Office, Sweden. Panes of 50. Designed by Czeslaw Slania and Ingalill Axelsson, Sweden.

1986, May 22 **Engr.** ***Perf. 12½***

146 A229 50c **dark green & henna brown** *(722,015)* .60 .65
First day cover 1.50
Inscription block of 4 2.50 —
147 A229 80c **dark green & yellow orange** *(750,945)* .90 .95
First day cover 1.50
First day cover, #146-147 1.75
Inscription block of 4 3.75 —

First day covers of Nos. 146-147 total 137,653.

Flags and Globe as Dove — G38

Peace in French — G39

International Peace Year. Printed by the Government Printing Bureau, Japan. Panes of 50. Designed by Renato Ferrini, Italy (No. 148), and Salahattin Kanidinc, US (No. 149).

1986, June 20 **Photo. & Embossed** ***Perf. 13½***

148 G38 45c **multicolored** *(620,978)* .60 .65
First day cover 1.00
Inscription block of 4 2.75 —
149 G39 1.40fr **multicolored** *(559,658)* 1.25 1.40
First day cover 1.60
First day cover, #148-149 3.00
Inscription block of 4 5.50 —

First day covers of Nos. 148-149 total 123,542.

WFUNA Anniversary Type
Souvenir Sheet

Printed by Johann Enschede and Sons, Netherlands. Designed by Rocco J. Callari, US.

Designs: 35c, Abstract by Benigno Gomez, Honduras. 45c, Abstract by Alexander Calder (1898-1976), US. 50c, Abstract by Joan Miro (b. 1893), Spain. 70c, Sextet with Dove, by Ole Hamann, Denmark.

1986, Nov. 14 **Litho.** ***Perf. 13x13½***

150 Sheet of 4 *(478,833)* 3.75 4.00
a. A232 35c **multicolored** .50 .55
b. A232 45c **multicolored** .70 .75
c. A232 50c **multicolored** .90 1.00
d. A232 70c **multicolored** 1.25 1.40
First day cover *(58,452)* 2.00

No. 150 has inscribed margin picturing UN and WFUNA emblems.

Trygve Lie Type

1987, Jan. 30 **Photo. & Engr.** ***Perf. 13½***

151 A233 1.40fr **multicolored** *(516,605)* 1.10 1.20
First day cover *(76,152)* 1.50
Inscription block of 4 5.50 —

Sheaf of Colored Bands, by Georges Mathieu — G40

Armillary Sphere, Palais des Nations — G41

Printed by Helio Courvoisier, Switzerland (No. 152), and the Government Printing Bureau, Japan (No. 153). Panes of 50. Designed by Georges Mathieu (No. 152) and Rocco J. Callari (No. 153), US.

Photo., Photo. & Engr. (#153)

1987, Jan. 30 ***Perf. 11½x12, 13½***

152 G40 90c **multicolored** *(1,600,000)+* .65 .70
First day cover 1.00
Inscription block of 4 3.00 —
153 G41 1.40fr **multicolored** *(1,600,000)+* 1.25 1.40
First day cover 1.00
First day cover, #152-153 2.00
Inscription block of 4 5.00 —

First day covers of Nos. 152-153 total 85,737.

Shelter for the Homeless Type

Designs: 50c, Cement-making and brick-making. 90c, Interior construction and decorating.

1987, Mar. 13 **Litho.** ***Perf. 13½x12½***

154 A234 50c **multicolored** *(564,445)* .50 .55
First day cover 1.00
Inscription block of 4 2.50 —
155 A234 90c **multicolored** *(526,646)* 1.00 1.10
First day cover 1.10
First day cover, #154-155 2.00
Inscription block of 4 4.25 —

First day covers of Nos. 154-155 total 100,366.

Fight Drug Abuse Type

Designs: 80c, Mother and child. 1.20fr, Workers in rice paddy.

1987, June 12 **Litho.** ***Perf. 14½x15***

156 A235 80c **multicolored** *(634,776)* .50 .55
First day cover 1.25
Inscription block of 4 3.00 —
157 A235 1.20fr **multicolored** *(609,475)* 1.00 1.10
First day cover 1.75
First day cover, #156-157 2.50
Inscription block of 4 4.75 —

First day covers of Nos. 156-157 total 95,247.

UN Day Type

Designed by Elisabeth von Janota-Bzowski (35c) and Fritz Oerter (50c).

Designs: Multinational people in various occupations.

1987, Oct. 23 **Litho.** ***Perf. 14½x15***

158 A236 35c **multicolored** *(1,114,756)* .55 .60
First day cover 1.60
Inscription block of 4 2.50 —
159 A236 50c **multicolored** *(1,117,464)* .80 .85
First day cover 1.90
Inscription block of 4 3.50 —
First day cover, #158-159 2.50
Panes of 12, #158-159 15.00

Immunize Every Child Type

Designs: 90c, Whooping cough. 1.70fr, Tuberculosis.

1987, Nov. 20 **Litho.** ***Perf. 15x14½***

160 A237 90c **multicolored** *(634,614)* 1.50 1.65
First day cover 1.00
Inscription block of 4 6.25 —
161 A237 1.70fr **multicolored** *(607,725)* 2.75 3.00
First day cover 1.25
First day cover, #160-161 2.50
Inscription block of 4 11.50 —

IFAD Type

Designs: 35c, Flocks, dairy products. 1.40fr, Fruit.

1988, Jan. 29 **Litho.** ***Perf. 13½***

162 A238 35c **multicolored** *(524,817)* .35 .40
First day cover 1.00
Inscription block of 4 1.90 —
163 A238 1.40fr **multicolored** *(499,103)* 1.40 1.50
First day cover 1.50
First day cover, #162-163 2.00
Inscription block of 4 7.00 —

For A Better World — G42

Printed by Heraclio Fournier, S.A., Spain. Panes of 50. Designed by Bjorn Wiinblad, Denmark.

1988, Jan. 29 **Photo.** ***Perf. 14***

164 G42 50c **multicolored** *(1,600,000)+* .80 .85
First day cover 2.00
Inscription block of 4 3.75 —

Survival of the Forests Type

Pine forest: 50c, Treetops, mountains. 1.10fr, Lake, tree trunks. Printed se-tenant in a continuous design.

1988, Mar. 18 **Litho.** ***Perf. 14x15***

165 A240 50c **multicolored** *(728,569)* 1.25 1.40
First day cover 4.00
166 A240 1.10fr **multicolored** *(728,569)* 3.50 3.75
First day cover 6.00
a. Pair, #165-166 5.50 6.00
First day cover, #166a 10.00
Inscription block of 4, 2 #166a 12.50 —
Pane of 12, #165-166 30.00

Intl. Volunteer Day Type

Designed by Christopher Magadini, US.
Designs: 80c, Agriculture, vert. 90c, Veterinary medicine, horiz.

1988, May 6 **Litho.** ***Perf. 13x14, 14x13***

167 A241 80c **multicolored** *(612,166)* .80 .85
First day cover 1.50
Inscription block of 4 4.00 —
168 A241 90c **multicolored** *(467,334)* 1.00 1.10
First day cover 1.75
First day cover, #167-168 3.60
Inscription block of 4 4.25 —

Health in Sports Type

Paintings by LeRoy Neiman, American sports artist: 50c, Soccer, vert. 1.40fr, Swimming.

1988, June 17 **Litho.** ***Perf. 13½x13, 13x13½***

169 A242 50c **multicolored** *(541,421)* .40 .45
First day cover 1.25
Inscription block of 4 3.00 —
170 A242 1.40fr **multicolored** *(475,445)* 1.40 1.50
First day cover 2.40
First day cover, #169-170 3.00
Inscription block of 4 10.00 —

Universal Declaration of Human Rights 40th Anniv. Type

1988, Dec. 9 **Photo. & Engr.** ***Perf. 12***

171 A243 90c **multicolored** *(745,508)* .70 .75
First day cover 2.50
Inscription block of 4 3.25 —

Souvenir Sheet

172 A243 2fr **multicolored** *(517,453)* 2.75 3.00
First day cover 4.00

World Bank Type

80c, Telecommunications. 1.40fr, Industry.

1989, Jan. 27 **Litho.** ***Perf. 13x14***

173 A244 80c multi *(524,056)* 1.00 1.10
First day cover 1.50
Inscription block of 4 4.50 —
174 A244 1.40fr multi *(488,058)* 2.00 2.20
First day cover 2.40
First day cover, #173-174 3.50
Inscription block of 4 9.00 —

First day covers of Nos. 173-174 total 111,004.

Peace-Keeping Force Type

1989, Mar. 17 ***Perf. 14x13½***

175 A245 90c **multicolored** *(684,566)* 1.25 1.40
First day cover *(52,463)* 1.00
Inscription block of 4 6.75 —

World Weather Watch Type

Satellite photographs: 90c, Europe under the influence of Arctic air. 1.10fr, Surface temperatures of sea, ice and land surrounding the Kattegat between Denmark and Sweden.

1989, Apr. 21 **Litho.** ***Perf. 13x14***

176 A247 90c **multicolored** *(864,409)* 1.25 1.40
First day cover 1.50
Inscription block of 4 5.50 —
177 A247 1.10fr **multicolored** *(853,556)* 2.00 2.20
First day cover 1.90
First day cover, #176-177 3.00
Inscription block of 4 9.00 —

First day covers of Nos. 176-177 total 83,343.

Offices in Vienna, 10th Anniv.
G43 G44

Printed by Government Printing Office, Austria. Panes of 25. Designed by Anton Lehmden (50c) and Arik Brauer (2fr), Austria.

1989, Aug. 23 **Photo., Photo. & Engr. (2fr)** ***Perf. 14***

178 G43 50c **multicolored** *(605,382)* .75 1.10
First day cover 1.25
Inscription block of 4 3.50 —
179 G44 2fr **multicolored** *(538,140)* 2.50 3.75
First day cover 2.75
Inscription block of 4 10.50 —
First day cover, #178-179 3.25
Panes of 25, #178-179 80.00

First day covers of Nos. 178-179 total 83,304.

Human Rights Type of 1989

Printed by Johann Enschede and Sons, the Netherlands. Panes of 12+12 se-tenant labels containing Articles 3 (35c) or 4 (80c) inscribed in English, French or German. Designed by Rocco J. Callari and Robert Stein, US.

Artwork: 35c, Young Mother Sewing, by Mary Cassatt. 80c, The Unknown Slave, sculpture by Albert Mangones.

1989, Nov. 17 **Litho.** ***Perf. 13½***

180 A250 35c **multicolored** *(1,923,818)* .35 .40
First day cover 1.25
Inscription block of 3 + 3 labels 1.60 —
181 A250 80c **multicolored** *(1,917,953)* 1.00 1.10
First day cover 3.00
Inscription block of 3 + 3 labels 4.50 —
First day cover, #180-181 4.50
Panes of 12, #180-181 17.50

First day covers of Nos. 180-181 total 134,469.
See Nos. 193-194, 209-210, 234-235.

Intl. Trade Center Type

1990, Feb. 2 **Litho.** ***Perf. 14½x15***

182 A251 1.50fr **multicolored** *(409,561)* 2.25 2.50
First day cover *(61,098)* 3.50
Inscription block of 4 11.00 —

G45

Printed by Heraclio Fournier, S.A., Spain. Designed by Guy Breniaux, France and Elizabeth White, US.

1990, Feb. 2 **Photo.** ***Perf. 14x13½***

183 G45 5fr **multicolored** *(1,600,000)+* 4.75 5.25
First day cover *(54,462)* 7.00
Inscription block of 4 21.00 —

G46

Fight AIDS Worldwide — G46a

Fight AIDS Type

Designed by Jacek Tofil, Poland (50c) and Lee Keun Moon, Korea (80c).

Designs: 50c, "SIDA." 80c, Proportional drawing of man like the illustration by Leonardo da Vinci.

1990, Mar. 16 **Litho.** ***Perf. 13½x12½***

184 G46 50c **multicolored** *(480,625)* 1.00 1.10
First day cover 1.25
Inscription block of 4 5.00 —
185 G46a 80c **multicolored** *(602,721)* 1.75 1.90
First day cover 1.50
First day cover, #184-185 2.00
Inscription block of 4 7.75 —

First day covers of Nos. 184-185 total 108,364.

Medicinal Plants Type

1990, May 4 **Photo.** **Granite Paper** ***Perf. 11½***

186 A253 90c Plumeria rubra *(625,522)* 1.00 1.10
First day cover 1.40
Inscription block of 4 5.00 —
187 A253 1.40fr Cinchona officinalis *(648,619)* 2.00 2.20
First day cover 2.25
First day cover, #186-187 3.50
Inscription block of 4 9.50 —

First day covers of Nos. 186-187 total 114,062.

UN 45th Anniv. Type

Designed by Fritz Henry Oerter and Ruth Schmidthammer, Federal Republic of Germany (90c), Michiel Mertens, Belgium (1.10fr), Robert Stein, US (No. 190).

"45," emblem and: 90c, Symbols of clean environment, transportation and industry. 1.10fr, Dove in silhouette.

1990, June 26 **Litho.** ***Perf. 14½x13***

188 A254 90c **multicolored** *(557,253)* 1.10 1.20
First day cover 1.40
Inscription block of 4 5.25 —
189 A254 1.10fr **multicolored** *(519,635)* 2.25 2.50
First day cover 2.00
First day cover, #188-189 3.00
Inscription block of 4 9.50 —

Souvenir Sheet

190 Sheet of 2, #188-189 *(401,027)* 6.00 6.50
First day cover 4.50

First day covers of Nos. 188-190 total 148,975.

Crime Prevention Type

1990, Sept. 13 **Photo.** ***Perf. 14***

191 A255 50c Official corruption *(494,876)* 1.25 1.40
First day cover 1.40
Inscription block of 4 5.50 —
192 A255 2fr Environmental crime *(417,033)* 3.00 3.25
First day cover 3.25
First day cover, #191-192 4.50
Inscription block of 4 15.00 —

First day covers of Nos. 191-192 total 76,605.

Human Rights Type of 1989

Panes of 12+12 se-tenant labels containing Articles 9 (35c) or 10 (90c) inscribed in French, German or English.

Artwork: 35c, The Prison Courtyard by Vincent Van Gogh. 90c, Katho's Son Redeems the Evil Doer From Execution by Albrecht Durer.

1990, Nov. 16 **Litho.** ***Perf. 13½***

193 A250 35c **multicolored** *(1,578,828)* .45 .50
First day cover 2.75
Inscription block of 3 + 3 labels 1.75 —
194 A250 90c **black & brown** *(1,540,200)* 1.25 1.40
First day cover 6.00
Inscription block of 3 + 3 labels 4.50 —
First day cover, #193-194 2.50
Panes of 12, #193-194 20.00

First day covers of Nos. 193-194 total 100,282.

Panes of 12+12 se-tenant labels containing Articles 9 (35c) or 10 (90c) inscribed in French, German or English.

Economic Commission for Europe Type

1991, Mar. 15 **Litho.** ***Perf. 14***

195 A256 90c Owl, gull *(643,143)+* 1.40 1.60
First day cover 3.00
196 A256 90c Bittern, otter *(643,143)+* 1.40 1.60
First day cover 3.00
197 A256 90c Swan, lizard *(643,143)+* 1.40 1.60
First day cover 3.00
198 A256 90c Great crested grebe *(643,143)+* 1.40 1.60
First day cover 3.00
a. Block of 4, #195-198 5.60 6.50
First day cover, #198a 5.50
Inscription block of 4, #198a 7.00 —
Pane of 40, #195-198 52.50

First day covers of Nos. 195-198a total 75,759.

Namibian Independence Type

1991, May 10 **Litho.** ***Perf. 14***

199 A257 70c Mountains *(328,014)* 1.00 1.10
First day cover 1.60
Inscription block of 4 4.25 —
200 A257 90c Baobab tree *(395,362)* 2.00 2.20
First day cover 2.25
First day cover, #199-200 5.00
Inscription block of 4 9.00 —

First day covers of Nos. 199-200 total 94,201.

Ballots Filling Ballot Box — G47

UN Emblem — G48

Printed by House of Questa, United Kingdom. Designed by Ran Banda Mawilmada, Sri Lanka (80c), Maurice Gouju, France (1.50fr).

1991, May 10 **Litho.** ***Perf. 15x14½***

201 G47 80c **multicolored** *(1,600,000)+* .75 .80
First day cover 1.75
Inscription block of 4 3.25 —
202 G48 1.50fr **multicolored** *(1,600,000)+* 2.00 2.20
First day cover 3.25
First day cover, #201-202 3.75
Inscription block of 4 9.00 —

First day covers of Nos. 201-202 total 77,590.

G49

Rights of the Child — G50

Printed by The House of Questa. Panes of 50. Designed by Ryuta Nakajima, Japan (80c) and David Popper, Switzerland (1.10fr).

1991, June 14 **Litho.** ***Perf. 14½***

203 G49 80c Hands holding infant *(469,962)* 1.00 1.10
First day cover 1.75
Inscription block of 4 5.00 —
204 G50 1.10fr Children, flowers *(494,382)* 2.00 2.20
First day cover 2.25
First day cover, #203-204 3.25
Inscription block of 4 9.50 —

First day covers of Nos. 203-204 total 97,732.

G51

Banning of Chemical Weapons — G52

Printed by Heraclio Fournier S.A. Panes of 50. Designed by Oscar Asboth, Austria (80c), Michel Granger, France (1.40fr).

1991, Sept. 11 **Litho.** ***Perf. 13½***

205 G51 80c **multicolored** *(345,658)* 2.00 2.20
First day cover 1.75
Inscription block of 4 8.50
206 G52 1.40fr **multicolored** *(366,076)* 3.00 3.25
First day cover 2.50
First day cover, #205-206 3.50
Inscription block of 4 13.50 —

First day covers of Nos. 205-206 total 91,887.

UN Postal Administration, 40th Anniv. Type

1991, Oct. 24 ***Perf. 14x15***

207 A263 50c UN NY No. 7 *(506,839)* .80 .85
First day cover 1.25
Inscription block of 4 3.75 —
208 A263 1.60fr UN NY No. 10 *(580,493)* 2.20 2.40
First day cover 3.00
Inscription block of 4 9.75 —
First day cover, #207-208 3.25
Panes of 25, #207-208 75.00

First day covers of Nos. 207-208 total 88,784.

Human Rights Type of 1989

Panes of 12+12 se-tenant labels containing Articles 15 (50c) or 16 (90c) inscribed in French, German or English.

Artwork: 50c, Early Morning in Rio...1925, by Paul Klee. 90c, Marriage of Giovanni (?) Arnolfini and Giovanna Cenami (?), by Jan Van Eyck.

1991, Nov. 20 **Litho.** ***Perf. 13½***

209 A250 50c **multicolored** *(1,295,172)* .75 .80
First day cover 3.25
Inscription block of 3 + 3 labels 2.40 —
210 A250 90c **multicolored** *(1,324,091)* 1.25 1.40
First day cover 6.75
Inscription block of 3 + 3 labels 3.80 —
First day cover, #209-210 2.00
Panes of 12, #209-210 25.00

First day covers of Nos. 209-210 total 139,904.

World Heritage Type of 1984

Designs: 50c, Sagarmatha Natl. Park, Nepal. 1.10fr, Stonehenge, United Kingdom.

1992, Jan. 24 **Litho.** ***Perf. 13***
Size: 35x28mm

211 G29 50c **multicolored** *(468,647)* .80 .85
First day cover 1.25
Inscription block of 4 3.75 —
212 G29 1.10fr **multicolored** *(369,345)* 1.90 2.10
First day cover 2.25
First day cover, #211-212 3.00
Inscription block of 4 8.00 —

First day covers of Nos. 211-212 total 77,034.

G53

Printed by The House of Questa. Panes of 50. Designed by Nestor Jose Martin, Argentina.

1992, Jan. 24 **Litho.** ***Perf. 15x14½***

213 G53 3fr **multicolored** *(1,600,000)+* 3.00 3.25
First day cover *(36,135)* 4.00
Inscription block of 4 12.00 —

Clean Oceans Type

1992, Mar. 13 **Litho.** ***Perf. 14***

214 A264 80c Ocean surface, diff. *(850,699)* .90 .95
215 A264 80c Ocean bottom, diff. *(850,699)* .90 .95
a. Pair, #214-215 1.80 *2.10*
First day cover, #215a 2.75
First day cover, #214-215, each 1.75
Inscription block of 4, 2 #215a 5.00 —
Pane of 12, #214-215 11.00

First day covers of Nos. 214-215a total 90,725.

Earth Summit Type

Designs: No. 216, Rainbow. No. 217, Two clouds shaped as faces. No. 218, Two sailboats. No. 219, Woman with parasol, boat, flowers.

1992, May 22 **Photo.** ***Perf. 11½***

216 A265 75c **multicolored** *(826,543)* 1.50 1.60
217 A265 75c **multicolored** *(826,543)* 1.50 1.60
218 A265 75c **multicolored** *(826,543)* 1.50 1.60
219 A265 75c **multicolored** *(826,543)* 1.50 1.60
a. Block of 4, #216-219 6.00 6.50
First day cover, #219a 4.00
First day cover, #216-219, each 6.00
Inscription block of 4, #216-219 6.50 —
Pane of 40, #216-219 60.00

First day covers of Nos. 216-219a total 74,629.

Mission to Planet Earth Type

Designs: No. 220, Space station. No. 221, Probes near Jupiter.

1992, Sept. 4 **Photo.** ***Rouletted 8***
Granite Paper

220 A266 1.10fr **multicolored** *(668,241)* 2.40 2.60
221 A266 1.10fr **multicolored** *(668,241)* 2.40 2.60
a. Pair, #220-221 5.00 5.25
First day cover, #221a 5.00
First day cover, #220-221, each 10.00
Inscription block of 4, 2 #220-221 11.00 —
Pane of 10, #220-221 25.00

First day covers of Nos. 220-221 total 76,060.

Science and Technology Type of 1992

Designs: 90c, Doctor, nurse. 1.60fr, Graduate seated before computer.

1992, Oct. 2 **Litho.** ***Perf. 14***

222 A267 90c **multicolored** *(438,943)* 1.25 1.40
First day cover 1.60
Inscription block of 4 5.00 —
223 A267 1.60fr **multicolored** *(400,701)* 3.00 3.25
First day cover 2.50
First day cover, #222-223 3.25
Inscription block of 4 12.00 —

First day covers of Nos. 222-223 total 75,882.

Human Rights Type of 1989

Panes of 12+12 se-tenant labels containing Articles 21 (50c) and 22 (90c) inscribed in French, German or English.

Artwork: 50c, The Oath of the Tennis Court, by Jacques Louis David. 90c, Rocking Chair I, by Henry Moore.

1992, Nov. 20 **Litho.** ***Perf. 13½***

224 A250 50c **multicolored,** *(1,201,788)* .75 .80
First day cover 7.00
Inscription block of 3 + 3 labels 2.75 —
225 A250 90c **multicolored,** *(1,179,294)* 1.25 1.40
First day cover 7.00
Inscription block of 3 + 3 labels 4.25 —
First day cover, #224-225 1.75
Panes of 12, #224-225 24.00

First day covers of Nos. 224-225 total 104,491.

Aging With Dignity Type

Designs: 50c, Older man coaching soccer. 1.60fr, Older man working at computer terminal.

1993, Feb. 5 **Litho.** ***Perf. 13***

226 A270 50c **multicolored** *(483,452)* .50 .55
First day cover 1.00
Inscription block of 4 2.75 —
227 A270 1.60fr **multicolored** *(331,008)* 1.50 1.65
First day cover 2.75
First day cover, #226-227 3.00
Inscription block of 4 7.50 —

First day covers of Nos. 226-227 total 61,361.

Endangered Species Type

Designed by Rocco J. Callari, US, and Betina Ogden, Australia.

Designs: No. 228, Pongidae (gorilla). No. 229, Falco peregrinus (peregrine falcon). No. 230, Trichechus inunguis (Amazonian manatee). No. 231, Panthera uncia (snow leopard).

1993, Mar. 2 **Litho.** ***Perf. 13x12½***

228 A271 80c **multicolored** *(1,200,000)+* 1.10 1.20
229 A271 80c **multicolored** *(1,200,000)+* 1.10 1.20
230 A271 80c **multicolored** *(1,200,000)+* 1.10 1.20
231 A271 80c **multicolored** *(1,200,000)+* 1.10 1.20
a. Block of 4, #228-231 4.50 4.80
First day cover, #231a 5.00
First day cover, #228-231, each 2.00
Inscription block of 4, #228-231 4.50 —
Pane of 16, #228-231 19.00

First day covers of Nos. 228-231a total 75,363.

Healthy Environment Type

1993, May 7 **Litho.** ***Perf. 15x14½***

232 A272 60c **Neighborhood** *(456,304)* .75 .80
First day cover 1.25
Inscription block of 4 3.50 —
233 A272 1fr **Urban skyscrapers** *(392,015)* 1.75 1.90
First day cover 2.00
First day cover, #232-233 3.25
Inscription block of 4 7.50 —

First day covers of Nos. 232-233 total 59,790.

Human Rights Type of 1989

Printed in panes of 12 + 12 se-tenant labels containing Article 27 (50c) and 28 (90c) inscribed in French, German or English.

Artwork: 50c, Three Musicians, by Pablo Picasso. 90c, Voice of Space, by Rene Magritte.

1993, June 11 **Litho.** ***Perf. 13½***

234 A250 50c **multicolored** *(1,166,286)* .75 .80
First day cover 3.50
Inscription block of 3 + 3 labels 2.50 —
235 A250 90c **multicolored** *(1,122,348)* 1.75 1.90
First day cover 4.50
Inscription block of 3 + 3 labels 5.50 —
First day cover, #234-235 2.00
Panes of 12, #234-235 25.00

First day covers of Nos. 234-235 total 83,432.

Intl. Peace Day Type

Denomination at: No. 236, UL. No. 237, UR. No. 238, LL. No. 239, LR.

1993, Sept. 21 **Litho. & Engr.** ***Rouletted 12½***

236 A274 60c **purple & multi** *(357,760)* 2.00 2.20
237 A274 60c **purple & multi** *(357,760)* 2.00 2.20
238 A274 60c **purple & multi** *(357,760)* 2.00 2.20
239 A274 60c **purple & multi** *(357,760)* 2.00 2.20
a. Block of 4, #236-239 8.00 9.00
First day cover, #239a 5.50

	First day cover, #236-239, each		5.00
	Inscription block of 4, #239a	9.50	—
	Pane of 40, #236-239	75.00	

First day covers of Nos. 236-239a total 47,207.

Environment-Climate Type

1993, Oct. 29 **Litho.** ***Perf. 14½***

240	A275 1.10fr Polar bears *(391,593)*	2.40	2.40
241	A275 1.10fr Whale sounding *(391,593)*	2.40	2.40
242	A275 1.10fr Elephant seal *(391,593)*	2.40	2.40
243	A275 1.10fr Penguins *(391,593)*	2.40	2.40
a.	Strip of 4, #240-243	9.75	10.75
	First day cover, #243a		7.25
	First day cover, #240-243, each		6.00
	Inscription block of 8, 2 #243a	22.50	—
	Pane of 24, #240-243	52.50	

First day covers of Nos. 240-243a total 41,819.

Intl. Year of the Family Type of 1993

Designs: 80c, Parents teaching child to walk. 1fr, Two women and child picking plants.

1994, Feb. 4 **Litho.** ***Perf. 13.1***

244	A276 80c **rose violet & multi** *(535,000)+*	1.00	1.10
	First day cover		1.75
	Inscription block of 4	4.75	—
245	A276 1fr **brown & multi** *(535,000)+*	1.40	1.50
	First day cover		2.00
	First day cover, #244-245		3.25
	Inscription block of 4	6.25	—

First day covers of Nos. 244-245 total 50,080.

Endangered Species Type of 1993

Designed by Rocco J. Callari (frame) and Leon Parson, US (stamps).

Designs: No. 246, Mexican prairie dog. No. 247, Jabiru. No. 248, Blue whale. No. 249, Golden lion tamarin.

1994, Mar. 18 **Litho.** ***Perf. 12.7***

246	A271 80c **multicolored** *(1,200,000)+*	1.10	1.20
247	A271 80c **multicolored** *(1,200,000)+*	1.10	1.20
248	A271 80c **multicolored** *(1,200,000)+*	1.10	1.20
249	A271 80c **multicolored** *(1,200,000)+*	1.10	1.20
a.	Block of 4, #246-249	4.50	5.00
	First day cover, #249a		5.50
	First day cover, #246-249, each		1.75
	Inscription block of 4, #246-249	4.75	—
	Pane of 16, #246-249	20.00	

First day covers of Nos. 246-249a total 82,043.

Protection for Refugees Type of 1994

Design: 1.20fr, Hand lifting figure over chasm.

1994, Apr. 29 **Litho.** ***Perf. 14.3x14.8***

250	A277 1.20fr **multicolored** *(550,000)+*	2.25	2.40
	First day cover *(33,805)*		2.50
	Inscription block of 4	10.00	—

Intl. Decade for Natural Disaster Reduction Type of 1994

Earth seen from space, outline map of: No. 251, North America. No. 252, Eurasia. No. 253, South America. No. 254, Australia and South Pacific region.

1994, May 27 **Litho.** ***Perf. 13.9x14.2***

251	A281 60c **multicolored** *(570,000)+*	1.75	1.90
252	A281 60c **multicolored** *(570,000)+*	1.75	1.90
253	A281 60c **multicolored** *(570,000)+*	1.75	1.90
254	A281 60c **multicolored** *(570,000)+*	1.75	1.90
a.	Block of 4, #251-254	7.00	7.75
	First day cover, #254a		7.00
	First day cover, #251-254, each		5.00
	Inscription block of 4, #254a	9.50	—
	Pane of 40, #251-254	75.00	

First day covers of Nos. 251-254a total 37,595.

Palais des Nations, Geneva — G54

Creation of the World, by Oili Maki — G55

Printed by House of Questa, United Kingdom. Designed by Rocco J. Callari, US.

1994, Sept. 1 **Litho.** ***Perf. 14.3x14.6***

255	G54 60c **multicolored** *(1,075,000)+*	.75	.80
	First day cover		1.10
	Inscription block of 4	3.25	—
256	G55 80c **multicolored** *(1,075,000)+*	1.00	1.10
	First day cover		1.50
	Inscription block of 4	4.25	—
257	G54 1.80fr **multi,** diff. *(1,075,000)+*	2.25	2.50
	First day cover		2.75
	Inscription block of 4	9.50	—
	First day cover, #255-257		4.50
	Nos. 255-257 (3)	4.00	4.40

First day covers of Nos. 255-257 total 51,637.

Population and Development Type of 1994

Designs: 60c, People shopping at open-air market. 80c, People on vacation crossing bridge.

1994, Sept. 1 **Litho.** ***Perf. 13.2x13.6***

258	A282 60c **multicolored** *(535,000)+*	1.00	1.10
	First day cover		1.25
	Inscription block of 4	4.50	—
259	A282 80c **multicolored** *(535,000)+*	1.25	1.40
	First day cover		1.75
	Inscription block of 4	6.50	—
	First day cover, #258-259		3.00

First day covers of Nos. 258-259 total 50,443.

UNCTAD Type of 1994

1994, Oct. 28

260	A283 80c **multi**, diff. *(535,000)+*	1.10	1.20
	First day cover		1.75
	Inscription block of 4	5.00	—
261	A283 1fr **multi**, diff. *(535,000)+*	1.50	1.65
	First day cover		2.00
	Inscription block of 4	6.75	—
	First day cover, #260-261		3.50
a.	Grayish green omitted	—	
	Inscription block of 4	—	

First day covers of Nos. 260-261 total 48,122.

UN 50th Anniv. Type of 1995

1995, Jan. 1 **Litho. & Engr.** ***Perf. 13.4***

262	A284 80c **multicolored** *(823,827)*	1.10	1.20
	First day cover *(38,988)*		3.00
	Inscription block of 4	5.00	—

Social Summit Type of 1995

1995, Feb. 3 **Photo. & Engr.** ***Perf. 13.6x13.9***

263	A285 1fr **multi**, diff. *(452,116)*	1.25	1.40
	First day cover *(35,246)*		2.00
	Inscription block of 4	6.00	—

Endangered Species Type of 1993

Designed by Sibylle Erni, Switzerland.

Designs: No. 264, Crowned lemur, Lemur coronatus. No. 265, Giant Scops owl, Otus gurneyi. No. 266, Zetek's frog, Atelopus varius zeteki. No. 267, Wood bison, Bison bison athabascae.

1995, Mar. 24 Litho. *Perf. 13x12½*

264	A271 80c **multicolored** *(730,000)+*	1.10	1.20
265	A271 80c **multicolored** *(730,000)+*	1.10	1.20
266	A271 80c **multicolored** *(730,000)+*	1.10	1.20
267	A271 80c **multicolored** *(730,000)+*	1.10	1.20
a.	Block of 4, 264-267	4.50	5.00
	First day cover, #267a		4.50
	First day cover, #264-267, each		1.60
	Inscription block of 4, #267a	5.25	—
	Pane of 16, #264-267	18.50	

First day covers of Nos. 264-267a total 71,907.

Intl. Youth Year Type of 1995

Designs: 80c, Farmer on tractor, fields at harvest time. 1fr, Couple standing by fields at night.

1995, May 26 Litho. *Perf. 14.4x14.7*

268	A286 80c **multicolored** *(294,987)*	1.25	1.40
	First day cover		1.75
	Inscription block of 4	5.50	—
269	A286 1fr **multicolored** *(264,823)*	2.00	2.20
	First day cover		2.00
	First day cover, #268-269		4.00
	Inscription block of 4	9.00	—

First day covers of Nos. 268-269 total 45,665.

UN, 50th Anniv. Type of 1995

Designs: 60c, Like No. 663. 1.80fr, Like No. 664.

1995, June 26 Engr. *Perf. 13.3x13.6*

270	A287 60c **maroon** *(352,336)*	.80	.85
	First day cover		.90
	Inscription block of 4	3.75	—
271	A287 1.80fr **green** *(377,391)*	3.00	3.25
	First day cover		3.00
	First day cover, #270-271		4.00
	Inscription block of 4	13.00	—

Souvenir Sheet
Litho. & Engr.
Imperf

272	Sheet of 2, #270-271 *(251,272)*	4.25	4.50
a.	A287 60c **maroon**	1.00	1.10
b.	A287 1.80fr **green**	3.25	3.40
	First day cover		8.00

First day covers of Nos. 270-272 total 72,666.

Conference on Women Type of 1995

Designs: 60c, Black woman, cranes flying above. 1fr, Women, dove.

1995, Sept. 5 Photo. *Perf. 12*

273	A288 60c **multicolored** *(342,336)*	1.00	1.10
	First day cover		1.25
	Inscription block of 4	4.50	—

Size: 28x50mm

274	A288 1fr **multicolored** *(345,489)*	2.00	2.20
	First day cover		2.25
	First day cover, #273-274		3.25
	Inscription block of 4	9.00	—

First day covers of Nos. 273-274 total 57,542.

UN People, 50th Anniv. Type of 1995

1995, Oct. 24 Litho. *Perf. 14*

275	Sheet of 12 *(216,832 sheets)*	14.00	15.00
	First day cover		20.00
a.-l.	A290 30c each	1.20	1.20
	First day cover, #275a-275l, each		7.00
276	Souvenir booklet, *(74,151 booklets)*	15.00	
a.	A290 30c Booklet pane of 3, vert. strip of 3 from UL of sheet	3.75	3.75
b.	A290 30c Booklet pane of 3, vert. strip of 3 from UR of sheet	3.75	3.75
c.	A290 30c Booklet pane of 3, vert. strip of 3 from LL of sheet	3.75	3.75
d.	A290 30c Booklet pane of 3, vert. strip of 3 from LR of sheet	3.75	3.75

First day covers of Nos. 275-276d total 53,245.

WFUNA, 50th Anniv. Type

Design: 80c, Fishing boat, fish in net.

1996, Feb. 2 Litho. *Perf. 13x13½*

277	A291 80c **multicolored** *(550,000)+*	1.25	1.40
	First day cover		2.00
	Inscription block of 4	6.50	—

The Galloping Horse Treading on a Flying Swallow, Chinese Bronzework, Eastern Han Dynasty (25-220 A.D.) — G56

Palais des Nations, Geneva — G57

Printed by House of Questa, UK.

1996, Feb. 2 Litho. *Perf. 14½x15*

278	G56 40c **multicolored** *(1,125,000)+*	.50	.55
	First day cover		1.25
	Inscription block of 4	2.50	—
279	G57 70c **multicolored** *(1,125,000+)*	.90	.95
	First day cover		1.50
	First day cover, #278-279		3.50
	Inscription block of 4	4.00	—

Endangered Species Type of 1993

Designs: No. 280, Paphiopedilum delenatii. No. 281, Pachypodium baronii. No. 282, Sternbergia lutea. No. 283, Darlingtonia californica.

1996, Mar. 14 Litho. *Perf. 12½*

280	A271 80c **multicolored** *(680,000)+*	1.00	1.10
281	A271 80c **multicolored** *(680,000)+*	1.00	1.10
282	A271 80c **multicolored** *(680,000)+*	1.00	1.10
283	A271 80c **multicolored** *(680,000)+*	1.00	1.10
a.	Block of 4, #280-283	4.00	4.50
	First day cover, #280-283, each		2.00
	First day cover, #283a		4.50
	Inscription block of 4, #283a	4.25	—
	Pane of 16, #280-283	16.00	

City Summit Type of 1996

Designs: No. 284, Asian family. No. 285, Oriental garden. No. 286, Fruit, vegetable vendor, mosque. No. 287, Boys playing ball. No. 288, Couple reading newspaper.

1996, June 3 Litho. *Perf. 14x13½*

284	A293 70c **multicolored** *(420,000)+*	1.50	1.65
285	A293 70c **multicolored** *(420,000)+*	1.50	1.65
286	A293 70c **multicolored** *(420,000)+*	1.50	1.65
287	A293 70c **multicolored** *(420,000)+*	1.50	1.65
288	A293 70c **multicolored** *(420,000)+*	1.50	1.65
a.	Strip of 5, #284-288	7.50	8.25
	First day cover, #288a		11.00
	First day cover, #284-288, each		5.00
	Inscription block of 10, 2 #288a	20.00	

Sport and the Environment Type

Designs: 70c, Cycling, vert. 1.10fr, Sprinters.

1996, July 19 Litho. *Perf. 14x14½, 14½x14*

289	A294 70c **multicolored** *(625,000)+*	1.00	1.10
	First day cover		1.50
	Inscription block of 4	4.75	—
290	A294 1.10fr **multicolored** *(625,000)+*	1.50	1.65
	First day cover		2.25
	First day cover, #289-290		4.50
	Inscription block of 4	7.50	—

Souvenir Sheet

291	A294 Sheet of 2, #289-290 *(345,000)+*	3.00	3.25
	First day cover		12.00

Plea for Peace Type

Designed by: 90c, Chen Yu, China. 1.10fr, Zhou Jing, China.

Designs: 90c, Tree filled with birds, vert. 1.10fr, Bouquet of flowers in rocket tail vase, vert.

1996, Sept. 17 **Litho.** ***Perf. 15x14½***

292 A295 90c **multicolored** *(550,000)+* 1.25 1.40
First day cover 1.50
Inscription block of 4 5.50 —
293 A295 1.10fr **multicolored** *(550,000)+* 1.50 1.65
First day cover 2.25
First day cover, #292-293 3.75
Inscription block of 4 7.50 —

UNICEF Type

Fairy Tales: 70c, The Sun and the Moon, South America. 1.80fr, Ananse, Africa.

1996, Nov. 20 **Litho.** ***Perf. 14½x15***

294 A296 70c **multicolored** *(1,000,000)+* .80 .85
First day cover 1.50
Pane of 8 + label 6.50
295 A296 1.80fr **multicolored** *(1,000,000)+* 2.00 2.20
First day cover 3.00
First day cover, #294-295 4.00
Pane of 8 + label 17.50

UN Flag — G58

Palais des Nations Under Construction by Massimo Campigli — G59

Printed by The House of Questa, Ltd., UK.

1997, Feb. 12 **Litho.** ***Perf. 14½***

296 G58 10c **multicolored** *(600,000)+* .25 .30
First day cover 1.25
Inscription block of 4 .55 —
297 G59 1.10fr **multicolored** *(700,000)+* 1.25 1.40
First day cover 2.25
First day cover, #296-297 3.50
Inscription block of 4 5.00 —

First day covers of Nos. 296-297 total 41,186.

Endangered Species Type of 1993

Designs: No. 298, Ursus maritimus (polar bear). No. 299, Goura cristata (blue-crowned pigeon). No. 300, Amblyrhynchus cristatus (marine iguana). No. 301, Lama guanicoe (guanaco).

1997, Mar. 13 **Litho.** ***Perf. 12½***

298 A271 80c **multicolored** *(620,000)+* .90 .95
299 A271 80c **multicolored** *(620,000)+* .90 .95
300 A271 80c **multicolored** *(620,000)+* .90 .95
301 A271 80c **multicolored** *(620,000)+* .90 .95
a. Block of 4, #298-301 3.60 3.90
First day cover, #301a 5.00
First day cover, #298-301, each 2.50
Inscription block of 4, #301a 4.00
Pane of 16 17.50

First day covers of Nos. 298-301 total 71,905.

Earth Summit Anniv. Type

Designs: No. 302, Person flying over mountain. No. 303, Mountain, person's face. No. 304, Person standing on mountain, sailboats. No. 305, Person, mountain, trees.
1.10fr, Combined design similar to Nos. 302-305.

1997, May 30 **Photo.** ***Perf. 11½***

Granite Paper

302 A299 45c **multicolored** *(227,187)* 1.00 1.10
303 A299 45c **multicolored** *(227,187)* 1.00 1.10
304 A299 45c **multicolored** *(227,187)* 1.00 1.10
305 A299 45c **multicolored** *(227,187)* 1.00 1.10
a. Block of 4, #302-305 4.00 4.50
First day cover, #305a 8.00
First day cover, #302-305, each 6.00
Inscription block of 4, #305a 6.25

Souvenir Sheet

306 A299 1.10fr **multicolored** *(176,386)* 4.00 4.25
First day cover 5.00

First day covers of Nos. 302-306 total 55,389.

Transportation Type of 1997

Air transportation: No. 307, Zeppelin, Fokker tri-motor. No. 308, Boeing 314 Clipper, Lockheed Constellation. No. 309, DeHavilland Comet. No. 310, Boeing 747, Illyushin jet. No. 311, Concorde.

1997, Aug. 29 **Litho.** ***Perf. 14x14½***

307 A300 70c **multicolored** *(271,575)* 1.00 1.10
308 A300 70c **multicolored** *(271,575)* 1.00 1.10
309 A300 70c **multicolored** *(271,575)* 1.00 1.10
310 A300 70c **multicolored** *(271,575)* 1.00 1.10
311 A300 70c **multicolored** *(271,575)* 1.00 1.10
a. Strip of 5, #307-311 5.00 5.50
First day cover, #311a 7.00
First day cover, #307-311, each 4.75
Margin block of 10, 2#311a 12.50

No. 311a has continuous design.
First day covers of Nos. 307-311 total 33,303.

Philately Type

Designs: 70c, No. 146. 1.10fr, No. 147.

1997, Oct. 14 **Litho.** ***Perf. 13½x14***

312 A301 70c **multicolored** *(254,406)* .80 .85
First day cover 1.75
Inscription block of 4 3.25 —
313 A301 1.10fr **multicolored** *(303,125)* 1.50 1.65
First day cover 2.25
First day cover, #312-313 6.00
Inscription block of 4 6.25 —

First day covers of Nos. 312-313 total 47,528.

World Heritage Convention Type

Terracotta warriors of Xian: 45c, Single warrior. 70c, Massed warriors. No. 316a, like NY No. 716. No. 316b, like NY No. 717. No. 316c, like Geneva No. 314. No. 316d, like Geneva No. 315. No. 316e, like Vienna No. 230. No. 316f, like Vienna No. 231.

1997, Nov. 19 **Litho.** ***Perf. 13½***

314 A302 45c **multicolored** *(409,820)* 1.25 1.40
First day cover 1.40
Inscription block of 4 5.50 —
315 A302 70c **multicolored** *(414,059)* 2.25 2.50
First day cover 1.50
First day cover, #314-315 4.00
Inscription block of 4 9.50 —
316 Souvenir booklet *(275,114 booklets)* 12.00
a.-f. A302 10c any single .45 .50
g. Booklet pane of 4 #316a 2.00 2.00
h. Booklet pane of 4 #316b 2.00 2.00
i. Booklet pane of 4 #316c 2.00 2.00
j. Booklet pane of 4 #316d 2.00 2.00
k. Booklet pane of 4 #316e 2.00 2.00
l. Booklet pane of 4 #316f 2.00 2.00

First day covers of Nos. 314-316 total 40,366.

Palais des Nations, Geneva — G60

Printed by The House of Questa, UK. Designed by UN (2fr).

1998, Feb. 13 **Litho.** ***Perf. 14½x15***

317 G60 2fr **multicolored** *(550,000)+* 1.50 1.65
First day cover 6.00
Inscription block of 4 6.00 —

Endangered Species Type of 1993

Designed by Rocco J. Callari, US and Suzanne Duranceau, Canada.

Designs: No. 318, Macaca thibetana (short-tailed Tibetan macaque). No. 319, Phoenicopterus ruber (Caribbean flamingo). No. 320, Ornithoptera alexandrae (Queen Alexandra's birdwing). No. 321, Dama mesopotamica (Persian fallow deer).

1998, Mar. 13 **Litho.** ***Perf. 12½***

318 A271 80c **multicolored** *(560,000)+* 1.00 1.10
319 A271 80c **multicolored** *(560,000)+* 1.00 1.10
320 A271 80c **multicolored** *(560,000)+* 1.00 1.10
321 A271 80c **multicolored** *(560,000)+* 1.00 1.10
a. Block of 4, #318-321 4.00 4.50
First day cover, #321a 6.00
First day cover, #318-321, each 5.00
Inscription block of 4, #321a 4.25 —
Pane of 16 16.00

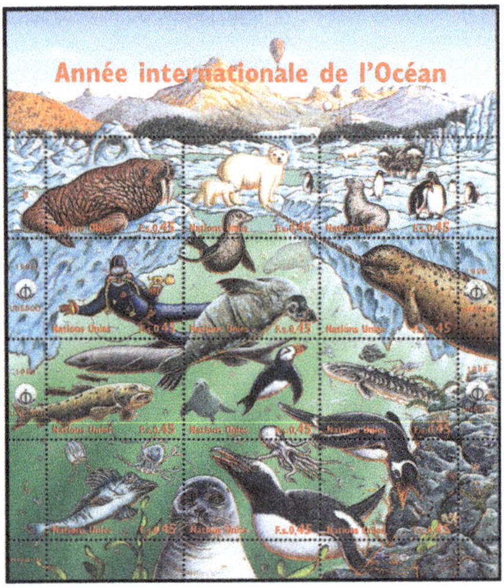

Intl. Year of the Ocean — G61

Designed by Jon Ellis, US.

1998, May 20 **Litho.** ***Perf. 13x13½***

322 G61 Pane of 12 *(270,000)+* 11.00 12.00
First day cover 10.00
a.-l. 45c any single .90 1.00
First day cover, #322a-322l, each 3.00

Rain Forests Type

1998, June 19 ***Perf. 13x13½***

323 A307 70c Orangutans *(430,000)+* .90 1.00
First day cover 5.00
Inscription block of 4 4.00 —

Souvenir Sheet

324 A307 3fr like #323 *(250,000)+* 4.00 *7.50*
First day cover 7.00

Peacekeeping Type

Designs: 70c, Soldier with two children. 90c, Two soldiers, children.

1998, Sept. 15 **Photo.** ***Perf. 12***

325 A308 70c **multicolored** *(400,000)+* .85 .90
First day cover 1.50
Inscription block of 4 3.50 —
326 A308 90c **multicolored** *(390,000)+* 1.40 1.50
First day cover 4.00
First day cover, #325-326 5.00
Inscription block of 4 6.00 —

Declaration of Human Rights Type of 1998

Designs: 90c, Stylized birds. 1.80fr, Stylized birds flying from hand.

1998, Oct. 27 **Litho. & Photo.** ***Perf. 13***

327 A309 90c **multicolored** *(400,000)+* .95 1.05
First day cover 2.00
Inscription block of 4 4.00 —
328 A309 1.80fr **multicolored** *(390,000)+* 2.00 2.20
First day cover 3.50
First day cover, #327-328 5.00
Inscription block of 4 8.00 —

Schönbrunn Palace Type

Designs: 70c, No. 331b, Great Palm House. 1.10fr, No. 331d, Blue porcelain vase, vert. No. 331a, Palace. No. 331c, The Gloriette (archway). No. 331e, Wall painting on fabric (detail), by Johann Wenzl Bergl, vert. No. 331f, Porcelain stove, vert.

1998, Dec. 4 **Litho.** ***Perf. 14***

329 A310 70c **multicolored** *(375,000)+* .90 1.00
First day cover 1.50
Inscription block of 4 3.75 —
330 A310 1.10fr **multicolored** *(375,000)+* 1.20 1.30
First day cover 2.25
First day cover, #329-330 5.00
Inscription block of 4 5.25 —

Souvenir Booklet

331 Booklet *(100,000)+* 21.50
a.-c. A310 10c any single .55 .55
d.-f. A310 30c any single 1.65 1.65
g. Booklet pane of 4 #331a 2.20 2.20
h. Booklet pane of 3 #331d 5.00 5.00
i. Booklet pane of 3 #331e 5.00 5.00
j. Booklet pane of 3 #331f 5.00 5.00
k. Booklet pane of 4 #331b 2.20 2.20
l. Booklet pane of 4 #331c 2.20 2.20

Palais Wilson, Geneva — G62

Designed and printed by Helio Courvoisier, SA, Switzerland.

1999, Feb. 5 **Photo.** ***Perf. 11½***

Granite Paper

332 G62 1.70fr **brown red** *(600,000)+* 1.75 1.90
First day cover *(25,568)* 3.50
Inscription block of 4 8.50 —

World Heritage, Australia Type

Designs: 90c, No. 335e, Kakadu Natl. Park. 1.10fr, No. 335c, Great Barrier Reef. No. 335a, Tasmanian Wilderness. No. 335b, Wet tropics of Queensland. No. 335d, Uluru-Kata Tjuta Natl. Park. No. 335f, Willandra Lakes region.

1999, Mar. 19 **Litho.** ***Perf. 13***

333 A313 90c **multicolored** *(420,000)+* 1.25 1.40
First day cover 2.00
Inscription block of 4 5.75 —
334 A313 1.10fr **multicolored** *(420,000)+* 1.50 1.65
First day cover 2.25
First day cover, #333-334 4.50
Inscription block of 4 8.00 —

Souvenir Booklet

335 Booklet *(90,000)+* 16.50
a.-c. A313 10c any single .45 .50
d.-f. A313 20c any single .90 1.00
g. Booklet pane of 4, #335a 1.80 2.00
h. Booklet pane of 4, #335d 3.60 4.00
i. Booklet pane of 4, #335b 1.80 2.00
j. Booklet pane of 4, #335e 3.60 4.00
k. Booklet pane of 4, #335c 1.80 2.00
l. Booklet pane of 4, #335f 3.60 4.00

First day covers of Nos. 333-335 total 44,622.

Endangered Species Type of 1993

Designed by Tim Barrall, US.

Designs: No. 336, Equus hemionus (Asiatic wild ass). No. 337, Anodorhynchus hyacinthinus (hyacinth macaw). No. 338, Epicrates subflavus (Jamaican boa). No. 339, Dendrolagus bennettianus (Bennetts' tree kangaroo).

1999, Apr. 22 **Litho.** ***Perf. 12½***

336	A271	90c **multicolored** *(488,000)+*	1.00	1.10
337	A271	90c **multicolored** *(488,000)+*	1.00	1.10
338	A271	90c **multicolored** *(488,000)+*	1.00	1.10
339	A271	90c **multicolored** *(488,000)+*	1.00	1.10
a.		Block of 4, #336-339	4.00	4.50
		First day cover, #339a		5.75
		First day cover, #336-339, each		2.00
		Inscription block of 4, #339a	4.50	—
		Pane of 16	16.00	

First day covers of Nos. 336-339 total 52,856.

UNISPACE III Type

Designs: No. 340, Farm, satellite dish. No. 341, City, satellite in orbit. No. 342, Composite of Nos. 340-341.

1999, July 7 **Photo.** ***Rouletted 8***

340	A314	45c **multicolored** *(925,000)+*	.90	1.00
341	A314	45c **multicolored** *(925,000)+*	.90	1.00
a.		Pair, #340-341	2.00	2.20
		First day cover, #341a		2.25
		First day cover, #340-341, each		14.00
		Inscription block of 4	5.00	—
		Pane of 10, #340-341	9.50	—

Souvenir Sheet

Perf. 14½

342	A314	2fr **multicolored** *(275,000)+*	4.50	5.00
		First day cover		6.00
a.		Ovptd. in sheet margin	9.50	10.50
		First day cover		19.00

No. 342a is ovptd. in violet blue "PHILEXFRANCE 99 / LE MONDIAL DU TIMBRE / PARIS / 2 AU 11 JUILLET 1999.
First day covers of Nos. 340-342 total 63,412.

UPU Type

Various people, early 20th century methods of mail transportation, denomination at: No. 343, UL. No. 344, UR. No. 345, LL. No. 346, LR.

1999, Aug. 23 **Photo.** ***Perf. 11¾***

343	A315	70c **multicolored** *(336,000)+*	.90	1.00
344	A315	70c **multicolored** *(336,000)+*	.90	1.00
345	A315	70c **multicolored** *(336,000)+*	.90	1.00
346	A315	70c **multicolored** *(336,000)+*	.90	1.00
a.		Block of 4, #343-346	3.60	4.00
		First day cover, #346a		3.50
		First day cover, #343-346, each		1.50
		Inscription block of 4, #346a	3.75	—

First day covers of Nos. 343-346 total 27,041.

In Memoriam Type

Designs: 1.10fr, 2fr, Armillary sphere, Palais de Nations. Size of 2fr stamp: 34x63mm.

1999, Sept. 21 **Litho.** ***Perf. 14½x14***

347	A316	1.10fr **multicolored** *(400,000)+*	1.25	1.40
		First day cover		3.00
		Inscription block of 4	5.50	—

Souvenir Sheet

Perf. 14

348	A316	2fr **multicolored** *(225,000)+*	3.00	3.25
		First day cover		3.50

First day covers of Nos. 347-348 total 46,527.

Education Type

90c, Rainbow over globe. 1.80fr, Fish, tree, globe, book.

1999, Nov. 18 **Litho.** ***Perf. 13½x13¾***

349	A317	90c Rainbow over globe *(350,000)+*	.75	.80
		First day cover		1.75
		Inscription block of 4	3.25	—
350	A317	1.80fr Fish, tree, globe, book *(370,000)+*	1.75	1.90
		First day cover		3.50
		First day cover, #349-350		4.50
		Inscription block of 4	7.25	—

First day covers of Nos. 349-350 total 37,925.

Intl. Year Of Thanksgiving Type

2000, Jan 1 **Litho.** ***Perf. 13¼x13½***

351	A318	90c **multicolored** *(450,000)+*	1.00	1.10
		First day cover		3.00
		Inscription block of 4	4.50	—

On No. 351 portions of the design were applied by a thermographic process producing a shiny, raised effect.

Endangered Species Type of 1993

Designed by Robert Hynes, US.

Designs: No. 352, Hippopotamus amphibius (hippopotamus). No. 353, Coscoroba coscoroba (Coscoroba swan). No. 354, Varanus prasinus (emerald monitor). No. 355, Enhydra lutris (sea otter).

2000, Apr. 6 **Litho.** ***Perf. 12¾x12½***

352	A271	90c **multicolored** *(488,000)+*	1.25	1.40
353	A271	90c **multicolored** *(488,000)+*	1.25	1.40
354	A271	90c **multicolored** *(488,000)+*	1.25	1.40
355	A271	90c **multicolored** *(488,000)+*	1.25	1.40
a.		Block of 4, #352-355	5.00	5.75
		First day cover, #355a		5.00
		First day cover, #352-355, each		1.90
		Inscription block of 4, #355a	5.25	—
		Pane of 16	20.00	

Our World 2000 Type

Winning artwork in Millennium painting competition: 90c, The Embrace, by Rita Adaimy, Lebanon. 1.10fr, Living Single, by Richard Kimanthi, Kenya, vert.

2000, May 30 **Litho.** ***Perf. 13x13½, 13½x13***

356	A319	90c **multicolored** *(330,000)+*	1.00	1.10
		First day cover		1.75
		Inscription block of 4	4.00	—
357	A319	1.10fr **multicolored** *(330,000)+*	1.25	1.40
		First day cover		2.25
		First day cover, #356-357		3.50
		Inscription block of 4	5.00	—

55th Anniversary Type

Designs: 90c, Trygve Lie, Harry S Truman, workers at cornerstone dedication ceremony, 1949. 1.40fr, Window cleaner on Secretariat Building, General Assembly Hall under construction, 1951.

2000, July 7 **Litho.** ***Perf. 13¼x13***

358	A320	90c **multicolored** *(370,000)+*	1.00	1.10
		First day cover		1.75
		Inscription block of 4	4.00	—
359	A320	1.40fr **multicolored** *(370,000)+*	1.50	1.65
		First day cover		2.60
		First day cover, #358-359		3.75
		Inscription block of 4	6.00	—

Souvenir Sheet

360	A320	Sheet of 2, #358-359 *(235,000)+*	3.50	3.75
		First day cover		3.25

The UN in the 21st Century — G63

Printed by Government Printing Office, Austria. Designed by Wilson McLean, UK.

No. 361: a, Two people, terraced rice paddy. b, Man carrying bricks on head. c, UN Peacekeeper with binoculars. d, Dam, doves. e, Men with shovels. f, People working on irrigation system.

2000, Sept. 15 **Litho.** ***Perf. 14***

361 G63 Pane of 6 *(266,000)+* 9.00 10.00
First day cover 7.50
a.-f. 50c any single 1.50 1.65
First day covers, each 5.00

World Heritage, Spain Type

Designs: Nos. 362, 364b, Walled Town of Cuenca. Nos. 363, 364e, Toledo. No. 364a, Alhambra, Generalife and Albayzin, Granada. No. 364c, Aqueduct of Segovia. No. 364d, Amphitheater of Mérida. No. 364f, Güell Park, Barcelona.

2000, Oct. 6 **Litho.** ***Perf. 14¾x14½***

362 A323 1fr **multicolored** *(340,000)+* 1.40 1.50
First day cover 1.90
Inscription block of 4 5.75 —
363 A323 1.20fr **multicolored** *(340,000)+* 1.60 1.75
First day cover 2.25
First day cover, #362-363 3.50
Inscription block of 4 6.50 —

Souvenir Booklet

364 Booklet *(64,000)+* 11.00
a.-c. A323 10c any single .30 .35
d.-f. A323 20c any single .60 .65
g. Booklet pane of 4, #364a 1.20 1.40
h. Booklet pane of 4, #364d 2.40 2.60
i. Booklet pane of 4, #364b 1.20 1.40
j. Booklet pane of 4, #364e 2.40 2.60
k. Booklet pane of 4, #364c 1.20 1.40
l. Booklet pane of 4, #364f 2.40 2.60

Respect for Refugees Type

Designs: 80c, 1.80fr, Refugee with cane, four other refugees.

2000, Nov. 9 **Litho.** ***Perf. 13¼x12¾***

365 A324 80c **multicolored** *(400,000)+* 1.25 1.40
First day cover 1.75
Inscription block of 4 4.50 —

Souvenir Sheet

366 A324 1.80fr **multicolored** *(215,000)+* 2.50 2.75
First day cover 3.00

Endangered Species Type of 1993

Printed by Johann Enschedé and Sons, the Netherlands. Designed by Higgins Bond, US.

Designs: No. 367, Felis lynx canadensis (North American lynx). No. 368, Pavo muticus (green peafowl). No. 369, Geochelone elephantopus (Galapagos giant tortoise). No. 370, Lepilemur spp. (sportive lemur).

2001, Feb. 1 **Litho.** ***Perf. 12¾x12½***

367 A271 90c **multicolored** *(448,000)+* 1.25 1.40
368 A271 90c **multicolored** *(448,000)+* 1.25 1.40
369 A271 90c **multicolored** *(448,000)+* 1.25 1.40
370 A271 90c **multicolored** *(448,000)+* 1.25 1.40
a. Block of 4, #367-370 5.00 5.75
First day cover, #370a 5.50
First day cover, #367-370 each 1.90
Inscription block of 4, #370a 5.25 —
Pane of 16 20.00

Intl. Volunteers Year — G64

Printed by Johann Enschedé and Sons, the Netherlands. Panes of 20. Designed by Rorie Katz and Robert Stein, US.

Paintings by: 90c, Ernest Pignon-Ernest, France. 1.30fr, Paul Siché, France.

2001, Mar. 29 **Litho.** ***Perf. 13¼***

371 G64 90c **multicolored** *(350,000)+* 1.10 1.20
First day cover 1.75
Inscription block of 4 4.50
372 G64 1.30fr **multicolored** *(340,000)+* 1.60 1.75
First day cover 2.40
First day cover, #371-372 3.50
Inscription block of 4 6.50

World Heritage, Japan Type

Designs: 1.10fr, No. 375b, Nara. 1.30fr, No. 375e, Itsukushima Shinto Shrine. No. 375a, Kyoto. No. 375c, Himeji-Jo. No. 375d, Shirakawa-Go and Gokayama. No. 375f, Nikko.

2001, Aug. 1 **Litho.** ***Perf. 12¾x13¼***

373 A328 1.10fr **multicolored** *(350,000)+* 1.30 1.40
First day cover 2.00
Inscription block of 4 5.75 —
374 A328 1.30fr **multicolored** *(350,000)+* 1.50 1.65
First day cover 2.40
First day cover, #373-374 3.75
Inscription block of 4 6.50 —

Souvenir Booklet

375 Booklet *(52,000)+* 15.00
a.-c. A328 10c any single .50 .55
d.-f. A328 30c any single .75 .80
g. Booklet pane of 4, #375a 2.00 2.20
h. Booklet pane of 4, #375d 3.00 3.20
i. Booklet pane of 4, #375b 2.00 2.20
j. Booklet pane of 4, #375e 3.00 3.20
k. Booklet pane of 4, #375c 2.00 2.20
l. Booklet pane of 4, #375f 3.00 3.20

Dag Hammarskjöld Type

2001, Sept. 18 **Engr.** ***Perf. 11x11¼***

376 A329 2fr **carmine lake** *(380,000)+* 2.50 2.75
First day cover 3.25
Inscription block of 4 10.00 —

UN Postal Administration, 50th Anniv. Types

2001, Oct. 18 **Litho.** ***Perf. 13½***

377 A330 90c Stamps, globe *(310,000)+* 1.00 1.10
First day cover 1.60
Inscription block of 4 4.25 —
378 A330 1.30fr Stamps, horns *(310,000)+* 1.75 1.90
First day cover 2.40
First day cover, #377-378 3.50
Inscription block of 4 8.00 —

Souvenir Sheet

379 A331 Sheet of 2 *(175,000)+* 12.50 13.50
a. 1.30fr **red & light blue,** 38mm diameter 5.00 5.50
b. 1.80fr **red & light blue,** 38mm diameter 7.50 8.00
First day cover 8.00

Climate Change Type

Designs: No. 380, Lizard, flowers, shoreline. No. 381, Windmills, construction workers. No. 382, Non-polluting factory. No. 383, Solar oven, city, village, picnickers.

2001, Nov. 16 **Litho.** ***Perf. 13¼***

380 A332 90c **multicolored** *(73,500)+* 1.10 1.20
381 A332 90c **multicolored** *(73,500)+* 1.10 1.20
382 A332 90c **multicolored** *(73,500)+* 1.10 1.20
383 A332 90c **multicolored** *(73,500)+* 1.10 1.20
a. Horiz. strip, #380-383 4.50 5.00
Inscription block of 8 9.00 —
First day cover, #383a 5.25
First day covers, #380-383, each 6.00
Pane of 24 26.00 —

Nobel Peace Prize Type

2001, Dec. 10 **Litho.** ***Perf. 13¼***

384 A333 90c **multicolored** *(840,000)+* 1.10 1.20
Inscription block of 4 4.50 —
First day cover 1.75
Pane of 12 13.50 —

Palais des Nations — G65

Printed by Government Printing Office, Austria. Panes of 20. Designed by Robert Stein, US.

2002, Mar. 1 **Litho.** ***Perf. 13¾***

385	G65	1.30fr **multicolored** *(630,000)+*	1.40	1.50
		First day cover		2.25
		Inscription block of 4	5.75	—

Endangered Species Type of 1993

Printed by Johann Enschedé and Sons, the Netherlands. Designed by Lori Anzalone, US.

Designs: No. 386, Cacajao calvus (white uakari). No. 387, Mellivora capensis (honey badger). No. 388, Otocolobus manul (manul). No. 389, Varanus exantematicus (Bosc's monitor).

2002, Apr. 4 **Litho.** ***Perf. 12¾x12½***

386	A271	90c **multicolored** *(420,000)+*	1.50	1.65
387	A271	90c **multicolored** *(420,000)+*	1.50	1.65
388	A271	90c **multicolored** *(420,000)+*	1.50	1.65
389	A271	90c **multicolored** *(420,000)+*	1.50	1.65
a.		Block of 4, #386-389	6.00	6.75
		First day cover, #389a		5.50
		First day cover, #386-389 each		1.90
		Inscription block of 4, #389a	6.25	—
		Pane of 16	24.00	—

Independence of East Timor Type

Designs: 90c, Wooden statue of male figure. 1.30fr, Carved wooden container.

2002, May 20 **Litho.** ***Perf. 14x14½***

390	A335	90c **multicolored** *(305,000)+*	1.25	1.40
		First day cover		1.90
		Inscription block of 4	5.00	—
391	A335	1.30fr **multicolored** *(295,000)+*	1.75	1.90
		First day cover		2.60
		First day cover, #390-391		3.75
		Inscription block of 4	7.00	—

Intl. Year of Mountains Type

Designs: No. 392, Weisshorn, Switzerland. No. 393, Mt. Fuji, Japan. No. 394, Vinson Massif, Antarctica. No. 395, Mt. Kamet, India.

2002, May 24 **Litho.** ***Perf. 13x13¼***

392	A336	70c **multicolored** *(1,230,000)+*	1.00	1.10
		First day cover		1.40
393	A336	70c **multicolored** *(1,230,000)+*	1.00	1.10
		First day cover		1.40
394	A336	1.20fr **multicolored** *(1,230,000)+*	1.75	1.90
		First day cover		2.40
		First day cover, #392, 394		3.25
395	A336	1.20fr **multicolored** *(1,230,000)+*	1.75	1.90
a.		Vert. strip or block of four, #392-395	8.50	9.50
		First day cover		2.40
		First day cover, #392, 395		3.25
		First day cover, #392-395		6.00
		Pane of 12, 3 each #392-395	22.50	—

World Summit on Sustainable Development (Peter Max) Type

Designs: No. 396, Sun, birds, flowers, heart. No. 397, Three faceless people, diff. No. 398, Three women, diff. No. 399, Sailboat, mountain.

2002, June 27 **Litho.** ***Perf. 14½x14***

396	A337	90c **multicolored** *(1,215,000)+*	1.25	1.40
		First day cover		1.90
397	A337	90c **multicolored** *(1,215,000)+*	1.25	1.40
		First day cover		1.90
398	A337	1.80fr **multicolored** *(1,215,000)+*	2.50	2.75
		First day cover		3.50
		First day cover, #396, 398		4.00
399	A337	1.80fr **multicolored** *(1,215,000)+*	2.50	2.75
a.		Vert. strip or block of four, #396-399	10.00	11.00
		First day cover		3.50
		First day cover, #397, 399		4.00
		First day cover, #396-399		8.00
		Pane of 12, 3 each #396-399	22.50	—

World Heritage, Italy Type

Designs: 90c, No. 402e, Pisa. 1.30fr, No. 402b, Aeolian Islands. No. 402a, Amalfi Coast. No. 402c, Rome. No. 402d, Florence. No. 402f, Pompeii.

2002, Aug. 30 **Litho.** ***Perf. 13½x13¼***

400	A338	90c **multicolored** *(355,000)+*	1.25	1.40
		First day cover		1.90
		Inscription block of 4	5.00	—
401	A338	1.30fr **multicolored** *(355,000)+*	2.00	2.20
		First day cover		2.75
		First day cover, #400-401		4.00
		Inscription block of 4	8.25	—

Souvenir Booklet

402		Booklet *(51,000)+*	29.00	
a.-c.	A338	10c any single	.60	.80
d.-f.	A338	20c any single	1.75	2.00
g.		Booklet pane of 4, #402d	7.00	8.00
h.		Booklet pane of 4, #402a	2.40	2.75
i.		Booklet pane of 4, #402e	7.00	8.00
j.		Booklet pane of 4, #402b	2.40	2.75
k.		Booklet pane of 4, #402f	7.00	8.00
l.		Booklet pane of 4, #402c	2.40	2.75

AIDS Awareness Type

2002, Oct. 24 **Litho.** ***Perf. 13½***

403	A339	1.30fr **multicolored** *(305,000)+*	2.00	2.20
		Inscription block of 4	7.75	—
		First day cover, #403		2.60
		Pane of 20	40.00	—

Entry of Switzerland into United Nations — G66

Printed by House of Questa, UK. Panes of 20. Designed by Thierry Clauson, Switzerland.

2002, Oct. 24 **Litho.** ***Perf. 14½x14¾***

404	G66	3fr **multicolored** *(580,000)+*	3.50	3.75
		Inscription block of 4	14.00	—
		First day cover, #404		5.00
		Pane of 20	70.00	—

Indigenous Art — G67

Printed by House of Questa, UK.

Designed by Rorie Katz and Robert Stein, US.

No. 405: a, Detail of Inca poncho, Peru. b, Bahia culture seated figure, Brazil. c, Blanket, Ecuador. d, Mayan stone sculpture, Belize. e, Embroidered fabric, Guatemala. f, Colima terra-cotta dog sculpture, Mexico.

2003, Jan. 31 **Litho.** ***Perf. 14¼***

405 G67 Pane of 6 *(168,000)+* 7.50 8.50
First day cover 9.75
a.-f. 90c Any single 1.25 1.35
First day cover, a.-f., each 2.50

New Inter-Parliamentary Union Headquarters, Geneva — G68

Printed by House of Questa, UK. Panes of 20. Designed by Cyril Wursten, Switzerland.

2003, Feb. 20 **Litho.** ***Perf. 14½x14***

406 G68 90c **multicolored** *(480,000)+* 1.75 1.75
Inscription block of 4 7.25 —
First day cover 2.00
Pane of 20 25.00 —

Endangered Species Type of 1993

Printed by Johann Enschedé and Sons, the Netherlands. Designed by James Hautman, US.

Designs: No. 407, Branta ruficollis (red-breasted goose). No. 408, Geronticus calvus (bald ibis). No. 409, Dendrocygna bicolor (fulvous whistling duck). No. 410, Ramphastos vitellinus (channel-billed toucan).

2003, Apr. 3 **Litho.** ***Perf. 12¾x12½***

407 A271 90c **multicolored** *(368,000)+* 1.25 1.25
408 A271 90c **multicolored** *(368,000)+* 1.25 1.25
409 A271 90c **multicolored** *(368,000)+* 1.25 1.25
410 A271 90c **multicolored** *(368,000)+* 1.25 1.25
a. Block of 4, #407-410 5.00 5.00
First day cover, #410a 6.25
First day cover, #407-410 each 2.10
Inscription block of 4, #410a 5.60 —
Pane of 16 22.50 —

International Year of Freshwater Type of 2003

2003, June 20 **Litho.** ***Perf. 14¼x14½***

411 A345 70c Waterfall *(255,000)+* 1.25 1.25
412 A345 1.30fr People, mountain *(255,000)+* 2.25 2.25
a. Horiz. pair, #411-412 5.00 5.00
First day cover, #412a 3.75
Inscription block of 4 10.50 —

Ralph Bunche Type

Litho. With Foil Application

2003, Aug. 7 ***Perf. 13½x14***

413 A346 1.80fr **brown red & multicolored** *(300,000)+* 2.75 2.75
First day cover 3.50
Inscription block of 4 12.50
Pane of 20 55.00

In Memoriam Type of 2003

2003, Oct. 24 **Litho.** ***Perf. 13¼x13***

414 A347 85c **multicolored** *(700,000)+* 1.50 1.50
First day cover 2.10
Inscription block of 4 6.00 —
Pane of 20 30.00 —

World Heritage Sites, United States Type

Designs: 90c, No. 417b, Great Smoky Mountains National Park. 1.30fr, No. 417f, Yellowstone National Park. No. 417a, Yosemite National Park. No. 417c, Olympic National Park. No. 417d, Hawaii Volcanoes National Park. No. 417e, Everglades National Park.

2003, Oct. 24 **Litho.** ***Perf. 14½x14¼***

415 A348 90c **multicolored** *(205,000)+* 1.50 1.50
First day cover 2.10
Inscription block of 4 6.25 —
416 A348 1.30fr **multicolored** *(205,000)+* 2.25 2.25
First day cover 3.25
First day cover, #415-416 4.50
Inscription block of 4 9.25 —

Souvenir Booklet

417 Booklet *(39,000)+* 12.00
a.-c. A348 10c any single .30 .30
d.-f. A348 30c any single .65 .65
g. Booklet pane of 4 #417a 1.20 1.20
h. Booklet pane of 4 #417d 2.60 2.60
i. Booklet pane of 4 #417b 1.20 1.20
j. Booklet pane of 4 #417e 2.60 2.60
k. Booklet pane of 4 #417c 1.20 1.20
l. Booklet pane of 4 #417f 2.60 2.60

Endangered Species Type of 1993

Printed by Johann Enschedé and Sons, the Netherlands. Designed by Yuan Lee, US.

Designs: No. 418, Ursus thibetanus (Asiatic black bear). No. 419, Hippocamelus antisensis (Northern Andean deer). No. 420, Macaca silenus (Lion-tailed macaque). No. 421, Bos gaurus (Gaur).

2004, Jan. 29 **Litho.** ***Perf. 12¾x12½***

418 A271 1fr **multicolored** *(300,000)+* 1.60 1.60
419 A271 1fr **multicolored** *(300,000)+* 1.60 1.60
420 A271 1fr **multicolored** *(300,000)+* 1.60 1.60
421 A271 1fr **multicolored** *(300,000)+* 1.60 1.60
a. Block of 4, #418-421 6.50 6.50
First day cover, #421a 7.50
First day cover, #418-421, each 2.50
Inscription block of 4, #421a 7.50 —
Pane of 16 27.50 —

Indigenous Art Type of 2003

Printed by Johann Enschedé and Sons, the Netherlands. Designed by Rorie Katz and Robert Stein, US.

No. 422: a, Decoration for cows, Switzerland. b, Stone Age terra cotta sculpture of seated woman, Romania. c, Butter stamps, France. d, Detail of herald's tabard, United Kingdom. e, Woodcut print of medieval Cologne, Germany. f, Mesolithic era terra cotta sculpture of mother and child, Serbia and Montenegro.

2004, Mar. 4 **Litho.** ***Perf. 13¼***

422 G67 Sheet of 6 *(102,000)+* 7.50 7.50
First day cover 12.00
a.-f. 1fr Any single 1.25 1.25

Road Safety Type

Road map art with: 85c, Man on hand. 1fr, Person, seat belt, vert.

2004, Apr. 7 **Litho.** ***Perf. 13x13¼, 13¼x13***

423 A354 85c **multicolored** *(185,000)+* 1.40 1.40
First day cover 2.10
Inscription block of 4 6.00 —
424 A354 1fr **multicolored** *(185,000)+* 1.75 1.75
First day cover 2.50
First day cover, #423-424 4.00
Inscription block of 4 7.25 —

See France No. 3011.

Japanese Peace Bell, 50th Anniv. Type

2004, June 3 **Litho. & Engr.** ***Perf. 13¼x13***

425 A355 1.30fr **multicolored** *(230,000)+* 2.00 2.00
First day cover 3.00
Inscription block of 4 8.50 —
Pane of 20 45.00

World Heritage Sites, Greece Type

Designs: 1fr, No. 428b, Delphi. 1.30fr, No. 428e, Pythagoreion and Heraion of Samos. No. 428a, Acropolis, Athens. No. 428c, Olympia. No. 428d, Delos. No. 428f, Mycenae and Tiryns.

2004, Aug. 12 **Litho.** ***Perf. 14x13¼***

426 A356 1fr **multicolored** *(180,000)+* 1.50 1.50
First day cover 2.25
Inscription block of 4 6.50 —
427 A356 1.30fr **multicolored** *(180,000)+* 2.00 2.00
First day cover 3.00
First day cover, #426-427 4.50
Inscription block of 4 8.50 —

Souvenir Booklet

428 Booklet *(33,000)+* 13.50
a.-c. A356 20c any single .30 .30
d.-f. A356 50c any single .80 .80
g. Booklet pane of 4 #428a 1.25 1.25
h. Booklet pane of 4 #428b 1.25 1.25
i. Booklet pane of 4 #428c 1.25 1.25
j. Booklet pane of 4 #428d 3.25 3.25
k. Booklet pane of 4 #428e 3.25 3.25
l. Booklet pane of 4 #428f 3.25 3.25

My Dream for Peace Type

Winning designs of Lions Club International children's global peace poster contest by: 85c, Anggun Sita Rustinya, Indonesia. 1.20fr, Amanda Nunez, Belize.

2004, Sept. 21	**Litho.**	***Perf. 14***	
429 A357 85c **multicolored** *(195,000)*+		1.40	1.40
First day cover			1.90
Inscription block of 4		5.75	
Pane of 20		28.00	
430 A357 1.20fr **multicolored** *(195,000)*+		2.00	2.00
First day cover			2.75
First day cover, #429-430			4.00
Inscription block of 4		8.25	
Pane of 20		40.00	

G69

Human Rights — G70

Printed by Banknote Corportation of America, US. Designed by Yuri Gervorgian, Armenia. Panes of 8.

2004, Oct. 14	**Litho.**	***Perf. 11¼***	
431 G69 85c **multicolored** *(408,000)*+		1.25	1.25
First day cover			2.10
Pane of 8		10.00	—
432 G70 1.30fr **multicolored** *(408,000)*+		2.25	2.25
First day cover			3.25
First day cover, #431-432			4.50
Pane of 8		18.00	—

Sports — G71

Printed by Cartor Security Printing, France. Designed by Roland Hirter, Switzerland. Panes of 20.

2004, Nov. 23	**Litho.**	***Perf. 13x13½***	
433 G71 180c **multicolored** *(216,000)*+		3.25	3.25
First day cover			4.00
Inscription block of 4		13.00	—
Pane of 20		65.00	—

See Switzerland No. 1196.

United Nations, 60th Anniv. Type of 2005

Printed by Banknote Corporation of America, US. Designed by Czeslaw Slania, Sweden.

2005, Feb. 4	**Litho. & Engr.**	***Perf. 11x11¼***	
434 A361 1.30fr **multicolored** *(270,000)*+		2.50	2.50
First day cover			3.50
Inscription block of 4		10.00	—
Pane of 20		50.00	—

Souvenir Sheet

Litho.

Imperf

435 A361 3fr **multicolored** *(125,000)*+		7.50	7.50
First day cover			6.75

Endangered Species Type of 1993

Printed by Johann Enschedé and Sons, the Netherlands. Designed by Boris Zlotsky, US.

Designs: No. 436, Laelia milleri. No. 437, Psygmorchis pusilla. No. 438, Dendrobium cruentum. No. 439, Orchis purpurea.

2005, Mar. 3	**Litho.**	***Perf. 12¾x12½***	
436 A271 1fr **multicolored** *(248,000)*+		2.00	2.00
437 A271 1fr **multicolored** *(248,000)*+		2.00	2.00
438 A271 1fr **multicolored** *(248,000)*+		2.00	2.00
439 A271 1fr **multicolored** *(248,000)*+		2.00	2.00
a. Block of 4, #436-439		8.00	8.00
First day cover, #439a			8.75
First day cover, #436-439, each			3.00
Inscription block of 4, #439a		8.75	—
Pane of 16		32.50	

Nature's Wisdom G72

Printed by Cartor Security Printing, France. Panes of 20. Designed by Robert Stein, US.

Designs: 1fr, Children collecting water, India. 80c, Ruby brittle star, Bahamas.

2005, Apr. 21	**Litho.**	***Perf. 13½x13¼***	
440 G72 1fr **multicolored** *(180,000)*+		1.75	1.75
First day cover			2.75
Inscription block of 4		7.25	—
Pane of 20		35.00	—
441 G72 1.30fr **multicolored** *(180,000)*+		2.00	2.00
First day cover			3.75
First day cover, #440-441			5.50
Inscription block of 4		9.25	—
Pane of 20		40.00	—

Intl. Year of Sport Type

Printed by Cartor Security Printing, France. Designed by Roland Hirter, Switzerland.

2005, June 3	**Litho.**	***Perf. 13x13¼***	
442 A368 1fr Wheelchair racing *(185,000)*+		1.75	1.75
First day cover			2.75
Inscription block of 4		7.75	—
Pane of 20		35.00	—

No.	Type	Description	Unused	Used
443	A368	1.30fr Cycling *(185,000)+*	2.25	2.25
		First day cover		3.75
		First day cover, #442-443		5.50
		Inscription block of 4	9.25	—
		Pane of 20	45.00	—

World Heritage Sites, Egypt Type

Printed by Johann Enschedé and Sons, the Netherlands. Panes of 20. Designed by Rorie Katz, US.

Designs: Nos. 444, 446b, Philae. Nos. 445, 446e, Islamic Cairo. No. 446a, Memphis and its Necropolis. No. 446c, Abu Mena. No. 446d, Ancient Thebes. No. 446f, St. Catherine area.

2005, Aug. 4 — Litho. — *Perf. 14x13¼*

No.	Type	Description	Unused	Used
444	A369	1fr **multicolored** *(180,000)+*	2.00	2.00
		First day cover		2.75
		Inscription block of 4	8.00	—
445	A369	1.30fr **multicolored** *(180,000)+*	2.50	2.50
		First day cover		3.75
		First day cover, #444-445		5.50
		Inscription block of 4	10.00	—

Souvenir Booklet

No.	Type	Description	Unused	Used
446		Booklet, #446g-446l *(31,000)+*	16.50	
a.-c.	A369	20c any single	.40	.40
d.-f.	A369	50c any single	.90	.90
g.		Booklet pane of 4 #446a	1.60	1.60
h.		Booklet pane of 4 #446b	1.60	1.60
i.		Booklet pane of 4 #446c	1.60	1.60
j.		Booklet pane of 4 #446d	3.75	3.75
k.		Booklet pane of 4 #446e	3.75	3.75
l.		Booklet pane of 4 #446f	3.75	3.75

My Dream for Peace Type

Winning designs of Lions Club International children's global peace poster contest by: 1fr, Marisa Harun, Indonesia. 1.30fr, Carlos Javier Parramón Teixidó, Spain.

2005, Sept. 21 — Litho. — *Perf. 14*

No.	Type	Description	Unused	Used
447	A357	1fr **multicolored** *(175,000)+*	1.75	1.75
		First day cover		2.60
		Inscription block of 4	7.25	
		Pane of 20	35.00	
448	A357	1.30fr **multicolored** *(175,000)+*	2.00	2.00
		First day cover		3.50
		First day cover, #447-448		5.00
		Inscription block of 4	8.25	
		Pane of 20	40.00	

Food for Life Type

Printed by Government Printing Office, Austria. Designed by Andrew Davidson, United Kingdom.

Designs: 1fr, Rye, airplane dropping parcels, camel caravan. 1.30fr, Sorghum, people carrying grain sacks, trucks.

2005, Oct. 20 — Litho. — *Perf. 13¾*

No.	Type	Description	Unused	Used
449	A370	1fr **multicolored** *(170,000)+*	1.90	1.90
		First day cover		2.60
		Inscription block of 4	7.75	—
		Pane of 20	38.00	—
450	A370	1.30fr **multicolored** *(170,000)+*	2.40	2.40
		First day cover		3.50
		First day cover, #449-450		5.00
		Inscription block of 4	9.75	—
		Pane of 20	48.00	—

Armillary Sphere, Palais des Nations — G73

Printed by Cartor Security Printing, France. Panes of 20. Designed by Rorie Katz, United States.

2006, Feb. 3 — Litho. with Hologram — *Perf. 13¼x13½*

No.	Type	Description	Unused	Used
451	G73	1.30fr **multicolored** *(280,000)+*	2.25	2.25
		First day cover		3.25
		Inscription block of 4	9.00	—
		Pane of 20	45.00	—

Indigenous Art Type of 2003

Printed by Johann Enschedé and Sons, the Netherlands.
Designed by Robert Stein, US.

No. 452 — Musical instruments: a, Bell, Benin. b, Drum, Swaziland. c, Sanza, Congo. d, Stringed instruments, Cape Verde. e, Caixixi, Ghana. f, Bells, Central Africa.

2006, Feb. 3 — Litho. — *Perf. 13¼*

No.	Type	Description	Unused	Used
452	G67	Pane of 6 *(91,000)+*	12.00	12.00
		First day cover		14.00
a.-f.		1.20fr Any single	2.00	2.00

Endangered Species Type of 1993

Printed by Johann Enschedé and Sons, the Netherlands.
Designed by John D. Dawson, US.

Designs: No. 453, Dyscophus antongilii. No. 454, Chamaeleo dilepsis. No. 455, Corallus caninus. No. 456, Phyllobates vittatus.

2006, Mar. 16 — Litho. — *Perf. 12¾x12½*

No.	Type	Description	Unused	Used
453	A271	1fr **multicolored** *(228,000)+*	1.75	1.75
454	A271	1fr **multicolored** *(228,000)+*	1.75	1.75
455	A271	1fr **multicolored** *(228,000)+*	1.75	1.75
456	A271	1fr **multicolored** *(228,000)+*	1.75	1.75
a.		Block of 4, #453-456	7.00	7.00
		First day cover, #456a		7.75
		First day cover, #453-456, each		2.60
		Inscription block of 4, #456a	7.00	—
		Pane of 16	28.00	

Intl. Day of Families Type

Printed by Johann Enschedé and Sons, the Netherlands. Designed by Shelly Bartek, US.

Designs: 1fr, Family reading together. 1.30fr, Family on motorcycle.

2006, May 27 — Litho. — *Perf. 14x13½*

No.	Type	Description	Unused	Used
457	A373	1fr **multicolored** *(150,000)+*	1.25	1.25
		First day cover		2.50
		Inscription block of 4	5.00	—
		Pane of 20	25.00	—
458	A373	1.30fr **multicolored** *(150,000)+*	1.75	1.75
		First day cover		3.25
		First day cover, #457-458		5.00
		Inscription block of 4	7.00	—
		Pane of 20	35.00	—

World Heritage Sites, France Type

Printed by Cartor Security Printing, France. Panes of 20. Designed by Robert Stein, US.

Eiffel Tower and: Nos. 459, 461b, Provins. Nos. 460, 461e, Mont Saint-Michel. No. 461a, Banks of the Seine. No. 461c, Carcasonne. No. 461d, Roman Aqueduct. No. 446f, Chateau de Chambord.

Litho. & Embossed with Foil Application

2006, June 17 — *Perf. 13½x13¼*

No.	Type	Description	Unused	Used
459	A374	1fr **multicolored** *(280,000)+*	1.75	1.75
		First day cover		2.50
		Inscription block of 4	7.00	—
460	A374	1.30fr **multicolored** *(280,000)+*	2.25	2.25
		First day cover		3.25
		First day cover, #444-445		5.00
		Inscription block of 4	9.00	—

Souvenir Booklet

No.	Type	Description	Unused	Used
461		Booklet, #461g-461l *(29,000)+*	15.00	
a.-c.	A374	20c any single	.35	.35
d.-f.	A374	50c any single	.85	.85
g.		Booklet pane of 4 #461a	1.40	1.40
h.		Booklet pane of 4 #461b	1.40	1.40
i.		Booklet pane of 4 #461c	1.40	1.40
j.		Booklet pane of 4 #461d	3.50	3.50
k.		Booklet pane of 4 #461e	3.50	3.50
l.		Booklet pane of 4 #461f	3.50	3.50

See France Nos. 3219-3220.

My Dream for Peace Type of 2004

Printed by Cartor Security Printing, France. Panes of 20.

Winning designs of Lions Club International children's global peace poster contest by: 85c, Ariam Boaglio, Italy. 1.20fr, Sierra Spicer, US.

2006, Sept. 21 Litho. *Perf. 13½x13*

No.	Description	Unused	Used
462	A357 85c **multicolored** *(160,000)+*	1.60	1.60
	First day cover		2.40
	Inscription block of 4	6.40	—
	Pane of 20	32.00	—
463	A357 1.20fr **multicolored** *(160,000)+*	2.25	2.25
	First day cover		3.25
	First day cover, #462-463		4.75
	Inscription block of 4	9.00	—
	Pane of 20	45.00	—

Flags and Coins Type

Printed by Cartor Security Printing, France. Designed by Rorie Katz, US.

No. 464 — Flag of: a, Uganda, 500 shilling coin. b, Luxembourg, 1 euro coin. c, Cape Verde, 20 escudo coin. d, Belgium, 1 euro coin. e, Italy, 1 euro coin. f, New Zealand, 1 dollar coin. g, Switzerland, 2 franc coin. h, Lebanon, 500 pound coin.

2006, Oct. 5 Litho. *Perf. 13¼x13*

No.	Description	Unused	Used
464	Pane of 8	15.00	15.00
a.-h.	A375 85c Any single	1.50	1.50
	First day cover		14.50
	First day cover, #464a-464h, each		5.00

A column of rouletting in the middle of the pane separates it into two parts.

Endangered Species Type of 1993

Printed by Johann Enschedé and Sons, the Netherlands. Designed by John Rowe, US.

Designs: No. 465, Theropithecus gelada. No. 466, Cercopithecus neglectus. No. 467, Varecia variegata. No. 468, Hylobates moloch.

2007, Mar. 15 Litho. *Perf. 12¾x12½*

No.	Description	Unused	Used
465	A271 1fr **multicolored** *(208,000)+*	1.75	1.75
466	A271 1fr **multicolored** *(208,000)+*	1.75	1.75
467	A271 1fr **multicolored** *(208,000)+*	1.75	1.75
468	A271 1fr **multicolored** *(208,000)+*	1.75	1.75
a.	Block of 4, #465-468	7.00	7.00
	First day cover, #468a		8.25
	First day cover, #465-468, each		2.75
	Inscription block of 4, #468a	7.00	—
	Pane of 16	28.00	—

Flags and Coins Type of 2006

Printed by Cartor Security Printing, France. Designed by Rorie Katz, US.

No. 469 — Flag of: a, Burkina Faso, 500 franc coin. b, France, 50 cent coin. c, Moldova, 50 bani coin. d, Papua New Guinea, 1 kina coin. e, Bolivia, 1 boliviano coin. f, Myanmar, 100 kyat coin. g, Mali, 500 franc coin. h, Tunisia, 5 dinar coin.

2007, May 3 Litho. *Perf. 13¼x13*

No.	Description	Unused	Used
469	Sheet of 8 *(125,000)+*	12.50	12.50
a.-h.	A375 85c Any single	1.50	1.50
	First day cover		14.50
	First day cover, #469a-469h, each		2.50

A column of rouletting in the middle of the sheet separates it into two parts.

Peaceful Visions Type of 2007

Printed by Lowe-Martin Company, Canada. Designed by Slavka Kolesar, Canada. Panes of 20.

Designs: 1.20fr, "Harvest for All." 1.80fr, "This Dream Has Wings."

2007, June 1 Litho. *Perf. 13x12½*

No.	Description	Unused	Used
470	A378 1.20fr **multicolored** *(156,000)+*	2.25	2.25
	First day cover		3.00
	Inscription block of 4	9.00	—
	Pane of 20	45.00	—
471	A378 1.80fr **multicolored** *(156,000)+*	3.25	3.25
	First day cover		4.50
	First day cover, #470-471		6.50
	Inscription block of 4	13.00	—
	Pane of 20	65.00	—

World Heritage Sites, South America Type

Printed by Lowe-Martin Group, Canada. Panes of 20. Designed by Rorie Katz, US.

Designs: Nos. 472, 474a, Tiwanaku, Bolivia. Nos. 473, 474f, Machu Picchu, Peru. No. 474b, Iguaçu National Park, Brazil. No. 474c, Galapagos Islands, Ecuador. No. 474d, Rapa Nui, Chile. No. 474e, Cueva de las Manos, Argentina.

2007, Aug. 9 Litho. *Perf. 13¼x13*

No.	Description	Unused	Used
472	A381 1fr **multicolored** *(150,000)+*	1.90	1.90
	First day cover		2.50
	Inscription block of 4	7.60	—
473	A381 1.80fr **multicolored** *(150,000)+*	3.25	3.25
	First day cover		4.50
	First day cover, #472-473		6.00
	Inscription block of 4	13.00	—

Souvenir Booklet

No.	Description	Unused	Used
474	Booklet, #474g-474l *(27,000)+*	16.00	
a.-c.	A381 20c Any single	.40	.40
d.-f.	A381 50c Any single	.90	.90
g.	Booklet pane of 4 #474a	1.60	1.60
h.	Booklet pane of 4 #474b	1.60	1.60
i.	Booklet pane of 4 #474c	1.60	1.60
j.	Booklet pane of 4 #474d	3.60	3.60
k.	Booklet pane of 4 #474e	3.60	3.60
l.	Booklet pane of 4 #474f	3.60	3.60

Humanitarian Mail Type

Printed by Lowe-Martin Group, Canada. Panes of 10.

2007, Sept. 6 Litho. *Perf. 12½x13¼*

No.	Description	Unused	Used
475	A382 1.80fr **multicolored** *(320,000)+*	3.00	3.00
	First day cover		4.25
	Inscription block of 4	12.00	—
	Pane of 10	30.00	—

Space for Humanity Type

Printed by Johann Enschedé and Sons, the Netherlands. Panes of 6. Designed by Donato Giancola, US.

Designs: 1fr, Astronaut spacewalking. 1.80fr, International Space Station, space probe, Jupiter.

3fr, Astronauts spacewalking.

2007, Oct. 25 Litho. *Perf. 13½x14*

No.	Description	Unused	Used
476	A383 1fr **multicolored** *(252,000)+*	1.90	1.90
	First day cover		2.50
	Inscription block of 4	7.60	—
	Pane of 6	11.40	—
477	A383 1.80fr **multicolored** *(252,000)+*	3.25	3.25
	First day cover		4.50
	First day cover, #476-477		6.00
	Inscription block of 4	13.00	—
	Pane of 6	19.50	—

Souvenir Sheet

No.	Description	Unused	Used
478	A383 3fr **multicolored** *(110,000)+*	7.50	7.50
	First day cover		6.50

Intl. Holocaust Remembrance Day Type

Printed by Lowe-Martin Company, Canada. Panes of 9. Designed by Matías Delfino, Argentina.

2008, Jan. 27 Litho. *Perf. 13*

No.	Description	Unused	Used
479	A384 85c **multicolored** *(495,000)+*	3.00	3.00
	First day cover		2.75
	Pane of 9	27.00	—

Endangered Species Type of 1993

Printed by Johann Enschedé and Sons, the Netherlands. Designed by Suzanne Duranceau, Canada.

Designs: No. 480, Odobenus rosmarus. No. 481, Platygyra daedalea. No. 482, Hippocampus bargibanti. No. 483, Delphinapterus leucas.

2008, Mar. 6 Litho. *Perf. 12¾x12½*

No.	Description	Unused	Used
480	A271 1fr **multicolored** *(172,000)+*	2.00	2.00
481	A271 1fr **multicolored** *(172,000)+*	2.00	2.00
482	A271 1fr **multicolored** *(172,000)+*	2.00	2.00
483	A271 1fr **multicolored** *(172,000)+*	2.00	2.00
a.	Block of 4, #480-483	8.00	8.00
	First day cover, #483a		9.00
	First day cover, #480-483, each		3.00
	Inscription block of 4, #483a	8.00	—
	Pane of 16	32.00	—

Flags and Coins Type of 2006

Printed by Cartor Security Printing, France. Designed by Rorie Katz, US.

No. 484 — Flag of: a, Madagascar, 1 ariary coin. b, Rwanda, 50 franc coin. c, Benin, 10 franc coin. d, Iran, 500 rial coin. e, Namibia, 5 dollar coin. f, Maldives, 1 rufiyaa coin. g, Albania, 10 lek coin. h, Turkey, 1 lira coin.

2008, May 8 **Litho.** ***Perf. 13¼x13***

484	Sheet of 8 *(100,000)*+	15.00	15.00
a.-h.	A375 85c Any single	1.75	1.75
	First day cover		17.00
	First day cover, #484a-484h		3.50

A column of rouletting in the middle of the sheet separates it into two parts.

Handshake — G74

Sign Language — G75

Printed by Johann Enschedé and Sons, the Netherlands. Panes of 20. Designed by Rorie Katz, US.

2008, June 6 **Litho. & Embossed** ***Perf. 14x13¼***

485	G74 1fr **orange & red** *(142,000)*+	2.25	2.25
	First day cover		3.00
	Inscription block of 4	9.00	—
	Sheet of 20	45.00	—
486	G75 1.80fr **red & orange** *(142,000)*+	4.00	4.00
	First day cover		5.25
	First day cover, #485-486		7.25
	Inscription block of 4	16.00	—
	Sheet of 20	80.00	—

Convention on the Rights of Persons with Disabilities.

Sport for Peace Type of 2008

Printed by Johann Enschedé and Sons, the Netherlands. Panes of 9 (Nos. 487-488). Designed by Romero Britto, Brazil.
Designs: 1fr, 3fr, Gymnast. 1.80fr, Tennis player.

2008, Aug. 8 **Litho.** ***Perf. 14½***

487	A393 1fr **multicolored** *(330,030)*+	2.25	2.25
	First day cover		3.00
	Inscription block of 4	9.00	—
	Pane of 9	21.00	—
488	A393 1.80fr **multicolored** *(330,030)*+	4.00	4.00
	First day cover		5.00
	First day cover, #487-488		7.00
	Inscription block of 4	16.00	—
	Pane of 9	36.00	—

Souvenir Sheet

Perf. 12¾x13¼

489	A393 3fr **multicolored** *(160,000)*+	9.00	9.00
	First day cover		7.50

2008 Summer Olympics, Beijing.

"We Can End Poverty" Type of 2008

Printed by Sweden Post, Sweden. Panes of 20.

Winning designs in children's art contest by: 1fr, Ranajoy Banerjee, India, vert. 1.80fr, Elizabeth Elaine Chun Nig Au, Hong Kong, vert.

2008, Sept. 18 **Litho.** ***Perf. 12½x12¾***

490	A395 1fr **multicolored** *(130,000)*+	2.25	2.25
	First day cover		3.00
	Inscription block of 4	9.00	—
	Sheet of 20	45.00	—
491	A395 1.80fr **multicolored** *(130,000)*+	3.75	3.75
	First day cover		5.00
	First day cover, #490-491		7.00
	Inscription block of 4	15.00	—
	Sheet of 20	75.00	—

Climate Change Types of New York and Vienna and

G76

Climate Change G77

Printed by Lowe-Martin Group, Canada. Panes of 4. Designed by Rorie Katz, US.
No. 492 — Polar bear with quarter of Earth in: a, LR. b, LL. c, UR. d, UL.
No. 493 — Ship and sea ice with quarter of Earth in: a, LR. b, LL. c, UR. d, UL.
No. 494: a, Like New York #969a. b, Like New York #969b. c, Like New York #969c. d, Like New York #969d. e, Like Geneva #493a. f, Like Geneva #493b. g, Like Geneva #493c. h, Like Geneva #493d. i, Like Vienna #434a. j, Like Vienna #434b. k, Like Vienna #434c. l, Like Vienna #434d. m, Like New York #968a. n, Like New York #968b, o, Like New York #968c, p, Like New York #968d. q, Like Geneva #492a. r, Like Geneva #492b. s, Like Geneva #492c. t, Like Geneva #492d. u, Like Vienna #435a. v, Like Vienna #435b. w, Like Vienna #435c. x, Like Vienna #435d.
All stamps have red panels inscribed "Changement de climat."

2008, Oct. 23 **Litho.** ***Perf. 13¼x13***

492	Sheet of 4 *(100,000)*+	10.50	10.50
a.-d.	G76 1.20fr Any single	2.60	2.60
	First day cover		11.00
493	Sheet of 4 *(100,000)*+	15.50	15.50
a.-d.	G77 1.80fr Any single	3.75	3.75
	First day cover		16.50
	First day cover, #492-493		27.50

Souvenir Booklet

494	Booklet, #494y-494ad *(22,000)*+	25.00	
a.-d.	A397 35c Any single	.75	.75
e.-h.	G77 35c Any single	.75	.75
i.-l.	V72 35c Any single	.75	.75
m.-p.	A396 50c Any single	1.00	1.00
q.-t.	G76 50c Any single	1.00	1.00
u.-x.	V73 50c Any single	1.00	1.00
y.	Booklet pane of 4, #494a-494d	3.00	3.00
z.	Booklet pane of 4, #494e-494h	3.00	3.00
aa.	Booklet pane of 4, #494i-494l	3.00	3.00
ab.	Booklet pane of 4, #494m-494p	4.25	4.25
ac.	Booklet pane of 4, #494q-494t	4.25	4.25
ad.	Booklet pane of 4, #494u-494x	4.25	4.25

U Thant Type of 2009

Printed by Johann Enschedé and Sons, the Netherlands. Panes of 20.

Litho. With Foil Application

2009, Feb. 6 *Perf. 14x13½*

495 A399 1.30fr **red & multi** *(150,000)+* 3.25 3.25
First day cover 3.50
Inscription block of 4 13.00 —
Sheet of 20 65.00 —

Endangered Species Type of 1993

Printed by Johann Enschedé and Sons, the Netherlands. Designed by Roger Kent, United Kingdom.

Designs: No. 496, Maculinea arion. No. 497, Dolomedes plantarius. No. 498, Cerambyx cerdo. No. 499, Coenagrion mercuriale.

2009, Apr. 16 **Litho.** *Perf. 12¾x12½*

496 A271 1fr **multicolored** *(144,000)+* 1.90 1.90
497 A271 1fr **multicolored** *(144,000)+* 1.90 1.90
498 A271 1fr **multicolored** *(144,000)+* 1.90 1.90
499 A271 1fr **multicolored** *(144,000)+* 1.90 1.90
a. Block of 4, #496-499 7.75 7.75
First day cover, #499a 8.50
First day cover, #496-499, each 2.75
Inscription block of 4, #499a 7.75 —
Pane of 16 31.00 —
b. Pane of 16, imperf. *5,000.*

World Heritage Sites, Germany Type of 2009

Printed by Johann Enschedé and Sons, the Netherlands. Panes of 20. Designed by Grit Fiedler, Germany.

Designs: Nos. 500, 502b, Wartburg Castle. Nos. 501, 502f, Monastic Island of Reichenau. No. 502a, Town Hall and Roland on the Marketplace, Bremen. No. 502c, Palaces and Parks of Potsdam and Berlin. No. 502d, Aachen Cathedral. No. 502e, Luther Memorials in Eisleben and Wittenberg.

2009, May 7 **Litho.** *Perf. 14x13½*

500 A400 1fr **multicolored** *(155,000)+* 2.25 2.25
First day cover 2.75
Inscription block of 4 0.00
501 A400 1.30fr **multicolored** *(155,000)+* 2.75 2.75
First day cover 3.50
First day cover, #500-501 5.50
Inscription block of 4 11.00 —

Souvenir Booklet

502 Booklet, #502g-502l *(22,000)+* 18.00
a.-c. A400 30c any single .55 .55
d.-f. A400 50c any single .90 .00
g. Booklet pane of 4 #502a 2.25 2.25
h. Booklet pane of 4 #502b 2.25 2.25
i. Booklet pane of 4 #502c 2.25 2.25
j. Booklet pane of 4 #502d 3.75 3.75
k. Booklet pane of 4 #502e 3.75 3.75
l. Booklet pane of 4 #502f 3.75 3.75

Economic and Social Council (ECOSOC) Type of 2009

Printed by Sweden Post, Sweden. Panes of 20. Designed by Rorie Katz, US.

Designs: 85c, Improving maternal health. 1.80fr, Access to essential medicines.

2009, Aug. 6 **Litho.** *Perf. 12¾x12½*

503 A411 85c **multicolored** *(130,000)+* 2.00 2.00
First day cover 2.40
Inscription block of 4 8.00 —
Sheet of 20 40.00 —
504 A411 1.80fr **multicolored** *(130,000)+* 4.00 4.00
First day cover 5.00
First day cover, #503-504 6.50
Inscription block of 4 16.00 —
Sheet of 20 80.00 —

Millennium Development Goals Type of 2009

Miniature Sheet

Printed by Lowe Martin Group, Canada.
Designed by Rorie Katz, US.

No. 505: a, Bowl of hot food. b, Pencil. c, Female symbol. d, Teddy bear. e, Pregnant woman, heart. f, Medicine bottle. g, Stylized tree. h, Conjoined people.

2009, Sept. 25 **Litho.** *Perf. 13¼*

505 A413 Sheet of 8 *(65,000)+* 18.00 18.00
First day cover 20.00
a.-h. 1.10fr Any single 2.25 2.25

Palais des Nations — G78

Palais des Nations — G79

Flags of United Nations and Switzerland — G80

Meeting Room — G81

Armillary Sphere — G82

2009, Oct. 2 **Litho.** *Perf. 13¼*

506 G78 1fr **multicolored** + label *6.00 6.00*
a. Perf. 11¼x11 + label *5.00 5.00*
507 G79 1fr **multicolored** + label *6.00 6.00*
a. Perf. 11¼x11 + label *5.00 5.00*
508 G80 1fr **multicolored** + label *6.00 6.00*
a. Perf. 11¼x11 + label *5.00 5.00*
509 G81 1fr **multicolored** + label *6.00 6.00*
a. Perf. 11¼x11 + label *5.00 5.00*

510	G82 1fr **multicolored** + label	*6.00*	*6.00*
a.	Perf. 11¼x11 + label	*5.00*	*5.00*
b.	Vert. strip of 5, #506-510, + 5 labels	*30.00*	*30.00*
	Sheet, 2 #510b	*60.00*	—
c.	Vert. strip of 5, #506a-510a, + 5 labels	*25.00*	*25.00*
	Sheet, 2 #510c	*50.00*	—

United Nations Postal Administration in Geneva, 40th anniv. The full sheets sold for €19.90 or $14.95. Labels could not be personalized. The sheet of No. 510c has "VER. 2" in the lower right selvage.

Miniature Sheet

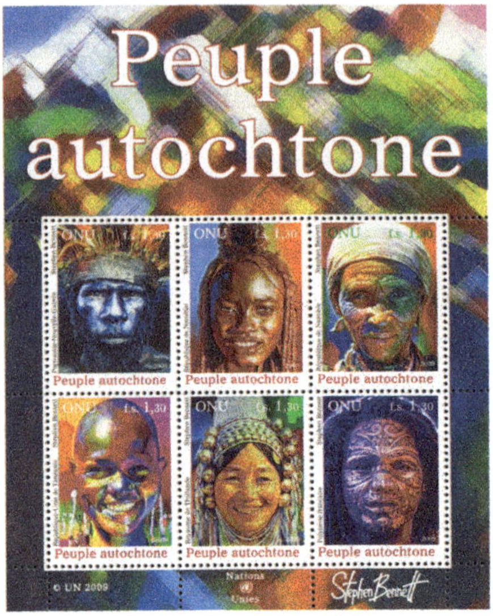

Indigenous People — G83

Printed by Lowe-Martin Group, Canada. Designed by Stephen Bennett, US.

No. 511 — Portraits of person from: a, Papua New Guinea. b, Namibia (young woman). c, Namibia (old man). d, Tanzania. e, Thailand. f, French Polynesia.

2009, Oct. 8 **Litho.** ***Perf. 12½***

511	G83 Sheet of 6 *(70,000)+*	16.00	16.00
a.-f.	1.30fr Any single	2.60	2.60
	First day cover		18.00

Flags and Coins Type of 2006

Printed by Cartor Security Printing, France. Designed by Rorie Katz, US.

No. 512 — Flag of: a, Equatorial Guinea, 100 franc coin. b, Laos, 20 kip coin. c, Seychelles, 5 rupee coin. d, Mauritania, 1 ougiya coin. e, Argentina, 1 peso coin. f, Morocco, 1 dirham coin. g, Sudan, 20 piaster coin. h, Brunei, 50 cent coin.

2010, Feb. 5 **Litho.** ***Perf. 13¼x13***

512	Sheet of 8 *(68,000)+*	15.00	15.00
a.-h.	A375 85c Any single	1.75	1.75
	First day cover		17.00

A column of rouletting in the middle of the sheet separates it into two parts.

Endangered Species Type of 1993

Printed by Johann Enschedé and Sons, the Netherlands. Designed by Rosie Sanders, United Kingdom.

Designs: No. 513, Fouquieria columnaris. No. 514, Aloe arborescens. No. 515, Galanthus krasnovii. No. 516, Dracaena draco.

2010, Apr. 15 **Litho.** ***Perf. 12¾x12½***

513	A271 1fr **multicolored** *(132,000)+*	2.25	2.25
514	A271 1fr **multicolored** *(132,000)+*	2.25	2.25
515	A271 1fr **multicolored** *(132,000)+*	2.25	2.25
516	A271 1fr **multicolored** *(132,000)+*	2.25	2.25
a.	Block of 4, #513-516	9.00	9.00
	First day cover, #516a		10.00
	First day cover, #513-516, each		3.25
	Inscription block of 4, #516a	9.00	—
	Pane of 16	36.00	—

Intl. Year of Biodiversity — G84

Printed by Lowe-Martin Group, Canada. Panes of 20. Designed by Deborah Halperin, US.

Drawings from Art Forms from Nature, by Ernst Heinrich: 1.60fr, Arachnid. 1.90fr, Starfish.

2010, Apr. 15 **Litho.** ***Perf. 13***

517	G84 1.60fr **multicolored** *(400,000)+*	3.75	3.75
	First day cover		4.50
	Inscription block of 4	15.00	—
	Sheet of 20	75.00	—
518	G84 1.90fr **multicolored** *(400,000)+*	4.25	4.25
	First day cover		5.25
	First day cover, #517-518		8.75
	Inscription block of 4	17.00	—
	Sheet of 20	85.00	—

One Planet, One Ocean Types of New York and Vienna and

G85

One Planet, One Ocean — G86

Printed by Johann Enschedé and Sons, the Netherlands. Designed by Robert Wyland, US.

No. 519: a, Turtles at left and top, fish at bottom. b, Hammerhead shark. c, Fish at left and center, corals. d, Fish at left, coral.

No. 520: a, Dolphins. b, Shark, head of fish at right, small fish in background. c, Ray and fish. d, Fish at bottom, coral and sponges.

No. 521: a, Like New York #1003a. b, Like New York #1003b, c, Like New York #1003c, d, Like New York #1003d. e, Like Vienna #471a. f, Like Vienna #471b. g, Like Vienna #471c, h, Like Vienna #471d. i, Like #519a. j, Like #519b, k, Like #519c. l, Like #519d. m, Like New York #1004a. n, Like New York #1004b. o, Like New York #1004c, p, Like New York #1004d. q, Like Vienna #472a. r, Like Vienna #472b. s, Like Vienna #472c. t, Like Vienna #472d. u, Like #520a. v, Like #520b. w, Like #520c. x, Like #520d.

2010, May 6 **Litho.** ***Perf. 14x13¼***

519	G85 Sheet of 4 *(65,000)+*	8.00	8.00
a.-d.	85c Any single	2.00	2.00
520	G86 Sheet of 4 *(65,000)+*	10.00	10.00
a.-d.	1fr Any single	2.50	2.50
	First day cover, #519-520		20.50

Souvenir Booklet

Perf. 13¼x13

521	Booklet, #521y-521z, 521aa-521ad *(22,000)*+	22.00	
a.-d.	A416 30c any single	.70	.70
e.-h.	V91 30c any single	.70	.70
i.-l.	G85 30c any single	.70	.70
m.-p.	A417 50c any single	1.10	1.10
q.-t.	V92 50c any single	1.10	1.10
u.-x.	G86 50c any single	1.10	1.10
y.	Booklet pane of 4 #521a-521d	2.80	2.80
z.	Booklet pane of 4 #521e-521h	2.80	2.80
aa.	Booklet pane of 4 #521i-521l	2.80	2.80
ab.	Booklet pane of 4 #521m-521p	4.40	4.40
ac.	Booklet pane of 4 #521q-521t	4.40	4.40
ad.	Booklet pane of 4 #521u-521x	4.40	4.40

Intl. Oceanographic Commission, 50th anniv.

United Nations, 65th Anniv. Type of 2010

Printed by Lowe-Martin Group, Canada. Designed by Rorie Katz, United States.

Litho. With Foil Application

2010, June 28 ***Perf. 13¼***

522	A422 1.90fr **red & gold** *(135,000)*+	4.00	4.00
	First day cover		5.00
	Inscription block of 4	16.00	—
	Pane of 15	60.00	—
a.	Souvenir sheet of 2 *(40,500)*+	8.00	8.00
	First day cover, #522a		8.75

G87

G88

G89

G90

United Nations Land Transport — G91

Printed by UAB Garsu Pasaulis, Lithuania. Designed by Simon Williams, United Kingdom.

2010, Sept. 2 **Litho.** ***Perf. 13¼x13***

523	G87 1fr **multicolored** *(120,000)*+	1.80	1.80
524	G88 1fr **multicolored** *(120,000)*+	1.80	1.80
525	G89 1fr **multicolored** *(120,000)*+	1.80	1.80
526	G90 1fr **multicolored** *(120,000)*+	1.80	1.80
527	G91 1fr **multicolored** *(120,000)*+	1.80	1.80
a.	Horiz. strip of 5, #523-527	9.00	9.00
	First day cover, #527a		11.50
	First day cover, #523-527, each		3.25
	Inscription block of 10	21.00	—
	Pane of 20	42.00	—

Miniature Sheet

Campaign Against Child Labor — G92

No. 528: a, Child, buildings, road, burning can. b, Child with full basket on back, children playing in background. c, Child working, children on school bus. d, Child with mining helmet, three other children. e, Child near tubs, children working, child being beaten. f, Child with hoo. g, Marionette, traffic light. h, Child carrying basket on head. i, Children on rock field near hills. j, Child holding bags in road.

2010, Sept. 2 **Litho.** ***Perf. 14¾***

528	G92 Sheet of 10 + 10 labels	32.50	32.50
a.-j.	1.90fr Any single + label	3.25	3.25

No. 528 sold for $14.95, 15fr and €11.46, each of which was far lower than the level at which 19fr, the total face value of the stamps on the sheet, was worth on the day of issue. Labels could not be personalized.

Miniature Sheet

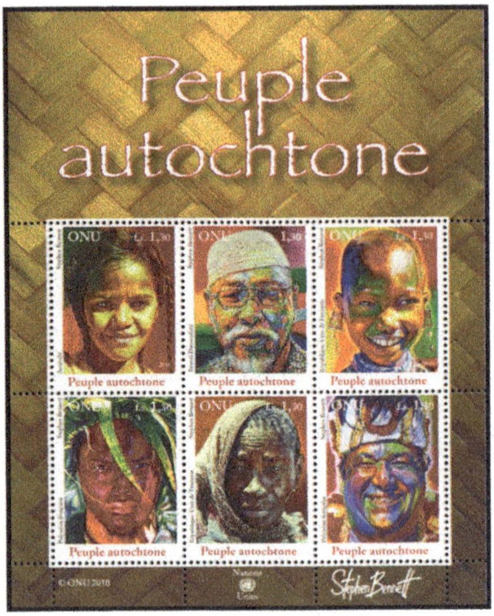

Indigenous People — G93

Printed by Lowe-Martin Group, Canada. Designed by Stephen Bennett, US.

No. 529 — Portraits of person from: a, Australia. b, Brunei. c, Tanzania (girl with bald head). d, French Polynesia (man with head-dress of leaves). e, Tanzania (man with headdress). f, French Polynesia (man with white headdress).

2010, Oct. 21 **Litho.** ***Perf. 13***

529	G93	Pane of 6 *(55,000)*+	14.50	14.50
a.-f.		1.30fr Any single	2.40	2.40
		First day cover		18.50

United Nations Headquarters, Geneva — G94

Printed by Cartor Security Printing, France. Panes of 20. Designed by Scott Solberg, US.

United Nations Headquarters, Geneva: 10c, Aerial view. 50c, Ground-level view.

2011, Feb. 4 **Litho.** ***Perf. 13***

530	G94	10c **multicolored** *(400,000)*+	.35	.35
		First day cover		1.25
		Inscription block of 4	1.40	—
		Pane of 20	7.00	—
531	G94	50c **multicolored** *(400,000)*+	1.25	1.25
		First day cover		2.75
		First day cover, #530-531		2.25
		Inscription block of 4	5.00	—
		Pane of 20	25.00	—

Flags and Coins Type of 2006

Printed by Cartor Security Printing, France. Designed by Rorie Katz, US.

No. 532 — Flag of: a, Mongolia, 500 tugrik coin. b, Senegal, 500 franc coin. c, Egypt, 100 piaster coin. d, Congo, 100 franc coin. e, Nicaragua, 1 Córdoba coin. f, Central African Republic, 100 franc coin. g, Algeria, 5 dinar coin. h, Ukraine, 5 hryvnia coin.

2011, Mar. 3 **Litho.** ***Perf. 13¼x13***

532		Sheet of 8 *(60,000)*+	15.00	15.00
a.-h.	A375	85c Any single	1.75	1.75
		First day cover		17.00

A column of rouletting in the middle of the sheet separates it into two parts.

Human Space Flight, 50th Anniv. — G95

Printed by Lowe-Martin Group, Canada. Designed by Peter Bollinger, US.

No. 533: Various parts of outer space scene.

No. 534, vert.: a, International Space Station. b, International Space Station, diff.

2011, Apr. 12 **Litho.** ***Perf. 13x13¼***

533	G95	Sheet of 16 *(55,000)*+	18.00	18.00
		First day cover		20.00
a.-p.		50c any single	1.10	1.10

Souvenir Sheet

534	G95	Sheet of 2	15.00	15.00
		First day cover		5.00
a.		85c **multicolored**	6.50	6.50
b.		1fr **multicolored**	8.50	8.50

No. 534 contains two 40x48mm stamps that were printed as part of a larger sheet of six stamps, Vienna No. 485c, which was broken up into its component two-stamp souvenir sheets, and also sold as one unit. Value, $90, complete unit.

UNESCO World Heritage Sites in Nordic Countries Type of 2011

Printed by Johann Enschedé and Sons, the Netherlands. Panes of 20. Designed by Rorie Katz, US.

Designs: 85c, Kronborg Castle, Denmark. 1fr, Suomenlinna Fortress, Finland.

2011, May 5 **Litho.** ***Perf. 14x13½***

535	A433	85c **multicolored** *(140,000)*+	1.90	1.90
		First day cover		2.75
		Inscription block of 4	7.60	—
		Pane of 20	30.00	—
536	A433	1fr **multicolored** *(140,000)*+	2.25	2.25
		First day cover		3.25
		First day cover, #535-536		5.00
		Inscription block of 4	9.00	—
		Pane of 20	45.00	—

AIDS Ribbon Type of 2011

Printed by Lowe-Martin Group, Canada. Panes of 4. Designed by Rorie Katz, US.

2011, June 3 **Litho.** ***Die Cut***

Self-Adhesive

537	A434	1.30fr **red & orange** *(220,000)*+	5.00	5.00
		Pane of 4	20.00	
		First day cover, pane of 4		14.50

ECOSOC Type of 2011

Printed by Cartor Security Printing, France. Panes of 20. Designed by Rorie Katz, US.

Education: 1fr, Girls taking notes. 1.30fr, Girls at computers.

2011, July 1 **Litho.** ***Perf. 14¼***

538	A435	1fr **multicolored** *(130,000)*+	3.00	3.00
		First day cover		3.50
		Inscription block of 4	12.00	—
		Pane of 20	60.00	—
539	A435	1.30fr **multicolored** *(130,000)*+	4.00	4.00
		First day cover		4.50
		First day cover, #538-539		7.00
		Inscription block of 4	16.00	—
		Pane of 20	80.00	—

Endangered Species Type of 1993

Printed by Johann Enschedé and Sons, the Netherlands. Designed by Wendy Wray, U.S.
Designs: No. 540, Strigops habroptilus (Kakapo). No. 541, Lophophorus impejanus (Himalayan monal). No. 542, Ciconia nigra (Black stork). No. 543, Pithecophaga jeffreyi (Philippine eagle).

2011, Sept. 7 **Litho.** ***Perf. 12¾x12½***

540 A271 1fr **multicolored** *(112,000)+* 2.60 2.60
541 A271 1fr **multicolored** *(112,000)+* 2.60 2.60
542 A271 1fr **multicolored** *(112,000)+* 2.60 2.60
543 A271 1fr **multicolored** *(112,000)+* 2.60 2.60
a. Block of 4, #540-543 10.40 10.40
First day cover, #543a 11.50
First day cover, #540-543, each 3.75
Inscription block of 4, #543a 10.40 —
Pane of 16 42.00 —

Intl. Year of Forests Type of 2011

Printed by Lowe-Martin Group, Canada. Panes of 8. Designed by Sergio Baradat, U.S.
Designs: 85c, Birds and butterflies, tree tops. 1.40fr, Fish and coral.

2011, Oct. 13 **Litho. With Foil Application** ***Perf. 12½***

544 85c **multicolored** *(88,000)+* 2.25 2.25
545 1.40fr **multicolored** *(88,000)+* 3.75 3.75
a. A436 Vert. pair, #544-545 6.00 6.00
First day cover, #545a 6.75
Pane of 8 24.00 —

Flags and Coins Type of 2006

Printed by Cartor Security Printing, France. Designed by Rorie Katz, US.
No. 546 — Flag of: a, Saudi Arabia, 100 halala coin. b, Georgia, 2 lari coin. c, Democratic People's Republic of Korea, 50 won coin. d, Lesotho, 50 lisente coin. e, Serbia, 5 dinar coin. f, Djibouti, 20 franc coin. g, Belize, 1 dollar coin. h, Liechtenstein, 20 centime coin.

2012, Feb. 3 **Litho.** ***Perf. 13¼x13***

546 Sheet of 8 *(48,000)+* 16.50 16.50
a.-h. A375 85c Any single 2.00 2.00
First day cover 18.50

A column of rouletting in the middle of the sheet separates it into two parts.

G96

Autism Awareness — G97

Printed by Joh. Enschedé Stamps Security Printers, Netherlands. Panes of 20.
Drawings by autistic people: No. 547, Victory, by J.A. Tan, Canada. No. 548, Untitled drawing, by Michael Augello, U.S.

2012, Apr. 2 **Litho.** ***Perf. 14x13½***

547 G96 1.40fr **multicolored** *(85,000)+* 3.50 3.50
548 G97 1.40fr **multicolored** *(85,000)+* 3.50 3.50
a. Pair, #547-548 7.00 7.00
First day cover, #547, 548 7.75
Inscription block of 4 14.00 —
Pane of 20 70.00 —

Endangered Species Type of 1993

Printed by Johann Enschedé and Sons, the Netherlands. Designed by Diana Marques, Portugal.
Designs: No. 549, Panthera tigris altaica. No. 550, Psitacella picta. No. 551, Iguana iguana. No. 552, Propithecus tattersalli.

2012, Apr. 19 **Litho.** ***Perf. 12¾x12½***

549 A271 1fr **multicolored** *(102,000)+* 2.40 2.40
550 A271 1fr **multicolored** *(102,000)+* 2.40 2.40
551 A271 1fr **multicolored** *(102,000)+* 2.40 2.40
552 A271 1fr **multicolored** *(102,000)+* 2.40 2.40
a. Block of 4, #549-552 9.75 9.75
First day cover, #552a 10.50
First day cover, #549-552, each 3.50
Inscription block of 4, #552a 9.75 —
Pane of 16 39.00 —

Rio + 20 Type of 2012

Printed by Lowe-Martin Group, Canada. Panes of 20. Designed by Shailesh Khandeparkar, India.

2012, June 1 **Litho.** ***Perf. 13x13¼***

553 A443 1.40fr **multicolored** *(116,000)+* 4.00 4.00
First day cover 4.50
Inscription block of 4 16.00 —
Pane of 20 80.00 —

Sport for Peace Type of 2012

Printed by Cartor Security Printing, France. Panes of 9. Designed by Daniel Stolle, Finland.
2012 Paralympics events: 1fr, Track. 1.40fr, Archery.

Litho. With Foil Application

2012, Aug. 17 ***Perf. 14½***

554 A444 1fr **multicolored** *(126,000)+* 2.40 2.40
First day cover 3.25
Inscription block of 4 9.60 —
Pane of 9 22.00 —
555 A444 1.40fr **multicolored** *(126,000)+* 3.50 3.50
First day cover 4.50
First day cover, #554-555 7.75
Inscription block of 4 14.00 —
Pane of 9 31.50
a. Souvenir sheet of 1 *(37,000)+* 3.50 3.50
First day cover 4.50

UNESCO World Heritage Sites in Africa Type of 2012

Printed by Lowe-Martin Group, Canada. Panes of 20. Designed by Rorie Katz, US.
Designs: 85c, Virunga National Park, Congo Democratic Republic. 1fr, Amphitheater of El Jem, Tunisia.

2012, Sept. 5 **Litho.** ***Perf. 13¼***

556 A445 85c **multicolored** *(120,000)+* 2.00 2.00
First day cover 3.00
Inscription block of 4 8.00 —
Pane of 20 40.00 —
557 A445 1fr **multicolored** *(120,000)+* 2.40 2.40
First day cover 3.25
First day cover, #556-557 5.25
Inscription block of 4 9.75 —
Pane of 20 48.00 —

Miniature Sheet

Indigenous People — G98

Printed by Lowe-Martin Group, Canada. Designed by Stephen Bennett, US.

No. 558 — Portrait of person from: a, China. b, Tibet, China. c, Mongolia. d, Mexico. e, Papua New Guinea. f, Haiti.

2012, Oct. 11 **Litho.** ***Perf. 13¼x13***

558 G98	Sheet of 6 *(39,000)*+	13.50	13.50
a.-f.	85c Any single	2.25	2.25
	First day cover		14.00

World Radio Day Type of 2013

Printed by Lowe-Martin Group, Canada. Panes of 20. Designed by Rorie Katz, US.

Designs: 1.40fr, Reporter with microphone and tape recorder. 1.90fr, Engineers in studio.

2013, Feb. 13 **Litho.** ***Perf. 13¼x13***

559 A448	1.40fr **multicolored** *(105,700)*+	3.50	3.50
	First day cover		4.25
	Inscription block of 4	14.00	—
	Pane of 20	70.00	—
560 A448	1.90fr **multicolored** *(105,700)*+	4.50	4.50
	First day cover		5.75
	First day cover, #559-560		9.00
	Inscription block of 4	18.00	—
	Pane of 20	90.00	—

Person on Leaf — G99

Dove and People — G100

Printed by Johann Enschedé and Sons, the Netherlands. Panes of 20. Designed by Sergio Baradat, US.

2013, Mar. 5 **Litho.** ***Perf. 14x13½***

561 G99	1fr **multicolored** *(200,000)*+	2.40	2.40
	First day cover		3.25
	Inscription block of 4	9.60	—
	Pane of 20	48.00	—

Perf. 13½x14

562 G100	1.40fr **multicolored** *(200,000)*+	3.50	3.50
	First day cover		4.50
	First day cover, #561-562		6.75
	Inscription block of 4	14.00	—
	Pane of 20	70.00	—

World Heritage Sites, China, Type of 2013

Printed by Johann Enschedé and Sons, the Netherlands. Panes of 20. Designed by Sergio Baradat, U.S.

Designs: Nos. 563, 565b, Potala Palace, Lhasa. Nos. 564, 565e, Mount Huangshan. No. 565a, Mogao Caves. No. 565c, Great Wall of China. No. 565d, Imperial Palace, Beijing. No. 565f, Mausoleum of the First Qing Emperor.

2013, Apr. 11 **Litho.** ***Perf. 14x13½***

563 A452	1.40fr **multicolored** *(128,600)*+	3.50	3.50
	First day cover		4.25
	Inscription block of 4	14.00	—
	Pane of 20	70.00	—
564 A452	1.90fr **multicolored** *(128,600)*+	4.50	4.50
	First day cover		5.75
	First day cover, #563-564		8.75
	Inscription block of 4	18.00	—
	Pane of 20	90.00	—

Souvenir Booklet

565	Booklet, #565g-565l *(20,000)*+	24.00	
a.-c.	A452 30c any single	.75	.75
d.-f.	A452 50c any single	1.25	1.25
g.	Booklet pane of 4 #565a	3.00	—
h.	Booklet pane of 4 #565b	3.00	—
i.	Booklet pane of 4 #565c	3.00	—
j.	Booklet pane of 4 #565d	5.00	—
k.	Booklet pane of 4 #565e	5.00	—
l.	Booklet pane of 4 #565f	5.00	—

World Oceans Day — G101

Printed by Lowe-Martin Group, Canada. Designed by Rorie Katz, US.

No. 566 — Fish from *One Fish, Two Fish, Red Fish, Blue Fish,* by Dr. Seuss: a, Three red fish facing right. b, Green fish, tail of yellow fish. c, Three red fish facing right, part of tail of red fish. d, Two entire green fish facing left, tail of bottom fish ends above "n" in "océan." e, Red fish with eye open facing left. f, Tail of red fish, yellow and red fish facing left. g, Red fish facing right, water droplets. h, Yellow and red fish facing right. i, Two green fish facing left, tail of bottom fish ends to right of "océan." j, Red fish and wave. k, Two green fish, red fish, wave. l, Yellow fish in car, wave.

2013, May 31 **Litho.** ***Perf. 13***

566	G101	Sheet of 12 *(48,000)+*	20.00	20.00
		First day cover		26.50
a.-l.		85c any single	1.60	1.60

Nebulae Type of 2013

Printed by UAB Garsu Pasaulis, Lithuania. Panes of 8. Designed by Sergio Baradat, U.S.

Designs: No. 567, NGC 2346. No. 568, Sh 2-106. 1fr, Messier 16.

2013, Aug. 9 **Litho.** ***Perf. 13¼***

567	A454	1.40fr **multicolored** *(112,000)+*	3.50	3.50
568	A454	1.40fr **multicolored** *(112,000)+*	3.50	3.50
a.		Pair, #567-568	7.00	7.00
		First day cover, #568a		7.75
		Inscription block of 4	14.00	—
		Pane of 8	28.00	—

Souvenir Sheet

569	A454	1fr **multicolored** *(31,000)+*	2.40	2.40
		First day cover		3.50

No. 569 contains one 44x44mm stamp.

Works of Disabled Artists Type of 2013

Printed by UAB Garsu Pasaulis, Lithuania. Panes of 20. Designed by Rorie Katz, U.S.

Designs: 1.40fr, See the Girl with the Red Dress On, by Sargy Mann, United Kingdom. 1.90fr, Performers in China Disabled People's Performing Art Troupe, People's Republic of China.

2013, Sept. 20 **Litho.** ***Perf. 13¼x13***

570	A456	1.40fr **multicolored** *(118,200)+*	3.50	3.50
		First day cover		4.25
		Inscription block of 4	14.00	—
		Pane of 20	70.00	—
571	A456	1.90fr **multicolored** *(118,200)+*	4.50	4.50
		First day cover		5.75
		First day cover, #570-571		9.00
		Inscription block of 4	18.00	—
		Pane of 20	90.00	—

Endangered Species Type of 1993

Printed by Johann Enschedé and Sons, the Netherlands. Designed by Sara Menon, Italy.

Designs: No. 572, Smutsia temminckii. No. 573, Perodicticus potto. No. 574, Tarsius syrichta. No. 575, Pteropus livingstonii.

2013, Oct. 10 **Litho.** ***Perf. 12¾x12½***

572	A271	1.40fr **multicolored** *(96,000)+*	3.25	3.25
573	A271	1.40fr **multicolored** *(96,000)+*	3.25	3.25
574	A271	1.40fr **multicolored** *(96,000)+*	3.25	3.25
575	A271	1.40fr **multicolored** *(96,000)+*	3.25	3.25
a.		Block of 4, #572-575	13.00	13.00
		First day cover, #575a		14.00
		First day cover, #572-575, each		4.25
		Inscription block of 4, #575a	13.00	—
		Pane of 16	52.00	—

Flags and Coins Type of 2006

Printed by Cartor Security Printing, France. Designed by Rorie Katz, US.

No. 576 — Flag of: a, Ivory Coast, 100 franc coin. b, Marshall Islands, 10 cent coin. c, Andorra, 20 cent coin. d, Guinea-Bissau, 100 franc coin. e, Kenya, 20 shilling coin. f, Antigua and Barbuda, 5 cent coin. g, Tajikistan, 50 diram coin. h, Micronesia, 5 cent coin.

2013, Nov. 6 **Litho.** ***Perf. 13¼x13***

576		Sheet of 8 *(40,000)+*	26.00	26.00
a.-h.	A375	1.40fr Any single	3.25	3.25
		First day cover		28.00

A column of rouletting in the middle of the sheet separates it into two parts.

International Day of Happiness Type of 2014

Printed by Lowe-Martin Group, Canada. Panes of 20. Designed by Rorie Katz, U.S.

Designs: 1fr, A Sweet Dog's Muzzle, photograph by Jaymi Heimbuch, "Heureux." 1.40fr, Two women making heart with hands, photograph by Glow Images, Chinese characters for "Happy."

2014, Mar. 17 **Litho.** ***Perf. 13¼x13***

577	A459	1fr **multicolored** *(90,000)+*	2.50	2.50
		First day cover		3.25
		Inscription block of 4	10.00	—
		Pane of 20	50.00	—
578	A459	1.40fr **multicolored** *(90,000)+*	3.50	3.50
		First day cover		4.50
		First day cover, #577-578		7.00
		Inscription block of 4	14.00	—
		Pane of 20	70.00	—

Miniature Sheet

International Year of Jazz — G102

Printed by Cartor Security Printing, France. Designed by Sergio Baradat, U.S.

No. 579: a, Woman behind microphone. b, Saxophone. c, Silhouette of pianist at grand piano. d, Cymbal and silhouette of man holding trumpet. e, Cymbal and clarinet. f, Clarinet and drum. g, Hi-hat. h, Silhouette of drummer and drum set. i, Trumpeter with hat. j, Microphone and cymbal stands. k, Clarinetist. l, Bass player.

2014, Apr. 30 **Litho.** ***Perf. 13x13¼***

579 G102 Sheet of 12 *(45,000)*+ 29.50 29.50
First day cover 31.00
a.-l. 1fr Any single 2.40 2.40

G103

G104

Printed by Lowe-Martin Group, Canada. Panes of 20. Designed by Sergio Baradat, U.S.

2014, June 6 **Litho.** ***Perf. 13¼x13***

580 G103 2.20fr **multicolored** *(106,000)*+ 5.50 5.50
First day cover 6.25
Inscription block of 4 22.00 —
Pane of 20 110.00 —
581 G104 2.60fr **multicolored** *(106,000)*+ 6.50 6.50
First day cover 7.50
First day cover, #580-581 13.00
Inscription block of 4 26.00 —
Pane of 20 130.00 —

Taj Mahal Types of 2014

Printed by Lowe-Martin Group, Canada. Panes of 20. Designed by Rorie Katz, U.S.

2014, July 16 **Engr.** ***Perf. 13¼x13***

582 A465 1.40fr **multicolored** *(110,000)*+ 3.50 3.50
First day cover 4.25
Inscription block of 4 14.00 —
Pane of 20 70.00 —
583 A467 1.90fr **multicolored** *(110,000)*+ 4.75 4.75
First day cover 5.75
First day cover, #582-583 9.25
Inscription block of 4 19.00 —
Pane of 20 95.00 —

Souvenir Booklet

584 Booklet, #584g-584l *(14,000)*+ 20.00
a. A463 30c multi .75 .75
b. A465 30c multi .75 .75
c. A466 50c multi 1.25 1.25
d. A464 50c multi 1.25 1.25
e. A467 30c multi .75 .75
f. A468 50c multi 1.25 1.25
g. Booklet pane of 4 #584a 2.50 —
h. Booklet pane of 4 #584b 2.50 —
i. Booklet pane of 4 #584c 2.50 —
j. Booklet pane of 4 #584d 4.00 —
k. Booklet pane of 4 #584e 4.00 —
l. Booklet pane of 4 #584f 4.00 —

International Year of Family Farming — G105

Printed by Lowe-Martin Group, Canada. Panes of 20. Designed by Sergio Baradat, U.S.

Designs: 1.30fr, African villagers harvesting produce. 1.60fr, Farming family, farm and animals.

2014, Aug. 21 **Litho.** ***Perf. 13x13¼***

585 G105 1.30fr **multicolored** *(90,000)*+ 3.25 3.25
First day cover 4.00
Inscription block of 4 13.00 —
Pane of 20 65.00 —
586 G105 1.60fr **multicolored** *(90,000)*+ 4.00 4.00
First day cover 5.00
First day cover, #585-586 8.25
Inscription block of 4 16.00 —
Pane of 20 80.00 —

G106

No. 587: a, Room with painted ceiling. b, Peacock with spread tail. c, Rows of flags, brown panel at bottom. d, Rows of flags near Palais des Nations, tan panel at top. e, Meeting hall with United nations emblem on rear wall. f, Armillary sphere and Palais des Nations. g, Meeting hall with movie screen on rear wall. h, Circular meeting hall. i, Farm animals on grass near buildings. j, Peacock with tail down.

2014, Sept. 12 **Litho.** ***Perf. 14¾***

587 G106 Sheet of 10 *35.00 35.00*
a.-j. 1.30fr Any single + label *3.50 3.50*

The full sheet sold for 14.95fr. The generic labels are shown. Labels could be personalized.

Global Education First Initiative Type of 2014

Printed by Lowe-Martin Group, Canada. Panes of 20. Designed by Oamul Lu, People's Republic of China.

Designs: No. 588, Students in art museum. No. 589, Student in library.

2014, Sept. 18 **Litho.** ***Perf. 13x13¼***

588 A470 1.90fr **multicolored** *(100,000)*+ 4.75 4.75
First day cover 5.75
Inscription block of 4 19.00 —
Pane of 20 95.00 —

Souvenir Sheet

Perf. 12½

589 A470 1.90fr **multicolored** *(34,000)*+ 4.75 4.75
First day cover 6.25

No. 589 contains one 32x32mm stamp.

Endangered Species Type of 2014

Printed by Johann Enschedé and Sons, the Netherlands. Designed by Amadeo Bachar, U.S.

Maps and: No. 590, Arapaima gigas. No. 591, Cetorhinus maximus. No. 592, Pristis pristis. No. 593, Acipenser baerii.

2014, Oct. 23	**Litho.**	***Perf. 12¾x12½***	
590 A471 1.40fr **multicolored** *(88,000)*+		3.50	3.50
591 A471 1.40fr **multicolored** *(88,000)*+		3.50	3.50
592 A471 1.40fr **multicolored** *(88,000)*+		3.50	3.50
593 A471 1.40fr **multicolored** *(88,000)*+		3.50	3.50
a. Block of 4, #590-593		14.00	14.00
First day cover, #593a			15.00
First day cover, #590-593, each			4.50
Inscription block of 4, #593a		14.00	—
Pane of 16		56.00	—

Flags and Coins Type of 2006

Printed by Cartor Security Printing, France. Designed by Rorie Katz, U.S.

No. 594 — Flag of: a, Vanuatu, 10 vatu coin. b, Nauru, 1 dollar coin. c, Eritrea, 100 cent coin. d, El Salvador, 1 colon coin. e, Mozambique, 50 centavo coin. f, Burundi, 1 franc coin. g, Turkmenistan, 10 tenge coin. h, Guinea, 1 franc coin.

2015, Feb. 6	**Litho.**	***Perf. 13¼x13***	
594 Sheet of 8 *(40,000)*+		16.50	16.50
a.-h. A375 90c Any single		2.00	2.00
First day cover			18.50

A column of rouletting in the middle of the sheet separates it into two parts.

Miniature Sheets

G107

World Poetry Day — G108

Printed by Cartor Security Printing, France. Designed by Sergio Baradat, U.S.

No. 595: a, Pen and gray circle. b, Li Bai quotation in Chinese, denomination in light blue green. c, Li Bai quotation in Chinese, denomination in red. d, Pen and red circle. e, Pen and orange circle. f, Li Bai quotation in Chinese, denomination in white.

No. 596: a, Pen and light green circle. b, Anais Nin quotation, denomination and "Journée mondiale de poésie" in light blue. c, As "b," with "Journée mondiale de poésie" in white, dark blue area below and to left of date. d, Pen and black circle. e, Pen and lilac circle. f, As "c," with dark blue area below and to right of date.

2015, Mar. 20	**Litho.**	***Perf. 14½x14¼***	
595 G107 Sheet of 6 *(37,000)*+		14.00	14.00
a.-f. 1fr Any single		2.25	2.25
596 G108 Sheet of 6 *(37,000)*+		19.50	19.50
a.-f. 1.40fr Any single		3.25	3.25
First day cover, #595-596			37.00

Endangered Species Type of 2015

Printed by Johann Enschedé and Sons, the Netherlands. Designed by John Keulemans and William Hart, United Kingdom.

Designs: No. 597, Diphyllodes respublica. No. 598, Ptiloris paradiseus. No. 599, Semioptera wallacii. No. 600, Paradisaea decora.

2015, Apr. 16	**Litho.**	***Perf. 12½x12¾***	
597 A476 1.40fr **multicolored** *(80,000)*+		3.25	3.25
598 A476 1.40fr **multicolored** *(80,000)*+		3.25	3.25
599 A476 1.40fr **multicolored** *(80,000)*+		3.25	3.25
600 A476 1.40fr **multicolored** *(80,000)*+		3.25	3.25
a. Block of 4, #597-600		13.00	13.00
First day cover, #600a			14.00
First day cover, #597-600, each			4.25
Inscription block of 4, #600a		13.00	—
Pane of 16		52.00	—
Nos. 597-600 (4)		13.00	13.00

World Heritage Sites, Southeast Asia, Type of 2015

Printed by Johann Enschedé and Sons, the Netherlands. Panes of 20. Designed by Sergio Baradat, U.S.

Designs: Nos. 601, 603b, Angkor Wat, Cambodia. Nos. 602, 603e, Cordillera, Philippines. No. 603a, Luang Prabang, Laos. No. 603c, Ayutthaya, Thailand. No. 565d, Borobudur Temple, Indonesia. No. 603f, Hué Monuments, Viet Nam.

2015, June 5	**Litho.**	***Perf. 14x13½***	
601 A480 1.40fr **multicolored** *(110,000)*+		3.25	3.25
First day cover			4.00
Inscription block of 4		13.00	—
Pane of 20		65.00	—
602 A480 1.90fr **multicolored** *(110,000)*+		4.50	4.50
First day cover			5.50
First day cover, #601-602			8.75
Inscription block of 4		18.00	—
Pane of 20		90.00	—

Souvenir Booklet

603 Booklet, #603g-603l *(13,000)*+		23.50	
a.-c. A480 30c any single		.70	.70
d.-f. A480 50c any single		1.25	1.25
g. Booklet pane of 4 #603a		2.80	—
h. Booklet pane of 4 #603b		2.80	—
i. Booklet pane of 4 #603c		2.80	—
j. Booklet pane of 4 #603d		5.00	—
k. Booklet pane of 4 #603e		5.00	—
l. Booklet pane of 4 #603f		5.00	—

End Violence Against Children Type of 2015

Printed by Cartor Security Printing, France. Panes of 20. Designed by Chris Sharp, U.S.

Designs: 1fr, Child marriage. 1.40fr, Child trafficking.

2015, Aug. 20	**Litho.**	***Perf. 14½x14¼***	
604 A481 1fr **multicolored** *(90,000)*+		2.40	2.40
First day cover			3.25
Inscription block of 4		9.60	—
Pane of 20		48.00	—
605 A481 1.40fr **multicolored** *(90,000)*+		3.25	3.25
First day cover			4.50
First day cover, #605-606			6.50
Inscription block of 4		13.00	—
Pane of 20		65.00	—

Miniature Sheet

G109

No. 606: a, Balcony above auditorium seats. b, Flags. c, Spiral staircase. d, Stylized horned mammal. e, Painting of trees. f, Auditorium seats facing stage with dais. g, Side view of auditorium seats, painting on wall. h, United Nations emblem. i, Armillary Sphere. j, Palais des Nations and flowers.

2015, Sept. 3 **Litho.** ***Perf. 14¾***

606	G109	Sheet of 10 + 10 labels	*35.00*	*35.00*
a.-j.		1.40fr Any single + label	*3.50*	*3.50*

The full sheet sold for $18.39 or 14.95fr. The generic labels are shown. Labels could be personalized. The personalization of labels was available only at UN Headquarters, and not through mail order.

Visitors Lobby — G110

ECOSOC Chamber G111

Façade of Secretariat G112

Chairs in ECOSOC Chamber G113

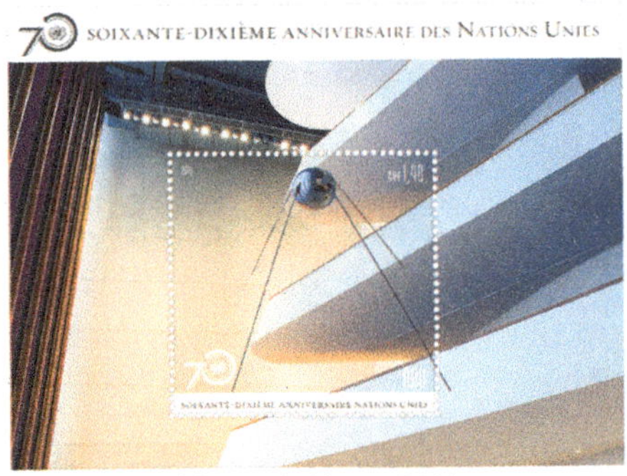

Visitors Lobby — G114

Printed by Cartor Security Printing, France. Panes of 6. Designed by Rorie Katz, U.S.

2015, Oct. 25 **Litho.** ***Perf. 13¾***

607	G110	1fr **multicolored** *(96,000)*+	2.40	2.40
608	G111	1fr **multicolored** *(96,000)*+	2.40	2.40
a.		Pair, #607-608	4.80	4.80
		First day cover, #607-608		5.25
		Inscription block of 4	9.60	—
		Pane of 6	14.50	—
609	G112	1.90fr **multicolored** *(96,000)*+	4.50	4.50
610	G113	1.90fr **multicolored** *(96,000)*+	4.50	4.50
a.		Pair, #609-610	9.00	9.00
		First day cover, #609-610		10.00
		Inscription block of 4	18.00	—
		Pane of 6	27.00	—
		Nos. 607-610 (4)	13.80	13.80

Souvenir Sheet

Perf. 13½

611	G114	1.40fr **multicolored** *(37,000)*+	4.50	4.50
		First day cover		4.25

United Nations, 70th anniv.

21st United Nations Climate Change Conference, Paris — G115

Printed by La Poste, France. Panes of 30. Designed by Rorie Katz, U.S.

2015, Nov. 24 **Litho.** ***Perf. 13¼***

612 G115 1.40fr **multicolored** *(84,000)+* 3.25 3.25
First day cover 4.25
Inscription block of 4 13.00 —
Pane of 30 97.50 —

Values are for stamps with surrounding selvage.

Free and Equal Type of 2016

Printed by Cartor Security Printing, France. Panes of 20. Designed by Sergio Baradat, U.S.

Designs: 1fr, Lesbians. 1.50fr, Gay family.

2016, Feb. 5 **Litho.** ***Perf. 13½x13¼***

613 A491 1fr **multicolored** *(90,000)+* 2.25 2.25
First day cover 3.00
Inscription block of 4 9.00 —
Pane of 20 45.00 —
614 A491 1.50fr **multicolored** *(90,000)+* 3.50 3.50
First day cover 4.50
First day cover, #613-614 6.50
Inscription block of 4 14.00 —
Pane of 20 70.00 —

HeForShe Type of 2016

Printed by Lowe-Martin Group, Canada. Panes of 20. Designed by Mirko Ilic, U.S.

Designs: 1fr, Man, blue background. 2fr, Woman, mauve background.

2016, Mar. 8 **Litho.** ***Perf. 12½x13***

615 A492 1fr **multicolored** *(90,000)+* 2.25 2.25
First day cover 3.00
Inscription block of 4 9.00 —
Pane of 20 45.00 —
616 A492 2fr **multicolored** *(90,000)+* 4.50 4.50
First day cover 5.75
First day cover, #615-616 7.75
Inscription block of 4 18.00 —
Pane of 20 90.00 —

Miniature Sheets

G116

International Dance Day — G117

Printed by Cartor Security Printing, France. Designed by Sergio Baradat, U.S.

No. 617 — Illustration of Swedish dancers by Karin Römark: a, Two male dancers. b, Male dancer on one knee with female dancer. c, Male dancer with yellow cap and female dancer. d, Male dancer with red cap and vest with female dancer. e, Three dancers, with woman with red skirt at LR. f, Three dancers, with woman with blue skirt at LR.

No. 618 — Illustration of African dancers by Rönmark: a, Four dancers with sticks. b, Three dancers with sticks. c, Dancers without sticks. d, Dancer with blue and white mask. e, Two masked dancers with sticks. f, Masked dancer with two sticks.

2016, Apr. 29 **Litho.** ***Perf. 13¼x13***

617 G116 Sheet of 6 *(30,000)+* 13.50 13.50
a.-f. 1fr Any single 2.25 2.25
618 G117 Sheet of 6 *(30,000)+* 20.00 20.00
a.-f. 1.50fr Any single 3.25 3.25
First day cover, #617-618 37.50

International Day of United Nations Peacekeepers Type of 2016

Printed by Lowe-Martin Group, Canada. Panes of 20. Designed by Sergio Baradat, U.S.

Designs: 1fr, Helmeted peacekeepers. 1.50fr, Peacekeeper with African women.

Litho. With Foil Application

2016, May 29 ***Perf. 13¼x13***

619 A496 1fr **multicolored** *(120,000)+* 2.25 2.25
First day cover 3.00
Inscription block of 4 9.00 —
Pane of 20 45.00 —
620 A496 1.50fr **multicolored** *(120,000)+* 3.50 3.50
First day cover 4.50
First day cover, #619-620 6.50
Inscription block of 4 14.00 —
Pane of 20 70.00 —

Sport for Peace Type of 2016

Printed by Cartor Security Printing, France. Panes of 6. Designed by Sergio Baradat and Linsey Thoeng, U.S.

Olympic rings and: No. 621, Rowers, denomination at UR. No. 622, Rowers, denomination at UL. No. 623, Rhythmic gymnast facing forward, eyes open. No. 624, Rhythmic gymnast facing left, eyes closed.

2016, July 22 **Litho.** ***Perf. 14¼***

621 A498 1fr **multicolored** *(90,000)+* 2.25 2.25
622 A498 1fr **multicolored** *(90,000)+* 2.25 2.25
a. Pair, #621-622 4.50 4.50
First day cover, #621-622 5.25
Inscription block of 4 9.00 —
Pane of 6 13.50 —
623 A498 2fr **multicolored** *(90,000)+* 4.50 4.50
624 A498 2fr **multicolored** *(90,000)+* 4.50 4.50
a. Pair, #623-624 9.00 9.00
First day cover, #623-624 10.50

Inscription block of 4 18.00 —
Pane of 6 27.00 —
Nos. 621-624 (4) 13.50 13.50

Souvenir sheets of three bearing three stamps, one from each office are listed under United Nations, Offices in New York as Nos. 1141, 1161, 1177-1178, 1203, and 1208.

World Heritage Sites, Czech Republic Type of 2016

Printed by Cartor Security Printing, France. Panes of 20. Designed by Sergio Baradat, U.S.

Designs: Nos. 625, 627b, Gardens and Castle at Kromeríz. Nos. 626, 627e, Lednice-Valtice Cultural Landscape. No. 627a, Historic Center of Prague. No. 627c, Historic Town Center of Kutná Hora. No. 627d, Holy Trinity Column, Olomouc. No. 627f, Historic Center of Cesky Krumlov.

2016, Sept. 8 Litho. *Perf. 14¼*

625 A500 1fr **multicolored** *(90,000)+* 2.25 2.25
First day cover 3.00
Inscription block of 4 9.00 —
Pane of 20 45.00 —
626 A500 1.50fr **multicolored** *(90,000)+* 3.50 3.50
First day cover 4.50
First day cover, #625-626 6.75
Inscription block of 4 14.00 —
Pane of 20 70.00 —

Souvenir Booklet

627 Booklet, #627g-627l 22.00
a.-c. A500 30c any single .65 .65
d.-f. A500 50c any single 1.10 1.10
g. Booklet pane of 4 #627a 2.75 —
h. Booklet pane of 4 #627b 2.75 —
i. Booklet pane of 4 #627c 2.75 —
j. Booklet pane of 4 #627d 4.50 —
k. Booklet pane of 4 #627e 4.50 —
l. Booklet pane of 4 #627f 4.50 —

Miniature Sheet

World Wildlife Conference, Johannesburg — G118

Printed by Cartor Security Printing, France. Designed by Sergio Baradat, U.S.

No. 628 — Part of map of Africa and: a, Grue royale (gray-crowned crane). b, Mantella madagascariensis. c, Gorille des montagnes (mountain gorilla). d, Avonia quinaria.

2016, Sept. 24 Litho. *Perf. 13x13½*

628 G118 Sheet of 4 *(30,000)+* 18.00 18.00
a.-d. 2fr Any single 4.50 4.50
First day cover 19.00

Sustainable Development Goals Type of 2016

Printed by Lowe-Martin, Canada. Designed by Lindsey Thoeng, U.S.

No. 629 — Inscription: a, 1 Pas de pauvreté. b, 2 Faim "zéro." c, 3 Bonne santé et bien-être. d, 4 Education de qualité. e, 5 Egalité entre les sexes. f, 6 Eau propre et assainissement. g, 7 Energie propre et d'un coût abordable. h, 8 Travail décent et croissance écononmique. i, 9 Industrie, innovation et infrastructure. j, 10 Inégalités réduites. k, 11 Villes et communautés durables. l, 12 Consommation et production responsables. m, 13 Mesures relatives à la lutte contre les changements climatiques. n, 14 Vie aquatique. o, 15 Vie terrestre. p, 16 Paix, justice et institutions efficaces. q, 17 Partneriats pour la réalisation des objectifs.

2016, Oct. 24 Litho. *Perf. 13¼*

629 Sheet of 17 + label *(28,000)+* 39.00 39.00
a.-q. A503 1fr Any single 2.25 2.25
First day cover 42.00

Miniature Sheets

G119

International Dance — G120

Printed by Cartor Security Printing. France. Designed by Sergio Baradat, U.S.

No. 630 — Illustration of Quadrille dancers by Jean François Martin: a, Female dancer wearing red mask facing right, striped pole. b, Male dancer wearing brown mask, harlequin costume, facing right. c, Masked male dancer with red mask facing right. d, Female dancer with brown mask facing left. e, Woman holding black mask facing right. f, Man wearing tan mask facing left.

No. 631 — Illustration of Japanese fan dancers by Martin: a, Dancer holding fan and other hand near her hair. b, Dancer with arm upraised at UR. c, Head of dancer, hand of dancer holding umbrella. d, Dancer, part of fan at LR, e, Dancer's hand holding fan. f, Face of dancer, no hands visible.

2017, Mar. 23 Litho. *Perf. 13¼x13*

630 G119 Sheet of 6 *(22,000)+* 13.00 13.00
a.-f. 1fr Any single 2.10 2.10

631	G120 Sheet of 6 *(22,000)*+	19.50	19.50
a.-f.	1.50fr Any single	3.25	3.25
	First day cover, #630-631		37.50

Endangered Species Type of 2017

Printed by Johann Enschedé and Sons, the Netherlands. Designed by Rorie Katz, U.S.

Designs: No. 632, Rhampholeon spp. No. 633, Mobula spp. No. 634, Adansonia grandidieri. No. 635, Scaphiophryne marmorata.

2017, May 11 **Litho.** ***Perf. 12¾x12½***

632	A509 1.50fr **multicolored** *(68,000)*+	3.25	3.25
633	A509 1.50fr **multicolored** *(68,000)*+	3.25	3.25
634	A509 1.50fr **multicolored** *(68,000)*+	3.25	3.25
635	A509 1.50fr **multicolored** *(68,000)*+	3.25	3.25
a.	Block of 4, #632-635	13.00	13.00
	First day cover, #635a		15.00
	First day cover, #632-635, each		5.00
	Inscription block of 4, #635a	13.00	—
	Pane of 16	52.00	—
	Nos. 632-635 (4)	13.00	13.00

World Environment Day Type of 2017

Printed by Lowe-Martin Group, Canada. Panes of 20. Designed by Sergio Baradat, U.S.

Designs: 1fr, Snowy owl, Quebec, Canada. 2fr, Red maple and aspen trees, Canada.

2017, June 5 **Litho.** ***Perf. 13¼***

636	A510 1fr **multicolored** *(80,000)*+	2.25	2.25
	First day cover		3.25
	Inscription block of 4	9.00	—
	Pane of 20	45.00	—
637	A510 2fr **multicolored** *(80,000)*+	4.50	4.50
	First day cover		6.50
	First day cover, #636-637		8.25
	Inscription block of 4	18.00	—
	Pane of 20	90.00	—

World Heritage Sites Along the Silk Roads Type of 2017

Printed by Cartor Security Printing, France. Panes of 20. Designed by Sergio Baradat, U.S.

Designs: Nos. 638, 640b, Historic Center of Bukhara, Uzbekistan. Nos. 639, 640e, Kunya-Urgench, Turkmenistan. No. 640a, Longmen Grottoes, People's Republic of China. No. 640c, Tabriz Historic Bazaar Complex, Iran. No. 640d, Sulaiman-Too Sacred Mountain, Kyrgyzstan. No. 640f, Safranbolu, Turkey.

2017, Aug. 3 **Litho.** ***Perf. 14¼***

638	A512 1fr **multicolored** *(80,000)*+	2.40	2.40
	First day cover		3.75
	Inscription block of 4	9.60	—
	Pane of 20	48.00	—
639	A512 1.50fr **multicolored** *(80,000)*+	3.50	3.50
	First day cover		5.50
	First day cover, #638-639		7.50
	Inscription block of 4	14.00	—
	Pane of 20	70.00	—

Souvenir Booklet

640	Booklet, #640g-640l *(8,500)*+	26.50	
a.-c.	A512 30c any single	.80	.80
d.-f.	A512 50c any single	1.40	1.40
g.	Booklet pane of 4 #640a	3.20	—
h.	Booklet pane of 4 #640b	3.20	—
i.	Booklet pane of 4 #640c	3.20	—
j.	Booklet pane of 4 #640d	5.60	—
k.	Booklet pane of 4 #640e	5.60	—
l.	Booklet pane of 4 #640f	5.60	—

Hare, Fox, and Dove — G121

Heads and Flowers — G122

Heads and Flowers — G123

Printed by Johann Enschedé and Sons, the Netherlands. Panes of 20. Designed by Stranger & Stranger, U.S.

2017, Sept. 21 **Litho.** ***Perf. 14¼x14***

641	G121 1fr **multicolored** *(80,000)*+	2.40	2.40
	First day cover		3.50
	Inscription block of 4	9.60	—
	Pane of 20	48.00	—
642	G122 2fr **multicolored** *(80,000)*+	4.75	4.75
	First day cover		7.00
	First day cover, #641-642		8.75
	Inscription block of 4	19.00	—
	Pane of 20	95.00	—

Souvenir Sheet

Perf. 14¼x13¾

643 G123 2fr **multicolored** *(25,000)+* 4.75 4.75
First day cover 6.25

International Day of Peace.

World Food Day Type of 2017

Printed by Royal Johann Enschedé. Panes of 20. Designed by Helen Dardik, Canada.

Designs: 1fr, Milk, yogurt and cheeses. 1.50fr, Fruits.

2017, Oct. 16 **Litho.** ***Perf. 13¼x14***

644 A516 1fr **multicolored** *(80,000)+* 2.40 2.40
First day cover 3.75
Inscription block of 4 9.60 —
Pane of 20 48.00 —
645 A516 1.50fr **multicolored** *(80,000)+* 3.50 3.50
First day cover 5.50
First day cover, #644-645 7.50
Inscription block of 4 14.00 —
Pane of 20 70.00 —

Endangered Species Type of 2018

Printed by Johann Enschedé Stamps Security Printers, the Netherlands. Designed by Rorie Katz, U.S.

Designs: No. 646, Saiga tatarica. No. 647, Uncarina grandidieri. No. 648, Polymita picta. No. 649, Carcharhinus falciformis.

2018, Mar. 2 **Litho.** ***Perf. 12¾x12½***

646 A519 1.50fr **multicolored** *(68,000)+* 3.50 3.50
647 A519 1.50fr **multicolored** *(68,000)+* 3.50 3.50
648 A519 1.50fr **multicolored** *(68,000)+* 3.50 3.50
649 A519 1.50fr **multicolored** *(68,000)+* 3.50 3.50
a. Block of 4, #646-649 14.00 14.00
First day cover, #649a 15.50
First day cover, #646-649, each 5.00
Inscription block of 4, #649a 14.00 —
Pane of 16 56.00 —
Nos. 646-649 (4) 14.00 14.00

World Health Day Type of 2018

Printed by Lowe-Martin Group, Canada. Panes of 20. Designed by Sergio Baradat, U.S.

Designs: 1fr, Microbes and microscope. 2fr, Child, apple, pencil, triangle, numbers, glass of milk.

2018, Apr. 6 **Litho.** ***Perf. 13x13¼***

650 A520 1fr **multicolored** *(80,000)+* 2.25 2.25
First day cover 3.50
Inscription block of 4 9.00 —
Pane of 20 45.00 —
651 A520 2fr **multicolored** *(80,000)+* 4.50 4.50
First day cover 6.75
First day cover, #650-651 8.50
Inscription block of 4 18.00 —
Pane of 20 90.00 —

Miniature Sheet

G124

No. 652: a, Cathedral of St. Lawrence belltower and buildings on hillside. b, Bank with curved glass facade. c, Table and chairs along footpath in city. d, Villa Saroli (yellow building). e, People near door of Santa Maria degli Angioli Church. f, Lugano Arts and Cultural Center (building with four large windows). g, Storefronts along hill on Via Cattedrale. h, Gates of Villa Ciani. i, Arches along Via della Posta. j, William Tell Monument.

2018, May 17 **Litho.** ***Perf. 14¾***

652 G124 Sheet of 10 + 10 labels *38.50 38.50*
a.-j. 1.50fr Any single + label *3.75 3.75*

The full sheet sold for $19.06 or 16.95fr. The generic labels are shown. Labels could be personalized. The personalization of labels was available only at UN Headquarters, and not through mail order.

UNISPACE + 50 Conferences Type of 2018

Printed by Johann Enschedé Stamps BV, Netherlands. Panes of 20. Designed by Sergio Baradat, U.S. Designs: 1fr, View of Earth from space. 1.50fr, Launch of Tiangong 1.

2fr, Widefield Infrared Survey Explorer photograph of Comet 65P/Gunn.

2018, June 20 **Litho.** ***Perf. 14x14¼***

653 A523 1fr **multicolored** *(70,000)+* 2.25 2.25
First day cover 3.75
Inscription block of 4 9.00 —
Pane of 20 45.00 —
654 A523 1.50fr **multicolored** *(70,000)+* 3.50 3.50
First day cover 5.50
First day cover, #653-654 7.25
Inscription block of 4 14.00 —
Pane of 20 70.00 —

Souvenir Sheet

Perf. 13¾

655 A523 2fr **multicolored** *(22,000)+* 4.50 4.50
First day cover 6.25

No. 655 contains one 45x45mm stamp.

Nelson Mandela (1918-2013), President of South Africa — G125

Printed by Lowe-Martin Group, Canada. Panes of 20. Designed by Martin Morck, Norway.

2018, July 18 **Litho.** ***Perf. 13¼***

656 G125 2fr **buff & black** *(260,000)+* 4.50 4.50
First day cover 6.25
Inscription block of 4 18.00 —
Pane of 20 90.00 —

World Heritage Sites in the United Kingdom Type of 2016

Printed by Cartor Security Printing, France. Panes of 20. Designed by Rorie Katz, U.S.

Designs: Nos. 657, 659b, Stonehenge. Nos. 658, 659e, Edinburgh. No. 659a, Giant's Causeway. No. 659c, Conwy Castle. No. 659d, Palace of Westminster. No. 659f, Maritime Greenwich.

2018, Aug. 15 **Litho.** ***Perf. 14¼***

657 A524 1fr **multicolored** *(74,000)+* 2.25 2.25
First day cover 3.50
Inscription block of 4 9.00 —
Pane of 20 45.00 —
658 A524 1.50fr **multicolored** *(74,000)+* 3.50 3.50
First day cover 5.50
First day cover, #657-658 7.25
Inscription block of 4 14.00 —
Pane of 20 70.00 —

Souvenir Booklet

659 Booklet, #659g-659l *(7,000)+* 23.50
a.-c. A524 30c any single .75 .75
d.-f. A524 50c any single 1.10 1.10
g. Booklet pane of 4 #659a 3.00 —
h. Booklet pane of 4 #659b 3.00 —
i. Booklet pane of 4 #659c 3.00 —
j. Booklet pane of 4 #659d 4.75 —
k. Booklet pane of 4 #659e 4.75 —
l. Booklet pane of 4 #659f 4.75 —

Miniature Sheet

International Music Day — G126

Printed by Johann Enschedé Stamps BV, the Netherlands. Designed by Sergio Baradat, U.S.

No. 660: a, Electric guitars with carved necks. b, Veena. c, Cello. d, Erhu. e, Ektara. f, Domra. g, Viola da gamba. h, Bazouki. i, Stringed instrument with bow. j, Violin with chin rest. k, Sitars. l, Zither.

2018, Oct. 1 **Litho.** ***Perf. 14x13¼***

660	G126	Sheet of 12 *(19,000)*+	27.00 27.00
		First day cover	29.00
a.-l.		1fr Any single	2.25 2.25

Miniature Sheet

World Languages — G127

Printed by Cartor Security Printing, France. Designed by Sergio Baradat, U.S.

No. 661 — Word bubbles with word for "Hello" in: a, French (Bonjour). b, Russian ("Langues du Monde" in lilac). c, Hebrew and Polish (Czesc), d, Hindi ("Langues du Monde" in white). e, Danish or Swedish (Hej). f, Japanese ("Langues du Monde" in dark gray).

2019, Feb. 21 **Litho.** ***Perf. 13¼x13***

661	G127	Sheet of 6 *(22,000)*+	13.50 13.50
a.-f.		1fr Any single	2.25 2.25
		First day cover, #661	17.00

Gender Equality — G128

Printed by Lowe-Martin Group, Canada. Panes of 20. Designed by Chris Gash, U.S.

2019, Mar.15 **Litho.** ***Perf. 13¼x13***

662	G128 1.50fr	**multicolored** *(170,000)*+	3.50 3.50
		First day cover	5.25
		Inscription block of 4	14.00 —
		Pane of 20	70.00 —

Endangered Species Type of 2019

Printed by Johann Enschedé Stamps Security Printers, the Netherlands. Designed by Rongliang Wang, People's Republic of China.

Designs: No. 663, Hippocampus kuda. No. 664, Dugong dugon. No. 665, Stylophora pistillata. No. 666, Lamna nasus.

2019, Apr. 26 **Litho.** ***Perf. 12¾x12½***

663	A534 1.50fr	**multicolored** *(56,000)*+	3.25 3.25
664	A534 1.50fr	**multicolored** *(56,000)*+	3.25 3.25
665	A534 1.50fr	**multicolored** *(56,000)*+	3.25 3.25
666	A534 1.50fr	**multicolored** *(56,000)*+	3.25 3.25
a.		Block of 4, #663-666	13.50 13.50
		First day cover, #666a	15.50
		First day cover, #663-666, each	5.25
		Inscription block of 4, #666a	13.50 —
		Pane of 16	54.00 —
		Nos. 663-666 (4)	13.00 13.00

Souvenir Sheet

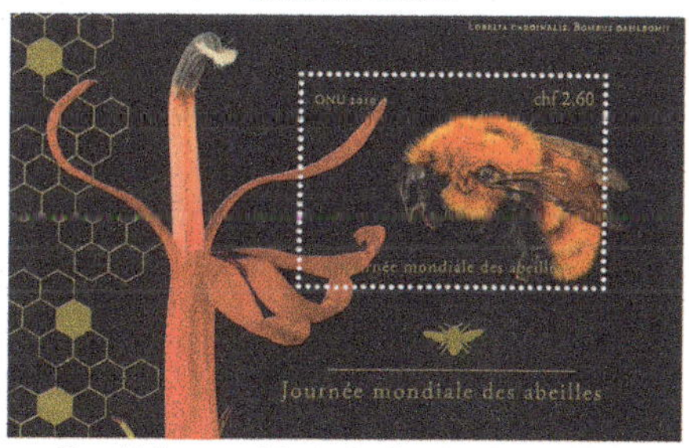

Bumblebee and Lobelia Cardinalis — G129

Printed by Lowe-Martin Group, Canada. Designed by Rorie Katz, U.S.

2019, May 20 **Litho. With Foil Application** ***Perf. 13***

667	G129 2.60fr	**multicolored** *(19,000)*+	6.00 6.00
		First day cover	8.75

World Bee Day.

G130

G131

G132

G133

International Labor Organization, Cent. — G134

Printed by Johann Enschedé Stamps BV, Netherlands. Sheets of 20. Designed by Owen Smith, U.S.

2019, June 28	**Litho.**	***Perf. 13½x14***	
668 G130 1fr **multicolored** *(72,000)+*		2.25	2.25
669 G131 1fr **multicolored** *(72,000)+*		2.25	2.25
670 G132 1fr **multicolored** *(72,000)+*		2.25	2.25
671 G133 1fr **multicolored** *(72,000)+*		2.25	2.25
672 G134 1fr **multicolored** *(72,000)+*		2.25	2.25
a. Horiz. strip of 5, #668-672		11.25	11.25
First day cover, #672a			13.00
Inscription block of 10		22.50	—
Pane of 20		45.00	—
Nos. 668-672 (5)		11.25	11.25

Climate Change Type of 2019

Printed by Cartor Security Printing, France. Panes of 20. Designed by Sergio Baradat, U.S.

Designs: 1fr, Fruit tree and burnt forest. 1.50fr, Field of flowers and traffic jam.

2fr, Clouds.

2019, Sept. 23	**Litho.**	***Perf. 14¼***	
673 A543 1fr **multicolored** *(70,000)+*		2.25	2.25
First day cover			3.75
Inscription block of 4		9.00	—
Pane of 20		45.00	—
674 A543 1.50fr **multicolored** *(70,000)+*		3.50	3.50
First day cover			5.50
First day cover, #673-674			7.50
Inscription block of 4		14.00	—
Pane of 20		70.00	—

Souvenir Sheet

Perf.

675 A543 2fr **multicolored** *(13,000)+*	4.50	4.50
First day cover		4.50

2019 United Nations Climate Change Conference, Madrid. No. 675 contains one 47mm diameter stamp.

Miniature Sheet

United Nations Postal Administration in Geneva, 50th Anniv. — G135

No. 676: a, Palais des Nations and Armillary Sphere, green panels. b, Palais des Nations and flags, gray panels. c, Assembly Hall, Palais des Nations, violet blue panels. d, Meeting room of Human Rights Council, light blue panels. e, Armillary Sphere in reflecting pond and Lake Geneva, violet black panels. f, Palais des Nations and flags, red panels. g, Palais des Nations and flags, orange yellow panels. h, Palais des Nations and United Nations flag, dark green panels. i, Peacock, blue green panels. j, Council Chamber, blue gray panels.

2019, Oct. 18	**Litho.**	***Perf. 14¾***	
676 G135 Sheet of 10 + 10 labels		*38.00*	*38.00*
a.-j. 1.50fr Any single + label		*3.75*	*3.75*

The full sheet sold for $18.80 or 16.95fr. The generic labels are shown. Labels could be personalized. The personalization of labels was available only at UN Headquarters, and not through mail order.

World Heritage Sites in Cuba Type of 2019

Printed by Cartor Security Printing, France. Panes of 20. Designed by Sergio Baradat, U.S.

Designs: Nos. 677, 679b, Trinidad. Nos. 678, 679e, Cienfuegos. No. 679a, Morro Castle. No. 679c, Camagüey. No. 679d, Vinales Valley. No. 679f, San Pedro de la Rosa Castle.

2019, Oct. 24	**Litho. With Foil Application**	***Perf. 14¼***	
677 A545 1fr **multicolored** *(70,000)+*		2.25	2.25
First day cover			3.75
Inscription block of 4		9.00	—
Pane of 20		45.00	—
678 A545 1.50fr **multicolored** *(70,000)+*		3.50	3.50
First day cover			5.50
First day cover, #677-678			7.50
Inscription block of 4		14.00	—
Pane of 20		70.00	—

Souvenir Booklet

679 Booklet, #679g-679l *(7,000)+*	24.50	
a.-c. A545 30c Any single	.75	.75
d.-f. A545 50c Any single	1.25	1.25
g. Booklet pane of 4 #679a	3.00	—
h. Booklet pane of 4 #679b	3.00	—
i. Booklet pane of 4 #679c	3.00	—
j. Booklet pane of 4 #679d	5.00	—
k. Booklet pane of 4 #679e	5.00	—
l. Booklet pane of 4 #679f	5.00	—

Complete booklet sold for $12.20.

Endangered Species Type of 2020

Printed by Johann Enschedé Stamps Security Printers, the Netherlands. Designed by Rorie Katz, U.S.

Designs: No. 680, Leucogeranus leucogeranus. No. 681, Addax nasomaculatus. No. 682, Falco cherrug. No. 683, Monodon monoceros.

2020, Feb. 17 **Litho.** *Perf. 12¾x12½*

680	A546 1.50fr **multicolored** *(52,000)*+		3.50	3.50
681	A546 1.50fr **multicolored** *(52,000)*+		3.50	3.50
682	A546 1.50fr **multicolored** *(52,000)*+		3.50	3.50
683	A546 1.50fr **multicolored** *(52,000)*+		3.50	3.50
a.	Block of 4, #680-683		14.00	14.00
	First day cover, #683a			15.50
	First day cover, #680-683, each			5.25
	Inscription block of 4, #683a		14.00	—
	Pane of 16		56.00	—
	Nos. 680-683 (4)		14.00	14.00

Blank Stamp On Which Stickers Can Be Applied — G136

Printed by Cartor Security Printing (No. 684) and La Poste (Nos. 684a, 684b), France. Designed by Rorie Katz, U.S.

2020, Mar. 19 **Litho.** *Die Cut*

Self-Adhesive

684	G136 2fr **multicolored,** with rounded corners, *(46,000)*+	4.75	4.75
a.	With perpendicular corners and black frame line	4.75	4.75
b.	Booklet pane of 6 #684a *(5,000)*+	28.50	
	First day cover, #684		6.50

No. 684 was issued as a souvenir sheet having two different sheet margins, each with different stickers. No. 684a was issued in a booklet containing six panes of one stamp, with each pane having different margins and stickers. Each booklet pane contained one sticker depicting Hello Kitty, a color wheel with Hello Kitty at the center, one of six different Sustainable Development Goal emblems, along with a variety of other stickers. The two souvenir sheets had the same sheet margin and stickers found on two of the panes of No. 684b. No. 684b was sold folded, without any means of separation between the individual panes.

Terre, Artwork by Mathilde Roussel — G137

Mermaids Hate Plastic, Photograph by Benjamin Von Wong — G138

Printed by La Poste, France. Panes of 10. Designed by Rorie Katz, U.S.

2020, Apr. 22 **Litho.** *Perf. 13¼*

685	G137 1fr **multicolored** *(90,000)*+	2.25	2.25
	First day cover		3.50
	Inscription block of 4	9.00	—
	Pane of 10	22.50	—
686	G138 2fr **multicolored** *(90,000)*+	4.50	4.50
	First day cover		7.00
	First day cover, #685-686		8.75
	Inscription block of 4	18.00	—
	Pane of 10	45.00	—

Earth Day, 50th anniv. Because of the COVID-19 pandemic, Nos. 685-686 were not available for sale on day of issue stated on the first-day covers as they had not yet been printed and delivered.

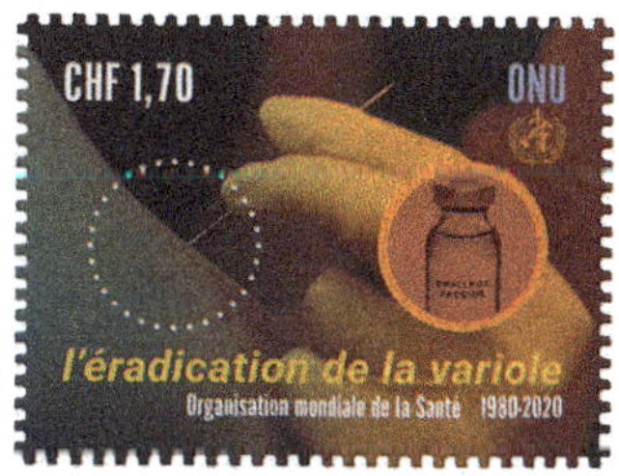

Eradication of Smallpox, 40th Anniv. — G139

Printed by Cartor Security Printing, France. Panes of 20. Designed by Sergio Baradat, U.S., and World Health Organization.

2020, May 8 **Litho.** *Perf. 13x13¼*

687	G139 1.70fr **multicolored** *(240,000)*+	4.00	4.00
	First day cover		5.75
	Inscription block of 4	16.00	—
	Pane of 20	80.00	—

World Heritage Sites in Russia Type of 2020

Printed by Cartor Security Printing, France. Panes of 20. Designed by Sergio Baradat, U.S.

Designs: Nos. 688, 690b, Kazan Kremlin. Nos. 689, 690e, Saint Petersburg. No. 690a, Lake Baikal. No. 690c, Novodevichy Convent. No. 690d, Kremlin and Red Square, Moscow. No. 690f, Kizhi Pogost.

2020, Sept. 11 **Litho.** *Perf. 14½x14¼*

688	A556 1fr **multicolored** *(70,000)*+	2.40	2.40
	First day cover		3.75
	Inscription block of 4	9.60	—
	Pane of 20	48.00	—
689	A556 1.50fr **multicolored** *(70,000)*+	3.75	3.75
	First day cover		5.75
	First day cover, #688-689		7.75
	Inscription block of 4	15.00	—
	Pane of 20	75.00	—

Souvenir Booklet

690	Booklet, #690g-690l *(6,500)*+	28.00	
a.-c.	A556 30c any single	.85	.85
d.-f.	A556 50c any single	1.40	1.40
g.	Booklet pane of 4 #690a	3.50	—
h.	Booklet pane of 4 #690b	3.50	—
i.	Booklet pane of 4 #690c	3.50	—
j.	Booklet pane of 4 #690d	5.75	—
k.	Booklet pane of 4 #690e	5.75	—
l.	Booklet pane of 4 #690f	5.75	—

Complete booklet sold for $13.21 or 11fr.

Souvenir Sheet

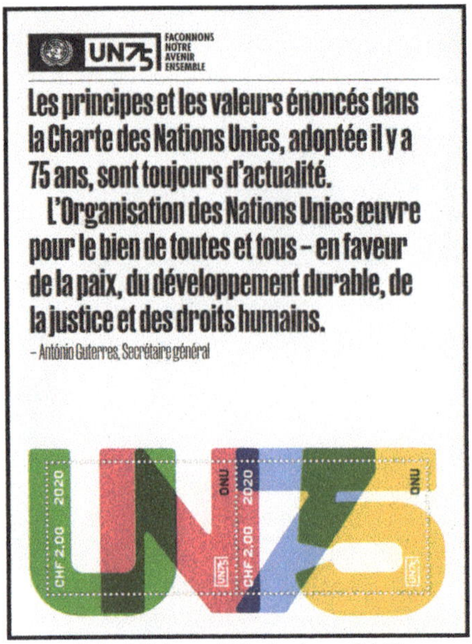

United Nations, 75th Anniv. — G140

Printed by La Poste. France. Designed by Matt Willey/Pentagram, U.S.

No. 691: a, Green "U," pink "N." b, Blue "7," yellow "5."

2020, Oct. 24 **Litho.** ***Perf. 13¼***

691	G140	Sheet of 2 *(32,000)*+	10.00	10.00
a.-b.		2fr Either single	5.00	5.00
		First day cover, #691		13.50

Souvenir Sheet

Palais des Nations and Emblem — G141

Printed by Royal Johann Enschedé, Netherlands. Designed by Sergio Baradat, U.S.

Litho. With Foil Application

2020, Nov. 24 ***Die Cut Perf. 11½***

Self-Adhesive

692	G141 8fr **multicolored** *(30,000)*+	19.50	19.50
	First day cover		21.00

Crypto stamp. Unused value is for sheets with unscratched panels at right.

International Day for the Elimination of Racial Discrimination — G142

Printed by Cartor Security Printing, France. Panes of 10. Designed by Rorie Katz, U.S.

2021, Mar. 19 **Litho.** ***Perf. 13¼x13***

693	G142 2fr **multicolored** *(100,000)*+	5.00	5.00
	First day cover		6.75
	Inscription block of 4	20.00	—
	Sheet of 10	50.00	—

Endangered Species Type of 2021

Printed by Johann Enschedé Stamps Security Printers, the Netherlands. Designed by Rorie Katz, U.S.

Designs: No. 694, Leontopithecus chrysomelas. No. 695, Macrotis lagotis. No. 696, Lemur catta. No. 697, Caladenia huegelii.

2021, Apr. 7 **Litho.** ***Perf. 12¾x12½***

694	A565 1.50fr **multicolored** *(44,000)*+	3.75	3.75
695	A565 1.50fr **multicolored** *(44,000)*+	3.75	3.75
696	A565 1.50fr **multicolored** *(44,000)*+	3.75	3.75
697	A565 1.50fr **multicolored** *(44,000)*+	3.75	3.75
a.	Block of 4, #694-697	15.00	15.00
	First day cover, #697a		17.00
	First day cover, #694-697, each		5.50
	Inscription block of 4, #697a	15.00	—
	Pane of 16	60.00	—
	Nos. 694-697 (4)	15.00	15.00

Two Judokas — G143

Judoka in Blue Judogi — G144

Judoka in White Judogi — G145

Female Diver — G146

Diver on Platform — G147

Diver Spinning — G148

Athlete Carrying Olympic Torch — G149

Printed by Royal Johann Enschedé, Netherlands. Sheets of 8. Designed by Satoshi Hashimoto, Japan.

2021, July 23 **Litho.** ***Perf. 13½***

698	G143	1fr	**multicolored** *(100,000)+*	2.50	2.50
699	G144	1fr	**multicolored** *(50,000)+*	2.50	2.50
700	G145	1fr	**multicolored** *(50,000)+*	2.50	2.50
a.			Horiz. strip of 3, #698-700	7.50	7.50
			First day cover, strip of 4, #700a, 698		11.50
			First day cover, pane of 8, 4 #698, 2 each #699-700		22.50
			Pane of 8, 4 #698 2 each #699-700	20.00	—
701	G146	1.50fr	**multicolored** *(100,000)+*	3.75	3.75
702	G147	1.50fr	**multicolored** *(50,000)+*	3.75	3.75
703	G148	1.50fr	**multicolored** *(50,000)+*	3.75	3.75
a.			Horiz. strip of 3, #701-703	11.25	11.25
			First day cover, strip of 4, #703a, 701		17.00
			First day cover, pane of 8, 4 #701, 2 each #702-703		33.50
			Pane of 8, 4 #701, 2 each #702-703	30.00	—
			Nos. 698-703 (6)	18.75	18.75

Souvenir Sheet

704	G149	2fr	**multicolored** *(24,000)+*	5.00	5.00
			First day cover		6.75

Sports for Peace, 2020 Summer Olympics, Tokyo. The 2020 Summer Olympics were postponed until 2021 because of the COVID-19 pandemic.

Waterways, Railways and Bridges World Heritage Sites Type of 2020

Printed by Cartor Security Printing, France. Panes of 20. Designed by Sergio Baradat, U.S.

Designs: Nos. 705, 707b, Rhaetian Railway, Switzerland and Italy. Nos. 706, 707e, Darjeeling Himalayan Railway, India. No. 707a, Rideau Canal, Canada. No. 707c, Forth Bridge, Scotland. No. 707d, Grand Canal, People's Republic of China. No. 707f, Old Bridge, Mostar, Bosnia and Herzegovina.

2021, Aug. 25 **Litho.** ***Perf. 14¼***

705	A575	1fr	**multicolored** *(70,000)+*	2.50	2.50
			First day cover		4.00
			Inscription block of 4	10.00	—
			Pane of 20	50.00	—
706	A575	1.50fr	**multicolored** *(70,000)+*	3.75	3.75
			First day cover		6.00
			First day cover, #705-706		8.00
			Inscription block of 4	15.00	—
			Pane of 20	75.00	—

Souvenir Booklet

707		Booklet, #707g-707l *(5,700)+*	28.00	
a.-c.	A575	30c any single	.85	.85
d.-f.	A575	50c any single	1.40	1.40
g.		Booklet pane of 4 #707a	3.50	—
h.		Booklet pane of 4 #707b	3.50	—
i.		Booklet pane of 4 #707c	3.50	—
j.		Booklet pane of 4 #707d	5.75	—
k.		Booklet pane of 4 #707e	5.75	—
l.		Booklet pane of 4 #707f	5.75	—

Complete booklet sold for $13.21 or 10.95fr.

Miniature Sheet

Celebrations — G150

No. 708: a, Birthday cake. b, Flower bouquet. c, Three balloons. d, Menorah. e, Heart and arrow. f, Christmas tree and ornament. g, "Merci." h, Champagne flutes. i, Diamond ring. j, Mosque.

2021, Nov. 4 **Litho.** ***Perf. 14½x14¼***

708 G150 Sheet of 10 *41.00 41.00*
a.-j. 1.50fr Any single + label *4.00 4.00*

The full sheet sold for $20.28. The generic labels are shown. Labels could be personalized. The personalization of labels was available only at UN Headquarters, and not through mail order.

World Toilet Day — G151

Printed by Cartor Security Printing, France. Panes of 20. Designed by Gail Armstrong, U.K.

2021, Nov. 19 **Litho.** ***Perf. 14¼***

709 G151 1fr **multicolored** *(100,000)+* 2.40 2.40
First day cover 4.25
Inscription block of 4 9.60 —
Sheet of 20 48.00 —

Feet of Figure Skater G152

Figure Skaters G153

Four-man Bobsled G154

Monobob G155

Printed by Cartor Security Printing, France. Panes of 6.

2022, Jan. 14 **Litho.** ***Perf. 14¼***

710 G152 1.10fr **multicolored** *(145,350)+* 2.25 2.25
711 G153 1.10fr **multicolored** *(145,350)+* 2.25 2.25
a. Horiz. pair, #710-711 5.50 5.50
First day cover, #710-711 7.25
Inscription block of 4 11.00 —
Pane of 6 16.50 —
712 G154 2fr **multicolored** *(137,550)+* 5.00 5.00
713 G155 2fr **multicolored** *(137,550)+* 5.00 5.00
a. Horiz. pair, #712-713 10.00 10.00
First day cover, #712-713 13.50
Inscription block of 4 20.00 —
Pane of 6 30.00 —
Nos. 710-713 (4) 14.50 14.50

Sports for Peace, 2022 Winter Olympics, Beijing.

Endangered Species Type of 2022

Printed by Johann Enschedé Stamps Security Printers, the Netherlands. Designed by Sergio Baradat, U.S.

Designs: No. 714, Acropora cervicornis. No. 715, Gonatodes daudini. No. 716, Mobula munkiana. No. 717, Oophaga arborea.

2022, Mar. 18 **Litho.** ***Perf. 12¾x12½***

714 A592 1.50fr **multicolored** *(40,000)+* 3.75 3.75
715 A592 1.50fr **multicolored** *(40,000)+* 3.75 3.75
716 A592 1.50fr **multicolored** *(40,000)+* 3.75 3.75
717 A592 1.50fr **multicolored** *(40,000)+* 3.75 3.75
a. Block of 4, #714-717 15.00 15.00
First day cover, #717a 17.50
First day cover, #714-717, each 6.50
Inscription block of 4, #717a 15.00 —
Pane of 16 60.00 —
Nos. 714-717 (4) 15.00 15.00

SEMI-POSTAL STAMP

AIDS Awareness Semi-postal Type

Souvenir Sheet

2002, Oct. 24 **Litho.** ***Perf. 14½***

B1 GSP1 90c + 30c **multicolored** *(171,000)+* 4.00 4.00
First day cover, #B1 5.00

GSP2

Photograph of John Lennon (1940-80), by Iain Macmillan — GSP3

Printed by Cartor Security Printing, France. Panes of 20. Designed by Rorie Katz, U.S.

2021, Sept. 21 **Litho.** ***Perf. 14¼***

B2 GSP2 1.50fr +50c **multicolored** *(150,000)*+ 5.00 5.00
First day cover 6.75
Inscription block of 4 20.00 —
Sheet of 20 100.00 —

Souvenir Sheet

Litho. With Foil Application

B3 GSP3 2.60fr +1fr **multicolored** *(20,000)*+ 8.75 8.75
First day cover 12.00

International Day of Peace. Surtax for United Nations peacekeeping efforts.

AIR LETTER SHEET

Used values for all postal stationery are for non-philatelic contemporaneous usages.

UN Type of 1968

Printed by Setelipaino, Finland. Designed by Robert Perrot.

1969, Oct. 4 **Litho.**

UC1 UC3 65c **ultra & light blue,** entire *(350,000)* .50 *1.50*
Entire, first day cancel *(52,000)* .75

POSTAL CARDS

UN Type of 1969 and Type of Air Post Postal Card, 1966

Printed by Courvoisier, S.A., Switzerland. Designed by John Mason (20c) and Olav S. Mathiesen (30c).

Wmk. Post Horn, Swiss Cross, "S" or "Z"

1969, Oct. 4 **Litho.**

UX1 PC2 20c **olive green & black,** *buff (415,000)* .25 .30
First day cancel *(51,500)* .50
UX2 APC2 30c **violet blue, blue, light & dark green,** *buff (275,000)* .25 .30
First day cancel *(49,000)* .50

No. UX2, although of design APC2, is not inscribed "Poste Aerienne" or "Air Mail."

UN Emblem — GPC1

UN Emblem and Ribbons — GPC2

Printed by Setelipaino, Finland. Designed by Veronique Crombez (40c) and Lieve Baeten (70c).

1977, June 27 **Litho.**

UX3 GPC1 40c **multicolored** *(500,000)* .30 .30
First day cancel *(65,000)* .55
UX4 GPC2 70c **multicolored** *(300,000)* .40 .40
First day cancel *(65,000)* .50

A second printing of No. UX3 was made in 1984. It was released after the Swiss postal card rate had been increased to 50c so instructions were issued that all cards must have a 10c stamp affixed before being sold. A few were sold in NY without the added stamp. The card stock differs from the original printing.

Emblem of the United Nations — GPC3

Peace Dove — GPC4

Printed by Johann Enschede en Zonen, Netherlands.
Designed by George Hamori, Australia (50c) and Ryszard Dudzicki, Poland (70c).

1985, May 10 **Litho.**

UX5 GPC3 50c **multicolored** *(300,000)* 1.00 3.50
First day cancel *(34,700)* 1.00
UX6 GPC4 70c **multicolored** *(300,000)* 3.25 3.25
First day cancel *(34,700)* 2.00

No. UX6 Surcharged in Lake

1986, Jan. 2 **Litho.**
UX7 GPC4 70c + 10c **multi** *(90,500)* 2.50 2.50
First day cancel *(8,000 est.)* 10.00

Type of 1990

Printed by Mercury-Walch, Australia.

1992, Sept. 4 **Litho.**
UX8 G45 90c **multicolored** *(150,000)*+ 1.75 1.75
First day cancel *(12,385)* 5.00

No. UX5 Surcharged in Lake like No. UX7

1993, May 7 **Litho.**
UX9 GPC3 50c +10c **multicolored** *(47,000)*+ 1.50 1.50
First day cancel 15.00

Palais des Nations — GPC5

Printed by Leigh Mardon Pty. Limited, Australia.

1993, May 7 **Litho.**
UX10 GPC5 80c **multicolored** *(200,000)*+ 3.00 3.00
First day cancel 4.50

#UX5, UX10 Surcharged in Carmine like #UX7

1996, Mar. 22 **Litho.**
UX11 GPC3 50c +20c **multi** 3.00 3.00
First day cancel 4.00
UX12 GPC5 80c +30c **multi** 3.00 3.00
First day cancel 4.00

Assembly Hall — GPC6

Palais des Nations — GPC7

Printed by Mercury-Walsh, Australia.

1998, May 20 **Litho.**
UX13 GPC6 70c **multicolored** *(80,000)*+ 2.50 2.00
First day cancel 3.00
UX14 GPC7 1.10fr **multicolored** *(80,000)*+ 3.00 3.00
First day cancel 3.25

Illustrations of the buildings are shown on the back of each card.

Type of 2002

Printed by Johann Enschedé and Sons, the Netherlands.

2002, Mar. 1 **Litho.**
UX15 G65 1.30fr **multicolored** *(68,000)*+ 1.75 1.75
First day cancel 2.00

Nos. UX8, UX13 and UX14 Surcharged Like No. UX7, But With Serifed Numerals

2004, Sept. 21 **Litho.**
UX16 GPC6 70c +15c **multicolored** 2.00 2.00
First day cancel 2.50
UX17 G45 90c +10c **multicolored** 2.25 2.25
First day cancel 2.75
UX18 GPC7 1.10fr +10c **multicolored** 2.50 2.50
First day cancel 3.00

Ceiling Sculpture, Human Rights and Alliance of Civilization Chamber — GPC8

The Broken Chair Memorial — GPC9

League of Nations Building — GPC10

2009, May 7 **Litho.**

UX19 GPC8 85c **multicolored**	2.25	2.25
First day cancel		3.00
UX20 GPC9 1fr **multicolored**	2.50	2.50
First day cancel		4.00
UX21 GPC10 1.80fr **multicolored**	4.25	4.25
First day cancel		6.00

No. UX21 Surcharged Like No. UX7, But With Serifed Numerals

2010 **Litho.**

UX22 GPC10 1.80fr +10c **multicolored**	4.00	4.00
First day cancel		6.00

No. UX15 Surcharged Like No. UX16

2016, July 20 **Litho.**

UX23 G65 1.30fr +20c **multicolored**	4.50	4.50
First day cancel		6.50

OFFICES IN VIENNA, AUSTRIA

For use only on mail posted at the Vienna International Center for the UN and the International Atomic Energy Agency.

100 Groschen = 1 Schilling
100 Cents = 1 Euro (2002)

Type of Geneva, 1978, UN Types of 1961-72 and

Donaupark, Vienna — V1

Aerial View — V2

Printed by Helio Courvoisier S.A., Switzerland. Panes of 50. Designed by Henryk Chylinski (4s); Jozsef Vertel (6s).

1979, Aug. 24 **Photo.** ***Perf. 11½***
Granite Paper

1 G8 50g **multicolored** *(3,500,000)+*	.25	.30
First day cover		1.00
Inscription block of 4	.40	—
2 A52 1s **multicolored** *(3,800,000)+*	.25	.30
First day cover		1.00
Inscription block of 4	.50	—
3 V1 4s **multicolored** *(3,500,000)+*	.25	.30
First day cover		1.00
Inscription block of 4	1.10	—
4 AP13 5s **multicolored** *(3,500,000)+*	.30	.35
First day cover		1.00
Inscription block of 4	1.40	—
5 V2 6s **multicolored** *(4,500,000)+*	.35	.35
First day cover		1.25
Inscription block of 4	1.75	—
6 A45 10s **multicolored** *(3,500,000)+*	.60	.70
First day cover		2.00
Inscription block of 4	3.25	—
Nos. 1-6 (6)	2.00	2.30

+ Printing orders to Mar. 1993.
No. 4 is not inscribed "Air Mail," No. 6 has no frame.
First day covers of Nos. 1-6 total 1,026,575.

New Economic Order Type of UN

1980, Jan. 11 **Litho.** ***Perf. 15x14½***

7 A178 4s **multicolored** *(1,418,418)*	.60	.70
First day cover		1.25
Inscription block of 4	*6.00*	—

Value for margin inscription block is for one from bottom of sheet. One from top is about twice the value shown.

Dove Type of UN

1980, Jan. 11 **Litho.** ***Perf. 14x13½***

8 A147 2.50s **multicolored** *(3,500,000)+*	.25	.30
First day cover		1.00
Inscription block of 4	1.25	—

First day covers of Nos. 7-8 total 336,229.

Women's Year Emblem on World Map — V3

United Nations Decade for Women

Printed by Questa Colour Security Printers, United Kingdom. Panes of 50. Designed by Gunnar Janssen.

1980, Mar. 7 **Litho.** ***Perf. 14½x15***

9 V3 4s **light green & dark green** *(1,569,080)*	.40	.45
First day cover		1.00
Inscription block of 4	1.75	—
10 V3 6s **bister brown** *(1,556,016)*	.75	.85
First day cover		1.25
First day cover, #9-10		1.50
Inscription block of 4	3.25	—

First day covers of Nos. 9-10 total 443,893.

Peace-keeping Operations Type of UN

1980, May 16 **Litho.** ***Perf. 14x13***

11 A182 6s **multicolored** *(1,719,852)*	.40	.45
First day cover *(323,923)*		1.00
Inscription block of 4	2.00	—

35th Anniversary Types of Geneva and UN

1980, June 26 **Litho.** ***Perf. 13x13½***

12 G16 4s **carmine rose & black** *(1,626,582)*	.35	.40
First day cover		1.00
Inscription block of 4	1.60	—
13 A184 6s **multicolored** *(1,625,400)*	.60	.65
First day cover		1.25
Inscription block of 4	2.75	—

Souvenir Sheet
Imperf

14 Sheet of 2 *(1,675,191)* .90 1.00
a. G16 4s carmine rose & black .25 .30
b. A184 6s multicolored .65 .30
First day cover 1.00

First day covers of Nos. 12-14 total 657,402.

ECOSOC Types of UN and Geneva

Printed by Ashton-Potter Ltd., Canada. Panes of 50. Designed by Dietman Kowall (4s), Angel Medina Medina (6s).

1980, Nov. 21 **Litho.** ***Perf. 13½x13***
15 A187 4s **multicolored** *(1,811,218)* .30 .35
First day cover 1.00
Inscription block of 4 1.50 —
16 G17 6s **multicolored** *(1,258,420)* .60 .30
First day cover 1.00
First day cover #15-16 1.25
Inscription block of 4 2.50 —

Economic and Social Council (ECOSOC).
First day covers of Nos. 15-16 total 224,631.

Palestinian Rights Type of UN

Printed by Courvoisier S.A., Switzerland. Panes of 50. Designed by David Dewhurst.

1981, Jan. 30 **Photo.** ***Perf. 12x11½***
17 A188 4s **multicolored** *(1,673,310)* .45 .50
First day cover *(208,812)* 1.00
Inscription block of 4 2.00 —

Disabled Type of UN and

Interlocking Stitches — V4

International Year of the Disabled.
Printed by Heraclio Fournier S.A., Spain. Panes of 50. Designed by Sophia van Heeswijk.

1981, Mar. 6 **Photo.** ***Perf. 14***
18 A189 4s **multicolored** *(1,508,719)* .40 .45
First day cover 1.00
Inscription block of 4 1.75 —
19 V4 6s **black & orange** *(1,569,385)* .60 .70
First day cover 1.00
First day cover, #18-19 1.25
Inscription block of 4 2.75 —

First day covers of Nos. 18-19 total 290,603.

Art Type of UN

1981, Apr. 15 **Photo.** ***Perf. 11½***
Granite Paper
20 A191 6s **multicolored** *(1,643,527)* .75 .85
First day cover *(196,916)* 1.00
Inscription block of 4 3.25 —

Energy Type of UN

1981, May 29 **Litho.** ***Perf. 13***
21 A193 7.50s **multicolored** *(1,611,130)* .70 .80
First day cover *(216,197)* 1.00
Inscription block of 4 3.00 —

Volunteers Program Types

1981, Nov. 13 **Litho.**
22 A195 5s **multicolored** *(1,582,780)* .40 .45
First day cover 1.00
Inscription block of 4 2.25 —
23 G18 7s **multicolored** *(1,516,139)* .90 1.00
First day cover 1.00
First day cover, #22-23 1.00
Inscription block of 4 4.25 —

First day covers of Nos. 22-23 total 282,414.

"For a Better World" — V5

Printed by Courvoisier, S.A., Switzerland. Sheets of 50. Designed by Eliezer Weishoff.

1982, Jan. 22 ***Perf. 11½x12***
24 V5 3s **multicolored** *(3,300,000)+* .35 .40
First day cover *(203,872)* 1.00
Inscription block of 4 1.75

Human Environment Types of UN and Geneva

10th Anniversary of United Nations Environment Program. Printed by Joh. Enschede en Zonen, Netherlands. Panes of 50. Designed by Peer-Ulrich Bremer (5s); Sybille Brunner (7s).

1982, Mar. 19 **Litho.** ***Perf. 13½x13***
25 A200 5s **multicolored** *(1,312,765)* .40 .45
First day cover 1.00
Inscription block of 4 1.90 —
26 G21 7s **multicolored** *(1,357,513)* .80 .90
First day cover 1.00
First day cover, #25-26 1.25
Inscription block of 4 3.75 —

First day covers of Nos. 25-26 total 248,576.

Outer Space Type of Geneva

Exploration and Peaceful Uses of Outer Space. Printed by Enschede. Panes of 50. Designed by George Hamori.

1982, June 11 **Litho.** ***Perf. 13x13½***
27 G22 5s **multicolored** *(1,339,038)* .60 .70
First day cover *(150,845)* 1.75
Inscription block of 4 3.00 —

Conservation & Protection of Nature Type

1982, Nov. 16 **Photo.** ***Perf. 14***
28 A202 5s Fish *(1,202,694)* .50 .60
First day cover 1.00
Inscription block of 4 2.50 —
29 A202 7s Animal *(1,194,403)* .70 .80
First day cover 1.00
First day cover, #28-29 1.40
Inscription block of 4 3.00 —

First day covers of Nos. 28-29 total 243,548.

World Communications Year Type

1983, Jan. 28 **Litho.** ***Perf. 13***
30 A203 4s **multicolored** *(1,517,443)* .40 .45
First day cover *(150,541)* 1.40
Inscription block of 4 2.10 —

Safety at Sea Types of Geneva and UN

1983, Mar. 18 **Litho.** ***Perf. 14½***
31 G23 4s **multicolored** *(1,506,052)* .40 .45
First day cover 1.00
Inscription block of 4 2.00 —
32 A206 6s **multicolored** *(1,527,990)* .65 .75
First day cover 1.00
First day cover, #31-32 2.25
Inscription block of 4 2.75 —

First day covers of Nos. 31-32 total 219,110.

World Food Program Type

1983, Apr. 22 **Engr.** ***Perf. 13½***

No.	Type	Description	Unused	Used
33	A207	5s **green** *(1,419,237)*	.45	.50
		First day cover		1.00
		Inscription block of 4	2.25	—
34	A207	7s **brown** *(1,454,227)*	.70	.80
		First day cover		1.00
		First day cover, #33-34		1.25
		Inscription block of 4	2.75	—

First day covers of Nos. 33-34 total 212,267.

UN Conference on Trade and Development Types of Geneva and UN

1983, June 6 **Litho.** ***Perf. 14***

No.	Type	Description	Unused	Used
35	G24	4s **multicolored** *(1,544,973)*	.30	.35
		First day cover		1.00
		Inscription block of 4	1.90	—
36	A209	8.50s **multicolored** *(1,423,172)*	.75	.85
		First day cover		1.00
		First day cover, #35-36		1.25
		Inscription block of 4	3.25	—

First day covers of Nos. 35-36 total 184,023.

The Second Skin — V6

Right to Think — V7

35th Anniversary of the Universal Declaration of Human Rights

Printed by Government Printing Office, Austria. Designed by Friedensreich Hundertwasser, Austria. Panes of 16 (4x4).

1983, Dec. 9 **Photo. & Engr.** ***Perf. 13½***

No.	Type	Description	Unused	Used
37	V6	5s **multicolored** *(2,163,419)*	.40	.45
		First day cover		1.25
		Inscription block of 4	2.00	
38	V7	7s **multicolored** *(2,163,542)*	.65	.75
		First day cover		1.25
		First day cover, #37-38		2.25
		Inscription block of 4	3.00	
		Panes of 16, #37-38	17.50	

First day covers of Nos. 37-38 total 246,440.

International Conference on Population Type

Printed by Bundesdruckerei, Federal Republic of Germany. Panes of 50. Designed by Marina Langer-Rosa and Helmut Langer, Federal Republic of Germany.

1984, Feb. 3 **Litho.** ***Perf. 14***

No.	Type	Description	Unused	Used
39	A212	7s **multicolored** *(1,135,791)*	.65	.75
		First day cover *(80,570)*		1.50
		Inscription block of 4	2.75	—

Field Irrigation — V8

Harvesting Machines — V9

World Food Day, Oct. 16

Printed by Walsall Security Printers, Ltd., United Kingdom. Panes of 50. Designed by Adth Vanooijen, Netherlands.

1984, Mar. 15 **Litho.** ***Perf. 14½***

No.	Type	Description	Unused	Used
40	V8	4.50s **multicolored** *(994,106)*	.40	.45
		First day cover		1.00
		Inscription block of 4	2.00	—
41	V9	6s **multicolored** *(1,027,115)*	.65	.75
		First day cover		1.00
		First day cover #40-41		2.25
		Inscription block of 4	2.50	—

First day covers of Nos. 40-41 total 194,546.

Serengeti Park, Tanzania — V10

Ancient City of Shiban, People's Democratic Rep. of Yemen — V11

World Heritage

Printed by Harrison and Sons, United Kingdom. Panes of 50. Designs adapted by Rocco J. Callari, US, and Thomas Lee, China.

1984, Mar. 15 **Litho.** ***Perf. 14***

No.	Type	Description	Unused	Used
42	V10	3.50s **multicolored** *(957,518)*	.25	.30
		First day cover		1.25
		Inscription block of 4	1.25	—
43	V11	15s **multicolored** *(928,794)*	1.25	1.40
		First day cover		1.75
		First day cover, #42-43		2.50
		Inscription block of 4	5.75	—

First day covers of Nos. 42-43 total 193,845.

V12

V13

Future for Refugees

Designed by Hans Erni, Switzerland.
Printed by Courvoisier. Panes of 50.

1984, May 29	**Photo.**	***Perf. 11½***	
44 V12 4.50s **multicolored** *(1,086,393)*		.45	.50
First day cover			1.25
Inscription block of 4		2.25	—
45 V13 8.50s **multicolored** *(1,109,865)*		1.25	1.40
First day cover			1.75
First day cover, #44-45			2.25
Inscription block of 4		5.75	—

First day covers of Nos. 44-45 total 185,349.

International Youth Year — V14

Printed by Waddingtons Ltd., United Kingdom. Panes of 50. Designed by Ruel A. Mayo, Phillipines.

1984, Nov. 15	**Litho.**	***Perf. 13½***	
46 V14 3.50s **multicolored** *(1,178,833)*		.45	.50
First day cover			1.25
Inscription block of 4		2.10	—
47 V14 6.50s **multicolored** *(1,109,337)*		.70	.80
First day cover			1.50
First day cover, #46-47			2.25
Inscription block of 4		3.25	—

First day covers of Nos. 46-47 total 165,762.

ILO Type of Geneva

Printed by the Government Printing Bureau, Japan. Panes of 50. Adapted from photographs by Rocco J. Callari, US, and Thomas Lee, China.

1985, Feb. 1	**Engr.**	***Perf. 13½***	
48 G34 7.50s U Thant Pavilion *(948,317)*		.75	.85
First day cover *(115,916)*			1.75
Inscription block of 4		3.50	—

UN University Type

Printed by Helio Courvoisier, Switzerland. Panes of 50. Designed by Moshe Pereg, Israel, and Hinedi Geluda, Brazil.

1985, Mar. 15	**Photo.**	***Perf. 11½***	
49 A221 8.50s Rural scene, lab researcher *(863,673)*		.75	.85
First day cover *(108,479)*			1.75
Inscription block of 4		3.75	—

Ship of Peace — V15

Shelter under UN Umbrella — V16

Printed by Carl Ueberreuter Druck and Verlag M. Salzer, Austria. Panes of 50. Designed by Ran Banda Mawilmada, Sri Lanka (4.50s), and Sophia van Heeswijk, Federal Republic of Germany (15s).

1985, May 10	**Litho.**	***Perf. 14***	
50 V15 4.50s **multicolored** *(2,000,000)+*		.30	.35
First day cover			.75
Inscription block of 4		1.50	—
51 V16 15s **multicolored** *(2,000,000)+*		2.00	2.25
First day cover			2.75
First day cover, #50-51			3.50
Inscription block of 4		9.50	—

First day covers of Nos. 50-51 total 142,687.

40th Anniversary Type

Designed by Rocco J. Callari, U.S., and Thomas Lee, China (No. 54).

1985, June 26	**Photo.**	***Perf. 12 x 11½***	
52 A224 6.50s **multicolored** *(984,820)*		.90	1.00
First day cover			1.25
Inscription block of 4		4.25	—
53 A225 8.50s **multicolored** *(914,347)*		1.40	1.60
First day cover			1.75
First day cover, #52-53			2.50
Inscription block of 4		6.25	—

Souvenir Sheet

Imperf

54	Sheet of 2 *(676,648)*	2.50	2.75
a.	A224 6.50s **multi**	1.00	1.10
b.	A225 8.50s **multi**	1.40	1.50
	First day cover		2.50

First day covers of Nos. 52-54 total 317,652.

UNICEF Child Survival Campaign Type

Printed by the Government Printing Bureau, Japan. Panes of 50. Designed by Mel Harris, United Kingdom (No. 55) and Vreni Wyss-Fischer, Switzerland (No. 56).

4s, Spoonfeeding children. 6s, Mother hugging infant.

1985, Nov. 22	**Photo. & Engr.**	***Perf. 13½***	
55 A226 4s multi *(889,918)*		.75	.85
First day cover			1.50
Inscription block of 4		3.50	—
56 A226 6s multi *(852,958)*		1.40	1.60
First day cover			1.50
First day cover, #55-56			2.50
Inscription block of 4		6.00	—

First day covers of Nos. 55-56 total 239,532.

Africa in Crisis Type

Printed by Helio Courvoisier, Switzerland. Panes of 50. Designed by Tesfaye Tessema, Ethiopia.

1986, Jan. 31	**Photo.**	***Perf. 11½x12***	
57 A227 8s **multicolored** *(809,854)*		.80	.90
First day cover *(99,996)*			2.75
Inscription block of 4		3.50	—

UN Development Program Type

Printed by the Government Printing Bureau, Japan. Panes of 40, 2 blocks of 4 horizontal and 5 blocks of 4 vertical. Designed by Thomas Lee, China.

Agriculture: No. 58, Developing crop strains. No. 59, Animal husbandry. No. 60, Technical instruction. No. 61, Nutrition education.

1986, Mar. 14 Photo. *Perf. 13½*

58 A228 4.50s multi *(730,691)* 1.40 1.60
59 A228 4.50s multi *(730,691)* 1.40 1.60
60 A228 4.50s multi *(730,691)* 1.40 1.60
61 A228 4.50s multi *(730,691)* 1.40 1.60
a. Block of 4, #58-61 6.25 7.00
First day cover, #61a 6.75
First day cover, #58-61, each 2.00
Inscription block of 4, #58-61 7.00 —
Pane of 40, #58-61 60.00

No. 61a has a continuous design.

First day covers of Nos. 58-61 total 227,664.

Stamp Collecting Type

Designs: 3.50s, UN stamps. 6.50s, Engraver. Printed by the Swedish Post Office, Sweden. Panes of 50. Designed by Czeslaw Slania and Ingalill Axelsson, Sweden.

1986, May 22 Engr. *Perf. 12½*

62 A229 3.50s **dk ultra & dk brown** *(874,119)* .40 .45
First day cover 1.50
Inscription block of 4 2.25 —
63 A229 6.50s **int blue & brt rose** *(877,284)* .90 1.00
First day cover 1.50
First day cover, #62-63 2.25
Inscription block of 4 4.50 —

First day covers of Nos. 62-63 total 150,836.

Olive Branch, Rainbow, Earth — V17

International Peace Year. Printed by the Government Printing Bureau, Japan. Panes of 50. Designed by Milo Schor, Israel (No. 64), and Mohammad Sardar, Pakistan (No. 65).

Photogravure & Embossed

1986, June 20 *Perf. 13½*

64 V17 5s shown *(914,699)* .75 .85
First day cover 1.50
Inscription block of 4 3.75 —
65 V17 6s Doves, UN emblem *(818,386)* 1.00 1.10
First day cover 1.50
First day cover, #64-65 2.50
Inscription block of 4 4.50 —

First day covers of Nos. 64-65 total 160,551.

WFUNA Anniversary Type
Souvenir Sheet

Printed by Johann Enschede and Sons, Netherlands. Designed by Rocco J. Callari, US.

Designs: 4s, White stallion by Elisabeth von Janota-Bzowski, Germany. 5s, Surrealistic landscape by Ernst Fuchs, Austria. 6s, Geometric abstract by Victor Vasarely (b. 1908), France. 7s, Mythological abstract by Wolfgang Hutter (b. 1928), Austria.

1986, Nov. 14 Litho. *Perf. 13x13½*

66 Sheet of 4 *(668,264)* 4.00 4.25
a. A232 4s **multicolored** .75 .80
b. A232 5s **multicolored** .85 .90
c. A232 6s **multicolored** 1.00 1.10
d. A232 7s **multicolored** 1.25 1.40
First day cover *(121,852)* 4.00

No. 66 has inscribed margin picturing UN and WFUNA emblems.

Trygve Lie Type

1987, Jan. 30 Photogravure & Engraved *Perf. 13½*

67 A233 8s **multicolored** *(778,010)* .70 .80
First day cover *(94,112)* 2.50
Inscription block of 4 3.50 —

Shelter for the Homeless Type

Designs: 4s, Family and homes. 9.50s, Family entering home.

1987, Mar. 13 Litho. *Perf. 13½x12½*

68 A234 4s **multicolored** *(704,922)* .50 .55
First day cover 1.25
Inscription block of 4 2.40 —
69 A234 9.50s **multicolored** *(671,200)* 1.10 1.25
First day cover 1.75
First day cover, #68-69 2.75
Inscription block of 4 4.75 —

First day covers of Nos. 68-69 total 117,941.

Fight Drug Abuse Type

Designs: 5s, Soccer players. 8s, Family.

1987, June 12 Litho. *Perf. 14½x15*

70 A235 5s **multicolored** *(869,875)* .40 .45
First day cover 1.40
Inscription block of 4 2.40 —
71 A235 8s **multicolored** *(797,889)* .90 1.00
First day cover 1.75
First day cover, #70-71 2.75
Inscription block of 4 4.00 —

First day covers of Nos. 70-71 total 117,964.

Donaupark, Vienna — V18

Peace Embracing the Earth — V19

Printed by The House of Questa, United Kingdom. Panes of 50. Designed by Henry Bencsath, US (2s), and Eliezer Weishoff, Israel (17s).

1987, June 12 Litho. *Perf. 14½x15*

72 V18 2s **multicolored** *(2,000,000)+* .30 .35
First day cover 1.25
Inscription block of 4 1.40 —
73 V19 17s **multicolored** *(2,000,000)+* 1.60 1.75
First day cover 2.50
First day cover, #72-73 3.50
Inscription block of 4 7.00 —

First day covers of Nos. 72-73 total 111,153.

UN Day Type

Designed by Elisabeth von Janota-Bzowski (5s) and Fritz Henry Oerter (6s), Federal Republic of Germany.

Designs: Multinational people in various occupations.

1987, Oct. 23 Litho. *Perf. 14½x15*

74 A236 5s **multicolored** *(1,575,731)* .75 .85
First day cover 1.40
Inscription block of 4 3.75 —
75 A236 6s **multicolored** *(1,540,523)* .90 1.00
First day cover 1.75
First day cover, #74-75 2.75
Inscription block of 4 4.25 —
Panes of 12, #74-75 22.00

Immunize Every Child Type

Designs: 4s, Poliomyelitis. 9.50s, Diphtheria.

1987, Nov. 20 Litho. *Perf. 15x14½*

76 A237 4s **multicolored** *(793,716)* .75 .85
First day cover 1.00
Inscription block of 4 4.00 —

77 A237 9.50s **multicolored** *(769,288)* 2.00 2.25
First day cover 1.90
First day cover, #76-77 2.75
Inscription block of 4 8.25 —

IFAD Type

Designs: 4s, Grains. 6s, Vegetables.

1988, Jan. 29 Litho. *Perf. 13½*
78 A238 4s **multicolored** *(697,307)* .40 .45
First day cover 1.25
Inscription block of 4 2.75 —
79 A238 6s **multicolored** *(701,521)* .90 1.00
First day cover 1.75
First day cover, #78-79 2.75
Inscription block of 4 4.25 —

Survival of the Forests Type

Deciduous forest in fall: 4s, Treetops, hills and dales. 5s, Tree trunks. Printed se-tenant in a continuous design.

1988, Mar. 18 Litho. *Perf. 14x15*
80 A240 4s **multicolored** *(990,607)* 2.25 2.40
First day cover 4.50
81 A240 5s **multicolored** *(990,607)* 3.00 3.25
First day cover 5.50
a. Pair, #80-81 5.25 5.75
First day cover, #81a 9.00
Inscription block of 4, #80-81 12.00 —
Pane of 12, #80-81 30.00

Intl. Volunteer Day Type

Designed by George Fernandez, U.S.
Designs: 6s, Medical care, vert. 7.50s, Construction.

1988, May 6 Litho. *Perf. 13x14, 14x13*
82 A241 6s **multicolored** *(701,167)* .75 .85
First day cover 1.40
Inscription block of 4 4.00 —
83 A241 7.50s **multicolored** *(638,240)* 1.00 1.10
First day cover 1.60
First day cover, #82-83 3.00
Inscription block of 4 5.75 —

Health in Sports Type

Paintings by LeRoy Neiman, American Sports artist: 6s, Skiing, vert. 8s, Tennis.

1988, June 17 Litho. *Perf. 13½x13, 13x13½*
84 A242 6s **multicolored** *(668,902)* .90 1.00
First day cover 1.40
Inscription block of 4 5.00 —
85 A242 8s **multicolored** *(647,915)* 1.40 1.60
First day cover 2.00
First day cover #84-85 4.00
Inscription block of 4 8.50 —

Universal Declaration of Human Rights 40th Anniv. Type

1988, Dec. 9 Photo. & Engr. *Perf. 11½*
86 A243 5s **multicolored** *(1,080,041)* .50 .55
First day cover 2.50
Inscription block of 4 3.00 —

Souvenir Sheet

87 A243 11s **multicolored** *(688,994)* 1.25 1.40
First day cover 4.75

No. 87 has multicolored decorative margin inscribed with preamble to the human rights declaration in German.

World Bank Type

1989, Jan. 27 Litho. *Perf. 13x14*
88 A244 5.50s Transportation *(682,124)* 1.10 1.25
First day cover 1.40
Inscription block of 4 5.25 —
89 A244 8s Health care, education *(628,649)* 1.75 1.90
First day cover 2.00
First day cover, #88-89 3.00
Inscription block of 4 8.25 —

First day covers of Nos. 88-89 total 135,964.

Peace-Keeping Force Type

1989, Mar. 17 *Perf. 14x13½*
90 A245 6s **multicolored** *(912,731)* .85 .95
First day cover *(81,837)* 2.00
Inscription block of 4 4.00 —

World Weather Watch Type

Satellite photograph and radar image: 4s, Helical cloud formation over Italy, the eastern Alps, and parts of Yugoslavia. 9.50s, Rainfall in Tokyo, Japan.

1989, Apr. 21 Litho. *Perf. 13x14*
91 A247 4s **multicolored** *(948,680)* 1.00 1.10
First day cover 1.40
Inscription block of 4 4.50 —
92 A247 9.50s **multicolored** *(880,138)* 2.10 2.25
First day cover 2.00
First day cover, #91-92 4.00
Inscription block of 4 10.50 —

First day covers of Nos. 91-92 total 116,846.

Offices in Vienna, 10th Anniv.
V20 V21

Printed by the Government Printing Office, Austria. Panes of 25. Designed by Gottfried Kumpf (5s) and Andre Heller (7.50s), Austria.

Photo. & Engr., Photo. (7.50s)

1989, Aug. 23 *Perf. 14*
93 V20 5s **multicolored** *(958,339)* 1.25 1.50
First day cover 1.25
Inscription block of 4 8.50 —
94 V21 7.50s **multicolored** *(785,517)* 1.25 1.50
First day cover 3.00
First day cover, #93-94 4.00
Inscription block of 4 8.50 —
Panes of 25, #93-94 *70.00*

First day covers of Nos. 93-94 total 210,746.

Human Rights Type of 1989

Panes of 12+12 se-tenant labels containing Articles 5 (4s) or 6 (6s) inscribed in German, English or French.
Paintings: 4s, The Prisoners, by Kathe Kollwitz. 6s, Justice, by Raphael.

1989, Nov. 17 Litho. *Perf. 13½*
95 A250 4s **multicolored** *(2,267,450)* .50 .55
First day cover 2.50
Inscription block of 3 + 3 labels 1.75 —
96 A250 6s **multicolored** *(2,264,876)* .75 .85
First day cover 3.50
First day cover, #95-96 3.00
Inscription block of 3 + 3 labels 2.50 —
Panes of 12, #95-96 15.00

First day covers of Nos. 95-96 total 183,199.
See Nos. 108-109, 123-124, 150-151.

Intl. Trade Center Type

1990, Feb. 2 Litho. *Perf. 14½x15*
97 A251 12s **multicolored** *(559,556)* 1.25 1.40
First day cover *(77,928)* 4.00
Inscription block of 4 5.50 —

Painting by Kurt Regschek — V22

Printed by the National Postage Stamps and Fiduciary Printing Works, France. Designed by Robert J. Stein, US.

1990, Feb. 2 Litho. ***Perf. 13x13½***

98 V22 1.50s **multicolored** *(1,000,000)+* .30 .35
First day cover *(64,622)* 2.50
Inscription block of 4 1.40 —

Fight AIDS Type — V23

Designed by Jacek Tofil, Poland (5s), Orlando Pelaez, Colombia (11s).
Designs: 5s, "SIDA." 11s, Stylized figures, ink blot.

1990, Mar. 16 Litho. ***Perf. 13½x12½***

99 V23 5s **multicolored** *(623,155)* 1.00 1.10
First day cover 1.50
Inscription block of 4 6.00 —
100 V23 11s **multicolored** *(588,742)* 2.25 2.40
First day cover 2.50
First day cover, #99-100 4.75
Inscription block of 4 11.50 —

First day covers of Nos. 99-100 total 123,657.

Medicinal Plants Type

1990, May 4 Photo. Granite Paper ***Perf. 11½***

101 A253 4.50s Bixa orellana *(709,840)* 1.25 1.40
First day cover 1.50
Inscription block of 4 5.50 —
102 A253 9.50s Momordica charantia *(732,883)* 2.50 2.75
First day cover 2.50
First day cover, #101-102 4.75
Inscription block of 4 10.50 —

First day covers of Nos. 101-102 total 117,545.

UN 45th Anniv. Type

Designed by Talib Nauman, Pakistan (7s), Marleen Bosmans (9s), Robert Stein, US (No. 105).
Designs: 7s, 9s, "45" and emblem.

1990, June 26 Litho. ***Perf. 14½x13***

103 A254 7s **multicolored** *(604,878)* 1.40 1.60
First day cover 1.75
Inscription block of 4 6.00 —
104 A254 9s **multicolored, diff.** *(550,902)* 2.40 2.75
First day cover 2.25
First day cover, #103-104 4.00
Inscription block of 4 10.50 —

Souvenir Sheet

105 Sheet of 2, #103-104 *(423,370)* 5.00 5.50
First day cover 3.50

First day covers of Nos. 103-105 total 181,174.

Crime Prevention Type

1990, Sept. 13 Photo. ***Perf. 14***

106 A255 6s Domestic violence *(661,810)* 1.00 1.10
First day cover 1.50
Inscription block of 4 5.50 —
107 A255 8s Crimes against cultural heritage *(607,940)* 2.25 2.50
First day cover 2.25
First day cover, #106-107 3.00
Inscription block of 4 11.00 —

First day covers of Nos. 106-107 total 112,193.

Human Rights Type of 1989

Panes of 12+12 se-tenant labels containing Articles 11 (4.50s) or 12 (7s) inscribed in German, English or French.
Paintings: 4.50s, Before the Judge, by Sandor Bihari. 7s, Young Man Greeted by a Woman Writing a Poem, by Suzuki Harunobu.

1990, Nov. 16 Litho. ***Perf. 13½***

108 A250 4.50s **multicolored** *(1,684,833)* .30 .35
First day cover 2.50
Inscription block of 3 + 3 labels 1.25 —
109 A250 7s **multicolored** *(1,541,022)* .90 1.00
First day cover 3.50
First day cover, #108-109 2.50
Inscription block of 3 + 3 labels 4.25 —
Panes of 12, #108-109 20.00

First day covers of Nos. 108-109 total 168,831.

Economic Commission for Europe Type

1991, Mar. 15 Litho. ***Perf. 14***

110 A256 5s Weasel, hoopoe *(727,436)* 1.40 1.60
111 A256 5s Warbler, swans *(727,436)* 1.40 1.60
112 A256 5s Badgers, squirrel *(727,436)* 1.40 1.60
113 A256 5s Fish *(727,436)* 1.40 1.60
a. Block of 4, #110-113 5.60 6.50
First day cover, No. 113a 5.00
First day cover, Nos. 110-113, each 3.25
Inscription block of 4, #110-113 6.50 —
Pane of 40, #110-113 57.50

First day covers of Nos. 110-113 total 81,624.

Namibian Independence Type

1991, May 10 Litho. ***Perf. 14***

114 A257 6s Mountains, clouds *(531,789)* 1.00 1.25
First day cover 2.50
Inscription block of 4 4.25 —
115 A257 9.50s Dune, Namib Desert *(503,735)* 2.25 2.50
First day cover 3.75
First day cover, #114-115 4.50
Inscription block of 4 9.50 —

First day covers of Nos. 114-115 total 111,184.

V24

Printed by House of Questa, United Kingdom. Designed by Marina Langer-Rosa, Germany.

1991, May 10 Litho. ***Perf. 15x14½***

116 V24 20s **multicolored** *(1,750,000)+* 1.75 2.00
First day cover *(60,843)* 4.00
Inscription block of 4 7.50 —

V25

Rights of the Child — V26

Printed by The House of Questa. Panes of 50. Designed by Anna Harmer, Austria (7s) and Emiko Takegawa, Japan (9s).

1991, June 14 **Litho.** ***Perf. 14½***

117 V25	7s Stick drawings *(645,145)*	1.00	1.25
	First day cover		1.75
	Inscription block of 4	4.25	—
118 V26	9s Child, clock, fruit *(568,214)*	1.50	1.75
	First day cover		2.25
	First day cover, #117-118		3.50
	Inscription block of 4	6.50	—

First day covers of Nos. 117-118 total 120,619.

V27

Banning of Chemical Weapons — V28

Printed by Heraclio Fournier, S.A. Panes of 50. Designed by Oscar Asboth, Austria (5s), Michel Granger, France (10s).

1991, Sept. 11 **Litho.** ***Perf. 13½***

119 V27	5s **multicolored** *(469,454)*	.75	.90
	First day cover		1.40
	Inscription block of 4	3.50	—
120 V28	10s **multicolored** *(525,704)*	1.75	2.00
	First day cover		2.50
	First day cover, #119-120		3.00
	Inscription block of 4	7.50	—

First day covers of Nos. 119-120 total 116,862.

UN Postal Administration, 40th Anniv. Type

1991, Oct. 24 **Litho.** ***Perf. 14x15***

121 A263	5s UN NY No. 8 *(564,450)*	.75	.90
	First day cover		1.40
	Inscription block of 4	4.00	—
122 A263	8s UN NY No. 5 *(609,830)*	1.50	1.75
	First day cover		2.10
	First day cover, #121-122		3.25
	Inscription block of 4	7.00	—
	Panes of 25, #121-122	57.50	

First day covers of Nos. 121-122 total 107,802.

Human Rights Type of 1989

Panes of 12+12 se-tenant labels containing Articles 17 (4.50s) or 18 (7s) inscribed in German, English or French.

Artwork: 4.50s, Pre-columbian Mexican pottery. 7s, Windows, by Robert Delaunay.

1991, Nov. 20 **Litho.** ***Perf. 13½***

123 A250	4.50s **black & brown** *(1,717,097)*	.50	.55
	First day cover		2.75
	Inscription block of 3 + 3 labels	3.00	—
124 A250	7s **multicolored** *(1,717,738)*	.80	.90
	First day cover		5.00
	First day cover, #123-124		1.75
	Inscription block of 3 + 3 labels	5.00	—
	Panes of 12+12 labels, #123-124	25.00	25.00

First day covers of Nos. 123-124 total 204,854.

World Heritage Type of 1984

Designs: 5s, Iguacu Natl. Park, Brazil. 9s, Abu Simbel, Egypt.

1992, Jan. 24 **Litho.** ***Perf. 13***

Size: 35x28mm

125 V10	5s **multicolored** *(586,738)*	.75	.90
	First day cancel		1.50
	Inscription block of 4	3.50	—
126 V10	9s **multicolored** *(476,965)*	1.60	1.80
	First day cancel		2.75
	First day cancel, #125-126		4.00
	Inscription block of 4	6.75	—

First day covers of Nos. 125-126 total 93,016.

Clean Oceans Type

1992, Mar. 13 **Litho.** ***Perf. 14***

127 A264	7s Ocean surface, diff. *(1,121,870)*	1.00	1.10
128 A264	7s Ocean bottom, diff. *(1,121,870)*	1.00	1.10
a.	Pair, #127-128	2.25	2.50
	First day cover, #128a		3.25
	First day cover, #127-128, any single		2.00
	Inscription block of 4, 2 each #127-128	5.00	—
	Pane of 12, #127-128	14.00	

First day covers of Nos. 127-128 total 128,478.

Earth Summit Type

1992, May 22 **Photo.** ***Perf. 11½***

129 A265	5.50s Man in space *(784,197)*	1.30	1.50
130 A265	5.50s Sun *(784,197)*	1.30	1.50
131 A265	5.50s Man fishing *(784,197)*	1.30	1.50
132 A265	5.50s Sailboat *(784,197)*	1.30	1.50
a.	Block of 4, #129-132	5.50	6.00
	First day cover, #132a		6.50
	First day cover, #129-132, any single		4.00
	Inscription block of 4, #129-132	7.00	—
	Pane of 40, #129-132	60.00	

First day covers of Nos. 129-132a total 82,920.

Mission to Planet Earth Type

Designs: No. 133, Satellite, person's mouth. No. 134, Satellite, person's ear.

1992, Sept. 4 **Photo.** ***Rouletted 8***

Granite Paper

133 A266	10s **multicolored** *(881,716)*	3.00	3.25
134 A266	10s **multicolored** *(881,716)*	3.00	3.25
a.	Pair, #133-134	6.00	6.50
	First day cover, #134a		5.00
	First day cover, #133-134, any single		10.00
	Inscription block of 4, #133-134	15.00	—
	Pane of 10, #133-134	35.00	

First day covers of Nos. 133-134 total 99,459.

Science and Technology Type of 1992

Designs: 5.50s, Woman emerging from computer screen. 7s, Green thumb growing flowers.

1992, Oct. 2 **Litho.** ***Perf. 14***

135 A267	5.50s **multicolored** *(482,830)*	.75	.85
	First day cover		1.75
	Inscription block of 4	3.75	—
136 A267	7s **multicolored** *(500,517)*	1.40	1.60
	First day cover		2.00
	First day cover, #135-136		4.00
	Inscription block of 4	6.75	—

First day covers of Nos. 135-136 total 98,091.

V29

Intl. Center, Vienna — V30

Printed by Walsall Secruity Printers, Ltd., UK. Designed by Gundi Groh, Austria (5.50s), Rocco J. Callari, US (7s).

1992, Oct. 2 **Litho.** ***Perf. 13x13½***

137 V29 5.50s **multicolored** *(2,100,000)+* .90 1.00
First day cover 1.25
Inscription block of 4 4.25 —

Perf. 13½x13

138 V30 7s **multicolored** *(2,100,000)+* 1.25 1.40
First day cover 2.00
First day cover, #137-138 3.50
Inscription block of 4 6.00 —

First day covers of Nos. 137-138 total 151,788.

Human Rights Type of 1989

Panes of 12+12 se-tenant labels containing Articles 23 (6s) and 24 (10s) inscribed in German, English or French.

Artwork: 6s, Les Constructeurs, by Fernand Leger. 10s, Sunday Afternoon on the Island of Le Grande Jatte, by Georges Seurat.

1992, Nov. 20 **Litho.** ***Perf. 13½***

139 A250 6s **multicolored,** *(1,536,516)* .75 .85
First day cover 5.00
Inscription block of 3 + 3 labels 3.00 —
140 A250 10s **multicolored,** *(1,527,861)* 1.25 1.40
First day cover 11.00
Inscription block of 3 + 3 labels 5.50 —
First day cover, #139-140 2.00
Panes of 12, #139-140 30.00 30.00

Aging With Dignity Type

Designs: 5.50s, Elderly couple, family working in garden. 7s, Older woman teaching.

1993, Feb. 5 **Litho.** ***Perf. 13***

141 A270 5.50s **multicolored** *(428,886)* .75 .85
First day cover 1.60
Inscription block of 4 4.50 —
142 A270 7s **multicolored** *(459,471)* 1.40 1.60
First day cover 2.00
First day cover, #141-142 3.00
Inscription block of 4 7.50 —

First day covers of Nos. 141-142 total 87,052.

Endangered Species Type

Designed by Rocco J. Callari and Steve Brennan, US.

Designs: No. 143, Equus grevyi (Grevy's zebra). No. 144, Spheniscus humboldti (Humboldt's penguins). No. 145, Varanus griseus (desert monitor). No. 146, Canis lupus (gray wolf).

1993, Mar. 2 **Litho.** ***Perf. 13x12½***

143 A271 7s **multicolored** *(1,200,000)+* .90 1.00
144 A271 7s **multicolored** *(1,200,000)+* .90 1.00
145 A271 7s **multicolored** *(1,200,000)+* .90 1.00
146 A271 7s **multicolored** *(1,200,000)+* .90 1.00
a. Block of 4, #143-146 3.60 4.00
First day cover, #146a 5.25
First day cover, #143-146, any single 1.75
Inscription block of 4, #146a 4.00 —
Pane of 16, #143-146 15.00

First day covers of Nos. 143-146a total 106,211.

Healthy Environment Type

1993, May 7 **Litho.** ***Perf. 15x14½***

147 A272 6s **Wave in ocean** *(517,433)* 1.25 1.40
First day cover 1.50
Inscription block of 4 5.25
148 A272 10s **Globe** *(453,123)* 2.00 2.25
First day cover 2.25
First day cover, #147-148 3.50
Inscription block of 4 8.75 —

First day covers of Nos. 147-148 total 79,773.

V31

Designed by Marek Kwiatkowski, Poland. Printed by Helio Courvoisier S.A., Switzerland.

1993, May 7 **Photo.** ***Perf. 11½***
Granite Paper

149 V31 13s **multicolored** *(1,500,000)+* 2.00 2.25
First day cover 1.25
Inscription block of 4 8.50 —

Human Rights Type of 1989

Printed in sheets of 12 + 12 se-tenant labels containing Article 29 (5s) and 30 (6s) inscribed in German, English or French.

Artwork: 5s, Lower Austrian Peasants' Wedding, by Ferdinand G. Waldmuller. 6s, Outback, by Sally Morgan.

1993, June 11 **Litho.** ***Perf. 13½***

150 A250 5s **multicolored** *(1,532,531)* .80 .90
First day cover 2.50
Inscription block of 3 + 3 labels 3.25 —
151 A250 6s **multicolored** *(1,542,716)* 1.00 1.10
First day cover 3.50
First day cover, #150-151 1.50
Inscription block of 3 + 3 labels 4.25 —
Panes of 12, #150-151 22.00 25.00

First day covers of Nos. 150-151 total 128,687.

Intl. Peace Day Type

Denomination at: No. 152, UL. No. 153, UR. No. 154, LL. No. 155, LR.

1993, Sept. 21 **Litho. & Engr.** ***Rouletted 12½***

152 A274 5.50s **green & multi** *(445,699)* 1.80 2.00
153 A274 5.50s **green & multi** *(445,699)* 1.80 2.00
154 A274 5.50s **green & multi** *(445,699)* 1.80 2.00
155 A274 5.50s **green & multi** *(445,699)* 1.80 2.00
a. Block of 4, #152-155 7.25 8.25
First day cover, #155a 4.00
First day cover, #152-155, any single 2.25
Inscription block of 4, #155a 8.75 —
Pane of 40, #152-155 80.00

First day covers of Nos. 152-155a total 67,075.

Environment-Climate Type

Designs: No. 156, Monkeys. No. 157, Bluebird, industrial pollution, volcano. No. 158, Volcano, nuclear power plant, tree stumps. No. 159, Cactus, tree stumps, owl.

1993, Oct. 29 **Litho.** ***Perf. 14½***

156 A275 7s **multicolored** *(484,517)* 2.50 2.75
157 A275 7s **multicolored** *(484,517)* 2.50 2.75
158 A275 7s **multicolored** *(484,517)* 2.50 2.75
159 A275 7s **multicolored** *(484,517)* 2.50 2.75
a. Strip of 4, #156-159 10.00 11.00
First day cover, #159a 9.50
First day cover, #156-159, any single 4.00
Inscription block of 8, 2 #159a 22.50 —
Pane of 24, #156-159 60.00

First day covers of Nos. 156-159a total 61,946.

Intl. Year of the Family Type of 1993

Designs: 5.50s, Adults, children holding hands. 8s, Two adults, child planting crops.

1994, Feb. 4 **Litho.** ***Perf. 13.1***

160 A276 5.50s **blue green & multi** *(650,000)+* 1.00 1.10
First day cover 1.60
Inscription block of 4 4.25 —

161 A276 8s **red & multi** *(650,000)+* 1.25 1.40
First day cover 2.25
First day cover, #160-161 3.00
Inscription block of 4 5.50 —

First day covers of Nos. 160-161 total 78,532.

Endangered Species Type of 1993

Designed by Rocco J. Callari, US (frame), and Paul Margocsy, Australia (stamps).
Designs: No. 162, Ocelot. No. 163, White-breasted silver-eye. No. 164, Mediterranean monk seal. No. 165, Asian elephant.

1994, Mar. 18 **Litho.** ***Perf. 12.7***
162 A271 7s **multicolored** *(1,200,000)+* 1.00 1.10
163 A271 7s **multicolored** *(1,200,000)+* 1.00 1.10
164 A271 7s **multicolored** *(1,200,000)+* 1.00 1.10
165 A271 7s **multicolored** *(1,200,000)+* 1.00 1.10
a. Block of 4, #162-165 4.00 4.40
First day cover, #165a 6.00
First day cover, #162-165, each 2.25
Inscription block of 4, #165a 4.50 —
Pane of 16, #162-165 16.50

First day covers of Nos. 162-165a total 104,478.

Protection for Refugees Type

Design: 12s, Protective hands surround group of refugees.

1994, Apr. 29 **Litho.** ***Perf. 14.3x14.8***
166 A277 12s **multicolored** *(650,000)+* 1.50 1.75
First day cover *(49,519)* 3.00
Inscription block of 4 8.00 —

V32

V33

V34

Designed by Masatoshi Hioki, Japan (No. 167), Ramon Alcantara Rodriguez, Mexico (No. 168), Eliezer Weishoff, Israel (No. 169).
Printed by Cartor, S.A., France.

1994, Apr. 29 **Litho.** ***Perf. 12.9***
167 V32 50g **multicolored** *(1,450,000)+* .25 .30
First day cover 1.25
Inscription block of 4 .40 —
168 V33 4s **multicolored** *(1,150,000)+* .40 .45
First day cover 1.25
Inscription block of 4 2.75 —
169 V34 30s **multicolored** *(560,000)+* 4.00 4.50
First day cover 5.00
Inscription block of 4 20.00 —
Nos. 167-169 (3) 4.65 5.25

First day covers of Nos. 167-169 total 74,558.

Intl. Decade for Natural Disaster Reduction Type

Earth seen from space, outline map of: No. 170, North America. No. 171, Eurasia. No. 172, South America. No. 173, Australia and South Asia.

1994, May 27 **Litho.** ***Perf. 13.9x14.2***
170 A281 6s **multicolored** *(690,000)+* 1.75 1.90
171 A281 6s **multicolored** *(690,000)+* 1.75 1.90
172 A281 6s **multicolored** *(690,000)+* 1.75 1.90
173 A281 6s **multicolored** *(690,000)+* 1.75 1.90
a. Block of 4, #170-173 7.00 7.75
First day cover, #173a 6.00
First day cover, #170-173, each 3.25
Inscription block of 4, #173a 8.50 —
Pane of 40, #170-173 82.50

First day covers of Nos. 170-173a total 52,502.

Population and Development Type

Designs: 5.50s, Women teaching, running machine tool, coming home to family. 7s, Family on tropical island.

1994, Sept. 1 **Litho.** ***Perf. 13.2x13.6***
174 A282 5.50s **multicolored** *(650,000)+* .90 1.00
First day cover 2.00
Inscription block of 4 3.75 —
175 A282 7s **multicolored** *(650,000)+* 1.50 1.75
First day cover 2.00
First day cover, #174-175 5.00
Inscription block of 4 6.50 —

First day covers of Nos. 174-175 total 67,423.

UNCTAD Type

1994, Oct. 28
176 A283 6s **multi, diff.** *(650,000)+* .90 1.00
First day cover 1.25
Inscription block of 4 4.25 —
177 A283 7s **multi, diff.** *(650,000)+* 1.50 1.75
First day cover 1.75
First day cover, #176-177 3.00
Inscription block of 4 7.00 —

First day covers of Nos. 176-177 total 67,064.

UN 50th Anniv. Type

1995, Jan. 1 **Litho. & Engr.** ***Perf. 13.4***
178 A284 7s **multicolored** *(742,052)* 1.25 1.40
First day cover *(118,537)* 2.00
Inscription block of 4 5.50 —

Social Summit Type

1995, Feb. 3 **Photo. & Engr.** ***Perf. 13.6x13.9***
179 A285 14s **multi, diff.** *(595,554)* 2.00 2.25
First day cover *(51,244)* 3.50
Inscription block of 4 9.00 —

Endangered Species Type of 1993

Designed by Salvatore Catalano, US.
Designs: No. 180, Black rhinoceros, Diceros bicornis. No. 181, Golden conure, Aratinga guarouba. No. 182, Douc langur, Pygathrix nemaeus. No. 183, Arabian oryx, Oryx leucoryx.

1995, Mar. 24 **Litho.** ***Perf. 13x12½***
180 A271 7s **multicolored** *(938,000)+* 1.00 1.10
181 A271 7s **multicolored** *(938,000)+* 1.00 1.10
182 A271 7s **multicolored** *(938,000)+* 1.00 1.10
183 A271 7s **multicolored** *(938,000)+* 1.00 1.10
a. Block of 4, 180-183 4.00 4.50
First day cover, #183a 4.50
First day cover, #180-183, each 2.00
Inscription block of 4, #183a 5.00 —
Pane of 16, #180-183 17.50

First day covers of Nos. 180-183a total 95,401.

Intl. Youth Year Type

Designs: 6s, Village in winter. 7s, Teepees.

1995, May 26 **Litho.** ***Perf. 14.4x14.7***
184 A286 6s **multicolored** *(437,462)* .80 .90
First day cover 1.50
Inscription block of 4 3.25 —
185 A286 7s **multicolored** *(409,449)* 1.00 1.10
First day cover 2.50
First day cover, #184-185 4.25
Inscription block of 4 4.25 —

First day covers of Nos. 184-185 total 60,979.

UN, 50th Anniv. Type

Designs: 7s, Like No. 663. 10s, Like No. 664.

1995, June 26 **Engr.** ***Perf. 13.3x13.6***

186 A287 7s **green** *(433,922)* 1.20 1.30
First day cover 2.00
Inscription block of 4 5.00 —
187 A287 10s **black** *(471,198)* 1.75 1.90
First day cover 1.75
First day cover, #186-187 4.00
Inscription block of 4 8.00 —

Souvenir Sheet
Litho. & Engr.
Imperf

188 Sheet of 2, #186-187 *(367,773)* 2.75 3.10
a. A287 7s **green** 1.10 1.25
b. A287 10s **black** 1.60 1.80
First day cover 6.50

First day covers of Nos. 186-188b total 171,765.

Conference on Women Type

Designs: 5.50s, Women amid tropical plants. 6s, Woman reading, swans on lake.

1995, Sept. 5 **Photo.** ***Perf. 12***

189 A288 5.50s **multicolored** *(549,951)* .80 .90
First day cover 1.50
Inscription block of 4 3.50 —

Size: 28x50mm

190 A288 6s **multicolored** *(556,569)* 1.20 1.30
First day cover 1.50
First day cover, #189-190 3.50
Inscription block of 4 5.25 —

First day covers of Nos. 189-190 total 71,976.

UN People, 50th Anniv. Type

1995, Oct. 24 **Litho.** ***Perf. 14***

191 Sheet of 12 *(280,528 sheets)* 9.00 10.00
First day cover 16.00
a.-l. A290 3s any single .75 .85
First day cover, #191a-191 l, each 1.25
192 Souvenir booklet, *(95,449 booklets)* 9.00
a. A290 3s Booklet pane of 3, vert. strip of 3 from UL of sheet 2.25 2.75
b. A290 3s Booklet pane of 3, vert. strip of 3 from UR of sheet 2.25 2.75
c. A290 3s Booklet pane of 3, vert. strip of 3 from LL of sheet 2.25 2.75
d. A290 3s Booklet pane of 3, vert. strip of 3 from LR of sheet 2.25 2.75

First day covers of Nos. 191-192d total 107,436.

WFUNA, 50th Anniv. Type

Design: 7s, Harlequin holding dove.

1996, Feb. 2 **Litho.** ***Perf. 13x13½***

193 A291 7s **multicolored** *(655,000)+* 1.00 1.10
First day cover 2.00
Inscription block of 4 4.50 —

UN Flag — V35

Abstract, by Karl Korab — V36

Printed by House of Questa, UK.

1996, Feb. 2 **Litho.** ***Perf. 15x14½***

194 V35 1s **multicolored** *(1,180,000)+* .25 .30
First day cover 1.25
Inscription block of 4 .80 —
195 V36 10s **multicolored** *(880,000)+* 1.60 1.75
First day cover 2.75
First day cover, #194-195 4.50
Inscription block of 4 7.00 —

Endangered Species Type of 1993

Designs: No. 196, Cypripedium calceolus. No. 197, Aztekium ritteri. No. 198, Euphorbia cremersii. No. 199, Dracula bella.

1996, Mar. 14 **Litho.** ***Perf. 12½***

196 A271 7s **multicolored** *(846,000)+* .75 .85
197 A271 7s **multicolored** *(846,000)+* .75 .85
198 A271 7s **multicolored** *(846,000)+* .75 .85
199 A271 7s **multicolored** *(846,000)+* .75 .85
a. Block of 4, #196-199 3.00 3.40
First day cover, #199a 4.50
First day cover, #196-199, each 2.00
Inscription block of 4, #199a 4.00 —
Pane of 16, #196-199 13.00

City Summit Type

Designs: No. 200, Arab family selling fruits, vegetables. No. 201, Women beside stream, camels. No. 202, Woman carrying bundle on head, city skyline. No. 203, Woman threshing grain, yoke of oxen in field. No. 204, Native village, elephant.

1996, June 3 **Litho.** ***Perf. 14x13½***

200 A293 6s **multicolored** *(500,000)+* 1.50 1.75
201 A293 6s **multicolored** *(500,000)+* 1.50 1.75
202 A293 6s **multicolored** *(500,000)+* 1.50 1.75
203 A293 6s **multicolored** *(500,000)+* 1.50 1.75
204 A293 6s **multicolored** *(500,000)+* 1.50 1.75
a. Strip of 5, #200-204 7.50 9.00
First day cover, #204a 11.50
First day cover, #200-204, each 4.50
Inscription block of 10, 2 #204a 16.00

Sport and the Environment Type

6s, Men's parallel bars (gymnastics), vert. 7s, Hurdles.

1996, July 19 **Litho.** ***Perf. 14x14½, 14½x14***

205 A294 6s **multicolored** *(730,000)+* .80 .90
First day cover 2.75
Inscription block of 4 3.75 —
206 A294 7s **multicolored** *(730,000)+* .90 1.00
First day cover 3.00
First day cover, #205-206 6.00
Inscription block of 4 4.25 —

Souvenir Sheet

207 A294 Sheet of 2, #205-206 *(500,000)+* 1.75 1.90
First day cover 10.00

Plea for Peace Type

Designed by: 7s, Du Keqing, China. 10s, Xu Kangdeng, China.

Designs: 7s, Dove and butterflies. 10s, Stylized dove, diff.

1996, Sept. 17 **Litho.** ***Perf. 14½x15***

208 A295 7s **multicolored** *(655,000)+* .80 .90
First day cover 1.50
Inscription block of 4 3.75 —
209 A295 10s **multicolored** *(655,000)+* 1.20 1.40
First day cover 2.50
First day cover, #208-209 5.00
Inscription block of 4 5.75 —

UNICEF Type

Fairy Tales: 5.50s, Hansel and Gretel, by the Brothers Grimm. 8s, How Maui Stole Fire from the Gods, South Pacific.

1996, Nov. 20 **Litho.** ***Perf. 14½x15***

210 A296 5.50s **multicolored** *(1,160,000)+* .90 1.00
First day cover 1.25
Pane of 8 + label 8.00
211 A296 8s **multicolored** *(1,160,000)+* 1.40 1.60
First day cover 2.00
First day cover, #210-211 4.00
Pane of 8 + label 12.00

V37

V38

Printed by The House of Questa, Ltd., UK.
Phoenixes Flying Down (Detail), by Sagenji Yoshida.

1997, Feb. 12 **Litho.** ***Perf. 14½***

212 V37 5s **multicolored** *(750,000)+* .80 .90
First day cover 1.25
Inscription block of 4 3.40 —
213 V38 6s **multicolored** *(1,050,000)+* .90 1.00
First day cover 1.50
First day cover, #212-213 4.00
Inscription block of 4 4.00 —

First day covers of Nos. 212-213 total 156,021.

Endangered Species Type of 1993

Designs: No. 214, Macaca sylvanus (Barbary macaque). No. 215, Anthropoides paradisea (blue crane). No. 216, Equus przewalskii (Przewalski horse). No. 217, Myrmecophaga tridactyla (giant anteater).

1997, Mar. 13 **Litho.** ***Perf. 12½***

214 A271 7s **multicolored** *(710,000)+* .75 .85
215 A271 7s **multicolored** *(710,000)+* .75 .85
216 A271 7s **multicolored** *(710,000)+* .75 .85
217 A271 7s **multicolored** *(710,000)+* .75 .85
a. Block of 4, #214-217 3.00 3.40
First day cover, #217a 6.00
First day cover, #214-217, each 3.75
Inscription block of 4, #217a 4.50
Pane of 16 13.50

First day covers of Nos. 214-217 total 86,406.

Earth Summit Anniv. Type

Designs: No. 218, Person running. No. 219, Hills, stream, trees. No. 220, Tree with orange leaves. No. 221, Tree with pink leaves. 11s, Combined design similar to Nos. 218-221.

1997, May 30 **Photo.** ***Perf. 11.5***

Granite Paper

218 A299 3.50s **multicolored** *(282,016)* 1.50 1.75
219 A299 3.50s **multicolored** *(282,016)* 1.50 1.75
220 A299 3.50s **multicolored** *(282,016)* 1.50 1.75
221 A299 3.50s **multicolored** *(282,016)* 1.50 1.75
a. Block of 4, #218-221 6.00 7.00
First day cover, #221a 10.00
First day cover, #218-221, each 4.75
Inscription block of 4, #221a 7.00

Souvenir Sheet

222 A299 11s **multicolored** *(221,434)* 2.40 2.60
First day cover 12.00

First day covers of Nos. 218-222 total 62,390.

Transportation Type

Ground transportation: No. 223, 1829 Rocket, 1901 Darraque. No. 224, Steam engine from Vladikawska Railway, trolley. No. 225, Double-decker bus. No. 226, 1950s diesel locomotive, semi-trailer. No. 227, High-speed train, electric car.

1997, Aug. 29 **Litho.** ***Perf. 14x14½***

223 A300 7s **multicolored** *(356,097)* 1.25 1.40
224 A300 7s **multicolored** *(356,097)* 1.25 1.40
225 A300 7s **multicolored** *(356,097)* 1.25 1.40
226 A300 7s **multicolored** *(356,097)* 1.25 1.40
227 A300 7s **multicolored** *(356,097)* 1.25 1.40
a. Strip of 5, #223-227 6.25 7.00
First day cover, #227a 16.00
First day cover, #223-227, each 4.75
Inscription block of 10, 2#227a 13.50

No. 227a has continuous design.

First day covers of Nos. 223-227 total 44,877.

Philately Type

Designs: 6.50s, No. 62. 7s, No. 63.

1997, Oct. 14 **Litho.** ***Perf. 13½x14***

228 A301 6.50s **multicolored** *(379,767)* .80 .90
First day cover 2.50
Inscription block of 4 4.00 —
229 A301 7s **multicolored** *(378,107)* .90 1.00
First day cover 3.50
First day cover, #228-229 6.00
Inscription block of 4 4.50 —

First day covers of Nos. 228-229 total 57,651.

World Heritage Convention Type

Terracotta warriors of Xian: 3s, Single warrior. 6s, Massed warriors. No. 232a, like No. 716. No. 232b, like No. 717. No. 232c, like Geneva No. 314. No. 232d, like Geneva No. 315. No. 232e, like Vienna No. 230. No. 232f, like Vienna No. 231.

1997, Nov. 19 **Litho.** ***Perf. 13½***

230 A302 3s **multicolored** *(528,352)* 1.00 1.10
First day cover 1.50
Inscription block of 4 4.25 —
231 A302 6s **multicolored** *(530,947)* 2.00 2.25
First day cover 2.75
First day cover, #230-231 5.00
Inscription block of 4 9.00 —
232 Souvenir booklet *(298,055 booklets)* 12.00
a.-f. A302 1s any single .50 .55
g. Booklet pane of 4 #232a 2.00 2.25
h. Booklet pane of 4 #232b 2.00 2.25
i. Booklet pane of 4 #232c 2.00 2.25
j. Booklet pane of 4 #232d 2.00 2.25
k. Booklet pane of 4 #232e 2.00 2.25
l. Booklet pane of 4 #232f 2.00 2.25

First day covers of Nos. 230-232 total 71,708.

Japanese Peace Bell, Vienna — V39

Vienna Subway, Vienna Intl. Center — V40

Printed by The House of Questa, UK. Panes of 20.
Designed by Heinz Pfeifer, Austria (6.50s), Pigneter, Austria (9s).

1998, Feb. 13 **Litho.** ***Perf. 15x14½***

233 V39 6.50s **multicolored** *(670,000)+* .80 .90
First day cover 3.25
Inscription block of 4 3.50 —
234 V40 9s **multicolored** *(770,000)+* 1.00 1.10
First day cover 4.50
First day cover, #233-234 3.00
Inscription block of 4 4.25 —

Endangered Species Type of 1993

Designed by Rocco J. Callari, US and Robert Hynes, US.
Designs: No. 235, Chelonia mydas (green turtle). No. 236, Speotyto cunicularia (burrowing owl). No. 237, Trogonoptera brookiana (Rajah Brooke's birdwing). No. 238, Ailurus fulgens (lesser panda).

1998, Mar. 13 **Litho.** ***Perf. 12½***

235 A271 7s **multicolored** *(620,000)+* .75 .85
236 A271 7s **multicolored** *(620,000)+* .75 .85
237 A271 7s **multicolored** *(620,000)+* .75 .85
238 A271 7s **multicolored** *(620,000)+* .75 .85
a. Block of 4, #235-238 3.00 3.40
First day cover, #238a 5.00
First day cover, #235-238, each 2.50
Inscription block of 4, #238a 3.50 —
Pane of 16 12.50

Intl. Year of the Ocean — V41

Designed by Yuan Lee, China.

1998, May 20 **Litho.** ***Perf. 13x13½***

239 V41 Sheet of 12 *(345,000)+* 9.50 10.75
a.-l. 3.50s any single .80 .90
First day cover, #239 17.00
First day cover, #239a-239l, each 3.00

Rain Forests Type

1998, June 19 ***Perf. 13x13½***

240 A307 6.50s Ocelot *(590,000)+* .90 1.00
First day cover 4.00
Inscription block of 4 4.75 —

Souvenir Sheet

241 A307 22s like #240 *(340,000)+* 3.00 3.25
First day cover 5.25

Peacekeeping Type of 1998

Designs: 4s, Soldier passing out relief supplies. 7.50s, UN supervised voting.

1998, Sept. 15 **Photo.** ***Perf. 12***

242 A308 4s multicolored *(555,000)+* .50 .60
First day cover 1.25
Inscription block of 4 2.00 —
243 A308 7.50s multicolored *(545,000)+* 1.00 1.10
First day cover 1.75
First day cover, #242-243 4.00
Inscription block of 4 4.25 —

Declaration of Human Rights Type

Designs: 4.50s, Stylized person. 7s, Gears.

1998, Oct. 27 **Litho. & Photo.** ***Perf. 13***

244 A309 4.50s multicolored *(555,000)+* .80 .90
First day cover 1.50
Inscription block of 4 3.25 —
245 A309 7s multicolored *(545,000)+* 1.25 1.40
First day cover 2.75
First day cover, #244-245 4.00
Inscription block of 4 5.00 —

Schönbrunn Palace Type

Designs: 3.50s, No. 248d, Palace. 7s, No. 248c, Porcelain stove, vert. No. 248a, Blue porcelain vase, vert. No. 248b, Wall painting on fabric (detail), by Johann Wenzl Bergl, vert. No. 248e, Great Palm House (conservatory). No. 248f, The Gloriette (archway).

1998, Dec. 4 **Litho.** ***Perf. 14***

246 A310 3.50s **multicolored** *(615,000)+* .60 .70
First day cover 2.00
Inscription block of 4 2.50 —
247 A310 7s **multicolored** *(615,000)+* 1.10 1.25
First day cover 2.75
First day cover, #246-247 4.00
Inscription block of 4 4.50 —

Souvenir Booklet

248 Booklet *(158,000)+* 20.00
a.-c. A310 1s any single .60 .70
d.-f. A310 2s any single 1.20 1.30
g. Booklet pane of 4 #248d 4.80 5.25
h. Booklet pane of 3 #248a 1.80 2.00
i. Booklet pane of 3 #248b 1.80 2.00
j. Booklet pane of 3 #248c 1.80 2.00
k. Booklet pane of 4 #248e 4.80 5.25
l. Booklet pane of 4 #248f 4.80 5.25

Volcanic Landscape — V42

Designed by Peter Pongratz, Austria. Printed by Johann Enschedé and Sons, the Netherlands.

1999, Feb. 5 **Litho.** ***Perf. 13x13½***

249 V42 8s **multicolored** *(660,000)+* 1.25 1.40
First day cover *(33,022)* 4.00
Inscription block of 4 7.50 —

World Heritage, Australia Type

Designs: 4.50s, No. 252d, Uluru-Kata Tjuta Natl. Park. 6.50s, No. 252a, Tasmanian Wilderness. No. 252b, Wet tropics of Queensland. No. 252c, Great Barrier Reef. No. 252e, Kakadu Natl. Park. No. 252f, Willandra Lakes region.

1999, Mar. 19 **Litho.** ***Perf. 13***

250 A313 4.50s **multicolored** *(540,000)+* .75 .85
First day cover 1.25
Inscription block of 4 3.00 —
251 A313 6.50s **multicolored** *(540,000)+* 1.10 1.25
First day cover 1.50
First day cover, #250-251 4.50
Inscription block of 4 4.50 —

Souvenir Booklet

252 Booklet *(116,000)+* 12.00
a.-c. A313 1s any single .35 .40
d.-f. A313 2s any single .65 .70
g. Booklet pane of 4, #252a 1.40 1.60
h. Booklet pane of 4, #252d 2.60 2.80
i. Booklet pane of 4, #252b 1.40 1.60
j. Booklet pane of 4, #252e 2.00 2.00
k. Booklet pane of 4, #252c 1.40 1.60
l. Booklet pane of 4, #252f 2.60 2.80

First day covers of Nos. 250-252 total 65,123.

Endangered Species Type of 1993

Designed by Jeffrey Terreson, US.

Designs: No. 253, Pongo pygmaeus (oran-utan). No. 254, Pelecanus crispus (Dalmatian pelican). No. 255, Eunectes notaeus (yellow anaconda). No. 256, Caracal.

1999, Apr. 22 **Litho.** ***Perf. 12½***

253 A271 7s **multicolored** *(552,000)+* .75 .85
254 A271 7s **multicolored** *(552,000)+* .75 .85
255 A271 7s **multicolored** *(552,000)+* .75 .85
256 A271 7s **multicolored** *(552,000)+* .75 .85
a. Block of 4, #253-256 3.00 3.40
First day cover, #256a 6.00
First day cover, #253-256, each 2.25
Inscription block of 4, #256a 3.75 —
Pane of 16 12.50

First day covers of Nos. 253-256 total 66,733.

UNISPACE III Type

Designs: No. 257, Satellite over ships. No. 258, Satellite up close. No. 259, Composite of Nos. 257-258.

1999, July 7 **Photo.** ***Rouletted 8***

257 A314 3.50s **multicolored** *(1,200,000)+* .75 .85
258 A314 3.50s **multicolored** *(1,200,000)+* .75 .85
a. Pair, #257-258 1.60 1.70
First day cover, #258a 3.00
First day cover, #257-258, each 2.50
Inscription block of 4 6.50 —
Pane of 10, #257-258 9.00 —

Souvenir Sheet

Perf. 14½

259 A314 13s **multicolored** *(350,000)+* 4.50 5.00
First day cover 5.00

First day covers of Nos. 257-259 total 72,143.

UPU Type

Various people, late 20th century methods of mail transportation, denomination at: No. 260, UL. No. 261, UR. No. 262, LL. No. 263, LR.

1999, Aug. 23 **Photo.** ***Perf. 11¾***

260 A315 6.50s **multicolored** *(417,000)+* 1.00 1.10
261 A315 6.50s **multicolored** *(417,000)+* 1.00 1.10
262 A315 6.50s **multicolored** *(417,000)+* 1.00 1.10
263 A315 6.50s **multicolored** *(417,000)+* 1.00 1.10
a. Block of 4, #260-263 4.00 4.50
First day cover, #263a 4.50
First day cover, #260-263, each 2.00
Inscription block of 4 4.50 —

First day covers of Nos. 260-263 total 38,453.

In Memoriam Type

Designs: 6.50s, 14s, Donaupark. Size of 14s stamp: 34x63mm.

1999, Sept. 21 **Litho.** ***Perf. 14½x14***

264 A316 6.50s **multicolored** *(530,000)+* .90 1.00
First day cover 3.00
Inscription block of 4 4.50 —

Souvenir Sheet

Perf. 14

265 A316 14s **multicolored** *(338,000)+* 3.00 3.25
First day cover 4.00

First day covers of Nos. 264-265 total 61,089.

Education Type

1999, Nov. 18 **Litho.** ***Perf. 13½x13¾***

266 A317 7s Boy, girl, book *(490,000)+* .75 .85
First day cover 1.60
Inscription block of 4 3.25 —
267 A317 13s Group reading *(490,000)+* 1.75 1.90
First day cover 3.00
First day cover, #266-267 4.00
Inscription block of 4 6.50 —

First day covers of Nos. 266-267 total 48,590.

Intl. Year of Thanksgiving Type

2000, Jan. 1 **Litho.** ***Perf. 13¼x13½***

268 A318 7s **multicolored** *(510,000)+* .80 .90
First day cover 3.00
Inscription block of 4 4.75 —

On No. 268 parts of the design were applied by a thermographic process producing a shiny, raised effect.

Endangered Species Type of 1993

Designed by Lori Anzalone, US.
Designs: No. 269, Panthera pardus (leopard). No. 270, Platalea leucorodia (white spoonbill). No. 271, Hippocamelus bisulcus (huemal). No. 272, Orcinus orca (killer whale).

2000, Apr. 6 **Litho.** ***Perf. 12¾x12½***

269 A271 7s **multicolored** *(548,000)+* 1.10 1.25
270 A271 7s **multicolored** *(548,000)+* 1.10 1.25
271 A271 7s **multicolored** *(548,000)+* 1.10 1.25
272 A271 7s **multicolored** *(548,000)+* 1.10 1.25
a. Block of 4, #269-272 4.50 5.00
First day cover, #272a 6.00
First day cover, #269-272, each 2.00
Inscription block of 4, #272a 4.75 —
Pane of 16 18.00

Our World 2000 Type

Winning artwork in Millennium painting competition: 7s, Tomorrow's Dream, by Voltaire Perez, Philippines. 8s, Remembrance, by Dimitris Nalbandis, Greece, vert.

2000, May 30 **Litho.** ***Perf. 13x13½, 13½x13***

273 A319 7s **multicolored** *(430,000)+* .60 .70
First day cover 1.75
Inscription block of 4 2.75 —
274 A319 8s **multicolored** *(430,000)+* .75 .85
First day cover 2.00
First day cover, #273-274 3.00
Inscription block of 4 3.25 —

55th Anniversary Type

Designs: 7s, Secretariat Building, unfinished dome of General Assembly Hall, 1951. 9s, Trygve Lie and Headquraters Advisory Committee at topping-out ceremony, 1949.

2000, July 7 **Litho.** ***Perf. 13¼x13***

275 A320 7s **multicolored** *(440,000)+* .90 1.00
First day cover 1.75
Inscription block of 4 4.50 —
276 A320 9s **multicolored** *(440,000)+* 1.25 1.40
First day cover 2.25
First day cover, #275-276 3.00
Inscription block of 4 6.00 —

Souvenir Sheet

277 A320 Sheet of 2, #275-276 *(300,000)+* 2.75 3.25
First day cover 3.25

The UN in the 21st Century — V43

Printed by Government Printing Office, Austria. Designed by Wilson McLean, UK.

No. 278: a, Farm machinery. b, UN Peacekeepers and children. c, Oriental farm workers. d, Peacekeepers searching for mines. e, Medical research. f, Handicapped people.

2000, Sept. 15 **Litho.** ***Perf. 14***

278 V43 Sheet of 6 *(330,000)+* 7.50 8.50
First day cover 5.00
a.-f. 3.50s any single 1.25 1.40
First day cover, #278a-278f, each 4.00

World Heritage, Spain Type

Designs: Nos. 279, 281c, Aqueduct of Segovia. Nos. 280, 281f, Güell Park, Barcelona. No. 281a, Alhambra, Generalife and Albayzin, Granada. No. 281b, Walled Town of Cuenca. No. 281d, Amphitheater of Mérida. No. 281e, Toledo.

2000, Oct. 6 **Litho.** ***Perf. 14¾x14½***

279 A323 4.50s **multicolored** *(430,000)+* .80 .90
First day cover 1.25
Inscription block of 4 3.00 —
280 A323 6.50s **multicolored** *(430,000)+* 1.20 1.40
First day cover 1.75
First day cover, #279-280 2.40
Inscription block of 4 4.00 —

Souvenir Booklet

281 Booklet *(92,000)+* 9.00
a.-c. A323 1s any single .25 .30
d.-f. A323 2s any single .50 .55
g. Booklet pane of 4, #281a 1.00 1.10

h. Booklet pane of 4, #281d 2.00 2.25
i. Booklet pane of 4, #281b 1.00 1.10
j. Booklet pane of 4, #281e 2.00 2.25
k. Booklet pane of 4, #281c 1.00 1.10
l. Booklet pane of 4, #281f 2.00 2.25

Respect for Refugees Type

Designs: 7s, 25s, Refugee with hat, three other refugees.

2000, Nov. 9 Litho. *Perf. 13¼x12¾*
282 A324 7s **multicolored** *(530,000)+* 1.10 1.25
First day cover 1.75
Inscription block of 4 4.50 —

Souvenir Sheet

283 A324 25s **multicolored** *(273,000)+* 3.75 4.25
First day cover 4.50

Endangered Species Type of 1993

Printed by Johann Enschedé and Sons, the Netherlands. Designed by Betina Ogden, Australia.

Designs: No. 284, Tremarctos ornatus (spectacled bear). No. 285, Anas laysanensis (Laysan duck). No. 286, Proteles cristatus (aardwolf). No. 287, Trachypithecus cristatus (silvered leaf monkey).

2001, Feb. 1 Litho. *Perf. 12¾x12½*
284 A271 7s **multicolored** *(540,000)+* 1.10 1.25
285 A271 7s **multicolored** *(540,000)+* 1.10 1.25
286 A271 7s **multicolored** *(540,000)+* 1.10 1.25
287 A271 7s **multicolored** *(540,000)+* 1.10 1.25
a. Block of 4, #284-287 4.50 5.00
First day cover, #287a 5.00
First day cover, #284-287 each 1.75
Inscription block of 4, #287a 4.25 —
Pane of 16 16.00

Intl. Volunteers Year — V44

Printed by Johann Enschedé and Sons, the Netherlands. Panes of 20. Designed by Rorie Katz and Robert Stein, US.

Paintings by: 10s, Nguyen Thanh Chuong, Viet Nam. 12s, Ikko Tanaka, Japan.

2001, Mar. 29 Litho. *Perf. 13¼*
288 V44 10s **multicolored** *(440,000)+* 1.40 1.60
First day cover 2.00
Inscription block of 4 5.75
289 V44 12s **multicolored** *(430,000)+* 1.75 1.90
First day cover 2.40
First day cover, #288-289 3.75
Inscription block of 4 7.00

World Heritage, Japan Type

Designs: 7s, No. 290c, Himeji-Jo. 15s, No. 291f, Nikko. No. 292a, Kyoto. No. 292b, Nara. No. 292d, Shirakawa-Go and Gokayama. No. 292e, Itsukushima Shinto Shrine.

2001, Aug. 1 Litho. *Perf. 12¾x13¼*
290 A328 7s **multicolored** *(440,000)+* 1.00 1.10
First day cover 1.40
Inscription block of 4 4.00 —
291 A328 15s **multicolored** *(440,000)+* 2.10 2.25
First day cover 3.00
First day cover, #290-291 3.75
Inscription block of 4 8.50 —

Souvenir Booklet

292 Booklet *(78,000)+* 11.50
a.-c. A328 1s any single .30 .35
d.-f. A328 2s any single .60 .70
g. Booklet pane of 4, #292a 1.20 1.40
h. Booklet pane of 4, #292d 2.40 2.75
i. Booklet pane of 4, #292b 1.20 1.40
j. Booklet pane of 4, #292e 2.40 2.75
k. Booklet pane of 4, #292c 1.20 1.40
l. Booklet pane of 4, #292f 2.40 2.75

Dag Hammarskjöld Type

2001, Sept. 18 Engr. *Perf. 11x11¼*
293 A329 7s **green** *(480,000)+* 1.00 1.10
First day cover 2.00
Inscription block of 4 4.25 —

UN Postal Administration, 50th Anniv. Types

2001, Oct. 18 Litho. *Perf. 13½*
294 A330 7s Stamps, balloons *(380,000)+* 1.00 1.10
First day cover 1.60
Inscription block of 4 4.00 —
295 A330 8s Stamps, cake *(380,000)+* 1.10 1.25
First day cover 1.75
First day cover, #294-295 2.75
Inscription block of 4 4.50 —

Souvenir Sheet

296 A331 Sheet of 2 *(225,000)+* 7.50 8.00
a. 7s **green & light blue,** 38mm diameter 2.50 2.75
b. 21s **green & light blue,** 38mm diameter 5.00 5.50
First day cover 7.00

Climate Change Type

Designs: No. 297, Solar panels, automobile at pump. No. 298, Blimp, bicyclists, horse and rider. No. 299, Balloon, sailboat, lighthouse, train. No. 300, Bird, train, traffic signs.

2001, Nov. 16 Litho. *Perf. 13¼*
297 A332 7s **multicolored** *(87,000)+* 1.00 1.10
298 A332 7s **multicolored** *(87,000)+* 1.00 1.10
299 A332 7s **multicolored** *(87,000)+* 1.00 1.10
300 A332 7s **multicolored** *(87,000)+* 1.00 1.10
a. Horiz. strip, #297-300 5.00 5.50
Inscription block of 8 8.25 —
First day cover, #300a 4.50
First day cover, #297-300 each 6.00
Pane of 24 30.00 —

Nobel Peace Prize Type

2001, Dec. 10 Litho. *Perf. 13¼*
301 A333 7s **multicolored** *(1,260,000)+* 1.00 .55
Inscription block of 4 5.00 —
First day cover 1.60
Pane of 12 14.00 —

100 Cents = 1 Euro (€)

Austrian Tourist Attractions — V45

Printed by House of Questa, UK. Panes of 20. Designed by Rorie Katz, US.

Designs: 7c, Semmering Railway. 51c, Pferdschwemme, Salzburg. 58c, Aggstein an der Donau Ruins. 73c, Hallstatt. 87c, Melk Abbey. €2.03, Kapitelschwemme, Salzburg.

2002, Mar. 1 Litho. *Perf. 14½x14*
302 V45 7c **multicolored** *(860,000)+* .25 .30
First day cover 1.25
Inscription block of 4 .75 —
303 V45 51c **multicolored** *(960,000)+* .90 1.25
First day cover 1.40
Inscription block of 4 4.00 —
304 V45 58c **multicolored** *(860,000)+* 1.00 1.10
First day cover 1.60
Inscription block of 4 4.25 —
305 V45 73c **multicolored** *(760,000)+* 1.25 1.40
First day cover 2.00
Inscription block of 4 5.50 —
306 V45 87c **multicolored** *(760,000)+* 1.75 2.00
First day cover 2.40
Inscription block of 4 7.25 —
307 V45 €2.03 **multicolored** *(710,000)+* 3.50 3.75
First day cover 5.50
First day cover, #288-289 10.50
Inscription block of 4 15.00 —
Nos. 302-307 (6) 8.65 9.80

Endangered Species Type of 1993

Printed by Johann Enschedé and Sons, the Netherlands. Designed by Tim Barrall, US.

Designs: No. 308, Hylobates syndactylus (siamang). No. 309, Spheniscus demersus (jackass penguin). No. 310, Prionodon linsang (banded linsang). No. 311, Bufo retiformis (Sonoran green toad).

2002, Apr. 4 **Litho.** ***Perf. 12¾x12½***

308 A271 51c **multicolored** *(500,000)+* 1.25 1.25
309 A271 51c **multicolored** *(500,000)+* 1.25 1.25
310 A271 51c **multicolored** *(500,000)+* 1.25 1.25
311 A271 51c **multicolored** *(500,000)+* 1.25 1.25
a. Block of 4, #308-311 5.00 5.00
First day cover, #311a 4.75
First day cover, #308-311 each 1.75
Inscription block of 4, #311a 5.25 —
Pane of 16 18.00 —

Independence of East Timor Type

Designs: 51c, Deer horn container with carved wooden stopper. €1.09, Carved wooden tai weaving loom.

2002, May 20 **Litho.** ***Perf. 14x14½***

312 A335 51c **multicolored** *(384,000)+* 1.00 1.00
First day cover 1.50
Inscription block of 4 4.50 —
313 A335 €1.09 **multicolored** *(374,000)+* 2.25 2.25
First day cover 3.25
First day cover, #312-313 4.00
Inscription block of 4 9.50 —

Intl. Year of Mountains Type

Designs: No. 314, Mt. Cook, New Zealand. No. 315, Mt. Robson, Canada. No. 316, Mt. Rakaposhi, Pakistan. No. 317, Mt. Everest (Sagarmatha), Nepal.

2002, May 24 **Litho.** ***Perf. 13x13¼***

314 A336 22c **multicolored** *(1,335,000)+* .40 .40
First day cover 1.25
315 A336 22c **multicolored** *(1,335,000)+* .40 .40
First day cover 1.25
316 A336 51c **multicolored** *(1,335,000)+* 1.00 1.00
First day cover 1.50
First day cover, #314, 316 2.25
317 A336 51c **multicolored** *(1,335,000)+* 1.00 1.00
a. Vert. strip or block of four, #314-317 12.50 12.50
First day cover 1.50
First day cover, #315, 317 2.25
First day cover, #314-317 3.75
Pane of 12, 3 each #314-317 10.00 —

World Summit on Sustainable Development (Peter Max) Type

Designs: No. 318, Rainbow. No. 319, Three women, diff. No. 320, Three faceless people. No. 321, Birds, wave.

2002, June 27 **Litho.** ***Perf. 14½x14***

318 A337 51c **multicolored** *(1,305,000)+* 1.00 1.00
First day cover 1.50
319 A337 51c **multicolored** *(1,305,000)+* 1.00 1.00
First day cover 1.50
320 A337 58c **multicolored** *(1,305,000)+* 1.25 1.25
First day cover 1.60
First day cover, #318, 320 2.50
321 A337 58c **multicolored** *(1,305,000)+* 1.25 1.25
a. Vert. strip or block of four, #318-321 10.00 8.50
First day cover 1.60
First day cover, #319, 321 2.50
First day cover, #318-321 3.75
Pane of 12, 3 each #318-321 13.50 —

World Heritage, Italy Type

Designs: 51c, No. 324f, Pompeii. 58c, No. 324c, Rome. No. 324a, Amalfi Coast. No. 324b, Aeolian Islands. No. 324d, Florence. No. 324e, Pisa.

2002, Aug. 30 **Litho.** ***Perf. 13½x13¼***

322 A338 51c **multicolored** *(400,000)+* 1.10 1.10
First day cover 1.75
Inscription block of 4 4.50 —
323 A338 58c **multicolored** *(400,000)+* 1.25 1.25
First day cover 2.00
First day cover, #322-323 3.00
Inscription block of 4 5.00 —

Souvenir Booklet

324 Booklet *(71,000)+* 15.00
a.-c. A338 7c any single .40 .40
d.-f. A338 15c any single .85 .85
g. Booklet pane of 4, #324d 3.40 3.40
h. Booklet pane of 4, #324a 1.60 1.60
i. Booklet pane of 4, #324e 3.40 3.40
j. Booklet pane of 4, #324b 1.60 1.60
k. Booklet pane of 4, #324f 3.40 3.40
l. Booklet pane of 4, #324c 1.60 1.60

AIDS Awareness Type

2002, Oct. 24 **Litho.** ***Perf. 13½***

325 A339 €1.53 **multicolored** *(370,000)+* 2.50 2.75
Inscription block of 4 13.00
First day cover, #325 4.00
Pane of 20 65.00

Indigenous Art — V46

Printed by House of Questa, UK.
Designed by Rorie Katz and Robert Stein, US.

No. 326: a, Mola, Panama. b, Mochican llama-shaped spouted vessel, Peru. c, Tarabuco woven cloth, Bolivia. d, Masks, Cuba. e, Aztec priest's feather headdress, Mexico. f, Bird-shaped staff head, Colombia.

2003, Jan. 31 **Litho.** ***Perf. 14¼***

326 V46 Sheet of 6 *(212,000)+* 7.50 7.50
First day cover 8.25
a.-f. 51c Any single 1.25 1.25
First day cover, a.-f., each 3.00

Austrian Tourist Attractions Type of 2002

Printed by House of Questa, UK. Designed by Rorie Katz, US. Panes of 20.

Designs: 25c, Kunsthistorisches Museum, Vienna. €1, Belvedere Palace, Vienna.

2003, Mar. 28 **Litho.** ***Perf. 14½x14***

327 V45 25c **multicolored** *(650,000)+* .55 .55
First day cover 1.25
Inscription block of 4 2.25 —
328 V45 €1 **multicolored** *(650,000)+* 2.25 2.25
First day cover 3.25
First day cover, #327-328 3.50
Inscription block of 4 9.00 —

Endangered Species Type of 1993

Printed by Johann Enschedé and Sons, the Netherlands. Designed by Robert Hautman, US.

Designs: No. 329, Anas formosa (Baikal teal). No. 330, Bostrychia hagedash (Hadada ibis). No. 331, Ramphastos toco (toco toucan). No. 332, Alopochen aegyptiacus (Egyptian goose).

2003, Apr. 3 **Litho.** ***Perf. 12¾x12½***

329 A271 51c **multicolored** *(432,000)+* 1.25 1.25
330 A271 51c **multicolored** *(432,000)+* 1.25 1.25
331 A271 51c **multicolored** *(432,000)+* 1.25 1.25
332 A271 51c **multicolored** *(432,000)+* 1.25 1.25
a. Block of 4, #329-332 5.00 5.00
First day cover, #332a 5.25
First day cover, #329-332 each 1.90
Inscription block of 4, #332a 5.50 —
Pane of 16 20.00 —

International Year of Freshwater Type of 2003

2003, June 20 **Litho.** ***Perf. 14¼x14½***

333 A345 55c Bridge, bird *(316,000)+* 3.00 3.00
334 A345 75c Horse, empty river *(316,000)+* 5.00 5.00
a. Horiz. pair, #333-334 8.00 8.00
First day cover, #334a 3.75
Inscription block of 4 15.00 —

Austrian Tourist Attractions Type of 2002

Printed by Johann Enschedé and Sons, the Netherlands. Panes of 20. Designed by Rorie Katz, US.
Design: 4c, Schloss Eggenberg, Graz.

2003, Aug. 7 Litho. *Perf. 14x13¼*
335 V45 4c **multicolored** *(650,000)+* .45 .45
First day cover 1.25
Inscription block of 4 1.80
Pane of 20 9.00

Ralph Bunche Type
Litho. With Foil Application

2003, Aug. 7 *Perf. 13½x14*
336 A346 €2.10 **olive green & multicolored** *(384,000)+* 3.50 3.50
First day cover 5.50
Inscription block of 4 15.00
Pane of 20 70.00

In Memoriam Type of 2003

2003, Oct. 24 Litho. *Perf. 13¼x13*
337 A347 €2.10 **multicolored** *(670,000)+* 5.00 5.00
First day cover 6.25
Inscription block of 4 22.00 —
Pane of 20 110.00 —

World Heritage Sites, United States Type

Designs: 55c, No. 340c, Olympic National Park. 75c, No. 340e, Everglades National Park. No. 340a, Yosemite National Park. No. 340b, Great Smoky Mountains National Park. No. 340d, Hawaii Volcanoes National Park. No. 340f, Yellowstone National Park.

2003, Oct. 24 Litho. *Perf. 14½x14¼*
338 A348 55c **multicolored** *(275,000)+* 1.50 .75
First day cover 2.10
Inscription block of 4 6.00 —
339 A348 75c **multicolored** *(275,000)+* 2.00 1.00
First day cover 2.75
First day cover, #338-339 4.25
Inscription block of 4 8.00 —

Souvenir Booklet

340 Booklet *(57,500)+* 14.50
a.-c. A348 15c any single .55 .55
d.-f. A348 20c any single .65 .65
g. Booklet pane of 4 #340a 2.10 2.10
h. Booklet pane of 4 #340d 2.60 2.60
i. Booklet pane of 4 #340b 2.10 2.10
j. Booklet pane of 4 #340e 2.60 2.60
k. Booklet pane of 4 #340c 2.10 2.10
l. Booklet pane of 4 #340f 2.60 2.60

Austrian Tourist Attractions Type of 2002

Printed by Imprimerie de Timbres-Poste, France.
Design: 55c, Schloss Schönbrunn, Vienna.

2004, Jan. 29 Litho. *Perf. 13x13¼*
341 V45 55c **multicolored** *(740,000)+* 1.50 1.50
First day cover 2.10
Inscription block of 4 6.00 —
Pane of 20 30.00 —

Endangered Species Type of 1993

Printed by Johann Enschedé and Sons, the Netherlands. Designed by Yuan Lee, U.S.

Designs: No. 342, Melursus ursinus (Sloth bear). No. 343, Cervus eldi (Eld's deer). No. 344, Cercocebus torquatus (Cherry-crowned mangabey). No. 345, Bubalus arnee (Wild water buffalo).

2004, Jan. 29 Litho. *Perf. 12¾x12½*
342 A271 55c **multicolored** *(376,000)+* 1.50 1.50
343 A271 55c **multicolored** *(376,000)+* 1.50 1.50
344 A271 55c **multicolored** *(376,000)+* 1.50 1.50
345 A271 55c **multicolored** *(376,000)+* 1.50 1.50
a. Block of 4, #342-345 6.00 6.00
First day cover, #345a 6.50
First day cover, #342-345, each 2.25
Inscription block of 4, #345a 7.00 —
Pane of 16 25.00 —

Indigenous Art Type of 2003

Printed by Johann Enschedé and Sons, the Netherlands.
Designed by Rorie Katz and Robert Stein, US.

No. 346: a, Illuminated illustration from the Book of Kells, Ireland. b, Easter eggs, Ukraine. c, Venus of Willendorf, Paleolithic age limestone statue, Austria. d, Flatatunga panel, Iceland. e, Neolithic era idol, Hungary. f, Illuminated illustration from medical treatise, Portugal.

2004, Mar. 4 Litho. *Perf. 13¼*
346 V46 Sheet of 6 *(133,000)+* 12.00 12.00
First day cover 10.50
a.-f. 55c Any single 2.00 2.00
First day cover, a.-f., each 2.75

Road Safety Type

Road map art with: 55c, Automobile, alcohol bottles. 75c, Road, clouds in traffic light colors, vert.

2004, Apr. 7 Litho. *Perf. 13x13¼, 13¼x13*
347 A354 55c **multicolored** *(225,000)+* 1.25 1.25
First day cover 2.10
Inscription block of 4 6.00 —
348 A354 75c **multicolored** *(225,000)+* 1.75 1.75
First day cover 2.75
First day cover, #338-339 4.25
Inscription block of 4 8.00 —

Japanese Peace Bell, 50th Anniv. Type

2004, June 3 Litho. & Engr. *Perf. 13¼x13*
349 A355 €2.10 **multicolored** *(280,000)+* 4.50 4.50
First day cover 6.25
Inscription block of 4 22.00 —
Pane of 20 110.00

World Heritage Sites, Greece Type

Designs: 55c, No. 352f, Mycenae and Tiryns. 75c, No. 352e, Olympia. No. 352a, Acropolis, Athens. No. 352b, Delos. No. 352c, Delphi. No. 352d, Pythagoreion and Heraion of Samos.

2004, Aug. 12 Litho. *Perf. 14x13¼*
350 A356 55c **multicolored** *(250,000)+* 1.75 1.75
First day cover 1.90
Inscription block of 4 7.25 —
351 A356 75c **multicolored** *(250,000)+* 2.25 2.25
First day cover 2.75
First day cover, #350-351 4.00
Inscription block of 4 9.25 —

Souvenir Booklet

352 Booklet *(49,000)+* 16.00
a.-d. A356 25c any single .60 .60
e.-f. A356 30c either single .70 .70
g. Booklet pane of 4 #352a 2.40 2.40
h. Booklet pane of 4 #352b 2.40 2.40
i. Booklet pane of 4 #352c 2.40 2.40
j. Booklet pane of 4 #352d 2.40 2.40
k. Booklet pane of 4 #352e 2.80 2.80
l. Booklet pane of 4 #352f 2.80 2.80

My Dream for Peace Type

Winning designs of Lions Club International children's global peace poster contest by: 55c, Henry Ulfe Renteria, Peru. €1, Michelle Fortaliza, Philippines.

2004, Sept. 21 Litho. *Perf. 14*
353 A357 55c **multicolored** *(235,000)+* 1.40 1.40
First day cover 1.90
Inscription block of 4 5.75
Pane of 20 28.00
354 A357 €1 **multicolored** *(235,000)+* 2.50 2.50
First day cover 3.50
First day cover, #353-354 4.50
Inscription block of 4 10.00
Pane of 20 50.00

V47

Human Rights — V48

Printed by Banknote Corporation of America, US. Designed by Yuri Gervorgian, Armenia. Panes of 8.

2004, Oct. 14 **Litho.** ***Perf. 11¼***

No.	Type	Description	Unused	Used
355	V47	55c **multicolored** *(480,000)+*	1.00	1.00
		First day cover		2.00
		Pane of 8	12.00	—
356	V48	€1.25 **multicolored** *(480,000)+*	3.00	3.00
		First day cover		4.50
		First day cover, #355-356		5.75
		Pane of 8	28.00	—

United Nations, 60th Anniv. Type of 2005

Printed by Banknote Corporation of America, US. Designed by Czeslaw Slania, Sweden.

2005, Feb. 4 **Litho. & Engr.** ***Perf. 11x11¼***

No.	Type	Description	Unused	Used
357	A361	55c **multicolored** *(310,000)+*	2.50	2.50
		First day cover		2.60
		Inscription block of 4	10.50	—
		Pane of 20	50.00	—

Souvenir Sheet

Litho.

Imperf

No.	Type	Description	Unused	Used
358	A361	€2.10 **multicolored** *(165,000)+*	6.50	6.50
		First day cover		6.25

International Center, Vienna — V49

Printed by Cartor Security Printing, France.

2005, Feb. 4 **Litho. with Hologram** ***Perf. 13½x13¼***

No.	Type	Description	Unused	Used
359	V49	75c **multicolored** *(360,000)+*	2.25	2.25
		First day cover		3.25
		Inscription block of 4	9.00	—
		Pane of 20	45.00	—

Endangered Species Type of 1993

Designs: No. 360, Ansellia africana. No. 361, Phragmipedium kovachii. No. 362, Cymbidium ensifolium. No. 363, Renanthera imschootiana.

2005, Mar. 3 **Litho.** ***Perf. 12¾x12½***

No.	Type	Description	Unused	Used
360	A271	55c multicolored	1.40	1.40
361	A271	55c multicolored	1.40	1.40
362	A271	55c multicolored	1.40	1.40
363	A271	55c multicolored	1.40	1.40
a.		Block of 4, #360-363	6.00	6.00
		First day cover, #363a		7.00
		First day cover, #360-363, each		2.25
		Inscription block of 4, #363a	6.25	—
		Pane of 16	24.00	—

Nature's Wisdom V50

Printed by Cartor Security Printing, France. Panes of 20. Designed by Robert Stein, US.

Designs: 55c, Desert landscape, China. 80c, Cheetah family, Africa.

2005, Apr. 21 **Litho.** ***Perf. 13½x13¼***

No.	Type	Description	Unused	Used
364	V50	55c **multicolored** *(230,000)+*	1.60	1.60
		First day cover		2.40
		Inscription block of 4	6.50	—
		Pane of 20	32.50	—
365	V50	75c **multicolored** *(230,000)+*	2.25	2.25
		First day cover		3.50
		First day cover, #364-365		4.75
		Inscription block of 4	9.00	—
		Pane of 20	45.00	—

Intl. Year of Sport Type

Printed by Cartor Security Printing, France. Designed by Roland Hirter, Switzerland.

2005, June 3 **Litho.** ***Perf. 13x13¼***

No.	Type	Description	Unused	Used
366	A368	55c Equestrian *(245,000)+*	1.60	1.60
		First day cover		2.25
		Inscription block of 4	6.50	—
		Pane of 20	32.50	—
367	A368	€1.10 Soccer *(245,000)+*	3.25	3.25
		First day cover		4.50
		First day cover, #366-367		6.00
		Inscription block of 4	13.00	—
		Pane of 20	65.00	—

World Heritage Sites, Egypt Type

Printed by Johann Enschedé and Sons, the Netherlands. Panes of 20. Designed by Rorie Katz, US.

Designs: Nos. 368, 370c, Abu Mena. Nos. 369, 370f, St. Catherine area. No. 370a, Memphis and its Necropolis. No. 370b, Philae. No. 370d, Ancient Thebes. No. 370e, Islamic Cairo.

2005, Aug. 4 **Litho.** ***Perf. 14x13¼***

No.	Type	Description	Unused	Used
368	A369	55c **multicolored** *(250,000)+*	1.60	1.60
		First day cover		2.40
		Inscription block of 4	6.50	—
369	A369	75c **multicolored** *(250,000)+*	2.25	2.25
		First day cover		3.25
		First day cover, #368-369		4.75
		Inscription block of 4	9.00	—

Souvenir Booklet

No.	Type	Description	Unused	Used
370		Booklet, #370g-370l *(45,000)+*	19.50	
a.-c.	A369	25c any single	.75	.75
d.-f.	A369	30c any single	.85	.85
g.		Booklet pane of 4 #370a	3.00	3.00
h.		Booklet pane of 4 #370b	3.00	3.00
i.		Booklet pane of 4 #370c	3.00	3.00
j.		Booklet pane of 4 #370d	3.50	3.50
k.		Booklet pane of 4 #370e	3.50	3.50
l.		Booklet pane of 4 #370f	3.50	3.50

No. 370 sold for €6.80.

My Dream for Peace Type

Winning designs of Lions Club International children's global peace poster contest by: 55c, Lee Min Gi, Republic of Korea. €1, Natalie Chan, US.

2004, Sept. 21 Litho. *Perf. 14*

371	A357	55c **multicolored** *(225,000)+*	1.60	1.60
		First day cover		2.25
		Inscription block of 4	6.50	
		Pane of 20	32.00	
372	A357	€1 **multicolored** *(225,000)+*	2.75	2.75
		First day cover		4.00
		First day cover, #371-372		5.25
		Inscription block of 4	11.00	
		Pane of 20	55.00	

Food for Life Type

Printed by Government Printing Office, Austria. Designed by Andrew Davidson, United Kingdom.

Designs: 55c, Corn, people with food bowls, teacher and students. €1.25, Rice, helicopter dropping food, elephant caravan.

2005, Oct. 20 Litho. *Perf. 13¾*

373	A370	55c **multicolored** *(210,000)+*	1.60	1.60
		First day cover		2.10
		Inscription block of 4	6.50	—
		Pane of 20	32.00	—
374	A370	€1.25 **multicolored** *(210,000)+*	3.50	3.50
		First day cover		4.75
		First day cover, #373-374		6.00
		Inscription block of 4	14.00	—
		Pane of 20	70.00	—

Indigenous Art Type of 2003

Printed by Johann Enschedé and Sons, the Netherlands. Designed by Robert Stein, US.

No. 375 — Musical instruments: a, Drum, Guinea. b, Whistle, Congo. c, Horn, Botswana. d, Drums, Burundi. e, Harp, Gabon. f, Bell, Nigeria.

2006, Feb. 3 Litho. *Perf. 13¼*

375	V46	Sheet of 6 *(117,000)+*	12.00	12.00
		First day cover		8.00
a.-f.		55c Any single	2.00	2.00
		First day cover, #375a-375f, each		4.50

Endangered Species Type of 1993

Printed by Johann Enschedé and Sons, the Netherlands. Designed by John D. Dawson, US.

Designs: No. 376, Dendrobates pumilio. No. 377, Furcifer lateralis. No. 378, Corallus hortulanus. No. 379, Dendrobates leucomelas.

2006, Mar. 16 Litho. *Perf. 12¾x12½*

376	A271	55c **multicolored** *(260,000)+*	1.50	1.50
377	A271	55c **multicolored** *(260,000)+*	1.50	1.50
378	A271	55c **multicolored** *(260,000)+*	1.50	1.50
379	A271	55c **multicolored** *(260,000)+*	1.50	1.50
a.		Block of 4, #376-379	6.00	6.00
		First day cover, #379a		6.75
		First day cover, #376-379, each		2.40
		Inscription block of 4, #379a	6.00	—
		Pane of 10	24.00	

Intl. Day of Families Type

Printed by Johann Enschedé and Sons, the Netherlands. Designed by Shelly Bartek, US.

Designs: 55c, Family at water pump. €1.25, Family preparing food.

2006, May 27 Litho. *Perf. 14x13½*

380	A373	55c **multicolored** *(190,000)+*	1.25	1.25
		First day cover		2.00
		Inscription block of 4	5.00	—
		Pane of 20	25.00	—
381	A373	€1.25 **multicolored** *(190,000)+*	2.50	2.50
		First day cover		4.50
		First day cover, #380-381		5.75
		Inscription block of 4	10.00	—
		Pane of 20	50.00	—

World Heritage Sites, France Type

Printed by Cartor Security Printing, France. Panes of 20. Designed by Robert Stein, US.

Eiffel Tower and: Nos. 382, 384c, Carcasonne. Nos. 383, 384f, Chateau de Chambord. No. 384a, Banks of the Seine. No. 384b, Provins. No. 384d, Roman Aqueduct. No. 384e, Mont Saint-Michel.

Litho. & Embossed with Foil Application

2006, June 17 *Perf. 13½x13¼*

382	A374	55c **multicolored** *(220,000)+*	1.50	1.50
		First day cover		2.25
		Inscription block of 4	6.00	—
383	A374	75c **multicolored** *(220,000)+*	2.00	2.00
		First day cover		3.00
		First day cover, #368-369		4.50
		Inscription block of 4	8.00	—

Souvenir Booklet

384		Booklet, #384g-384l *(41,000)+*	18.00	
a.-c.	A374	25c any single	.65	.65
d.-f.	A374	30c any single	.80	.80
g.		Booklet pane of 4 #384a	2.60	2.60
h.		Booklet pane of 4 #384b	2.60	2.60
i.		Booklet pane of 4 #384c	2.60	2.60
j.		Booklet pane of 4 #384d	3.25	3.25
k.		Booklet pane of 4 #384e	3.25	3.25
l.		Booklet pane of 4 #384f	3.25	3.25

No. 384 sold for €6.80.

My Dream for Peace Type of 2004

Printed by Cartor Security Printing, France. Panes of 20.

Winning designs of Lions Club International children's global peace poster contest by: 55c, Klara Thein, Germany. €1, Laurensia Levina, Indonesia.

2006, Sept. 21 Litho. *Perf. 13½x13*

385	A357	55c **multicolored** *(200,000)+*	1.60	1.60
		First day cover		2.25
		Inscription block of 4	6.40	—
		Pane of 20	32.00	—
386	A357	€1 **multicolored** *(200,000)+*	3.00	3.00
		First day cover		4.00
		First day cover, #385-386		5.50
		Inscription block of 4	12.00	—
		Pane of 20	60.00	—

Flags and Coins Type

Printed by Cartor Security Printing, France. Designed by Rorie Katz, US.

No. 387 — Flag of: a, Gambia, 1 dalasi coin. b, Pakistan, 1 rupee coin. c, Afghanistan, 2 afghani coin. d, Austria, 1 euro coin. e, Germany, 50 cent coin. f, Haiti, 50 centimes coin. g, Denmark, 20 krone coin. h, Netherlands, 1 euro coin.

2006, Oct. 5 Litho. *Perf. 13¼x13*

387		Sheet of 8	14.00	14.00
a.-h.	A375	55c Any single	1.75	1.75
		First day cover		14.50
		First day cover, #387a-387h, each		5.00

A column of rouletting in the middle of the sheet separates it into two parts.

Endangered Species Type of 1993

Printed by Johann Enschedé and Sons, the Netherlands. Designed by John Rowe, US.

Designs: No. 388, Chlorocebus aethiops. No. 389, Nasalis larvatus. No. 390, Papio hamadryas. No. 391, Erythrocebus patas.

2007, Mar. 15 Litho. *Perf. 12¾x12½*

388	A271	55c **multicolored** *(256,000)+*	1.60	1.60
389	A271	55c **multicolored** *(256,000)+*	1.60	1.60
390	A271	55c **multicolored** *(256,000)+*	1.60	1.60
391	A271	55c **multicolored** *(256,000)+*	1.60	1.60
a.		Block of 4, #388-391	6.40	6.40
		First day cover, #391a		7.50
		First day cover, #388-391, each		2.60
		Inscription block of 4, #391a	6.40	—
		Pane of 16	26.00	—

Flags and Coins Type of 2006

Printed by Cartor Security Printing, France. Designed by Rorie Katz, US.

No. 392 — Flag of: a, Trinidad and Tobago, 50 cent coin. b, Sierra Leone, 10 cent coin. c, Hungary, 100 forint coin. d, San Marino, 2 euro coin. e, Croatia, 1 kuna coin. f, Spain, 1 euro coin. g, Kazakhstan, 100 tenge coin. h, Ireland, 5 cent coin.

2007, May 3 Litho. *Perf. 13¼x13*

392		Sheet of 8 *(155,000)+*	13.00	13.00
a.-h.	A375	55c Any single	1.60	1.60
		First day cover		15.00
		First day cover, #392a-392h, each		5.00

A column of rouletting in the middle of the sheet separates it into two parts.

Five 55c stamps depicting views of the Vienna International Center and the United Nations flag were released May 3, 2007. The editors have reason to believe that these stamps were not sold at the UN Post Office in Vienna. Value, strip of 5 with labels $45, sheet of 10 $90.

Peaceful Visions Type of 2007

Printed by Lowe-Martin Company, Canada. Designed by Slavka Kolesar. Panes of 20.
Designs: 55c, "The Sowers." €1.25, "We All Thrive Under the Same Sky."

2007, June 1 **Litho.** ***Perf. 13x12½***

398 A378 55c **multicolored** *(200,000)+* 1.60 1.60
First day cover 2.25
Inscription block of 4 6.40 —
Pane of 20 32.00 —
399 A378 €1.25 **multicolored** *(200,000)+* 3.75 3.75
First day cover 5.00
First day cover, #398-399 6.25
Inscription block of 4 15.00 —
Pane of 20 75.00 —

World Heritage Sites, South America Type

Printed by Lowe-Martin Group, Canada. Panes of 20. Designed by Rorie Katz, US.
Designs: Nos. 400, 402e, Iguaçu National Park, Brazil. Nos. 401, 402b, Cueva de las Manos, Argentina. No. 402a, Rapa Nui, Chile. No. 402c, Machu Picchu, Peru. No. 402d, Tiwanaku, Bolivia. No. 474f, Galapagos Islands, Ecuador.

2007, Aug. 9 **Litho.** ***Perf. 13¼x13***

400 A381 55c **multicolored** *(210,000)+* 2.00 2.00
First day cover 2.50
Inscription block of 4 8.00 —
401 A381 75c **multicolored** *(210,000)+* 2.75 2.75
First day cover 3.50
First day cover, #400-401 5.00
Inscription block of 4 11.00 —

Souvenir Booklet

402 Booklet, #402g-402l *(37,000)+* 20.00
a.-c. A381 25c Any single .75 .75
d.-f. A381 30c Any single .90 .90
g. Booklet pane of 4 #402a 3.00 3.00
h. Booklet pane of 4 #402b 3.00 3.00
i. Booklet pane of 4 #402c 3.00 3.00
j. Booklet pane of 4 #402d 3.60 3.60
k. Booklet pane of 4 #402e 3.60 3.60
l. Booklet pane of 4 #402f 3.60 3.60

Humanitarian Mail Type

Printed by Lowe-Martin Group, Canada. Panes of 10.

2007, Sept. 6 **Litho.** ***Perf. 12½x13¼***

403 A382 75c **multicolored** *(310,000)+* 2.25 2.25
First day cover 3.25
Inscription block of 4 9.00 —
Pane of 10 22.50 —

Five 65c stamps depicting the International Space Station, astronauts and planets were released Oct. 1, 2007. The editors have reason to believe that these stamps were not sold at the UN Post Office in Vienna. Value, strip of 5 with labels $35, sheet of 10 $65.

Space for Humanity Type

Printed by Johann Enschedé and Sons, the Netherlands. Panes of 6. Designed by Donato Giancola, US.
Designs: 65c, Space stations. €1.15, Space Station. €2.10, Space probe, Jupiter.

2007, Oct. 25 **Litho.** ***Perf. 13½x14***

409 A383 65c **multicolored** *(306,000)+* 2.00 2.00
First day cover 2.60
Inscription block of 4 8.00 —
Pane of 6 12.00 —
410 A383 €1.15 **multicolored** *(306,000)+* 3.50 3.50
First day cover 4.75
First day cover, #409-410 6.25
Inscription block of 4 14.00 —
Pane of 6 21.00 —

Souvenir Sheet

411 A383 €2.10 **multicolored** *(130,000)+* 8.00 8.00
First day cover 7.25

Intl. Holocaust Remembrance Day Type

Printed by Lowe-Martin Company, Canada. Panes of 9. Designed by Matías Delfino, Argentina.

2008, Jan. 27 **Litho.** ***Perf. 13***

412 A384 65c **multicolored** *(540,000)+* 3.00 3.00
First day cover 3.25
Pane of 9 27.00 —

Johann Strauss Memorial, Vienna — V61

Pallas Athene Fountain, Vienna — V62

Pegasus Fountain, Salzburg — V63

Statue, Belvedere Palace Gardens, Vienna — V64

Printed by Johann Enschedé and Sons, the Netherlands. Panes of 20. Designed by Rorie Katz, US.

2008, Jan. 28 **Litho.** ***Perf. 13½x14***

413 V61 10c **black** *(320,000)+* .35 .35
First day cover .50
Inscription block of 4 1.40 —
Pane of 20 7.00 —

Perf. 14x13½

414 V62 15c **black** *(320,000)+* .50 .50
First day cover .75
Inscription block of 4 2.00 —
Pane of 20 10.00 —
415 V63 65c **black** *(320,000)+* 2.25 2.25
First day cover 3.25
Inscription block of 4 9.00 —
Pane of 20 45.00 —
416 V64 €1.40 **black** *(320,000)+* 4.75 4.75
First day cover 7.00
Inscription block of 4 19.00 —
Pane of 20 95.00 —
Nos. 413-416 (4) 7.85 7.85

Endangered Species Type of 1993

Printed by Johann Enschedé and Sons, the Netherlands. Designed by Suzanne Duranceau, Canada.

Designs: No. 4170, Mirounga angustirostris. No. 418, Millepora alcicornis. No. 419, Hippocampus histrix. No. 420, Physeter catodon.

2008, Mar. 6 Litho. *Perf. 12¾x12½*

417 A271 65c **multicolored** *(212,000)+*	2.50	2.50
418 A271 65c **multicolored** *(212,000)+*	2.50	2.50
419 A271 65c **multicolored** *(212,000)+*	2.50	2.50
420 A271 65c **multicolored** *(212,000)+*	2.50	2.50
a. Block of 4, #417-420	10.00	10.00
First day cover, #420a		9.50
First day cover, #417-420, each		3.25
Inscription block of 4, #420a	10.50	—
Pane of 16	40.00	—

Flags and Coins Type of 2006

Printed by Cartor Security Printing, France. Designed by Rorie Katz, US.

No. 421 — Flag of: a, Poland, 5 zloty coin. b, Latvia, 1 lat coin. c, Portugal, 1 euro coin. d, Armenia, 500 dram coin. e, Sweden, 1 krona coin. f, Cyprus, 1 euro coin. g, Slovakia, 1 koruna coin. h, Qatar, 50 dirham coin.

2008, May 8 Litho. *Perf. 13¼x13*

421 Sheet of 8 *(120,000)+*	18.00	18.00
a.-h. A375 65c Any single	2.25	2.25
First day cover		20.00

A column of rouletting in the middle of the sheet separates it into two parts.

Five 65c stamps depicting the Vienna International Center and its artwork were released May 12, 2008. The editors have reason to believe that these stamps were not sold at the UN Post Office in Vienna. Value, strip of 5 with labels $30, sheet of 10 $60.

Graduate — V70

Stylized Person, Heart, Brain, Hands — V71

Printed by Johann Enschedé and Sons, the Netherlands. Panes of 20. Designed by Rorie Katz, US.

2008, June 6 Litho. & Embossed *Perf. 14x13¼*

427 V70 55c **green & violet** *(186,000)+*	2.00	2.00
First day cover		2.50
Inscription block of 4	8.00	—
Sheet of 20	40.00	—
428 V71 €1.40 **violet & green** *(186,000)+*	5.00	5.00
First day cover		6.50
First day cover, #427-428		7.75
Inscription block of 4	20.00	—
Sheet of 20	100.00	—

Convention on the Rights of Persons with Disabilities.

Sport for Peace Type of 2008

Printed by Johann Enschedé and Sons, the Netherlands. Panes of 9 (Nos. 429-430). Designed by Romero Britto, Brazil.

Designs: 65c, Man on rings. €1.30, €2.10, Swimmer.

2008, Aug. 8 Litho. *Perf. 14½*

429 A393 65c **multicolored** *(435,600)+*	2.25	2.25
First day cover		3.00
Inscription block of 4	9.00	—
Pane of 9	21.00	—
430 A393 €1.30 **multicolored** *(435,600)+*	4.50	4.50
First day cover		6.00
First day cover, #429-430		7.75
Inscription block of 4	18.00	—
Pane of 9	41.00	—

Souvenir Sheet

Perf. 12¾x13¼

431 A393 €2.10 **multicolored** *(200,000)+*	9.00	9.00
First day cover		8.00
a. Overprinted in sheet margin	10.00	10.00
First day cover		8.00

2008 Summer Olympics, Beijing. No. 431a is overprinted in black "Peking 2008" and medals with UN emblem.

"We Can End Poverty" Type of 2008

Printed by Sweden Post, Sweden. Panes of 20.

Winning designs in children's art contest: 65c, By Mariam Marukian, Armenia. 75c, By Rufaro Duri, Zimbabwe, vert.

2008, Sept. 18 Litho. *Perf. 12¾x12½*

432 A395 65c **multicolored** *(160,000)+*	2.25	2.25
First day cover		3.25
Inscription block of 4	9.00	—
Sheet of 20	45.00	—

Perf. 12½x12¾

433 A395 75c **multicolored** *(160,000)+*	2.60	2.60
First day cover		3.75
First day cover, #432-433		5.75
Inscription block of 4	10.50	—
Sheet of 20	52.00	—

Five €1.40 stamps depicting views of the Vienna International Center and its artwork were released Sept. 18, 2008. The editors have reason to believe that these stamps were not sold at the UN Post Office in Vienna. Value, strip of 5 with labels $40, sheet of 10 $80.

Climate Change Types of New York and Geneva and

V72

Climate Change
V73

Printed by Lowe-Martin Group, Canada. Panes of 4. Designed by Rorie Katz, US.

No. 434 — Smokestacks with quarter of Earth in: a, LR. b, LL. c, UR. d, UL.

No. 435 — Cut trees with quarter of Earth in: a, LR. b, LL. c, UR. d, UL.

No. 436: a, Like New York #969a. b, Like New York #969b. c, Like New York #969c. d, Like New York #969d. e, Like Geneva #493a. f, Like Geneva #493b. g, Like Geneva #493c. h, Like Geneva #493d. i, Like Vienna #434a. j, Like Vienna #434b. k, Like Vienna #434c. l, Like Vienna #434d. m, Like New York #968a. n, Like New York #968b, o, Like New York #968c, p, Like New York #968d. q, Like Geneva #492a. r, Like Geneva#492b. s, Like Geneva #492c. t, Like Geneva #492d. u, Like Vienna #435a. v, Like Vienna #435b. w, Like Vienna #435c. x, Like Vienna #435d.

All stamps have green panels inscribed "Klimawandel."

2008, Oct. 23 Litho. *Perf. 13¼x13*

434	Sheet of 4 *(120,000)*+	9.00	9.00
a.-d.	V72 65c Any single	2.25	2.25
	First day cover		9.75
435	Sheet of 4 *(120,000)*+	16.00	16.00
a.-d.	V73 €1.15 Any single	4.00	4.00
	First day cover		17.00
	First day cover, #434-435		27.00

Souvenir Booklet

436	Booklet, #436y-436ad *(31,000)*+	27.00	
a.-d.	A397 30c Any single	1.00	1.00
e.-h.	G77 30c Any single	1.00	1.00
i.-l.	V72 30c Any single	1.00	1.00
m.-p.	A396 35c Any single	1.10	1.10
q.-t.	G76 35c Any single	1.10	1.10
u.-x.	V73 35c Any single	1.10	1.10
y.	Booklet pane of 4, #436a-436d	4.25	4.25
z.	Booklet pane of 4, #436e-436h	4.25	4.25
aa.	Booklet pane of 4, #436i-436l	4.25	4.25
ab.	Booklet pane of 4, #436m-436p	4.75	4.75
ac.	Booklet pane of 4, #436q-436t	4.75	4.75
ad.	Booklet pane of 4, #436u-436x	4.75	4.75

U Thant Type of 2009

Printed by Johann Enschedé and Sons, the Netherlands. Panes of 20.

Litho. With Foil Application

2009, Feb. 6 *Perf. 14x13½*

437	A399 €1.15 **green & multicolored** *(180,000)*+	4.50	4.50
	First day cover		4.25
	Inscription block of 4	18.00	—
	Sheet of 20	90.00	—

Endangered Species Type of 1993

Printed by Johann Enschedé and Sons, the Netherlands. Designed by Roger Kent, United Kingdom.

Designs: No. 438, Trogonoptera brookiana. No. 439, Pandinus imperator. No. 440, Carabus intricatus. No. 441, Brachypelma smithi.

2009, Apr. 16 Litho. *Perf. 12¾x12½*

438	A271 65c **multicolored** *(184,000)*+	2.00	2.00
439	A271 65c **multicolored** *(184,000)*+	2.00	2.00
440	A271 65c **multicolored** *(184,000)*+	2.00	2.00
441	A271 65c **multicolored** *(184,000)*+	2.00	2.00
a.	Block of 4, #438-441	8.00	8.00
	First day cover, #441a		8.50
	First day cover, #438-441, each		2.75
	Inscription block of 4, #441a	8.00	—
	Pane of 16	32.00	—

World Heritage Sites, Germany Type of 2009

Printed by Johann Enschedé and Sons, the Netherlands. Panes of 20. Designed by Grit Fiedler, Germany.

Designs: Nos. 442, 444c, Palaces and Parks of Potsdam and Berlin. Nos. 443, 444e, Luther Memorials in Eisleben and Wittenberg. No. 444a, Town Hall and Roland on the Marketplace, Bremen. No. 444b, Wartburg Castle. No. 444d, Aachen Cathedral. No. 444f, Monastic Island of Reichenau.

2009, May 7 Litho. *Perf. 14x13½*

442	A400 65c **multicolored** *(190,000)*+	1.90	1.90
	First day cover		2.50
	Inscription block of 4	7.75	—
443	A400 €1.40 **multicolored** *(320,000)*+	4.00	4.00
	First day cover		5.25
	First day cover, #500-501		6.75
	Inscription block of 4	16.00	—

Souvenir Booklet

444	Booklet, #444g-444l *(32,000)*+	20.00	
a.-c.	A400 30c any single	.75	.75
d.-f.	A400 35c any single	.90	.90
g.	Booklet pane of 4 #444a	3.00	3.00
h.	Booklet pane of 4 #444b	3.00	3.00
i.	Booklet pane of 4 #444c	3.00	3.00
j.	Booklet pane of 4 #444d	3.60	3.60
k.	Booklet pane of 4 #444e	3.60	3.60
l.	Booklet pane of 4 #444f	3.60	3.60

Memorial Plaza, Vienna International Center — V74

The First Swallows, Sculpture by Juozas Mikenas — V75

Conference Building, Vienna International Center — V76

Butterfly Tree, by Rudolf Hausner — V77

Flags in Memorial Plaza — V78

2009, May 7	**Litho.**	***Perf. 13¼***	
445 V74 65c **multicolored** + label		*5.00*	*5.00*
a. Perf. 11¼x11		*10.00*	*10.00*
446 V75 65c **multicolored** + label		*5.00*	*5.00*
a. Perf. 11¼x11		*10.00*	*10.00*
447 V76 65c **multicolored** + label		*5.00*	*5.00*
a. Perf. 11¼x11		*10.00*	*10.00*
448 V77 65c **multicolored** + label		*5.00*	*5.00*
a. Perf. 11¼x11		*10.00*	*10.00*
449 V78 65c **multicolored** + label		*5.00*	*5.00*
a. Perf. 11¼x11		*10.00*	*10.00*
b. Vert. strip of 5, #445-449, + 5 labels		*25.00*	*25.00*
Sheet, 2 #449b		*50.00*	—
c. Vert. strip of 5, #445a-449a, + 5 labels		*50.00*	*50.00*
Sheet, 2 #449c		*100.00*	—

The full sheets sold for €11.69 or $14.95. Labels could not be personalized. The sheet of No. 449c has "ver. 2" in the lower right selvage.

Economic and Social Council (ECOSOC) Type of 2009

Printed by Sweden Post, Sweden. Panes of 20. Designed by Rorie Katz, US.

Designs: 55c, Combat HIV/AIDS, malaria and other diseases. 65c, Reduce child mortality.

2009, Aug. 6	**Litho.**	***Perf. 12¾x12½***	
450 A411 55c **multicolored** *(160,000)*+		2.25	2.25
First day cover			2.60
Inscription block of 4		9.00	—
Sheet of 20		45.00	—
451 A411 65c **multicolored** *(160,000)*+		3.50	3.50
First day cover			3.00
First day cover, #450-451			4.75
Inscription block of 4		14.00	—
Sheet of 20		70.00	—

V79

V80

V81

V82

Vienna International Center, 30th Anniv. — V83

2009, Aug. 24	**Litho.**	***Perf. 13¼***	
452 V79 €1.40 **multicolored** + label		*6.00*	*6.00*
a. Perf. 11¼x11		*20.00*	*20.00*
453 V80 €1.40 **multicolored** + label		*6.00*	*6.00*
a. Perf. 11¼x11		*20.00*	*20.00*
454 V81 €1.40 **multicolored** + label		*6.00*	*6.00*
a. Perf. 11¼x11		*20.00*	*20.00*
455 V82 €1.40 **multicolored** + label		*6.00*	*6.00*
a. Perf. 11¼x11		*20.00*	*20.00*
456 V83 €1.40 **multicolored** + label		*6.00*	*6.00*
a. Perf. 11¼x11		*20.00*	*20.00*
b. Vert. strip of 5, #452-456, + 5 labels		*30.00*	*30.00*
Sheet, 2 #456b		*60.00*	—
c. Vert. strip of 5, #452a-456a, + 5 labels		*100.00*	*100.00*
Sheet, 2 #456c		*200.00*	—

The full sheets sold for €19.90 or $27.75. Labels could not be personalized. The sheet of No. 456c has "ver. 2" in the lower right selvage.

Millennium Development Goals Type of 2009
Miniature Sheet

Printed by Lowe Martin Group, Canada.
Designed by Rorie Katz, US.

No. 457: a, Bowl of hot food. b, Pencil. c, Female symbol. d, Teddy bear. e, Pregnant woman, heart. f, Medicine bottle. g, Stylized tree. h, Conjoined people.

2009, Sept. 25	**Litho.**	***Perf. 13¼***	
457 A413 Sheet of 8 *(75,000)*+		16.00	16.00
First day cover			18.00
a.-h. 65c Any single		2.00	2.00

Miniature Sheet

Indigenous People — V84

Printed by Lowe-Martin Group, Canada. Designed by Stephen Bennett, US.

No. 458 — Portraits of person from: a, Tanzania. b, Australia. c, Namibia (small child). d, Indonesia. e, Namibia (young girl). f, Untied Arab Emirates.

2009, Oct. 8 **Litho.** ***Perf. 12½***

458	V84 Sheet of 6 *(80,000)*+	12.00	12.00
a.-f.	65c Any single	2.00	2.00
	First day cover		14.00

Flags and Coins Type of 2006

Printed by Cartor Security Printing, France. Designed by Rorie Katz, US.

No. 459 — Flag of: a, Romania, 1 ban coin. b, Slovenia, 5 cent coin. c, Azerbaijan, 10 giapik coin. d, Bangladesh, 5 taka coin. e, Belarus, 1 ruble coin. f, Malta, 1 euro coin. g, Swaziland, 1 lilangeni coin. h, Jordan, 10 piaster coin.

2010, Feb. 5 **Litho.** ***Perf. 13¼x13***

459	Sheet of 8 *(88,000)*+	16.00	16.00
a.-h.	A375 65c Any single	2.00	2.00
	First day cover		19.50

A column of rouletting in the middle of the sheet separates it into two parts.

People Pulling Rope — V85

Person With Hands Over Eyes — V86

Woman Touching Her Shoulder — V87

Man With Wheelbarrow — V88

Blue Heart — V89

Designed by Rorie Katz, US.

2010, Feb. 5 **Litho.** ***Perf. 11¼x11***

460	V85 65c **multicolored** + label	*4.50*	*4.50*
461	V86 65c **multicolored** + label	*4.50*	*4.50*
462	V87 65c **multicolored** + label	*4.50*	*4.50*
463	V88 65c **multicolored** + label	*4.50*	*4.50*
464	V89 65c **multicolored** + label	*4.50*	*4.50*
a.	Vert. strip of 5, #460-464, + 5 labels	*22.50*	*22.50*
	Sheet, 2 #464a	*45.00*	—

The full sheet sold for $14.95 or €19.90. The labels could not be personalized.

Endangered Species Type of 1993

Printed by Johann Enschedé and Sons, the Netherlands. Designed by Rosie Sanders, United Kingdom.

Designs: No. 465, Mammillaria zeilmanniana. No. 466, Hoodia gordonii. No. 467, Welwitschia mirabilis. No. 468, Euphorbia milii.

2010, Apr. 15 **Litho.** ***Perf. 12¾x12½***

465	A271 65c **multicolored** *(148,000)*+	2.25	2.25
466	A271 65c **multicolored** *(148,000)*+	2.25	2.25
467	A271 65c **multicolored** *(148,000)*+	2.25	2.25

468	A271 65c **multicolored** *(148,000)+*	2.25	2.25
a.	Block of 4, #465-468	9.00	9.00
	First day cover, #468a		9.75
	First day cover, #465-468, each		3.25
	Inscription block of 4, #468a	9.00	—
	Pane of 16	36.00	—

Intl. Year of Biodiversity — V90

Printed by Lowe-Martin Group, Canada. Panes of 20. Designed by Deborah Halperin, US.

Drawings from Art Forms from Nature, by Ernst Heinrich: 5c, Colonial algae. 20c, Boxfish.

2010, Apr. 15 **Litho.** ***Perf. 13***

469	V90 5c **multicolored** *(400,000)+*	.25	.25
	First day cover		1.90
	Inscription block of 4	.80	—
	Sheet of 20	4.00	—
470	V90 20c **multicolored** *(400,000)+*	.70	.70
	First day cover		2.25
	First day cover, #469-470		1.90
	Inscription block of 4	2.80	—
	Sheet of 20	14.00	—

One Planet, One Ocean Types of New York and Geneva and

V91

One Planet, One Ocean — V92

Printed by Johann Enschedé and Sons, the Netherlands. Designed by Robert Wyland, US.

No. 471: a, Dolphin at left, fish at right. b, Fish at top, shark in center. c, Dolphin at left, fish at right and bottom. d, Fish at left, top and right.

No. 472: a, Dolphins. b, Shark and fish at center, ray at bottom. c, Fish at left, turtle at bottom. d, Fish and coral.

No. 473: a, Like New York #1003a. b, Like New York #1003b, c, Like New York #1003c, d, Like New York #1003d. e, Like #471a. f, Like #471b. g, Like #471c, h, Like #471d. i, Like Geneva # 519a. j, Like Geneva #519b, k, Like Geneva # 519c. l, Like Geneva #519d. m, Like New York #1004a. n, Like New York #1004b. o, Like New York #1004c, p, Like New York #1004d. q, Like #472a. r, Like #472b. s, Like #472c. t, Like #472d. u, Like Geneva #520a. v, Like Geneva #520b. w, Like Geneva #520c. x, Like Geneva #520d.

2010, May 6 **Litho.** ***Perf. 14x13¼***

471	V91 Sheet of 4 *(75,000)+*	7.75	7.75
a.-d.	55c Any single	1.90	1.90
472	V92 Sheet of 4 *(75,000)+*	9.00	9.00
a.-d.	65c Any single	2.25	2.25
	First day cover, #471-472		20.00

Souvenir Booklet

Perf. 13¼x13

473	Booklet, #473y-473z, 473aa-473ad *(32,000)+*	27.00	
a.-d.	A416 30c any single	1.00	1.00
e.-h.	V91 30c any single	1.00	1.00
i.-l.	G85 30c any single	1.00	1.00
m.-p.	A417 35c any single	1.25	1.25
q.-t.	V92 35c any single	1.25	1.25
u.-x.	G86 35c any single	1.25	1.25
y.	Booklet pane of 4 #473a-473d	4.00	4.00
z.	Booklet pane of 4 #473e-473h	4.00	4.00
aa.	Booklet pane of 4 #473i-473l	4.00	4.00
ab.	Booklet pane of 4 #473m-473p	5.00	5.00
ac.	Booklet pane of 4 #473q-473t	5.00	5.00
ad.	Booklet pane of 4 #473u-473x	5.00	5.00

Intl. Oceanographic Commission, 50th anniv.

United Nations, 65th Anniv. Type of 2010

Printed by Lowe-Martin Group, Canada. Designed by Rorie Katz, United States.

Litho. With Foil Application

2010, June 28 ***Perf. 13¼***

474	A422 75c **green & gold** *(150,000)+*	3.00	3.00
	First day cover		3.25
	Inscription block of 4	12.50	—
	Pane of 15	45.00	—
a.	Souvenir sheet of 2 *(50,500)+*	6.00	6.00
	First day cover, #474a		6.50

V93

V94

V95

V96

United Nations Air Transport — V97

Printed by UAB Garsu Pasaulis, Lithuania. Designed by Simon Williams, United Kingdom.

2010, Sept. 2	**Litho.**	***Perf. 13¼x13***	
475 V93 65c **multicolored** *(132,000)+*		1.90	1.90
476 V94 65c **multicolored** *(132,000)+*		1.90	1.90
477 V95 65c **multicolored** *(132,000)+*		1.90	1.90
478 V96 65c **multicolored** *(132,000)+*		1.90	1.90
479 V97 65c **multicolored** *(132,000)+*		1.90	1.90
a. Horiz. strip of 5, #475-479		9.50	9.50
First day cover, #479a			10.50
First day cover, #475-479, each			3.25
Inscription block of 10		19.00	—
Pane of 20		38.00	—

Miniature Sheet

Indigenous People — V98

Printed by Lowe-Martin Group, Canada. Designed by Stephen Bennett, US.

No. 480 — Portraits of person from: a, French Polynesia (denomination in white). b, Tanzania (child with cloth head covering). c, Malaysia. d, French Polynesia (denomination in white and green). e, Namibia. f, Tanzania (man with band around forehead).

2010, Oct. 21	**Litho.**	***Perf. 13***	
480 V98 Pane of 6 *(65,000)+*		11.50	11.50
a.-f. 65c Any single		1.90	1.90
First day cover			13.50

United Nations Headquarters, Vienna — V99

Printed by Cartor Security Printing, France. Panes of 20. Designed by Scott Solberg, US.

United Nations Headquarters, Geneva: €1.25, Aerial view. €2.85, Ground-level view.

2011, Feb. 4	**Litho.**	***Perf. 13***	
481 V99 €1.25 **multicolored** *(400,000)+*		3.75	3.75
First day cover			4.25
Inscription block of 4		15.00	—
Pane of 20		75.00	—
482 V99 €2.85 **multicolored** *(400,000)+*		8.25	8.25
First day cover			9.50
First day cover, #481-482			13.00
Inscription block of 4		33.00	—
Pane of 20		165.00	—

Flags and Coins Type of 2006

Printed by Cartor Security Printing, France. Designed by Rorie Katz, US.

No. 483 — Flag of: a, Lithuania, 2 lita coin. b, Greece, 1 euro coin. c, Kyrgyzstan, 50 tyiyn coin. d, Oman, 100 baisa coin. e, Estonia, 2 euro coin. f, Czech Republic, 5 koruna coin. g, Uzbekistan, 100 som coin. h, Monaco, 1 euro coin.

2011, Mar. 3	**Litho.**	***Perf. 13¼x13***	
483 Sheet of 8 *(70,000)+*		15.00	15.00
a.-h. A375 65c Any single		1.75	1.75
First day cover			17.00

A column of rouletting in the middle of the sheet separates it into two parts.

Human Space Flight, 50th Anniv. — V100

Printed by Lowe-Martin Group, Canada. Designed by Peter Bollinger, US.
No. 484: Various parts of outer space scene.
No. 485, vert.: a, Space Shuttle. b, Space Station.

2011, Apr. 12 **Litho.** ***Perf. 13x13¼***

484	V100	Sheet of 16 *(65,000)*+	16.50	16.50
		First day cover		18.50
a.-p.		35c any single	1.00	1.00

Souvenir Sheet

485	V100	Sheet of 2	12.00	12.00
		First day cover		4.50
a.		55c **multicolored**	5.50	5.50
b.		65c **multicolored**	6.50	6.50
c.		Souvenir sheet of 6, New York #1025a-1025b, Geneva #534a-b, Vienna #485a-485b *(68,000)*+	42.50	42.50
		First day cover, #485c		13.00

No. 485 contains two 40x48mm stamps that were printed as part of a larger sheet of six stamps, No. 485c, which was broken up into its component two-stamp souvenir sheets, and also sold as one unit. Value $90, complete unit.

Vienna International Center and Flagpoles — V101

Fish-eye View of Vienna International Center and Flagpole — V102

Vienna International Center and Train — V103

Aerial View of Vienna International Center — V104

Vienna International Center and Water — V105

Detail From La Pioggia, Stadt Unter de Regen, by Friedensreich Hundertwasser — V106

Hand in Hand, by Hans Dietrich — V107

The Scholars Pavilion — V108

Detail From Grupo Expectante, by Alfredo Sosabravo — V109

Yes to Life, No to Drugs, by Sami Burhan — V110

2011, May 1 **Litho.** ***Perf. 14¾***

486	V101 62c **multicolored** + label	*2.50*	*2.50*
487	V102 62c **multicolored** + label	*2.50*	*2.50*
488	V103 62c **multicolored** + label	*2.50*	*2.50*
489	V104 62c **multicolored** + label	*2.50*	*2.50*
490	V105 62c **multicolored** + label	*2.50*	*2.50*
a.	Vert. strip of 5, #486-490, + 5 labels	*15.00*	*15.00*
	Sheet, 4 #490a	*60.00*	—
491	V106 70c **multicolored** + label	*3.00*	*3.00*
492	V107 70c **multicolored** + label	*3.00*	*3.00*
493	V108 70c **multicolored** + label	*3.00*	*3.00*
494	V109 70c **multicolored** + label	*3.00*	*3.00*
495	V110 70c **multicolored** + label	*3.00*	*3.00*
a.	Vert. strip of 5, #491-495, + 5 labels	*17.50*	*17.50*
	Sheet, 2 #495a	*35.00*	—
	Nos. 486-495 (10)	*25.50*	*25.50*

The full sheet of Nos. 486-490 sold for $21.45 or €12.40. The full sheet of Nos. 491-495 sold for $14.26 or €9.90. The labels could be personalized.

UNESCO World Heritage Sites in Nordic Countries Type of 2011

Printed by Johann Enschedé and Sons, the Netherlands. Panes of 20. Designed by Rorie Katz, US.

Designs: 62c, Urnes Stave Church, Norway. 70c, Struve Geodetic Arc, Norway, Finland and Sweden.

2011, May 5 **Litho.** ***Perf. 14x13½***

496	A433 62c **multicolored** *(160,000)+*	1.90	1.90
	First day cover		2.75
	Inscription block of 4	7.60	—
	Pane of 20	30.00	—
497	A433 70c **multicolored** *(160,000)+*	2.10	2.10
	First day cover		3.00
	First day cover, #496-497		4.75
	Inscription block of 4	8.40	—
	Pane of 20	42.00	—

AIDS Ribbon Type of 2011

Printed by Lowe-Martin Group, Canada. Panes of 4. Designed by Rorie Katz, US.

2011, June 3 **Litho.** ***Die Cut***

Self-Adhesive

498	A434 70c **red & green** *(260,000)+*	2.40	2.40
	Pane of 4	9.75	
	First day cover, pane of 4		10.50

ECOSOC Type of 2011

Printed by Cartor Security Printing, France. Panes of 20. Designed by Rorie Katz, US.

Education: 62c, Children with musical instruments. 70c, Woman teaching reading to old man.

2011, July 1 **Litho.** ***Perf. 14¼***

499	A435 62c **multicolored** *(150,000)+*	3.00	3.00
	First day cover		3.00
	Inscription block of 4	12.00	—
	Pane of 20	60.00	—
500	A435 70c **multicolored** *(150,000)+*	4.00	4.00
	First day cover		3.50
	First day cover, #499-500		5.50
	Inscription block of 4	16.00	—
	Pane of 20	80.00	—

Endangered Species Type of 1993

Printed by Johann Enschedé and Sons, the Netherlands. Designed by Wendy Wray, U.S.

Designs: No. 501, Cyanoramphus novaezelandiae (Red-fronted parakeet). No. 502, Haliaeetus albicilla (White-tailed eagle). No. 503, Probosciger aterrimus (Black palm cockatoo). No. 504, Caloenas nicobarica (Nicobar pigeon).

2011, Sept. 7 **Litho.** ***Perf. 12¾x12½***

501	A271 70c **multicolored** *(132,000)+*	2.50	2.50
502	A271 70c **multicolored** *(132,000)+*	2.50	2.50
503	A271 70c **multicolored** *(132,000)+*	2.50	2.50
504	A271 70c **multicolored** *(132,000)+*	2.50	2.50
a.	Block of 4, #501-504	10.00	10.00
	First day cover, #504a		9.75
	First day cover, #501-504, each		3.25
	Inscription block of 4, #504a	10.00	—
	Pane of 16	40.00	—

Intl. Year of Forests Type of 2011

Printed by Lowe-Martin Group, Canada. Panes of 8. Designed by Sergio Baradat, U.S.

Designs: 62c, Tree top, crosses, circles and ovals. 70c, Stylized people and trees.

2011, Oct. 13 **Litho. With Foil Application** ***Perf. 12½***

505	62c **multicolored** *(100,000)+*	2.00	2.00
506	70c **multicolored** *(100,000)+*	2.25	2.25
a.	A436 Vert. pair, #505-506	4.25	4.25
	First day cover, #506a		5.25
	Pane of 8	17.00	—

Flags and Coins Type of 2006

Printed by Cartor Security Printing, France. Designed by Rorie Katz, US.

No. 507 — Flag of: a, Cameroun, 100 franc coin. b, Samoa, 2 tala coin. c, Surinam, 5 cent coin. d, Macedonia, 50 denar coin. e, Bulgaria, 50 stotinka coin. f, Tanzania, 100 shilling coin. g, Finland, 1 euro coin. h, Cuba, 1 peso coin.

2012, Feb. 3 **Litho.** ***Perf. 13¼x13***

507	Sheet of 8 *(56,000)+*	16.50	16.50
a.-h.	A375 70c Any single	2.00	2.00
	First day cover		18.50

A column of rouletting in the middle of the sheet separates it into two parts.

V111

Autism Awareness — V112

Printed by Johann Enschedé Stamps Security Printers, Netherlands. Panes of 20.

Drawings by autistic people: No. 508, The Path, by Ryan Smoluk, Canada. No. 509, Untitled drawing, by Colm Isherwood, Ireland.

2012, Apr. 2 **Litho.** ***Perf. 14x13½***

508 V111 70c **multicolored** *(90,000)+* 2.25 2.25
509 V112 70c **multicolored** *(90,000)+* 2.25 2.25
a. Pair, #508-509 4.50 4.50
First day cover, #508, 509 5.25
Inscription block of 4 9.00 —
Pane of 20 45.00 —

UN Emblem — V113

2012, Apr. 12 **Litho.** ***Perf. 14½***

510 V113 70c **purple, black** + label *3.50 3.50*
Sheet of 10 + 10 labels *35.00 35.00*

The full sheet sold for $14.52 or €9.90. The labels could be personalized.

Endangered Species Type of 1993

Printed by Johann Enschedé and Sons, the Netherlands. Designed by Diana Marques, Portugal.

Designs: No. 511, Panthera uncia. No. 512, Polyplectron schleiermacheri. No. 513, Tyto novaehollandiae. No. 514, Ambystoma mexicanum.

2012, Apr. 19 **Litho.** ***Perf. 12¾x12½***

511 A271 70c **multicolored** *(121,600)+* 2.25 2.25
512 A271 70c **multicolored** *(121,600)+* 2.25 2.25
513 A271 70c **multicolored** *(121,600)+* 2.25 2.25
514 A271 70c **multicolored** *(121,600)+* 2.25 2.25
a. Block of 4, #511-514 9.00 9.00
First day cover, #514a 9.25
First day cover, #511-514, each 3.00
Inscription block of 4, #514a 9.00 —
Pane of 16 36.00 —

Rio + 20 Type of 2012

Printed by Lowe-Martin Group, Canada. Panes of 20. Designed by Fei, People's Republic of China.

2012, June 1 **Litho.** ***Perf. 13x13¼***

515 A443 70c **multicolored** *(136,000)+* 2.10 2.10
First day cover 3.25
Inscription block of 4 8.40 —
Pane of 20 42.00 —

Sport for Peace Type of 2012

Printed by Cartor Security Printing, France. Panes of 9. Designed by Daniel Stolle, Finland.

2012 Paralympics events: 62c, Wheelchair basketball. 70c, Paralympic table tennis.

Litho. With Foil Application

2012, Aug. 17 ***Perf. 14½***

516 A444 62c **multicolored** *(153,000)+* 1.90 1.90
First day cover 2.75
Inscription block of 4 7.60 —
Pane of 9 17.50 —
517 A444 70c **multicolored** *(153,000)+* 2.10 2.10
First day cover 3.25
First day cover, #516-517 5.00
Inscription block of 4 8.40 —
Pane of 9 42.00 —
a. Souvenir sheet of 1 *(43,000)+* 2.10 2.10
First day cover 3.25

UNESCO World Heritage Sites in Africa Type of 2012

Printed by Lowe-Martin Group, Canada. Panes of 20. Designed by Rorie Katz, US.

Designs: 62c, Kenya Lake System, Kenya. 70c, Medina of Marrakesh, Morocco.

2012, Sept. 5 **Litho.** ***Perf. 13¼***

518 A445 62c **multicolored** *(140,000)+* 1.75 1.75
First day cover 2.60
Inscription block of 4 7.00 —
Pane of 20 35.00 —
519 A445 70c **multicolored** *(140,000)+* 2.00 2.00
First day cover 3.00
First day cover, #518-519 4.75
Inscription block of 4 8.00 —
Pane of 20 40.00 —

Miniature Sheet

Indigenous People — V114

Printed by Lowe-Martin Group, Canada. Designed by Stephen Bennett, US.

No. 520 — Portrait of person from: a, Chile. b, Malaysia. c, China (woman with black hair). d, China (woman with flower in hair). e, Tanzania. f, Mongolia.

2012, Oct. 11 **Litho.** ***Perf. 13¼x13***

520	V114	Sheet of 6 *(49,000)+*	11.50	11.50
a.-f.		70c Any single	1.90	1.90
		First day cover		13.50

World Radio Day Type of 2013

Printed by Lowe-Martin Group, Canada. Panes of 20. Designed by Rorie Katz, US.

Designs: 70c, Microphone and scripts. €1.70, Boy with radio.

2013, Feb. 13 **Litho.** ***Perf. 13¼x13***

521	A448	70c **multicolored** *(126,700)+*	2.00	2.00
		First day cover		2.60
		Inscription block of 4	8.00	—
		Pane of 20	40.00	—
522	A448	€1.70 **multicolored** *(126,700)+*	5.00	5.00
		First day cover		6.25
		First day cover, #521-522		8.00
		Inscription block of 4	20.00	—
		Pane of 20	100.00	—

People in Handprint V115

People in Heart — V116

Printed by Johann Enschedé and Sons, the Netherlands. Panes of 20. Designed by Sergio Baradat, US.

2013, Mar. 5 **Litho.** ***Perf. 14x13½***

523	V115	62c **multicolored** *(200,000)+*	1.90	1.90
		First day cover		2.25
		Inscription block of 4	7.60	—
		Pane of 20	38.00	—

Perf. 13½x14

524	V116	€2.20 **multicolored** *(200,000)+*	6.50	6.50
		First day cover		7.75
		First day cover, #523-524		9.00
		Inscription block of 4	26.00	—
		Pane of 20	130.00	—

World Heritage Sites, China, Type of 2013

Printed by Johann Enschedé and Sons, the Netherlands. Panes of 20. Designed by Sergio Baradat, U.S.

Designs: Nos. 525, 527c, Great Wall of China. Nos. 526, 527f, Mausoleum of the First Qing Emperor. No. 527a, Mogao Caves. No. 527b, Potala Palace, Lhasa. No. 527d, Imperial Palace, Beijing. No. 527e, Mount Huangshan.

2013, Apr. 11 **Litho.** ***Perf. 14x13½***

525	A452	70c **multicolored** *(150,000)+*	2.00	2.00
		First day cover		2.60
		Inscription block of 4	8.00	—
		Pane of 20	40.00	—
526	A452	€1.70 **multicolored** *(150,000)+*	5.00	5.00
		First day cover		6.25
		First day cover, #525-526		8.00
		Inscription block of 4	20.00	—
		Pane of 20	100.00	—

Souvenir Booklet

527		Booklet, #527g-527l *(27,000)+*	25.00	
a.-c.	A452	30c any single	.85	.85
d.-f.	A452	40c any single	1.10	1.10
g.		Booklet pane of 4 #527a	3.50	—
h.		Booklet pane of 4 #527b	3.50	—
i.		Booklet pane of 4 #527c	3.50	—
j.		Booklet pane of 4 #527d	4.75	—
k.		Booklet pane of 4 #527e	4.75	—
l.		Booklet pane of 4 #527f	4.75	—

World Oceans Day — V117

Printed by Lowe-Martin Group, Canada. Designed by Rorie Katz, US.

No. 528 — Fish from *One Fish, Two Fish, Red Fish, Blue Fish,* by Dr. Seuss: a, Green fish facing left, wave. b, Red fish facing right. c, Three green fish on plate. d, Red fish, back half of red fish, wave. e, Red fish facing left, front half of red fish facing right. f, Two red fish facing left. g, Two green fish facing right, wave. h, Red fish facing right, head of blue fish wearing hat. i, Yellow fish with green star, wave. j, Yellow fish, back of blue fish, wave. k, Two red fish, body of blue fish. l, Tail of yellow fish, two green fish facing left, wave.

2013, May 31 **Litho.** ***Perf. 13***

528	V117	Sheet of 12 *(53,000)+*	24.00	24.00
		First day cover		26.00
a.-l.		70c any single	2.00	2.00

Nebulae Type of 2013

Printed by UAB Garsu Pasaulis, Lithuania. Panes of 8. Designed by Sergio Baradat, U.S.

Designs: No. 529, NGC 7293. No. 530, NGC 1850. 62c, Eagle Nebula.

2013, Aug. 9 **Litho.** ***Perf. 13¼***

529	A454	€1.70 **multicolored** *(136,000)+*	5.00	5.00
530	A454	€1.70 **multicolored** *(136,000)+*	5.00	5.00
a.		Pair, #529-530	10.00	10.00
		First day cover, #5308a		11.00
		Inscription block of 4	20.00	—
		Pane of 8	40.00	—

Souvenir Sheet

531	A454	62c **multicolored** *(37,000)+*	1.90	1.90
		First day cover		2.75

No. 531 contains one 44x44mm stamp.

Works of Disabled Artists Type of 2013

Printed by UAB Garsu Pasaulis, Lithuania. Panes of 20. Designed by Rorie Katz, U.S.

Designs: 70c, Electro Man, by Pete Eckert, U.S. €1.70, Dive Bomb, by Matt Sesow, U.S.

2013, Sept. 20 **Litho.** ***Perf. 13¼x13***

532 A456 70c **multicolored** *(129,500)+* 2.00 2.00
First day cover 2.60
Inscription block of 4 8.00 —
Pane of 20 40.00 —
533 A456 €1.70 **multicolored** *(129,500)+* 5.00 5.00
First day cover 6.25
First day cover, #532-533 8.00
Inscription block of 4 20.00 —
Pane of 20 100.00 —

Endangered Species Type of 1993

Printed by Johann Enschedé and Sons, the Netherlands. Designed by Emily S. Damstra, Canada.

Designs: No. 534, Hemigalus derbyanus. No. 535, Bubo ascalaphus. No. 536, Nycticebus coucang. No. 537, Zaglossus spp.

2013, Oct. 10 **Litho.** ***Perf. 12¾x12½***

534 A271 70c **multicolored** *(120,000)+* 2.00 2.00
535 A271 70c **multicolored** *(120,000)+* 2.00 2.00
536 A271 70c **multicolored** *(120,000)+* 2.00 2.00
537 A271 70c **multicolored** *(120,000)+* 2.00 2.00
a. Block of 4, #534-537 8.00 8.00
First day cover, #537a 9.00
First day cover, #534-537, each 3.00
Inscription block of 4, #537a 8.00 —
Pane of 16 32.00 —

UN Emblem — V118

2013, Oct. 24 **Litho.** ***Perf. 14½***

538 V118 70c **gray blue & blue** + label *4.00 4.00*
Sheet of 10 + 10 labels *30.00* —

The full sheet sold for $14.20 or €9.90. The labels could be personalized.

Flags and Coins Type of 2006

Printed by Cartor Security Printing, France. Designed by Rorie Katz, US.

No. 539 — Flag of: a, Malaysia, 50 sen coin. b, Nigeria, 1 naira coin. c, Zambia, 20 ngwee coin. d, Togo, 100 franc coin. e, Dominica, 5 cent coin. f, Chad, 100 franc coin. g, St. Vincent and the Grenadines, 5 cent coin. h, Syria, 25 pound coin.

2013, Nov. 6 **Litho.** ***Perf. 13¼x13***

539 Sheet of 8 *(48,000)+* 16.00 16.00
a.-h. A375 70c Any single 2.00 2.00
First day cover 18.00

A column of rouletting in the middle of the sheet separates it into two parts.

International Day of Happiness Type of 2014

Printed by Lowe-Martin Group, Canada. Panes of 20. Designed by Rorie Katz, U.S.

Designs: 90c, Happy Asian Boy at the Park, photograph by Alan Levenson, Russian word for "Happy." €1.70, Barbary Macacque with Baby, photograph by Gerhard Schulz, Arabic word for "Happy."

2014, Mar. 17 **Litho.** ***Perf. 13¼x13***

540 A459 90c **multicolored** *(100,000)+* 2.75 2.75
First day cover 3.50
Inscription block of 4 11.00 —
Pane of 20 55.00 —
541 A459 €1.70 **multicolored** *(100,000)+* 5.25 5.25
First day cover 6.50
First day cover, #540-541 8.75
Inscription block of 4 21.00 —
Pane of 20 105.00 —

Miniature Sheet

International Year of Jazz — V119

Printed by Cartor Security Printing, France. Designed by Sergio Baradat, U.S.

No. 542: a, Silhouette of saxophonist in blue. b, Woman singing. c, Silhouette of man in red, neon lights. d, Bass player. e, Trombone in gold. f, Silhouette of saxophonist in black, silhouette of man holding trombone. g, "Cocktails" neon sign . h, Silhouette of bass player in orange. i, Stack of record albums. j, Cymbal. k, Trombone in silver. l, Silhouette of clarinetist in black.

2014, Apr. 30 **Litho.** ***Perf. 13x13¼***

542 V119 Sheet of 12 *(50,000)+* 24.00 24.00
First day cover 27.00
a.-l. 70c Any single 2.00 2.00

Vienna International Center, 35th Anniv. — V120

Designed by Eduardo Sinoy, U.S.

No. 543: a, Vienna International Center under construction (towers and shadows), red panel. b, Vienna International Center, street light at left, green panel. c, Vienna International Center, curved building at left, green panel. d, Vienna International Center under construction (arch in foreground, cranes at right), red panel. e, Vienna International Center under construction (cranes at left, center and right), red panel. f, Doorway to Vienna International Center, green panel. g, View of curved buildings of Vienna International Center looking up from ground, green panel. h, Vienna International Center under construction (two cranes on central tower), red panel. i, Completed Vienna International Center, red panel. j, Flags in front of Vienna International Center.

2014, May 8 **Litho.** ***Perf. 14¾***

543 V120 Sheet of 10 + 10 labels *30.00 30.00*
a.-j. 70c Any single + label *3.00 3.00*

The full sheet sold for $14.80 or €9.90. The generic labels are shown. Labels could be personalized.

V121

V122

Printed by Lowe-Martin Group, Canada. Panes of 20. Designed by Sergio Baradat, U.S.

2014, June 6	**Litho.**		*Perf. 13¼x13*	
544 V121	70c **multicolored** *(116,000)+*		2.10	2.10
	First day cover			2.75
	Inscription block of 4		8.40	—
	Pane of 20		42.00	—
545 V122	€1.70 **multicolored** *(116,000)+*		5.25	5.25
	First day cover			6.50
	First day cover, #544-545			8.25
	Inscription block of 4		21.00	—
	Pane of 20		105.00	—

Taj Mahal Types of 2014

Printed by Lowe-Martin Group, Canada. Panes of 20. Designed by Rorie Katz, U.S.

2014, July 16	**Engr.**		*Perf. 13¼x13*	
546 A466	90c **multicolored** *(120,000)+*		2.75	2.75
	First day cover			3.50
	Inscription block of 4		11.00	—
	Pane of 20		55.00	—
547 A468	€1.70 **multicolored** *(120,000)+*		5.25	5.25
	First day cover			6.50
	First day cover, #546-547			8.75
	Inscription block of 4		21.00	—
	Pane of 20		105.00	—

Souvenir Booklet

548	Booklet, #548g-548l *(18,000)+*	25.00	
a.	A463 30c multi	.85	.85
b.	A465 30c multi	.85	.85
c.	A466 30c multi	.85	.85
d.	A464 40c multi	1.20	1.20
e.	A467 40c multi	1.20	1.20
f.	A468 40c multi	1.20	1.20
g.	Booklet pane of 4 #548a	3.40	—
h.	Booklet pane of 4 #548b	3.40	—
i.	Booklet pane of 4 #548c	3.40	—
j.	Booklet pane of 4 #548d	4.80	—
k.	Booklet pane of 4 #548e	4.80	—
l.	Booklet pane of 4 #548f	4.80	—

International Year of Family Farming — V123

Printed by Lowe-Martin Group, Canada. Panes of 20. Designed by Sergio Baradat, U.S.

Designs: 62c, Indian farmers collecting harvested straw and grain. €1.70, Asian farmers, bull, terraced fields.

2014, Aug. 21	**Litho.**	*Perf. 13x13¼*	
549 V123	62c **multicolored** *(100,000)+*	1.90	1.90
	First day cover		2.40
	Inscription block of 4	7.60	—
	Pane of 20	38.00	—
550 V123	€1.70 **multicolored** *(100,000)+*	5.25	5.25
	First day cover		6.50
	First day cover, #549-550		8.00
	Inscription block of 4	21.00	—
	Pane of 20	105.00	—

Global Education First Initiative Type of 2014

Printed by Lowe-Martin Group, Canada. Panes of 20. Designed by Oamul Lu, People's Republic of China.

Designs: €1.70, Children boarding school bus. €2, Tree growing from book held by students.

2014, Sept. 18	**Litho.**	*Perf. 13x13¼*	
551 A470	€1.70 **multicolored** *(110,000)+*	5.25	5.25
	First day cover		6.25
	Inscription block of 4	21.00	—
	Pane of 20	105.00	—

Souvenir Sheet

Perf. 12½

552 A470	€2 **multicolored** *(42,000)+*	6.00	6.00
	First day cover		6.25

No. 552 contains one 32x32mm stamp.

Endangered Species Type of 2014

Printed by Johann Enschedé and Sons, the Netherlands. Designed by Amadeo Bachar, U.S.

Maps and: No. 553, Cheilinus undulatus. No. 554, Carcharodon carcharias. No. 555, Manta birostris. No. 556, Polyodon spathula.

2014, Oct. 23	**Litho.**	*Perf. 12¾x12½*	
553 A471	70c **multicolored** *(108,000)+*	2.10	2.10
554 A471	70c **multicolored** *(108,000)+*	2.10	2.10
555 A471	70c **multicolored** *(108,000)+*	2.10	2.10
556 A471	70c **multicolored** *(108,000)+*	2.10	2.10
a.	Block of 4, #553-556	8.50	8.50
	First day cover, #556a		9.50
	First day cover, #553-556, each		3.00
	Inscription block of 4, #556a	8.50	—
	Pane of 16	34.00	—

Miniature Sheet

V124

Designed by Rorie Katz, U.S.

No. 557: a, Flag on pole as seen from base of pole. b, Vienna International Center, structure in shadow at bottom. c, Persian Scholars Pavilion. d, Vienna International Center and fountain. e, Sailboat and Vienna International Center. f, Rowboat on water near Vienna International Center. g, Vienna International Center, flags and sculpture. h, Entrance to Vienna International Center. i, Woman Free sculpture near Vienna International Center. j, Aerial view of Vienna International Center.

2015, Jan. 23	**Litho.**	***Perf. 14¾***	
557	V124 Sheet of 10	*30.00*	*30.00*
a.-j.	80c Any single + label	*3.00*	*3.00*

The full sheet sold for $15 or €10.90. The generic labels are shown. Labels could be personalized.

Flags and Coins Type of 2006

Printed by Cartor Security Printing, France. Designed by Rorie Katz, U.S.

No. 558 — Flag of: a, Tuvalu, 10 cent coin. b, Malawi, 1 kwacha coin. c, Iraq, 50 dinar coin. d, St. Thomas and Prince Islands, 250 dobra coin. e, Botswana, 10 thebe coin. f, Uruguay, 5 peso coin. g, Bosnia and Herzegovina, 20 pfennig coin. h, Somalia, 25 shilling coin.

2015, Feb. 6	**Litho.**	***Perf. 13¼x13***	
558	Sheet of 8 *(45,000)*+	18.00	18.00
a.-h.	A375 80c Any single	2.25	2.25
	First day cover		20.00

A column of rouletting in the middle of the sheet separates it into two parts.

Miniature Sheets

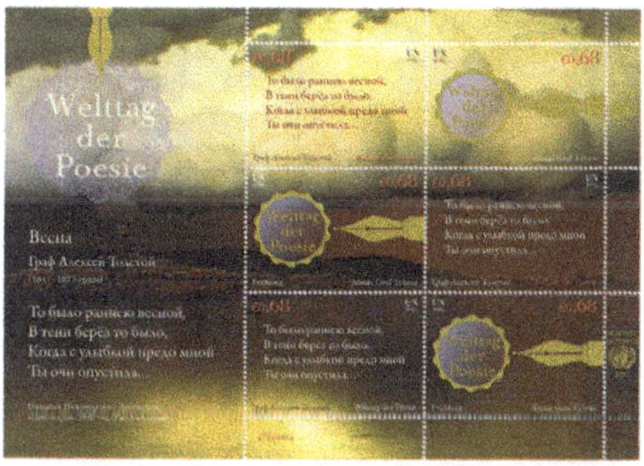

V125

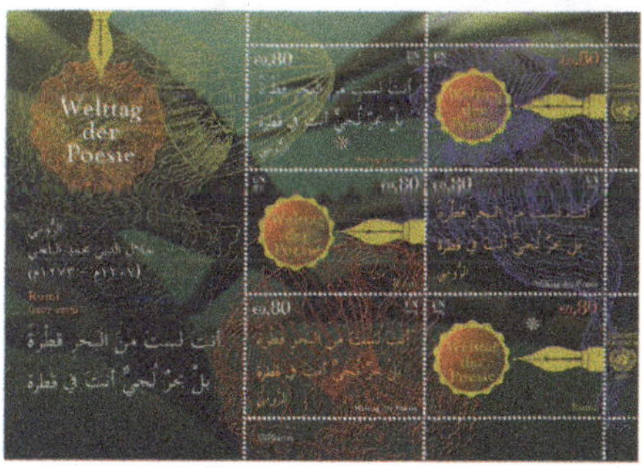

World Poetry Day — V126

Printed by Cartor Security Printing, France. Designed by Sergio Baradat, U.S.

No. 559: a, Aleksey Tolstoy quotation in Russian in red brown, date in purple, "Welttag der Poesie" in red. b, Pen and circle, date in black, "Frühling" in purple. c, Pen and circle, date and "Frühling" in white, clouds above land in background. d, Tolstoy quotation in Russian in white, date in white, "Welttag der Poesie" in red. e, Tolstoy quotation in white, date and "Welttag der Poesie" in white. f, As "c," brown background.

No. 560: a, Rumi quotation in Arabic in light blue. b, Pen and red brown circle, denomination in red, purple jellyfish in background. c, Pen and red brown circle, denomination in white. d, Rumi quotation in orange, purple jellyfish tentacles in background. e, Rumi quotation in orange, red jellyfish tentacles in background. f, Pen and red brown circle, red denomination, red and purple jellyfish tentacles in background.

2015, Mar. 20	**Litho.**	***Perf. 14½x14¼***	
559	V125 Sheet of 6 *(42,000)*+	11.50	11.50
a.-f.	68c Any single	1.90	1.90
560	V126 Sheet of 6 *(42,000)*+	13.50	13.50
a.-f.	80c Any single	2.25	2.25
	First day cover, #559-560		28.50

Endangered Species Type of 2015

Printed by Johann Enschedé and Sons, the Netherlands. Designed by John Keulemans and William Hart, United Kingdom.

Designs: No. 561, Pteridophora alberti. No. 562, Astrapia splendidissima. No. 563, Paradisaea apoda. No. 564, Lophorina superba.

2015, Apr. 16	**Litho.**	***Perf. 12½x12¾***	
561	A476 80c **multicolored** *(100,000)*+	2.00	2.00
562	A476 80c **multicolored** *(100,000)*+	2.00	2.00
563	A476 80c **multicolored** *(100,000)*+	2.00	2.00
564	A476 80c **multicolored** *(100,000)*+	2.00	2.00
a.	Block of 4, #561-564	8.00	8.00
	First day cover, #564a		9.00
	First day cover, #561-564, each		3.00
	Inscription block of 4, #564a	8.00	—
	Pane of 16	32.00	—
	Nos. 561-564 (4)	8.00	8.00

V127

V128

Printed by Lowe-Martin Group, Canada. Panes of 20. Designed by Sergio Baradat, U.S.

2015, May 7	**Litho.**	***Perf. 13¼x13***	
565	V127 68c **multicolored** *(110,000)*+	1.75	1.75
	First day cover		2.50
	Inscription block of 4	7.00	—
	Pane of 20	35.00	—
566	V128 80c **multicolored** *(110,000)*+	2.00	2.00
	First day cover		3.00
	First day cover, #565-566		4.75
	Inscription block of 4	8.00	—
	Pane of 20	40.00	—

World Heritage Sites, Southeast Asia Type of 2015

Printed by Johann Enschedé and Sons, the Netherlands. Panes of 20. Designed by Sergio Baradat, U.S.

Designs: Nos. 567, 569c, Ayutthaya, Thailand. Nos. 568, 569f, Hué Monuments, Viet Nam. No. 569a, Luang Prabang, Laos. No. 569b, Angkor Wat, Cambodia. No. 569d, Borobudur Temple, Indonesia. No. 569e, Cordillera, Philippines.

2015, June 5 **Litho.** ***Perf. 14x13½***

567 A480	80c **multicolored** *(120,000)+*	2.00	2.00
	First day cover		2.60
	Inscription block of 4	8.00	—
	Pane of 20	40.00	—
568 A480	€1.70 **multicolored** *(120,000)+*	4.25	4.25
	First day cover		5.50
	First day cover, #567-568		7.25
	Inscription block of 4	17.00	—
	Pane of 20	85.00	—

Souvenir Booklet

569	Booklet, #569g-569l *(17,000)+*	21.00	
a.-c.	A480 30c any single	.75	.75
d.-f.	A480 40c any single	1.00	1.00
g.	Booklet pane of 4 #569a	3.00	—
h.	Booklet pane of 4 #569b	3.00	—
i.	Booklet pane of 4 #569c	3.00	—
j.	Booklet pane of 4 #569d	4.00	—
k.	Booklet pane of 4 #569e	4.00	—
l.	Booklet pane of 4 #569f	4.00	—

End Violence Against Children Type of 2015

Printed by Cartor Security Printing, France. Panes of 20. Designed by Chris Sharp, U.S.

Designs: 68c, Gender-based violence. 80c, Child labor.

2015, Aug. 20 **Litho.** ***Perf. 14½x14¼***

570 A481	68c **multicolored** *(100,000)+*	1.75	1.75
	First day cover		2.50
	Inscription block of 4	7.00	—
	Pane of 20	35.00	—
571 A481	80c **multicolored** *(100,000)+*	2.00	2.00
	First day cover		3.00
	First day cover, #570-571		4.75
	Inscription block of 4	8.00	—
	Pane of 20	40.00	—

ECOSOC Chamber V129

Trusteeship Council V130

Visitors Lobby — V131

General Assembly Hall — V132

Trusteeship Council — V133

Printed by Cartor Security Printing, France. Panes of 6. Designed by Rorie Katz, U.S.

2015, Oct. 25 **Litho.** ***Perf. 13¾***

572 V129	80c **multicolored** *(111,000)+*	2.00	2.00
573 V130	80c **multicolored** *(111,000)+*	2.00	2.00
a.	Pair, #572-573	4.00	4.00
	First day cover, #572-573		4.75
	Inscription block of 4	8.00	—
	Pane of 6	12.00	—
574 V131	€1.70 **multicolored** *(111,000)+*	4.25	4.25
575 V132	€1.70 **multicolored** *(111,000)+*	4.25	4.25
a.	Pair, #574-575	8.50	8.50
	First day cover, #574-575		9.75
	Inscription block of 4	17.00	—
	Pane of 6	25.50	—
	Nos. 572-575 (4)	12.50	12.50

Souvenir Sheet

Perf. 13½

576 V133	€1.70 **multicolored** *(42,000)+*	4.25	4.25
	First day cover		5.25

United Nations, 70th anniv.

United Nations, 70th Anniv. Type of 2015

Designed by Sergio Baradat, U.S.

2015, Nov. 5 **Litho.** ***Perf. 14¾***

577 A482 80c **multicolored** + label *4.00 4.00*
Sheet of 10 + 10 labels *40.00 —*

The full sheet sold for $13.45 or €10.90. The sheet contains ten different generic labels. Labels could be personalized. The personalization of labels was available only at UN Headquarters, and not through mail order.

21st United Nations Climate Change Conference, Paris — V134

Printed by La Poste, France. Panes of 30. Designed by Rorie Katz, U.S.

2015, Nov. 24 **Litho.** ***Perf. 13¼***

578 V134 80c **multicolored** *(90,000)*+ 3.00 3.00
First day cover 3.50
Inscription block of 4 12.00 —
Pane of 30 60.00 —

Values are for stamps with surrounding selvage.

Free and Equal Type of 2016

Printed by Cartor Security Printing, France. Panes of 20. Designed by Sergio Baradat, U.S.
Designs: 68c, Person coming out of closet. 80c, Gay men.

2016, Feb. 5 **Litho.** ***Perf. 13½x13¼***

579 A491 68c **multicolored** *(100,000)*+ 1.75 1.75
First day cover 2.50
Inscription block of 4 7.00 —
Pane of 20 35.00 —
580 A491 80c **multicolored** *(100,000)*+ 2.00 2.00
First day cover 3.00
First day cover, #579-580 4.50
Inscription block of 4 8.00 —
Pane of 20 40.00 —

HeForShe Type of 2016

Printed by Lowe-Martin Group, Canada. Panes of 20. Designed by Mirko Ilic, U.S.
Designs: 1fr, Man, red background. 2fr, Woman, orange brown background.

2016, Mar. 8 **Litho.** ***Perf. 12½x13***

581 A492 68c **multicolored** *(100,000)*+ 1.75 1.75
First day cover 2.25
Inscription block of 4 7.00 —
Pane of 20 35.00 —
582 A492 80c **multicolored** *(100,000)*+ 2.00 2.00
First day cover 2.75
First day cover, #581-582 4.25
Inscription block of 4 8.00 —
Pane of 20 40.00 —

Miniature Sheets

V135

International Dance Day — V136

Printed by Cartor Security Printing. France. Designed by Sergio Baradat, U.S.
No. 583 — Illustration of Spanish dancers by Allison Seiffer: a, Female dancer with fan. b, Male dancer with crossed arms. c, Red dress of dancer. d, Female dancer with male guitarist. e, Feet of dancer in ochre and green dress. f, Feet of male and female dancers, rose on floor.
No. 584 — Illustration of Middle Eastern dancers by Seiffer: a, Head of female dancer, "Welttanztag" in red, denomination in yellow. b, Head of female dancer, "Welttanztag" and denomination in red. c, Torso of dancer. d, Dancer, "Welttanztag" in black, denomination in yellow. e, Feet of dancer, "Welttanztag" in black. f, Feet of dancer and drum, "Welttanztag" in yellow.

2016, Apr. 29 **Litho.** ***Perf. 13¼x13***

583 V135 Sheet of 6 *(35,000)*+ 10.00 10.00
a.-f. 68c Any single 1.60 1.60
584 V136 Sheet of 6 *(35,000)*+ 12.00 12.00
a.-f. 80c Any single 2.00 2.00
First day cover, #583-584 25.50

United Nations Industrial Development Organization, 50th Anniv. — V137

2016, May 12 **Litho.** ***Perf. 14¾***

585 V137 80c **multicolored** + label	*2.60*	*2.60*
Sheet of 10 + 10 labels	*26.50*	—

The full sheet sold for $13.12 and €10.90. One of the ten different generic labels is shown. Labels could be personalized. The personalization of labels was available only at UN Headquarters, and not through mail order.

International Day of United Nations Peacekeepers Type of 2016

Printed by Lowe-Martin Group, Canada. Panes of 20. Designed by Sergio Baradat, U.S.

Designs: 68c, Peacekeepers and African children. 80c, Peacekeepers in tank, Africans.

Litho. With Foil Application

2016, May 29 ***Perf. 13¼x13***

586 A496 68c **multicolored** *(130,000)*+	1.75	1.75
First day cover		2.50
Inscription block of 4	7.00	—
Pane of 20	35.00	—
587 A496 80c **multicolored** *(130,000)*+	2.00	2.00
First day cover		3.00
First day cover, #586-587		4.50
Inscription block of 4	8.00	—
Pane of 20	40.00	—

Sport for Peace Type of 2016

Printed by Cartor Security Printing, France. Panes of 6. Designed by Sergio Baradat and Linsey Thoeng, U.S.

Olympic rings and: No. 588, Weight lifting, denomination at LR. No. 589, Weight lifting, denomination at LL. No. 590, Fencing, denomination at UR. No. 591, Fencing, denonomiation at UL.

2016, July 22 **Litho.** ***Perf. 14¼***

588 A498 68c **multicolored** *(105,000)*+	1.75	1.75
589 A498 68c **multicolored** *(105,000)*+	1.75	1.75
a. Pair, #588-589	3.50	3.50
First day cover, #588-589		4.00
Inscription block of 4	7.00	—
Pane of 6	10.50	—
590 A498 €1.70 **multicolored** *(105,000)*+	4.25	4.25
591 A498 €1.70 **multicolored** *(105,000)*+	4.25	4.25
a. Pair, #590-591	8.50	8.50
First day cover, #590-591		9.75
Inscription block of 4	17.00	—
Pane of 6	25.50	—
Nos. 588-591 (4)	12.00	12.00

Souvenir sheets of three bearing three stamps, one from each office are listed under United Nations, Offices in New York as Nos. 1141, 1161, 1177-1178, 1203, and 1208.

World Heritage Sites, Czech Republic Type of 2016

Printed by Cartor Security Printing, France. Panes of 20. Designed by Sergio Baradat, U.S.

Designs: Nos. 592, 594c, Historic Town Center of Kutná Hora. Nos. 593, 594f, Historic Center of Cesky Krumlov. No. 594a, Historic Center of Prague. No. 594b, Gardens and Castle at Kromeríz. No. 594d, Holy Trinity Column, Olomouc. Nos. 594e, Lednice-Valtice Cultural Landscape.

2016, Sept. 8 **Litho.** ***Perf. 14¼***

592 A500 68c **multicolored** *(100,000)*+	1.75	1.75
First day cover		2.25
Inscription block of 4	7.00	—
Pane of 20	35.00	—
593 A500 €1.70 **multicolored** *(100,000)*+	4.25	4.25
First day cover		5.50
First day cover, #592-593		6.75
Inscription block of 4	17.00	—
Pane of 20	85.00	—

Souvenir Booklet

594 Booklet, #594g-594l	20.50	
a.-c. A500 30c any single	.65	.65
d.-f. A500 40c any single	1.00	1.00
g. Booklet pane of 4 #594a	2.75	—
h. Booklet pane of 4 #594b	2.75	—
i. Booklet pane of 4 #594c	2.75	—
j. Booklet pane of 4 #594d	4.00	—
k. Booklet pane of 4 #594e	4.00	—
l. Booklet pane of 4 #594f	4.00	—

Comprehensive Nuclear Test-Ban Treaty Organization, 20th Anniv. — V138

2016, Sept. 23 **Litho.** ***Perf. 14¾***

595 V138 80c **multicolored** + label	*4.00*	*4.00*
Sheet of 10 + 10 labels	*40.00*	—

The full sheet sold for $13.27 and €10.90. One of the ten different generic labels is shown. Labels could be personalized. The personalization of labels was available only at UN Headquarters, and not through mail order.

Miniature Sheet

World Wildlife Conference, Johannesburg — V139

Printed by Cartor Security Printing, France. Designed by Sergio Baradat, U.S.

No. 596 — Part of map of Africa and: a, Nilkrokodil (Nile crocodile). b, Kapgeier (Cape vulture). c, Steppenschuppentier (Cape pangolin). d, Mystacidium capense.

2016, Sept. 24 **Litho.** ***Perf. 13x13½***

596 V139 Sheet of 4 *(35,000)*+	17.00	17.00
a.-d. €1.70 Any single	4.25	4.25
First day cover		17.50

Sustainable Development Goals Type of 2016

Printed by Lowe-Martin, Canada. Designed by Lindsey Thoeng, U.S.

No. 597 — Inscription: a, 1 Keine armut. b, 2 Kein hunger. c, 3 Gesundheit und wohlergehen. d, 4 Hochwertige bildung. e, 5 Geschlechter-gleighheit. f, 6 Sauberes wasser und sanitär-einrichtungen. g, 7 Bezahlbare und saubere energie. h, 8 Menschenwürdige arbeit und wirtschafts-wachstum. i, 9 Industrie, innovation und infrastruktur. j, 10 Weniger ungleichheiten. k, 11 Nachhaltige städte und gemeinden. l, 12 Nachhaltige/r konsum und produktion. m, 13 Massnahmen zum klimaschutz. n, 14 Leben unter wasser. o, 15 Leben an land. p, 16 Frieden, gerechtigkeit und starke institutionen. q, 17 Partnerschaften zur erreichung der ziele.

2016, Oct. 24	**Litho.**	***Perf. 13¼***	
597	Sheet of 17 + label *(30,000)+*	28.50	28.50
a.-q.	A503 68c Any single	1.60	1.60
	First day cover		32.00

Miniature Sheet

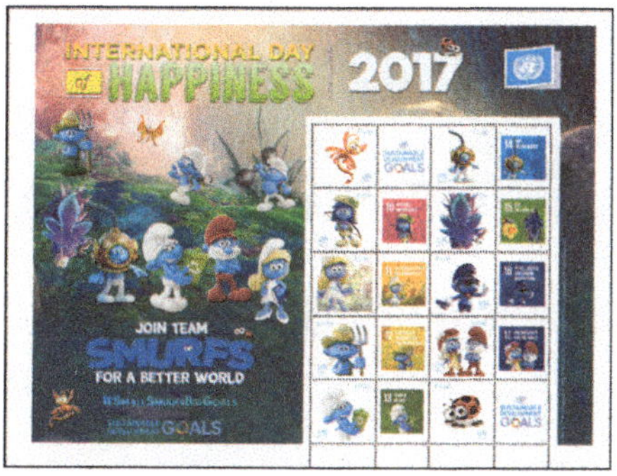

V140

No. 598: a, Insect. b, Smurf wearing diving helmet. c, Smurf holding archery bow. d, Flower with eyes. e, Smurf in park. f, Smurf with police hat, whistle and baton. g, Smurf holding pitchfork. h, Two Smurfs wearing red caps. i, Smurf holding garbage can. j, Ladybug.

2017, Mar. 20	**Litho.**	***Perf. 14¾***	
598	V140 Sheet of 10 + 10 labels	*30.00*	*30.00*
a.-j.	80c Any single + label	*3.00*	*3.00*

The full sheet sold for $14.95. The generic labels are shown. Labels could be personalized.

Miniature Sheets

V141

International Dance — V142

Printed by Cartor Security Printing, France. Designed by Sergio Baradat, U.S.

No. 599 — Illustration of Samba dancers by Victo Ngai: a, Lion's head. b, Black and tan female dancers. c, Dancers holding drums. d, Black female dancer. e, White female dancer. f, Brown female dancer.

No. 600 — Illustration of Ballet dancers by Ngai: a, Blue dancer with hand bent downward. b, Blue dancer with arm raised above head. c, Blue dancer with arms extended to side. d, Dancer with black dress. e, Head of dancer, tip of dress at bottom. f, Head of dancer facing right.

2017, Mar. 23	**Litho.**	***Perf. 13¼x13***	
599	V141 Sheet of 6 *(28,000)+*	9.75	9.75
a.-f.	68c Any single	1.60	1.60
599g	As #599, with Brasilia 2017 World Stamp Exhibition emblem overprinted in sheet margin	10.50	10.50
600	V142 Sheet of 6 *(28,000)+*	11.50	11.50
a.-f.	80c Any single	1.90	1.90
	First day cover, #599-600		25.50

Issued: No. 599g, 10/24.

Endangered Species Type of 2017

Printed by Johann Enschedé and Sons, the Netherlands. Designed by Rorie Katz, U.S.

Designs: No. 601, Capra caucasica. No. 602, Nautilidae spp. No. 603, Siphonochilus aethiopicus. No. 604, Lygodactylus williamsi.

2017, May 11	**Litho.**	***Perf. 12¾x12½***	
601	A509 80c **multicolored** *(76,000)+*	1.90	1.90
602	A509 80c **multicolored** *(76,000)+*	1.90	1.90
603	A509 80c **multicolored** *(76,000)+*	1.90	1.90
604	A509 80c **multicolored** *(76,000)+*	1.90	1.90
a.	Block of 4, #601-604	7.75	7.75
	First day cover, #604a		9.25
	First day cover, #601-604, each		3.50
	Inscription block of 4, #604a	7.75	—
	Pane of 16	31.00	—
	Nos. 601-604 (4)	7.60	7.60

World Environment Day Type of 2017

Printed by Lowe-Martin Group, Canada. Panes of 20. Designed by Sergio Baradat, U.S.

Designs: 68c, Supreme Court, Ottawa, Ontario, Canada. €1.70, Moraine Lake, Canada.

2017, June 5	**Litho.**	***Perf. 13¼***	
605	A510 68c **multicolored** *(90,000)+*	1.60	1.60
	First day cover		2.60
	Inscription block of 4	6.40	—
	Pane of 20	32.00	—
606	A510 €1.70 **multicolored** *90,000)+*	4.00	4.00
	First day cover		6.50
	First day cover, #605-606		7.25
	Inscription block of 4	16.00	—
	Pane of 20	80.00	—

World Heritage Sites Along the Silk Roads Type of 2017

Printed by Cartor Security Printing, France. Panes of 20. Designed by Sergio Baradat, U.S.

Designs: Nos. 607, 609c, Tabriz Historic Bazaar Complex, Iran. Nos. 608, 609f, Safranbolu, Turkey. No. 609a, Longmen Grottoes, People's Republic of China. No. 609b, Historic Center of Bukhara, Uzbekistan. No. 609d, Sulaiman-Too Sacred Mountain, Kyrgyzstan. No. 609e, Kunya-Urgench, Turkmenistan.

2017, Aug. 3 **Litho.** ***Perf. 14¼***

607 A512	80c **multicolored** *(90,000)+*	2.00	2.00
	First day cover		3.25
	Inscription block of 4	8.00	—
	Pane of 20	40.00	—
608 A512	€1.70 **multicolored** *(90,000)+*	4.25	4.25
	First day cover		6.75
	First day cover, #607-608		8.00
	Inscription block of 4	17.00	—
	Pane of 20	85.00	—

Souvenir Booklet

609	Booklet, #609g-609l *(10,500)+*	23.50	
a.-c.	A512 30c any single	.85	.85
d.-f.	A512 40c any single	1.10	1.10
g.	Booklet pane of 4 #609a	3.40	—
h.	Booklet pane of 4 #609b	3.40	—
i.	Booklet pane of 4 #609c	3.40	—
j.	Booklet pane of 4 #609d	4.40	—
k.	Booklet pane of 4 #609e	4.40	—
l.	Booklet pane of 4 #609f	4.40	—

Miniature Sheet

V143

No. 610: a, Traunsee with ships and lakeshore buildings. b, Ort Castle and bridge at dusk. c, Aerial view of Cumberland Castle. d, Street in Gmunden, Austria. e, Gmunden City Hall. f, Ort Castle and bridge. g, Sailboat near Ort Castle. h, Villa Toscana. i, Aerial view of Traunsee. j, Ships on Traunsee.

2017, Aug. 24 **Litho.** ***Perf. 14¾***

610 V143	Sheet of 10 + 10 labels	*27.50*	*27.50*
a.-j.	68c Any single + label	*2.75*	*2.75*

United Nations Postal Administration on the Traunsee, 35th anniv. The full sheet sold for $13.64. The generic labels are shown. Labels could be personalized.

Hands and Flower V144

Handshake and Flowers — V145

Handshake and Flowers — V146

Printed by Johann Enschedé and Sons, the Netherlands. Panes of 20. Designed by Stranger and Stranger, U.S.

2017, Sept. 21 **Litho.** ***Perf. 14x14¼***

611 V144	68c **multicolored** *(90,000)+*	1.75	1.75
	First day cover		2.75
	Inscription block of 4	7.00	—
	Pane of 20	35.00	—
612 V145	€1.70 **multicolored** *(90,000)+*	4.25	4.25
	First day cover		6.75
	First day cover, #611-612		7.75
	Inscription block of 4	17.00	—
	Pane of 20	85.00	—

Souvenir Sheet

Perf. 14¼x13¾

613 V146	€1.70 **multicolored** *(33,000)+*	4.25	4.25
	First day cover		6.00

International Day of Peace.

World Food Day Type of 2017

Printed by Royal Johann Enschedé. Panes of 20. Designed by Helen Dardik, Canada.

Designs: 68c, Breads and grains. 80c, Steak, fish, chicken drumstick, shrimp, egg, beans, lemon slice.

2017, Oct. 16 **Litho.** ***Perf. 13¼x14***

614 A516	68c **multicolored** *(90,000)+*	1.75	1.75
	First day cover		3.25
	Inscription block of 4	7.00	—
	Pane of 20	35.00	—
615 A516	80c **multicolored** *(90,000)+*	2.00	2.00
	First day cover		4.00
	First day cover, #614-615		5.50
	Inscription block of 4	8.00	—
	Pane of 20	40.00	—

Endangered Species Type of 2018

Printed by Johann Enschedé Stamps Security Printers, the Netherlands. Designed by Rorie Katz, U.S.

Designs: No. 616, Hoodia pilifera. No. 617, Mantella madagascariensis. No. 618, Pangshua sylhetensis. No. 619, Hippocampus zebra.

2018, Mar. 2 Litho. *Perf. 12¾x12½*

616 A519 80c **multicolored** *(76,000)+*	2.00	2.00
617 A519 80c **multicolored** *(76,000)+*	2.00	2.00
618 A519 80c **multicolored** *(76,000)+*	2.00	2.00
619 A519 80c **multicolored** *(76,000)+*	2.00	2.00
a. Block of 4, #616-619	8.00	8.00
First day cover, #619a		10.50
First day cover, #616-619, each		3.75
Inscription block of 4, #619a	8.00	—
Pane of 16	32.00	—
Nos. 616-619 (4)	8.00	8.00

World Health Day Type of 2018

Printed by Lowe-Martin Group, Canada. Panes of 20. Designed by Sergio Baradat, U.S.

Designs: 68c, Medical worker, people, globe, caduceus. €1.70, Coins entering piggy bank with white cross.

2018, Apr. 6 Litho. *Perf. 13x13¼*

620 A520 68c **multicolored** *(90,000)+*	1.90	1.90
First day cover		2.75
Inscription block of 4	7.60	—
Pane of 20	38.00	—
621 A520 €1.70 **multicolored** *(90,000)+*	4.50	4.50
First day cover		7.00
First day cover, #620-621		8.00
Inscription block of 4	18.00	—
Pane of 20	90.00	—

United Nations Emblem — V147

2018 Litho. *Perf. 14¾*

622 V147 80c **multicolored** + label	*2.75*	*2.75*
Sheet of 10 + 10 labels	*29.00*	—
a. Less distinct year date and frame, lighter blue emblem	*2.75*	*2.75*
Sheet of 10 #622a + 10 labels	*29.00*	—

Issued: No. 622, 5/26; No. 622a, 7/30. The full sheet sold for $14.32 and €10.90. One of the ten different generic labels is shown. Labels could be personalized. The personalization of labels was available only at UN Headquarters, and not through mail order.

UNISPACE + 50 Conferences Type of 2018

Printed by Johann Enschedé Stamps BV, Netherlands. Panes of 20. Designed by Sergio Baradat, U.S. Designs: 68c, Great Red Spot of Jupiter. 80c, Aurora Australis from International Space Station.

€1.70, View of river delta from Copernicus Sentinel satellite.

2018, June 20 Litho. *Perf. 14x14¼*

623 A523 68c **multicolored** *(80,000)+*	1.90	1.90
First day cover		3.50
Inscription block of 4	7.60	—
Pane of 20	45.00	—
624 A523 80c **multicolored** *(80,000)+*	2.25	2.25
First day cover		4.00
First day cover, #623-624		5.75
Inscription block of 4	9.00	—
Pane of 20	45.00	—

Souvenir Sheet

Perf. 13¾

625 A523 €1.70 **multicolored** *(27,000)+*	4.50	4.50
First day cover		6.25

No. 625 contains one 45x45mm stamp.

World Heritage Sites In the United Kingdom Type of 2018

Printed by Cartor Security Printing, France. Panes of 20. Designed by Rorie Katz, U.S.

Designs: Nos. 626, 628c, Conwy Castle. Nos. 627, 628f, Maritime Greenwich. No. 628a, Giant's Causeway. No. 628b, Stonehenge. No. 628d, Palace of Westminster. No. 628e, Edinburgh.

2018, Aug. 15 Litho. *Perf. 14¼*

626 A524 90c **multicolored** *(80,000)+*	2.40	2.40
First day cover		3.25
Inscription block of 4	9.60	—
Pane of 20	48.00	—
627 A524 €1.80 **multicolored** *(90,000)+*	4.75	4.75
First day cover		6.75
First day cover, #626-627		8.00
Inscription block of 4	19.00	—
Pane of 20	95.00	—

Souvenir Booklet

628 Booklet, #628g-628l *(9,000)+*	25.50	
a.-c. A524 35c any single	1.00	1.00
d.-f. A524 40c any single	1.10	1.10
g. Booklet pane of 4 #628a	4.00	—
h. Booklet pane of 4 #628b	4.00	—
i. Booklet pane of 4 #628c	4.00	—
j. Booklet pane of 4 #628d	4.50	—
k. Booklet pane of 4 #628e	4.50	—
l. Booklet pane of 4 #628f	4.50	—

Miniature Sheet

International Music Day — V148

Printed by Johann Enschedé Stamps BV, the Netherlands. Designed by Sergio Baradat, U.S.

No. 629: a, Kalimba with three holes. b, Snare drum. c, Shekere. d, Castanets. e, Gong. f, Hourglass drum. g, Castanet with handles and tambourine stick. h, Cymbals. i, Djembe drum. j, Kalimba with one hole. k, Button accordion. l, Maracas and decorated stick.

2018, Oct. 1 Litho. *Perf. 14x13¼*

629 V148 Sheet of 12 *(24,000)+*	24.50	24.50
First day cover		27.00
a.-l. 80c Any single	2.00	2.00

V149

Non-Violence, Sculpture by Carl Fredrik Reuterswärd — V150

Printed by Johann Enschedé Stamps BV, the Netherlands. Panes of 20. Designed by Martin Mörck, Norway.

2018, Oct. 2 **Litho.** ***Perf. 14x14¼***

630 V149	90c **multicolored** *(300,000)*+	2.40	2.40
	First day cover		3.25
	Inscription block of 4	9.60	—
	Pane of 20	48.00	—
631 V150	€2.30 **multicolored** *(200,000)*+	6.00	6.00
	First day cover		8.25
	First day cover, #630-631		10.00
	Inscription block of 4	24.00	—
	Pane of 20	120.00	—

Miniature Sheet

World Languages — V151

Printed by Cartor Security Printing, France. Designed by Sergio Baradat, U.S.

No. 632 — Word bubbles with word for "Hello" in: a, Serbian or Croatian ("Sprachen der Welt" and denomination in red). b, Arabic ("Sprachen der Welt" and denomination in white). c, Korean ("Sprachen der Welt" in white, denomination in black), d, Dutch or German or Norwegian (Hallo). e, Greek and Turkish (Merhaba). f, Spanish (Hola).

2019, Feb. 21 **Litho.** ***Perf. 13¼x13***

632 V151	Sheet of 6 *(28,000)*+	12.50	12.50
a.-f.	80c Any single	2.00	2.00
	First day cover, #632		15.50

Migration — V152

Printed by Lowe-Martin Group, Canada. Panes of 20. Designed by Chris Gash, U.S.

2019, Mar.15 **Litho.** ***Perf. 13¼x13***

633 V152	€1.80 **multicolored** *(170,000)*+	4.75	4.75
	First day cover		6.50
	Inscription block of 4	19.00	—
	Pane of 20	95.00	—

Endangered Species Type of 2019

Printed by Johann Enschedé Stamps Security Printers, the Netherlands. Designed by Rongliang Wang, People's Republic of China.

Designs: No. 634, Anguilla anguilla. No. 635, Dermochelys coriacea. No. 636, Acropora spp. No. 637, Huso huso.

2019, Apr. 26 **Litho.** ***Perf. 12¾x12½***

634 A534	90c **multicolored** *(60,000)*+	2.25	2.25
635 A534	90c **multicolored** *(60,000)*+	2.25	2.25
636 A534	90c **multicolored** *(60,000)*+	2.25	2.25
637 A534	90c **multicolored** *(60,000)*+	2.25	2.25
a.	Block of 4, #634-637	9.25	9.25
	First day cover, #637a		11.00
	First day cover, #634-637, each		4.25
	Inscription block of 4, #637a	9.25	—
	Pane of 16	37.00	—
	Nos. 634-637 (4)	9.00	9.00

Souvenir Sheet

Long-horned Bee and Scutellaria Lateriflora — V153

Printed by Lowe-Martin Group, Canada. Designed by Rorie Katz, U.S.

2019, May 20 **Litho. With Foil Application** ***Perf. 13***

638 V153	€2.70 **multicolored** *(21,000)*+	7.00	7.00
	First day cover		9.75

World Bee Day.

V154

V155

V156

V157

International Labor Organization, Cent. — V158

Printed by Johann Enschedé Stamps BV, Netherlands. Sheets of 20. Designed by Owen Smith, U.S.

2019, June 28 **Litho.** ***Perf. 13½x14***

639	V154 80c **multicolored** *(80,000)*+	2.00	2.00
640	V155 80c **multicolored** *(80,000)*+	2.00	2.00
641	V156 80c **multicolored** *(80,000)*+	2.00	2.00
642	V157 80c **multicolored** *(80,000)*+	2.00	2.00
643	V158 80c **multicolored** *(80,000)*+	2.00	2.00
a.	Horiz. strip of 5, #639-643	10.00	10.00
	First day cover, #643a		12.00
	Inscription block of 10	20.00	—
	Pane of 20	40.00	—
	Nos. 639-643 (5)	10.00	10.00

V159

V160

V161

V162

United Nations Postal Administration in Vienna, 40th Anniv. V163

2019, Aug. 23 **Litho.** ***Perf. 14¾***

644	V159 90c **multicolored** + label	3.00	3.00
645	V160 90c **multicolored** + label	3.00	3.00
646	V161 90c **multicolored** + label	3.00	3.00
647	V162 90c **multicolored** + label	3.00	3.00
648	V163 90c **multicolored** + label	3.00	3.00
a.	Vert. strip of 5, #644-648, + 5 labels	15.00	15.00
	Sheet, 2 #648a	30.00	—
	Nos. 644-648 (5)	15.00	15.00

The full sheets sold for $14.94 or €15.33. The generic labels are shown. Labels could be personalized. The personalization of labels was available only at UN Headquarters, and not through mail order.

Climate Change Type of 2019

Printed by Cartor Security Printing, France. Panes of 20. Designed by Sergio Baradat, U.S.

Designs: 80c, Canyon and mining operation. 90c, Clouds and smokestack.

€1.80, Fish and corals.

2019, Sept. 23 **Litho.** ***Perf. 14¼***

649	A543 80c **multicolored** *(70,000)*+	2.00	2.00
	First day cover		3.75
	Inscription block of 4	8.00	—
	Pane of 20	40.00	—
650	A543 90c **multicolored** *(70,000)*+	2.25	2.25
	First day cover		4.25
	First day cover, #649-650		6.00
	Inscription block of 4	9.00	—
	Pane of 20	45.00	—

Souvenir Sheet

Perf.

651 A543 €1.80 **multicolored** *(15,000)+* 4.50 4.50
First day cover 4.50

2019 United Nations Climate Change Conference, Madrid. No. 651 contains one 47mm diameter stamp.

World Heritage Sites in Cuba Type of 2019

Printed by Cartor Security Printing, France. Panes of 20. Designed by Sergio Baradat, U.S.

Designs: Nos. 652, 654c, Camagüey. Nos. 653, 654f, San Pedro de la Rosa Castle. No. 654a, Morro Castle. No. 654b, Trinidad. No. 654d, Vinales Valley. No. 654e, Cienfuegos.

2019, Oct. 24 Litho. With Foil Application *Perf. 14¼*

652 A545 90c **multicolored** *(70,000)+* 2.25 2.25
First day cover 3.50
Inscription block of 4 9.00 —
Pane of 20 45.00 —
653 A545 €1.80 **multicolored** *(70,000)+* 4.50 4.50
First day cover 7.00
First day cover, #652-653 8.50
Inscription block of 4 18.00 —
Pane of 20 90.00 —

Souvenir Booklet

654 Booklet, #654g-654l *(10,000)+* 25.00
a.-c. A545 35c Any single .95 .95
d.-f. A545 40c Any single 1.10 1.10
g. Booklet pane of 4 #654a 3.80 —
h. Booklet pane of 4 #654b 3.80 —
i. Booklet pane of 4 #654c 3.80 —
j. Booklet pane of 4 #654d 4.40 —
k. Booklet pane of 4 #654e 4.40 —
l. Booklet pane of 4 #654f 4.40 —

Complete booklet sold for $12.27.

Endangered Species Type of 2020

Printed by Johann Enschedé Stamps Security Printers, the Netherlands. Designed by Rorie Katz, U.S.

Designs: No. 655, Panthera leo. No. 656, Pelecanus crispus. No. 657, Phocoena phocoena. No. 658, Equus africanus.

2020, Feb. 17 Litho. *Perf. 12¾x12½*

655 A546 90c **multicolored** *(58,000)+* 2.25 2.25
656 A546 90c **multicolored** *(58,000)+* 2.25 2.25
657 A546 90c **multicolored** *(58,000)+* 2.25 2.25
658 A546 90c **multicolored** *(58,000)+* 2.25 2.25
a. Block of 4, #655-658 9.00 9.00
First day cover, #658a 11.00
First day cover, #655-658, each 4.00
Inscription block of 4, #658a 9.00 —
Pane of 16 36.00 —
Nos. 655-658 (4) 9.00 9.00

Blank Stamp On Which Stickers Can Be Applied — V164

Printed by Cartor Security Printing (No. 659) and La Poste (Nos. 659a, 659b), France. Designed by Rorie Katz, U.S.

2020, Mar. 19 Litho. *Die Cut*

Self-Adhesive

659 V164 €1.80 **multicolored,** with rounded corners, *(52,000)+* 4.50 4.50
a. With perpendicular corners and black frame line 4.50 4.50
b. Booklet pane of 6 #659a *(5,000)+* 27.00
First day cover, #659 6.25

No. 659 was issued as a souvenir sheet having two different sheet margins, each with different stickers. No. 659a was issued in a booklet containing six panes of one stamp, with each pane having different margins and stickers. Each booklet pane contained one sticker depicting Hello Kitty, a color wheel with Hello Kitty at the center, one of six different Sustainable Development Goal emblems, along with a variety of other stickers. The two souvenir sheets had the same sheet margin and stickers found on two of the panes of No. 659b. No. 659b was sold folded, without any means of separation between the individual panes.

Lepidopterist, Artwork by Paul Villinski — V165

Ruth, Costume by Nicole Dextras — V166

Printed by La Poste, France. Panes of 10. Designed by Rorie Katz, U.S.

2020, Apr. 22 Litho. *Perf. 13¼*

660 V165 85c **multicolored** *(100,000)+* 2.10 2.10
First day cover 3.50
Inscription block of 4 8.40 —
Pane of 10 21.00 —
661 V166 €1.35 **multicolored** *(100,000)+* 3.50 3.50
First day cover 5.50
First day cover, #660-661 7.25
Inscription block of 4 14.00 —
Pane of 10 35.00 —

Earth Day, 50th anniv. Because of the COVID-19 pandemic, Nos. 660-661 were not available for sale on day of issue stated on the first-day covers as they had not yet been printed and delivered.

Florence Nightingale (1820-1910), Nurse — V167

Printed by Johann Enschedé Stamps Security Printers, the Netherlands. Panes of 20. Designed by Rorie Katz, U.S.

2020, May 12 **Litho.** ***Perf. 14***

662 V167 €1.35 **multicolored** *(240,000)+*	3.50	3.50
First day cover		5.25
Inscription block of 4	14.00	—
Pane of 20	70.00	—

International Year of the Nurse and the Midwife.

World Heritage Sites in Russia Type of 2020

Printed by Cartor Security Printing, France. Panes of 20. Designed by Sergio Baradat, U.S.

Designs: Nos. 663, 665c, Novodevichy Convent. Nos. 664, 665f, Kizhi Pogost. No. 665a, Lake Baikal. No. 665b, Kazan Kremlin. No. 665d, Kremlin and Red Square, Moscow. No. 665e, Saint Petersburg.

2020, Sept. 11 **Litho.** ***Perf. 14½x14¼***

663 A556 €1 **multicolored** *(70,000)+*	2.60	2.60
First day cover		4.00
Inscription block of 4	10.40	—
Pane of 20	52.00	—
664 A556 €1.80 **multicolored** *(70,000)+*	4.75	4.75
First day cover		7.00
First day cover, #663-664		9.00
Inscription block of 4	19.00	—
Pane of 20	95.00	—

Souvenir Booklet

665 Booklet, #665g-665l *(9,000)+*	27.00	
a.-c. A556 35c any single	1.00	1.00
d.-f. A556 40c any single	1.25	1.25
g. Booklet pane of 4 #665a	4.00	—
h. Booklet pane of 4 #665b	4.00	—
i. Booklet pane of 4 #665c	4.00	—
j. Booklet pane of 4 #665d	5.00	—
k. Booklet pane of 4 #665e	5.00	—
l. Booklet pane of 4 #665f	5.00	—

Complete booklet sold for $12.94 or €10.

United Nations Emblem — V168

2020, Oct. 2 **Litho.** ***Perf. 14¾***

666 V168 €1 **multicolored** + label	*3.25*	*3.25*
Sheet of 10 + 10 labels	*33.50*	—

The full sheet sold for $16.70 or €12.90. One of the ten different generic labels is shown. Labels could be personalized. The personalization of labels was available only at UN Headquarters, and not through mail order.

Souvenir Sheet

United Nations, 75th Anniv. — V169

Printed by La Poste. France. Designed by Matt Willey/Pentagram, U.S.

No. 667: a, Red "U," blue "N." b, Pink "7," green "5."

2020, Oct. 24 **Litho.** ***Perf. 13¼***

667 V169 Sheet of 2 *(35,000)+*	9.50	9.50
a.-b. €1.80 Either single	4.75	4.75
First day cover, #667		13.00

Souvenir Sheet

Vienna International Center and Emblem — V170

Printed by Royal Johann Enschedé, Netherlands. Designed by Sergio Baradat, U.S.

Litho. With Foil Application

2020, Nov. 24 ***Die Cut Perf. 11½***

Self-Adhesive

668 V170 €7 **multicolored** *(30,000)+*	18.50	18.50
First day cover		20.00

Crypto stamp. Unused value is for sheets with unscratched panels at right.

International Day for the Elimination of Racial Discrimination — V171

Printed by Cartor Security Printing, France. Panes of 10. Designed by Rorie Katz, U.S.

2021, Mar. 19 **Litho.** ***Perf. 13¼x13***

669 V171 €1.80 **multicolored** *(100,000)*+	5.00	5.00
First day cover		6.75
Inscription block of 4	20.00	—
Sheet of 10	50.00	—

Endangered Species Type of 2021

Printed by Johann Enschedé Stamps Security Printers, the Netherlands. Designed by Rorie Katz, U.S.

Designs: No. 670, Neophema chrysogaster. No. 671, Babyrousa babyrussa. No. 672, Onychogalea fraenata. No. 673, Lepanthes telipogoniflora.

2021, Apr. 7 **Litho.** ***Perf. 12¾x12½***

670 A565 90c **multicolored** *(50,000)*+	2.50	2,50
671 A565 90c **multicolored** *(50,000)*+	2.50	2.50
672 A565 90c **multicolored** *(50,000)*+	2.50	2.50
673 A565 90c **multicolored** *(50,000)*+	2.50	2,50
a. Block of 4, #670-673	10.00	10.00
First day cover, #673a		11.50
First day cover, #670-673, each		4.25
Inscription block of 4, #673a	10.00	—
Pane of 16	40.00	—
Nos. 670-673 (4)	10.00	5.50

Rider on Orange Horse — V172

Rider on Brown Horse — V173

Rider on White Horse — V174

Golfer Contemplating Putt — V175

Golfer and Ball on Hill — V176

Female Golfer — V177

Doves and Olympic Flame — V178

Printed by Royal Johann Enschedé, Netherlands. Sheets of 8. Designed by Satoshi Hashimoto, Japan.

2021, July 23 **Litho.** ***Perf. 13½***

674 V172 85c **multicolored** *(112,000)*+ 2.25 2.25
675 V173 85c **multicolored** *(56,000)*+ 2.25 2.25
676 V174 85c **multicolored** *(56,000)*+ 2.25 2.25
a. Horiz. strip of 3, #674-676 6.75 6.75
First day cover, strip of 4, #676a, 674 11.00
First day cover, pane of 8, 4 #674, 2 each #675-676 21.50
Pane of 8, 4 #674 2 each #675-676 18.00 —
677 V175 €1 **multicolored** *(112,000)*+ 2.75 2.75
678 V176 €1 **multicolored** *(56,000)*+ 2.75 2.75
679 V177 €1 **multicolored** *(56000)*+ 2.75 2.75
a. Horiz. strip of 3, #677-679 8.25 8.25
First day cover, strip of 4, #679a, 677 13.00
First day cover, pane of 8, 4 #677, 2 each #678-679 25.00
Pane of 8, 4 #677, 2 each #678-679 22.00 —
Nos. 674-679 (6) 15.00 15.00

Souvenir Sheet

680 V178 €1.80 **multicolored** *(26,000)*+ 5.00 5.00
First day cover 6.75

Sports for Peace, 2020 Summer Olympics, Tokyo. The 2020 Summer Olympics were postponed until 2021 because of the COVID-19 pandemic.

Waterways, Railways and Bridges World Heritage Sites Type of 2020

Printed by Cartor Security Printing, France. Panes of 20. Designed by Sergio Baradat, U.S.

Designs: Nos. 681, 683c, Forth Bridge, Scotland. Nos. 682, 683f, Old Bridge, Mostar, Bosnia and Herzegovina. No. 683a, Rideau Canal, Canada. No. 683b, Rhaetian Railway, Switzerland and Italy. No. 683d, Grand Canal, People's Republic of China. No. 683e, Darjeeling Himalayan Railway, India.

2021, Aug. 25 **Litho.** ***Perf. 14¼***

681 A575 €1 **multicolored** *(70,000)*+ 2.75 2.75
First day cover 4.00
Inscription block of 4 11.00 —
Pane of 20 55.00 —
682 A575 €1.80 **multicolored** *(70,000)*+ 5.00 5.00
First day cover 7.25
First day cover, #681-682 9.50
Inscription block of 4 20.00 —
Pane of 20 100.00 —

Souvenir Booklet

683 Booklet, #683g-683l *(6,700)*+ 27.00
a.-c. A575 35c any single 1.00 1.00
d.-f. A575 40c any single 1.25 1.25
g. Booklet pane of 4 #683a 4.00 —
h. Booklet pane of 4 #683b 4.00 —
i. Booklet pane of 4 #683c 4.00 —
j. Booklet pane of 4 #683d 5.00 —
k. Booklet pane of 4 #683e 5.00 —
l. Booklet pane of 4 #683f 5.00 —

Complete booklet sold for $12.94 or €10.

Miniature Sheet

Comprehensive Nuclear Test Ban Treaty, 25th Anniv. — V179

No. 684: a, Hydroacoustic Station HA4, Crozet Islands, and penguins. b, Hydroacoustic Station HA3, Chile, with red sphere. c, Radionuclide Station RN68, Tristan da Cunha, in fenced enclosure. d, Radionuclide Station RN33, Germany, with green base. e, Large group of technicians at Infrasound Station IS33, Madagascar. f, Two technicians near antenna at Infrasound Station IS55, Antarctica. g, Two technicians at Auxiliary Seismic Station AS74, Oman. h, Vehicle and technician at Auxiliary Seismic Station AS69, New Zealand. i, Technician in protective clothing carrying equipment for field exercise, Kazakhstan. j, Technician for field exercise in aircraft above Jordan.

2021, Aug. 27 **Litho.** ***Perf. 14½***

684 V179 Sheet of 10 + 10 labels *24.00 24.00*
a.-j. €1 Any single + label *2.40 2.40*

The full sheet sold for $12.00 or €12.90. The generic labels are shown. Labels could be personalized.

Miniature Sheet

Celebrations — V180

No. 685: a, Birthday cake. b, Flower bouquet. c, Three balloons. d, Menorah. e, Heart and arrow. f, Christmas tree and ornament. g, "Danke." h, Champagne flutes. i, Diamond ring. j, Mosque.

2021, Nov. 4 **Litho.** ***Perf. 14½x14¼***

685 V180 Sheet of 10 *34.00 34.00*
a.-j. €1 Any single + label *3.25 3.25*

The full sheet sold for $16.93. The generic labels are shown. Labels could be personalized. The personalization of labels was available only at UN Headquarters, and not through mail order.

World Toilet Day — V181

Printed by Cartor Security Printing, France. Panes of 20. Designed by Gail Armstrong, U.K.

2021, Nov. 19 **Litho.** ***Perf. 14¼***

686 V181 €1 **multicolored** *(100,000)*+ 2.75 2.75
First day cover 4.50
Inscription block of 4 11.00 —
Pane of 20 55.00 —

Curler Delivering Stone — V182

Curling Stones and Brooms V183

Skier in Air V184

Skier On Snow V185

Printed by Cartor Security Printing, France. Panes of 6.

2022, Jan. 14	**Litho.**	***Perf. 14¼***	
687 V182	85c **multicolored** *(145,950)+*	2.10	2.10
688 V183	85c **multicolored** *(145,950)+*	2.10	2.10
a.	Horiz. pair, #687-688	4.25	4.25
	First day cover, #687-688		6.00
	Inscription block of 4	8.50	—
	Pane of 6	13.00	—
689 V184	€1.80 **multicolored** *(145,650)+*	4.50	4.50
690 V185	€1.80 **multicolored** *(145,650)+*	4.50	4.50
a.	Horiz. pair, #689-690	9.00	9.00
	First day cover, #689-690		13.00
	Inscription block of 4	18.00	—
	Pane of 6	27.00	—
	Nos. 687-690 (4)	13.20	13.20

Sports for Peace, 2022 Winter Olympics, Beijing.

Endangered Species Type of 2022

Printed by Johann Enschedé Stamps Security Printers, the Netherlands. Designed by Sergio Baradat, U.S.

Designs: No. 691, Dynastes satanas. No. 692, Hylocereus triangularis. No. 693, Cedrela odorata. No. 694, Acanthocereus tetragonus.

2022, Mar. 18	**Litho.**	***Perf. 12¾x12½***	
691 A592	€1 **multicolored** *(44,000)+*	2.50	2.50
692 A592	€1 **multicolored** *(44,000)+*	2.50	2.50
693 A592	€1 **multicolored** *(44,000)+*	2.50	2.50
694 A592	€1 **multicolored** *(44,000)+*	2.50	2.50
a.	Block of 4, #691-694	10.00	10.00
	First day cover, #694a		13.00
	First day cover, #691-694, each		5.25
	Inscription block of 4, #694a	10.00	—
	Pane of 16	40.00	—
	Nos. 691-694 (4)	10.00	10.00

SEMI-POSTAL STAMP

AIDS Awareness Semi-postal Type

Souvenir Sheet

2002, Oct. 24	**Litho.**	***Perf. 14½***	
B1 SP1	51c + 25c **multicolored** *(220,000)+*	3.50	3.50
	First day cover, #B1		3.50

VSP1

Photograph of John Lennon (1940-80), by David Nutter — VSP2

Printed by Cartor Security Printing, France. Panes of 20. Designed by Rorie Katz, U.S.

2021, Sept. 21	**Litho.**	***Perf. 14¼***	
B2 VSP1	€1 +50c **multicolored** *(150,000)+*	4.00	4.00
	First day cover		5.75
	Inscription block of 4	16.00	—
	Sheet of 20	80.00	—

Souvenir Sheet
Litho. With Foil Application

B3 VSP2 €2.85 +€1 **multicolored** *(20,000)+* 10.50 10.50
First day cover 12.00

International Day of Peace. Surtax for United Nations peacekeeping efforts.

ENVELOPES

Used values for all postal stationery are for non-philatelic contemporaneous usages.

Donaupark, Vienna — VU1

Printed by Mercury-Walch Pty. Ltd. (Australia). Designed by Hannes Margreiter (Austria).

Design: 7s, Landscape. Design at lower left shows Vienna landmarks (6s), river scene (7s).

1995, Feb. 3 **Litho.**

U1 VU1 6s **multicolored,** entire *(128,000)+* 2.00 2.00
First day cancel *(14,132)* 2.75
U2 VU1 7s **multicolored,** entire *(128,000)+* 2.00 2.00
First day cancel *(9,684)* 3.50

VU2

Printed by Mercury-Walch Pty. Ltd. (Australia).

1998, Mar. 13 **Litho.**

U3 VU2 13s **multicolored,** entire *(87,000)+* 3.50 3.00
Entire, first day cancel 3.50

VU3

Vienna International Center — VU4

Printed by Australia Post Sprintpak (Australia). Designed by Robert Stein (US).

2002, June 27 **Litho.**

U4 VU3 51c **multicolored,** entire *(93,000)+* 2.00 2.00
Entire, first day cancel 2.00
U5 VU4 €1.09 **multicolored,** entire *(88,000)+* 2.60 2.60
Entire, first day cancel 3.25

Nos. U4-U5 Surcharged

2003, June 2 **Litho.**

U6 VU3 51c +4c **multicolored,** entire 4.00 *6.00*
Entire, first day cancel 3.75
U7 VU4 €1.09 +16c **multicolored,** entire 5.25 *8.00*
Entire, first day cancel 4.75

UN Flag — VU5

Dove With Olive Branch — VU6

Printed by Government Printing Office, Austria. Designed by Rorie Katz, US.

2004, June 3 **Litho.**

U8 VU5 55c **multicolored,** entire *(53,000)+* 2.25 1.75
Entire, first day cancel 2.50
U9 VU6 €1.25 **multicolored,** entire *(48,000)+* 4.00 2.75
Entire, first day cancel 4.00

Nos. U8-U9 Surcharged Like No. U6

2007, Sept. 3 **Litho.**

U10 VU5 55c +10c **multicolored,** entire 3.25 *4.00*
Entire, first day cancel 3.75
U11 VU6 €1.25 +15c **multicolored,** entire 5.00 *6.00*
Entire, first day cancel 5.00

Vienna International Center VU7

Vienna International Center — VU8

Designed by Rorie Katz, US.

2009, May 7 **Litho.**

U12 VU7 65c **multicolored,** entire 3.25 3.25
Entire, first day cancel 3.00
U13 VU8 €1.40 **multicolored,** entire 5.00 5.00
Entire, first day cancel 5.00

Nos. U12-U13 Surcharged Like No. U6

2011, May 5 **Litho.**

U14 VU7 65c +5c **multicolored,** entire 3.50 *4.00*
Entire, first day cancel 4.50
U15 VU8 €1.40 +30c **multicolored,** entire 6.50 *8.00*
Entire, first day cancel 7.50

Surcharges on Nos. U14-U15 are vertical, reading up.

United Nations Emblem — VU9

Printed by Lowe-Martin Group, Canada. Designed by Sergio Baradat, U.S.

2015, May 7 **Litho.**

U16 VU9 68c **dull orange,** entire *(9,000)+* 3.00 3.00
Entire, first day cancel 3.00
U17 VU9 80c **yellow green,** entire *(9,000)+* 3.25 3.25
Entire, first day cancel 3.25
U18 VU9 €1.70 **lilac,** entire *(9,000)+* 5.50 5.50
Entire, first day cancel 5.50
Nos. U16-U18 (3) 11.75 11.75

Vienna International Center — VU10

Printed by Goessler, Austria. Designed by Adolf Tuma, Austria.

2016, July 20 **Litho.**

U19 VU10 68c **multicolored** *(8,000)+* 3.50 3.50
First day cancel 4.50

Vienna International Center VU11

Designed by Kurt Regschek, Austria.

2019, Aug. 24 **Litho.**

U20 VU11 90c **multicolored** *(10,000)+* 3.75 3.75
First day cancel 3.75

AIR LETTER SHEETS

VLS1

Printed by Joh. Enschede and Sons. Designed by Ingrid Ousland.

1982, Apr. 28 **Litho.**

UC1 VLS1 9s **multi,** *light green,* entire *(650,000)* 1.50 1.50
First day cancel *(120,650)* 1.50

No. UC1 Surcharged in Lake

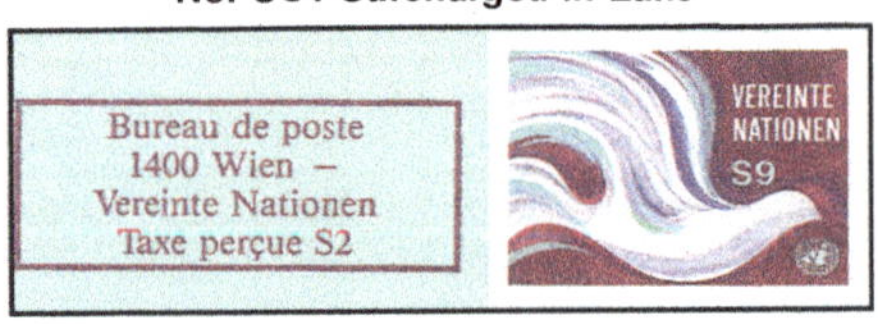

1986, Feb. 3 **Litho.**

UC2 VLS1 9s +2s **multi,** *light green,* entire *(131,190)* 45.00 *75.00*
First day cancel *(18,500)* 10.00

Birds in Flight, UN Emblem — VLS2

Printed by Mercury-Walch, Australia. Designed by Mieczyslaw Wasiliewski, Poland.

1987, Jan. 30 **Litho.**

UC3 VLS2 11s **bright blue,** entire *(414,000)* 2.00 2.00
First day cancel *(48,348)* 4.00

No. UC3 Surcharged

1992, Jan. 1 **Litho.**

UC4 VLS2 11s +1s **bright blue,** entire *(80,000)* 45.00 *75.00*
First day cancel 30.00

Donaupark, Vienna — VLS3

Designed by Rocco J. Callari. Printed by Mercury-Walch, Australia.

1992, Sept. 4 **Litho.**

UC5 VLS3 12s **multicolored,** entire *(200,000)*+ 6.50 6.50
First day cancel *(16,261)* 27.50

POSTAL CARDS

Olive Branch — VPC1

Bird Carrying Olive Branch — VPC2

Printed by Courvoisier. Designed by Rolf Christianson (3s), M.A. Munnawar (5s).

1982, Apr. 28 **Photo.**

UX1 VPC1 3s **multicolored,** *cream (500,000)* .80 .90
First day cancel *(93,010)* 1.65
UX2 VPC2 5s **multicolored** *(500,000)* .75 1.00
First day cancel *(89,502)* 1.65

Emblem of the United Nations — VPC3

Printed by Johann Enschede en Zonen, Netherlands. Designed by George Hamori, Australia.

1985, May 10 **Litho.**

UX3 VPC3 4s **multicolored** *(350,000)* 1.50 3.50
First day cancel *(53,450)* 3.00

No. UX2 Surcharged

1992, Jan. 1 **Photo.**

UX4 VPC2 5s +1s **multicolored** *(71,700)* 25.00 *30.00*
First day cancel 25.00

Type of 1990

Printed by Mercury-Walch, Australia.

1992, Sept. 4 **Litho.**

UX5 V22 6s **multicolored** *(445,000)*+ 1.75 2.75
First day cancel *(16,359)* 10.00

See No. UX9.

Type of 1985

Printed by Leigh Mardon Pty. Limited, Australia.

1993, May 7 **Litho.**

UX6 A222 5s **multicolored** *(450,000)* 19.00 19.00
First day cancel 10.00

Donaupark, Vienna — VPC4

Printed by Leigh Mardon Pty. Limited, Australia.

1993, May 7 **Litho.**
UX7 VPC4 6s **multicolored** *(450,000)+* 4.00 4.00
First day cancel 6.00

See No. UX10.

No. UX6 with design of Vienna No.1 Added

1994, Jan. 1 **Litho.**
UX8 A222+G8 5s +50g **multi** *(350,000)+* 2.50 *5.00*
First day cancel 4.00

No. UX5 with design of Vienna #167 Added

1997, July 1 **Litho.**
UX9 V22+V32 6s +50g **multi** 2.50 *3.00*
First day cancel 3.50

No. UX7 with design of Vienna #194 Added

UX10 VPC4+V35 6s +1s **multi** 3.00 *4.00*
First day cancel 4.00

VPC5

Designed by Günter Leidenfrost.

1998, May 20 **Litho.**
UX11 VPC5 6.50s **multicolored** *(137,000)+* 1.50 1.50
First day cancel 2.00

The Gloriette — VPC6

1999, Feb. 5 **Litho.**
UX12 VPC6 7s **multicolored** *(136,000)+* 2.00 2.00
First day cancel 2.50

Type of 1983

2000, June 2 **Litho.**
UX13 V7 7s **multicolored** 2.25 2.25
First day cancel 2.25

Clock Tower, Graz, Austria — VPC7

Printed by Johann Enschedé and Sons, the Netherlands. Designed by Robert Stein, US.

2002, Mar. 1 **Litho.**
UX14 VPC7 51c **multicolored** *(83,000)+* 1.50 1.50
First day cancel 1.50

No. UX14 Surcharged

2003, June 2 **Litho.**
UX15 VPC7 51c +4c **multicolored** 2.75 *4.00*
First day cancel 2.75

Vienna International Center — VPC8

Printed by Government Printing Office, Austria. Designed by Rorie Katz, US.

2004, June 3 **Litho.**

UX16 VPC8 55c **multicolored** *(63,000)+* 2.60 1.25
First day cancel 3.00

No. UX16 Surcharged Like No. UX15

2007, Sept. 3 **Litho.**

UX17 VPC8 55c +10c **multicolored,** entire 3.75 *5.00*
Entire, first day cancel 4.00

Vienna International Center — VPC9

2009, May 7 **Litho.**

UX18 VPC9 65c **multicolored** 3.50 3.50
First day cancel 3.50

Vienna International Center and Flagpoles — VPC10

Designs: 70c, Fish-eye view of Vienna International Center and flagpole. €1.70, Vienna International Center at night.

2011, May 5 **Litho.**

UX19 VPC10 62c **multicolored** 3.75 3.75
First day cancel 3.75
UX20 VPC10 70c **multicolored** 4.25 4.25
First day cancel 4.50
UX21 VPC10 €1.70 **multicolored** 8.00 8.00
First day cancel 8.00
Nos. UX19-UX21 (3) 13.25 13.25

Dove and Vienna International Center — VPC11

Vienna International Center — VPC12

Woman Free, Sculpture by Edwina Sandys — VPC13

Printed by Lowe-Martin Group, Canada. Designed by Sergio Baradat, U.S.

2015, May 7 **Litho.**

UX22 VPC11 68c **multicolored** *(11,000)+* 3.00 3.00
First day cancel 3.00
UX23 VPC12 80c **multicolored** *(11,000)+* 3.25 3.25
First day cancel 3.25
UX24 VPC13 €1.70 **multicolored** *(11,000)+* 5.50 5.50
First day cancel 5.50
Nos. UX22-UX24 (3) 11.75 11.75

Nos. UX22, UX24 Surcharged With Vertical Surcharge Similar to No. UX15

2018, Aug. 23 **Litho.**

UX25 VPC11 68c+22c **multicolored,** entire (#UX22) 3.75 *3.75*
Entire, first day cancel 3.75
UX26 VPC13 €1.70+10c **multicolored,** entire (#UX24) 6.25 *6.25*
Entire, first day cancel 6.25

U.N. SOUVENIR CARDS

No. 39

These cards were issued by the United Nations Postal Administration and were not valid for postage.

Each card bears reproductions of UN stamps and a statement by the Secretary-General in English.

Values are for mint cards without cancels.

SC1	World Health Day, Apr. 7, 1972. Card of 5: #43, 102, 156, 207, 228.	.65

A second printing shows several minor differences.

SC2	Art on UN Stamps, Nov. 17, 1972. Card of 11: #170, 171, 173, 174, 180, 183, 201, 202, 203, 224, 232. #201, 202 form a simulated se-tenant pair	.45
SC3	Disarmament Decade, Mar. 9, 1973. Card of 5: #133, 147, 177, 227, 234	.50
SC4	Declaration of Human Rights, 25th Anniversary, Nov. 16, 1973. Card of 10: #13, 22, 29, 39, 47, 58, 68, 121, 190, 242	.75
SC5	UPU centenary, Mar. 22, 1974. Card of 7: #17, 18, 219, 246; Geneva 18, 39, 40.	.75
SC6	World Population Year, Oct. 18, 1974. Card of 7: #151, 152, 153, 252, 253; Geneva 43, 44.	2.50
SC7	Peaceful Uses of Outer Space, Mar. 14, 1975. Card of 6: #112, 113, 256, 257; Geneva 46, 47.	2.00
SC8	UN Peace Keeping Operations, Nov. 21, 1975. Card of 9: #52, 111, 118, 139, 160, 265, 266; Geneva 55, 56.	2.00
SC9	World Federation of United Nations Associations, Mar. 12, 1976. Card of 5: #154, 155, 272, 273; Geneva 57.	2.00
SC10	World Food Council, Nov. 19, 1976. Card of 6: #116, 117, 218, 280; Geneva 17, 63.	2.50
SC11	World Intellectual Property Organization (WIPO), Mar. 11, 1977. Card of 15: #17, 23, 25, 31, 33, 41, 43, 49, 59, 86, 90, 123, 281, 282; Geneva 64.	2.50
SC12	Combat Racism, Sept. 19, 1977. Card of 8: #220, 221, 287, 288; Geneva 19, 20, 69, 70.	2.50
SC13	Namibia, May 5, 1978. Card of 10: #240, 241, 263, 264, 296, 297; Geneva 34, 53, 54, 76.	1.00
SC14	Intl. Civil Aviation Organization, June 12, 1978. Card of 6: #31, 32, 298, 299; Geneva 77, 78.	2.50
SC15	Intl. Year of the Child, May 4, 1979. Card of 9: #5, 97, 161, 162, 163, 310, 311; Geneva 84, 85.	.75
SC16	Intl. Court of Justice, Nov. 9, 1979. Card of 6: #88, 89, 314, 315; Geneva 87, 88.	.75
SC17	UN Decade for Women, Mar. 7, 1980. Card of 4: #258, 318; Geneva 90; Vienna 9.	7.50
SC18	Economic and Social Council, Nov. 7, 1980. Card of 8; #65, 66, 341, 342; Geneva 96, 97; Vienna 15, 16.	.75
SC19	Intl. Year of Disabled Persons, Mar. 6, 1981. Card of 6; #344, 345; Geneva 99, 100; Vienna 18, 19.	.65
SC20	New and Renewable Sources of Energy, May 29, 1981. Card of 4; #348, 349; Geneva 102; Vienna 21.	1.00
SC21	Human Environment, Mar. 19, 1982. Card of 5: #230, 371; Geneva 26, 107; Vienna 25	.75
SC22	Exploration and Peaceful Uses of Outer Space, June 11, 1982. Card of 7: #112, 256, 373; Geneva 46, 109, 110; Vienna 27.	1.40
SC23	Safety at Sea, Mar. 18, 1983. Card of 8: #123, 124, 394, 395; Geneva 114, 115; Vienna 31, 32.	1.10
SC24	Trade and Development, June 6, 1983. Card of 11: #129, 130, 274, 275, 397, 398; Geneva 58, 117, 118; Vienna 31, 32.	1.50
SC25	Intl. Conference on Population, Feb. 3, 1984. Card of 10: #151, 153, 252, 253, 417, 418; Geneva 43, 44, 121; Vienna 39.	2.00
SC26	Intl. Youth Year, Nov. 15, 1984. Card of 5: #441, 442; Geneva 128; Vienna 46, 47.	3.00
SC27	ILO Turin Center, Feb. 1, 1985. Card of 8: #25, 200, 244, 443; Geneva 37, 129, 130; Vienna 48.	2.75
SC28	Child Survival Campaign, Nov. 22, 1985. Card of 6: #466, 467; Geneva 138, 139; Vienna 55, 56.	3.00
SC29	Stamp Collecting, May 22, 1986. Card of 5: #278, 473; Geneva 61, 147; Vienna 63.	*8.25*

No. 29 with stitch marks has been removed from the Ameripex program. Value is one-half that of unstitched card.

SC30	Intl. Peace Year, June 20, 1986. Card of 6: #475, 476; Geneva 148, 149; Vienna 64, 65.	4.00
SC31	Shelter for the Homeless, Mar. 13, 1987. Card of 6: #495, 496; Geneva 154, 155; Vienna 68, 69.	2.50
SC32	Immunize Every Child, Nov. 20, 1987. Card of 13: #44, 103, 157, 208, 294, 517, 518; Vienna 76, 77.	3.00
SC33	Intl. Volunteer Day, May 6, 1988. Card of 10; #239, 367, 524, 525; Geneva 103, 167, 168; Vienna 23, 82, 83.	4.00
SC34	Health in Sports, June 17, 1988. Card of 6; #526, 527; Geneva 169, 170; Vienna 84, 85.	5.00
SC35	World Bank, Jan. 27, 1989. Card of 8; #86-87, 546-547; Geneva 173-174; Vienna 88-89.	5.00
SC36	World Weather Watch, Apr. 21, 1989. Card of 10; #49-50, 188-189, 550-551; Geneva 176-177; Vienna 91-92.	5.00
SC37	Fight AIDS Worldwide, Mar. 16, 1990. Card of 6, #573-574; Geneva 184-185; Vienna 99-100	6.50
SC38	Crime Prevention, Sept. 13, 1990. Card of 6; #580-581; Geneva 191-192; Vienna 106-107.	6.00
SC39	Economic Commission for Europe, Mar. 15, 1991. Card of 12; #584-587; Geneva 195-198; Vienna 110-113.	6.00
SC40	Rights of the Child, June 14, 1991. Card of 6; #593-594; Geneva 203-204; Vienna 117-118.	7.00
SC41	Mission to Planet Earth, Sept. 4, 1992, Card of 6, #609-610; Geneva 220-221; Vienna 133-134	14.00
SC42	Science and Technology for Development, Oct. 2, 1992, Card of 6, #611-612; Geneva 222-223; Vienna 135-136	15.00
SC43	Healthy Environment, May 7, 1993, Card of 6, #624-625; Geneva #232-233; Vienna #147-148	14.00
SC44	Peace, Sept. 21, 1993, Card of 12, #629-632; Geneva #236-239; Vienna #152-155	16.00

No. 44 exists overprinted in gold with Hong Kong '94 emblem.

SC45	Intl. Year of the Family, Feb. 4, 1994, Card of 6, #637-638; Geneva #244-245; Vienna #160-161	13.50
SC46	Population & Development, 1994, Card of 9, #151, 651-652; Geneva #43, 258-259; Vienna #39, 174-175	12.50
SC47	World Summit for Social Development, 1995, Card of 3, #656; Geneva #263; Vienna #179	10.50
SC48	Intl. Youth Year, 1995, Card of 9, #441, 661-662; Geneva #128, 268-269; Vienna #46, 184-185	14.00
SC49	WFUNA, 1996, Card of 3, #671; Geneva #277; Vienna #193	12.00
SC50	UNICEF, 1996, Card of 6, #688-689; Geneva #294-295; Vienna #210-211	9.00
SC51	Philately, 1997, Card of 6, #714-715; Geneva #312-313; Vienna #228-229	12.50
SC52	Peacekeeping, #737-738; Geneva #325-326; Vienna #242-243	9.00
SC53	Universal Declaration of Human Rights, #739-740; Geneva #327-328; Vienna #244-245	9.00
SC54	UPU, #767a; Geneva #346a; Vienna #263a	5.00
SC55	Respect for Refugees, #787; Geneva #365; Vienna #282	6.00
SC56	Intl. Volunteers Year, #793-794; Geneva #371-372; Vienna #288-289	4.00
SC57	Johannesburg Summit on Sustainable Development, #828-831; Geneva #396-399; Vienna #318-321	5.00
SC58	International Year of Freshwater, #846-8471; Geneva #411-412; Vienna #333-334	5.00
SC59	Japanese Peace Bell, 50th Anniv., #865; Geneva #425; Vienna #349	6.50
SC60	Nature's Wisdom, #885-886; Geneva #440-441; Vienna #364-365	5.00
SC61	Intl. Day of Families, #913-914, Geneva #457-458, Vienna #380-381	5.00
SC62	As #SC61, with Washington 2006 World Philatelic Exhibition emblem and text	*22.50*

No. SC62 was only sold canceled.

0000	Peaceful Visions, #932, Geneva #470-471, Vienna #398-399	6.50

A "souvenir card" depicting no stamps was released in 2008 with the "We Can End Poverty" set. It sold for $1.75. Value, $5.

2009

SC64	Economic and Social Council (ECOSOC), #992-993, Geneva #503-504, Vienna #450-451	7.50

2010

SC65	International Year of Biodiversity, #1017-1018, Geneva #517-518, Vienna #469-470	12.00

2011

SC66	AIDS Ribbon, #1028, Geneva #537, Vienna #498	5.50

2012

SC67	Rio + 20, #1048, Geneva #553, Vienna #515	7.50

2013

SC68	Works of Disabled Artists, #1072-1073, Geneva #570-571, Vienna #532-533	6.50

A "souvenir card" depicting no stamps was released in 2014 with the "International Year of Jazz" set. It sold for $1.75. Value, $5.

2016

SC69	Free and Equal, #1127-1128, Geneva #613-614, Vienna #579-580	4.25

A "souvenir card" depicting no stamps was issued in 2017 with the "World Environment Day" set. It sold for $2. Value, $4.

2019

SC70	International Labor Organization, Cent., vignette details from #1221-1223, Geneva #668-669, 671-672	4.00

A "souvenir card" depicting no stamps was released in 2020 with the "United Nations, 75th Anniversary" set. It sold for $2. Value, $4.

A "souvenir card" depicting no stamps was released in 2021 with the International Day for the Elimination of Racial Discrimination set. It sold for $2. Value, $4.

U.N. PROOFS

Proofs of United Nations stamps are known in four basic types: Die Proofs, Trial Color Proofs, Progressive Color Proofs, and Imperforate Plate Proofs on gummed stamp paper.

Die Proofs (PD suffix) for United Nations stamps show the design of the issued stamp. They are usually imperforate singles printed on stamp paper, that are either affixed to a backing paper that is a component of a printer's card, or affixed directly to a printer's card. These cards usually have a handstamp denoting the status of the proof (approved, approved with corrections, not approved, etc.). Many cards have signatures of UN Postal Administration officials. Cards with an "approved" handstamp and/or signature do not always contain proofs having the designs of the actual stamp produced for sale. As most proof cards have a handstamp, the listings mention specific handstamps only when it is critical to distinguishing items. Items not affixed to cards that are indistinguishable from imperforate singles of the issued stamps are not listed, even though they may have come from "stock sheet style" proof cards that have approval handstamps. Items affixed to art boards available to the general public are not considered to be proofs unless they are identified, usually by handstamps, that they are proofs. Die proofs of sheet layouts showing marginal inscriptions only exist, but are beyond the scope of these listings.

Trial Color Proofs (TC suffix) show the design of the stamp, but with one or more colors differing from that of the actual stamp. Items will be listed as trial color proofs when they differ significantly from the issued color. As evidenced by printer's identification numbers on some trial color proof cards, shades of individual items may differ slightly, but two similar yet discrete shades may fall under one color description. Trial colors can sometimes be found on cards with die proofs.

Progressive Color Proofs (PP suffix) are a set of color proofs containing the number of items stated in the listing. Values, therefore, are for the set of singles (unless otherwise mentioned in the description), not a single progressive color proof from that set. Numbers in parentheses represent the total number of complete sets that were created. Partial sets are not listed if complete sets are known.

Imperforate Plate Proofs (PI suffix) are usually found on gummed stamp paper. Any exceptions are noted in the listing description. Numbers in parentheses represent the total number of imperforate proof stamps created. Many items have inked fingerprints on the reverse as a security device. Values are for pairs unless otherwise stated. Many gutter pairs will have creases. Some gutter pairs will have marginal inscriptions. These are worth more.

Organization of listings Listings have all of the New York, Geneva and Vienna stamps and souvenir cards for any set all together. The first part of an item's catalogue number is the same catalogue number as shown in the listings for stamps and postal stationery. The prefix "G" is before the catalogue number for items from Geneva; prefix "V" for items from Vienna. Items with prefix "SC" are souvenir cards, and catalogue numbers without prefix are from New York. The suffix describing the type of proof follows the catalogue number. Die proofs (suffix PD) are the first proof category in the listings, and will be followed by the other categories in the same order as listed above. Each proof category will list New York items first, followed by Geneva items, Vienna items, and then souvenir cards.

Often cards of proofs will contain all of the items in an issued set. The catalogue numbers for cards that contain New York, Geneva and Vienna proofs are organized by the highest New York catalogue number of the various die proof items in the set. If there are no New York items in the card, then the numbering will be organized by the highest Geneva or Vienna catalogue number in the card of die proofs. Cards that contain both die proofs and trial color proofs are catalogued under the die proofs.

Numbers in parentheses represent the total number of items created. The number of items coming in part or in total from printer's archives are approximations. Listings for single proofs affixed to cards do not usually mention that they are affixed to a card. Cards containing more than one proof will have a minor letter following the PD suffix, and the listing will detail the component parts, as some cards may in the future be broken down by owners into individual proof items. Cutting up cards, however, may destroy their value, as listings are often based on the presence of the handstamp. Removing proofs from the card will lower their value, as it may then be impossible to distinguish them from imperforate singles.

No. 303PDa — A Typical Die Proof Card

No. U1TC in Black — A Typical Trial Color Proof

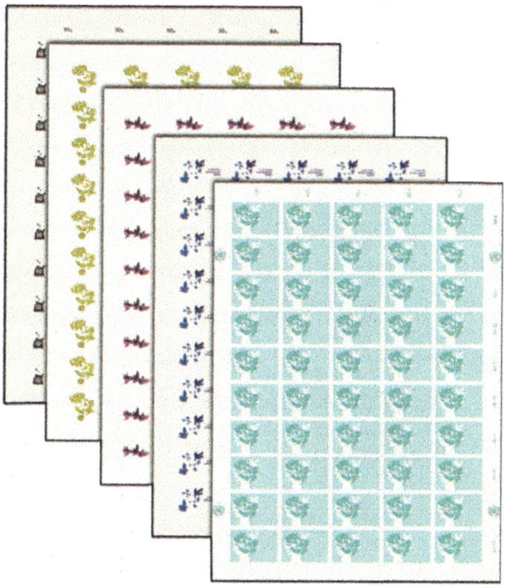

Sheets of 50 of No. V1PP — A Typical Progressive Proof Set

No. 1PI — A Typical Pair of Imperforate Plate Proofs

New York #1-11
Definitives

1951

1PD	(1)	600.
2PD	(3)	500.
3PD	(3)	450.
3PDa	Card, #3PD, 3TC blue violet (1)	575.
4PD	(1)	600.
5PD	(1)	575.
5PDa	Card, #5PD, 5TC dark blue violet	1,150.
6PD	(1)	600.
6PDa	Card, #1PD, 6PD (3)	3,100.
7PD	(1)	600.
8PD	(4)	300.
9PD	(1)	600.
9PDa	Card, #4PD, 7PD, 9PD, essays of #7, 9 (1)	1,850.
9PDb	Card, #9PD, 9TC green (1)	825.
10PD	(1)	500.
11PD	(4)	475.
2TC	indigo (1)	—
3TC	red violet (2)	
3TC	dark red (2)	350.
3TC	red orange (1)	450.
3TC	carmine (3)	—
3TC	orange red (3)	—
3TCa	Card, #3TC carmine, #3TC orange red (1)	700.
5TC	orange red (1)	750.
5TC	brown (1)	750.
5TC	bright blue (1)	—
5TC	light blue (1)	—
5TC	dark blue (1)	—
5TC	black (1)	—
5TC	red orange (1)	—
5TCa	Card, #5TC black, 5TC brown (1)	925.
10TC	black (1)	—
10TC	dark green (1)	—
10TCa	Card, #10TC blue green , #10TC yellow green (1)	—
11TC	dark red, 2 impressions side by side (1)	—
11TC	purple, 2 impressions side by side (1)	—
11TCa	dark blue (2 impressions side by side below two impressions of #5TC (1)	—
1PI	Pair (25)	1,000.
2PI	Pair (5)	—
5PI	Pair (42)	350.
	Vert. pair with horiz. gutter (8)	—
6PI	Pair (25)	375.
8PI	Pair (50)	500.
11PI	Pair (3)	800.

Imperforate printer's waste has impression of No. 6 with stamps of other countries.

New York #12
Signing of UN Charter, 7th Anniv.

1952

12PD	(3)	—
12TC	dark blue (2)	—
12TC	black (2)	—
12TC	green (2)	—
12TC	light blue (1)	—

New York #13-14
Universal Declaration of Human Rights, 4th Anniv.

1952

13PDa	Card, #13PD and two #13TC in slightly different shades (1)	975.
14PDa	Card, #14PD and two #14TC in slightly different shades (1)	975.
14PDb	Card, #13PD, 14PD (1)	—

New York #15-16
Protection for Refugees

1953

15PD	(1)	450.
16PD	(1)	450.
16PDa	Card, #15PD, 16PD (3)	775.
16PDb	Card, #15PD, 16PD, 16TC indigo (1)	875.
16PDc	Card, #16PDb and card, #15PD, 15TC, 16PD (some staining) (1)	575.
15PI	Pair (80)	400.
	Vert. pair with horiz. gutter (20)	—
16PI	Pair (80)	400.
	Vert. pair with horiz. gutter (20)	—

New York #17-18
Universal Postal Union

1953

17PDa	Card, #17PD, 17TC red brown, 17TC ultramarine, 17TC blue	2,000.
17PDb	Card, #17PD, 17TC violet brown (1)	—
18PDa	Card, #18PD, 18TC bright blue (1)	—
18PDb	Card, #17PDa, 18PDa (1)	—
17PI	Pair (82)	200.
	Horiz. pair with vert. gutter (8)	—
18PI	Pair (84)	200.
	Horiz. pair with vert. gutter (6)	—

Approximately half of PI items are stained and glued on cardboard. Imperforate printer's waste has No. 17 with No. 18 and impressions of other items on the reverse.

New York #19-20
Technical Assistance

1953

20PDa	Card, #19PD-20PD, #19TC-20TC in slightly different shades (2)	1,250.

New York #21-22
Human Rights Day

1953

22PDa	Card, #23PD-24PD, two #23TC, two #24TC in slightly different shades (2)	1,600.
21PI	Pair (40)	350.
	Vert. pair with horiz. gutter (10)	—
22PI	Pair (40)	350.
	Vert. pair with horiz. gutter (10)	—

New York #23-24
Food and Agricultural Organization

1954

24PDa	Card, #23PD-24PD, two #23TC-24TC in slightly different colors (2)	1,600.
23PI	Pair (40)	225.
	Vert. pair with horiz. gutter (10)	—
24PI	Pair (40)	225.
	Vert. pair with horiz. gutter (120)	—

New York #25-26
International Labor Organization

1954

25PDa	Card, #25PD, two #25TC in slightly different shades, three #26TC in purple shades (2)	2,400.
26PDa	Card, #25PD-26PD, #26TC in slightly different shade (2)	—
25PI	Pair (40)	350.
	Vert. pair with horiz. gutter (10)	—
26PI	Pair (40)	350.
	Vert. pair with horiz. gutter (10)	—

New York #27-28
United Nations Day

1954

27PI	Pair (40)	300.
	Horiz. pair with vert. gutter (10)	—
28PI	Pair (40)	300.
	Horiz. pair with vert. gutter (10)	—

New York #29-30
Human Rights Day

1954

29PD	(5)	350.
30PD	(5)	350.
29PI	Pair (40)	350.
	Vert. pair with horiz. gutter (10)	—
30PI	Pair (40)	—
	Vert. pair with horiz. gutter (10)	—

New York #31-32
International Civil Aviation Organization

1955

31PDa	Card, #31PD, two #31TC in different blue shades (3)	—
32PDa	Card, #32PD, three #32TC in different red shades (3)	1,400.
32PDb	Card, #31PD-32PD, #31TC-#32TC in different shades, three essays of #31-32 (1)	1,650.
31TC	black (1)	—
32TC	black (1)	—
31PI	Pair (171)	225.
	Horiz. pair with vert. gutter (26)	—
32PI	Pair (130)	225.
	Horiz. pair with vert. gutter (20)	—

No. 31PI exists with and without punch holes.

New York #33-34
UN Educational, Scientific and Cultural Organization

1955

33PD	(1)	—
33PDa	Card, #33PD, two #33TC in different shades (3)	700.
34PD	(1)	—
34PDa	Card, #34PD, two #34TC in different shades (3)	700.
33TC	black (1)	—
34TC	black (1)	—
33PI	Pair (128)	—
	Horiz. pair with vert. gutter (16)	—
34PI	Pair (90)	—
	Horiz. pair with vert. gutter (10)	—

No. 33PI exists with and without punch holes.

New York #35-38
UN, 10th Anniv.

1955

35PDa	Card, #35PD, two #35TC in different shades (2)	2,400.
35PDb	Card, #35PD, #35TC in lighter shade (1)	—
36PDa	Card, #36PD, two #36TC in different shades (3)	—
37PDa	Card, #37PD, two #37TC in different shades (3)	—
38PD	Sheet of #38 with security punches (2)	1,950.
38bPD	Watermarked sheet of nine #38b and nine #38c with security punches (1)	4,250.
38cPD	Watermarked sheet of nine #38c with security punches (1)	5,000.
35TC	carmine (1)	—
35TC	black (1)	—
36TC	black (1)	—
37TC	black (1)	—
38PP	4 items (9 souvenir sheets)	—
38PP	Retouch, 2 items (9 souvenir sheets)	—
35PI	Pair (130)	325.
	Horiz. pair with vert. gutter (20)	—
36PI	Pair (130)	325.
	Horiz. pair with vert. gutter (20)	—
37PI	Pair (180)	325.
	Horiz. pair with vert. gutter (30)	—
38PI	Pairs of souvenir sheets (16)	3,000.
	Single with sheet margin (4)	850.
38PI	Retouch Pairs of souvenir sheets (4)	—
	Retouch, single with sheet margin (1)	—

No. 37PI exists with and without punch holes.

New York #39-40
Human Rights Day

1955

39PDa	Card, #39PD, two #39TC in different shades (2)	850.
40PDa	Card, #40PD, two #40TC in different shades (2)	850.
39TC	black (1)	—
40TC	black (1)	—
40TCa	Card, #39TC in aquamarine, #40TC in dark green and two essays (1)	1,250.
39PI	Pair (180)	425.
	Vert. pair with horiz. gutter (20)	—
40PI	Pair (130)	425.
	Vert. pair with horiz. gutter (20)	—

No. 39PI exists with and without punch holes.

New York #41-42
International Telecommunication Union

1956

41PD	(2)	300.
42PD	(2)	300.
41PI	Pair (40)	350.
	Horiz. pair with vert. gutter (10)	—
42PI	Pair (40)	350.
	Horiz. pair with vert. gutter (10)	—

New York #43-44
World Health Organization

1956

43PD	(2)	225.
44PD	(2)	225.
43PI	Pair (40)	250.
	Vert. pair with horiz. gutter (10)	—
44PI	Pair (40)	250.
	Vert. pair with horiz. gutter (10)	—

Nos. 43PI-44PI have "Colour approved" handstamped in margin.

New York #45-46
General Assembly

1956

45PD	(7)	275.
46PD	(7)	275.
45PI	Pair (40)	350.
	Horiz. pair with vert. gutter (10)	—
46PI	Pair (40)	350.
	Horiz. pair with vert. gutter (10)	—

New York #47-48
Human Rights Day

1956

47PD	(2)	375.
48PD	(2)	375.
47TC	red (3)	400.
47TC	carmine (3)	—
48TC	blue (6)	400.
47PI	Pair (40)	300.
	Horiz. pair with vert. gutter (10)	—
48PI	Pair (40)	300.
	Horiz. pair with vert. gutter (10)	—

New York #49-50
World Meteorological Organization

1957

49PD	(2)	275.
50PD	(2)	275.
49TC	blue (3)	250.
50TC	carmine rose (3)	250.
49PI	Pair (40)	—
	Vert. pair with horiz. gutter (10)	—
50PI	Pair (40)	—
	Vert. pair with horiz. gutter (10)	—

Nos. 49PI-50PI have "Colour approved" handstamped in margin.

New York #51-52
UN Emergency Force

1957

51PD	(7)	275.
52PD	(7)	275.
51PI	Pair (40)	—
	Horiz. pair with vert. gutter (10)	—
52PI	Pair (40)	—
	Horiz. pair with vert. gutter (10)	—

New York #55-56
Security Council

1957

55PD	(6)	275.
56PD	(11)	275.
55TC	golden brown (6)	—
55TC	brown (5)	—
55PI	Pair (40)	—
	Vert. pair with horiz. gutter (10)	—
56PI	Pair (40)	—
	Vert. pair with horiz. gutter (10)	—

New York #57-58
Human Rights Day

1957

57PD	(12)	275.
58PD	(9)	275.
57TC	light red brown (1)	300.
58TC	dark blue (3)	—
58TC	gray green (6)	300.
57PI	Pair (50)	—
58PI	Pair (50)	—

Nos. 57TC-58TC have handstamps with "Approved" crossed out.

New York #59-60
International Atomic Energy Agency

1958

59PD	(12)	250.
60PD	(13)	250.
59TC	emerald (7)	—
59TC	black (7)	350.
60TC	black (8)	350.
59PI	With security punch (358 pairs)	—
	Cross gutter block, with security punch (4)	—
	Horiz. pair with vert. gutter, with security punch (52)	—
	Vert. pair with horiz. gutter, with security punch (32)	—
60PI	Pair with security punch (358)	—
	Cross gutter block, with security punch (4)	—
	Horiz. pair with vert. gutter, with security punch (52)	—
	Vert. pair with horiz. gutter, with security punch (32)	—

New York #61-62
Central Hall, Site of First General Assembly Meeting

1958

61PD	(8)	275.
62PD	(8)	275.
61TC	black (3)	275.
62TC	black (3)	275.
61PI	With security punch (358 pairs)	—
	Cross gutter block, with security punch (4)	—
	Horiz. pair with vert. gutter, with security punch (32)	—
	Vert. pair with horiz. gutter, with security punch (52)	—
62PI	Pair with security punch (358)	—
	Cross gutter block, with security punch (4)	—
	Horiz. pair with vert. gutter, with security punch (32)	—
	Vert. pair with horiz. gutter, with security punch (52)	—

New York #63-64
UN Emblem

1958

63PD	(21)	250.
64PD	(7)	250.
64PDa	Card, #64PD, #64TC Prussian blue, #64TC ultramarine (2)	975.
63TC	brown orange (3)	300.
64TC	light blue (1)	300.
64TC	ultramarine (1)	500.
63PI	Pair (80)	—
	Vert. pair with horiz. gutter (20)	—
64PI	Pair (80)	—
	Vert. pair with horiz. gutter (20)	—

No. 63TC is affixed to cards inscribed "D."

New York #65-66
Economic and Social Council

1958

65PD	(8)	250.
66PD	(7)	250.
65TC	black (2)	325.
65TC	orange brown (1)	—
65TC	green (1)	—
65TC	red orange (1)	—
66TC	black (2)	325.
65PI	Pair with security punch (358)	—
	Cross gutter block, with security punch (4)	—
	Horiz. pair with vert. gutter, with security punch (32)	—
	Vert. pair with horiz. gutter, with security punch (52)	—
66PI	Pair with security punch (358)	—
	Cross gutter block, with security punch (4)	—
	Horiz. pair with vert. gutter, with security punch (32)	—
	Vert. pair with horiz. gutter, with security punch (52)	—

New York #67-68
Human Rights Day

1958

67PD	(5)	300.
68PD	(5)	300.
67TC	black (2)	425.
68TC	black (1)	425.
67PI	Pair (358)	—
	Cross gutter block, with security punch and "SPECIMEN" ovpt. (4)	—
	Horiz. pair with vert. gutter, with security punch and "SPECIMEN" ovpt. (52)	—
	Vert. pair with horiz. gutter, with security punch and "SPECIMEN" ovpt. (32)	—
68PI	Pair (358)	—
	Cross gutter block, with security punch and "SPECIMEN" ovpt. (4)	—
	Horiz. pair with vert. gutter, with security punch and "SPECIMEN" ovpt. (52)	—
	Vert. pair with horiz. gutter, with security punch and "SPECIMEN" ovpt. (32)	—

Essays of Nos. 67 and 68 without denominations exist in issued colors and black.

New York #69-70
New York City Building, Flushing Meadows

1959

69PD	(7)	300.
70PD	(7)	300.
69PI	Pair (216)	—
	Cross gutter block (3)	—
	Horiz. pair with vert. gutter (54)	—
	Vert. pair with horiz. gutter (24)	—
70PI	Pair (216)	—
	Cross gutter block (3)	—
	Horiz. pair with vert. gutter (54)	—
	Vert. pair with horiz. gutter (24)	—

New York #71-72
Economic Commission for Europe

1959

71PD	(7)	275.
72PD	(7)	275.
71PI	Pair (216)	—
	Cross gutter block (3)	—
	Horiz. pair with vert. gutter (24)	—
	Vert. pair with horiz. gutter (54)	—

72PI	Pair (216)	—
	Cross gutter block (3)	—
	Horiz. pair with vert. gutter (24)	—
	Vert. pair with horiz. gutter (54)	—

New York #73-74
Trusteeship Council

1959

73PD	(5)	300.
74PD	(5)	300.
73TC	orange red (2)	—
73PI	Pair (216)	—
	Cross gutter block (3)	—
	Horiz. pair with vert. gutter (24)	—
	Vert. pair with horiz. gutter (54)	—
74PI	Pair (216)	—
	Cross gutter block (3)	—
	Horiz. pair with vert. gutter (24)	—
	Vert. pair with horiz. gutter (54)	—

No. 73TC has handstamps with words "Color and" crossed out.

New York #75-76
World Refugee Year

1959

75PD	(6)	300.
76PD	(5)	300.
75TC	purple & red (3)	—
76TC	olive & Prussian blue (2)	—
76TC	purple & green (3)	—
75PI	Pair (216)	—
	Cross gutter block (3)	—
	Horiz. pair with vert. gutter (54)	—
	Vert. pair with horiz. gutter (24)	—
76PI	Pair (216)	—
	Cross gutter block (3)	—
	Horiz. pair with vert. gutter (54)	—
	Vert. pair with horiz. gutter (24)	—

New York #77-78
Chaillot Palace

1960

77PD	(4)	250.
78PD	(4)	250.
78TC	brown & blue green(1)	325.
78TC	blue & red (1)	325.
78TCa	Card, #78TC brown & blue green, #78TC blue &red (1)	—
77PI	Pair (25)	—
78PI	Pair (25)	—

New York #79-80
Economic Commission for Asia and the Far East

1960

79PD	(1)	—
80PDa	Card, #79PD, #80PD (1)	—
80PDb	Card, two #79PD, two #80PD (1)	1,250.
79PI	Pair (50)	—
80PI	Pair (50)	—

New York #81-82
World Forestry Congress

1960

81PD	(2)	425.
82PDa	Card, #81PD-82PD (3)	350.
81PI	Pair (100)	—
82PI	Pair (100)	—

New York #83-85
UN, 15th Anniv.

1960

83PD	(5)	325.
84PD	(6)	325.
85PD	(2)	700.
83TC	black (1)	—
83TC	bright blue (2)	—
83PI	Pair (144)	—
	Cross gutter block (2)	—
	Horiz. pair with vert. gutter (36)	—
	Vert. pair with horiz. gutter (16)	—
84PI	Pair (119)	—
	Cross gutter block (2)	—
	Horiz. pair with vert. gutter (36)	—
	Vert. pair with horiz. gutter (16)	—
85PI	Pair (16)	—
	Cross gutter block (2)	—
	Horiz. pair with vert. gutter (8)	—
	Vert. pair with horiz. gutter (8)	—

An essay in blue has diagonal lines in background rather than cross-hatching.

New York #86-87
International Bank for Reconstruction and Development

1960

87PDa	Card, 2 #86PD, 2 #87PD (2)	1,150.
87PDb	Card, #86PD-87PD with simulated perforations (1)	—
86PI	Pair (100)	—
87PI	Pair (100)	—

New York #88-89
International Court of Justice

1961

89PDa	Card, #88PD-89PD affixed, dated 10/31/61 (2)	450.
89PDb	Card, 2 #88PD, 2 #89PD, disapproved (2)	—
88PI	Pair (100)	—
89PI	Pair (100)	—

New York #90-91
International Monetary Fund

1961

91PDa	Card with 2 #90PD, 2 #91PD in slightly different shades (1)	1,300.
90PI	Pair (100)	—
91PI	Pair (50)	—

New York #92
Abstract Flags

1961

92PI	Pair (80)	—
	Horiz. pair with vert. gutter (20)	—

New York #93-94
Economic Commission for Latin America

1961

93PDa	Card, 2 #93PD, 2 essays of #94 (2)	—
94PDa	Card, 2 #94PD (1)	400.

Essays of No. 94 lack serifs in "1's."

New York #95-96
Economic Commission for Africa

1961

96PDa	Card with #95PD-96PD affixed (8)	500.
95PP	4 items (100)	—
96PP	8 items (100)	—
95PI	Pair (100)	—
96PI	Pair (100)	—

New York #97-99
UN Children's Fund (UNICEF)

1961

99PDa	Card, #97PD-99PD, with approval handstamp (3)	1,050.
99PDb	Card, #97PD-99PD, no approval handstamp (5)	600.
97PP	4 items (80)	—
	Vert. pair with horiz. gutter (10)	—
98PP	4 items (80)	—
	Vert. pair with horiz. gutter (10)	—
99PP	4 items (80)	—
	Vert. pair with horiz. gutter (10)	—
97PI	Pair (80)	—
	Vert. pair with horiz. gutter (20)	—
98PI	Pair (80)	—
	Vert. pair with horiz. gutter (20)	—
99PI	Pair (80)	—
	Vert. pair with horiz. gutter (20)	—

New York #100-101
Housing and Urban Development Program

1962

100PD	With approval handstamp (3)	200.
101PD	With approval handstamp (3)	200.
100PI	Pair with oval "Harrison's Photogravure Specimen" handstamp (25)	350.
101PI	Pair with oval "Harrison's Photogravure Specimen" handstamp (25)	350.

Three essays each of Nos. 100 and 101 have larger numerals than issued stamps are are on cards marked "disapproved."

New York #102-103
Malaria Eradication Campaign

1962

102PD	(5)	400.
103PD	(5)	400.

New York #104-107
Definitives

1962

104PD	(5)	400.
105PD	(7)	425.
106PD	With approval handstamp & signature (2)	400.
107PD	(3)	500.
104PI	Pair with oval "Harrison's Photogravure Specimen" handstamp (25)	250.
105PI	Pair with oval "Harrison's Photogravure Specimen" handstamp (25)	250.
107PI	Pair with oval "Harrison's Photogravure Specimen" handstamp (25)	250.
	Same, without handstamp (25)	400.

Three essays of No. 106 have indistinct line between "U" and "N," and are on cards marked "disapproved."

New York #108-109
Death of Dag Hammarskjold, 1st Anniv.

1962

108PDa	Card, #108PD, essay of #109 (1)	—
109PDa	Card, #109PD, essay of #108 (1)	—
109PDb	Card, #108PD-#109PD (2)	600.
108PI	Pair (80)	—
	Vert. pair with horiz. gutter (20)	—
109PI	Pair (80)	—
	Vert. pair with horiz. gutter (20)	—

Essays of Nos 108-109 lack denomination.

New York #110-111
UN Operation in the Congo

1962

111PDa	Card, 3 #110PD, 3 #111PD (1)	1,150.
111PDb	Card, #111PD, essay of #110 (2)	550.
110PP	4 items (80)	—
	Horiz. pair with vert. gutter (10)	—
111PP	4 items (80)	—
	Horiz. pair with vert. gutter (10)	—
110PI	Pair (80)	—
	Horiz. pair with vert. gutter (20)	—
111PI	Pair (80)	—
	Horiz. pair with vert. gutter (20)	—

Essays of No. 110 have 5c denomination.

New York #112-113
Committee on Peaceful Uses of Outer Space

1962

112PD	(2)	—
113PD	(1)	—
113PDa	Card, #112PD-113PD (3)	500.

Essays similar to Nos. 112PD-113PD have text in white panel below palm frond.

New York #114-115
UN Development Decade

1963

115PDa	Card, #114PD, 2 #115PD (one in slightly different shade) with approval handstamp (3)	875.
115PDb	Card, #114PD-115PD (3)	400.
114PP	4 items (80)	—
	Vert. pair with horiz. gutter (10)	—
115PP	4 items (80)	—
	Vert. pair with horiz. gutter (10)	—
114PI	Pair (80)	—
	Vert. pair with horiz. gutter (20)	—
115PI	Pair (80)	—
	Vert. pair with horiz. gutter (20)	—

New York #116-117
Freedom from Hunger Campaign

1963

116PD	(1)	—
117PD	(1)	—
117PDa	Card, #116PD-117PD (5)	500.
116PP	3 items (80)	—
	Horiz. pair with vert. gutter (10)	—
117PP	3 items (80)	—
	Horiz. pair with vert. gutter (10)	—
116PI	Pair (80)	—
	Horiz. pair with vert. gutter (20)	—
117PI	Pair (80)	—
	Horiz. pair with vert. gutter (20)	—

Essays similar to Nos. 116PD-117PD have taller numerals and lettering.

New York #118
UN Temporary Executive Authority in West New Guinea

1963

118PD	With approval handstamp (2)	400.
118PDa	Card, #118PD (approved), #118TC (not approved) (3)	500.
118TCa	Card, 2 #118TC (disapproved or with instructions to printer) (3)	500.
118PP	3 items (100)	—
	Horiz. pair with vert. gutter (10)	—
118PI	Pair (100)	—
	Horiz. pair with vert. gutter (20)	—

No. 118TC has right side of map in a lighter shade of green.

New York #119-120
General Assembly Building, New York

1963

120PDa	Card, #119PD-120PD (2)	400.

New York #121-122
Universal Declaration of Human Rights, 15th Anniv.

1963

121PD	(2)	250.
122PD	(2)	250.
121PI	Pair (100)	—
122PI	Pair (100)	—

Essays similar to Nos. 121PD-122PD have top line of frame text flush left rather than centered, and are on a disapproved card.

New York #123-124
Intergovernmental Maritime Consultative Organization

1964

124PDa	Card, #123PD-124PD (3)	550.
123PP	4 items (80)	—
	Horiz. pair with vert. gutter (10)	—
124PP	4 items (80)	—
	Horiz. pair with vert. gutter (10)	—
123PI	Pair (80)	—
	Horiz. pair with vert. gutter (20)	—
124PI	Pair (80)	—
	Horiz. pair with vert. gutter (20)	—

New York #125-128
Definitives

1964

125PD	(3)	275.
125PDa	Card, #125 perforated with approval handstamp (1)	—
126PD	(3)	240.
127PDa	Card, #126PD-127PD with approval handstamp (3)	550.
127PDb	Card, #127PD (approved), #127PD (not approved, in slightly different shade, #126PD (disapproved in slightly different shade (3)	925.
128PD	(3)	240.
125PP	3 items (100)	—
126PI	3 items (80)	—
	Vert. pair with horiz. gutter (10)	—
127PP	4 items (80)	—
	Horiz. pair with vert. gutter (10)	—

128PP	4 items (80)	—
	Horiz. pair with vert. gutter (10)	—
125PI	Pair (65)	—
	Horiz. pair with vert. gutter (10)	—
126PI	Pair (80)	—
	Vert. pair with horiz. gutter (20)	—
127PI	Pair (80)	—
	Horiz. pair with vert. gutter (20)	—
128PI	Pair (80)	—
	Horiz. pair with vert. gutter (20)	—

Essays similar to No. 125PD have larger numerals and blue text.

New York #129-130
UN Conference on Trade and Development

1964

129PD	(6)	250.
130PD	(6)	250.
129PI	Pair (25)	—
130PI	Pair (25)	—

New York #131-132
Narcotics Control

1964

131PD	(2)	250.
132PD	(2)	250.
132PDa	Card, #131PD-132PD (3)	600.

New York #133
Nuclear Test Ban Treaty

1964

133TC	dark red & black, perforated, litho. & engr. (1)	300.
133TC	lilac, perforated, engr. (20)	—
133TCa	Card, 2 #133TC dark red & dark brown, litho. & vignette essay, litho. (1)	—
133TCb	Card, #133TC dark red & black, engr. & 5 vignette essays, engr. (1)	—
133TCc	Card, 11 #133TC in red, claret, brown rose, brown, dark brown, dull blue, blue, blue violet, gray, dark gray, black, engr. (1)	—

New York #134-136
Education for Progress Campaign

1964

135PD	(1)	—
136PDa	Card, #134PD-136PD, with approval stamp (3)	—
136PDb	Card, #134PD-136PD, without approval stamp (2)	300.
136PDc	Card, #134PD, #136PD, without approval stamp (1)	450.
134PP	4 items (80)	—
	Horiz. pair with vert. gutter (10)	—
135PP	4 items (80)	—
	Horiz. pair with vert. gutter (10)	—
136PP	4 items (80)	—
	Horiz. pair with vert. gutter (10)	—
134PI	Pair (80)	—
	Horiz. pair with vert. gutter (20)	—
135PI	Pair (80)	—
	Horiz. pair with vert. gutter (20)	—
136PI	Pair (80)	—
	Horiz. pair with vert. gutter (20)	—

New York #137-138
Special Fund Program

1965

137PD	(2)	225.
138PD	(2)	225.
138PDa	Card, #137PD-138PD, with approval stamp (1)	500.
138PDb	Card, #137PD-138PD, without approval stamp (1)	—

New York #139-140
UN Peace-Keeping Force in Cyprus

1965

140PDa	Card #139PD-140PD, with approval stamp (5)	500.
140PP	3 items (80)	—
	Vert. pair with horiz. gutter (10)	—
139PI	Pair (40)	—
	Vert. pair with horiz. gutter (10)	—
140PI	Pair (40)	—
	Vert. pair with horiz. gutter (10)	—

Smaller-size essays (30x38mm) of Nos. 139-140 are in three cards with approval stamps.

New York #141-142
International Telecommunication Union

1965

142PDa	Card, #141PD-142PD, with approval stamp (3)	500.
142PDb	Card, #141PD-142PD, no approval stamp (3)	450.
142PDc	Card, #141PD-142PD, #141TC dated "8.2.65" (3)	925.
141PP	4 items (80)	—
	Horiz. pair with vert. gutter (10)	—
142PP	4 items (80)	—
	Horiz. pair with vert. gutter (10)	—
141PI	Pair (80)	—
	Horiz. pair with vert. gutter (20)	—
142PI	Pair (80)	—
	Horiz. pair with vert. gutter (20)	—

No. 141TC has orange yellow lines instead of orange lines.

New York #143-145
UN, 20th Anniv. and International Cooperation Year

1965

143PD	(3)	275.
143PDa	Card, #143PD, 144TC orange red (3)	825.
144PD	(3)	275.
144PDa	Card, #143PD-144PD, with approval stamp (7)	500.
145PD	Imperforate sheet with manuscript printer's instructions (4)	—
	Issued souvenir sheet, perforated (on printer's card) (1)	110.
145PDa	#143PD, #144PD affixed to #145 souvenir sheet margin (5)	600.

New York #146-150
Definitives

1965-66

146PD	(7)	200.
148PDa	Block of 12 perforated stamps with approval handstamp in margin (2)	140.
148PDb	Card, #147-148 perforated, with approval handstamp (3)	500.
149PD	Perforated, with approval handstamp (2)	250.
149PDa	Card, #149PD (2nd printing), #149PD, first printing, perforated, with approval handstamp (2)	600.
150PD	(3)	240.
149TC	Prussian blue & dark blue, perforated (1)	—
150PP	3 items (80), affixed on cards	—
	Horiz. pair with vert. gutter (10)	—
150PI	Pair (161)	375.
	Horiz. pair with vert. gutter (19)	—

Two cards without approval handstamp have perforated essays of both Nos. 147 and 148. The essay of No. 147 has larger numerals and the essay of No. 148 has bright yellow text at bottom. No. 150PI has had extra glue applied.

New York #151-153
Population Trends and Development

1965

152PDa	Card, #151PD-152PD, 153TC, perforated, with approval handstamp (2)	825.

No. 153TC has "Nations Unies" in black instead of gray.

New York #154-155
World Federation of United Nations Associations

1966

155PDa	Card, #154-155PD with approval handstamp (3)	500.
154PP	4 items (80)	—
	Vert. pair with horiz. gutter (10)	—
155PP	4 items (80)	—
	Vert. pair with horiz. gutter (10)	—
154PI	Pair (80)	—
	Vert. pair with horiz. gutter (20)	—
155PI	Pair (80)	—
	Vert. pair with horiz. gutter (20)	—

New York #156-157
World Health Organization

1966

157TCa	Card, #156TC-157TC, with approval handstamp (3)	500.
156PP	4 items (50)	—
157PP	4 items (80)	—
	Horiz. pair with vert. gutter (10)	—
156PI	Pair (65)	—
	Horiz. pair with vert. gutter (10)	—
157PI	Pair (80)	—
	Horiz. pair with vert. gutter (20)	—

Nos. 156TC and 157TC have side and front of building the same shade of blue.

New York #158-159
International Coffee Agreement of 1962

1966

159PDa	Card, #158PD-159PD (3)	625.

New York #160
UN Observers

1964

160PD	(2) on cards dated "3.2.1966"	125.
160PP	4 items (50)	—
160PI	Pair (65)	—
	Vert. pair with horiz. gutter (10)	—

Two essays of No. 160 with white text lines larger and closer together are on cards dated "17.1.1966."

New York #161-163
UNICEF, 20th Anniv.

1966

161PD	(3)	250.
162PD	(3)	250.
163PD	(3)	250.
161PI	Pair (72)	—
	Cross gutter block (1)	—
	Horiz. pair with vert. gutter (18)	—
	Vert. pair with horiz. gutter (8)	—
162PI	Pair (72)	—
	Cross gutter block (1)	—
	Horiz. pair with vert. gutter (18)	—
	Vert. pair with horiz. gutter (8)	—
163PI	Pair (72)	—
	Cross gutter block (1)	—
	Horiz. pair with vert. gutter (18)	—
	Vert. pair with horiz. gutter (8)	—

New York #164-165
UN Development Program

1967

165PDa	Card, # 164PD-165PD, dated "6.9. 1966" (3)	725.
165PDb	Card, #165PD, 2 #164PD, with approval handstamp, dated "4.10.66" (6)	925.
164PI	Pair (40)	—
	Horiz. pair with vert. gutter (10)	—
165PI	Pair (40)	—
	Horiz. pair with vert. gutter (10)	—

New York #166-167
Definitives

1967

166PD	(6)	225.
166PDa	Card, 2 #166PD (3)	575.
167PD	(3)	200.
167TC	With brown line separating "UN" in vignette, on card dated "27.4.1966" (3)	250.
166PP	4 items (80)	—
	Vert. pair with horiz. gutter (10)	—
167PP	3 items (80)	—
	Horiz. pair with vert. gutter (10)	—
166PI	Pair (80)	—
	Vert. pair with horiz. gutter (20)	—
167PI	Pair (80)	—
	Horiz. pair with vert. gutter (20)	—

New York #168-169
Independence

1967

168PD	(2)	250.
169PD	(3)	250.

New York #170-174
EXPO '67

1967

170PD	(1)	300.
171PD	(1)	300.
172PD	(3)	300.
173PD	(1)	300.
174PD	(3)	300.
170PP	2 items (144)	—
	Cross gutter block (1)	—
	Horiz. pair with vert. gutter (8)	—
	Vert. pair with horiz. gutter (18)	—
171PP	2 items (144)	—
	Cross gutter block (1)	—
	Horiz. pair with vert. gutter (8)	—
	Vert. pair with horiz. gutter (18)	—
172PP	3 items (144)	—
	Cross gutter block (1)	—
	Horiz. pair with vert. gutter (18)	—
	Vert. pair with horiz. gutter (8)	—
173PP	2 items (144)	—
	Cross gutter block (1)	—
	Horiz. pair with vert. gutter (8)	—
	Vert. pair with horiz. gutter (18)	—
174PP	2 items (144)	—
	Cross gutter block (1)	—
	Horiz. pair with vert. gutter (8)	—
	Vert. pair with horiz. gutter (18)	—
170PI	Pair (72)	—
	Cross gutter block (1)	—
	Horiz. pair with vert. gutter (8)	—
	Vert. pair with horiz. gutter (18)	—
171PI	Pair (72)	—
	Cross gutter block (1)	—
	Horiz. pair with vert. gutter (8)	—
	Vert. pair with horiz. gutter (18)	—
172PI	Pair (72)	—
	Cross gutter block (1)	—
	Horiz. pair with vert. gutter (18)	—
	Vert. pair with horiz. gutter (8)	—
173PI	Pair (72)	—
	Cross gutter block (1)	—
	Horiz. pair with vert. gutter (8)	—
	Vert. pair with horiz. gutter (18)	—
174PI	Pair (72)	—
	Cross gutter block (1)	—
	Horiz. pair with vert. gutter (8)	—
	Vert. pair with horiz. gutter (18)	—

New York #175-176
International Tourist Year

1967

176PDa	#175-176, perforated, affixed to printer's card (2)	600.

New York #177-178
Towards Disarmament

1967

177PD	(3)	—
178PD	(3)	200.
178TC	Wall text in copper, gold lines in wall (1)	110.
178TC	Wall text in copper, blue gray lines in wall (3)	110.
178TC	Wall text in brown, silver lines in wall (1)	110.
178TC	Wall text in brown, blue gray lines in wall (3)	110.

New York #179-180
Chagall Stained Glass Windows

1967

179PP	8 items (29)	—
180PP	8 items (29)	—
179PI	Pair on card stock (24)	1,050.
180PI	Pair on card stock (135)	650.
	Horiz. pair with vert. gutter, on card stock (15)	—
180PI	Pair on stamp paper (75)	525.

Essays of Nos. 179-180 in 5c denomination exist.

New York #181-182
UN Secretariat

1968

181PD	(1)	110.
182PD	(1)	110.
182PDa	Card, #181PD-182PD (1)	—
181PP	5 items (160)	—
	Horiz. pair with vert. gutter (20)	—
182PP	5 items (160)	—
	Horiz. pair with vert. gutter (20)	—

181PI	Pair (80)	—
	Horiz. pair with vert. gutter (20)	—
182PI	Pair (80)	—
	Horiz. pair with vert. gutter (20)	—

New York #183-184
Art at the UN

1968

183PD	(1)	250.
184PD	(1)	250.
184PDa	Card, #183PD-184PD, dated "5.12.67" (2)	—
184TCa	Card, #183TC-184TC, dated "10.XI.67" (3)	725.
183PP	5 items (80)	—
	Vert. pair with horiz. gutter (10)	—
184PP	5 items (80)	—
	Vert. pair with horiz. gutter (10)	—
183PI	Pair (65)	—
	Vert. pair with horiz. gutter (10)	—
184PI	Pair (80)	—
	Vert. pair with horiz. gutter (20)	—

No. 183TC has a bright blue frame; No. 184TC a birght red frame.

New York #185-186
UN Industrial Development Orgainzation

1968

185PD	(4)	325.
186PD	(3)	500.
186TC	brown frame, deep blue "ONUDI" (2)	—
185PP	4 items, affixed to cards (3)	—
186PP	4 items, affixed to cards (3)	—
185PI	Pair with security punch (25)	250.
186PI	Pair with security punch (25)	250.

New York #187
UN Headquarters

1964

187TC	light gray roof in foreground, numbered 34 or 38, dated July 7, 1967 (2)	140.
187TC	With wide curved white line under window of General Assembly building, numbered 397 or 404, dated 11.8.1967 (2)	125.
187TC	With halo around UN emblem, dated Feb. 12, 1968 (2)	240.
187PP	11 items, on card with staple holes (3)	—
187PI	Pair with "Specimen" overprint (80)	250.
	Vert. pair with horiz. gutter, with "Specimen" overprint (20)	—
187PI	Pair without "Specimen" overprint (80)	375.
	Vert. pair with horiz. gutter, without "Specimen" overprint (20)	—

New York #188-189
World Weather Watch

1968

189PDa	Card, #188PD-189PD (1)	500.
188PP	5 items (100)	—
189PP	5 items (100)	—

New York #190-191
International Human Rights Year

1968

190PD	(6)	210.
191PD	(6)	210.
190PP	4 items (100)	—
191PP	4 items (100)	—
190PI	Pair (50)	—
191PI	Pair (50)	—

New York #192-193
UN Institute for Training and Research

1969

193PDa	Card, #192PD-193PD (2)	425.
192PP	6 items (50)	—
193PP	6 items (100)	—
192PI	Pair (15)	425.
193PI	Pair (15)	425.

New York #194-195
Economic Commission for Latin America

1969

195PDa	#194-195, perforated, affixed to printer's card (4)	425.

New York #196
"UN" and Emblem

1969

196PD	With approval handstamp (2)	250.
196TC	Card, #196PD, 196TC dark blue background (2)	—
196PP	3 items (100)	—

New York #197-198
UN International Law Commission

1969

198PDa	Card, #197PD-198PD (9)	650.
197PP	4 items (80)	—
	Horiz. pair with vert. gutter (10)	—
198PP	4 items (80)	—
	Horiz. pair with vert. gutter (10)	—
197PI	(40 pairs)	—
	Horiz. pair with vert. gutter (10)	—
198PI	(40 pairs)	—
	Horiz. pair with vert. gutter (10)	—

New York #199-200
Labor and Development

1969

199PD	With approval handstamp (1)	—
200PD	(1)	—
200PDa	Card, #199PD-200PD, with approval handstamp (1)	425.
199TC	Men in dark blue, perforated (3)	—
200TC	Rose pink background, perforated (3)	—
200PP	4 items (91)	—

Geneva #1-14
Definitives

1969-70

G1PD	(2)	200.
G3PD	(1)	—
G3PDa	Card, 2 #G3PD, with approval handstamp (2)	—
G4PD	(2)	—
G5PD	(3)	325.
G7PD	(1)	250.
G8PD	Perforated, on card with approval handstamp (2)	275.
G8PDa	Perforated layout sheet proof with 4 #G8PD affixed (1)	—
G8PDb	Partial perforated layout sheet proof with 2 #G8PD affixed (1)	—
G9PD	(1)	275.
G10PD	(1)	200.
G11PD	(1)	—
G12PD	(1)	225.
G13PD	(4)	240.
G14PD	(3)	225.
G1TC	Black panel behind "UN" (1)	—
G6TCa	Card, #G6PD, #G6TC pewter emblem, dated "7.10.69" (3)	—
G6TCb	Card, #G6TC silver emblem, 2 #G6PD dated "17.9.69" (3)	—
G6TCc	Card, #G6PD, #G6TC orange denomination, dated "27.8.69" (3)	—
G12TC	gray background, on card marked "Rejected" (2)	325.
G1PP	3 items, perforated (100)	—
G2PP	5 items (160)	—
	Horiz. pair with vert. gutter (20)	—
G3PP	5 items (160)	—
	Horiz. pair with vert. gutter (20)	—
G4PP	5 items (151)	—
	Horiz. pair with vert. gutter (20)	—
G5PP	4 items (160)	—
	Vert. pair with horiz. gutter (20)	—
G6PP	3 items (160)	—
	Horiz. pair with vert. gutter (20)	—
G7PP	4 items (100)	—
G8PP	8 items (150)	—
G9PP	6 items (100)	—
G10PP	8 items (100)	—
G12PP	6 items (100)	—
G13PP	5 items (160)	—
	Vert. pair with horiz. gutter (20)	—
G2PI	Pair (80)	—
	Horiz. pair with vert. gutter (20)	—
G3PI	Pair (80)	—
	Horiz. pair with vert. gutter (20)	—
G4PI	Pair (73)	—
	Horiz. pair with vert. gutter (20)	—
G5PI	Pair (80)	—
	Vert. pair with horiz. gutter (20)	—
G6PI	Pair (80)	—
	Horiz. pair with vert. gutter (20)	—

G7PI	Pair (50)	—
G8PI	Pair (75)	—
G9PI	Pair (50)	—
G10PI	Pair (50)	—
G13PI	Pair (80)	—
	Vert. pair with horiz. gutter (20)	—

Four essays of No. G2 exist, having "0" below "F" jutting out to left. Two essays of No. G10 with small "F.S." are on rejected cards.

New York #201-202
Mosaic Art at the UN

1969

201PD	(3)	210.
202PD	(3)	210.
202PDa	Card, #201PD-202PD (2)	—
201PP	8 items (100)	—
202PP	8 items (100)	—
201PI	Pair (50)	—
202PI	Pair (50)	—

New York #203-204
Peace Bell

1970

204PDa	Card, 2 each #203PD-204PD (2)	1,300.
203PP	5 items (100)	—
204PP	5 items (100)	—

About half of Nos. 203PP and 204PP have faults.

New York #205-206
Lower Mekong Basin Development Project

1970

205PD	(2)	250.
206PD	(2)	250.
205PP	10 items (100)	—
206PP	10 items (100)	—
205PI	Pair (50)	—
206PI	Pair (50)	—

New York #207-208
Fight Cancer

1970

207PD	Perforated, non-glossy paper, on piece of printer's card (1)	—
208PD	Perforated, non-glossy paper, on piece of printer's card (1)	—
208PDa	Card, #207PD-208PD, perforated, non-glossy paper (1)	—
208PDb	Card, 2 #207PD-208PD, perforated, non-glossy paper, with approval handstamp (1)	1,050.
208PDc	#207-208, perforated, glossy paper, on printer's card (2)	—
207PP	2 items (50)	—
208PP	2 items (50)	—
207PI	Pair (50)	—
208PI	Pair (50)	—

New York #209-212
UN, 25th Anniv.

1970

209PD	(2)	—
210PD	(2)	—
211PD	On card (3)	—
211PDa	Card, #209PD-211PD (2)	750.
212PD	(1)	275.
212PDa	Card, #209PD-212PD (1)	—
209PP	4 items (180)	—
	Horiz. pair with vert. gutter (10)	—
210PP	5 items (180)	—
	Horiz. pair with vert. gutter (10)	—
211PP	3 items (180)	—
	Vert. pair with horiz. gutter (10)	—
212PP	5 items (22)	—
209PI	Pair (80)	—
	Horiz. pair with vert. gutter (20)	—
210PI	Pair (80)	—
	Horiz. pair with vert. gutter (20)	—
211PI	Pair (80)	—
	Vert. pair with horiz. gutter (20)	—
212PI	Pair (12)	—

New York #213-214
Peace, Justice and Progress

1970

214PDa	Card, #213PD-214PD (3)	600.
214PDb	Card, 2 each #213PD-214PD (2)	1,300.
213PP	4 items (50)	—
214PP	4 items (50)	—

New York #215, Geneva #15
Peaceful Uses of the Sea Bed

1971

215PD	(2)	200.
G15PD	(1)	—
215PP	6 items (100)	—
G15PP	6 items (100)	—
215PI	Pair (50)	—
G15PI	Pair (50)	—

New York #216-217, Geneva #16
International Support for Refugees

1971

217PDa	Card, #216PD-217PD, #G16PD (2)	775.
216PP	4 items (80)	—
	Horiz. pair with vert. gutter (10)	—
217PP	4 items (80)	—
	Horiz. pair with vert. gutter (10)	—
G16PP	4 items (160)	—
	Horiz. pair with vert. gutter (20)	—
216PI	Pair (80)	—
	Horiz. pair with vert. gutter (20)	—
217PI	Pair (80)	—
	Horiz. pair with vert. gutter (20)	—
G16PI	Pair (80)	—
	Horiz. pair with vert. gutter (20)	—

New York #218, Geneva #17
World Food Program

1971

218PD	(4)	225.
G17PD	(4)	225.
G17TC	(1)	375.
218PP	6 items (100)	—
G17PP	6 items (100)	—
218PI	Pair (50)	—
G17PI	Pair (50)	—

New York #219, Geneva #18
Universal Postal Union

1971

219PDa	Card, #219PD, #G18PD (3)	550.
219PP	5 items (130)	—
	Horiz. pair with vert. gutter (10)	—
G18PP	5 items (150)	—
219PI	Pair (80)	—
	Horiz. pair with vert. gutter (20)	—
G18PI	Pair (80)	—
	Horiz. pair with vert. gutter (20)	—

New York #220-221, Geneva #19-20
International Year Against Racial Discrimination

1971

221PDa	Card, #220PD-221PD, #G19PD-G20PD and 4 similar items with slightly different colors (1)	2,400.
221PDb	Card with affixed plastic sheet with #220PD-221PD, #G19PD-G20PD affixed (1)	600.
221PDc	Cut-up card, #220PD-221PD, G19PD-G20PD (1)	—
220PP	5 items (100)	—
221PP	5 items (75)	—
G19PP	5 items (100)	—
G20PP	5 items (100)	—

New York #222-223
UN Headquarters, New York

1971

222PD	(4)	275.
223PD	(2)	275.
222PP	8 items (91)	—
223PP	5 items (92)	—
222PI	Pair (175)	—

Two sheets of 50 of No. 222PI are "approved."

New York #224-225, Geneva #21
UN International School

1971

225PDa	Card, #224PD-225PD, G21PD, with approval stamp (2)	750.
225PDb	Card or sheet, #224PD-225PD, 1fr essay of #G21 (3)	925.
224PP	5 items (180)	—
	Vert. pair with horiz. gutter (10)	—
225PP	5 items (100)	—
	Vert. pair with horiz. gutter (10)	—
G21PP	5 items (180)	—
	Vert. pair with horiz. gutter (10)	—
224PI	Pair (80)	—
	Vert. pair with horiz. gutter (20)	—
225PI	Pair (80)	—
	Vert. pair with horiz. gutter (20)	—
G21PI	Pair (80)	—
	Vert. pair with horiz. gutter (20)	—

New York #226, Geneva #22
Definitives

1972

226PD	Perforated on printer's card (3)	225.
G22PD	(5)	225.
226PP	4 items (100)	—
G22PP	4 items (180)	—
	Horiz. pair with vert. gutter (10)	—
226PI	Pair (50)	—
G22PI	Pair (80)	—
	Horiz. pair with vert. gutter (20)	—

New York #227, Geneva #23
Non-proliferation of Nuclear Weapons

1972

227PD	(2)	200.
G23PD	(2)	225.
227PP	6 items (100)	—
G23PP	6 items (100)	—
227PI	Pair (50)	—
G23PI	Pair (50)	—

Two essays each of Nos. 227 and G23 lacking strong gray billowing in center of cloud exist on cards dated "22.Set.1971."

New York #228, Geneva #24, Souvenir Card #1
World Health Day

1972

228PDa	Card, #228PD, #G24PD with approval handstamp (1)	500.
G24PD	(1)	—
SC1PD	Card with stamps with simulated perforations and cancels (2)	600.
228PP	8 items (80)	—
	Vert. pair with horiz. gutter (10)	—
G24PP	8 items (160)	—
	Vert. pair with horiz. gutter (20)	—
G24PI	Pair (180)	—
	Vert. pair with horiz. gutter (20)	—

New York #229-230, Geneva #25-26
UN Conference on Human Environment

1972

229PD	(1)	—
230PDa	Card, #229PD-230PD, #G25PD-G26PD (3)	450.
230PDb	Card, #230PD, #G25PD-G26PD (1)	—
229PP	6 items (288)	—
	Cross gutter block (2)	—
	Horiz. pair with vert. gutter (16)	—
	Vert. pair with horiz. gutter (36)	—
230PP	6 items (288)	—
	Cross gutter block (2)	—
	Horiz. pair with vert. gutter (16)	—
	Vert. pair with horiz. gutter (36)	—
G25PP	6 items (288)	—
	Cross gutter block (2)	—
	Horiz. pair with vert. gutter (16)	—
	Vert. pair with horiz. gutter (36)	—
G26PP	6 items (288)	—
	Cross gutter block (2)	—
	Horiz. pair with vert. gutter (16)	—
	Vert. pair with horiz. gutter (36)	—
229PI	Pair (144)	—
	Cross gutter block (2)	—
	Horiz. pair with vert. gutter (16)	—
	Vert. pair with horiz. gutter (36)	—
230PI	Pair (144)	—
	Cross gutter block (2)	—
	Horiz. pair with vert. gutter (16)	—
	Vert. pair with horiz. gutter (36)	—
G25PI	Pair (144)	—
	Cross gutter block (2)	—
	Horiz. pair with vert. gutter (16)	—
	Vert. pair with horiz. gutter (36)	—
G26PI	Pair (144)	—
	Cross gutter block (2)	—
	Horiz. pair with vert. gutter (16)	—
	Vert. pair with horiz. gutter (36)	—

New York #231, Geneva #27
Economic Commission for Europe

1972

231PDa	Card, #231PD, #G27PD (4)	550.
231PP	8 items (100)	—
G27PP	8 items (50)	—

New York #232-233, Geneva #28-29, Souvenir Card #2
Art at the UN

1972

232PDa	Card, #232PD, #233TC text in dull blue green, #G28PD-G29PD (1)	975.
G28PD	(1)	—
G29PDa	Card, #G28PD-G29PD, #233TC text in dull blue green (1)	—
G29PDb	Card, #G29PD, #233TC text in dull blue green (1)	—
SC2PD	(25)	—
SC2PDa	Defaced card, with corrections marked in blue (8)	—
SC2TC	Untrimmed card, signature in light blue(3)	160.
G28PP	3 items (50)	—
G29PP	3 items (50)	—
232PI	Pair (80)	—
	Vert. pair with horiz. gutter (20)	—
233PI	Pair (80)	—
	Vert. pair with horiz. gutter (20)	—
G28PI	Pair (80)	—
	Vert. pair with horiz. gutter (20)	—
G29PI	Pair (80)	—
	Vert. pair with horiz. gutter (20)	—

New York #234-235, Geneva #30-31, Souvenir Card #3
Disarmament Decade

1973

235PDa	Card, #234PD-235PD, #G30PD-G31PD, with approval handstamp (1)	825.
SC3PD	With printer's stamp or approval handstamp (9)	110.
234PP	8 items (130)	—
	Horiz. pair with vert. gutter (20)	—
235PP	8 items (100)	—
G30PP	8 items (130)	—
	Horiz. pair with vert. gutter (20)	—
G31PP	8 items (100)	—
234PI	Pair (230)	—
	Horiz. pair with vert. gutter (20)	—
235PI	Pair (230)	—
	Horiz. pair with vert. gutter (20)	—
G30PI	Pair (205)	—
	Horiz. pair with vert. gutter (20)	—
G31PI	Pair (230)	—
	Horiz. pair with vert. gutter (20)	—

Two examples of #SC3PD are cut in half.

New York #236-237, Geneva #32
Fight Against Drug Abuse

1973

236PD	(1)	—
237PDa	Card, #236PD-237PD, #G32PD with approval handstamp (4)	725.
237PDb	Card, #237PD, #G32PD with approval handstamp (1)	—
237PDc	Card, #237PD, #G32PD, 9c essay of #236 (6)	—
236PP	8 items (75)	—
237PP	8 items (100)	—
G32PP	8 items (50)	—
236PI	Pair (50)	—
237PI	Pair (50)	—
G32PI	Pair (50)	—

New York #238-239, Geneva #33
UN Volunteer Program

1973

239PDa	Card, #238PD-239PD, #G33PD (9)	600.
238PP	8 items (80)	—
239PP	8 items (100)	—
G33PP	8 items (50)	—
238PI	Pair (50)	—
239PI	Pair (50)	—
G33PI	Pair (25)	—

New York #240-241, Geneva #34
Namibia

1973

241PDa	Card, #240PD-241PD, #G34PD (1)	—
241PDb	Card, #240PD-241PD, #G34PD, essays of #240-241, #G34 with Africa outlined in gold (3)	1,400.
240PP	8 items (100)	—
241PP	8 items (100)	—
G34PP	8 items (50)	—
240PI	Pair (50)	—
241PI	Pair (50)	—
G34PI	Pair (50)	—

Two cards containing only the essays exist.

New York #242-243, Geneva #35-36, Souvenir Card #4
Universal Declaration of Human Rights, 25th Anniv.

1973

242PD	(9)	275.
243PDa	Card, #242PD-243PD, #G35PD-G36PD (6)	1,300.
243PDb	Card, #242PD-243PD (9)	725.
243PDc	Card, #243PD, #G35PD-G36PD (1)	—
SC4PD	With approval handstamp (3)	—
242PP	5 items (100)	—
243PP	5 items (100)	—
G35PP	5 items (100)	—
G36PP	5 items (50)	—
SC4PP	2 items (1)	—
SC4PI	untrimmed card (1)	—

No. SC4PP may not be a complete set of progressive proofs.

New York #244-245, Geneva #37-38
New International Labor Organization Headquarters

1974

245PDa	Card, #245PD, #G37PD-G38PD, 8c essay of #244 (4)	1,200.
244PP	8 items (75)	—
245PP	8 items (75)	—
G37PP	8 items (50)	—
G38PP	8 items (50)	—
244PI	Pair (50)	—
245PI	Pair (50)	—
G37PI	Pair (50)	—
G38PI	Pair (50)	—

New York #246, Geneva #39-40, Souvenir Card #5
Universal Postal Union, Cent.

1974

246PD	(1)	—
246PDa	Card, #246PD, #G39PD-G40PD (7)	925.
G40PDa	Card, #G39PD-G40PD (1)	—
SC5PD	Affixed to card (5)	400.
SC5PDa	Card with printer instructions in ink (1)	—
SC5PDb	Progressive proof sheet with printer instructions in ink (1)	400.
246PP	6 items (100)	—
G39PP	5 items (50)	—
G40PP	5 items (50)	—
246PI	Pair (25)	—
G39PI	Pair (25)	—
G40PI	Pair (25)	—

New York #247-248, Geneva #41-42
Art at the UN

1974

247PDa	Card, #247PD, #G41PD-G42PD, 15c essay of #248 (5)	1,250.
248PDa	Card, #247PD-248PD, #G41PD-G42PD (3)	925.
247PP	8 items (100)	—
248PP	8 items (100)	—
G41PP	8 items (50)	—
G42PP	8 items (50)	—
247PI	Pair (50)	—
248PI	Pair (50)	—
G41PI	Pair (50)	—
G42PI	Pair (50)	—

New York #249-251
Definitives

1974

249PD	Affixed on perforated blank (1)	—
250PD	Affixed on perforated blank (1)	—
250PDa	Taped to card (1)	—
250PDb	Card, #250PD, 251TC with darker brown background, essay of #249 with flat top "S," with "21.DIC.1973" date and approval stamp (2)	—
251PD	Affixed on perforated blank (1)	125.
251PDa	Card, #249PD, #251PD, with "17.ENE.1974" date and approval stamp (3)	500.
251TCa	Darker brown background, on cards dated "21.DIC.1973" (3)	—
250PP	10 items (50)	—
251PP	8 items (35)	—
249PI	Pair (200)	—
250PI	Pair (50)	—
251PI	Pair (100)	—

New York #252-253, Geneva #43-44, Souvenir Card #6
World Population Year

1974

252PDa	Card, #252PD, #G44PD, 21c essay of #253, 40c essay of #G43 in se-tenant strip (5)	725.
253PDa	Card, #252PD-253PD, G44PD, 40c essay of #G43 in se-tenant strip (4)	800.
SC6PD	With approval handstamp (10)	—
252PP	10 items (50)	—
253PP	10 items (50)	—
G43PP	10 items (50)	—
G44PP	10 items (50)	—
252PI	Pair (50)	—
253PI	Pair (50)	—
G43PI	Pair (50)	—
G44PI	Pair (50)	—

All examples of No. SC6PD show the 40c essay.

New York #254-255, Geneva #45
Law of the Sea

1974

255PDa	Card, #254PD-255PD, #G45TC with blue green sky (3)	800.
254PP	10 items (50)	—
255PP	10 items (50)	—
G45PP	10 items (50)	—
254PI	Pair (50)	—
255PI	Pair (50)	—
G45PI	Pair (50)	—

New York #256-257, Geneva #46-47, Souvenir Card #7
Peaceful Uses of Outer Space

1975

256PDa	Card, #256PD, #G46PD-G47PD (1)	—
257PD	Cut from #256PDa (1)	—
257PDa	Card, #256PD-257PD, G46PD-G47PD (3)	825.
SC7PD	with approval handstamp (4)	—
256PP	8 items (150)	—
257PP	8 items (150)	—
G46PP	8 items (50)	—
G47PP	8 items (50)	—
256PI	Pair (100)	—
257PI	Pair (100)	—
G46PI	Pair (50)	—
G47PI	Pair (50)	—

New York #258-259, Geneva #48-49
International Women's Year

1975

258PD	On card dated "16 Oct. 1974" (4)	250.
259PD	(4)	250.
G48PD	On card dated "16 Oct. 1974" (4)	325.
G49PD	(4)	325.
258TC	bright blue background (on cards dated "17 Sep. 1974") (4)	—
G48TC	red brown background (on cards dated "17 Sep. 1974") (4)	—

258PP	6 items (50)	—
259PP	6 items (50)	—
G48PP	6 items (50)	—
G49PP	6 items (50)	—
258PI	Pair (50)	—
259PI	Pair (50)	—
G48PI	Pair (50)	—
G49PI	Pair (50)	—

Six essays of the 18c stamp with "Nations Unies" inscription, and six essays of the 90c stamp with "United Nations" inscription exist.

New York #260-262, Geneva #50-52
UN, 30th Anniv.

1975

261PDa	Card, #260PD-261PD, #G51PD, #G50TC in olive green, se-tenant (4)	1,200.
262PD	(5)	500.
G52PD	(1)	—
G52TC	With #G52aTC olive green (5)	700.
260PP	6 items (50)	—
261PP	6 items (50)	—
262PP	10 items (6)	—
G50PP	6 items (50)	—
G51PP	6 items (50)	—
G52PP	10 items (6)	—
260PI	Pair (50)	—
261PI	Pair (50)	—
262PI	Pair of souvenir sheets (26)	—
G50PI	Pair (50)	—
G51PI	Pair (50)	—
G52PI	Pair of souvenir sheets (26)	—

New York #263-264, Geneva #53-54
Namibia

1975

264PDa	Card, #263PD-264PD, #G53PD-G54PD (9)	975.
263PP	8 items (50)	—
264PP	8 items (50)	—
G53PP	8 items (50)	—
G54PP	7 items (50)	—
263PI	Pair (50)	—
264PI	Pair (50)	—
G53PI	Pair (50)	—
G54PI	Pair (50)	—

New York #265-266, Geneva #55-56, Souvenir Card #8
UN Peacekeeping Operations

1975

266PDa	Card, #265PD-266PD, #G55PD-G56PD (3)	1,300.
266PDb	Card, #266PD, #G55PD-G56PD, 10c essay of #265 (5)	1,200.
SC8PD	With approval handstamp (5)	—
265PI	Pair (25)	—
266PI	Pair (25)	—
G55PI	Pair (25)	—
G56PI	Pair (25)	—

New York #267-271
Definitives

1976

267PD	(4)	225.
268PD	(3)	350.
269PD	(5)	110.
270PD	(8)	225.
271PD	(4)	200.
271TC	Dark green background (not approved cards dated "30 June 1975" (5)	—
267PP	10 items (25)	—
268PP	8 items (50)	—
269PP	3 items (50)	—
270PP	6 items (50)	—
271PP	10 items (25)	—
267PI	Pair (50)	—
268PI	Pair (50)	—
269PI	Pair (50)	—
270PI	Pair (50)	—
271PI	Pair (50)	—

New York #272-273, Geneva #57, Souvenir Card #9
World Federation of United Nations Associations

1976

273PDa	Card, #272PD-273PD, #G57PD (4)	825.
SC9PD	With approval handstamp dated "18 Sep 1975" (4)	—
SC9TC	With light blue denominations on 1966 stamp (not approved) (5)	—
272PP	6 items (50)	—
273PP	6 items (50)	—
G57PP	6 items (50)	—
272PI	Pair (50)	—
273PI	Pair (50)	—
G57PI	Pair (50)	—

New York #274-275, Geneva #58
UN Conference on Trade and Development

1976

G58PDa	Card, #G58PD, non-denominated essays of #274-275 (5)	725.
274PP	5 items (130)	—
	Vert. pair with horiz. gutter (10)	—
275PP	5 items (130)	—
	Vert. pair with horiz. gutter (10)	—
G58PP	5 items (150)	—
274PI	Pair (80)	—
	Vert. pair with horiz. gutter (20)	—
275PI	Pair (80)	—
	Vert. pair with horiz. gutter (20)	—
G58PI	Pair (80)	—
	Vert. pair with horiz. gutter (20)	—

New York #276-277, Geneva #59-60
UN Conference on Human Settlements

1976

277PDa	Card, #276PD-277PD, #G59PD-G60PD (4)	1,100.
276PP	12 items (50)	—
277PP	12 items (50)	—
G59PP	12 items (50)	—
G60PP	12 items (50)	—
276PI	Pair (50)	—
277PI	Pair (50)	—
G59PI	Pair (50)	—
G60PI	Pair (50)	—

New York #278-279, Geneva #61-62
UN Postal Administration, 25th Anniv.

1976

279PDa	Card, #278PD-279PD, #G61PD-G62PD (5)	700.
278PP	5 items (64)	—
	Horiz. pair with vert. gutter (4)	—
	Vert. pair with horiz. gutter (4)	—
279PP	5 items (64)	—
	Horiz. pair with vert. gutter (4)	—
	Vert. pair with horiz. gutter (4)	—
G61PP	5 items (72)	—
	Horiz. pair with vert. gutter (4)	—
G62PP	5 items (63)	—
	Horiz. pair with vert. gutter (4)	—
	Vert. pair with horiz. gutter (4)	—

New York #280, Geneva #63, Souvenir Card #10
World Food Council

1976

280PD	(5)	200.
G63PD	(5)	200.
SC10PD	With approval handstamp (12)	—
280PP	2 items (50)	—
G63PP	2 items (50)	—
280PI	Pair (50)	—
G63PI	Pair (50)	—

New York #281-282, Geneva #64, Souvenir Card #11
World Intellectual Property Organization

1977

282PDa	Card, #281PD-282PD, #G64PD (4)	650.
SC11PD	With approval handstamp (4)	—
281PP	8 items (50)	—
282PP	8 items (50)	—
G64PP	8 items (50)	—
281PI	Pair (50)	—
282PI	Pair (50)	—
G64PI	Pair (50)	—

New York #283-284, Geneva #65-66
UN Water Conference

1977

283PD	Cut out from #284PDb (1)	—
284PDa	Card, #283PD-284PD, #G65PD-G66PD (2)	925.
284PDb	Card, #284PD, #G65PD-G66PD (1)	—
284PDc	Card, #284PD, #G66PD (1)	—
283PP	6 items (50)	—
284PP	6 items (50)	—

G65PP 5 items (50) —
G66PP 5 items (50) —
283PI Pair (50) —
284PI Pair (50) —
G65PI Pair (50) —
G66PI Pair (50) —

New York #285-286, Geneva #67-68
UN Security Council

1977

286PDa Card, #285PD-286PD, essays of #G67-G68 with small top Chinese character (4) 975.
G68PDa Card, #G67PD-G68PD (large Chinese character) (4) 450.
286PP 8 items (50) —
G67PP 8 items (50) —
G68PP 8 items (50) —
285PI Pair (50) —
286PI Pair (50) —
G67PI Pair (50) —
G68PI Pair (50) —

A card with the two essays only (a cutout of No. 286PDa) with "not approved" handstamp exists.

New York #287-288, Geneva #69-70, Souvenir Card #12
Combat Racism

1977

288PDa Card, #287PD-288PD (4) 425.
G70PDa Card, #G69PD-G70PD (4) 500.
SC12PD With approval handstamp and specimen perfin (5) —
287PP 3 items (50) —
288PP 3 items (50) —
G69PP 6 items (150) —
G70PP 6 items (150) —
287PI Pair (175) —
288PI Pair (175) —
G69PI Pair (225) —
G70PI Pair (225) —

New York #289-290, Geneva #71-72
Peaceful Uses of Atomic Energy

1977

290PDa Card, #289PD-290PD, #G71PD-G72PD (4) 1,100.
290PDb Card, #289PD-290PD, #G71PD, essay of #G72 with capital "F" in "Fins" (6) 975.
289PP 8 items (50) —
290PP 8 items (50) —
G71PP 6 items (50) —
G72PP 6 items (50) —
289PI Pair (50) —
290PI Pair (50) —
G71PI Pair (50) —
G72PI Pair (50) —

New York #291-293, Geneva #73
Definitives

1978

291PD (4) 200.
292PD (5) 225.
293PD (4) 200.
G73PD With approval handstamp (4) 225.
G73TC Tree in deep brown (with "not approved" handstamp (6) 175.
G73PP 6 items (50) —
291PI Pair (50) —
292PI Pair (50) —
293PI Pair (75) —
G73PI Pair (50) —

Six essays of No. 293 having "C" in Naciones not even with "A" exist on card with "not approved" handstamp.

New York #294-295, Geneva #74-75
Global Eradication of Smallpox

1978

295PDa Card, #294PD-295PD, #G74PD-G75PD (5) 1,000.
294PP 2 items (50) —
295PP 2 items (50) —
G74PP 4 items (50) —
G75PP 4 items (50) —
294PI Pair (50) —
295PI Pair (50) —
G74PI Pair (50) —
G75PI Pair (50) —

New York #296-297, Geneva #76, Souvenir Card #13
Liberation, Justice and Cooperation for Namibia

1978

296PD On perforated sheet layout (2) —
297PD On perforated sheet layout (1) —
297PDa Card, #296-297, #G76, perforated (4) 725.
297PDb Card, #296-297 perforated, essay of #G76 ("F." and "S." same size, not approved) (5) 725.
G76PD On perforated sheet layout (9) —
SC13PD With approval handstamp (5) 110.
296PP 6 items (50) —
297PP 6 items (50) —
G76PP 6 items (50) —
296PI Pair (50) —
297PI Pair (50) —
G76PI Pair (50) —

The essay of No. G76 exists on a not approved perforated sheet layout.

New York #298-299, Geneva #77-78, Souvenir Card #14
Safety in the Air

1978

298PDa Card, #298PD, #G77PD-G78PD (1) —
299PD Cut out from #298PDa (1) —
299PDa Card, #298PD-299PD, #G77PD-G78PD (3) 875.
SC14PD With approval handstamp (4) —
298PP 10 items (50) —
299PP 10 items (50) —
G77PP 6 items (50) —
G78PP 6 items (50) —
298PI Pair (50) —
299PI Pair (50) —
G77PI Pair (50) —
G78PI Pair (50) —

New York #300-301, Geneva #79-80
UN General Assembly

1978

301PDa Card, #300PD-301PD, #G79PD-G80PD (4) 975.
300PP 4 items (50) —
301PP 5 items (50) —
G79PP 6 items (50) —
G80PP 6 items (50) —
300PI Pair (25) —
301PI Pair (25) —
G79PI Pair (25) —
G80PI Pair (25) —

New York #302-303, Geneva #81
Technical Cooperation Conference

1978

303PDa Card, #302PD-303PD, #G81PD (3) 975.
302PP 10 items (50) —
303PP 10 items (50) —
G81PP 8 items (50) —
302PI Pair (50) —
303PI Pair (50) —
G81PI Pair (50) —

Five not approved cards have essays of the set showing black behind closer cogwheels and text close to bottom frame. Value $725.

New York #304-307
Definitives

1979

304PD (1) —
304PDa Card, #304PD-307PD (9) —
304PDb Card, #304PD, essays of #305, 306, 307 with inked-in corrections for printer (2) 875.
307PDa Card, #305PD-307PD (3) 725.
304PP 8 items (50) —
305PP 8 items (50) —
306PP 6 items (50) —
307PP 4 items (50) —
304PI Pair (50) —
305PI Pair (50) —
306PI Pair (75) —
307PI Pair (75) —

Three cut-up not approved cards exist containing the three essays with inked-in corrections.

Nos. 306PI and 307PI include 25 pairs of reprints.

New York #308-309, Geneva #82-83
UN Disaster Relief Coordinator

1979		
309PDa	Card, #308PD-309PD (4)	425.
G83PDa	Card, #G82PD-G83PD (1)	—
G83PDb	Card, #G82PD-G83PD, essays of #308-309 with inked-in corrections for printer (3)	875.
308PP	9 items (50)	—
309PP	9 items (50)	—
G82PP	4 items (50)	—
G83PP	4 items (50)	—
308PI	Pair (50)	—
309PI	Pair (50)	—
G82PI	Pair (50)	—
G83PI	Pair (50)	—

Two not approved cards contain the essays with inked-in corrections for printer.

New York #310-311, Geneva #84-85, Souvenir Card #15
International Year of the Child

1979		
310PDa	Card, #310PD, essays of #G84-G85 (with IYC emblem above bottom of children's feet) (1)	—
311PD	Cut out from #310PDa (1)	—
311PDa	Card, #310PD-311PD, essays #G84-G85 (2)	1,350.
G85PDa	Card, #G84PD-G85PD (4)	625.
SC15PD	With manuscript approval (4)	—
310PP	9 items (20)	—
311PP	9 items (20)	—
G84PP	8 items (20)	—
G85PP	10 items (20)	—
310PI	Pair (40)	140.
311PI	Pair (40)	140.
G84PI	Pair (20)	140.
G85PI	Pair (20)	140.

One cut up not approved card contains the two essays. Five essays of No. SC15 marked "not approved" show the stamp essays.

Vienna #1-6
Definitives

1979		
V6PDa	Card, #V1PD-V6PD (5)	2,000.
V1PP	5 items (50)	—
V2PP	5 items (150)	—
V3PP	5 items (50)	—
V4PP	5 items (50)	—
V5PP	5 items (50)	—
V6PP	5 items (50)	—
V1PI	Pair (50)	—
V2PI	Pair (150)	—
V3PI	Pair (50)	—
V4PI	Pair (50)	—
V5PI	Pair (50)	—
V6PI	Pair (50)	—

New York #312-313, Geneva #86
Namibia

1979		
313PDa	Card, #312PD-313PD, #G86PD (4)	825.
312PP	8 items (50)	—
313PP	8 items (50)	—
G86PP	8 items (50)	—
312PI	Pair (50)	—
313PI	Pair (50)	—
G86PI	Pair (50)	—

One card of No. 313PDa is badly damaged.

New York #314-315, Geneva #87-88, Souvenir Card #16
International Court of Justice

1979		
315PDa	Card, #314PD-315PD, #G87PD-G88PD 2 each (4)	1,650.
SC16PD	With "not approved" handstamp and "Specimen" perfin (5)	—
314PP	4 items (50)	—
315PP	4 items (50)	—
G87PP	6 items (50)	—
G88PP	7 items (50)	—
314PI	Pair (50)	—
315PI	Pair (50)	—
G87PI	Pair (50)	—
G88PI	Pair (50)	—

New York #316-317, Geneva #89, Vienna #7
New International Economic Order

1980		
316PD	(11)	225.
317PD	(5)	200.
G89PD	With approval handstamp (5)	175.
V7PD	(5)	225.
316PP	4 items (50)	—
317PP	4 items (50)	—
G89PP	4 items (50)	—
V7PP	5 items (50)	—
316PI	Pair (50)	—
317PI	Pair (50)	—
G89PI	Pair (50)	—
V7PI	Pair (50)	—

Five cards of No. 316PD are marked "not approved" but there are no discernable differences between it and approved proofs. Six "not approved" cards have essays of No. G89 with text "Nouvel International Economique Ordre." Six "not approved" cards have essays of No. V7 with the same text.

Vienna #8
Definitive

1980		
V8PD	(4)	200.
V8PP	11 items, perforated (250)	—
V8PI	Pair (25)	—

New York #318-319, Geneva #90-91, Vienna #9-10, Souvenir Card #17
Decade for Women

1980		
318PD	(13)	225.
319PD	(11)	200.
G90PD	(13)	225.
G91PD	(5)	225.
V9PD	(5)	175.
V10PD	(5)	200.
SC17PD	With approval handstamp (5)	175.
318PP	4 items (50)	—
319PP	4 items (50)	—
G90PP	4 items (50)	—
G91PP	4 items (50)	—
V9PP	3 items (50)	—
V10PP	2 items (50)	—
318PI	Pair (50)	—
319PI	Pair (50)	—
G90PI	Pair (50)	—
G91PI	Pair (50)	—
V9PI	Pair (50)	—
V10PI	Pair (50)	—

New York #320-321, Geneva #92, Vienna #11
UN Peace-keeping Operations

1980		
321PDa	Card, #320PD-321PD, #V11PD, essay of #G92 with "de" on top line (3)	975.
G92PD	(4)	240.
320PP	2 items (50)	—
321PP	8 items (50)	—
G92PP	4 items (50)	—
V11PP	12 items (50)	—
320PI	Pair (50)	—
321PI	Pair (50)	—
G92PI	Pair (50)	—
V11PI	Pair (50)	—

New York #322-324, Geneva #93-95, Vienna #12-14
UN, 35th Anniv.

1980		
324PDa	Card, #324PD, #G95D, #V14PD (4)	1,050.
324PDb	Card, #322PD-324PD, #G93PD-G94PD, #V12PD-V14PD, essay of #G95 with incomplete marginal inscription (3)	1,050.
322PP	8 items (50)	—
323PP	8 items (50)	—
G93PP	6 items (300)	—
G94PP	13 items (650)	—
V12PP	3 items (50)	—
V13PP	8 items (50)	—
322PI	Pair (100)	—
323PI	Pair (100)	—
G93PI	Pair (100)	—
G94PI	Pair (100)	—
V12PI	Pair (175)	—
V13PI	Pair (100)	—

New York #325-340
Flags

1980

325PD	Cut from #340PDa (1)	—
332PD	Cut from #340PDa (1)	—
340PDa	Card, #325PD-340PD (4)	3,500.
340PDb	Card, #326PD-331PD, #333PD-340PD (1)	—
325-340PP	Set of 20 sheets (1)	—
325-340PI	Set of 4 sheets (2)	—

On Nos. 325-340PP, there are five progressive proof sheets per issued sheet.

New York #341-342, Geneva #96-97, Vienna #15-16, Souvenir Card #18
Economic and Social Council

1980

342PDa	Sheet, #341PD-342PD, #G96PD-G97PD, #V15PD-V16PD (4)	110.
G96PD	(4)	—
G97PD	(4)	—
V15PD	(4)	—
V16PD	(4)	—
SC18PD	(4)	—
341PP	6 items (50)	—
342PP	6 items (50)	—
G96PP	6 items (50)	—
G97PP	6 items (50)	—
V15PP	6 items (50)	—
V16PP	6 items (50)	—
341PI	Pair (50)	—
342PI	Pair (50)	—
G96PI	Pair (50)	—
G97PI	Pair (50)	—
V15PI	Pair (50)	—
V16PI	Pair (50)	—

An essay of No. SC18 with curved cancel on 4s stamp has "not approved" handstamp.

New York #343, Geneva #98, Vienna #17
Inalienable Rights of the Palestinian People

1981

343TCa	Card, #343TC blue, #G98PD, #V17PD (1)	625.
G98PD	(5)	—
V17PD	(5)	—
343PP	4 items (50)	—
G98PP	5 items (50)	—
V17PP	4 items (50)	—
343PI	Pair (50)	—
G98PI	Pair (50)	—
V17PI	Pair (50)	—

New York #344-345, Geneva #99-100, Vienna #18-19, Souvenir Card #19
Intl. Year of the Disabled

1980

344PD	Cut out from #G100PDa (1)	—
344PDa	Card, #344PD, #G99PD-G100PD, #V18PD-V19PD, 31c essay of #345 (4)	1,450.
344PDb	Card, #344PD, #G100PD, #V18PD-V19PD (4)	—
G100PDa	Card, #G100PD, #V18PD-V19PD (1)	—
SC19PD	With "not approved" handstamp (9)	110.
344PP	6 items (50)	—
345PP	2 items (50)	—
G99PP	2 items (50)	—
G100PP	2 items (50)	—
V18PP	6 items (50)	—
V19PP	2 items (50)	—
344PI	Pair (50)	—
345PI	Pair (50)	—
G99PI	Pair (50)	—
G100PI	Pair (50)	—
V18PI	Pair (50)	—
V19PI	Pair (50)	—

All die proof cards are stamped "not approved." One example of No. SC19PD has "35c" covering "31c."

New York #346-347, Geneva #101, Vienna #20
Art at the UN

1981

347PDa	Card, #346PD-347PD, #G101PD, #V20PD (1)	1,050.
347PDb	Card, #347PD, #G101PD, #V20PD, 15c essay of #346 (not approved) (6)	—
346PP	5 items (50)	—
347PP	5 items (50)	—
G101PP	5 items (50)	—
V20PP	5 items (50)	—
346PI	Pair (50)	—
347PI	Pair (50)	—
G101PI	Pair (50)	—
V20PI	Pair (50)	—

New York #348-349, Geneva #102, Vienna #21, Souvenir Card #20
Conference on New and Renewable Sources of Energy

1981

348PDa	Card, #348PD, #G102PD, #V21PD, 31c essay of #349 (3)	925.
SC20PD	With approval and specimen handstamps (4)	—
348PP	6 items (50)	—
349PP	4 items (50)	—
G102PP	6 items (50)	—
V21PP	4 items (50)	—
348PI	Pair (50)	—
349PI	Pair (50)	—
G102PI	Pair (50)	—
V21PI	Pair (50)	—

All examples of No. SC20PD have the 31c essay.

New York #350-365
Flags

1981

357PDa	Card, #350PD-357PD (5)	—
365PDa	Card, #358PD-365PD (5)	2,300.
350-365PP	Set of 19 sheets (1)	—
350-365PI	Set of 4 sheets (2)	4,600.

On Nos. 350-365PP, there are four progressive sheets for the issued sheet containing Nos. 354-357, and five progressive proof sheets per issued sheet for the issued sheets containing Nos. 350-353, 358-361 and 362-365. Two sets of imperforate sheets of Nos. 350-353 and two sets of imperforate sheets of Nos. 354-357 exist with 15c denominations are essays.

New York #366-367, Geneva #103-104, Vienna #22-23
Volunteers Program, 10th Anniv.

1981

367PDa	Card, #367PD, #G103PD-G104PD, #V22PD-V23PD, 20c essay of #366 (3)	1,450.
G103TC	white background (1)	—
V22TC	white background (1)	—
V23TC	white background (1)	—
366PI	Pair (50)	—
367PI	Pair (50)	—
G103PI	Pair (50)	—
G104PI	Pair (50)	—
V22PI	Pair (50)	—
V23PI	Pair (50)	—

New York #368-370, Geneva #105-106, Vienna #24
Definitives

1982

370PDa	Card, #368PD-370PD, #G106PD, #V24PD, essay of #G105 with no "l'" before "apartheid" (5)	1,450.
368PP	5 items (50)	—
369PP	5 items (50)	—
370PP	5 items (50)	—
G105PP	4 items (50)	—
G106PP	5 items (50)	—
V24PP	5 items (50)	—
368PI	Pair (50)	—
369PI	Pair (50)	—
370PI	Pair (50)	—
G105PI	Pair (50)	—
C106PI	Pair (50)	—
V24PI	Pair (50)	—

One example of No. 370PDa has all stamps canceled and #G105 altered.

New York #371-372, Geneva #107-108, Vienna #25-26, Souvenir Card #21
Environment Program, 10th Anniv.

1982

372PDa	Card, #371PD-372PD, #G107PD, #V25PD-V26PD, 1.30fr essay of #G108 (5)	1,600.

372PDb	Card, #372PD, #G107PD-G108PD, #V25PD-V26PD, 18c essay of #371 (4)	1,450.
SC21PD	(5)	—
371PP	8 items (50)	—
372PP	7 items (50)	—
G107PP	12 items (50)	—
G108PP	8 items (50)	—
V25PP	7 items (50)	—
V26PP	11 items (50)	—
371PI	Pair (50)	—
372PI	Pair (50)	—
G107PI	Pair (50)	—
G108PI	Pair (50)	—
V25PI	Pair (50)	—
V26PI	Pair (50)	—

One example of No. 372PDb has had some stamps defaced. Five essays of No. SC21PD show the 18c essay, with one altered to change 18c to 20c.

New York #373, Geneva #109-110, Vienna #27, Souvenir Card #22
Exploration and Peaceful Uses of Outer Space

1982

373PDa	Card, #373PD, #G109PD-G110PD, #V27PD (4)	925.
G109PD	(4)	—
G110PD	(4)	—
V27PD	(4)	—
SC22PD	(4)	—
373PP	6 items (50)	—
G109PP	6 items (50)	—
G110PP	14 items (50)	—
V27PP	14 items (50)	—
373PI	Pair (50)	—
G109PI	Pair (50)	—
G110PI	Pair (50)	—
V27PI	Pair (50)	—

New York #374-389
Flags

1982

381PDa	Card, #374PD-381PD (5)	2,000.
389PDa	Card, #382PD-389PD (4)	2,000.
374-389PP	Set of 20 sheets (1)	—
374-389PI	Set of 4 sheets (2)	5,250.

On Nos. 374-389PP, there are five progressive proof sheets per issued sheet.

New York #390-391, Geneva #111-112, Vienna #28-29
Conservation and Protection of Nature

1982

390PDa	Card, #390PD, #G111PD, #V29PD, essays of #G112 and #V28 (1)	—
391PD	(1)	—
391PDa	Card, #390PD-391PD, #G111PD, #V29PD, essays of #G112 and #V28 (3)	1,400.
G112PD	(3)	250.
V29PD	(3)	200.
390PP	10 items (50)	—
391PP	10 items (50)	—
G111PP	10 items (50)	—
G112PP	10 items (50)	—
V28PP	10 items (50)	—
V29PP	10 items (50)	—
390PI	Pair (50)	—
391PI	Pair (50)	—
G111PI	Pair (50)	—
G112PI	Pair (50)	—
V28PI	Pair (50)	—
V29PI	Pair (50)	—

Essays of No. G112 have snake with lighter stripes. Essays of No. V28 have umlaut missing one dot.

New York #392-393, Geneva #113, Vienna #30
World Communications Year

1983

392PD	(5)	225.
393PD	(4)	200.
G113PD	(4)	200.
V30PD	(5)	200.
392TC	Dark blue and green colors switched (4)	300.
V30TC	Dark blue and green colors switched (3)	325.
392PP	10 items (50)	—
393PP	15 items (50)	—
G113PP	15 items (50)	—
V30PP	10 items (50)	—
392PI	Pair (50)	—
393PI	Pair (50)	—
G113PI	Pair (50)	—
V30PI	Pair (50)	—

New York #394-395, Geneva #114-115, Vienna #31-32, Souvenir Card #23
Safety at Sea

1983

395PDa	Card, #394PD-395PD, #G114PD-G115PD, #V31PD-V32PD, #394TC-395TC, #G114TC (1)	—
395PDb	Card, #394PD-395PD, #G114PD (4)	750.
G115PDa	Card, #G115PD, #V31PD-V32PD, #394TC-395TC,#G114TC(10)	—
SC23PD	(5)	—
SC23TC	(6)	—
394PP	10 items (50)	—
395PP	8 items (50)	—
G114PP	11 items (50)	—
G115PP	5 items (50)	—
V31PP	5 items (50)	—
V32PP	8 items (50)	—
394PI	Pair (50)	—
395PI	Pair (50)	—
G114PI	Pair (50)	—
G115PI	Pair (50)	—
V31PI	Pair (50)	—
V32PI	Pair (50)	—

Nos. 394TC and G114TC have orange buoy lights instead of red, and No. 395TC has red violet line in ship instead of orange. These appear on No. SC23TC.

New York #396, Geneva #116, Vienna #33-34
World Food Program

1983

396PD	(3)	225.
G116PD	(3)	225.
V33PD	(3)	200.
V34PD	(3)	225.
396PI	Pair (25)	—
G116PI	Pair (25)	—
V33PI	Pair (25)	—
V34PI	Pair (25)	—

New York #397-398, Geneva #117-118, Vienna #35-36, Souvenir Card #24
UN Conference on Trade and Development

1983

398PDa	Card, #397PD-398PD, #G117PD-G118PD, #V35PD-V36PD, approval handstamp (4)	—
398PDb	Card, #397PD-398PD, #G117PD, #V36PD, essays of #G118 and #V35, (not approved, undated) (5)	1,300.
398PDc	As #398PDb, with red dot essays (not approved, dated) (5)	—
SC24PD	With approval handstamp (4)	—
SC24TC	With "not approved" handstamp (5)	—
397PP	5 items (50)	—
398PP	7 items (50)	—
G117PP	5 items (50)	—
G118PP	6 items (50)	—
V35PP	6 items (50)	—
V36PP	7 items (50)	—
397PI	Pair (50)	—
398PI	Pair (50)	—
G117PI	Pair (50)	—
G118PI	Pair (50)	—
V35PI	Pair (50)	—
V36PI	Pair (50)	—

Essays of Nos. G118 and V35 have blue rectangle instead of blue and yellow triangles on bottom row of flags, along with other differences. No. 398PDb has essays showing flag with green dot in 3rd row; No. 398PDc has red dot on this flag. No. SC24TC has Nos. G118 and V35 with lighter box bottom.

New York #399-414
Flags

1983

403PD	With approval handstamp (1)	240.
406PDa	Card, #399PD-402PD, 404PD-406PD, #403 essay (5)	1,600.

414PDa	Card, #407PD, 409PD-414PD, #408 essay (5)	2,100.
399-414PP	Set of 20 sheets (1)	—
399-414PI	Set of 4 sheets (2)	5,000.

The essay of No. 403 has fewer sun rays than on the issued stamp. The essay of No. 408 has incomplete ring above crest and thinner garlands at left and right. Nos. 413PD-414PD are marked "not approved" on No. 414PDa, but there is no appreciable difference between these and the issued stamps. On Nos. 399-414PP, there are five progressive proof sheets per issued sheet.

New York #415-416, Geneva #119-120, Vienna #37-38 Universal Declaration of Human Rights, 35th Anniv.

1983

415PD	mounted on presentation folder, perforated	450.
416PD	mounted on presentation folder, perforated	450.
G120PDa	Card, #G119PD-G120PD (10)	500.
V37PD	mounted on presentation folder, perforated	325.
V38PD	mounted on presentation folder, perforated	400.
415PP	7 items, with "Muster" overprint (32)	—
415PPa	6 items, without "Muster" overprint (24)	—
	Horiz. pair with vert. gutter, without "Muster" overprint (4)	—
416PP	7 items, with "Muster" overprint (24)	—
	Horiz. pair with vert. gutter, with "Muster" overprint (16)	—
416PPa	6 items, without "Muster" overprint (24)	—
	Horiz. pair with vert. gutter, without "Muster" overprint (4)	—
G119PP	7 items, with "Muster" overprint (24)	—
	Horiz. pair with vert. gutter, with "Muster" overprint (16)	—
G119PPa	6 items, without "Muster" overprint (24)	—
	Horiz. pair with vert. gutter, without "Muster" overprint (4)	—
G120PP	7 items, with "Muster" overprint (24)	—
	Horiz. pair with vert. gutter, with "Muster" overprint (16)	—
G120PPa	6 items, without "Muster" overprint (24)	—
	Horiz. pair with vert. gutter, without "Muster" overprint (4)	—
V37PP	7 items, with "Muster" overprint (24)	—
	Horiz. pair with vert. gutter, with "Muster" overprint (16)	—
V37PPa	6 items, without "Muster" overprint (24)	—
	Horiz. pair with vert. gutter, without "Muster" overprint (4)	—
V38PP	7 items, with "Muster" overprint (24)	—
	Horiz. pair with vert. gutter, with "Muster" overprint (16)	—
V38PPa	6 items, without "Muster" overprint (24)	—
	Horiz. pair with vert. gutter, without "Muster" overprint (4)	—
415PI	Pair (64)	—
	Horiz. pair with vert. gutter (16)	—
416PI	Pair (64)	—
	Horiz. pair with vert. gutter (16)	—
G119PI	Pair (64)	—
	Horiz. pair with vert. gutter (10)	—
G120PI	Pair (64)	—
	Horiz. pair with vert. gutter (16)	—
V37PI	Pair (64)	—
	Horiz. pair with vert. gutter (16)	—
V38PI	Pair (64)	—
	Horiz. pair with vert. gutter (16)	—

On Nos. 415PP-416PP, G119PP-G120PP, V37PP-V38PP, one of the items with "Muster" overprint is a finished imperforate.

New York #417-418, Geneva #121, Vienna #39, Souvenir Card #25 Intl. Conference on Population

1984

417PD	(4)	240.
418PD	(4)	250.
G121PD	(4)	250.
V39PD	(4)	250.
SC25PD	With "not approved" handstamp (9)	—
417PP	8 items (50)	—
418PP	7 items (50)	—
G121PP	8 items (50)	—
V39PP	8 items (50)	—
417PI	Pair (50)	—
418PI	Pair (50)	—
G121PI	Pair (50)	—
V39PI	Pair (50)	—

No. 418PP does not include the blue progressive proof found in No. 417PP.

New York #419-420, Geneva #122-123, Vienna #40-41 World Food Day

1984

419PD	(5)	—
420PDa	Card, #419PD-420PD, #G122PD-G123PD, #V40PD-V41PD with "not approved" handstamp (8)	1,500.
419PP	6 items (50)	—
420PP	6 items (50)	—
G122PP	6 items (50)	—
G123PP	6 items (50)	—
V40PP	6 items (50)	—
V41PP	6 items (50)	—
419PI	Pair (50)	—
420PI	Pair (50)	—
G122PI	Pair (50)	—
G123PI	Pair (50)	—
V40PI	Pair (50)	—
V41PI	Pair (50)	—

There is no appreciable difference between approved and not approved examples of No. 419PD.

New York #421-422, Geneva #124-125, Vienna #42-43 World Heritage Sites

1984

422PDa	Card, #421PD-422PD, with approval handstamp (4)	875.
G125PDa	Card, #G124PD-G125PD, with approval handstamp (4)	625.
V43PDa	Card, #V42PD-V43PD, with approval handstamp (4)	625.
V43TCa	Card, #V42PD (darker sky), V43PD prussian blue sky, "not approved" handstamp (8)	875.
421PP	6 items (80)	—
	Horiz. pair with vert. gutter (10)	—
422PP	6 items (80)	—
	Horiz. pair with vert. gutter (10)	—
G124PP	6 items (80)	—
	Horiz. pair with vert. gutter (10)	—
G125PP	6 items (80)	—
	Horiz. pair with vert. gutter (10)	—
V42PP	6 items (80)	—
	Horiz. pair with vert. gutter (10)	—
V43PP	6 items (80)	—
	Horiz. pair with vert. gutter (10)	—
421PI	Pair (80)	—
	Horiz. pair with vert. gutter (20)	—
422PI	Pair (80)	—
	Horiz. pair with vert. gutter (20)	—
G124PI	Pair (80)	—
	Horiz. pair with vert. gutter (20)	—
G125PI	Pair (80)	—
	Horiz. pair with vert. gutter (20)	—
V42PI	Pair (80)	—
	Horiz. pair with vert. gutter (20)	—
V43PI	Pair (80)	—
	Horiz. pair with vert. gutter (20)	—

Four cards like No. 422PDa with "not approved" handstamp contain essays with slightly different vignettes having taller sky area that is brighter blue and with less distinct designs. Four cards like No. G125PDa contain essays lacking "F.S." before denominations.

New York #423-424, Geneva #126-127, Vienna #44-45 Future for Refugees

1984

424PDa	Card, #423PD-424PD, #G126PD-G127PD, #V44PD-V45PD (2)	—
424PDb	Card, #423PD, #G127PD, 2 each #424PD, #G126PD, #V44PD-V45PD (3)	—
424PDc	Card, #423PD-424PD, #G126PD-G127PD, #V44PD-V45PD, #423TC-424TC, #G126TC-G127TC, V44TC-V45TC (5)	2,750.
424TCa	Card, #423TC-424TC, #G126TC-G127TC, #V44TC-V45TC (1)	—
423PP	2 items (50)	—
G126PP	2 items (50)	—
G127PP	2 items (50)	—
V44PP	2 items (50)	—
V45PP	2 items (50)	—
423PI	Pair (50)	—
424PI	Pair (25)	—
G126PI	Pair (50)	—
G127PI	Pair (50)	—
V44PI	Pair (50)	—
V45PI	Pair (50)	—

Trial color items have backgrounds in buff.

New York #425-440
Flags

1984

432PDa	Card, #429PD-432PD (1)	925.
432PDb	Card, 2 each #429PD-432PD (2)	—
436PDa	Card, #425PD, 427PD, 433PD-436PD, essays of #426, 428 (5)	1,850.
440PDa	Card, #437PD-440PD (1)	925.
440PDb	Card, 2 each #437PD-440PD (2)	—
425-440PP	Set of 21 sheets (1)	—
425-440PI	Set of 4 sheets (2)	4,250.

Essays of Nos. 426 and 428 have country name in smaller type. On Nos. 425-440PP, there are six progressive proof sheets for the issued sheet containing Nos. 429-432, and five progressive proof sheets for the issued sheets containing Nos. 425-428, 433-436 and 437-440.

New York #441-442, Geneva #128, Vienna #46-47, Souvenir Card #26
Intl. Youth Year

1984

441PD	With approval handstamp (4)	350.
442PD	With approval handstamp (3)	240.
G128PD	With approval handstamp (4)	300.
V46PD	(4)	250.
V47PD	(4)	300.
SC26PD	With approval handstamp (4)	—
G128TC	Greenish black strand in center (not approved) (5)	325.
SC26TC	With #G128TC "not approved" handstamp (5)	—
441PP	7 items (50)	—
442PP	9 items (50)	—
G128PP	9 items (50)	—
V46PP	7 items (50)	—
V47PP	7 items (50)	—
441PI	Pair (50)	—
442PI	Pair (50)	—
G128PI	Pair (50)	—
V46PI	Pair (50)	—
V47PI	Pair (50)	—

Five "not approved" essays of No. 441 and four of No. 442 have "N" in "Nations" not touching white frame at bottom. A card with a cutout version of the approved No. 442, but with a "not approved" handstamp, and a card with a cutout essay of No. 442 with an "approved" handstamp exist, probably in error.

New York #443, Geneva #129-130, Vienna #48, Souvenir Card #27
Intl. Labor Organization

1985

443PD	Card, imperforate sheet of 50 stamps (1)	—
443PDa	Card, #443PD (single), #G129PD (single) (4)	500.
G130PDa	Card, #G130PD (single), #V48PD (single) (4)	550.
V48PD	Card, imperforate sheet of 50 stamps (4)	—
SC27PD	With approval handstamp (4)	—
443PI	Pair (50)	—
G129PI	Pair (50)	—
G130PI	Pair (50)	—
V48PI	Pair (50)	—

Essays of No. SC27 exist which have the 1954 stamp with a buff background.

New York #444, Geneva #131-132, Vienna #49
UN University

1985

444PDa	Card, #444PD, #G131PD-G132PD, #V49PD, with approval handstamp (5)	1,150.
G132TC	Bright colors in background ("not approved" handstamp) (6)	400.
444PP	6 items (50)	—
G131PP	6 items (50)	—
G132PP	6 items (50)	—
V49PP	6 items (50)	—
444PI	Pair (50)	—
G131PI	Pair (50)	—
G132PI	Pair (50)	—
V49PI	Pair (50)	—

New York #445-446, Geneva #133-134, Vienna #50-51
Definitives

1985

445PDa	Card, #445PD, #G133PD-G134PD, #V50PD-V51PD, #446TC ("not approved handstamp") (4)	1,600.
446PDa	Card, #445PD-446PD, #G134PD (4)	775.
445PP	4 items (50)	—
446PP	5 items (50)	—
G133PP	7 items (50)	—
G134PP	3 items (50)	—
V50PP	5 items (50)	—
V51PP	5 items (50)	—
V50PI	Pair (50)	—
V51PI	Pair (50)	—

No. 446TC has a lighter blue emblem. Other items in No. 445PDa were declared "not approved," but do not have any appreciable difference from approved items.

New York #447-449, Geneva #135-137, Vienna #52-54
UN, 40th Anniv.

1985

447PDa	Card, 4 each #447PD, #G135PD, #V52PD (1)	—
448PDa	Card, 4 each #448PD, #G136PD, #V53PD (1)	—
449PDa	Card, #447PD-449PD, #G135PD-G137PD, #V52PD-V54PD (1)	1,850.
449PDb	Card, #449PD, #G137PD, #V54PD (4)	—
447PP	5 items (50)	—
448PP	5 items (50)	—
449PP	6 items (36)	—
G135PP	5 items (50)	—
G136PP	5 items (50)	—
G137PP	6 items (36)	—
V52PP	5 items (50)	—
V53PP	5 items (50)	—
V54PP	6 items (36)	—
447PI	Pair (50)	—
448PI	Pair (50)	—
449PI	Pair of souvenir sheets (27)	—
G135PI	Pair (50)	—
G136PI	Pair (50)	—
G137PI	Pair of souvenir sheets (27)	—
V52PI	Pair (50)	—
V53PI	Pair (50)	—
V54PI	Pair of souvenir sheets (27)	—

New York #450-465
Flags

1985

465PDa	Card, #450PD-455PD, 457PD-465PD, essay of #456 (5)	2,900.
450-465PP	Set of 24 sheets (1)	—
450-465PI	Set of 4 sheets (2)	4,000.

Essay of Nos. 456 has thin-lined star. On Nos. 425-440PP, there are six progressive proof sheets per issued sheet.

New York #466-467, Geneva #138-139, Vienna #55-56, Souvenir Card #28
UNICEF Child Survival Campaign

1985

466PD	(4)	300.
466PDa	Card, with cut-up pane of 50 (1)	—
467PD	(4)	—
467PDa	Card, with cut-up pane of 50 (1)	—
G138PD	(4)	300.
G138PDa	Card, with cut-up pane of 50 (1)	—
G139PD	(4)	225.
G139PDa	Card, with cut-up pane of 50 (1)	—
V55PD	(4)	300.
V55PDa	Card, with cut-up pane of 50 (1)	—
V56PD	(4)	250.
V56PDa	Card, with cut-up pane of 50 (1)	—
SC28PD	(4)	—
466PP	5 items (50)	—
467PP	5 items (50)	—
G138PP	5 items (50)	—
G139PP	5 items (50)	—
V55PP	5 items (50)	—
V56PP	5 items (50)	—
466PI	Pair (50)	—
467PI	Pair (50)	—
G138PI	Pair (50)	—
G139PI	Pair (50)	—
V55PI	Pair (50)	—
V56PI	Pair (50)	—

New York #468, Geneva #140, Vienna #57
Africa in Crisis

1986

468PDa	Card, #468PD, #G140PD, essay of #V57 (4)	—
468PP	5 items (50)	—
G140PP	4 items (50)	—
V57PP	4 items (50)	—
468PI	Pair (50)	—
G140PI	Pair (50)	—
V57PI	Pair (50)	—

One example of No. 468PDa has essay of No. V57 corrected to show small loop of "8" at top as in the issued stamp.

New York #472a, Geneva #144a, Vienna #61a
UN Development Program

1986

472aPD	(4)	825.
472aPDa	Card, pane of 10 blocks (2)	—
G144aPD	(4)	825.
G144aPDa	Card, pane of 10 blocks (2)	—
V61aPD	(4)	825.
V61aPDa	Card, pane of 10 blocks (2)	—
472aPP	6 items (10 blocks)	—
G144aPP	6 items (10 blocks)	—
V61aPP	6 items (10 blocks)	—
472aPI	Pair (20)	—
G144aPI	Pair (20)	—
V61aPI	Pair (20)	—

Geneva #145
Definitive

1986

G145PD	(5)	—
G145PP	5 items (50)	—
G145PI	Pair (50)	—

New York #473-474, Geneva #146-147, Vienna #62-63, Souvenir Card #29
Philately

1986

473PDa	Partial pane of 39 with approval handstamp on reverse (1)	—
473PDb	Full pane of 50 with approval handstamp on reverse (3)	—
474PDa	Imperforate pane of 50 with approval handstamp on reverse (4)	—
G146PDa	Imperforate pane of 50 with approval handstamp on reverse (4)	—
G147PDa	Partial pane of 41 with approval handstamp on reverse (1)	—
G147PDb	Full pane of 50 with approval handstamp on reverse (3)	—
V62PDa	Imperforate pane of 50 with approval handstamp on reverse (4)	—
V63PDa	Partial pane of 41 with approval handstamp on reverse (1)	—
V63PDb	Full pane of 50 with approval handstamp on reverse (4)	—
SC29PD	(3)	—
473TC	greenish black (5)	725.
474TC	purple (1)	725.
474TC	blue (1)	725.
474TC	red brown (1)	725.
474TC	olive brown (1)	725.
474TC	dark green (1)	725.
G146TC	purple (1)	725.
G146TC	blue (1)	725.
G146TC	reddish purple (1)	725.
G146TC	greenish black (1)	725.
G146TC	dark olive brown (1)	725.
G147TC	dark blue (5)	775.
V62TC	purple (1)	725.
V62TC	blue (1)	725.
V62TC	red brown (1)	725.
V62TC	greenish black (1)	725.
V62TC	dark olive brown (1)	725.
V63TC	greenish black (5)	775.

New York #475-476, Geneva #148-149, Vienna #64-65, Souvenir Card #30
International Peace Year

1986

475PD	(4)	300.
475PDa	Card, imperforate pane of 50 (1)	—
476PD	(4)	250.
476PDa	Card, imperforate pane of 50 (1)	—
G148PD	(4)	450.
G148PDa	Card, imperforate pane of 50 (1)	—
G149PD	(4)	250.
V64PD	(1)	300.
V65PD	(4)	—
V65PDa	Card, imperforate pane of 50 (1)	—
SC30PD	(4)	—
475PP	4 items (50)	—
476PP	4 items (50)	—
G148PP	4 items (50)	—
G149PP	4 items (50)	—
V64PP	4 items (50)	—
V65PP	3 items (50)	—
475PI	Pair (50)	—
476PI	Pair (50)	—
G148PI	Pair (50)	—
G149PI	Pair (50)	—
V64PI	Pair (50)	—
V65PI	Pair (50)	—

Essays of No. V64 with 7s denominations exist in three cards with singles and one card with an imperforate pane of 50.

New York #477-492
Flags

1986

492PDa	Card, #477PD-492PD (5)	3,250.
477-492PP	Set of 24 sheets (1)	—
477-492PI	Set of 4 sheets (2)	4,000.

On Nos. 477-492PP, there are six progressive proof sheets per issued sheet.

New York #493, Geneva #150, Vienna #66
World Federation of UN Associations, 40th Anniv.

1986

493PD	(3)	525.
493PDa	Imperforate souvenir sheet with cancel lines added (1)	—
G150PD	(3)	300.
G150PDa	Imperforate souvenir sheet with cancel lines added (1)	—
V66PD	(3)	400.
V66PDa	Imperforate souvenir sheet with cancel lines added (1)	—
493PP	8 items (16)	—
G150PP	11 items (16)	—
V66PP	6 items (16)	—
493PI	souvenir sheets (32)	—
G150PI	souvenir sheets (32)	—
V66PI	souvenir sheets (32)	—

Now York #494, Geneva #151, Vienna #67
Trygve Lie

1987

494PD	On imperforate sheet layout (1)	—
494PDa	Card, #494PD, #G151PD, V67PD (4)	725.
G151PD	On imperforate sheet layout (1)	—
V67PD	On imperforate sheet layout (1)	—
494PP	10 items (50)	—
G151PP	10 items (50)	—
V67PP	10 items (50)	—
494PI	Pair (50)	—
G151PI	Pair (100)	—
V67PI	Pair (50)	—

Geneva #152-153
Definitives

1987

G152PD	(1)	375.
G153PD	(4)	—
G153TCa	Card, 2 #G153TC dark blue panel (5)	—
G153TCb	Card, imperforate pane of 50 #G153TC dark blue panel (2)	525.
G152PP	6 items (50)	—
G153PP	5 items (50)	—
G152PI	Pair (50)	—
G153PI	Pair (50)	—

Six essays of No. G152 with design 33mm high exist on cards marked "approved text only."

New York #495-496, Geneva #154-155, Vienna #68-69, Souvenir Card #31
International Year of Shelter for the Homeless

1987

496PDa	Card, #495PD-496PD, #G154PD-G155PD, #V68PD-V69PD (4)	1,350.
SC31PD	(3)	—
495PP	6 items (80)	—
	Horiz. pair with vert. gutter (10)	—

496PP	6 items (80)	—
	Horiz. pair with vert. gutter (10)	—
G154PP	6 items (80)	—
	Horiz. pair with vert. gutter (10)	—
G155PP	6 items (80)	—
	Horiz. pair with vert. gutter (10)	—
V68PP	6 items (80)	—
	Horiz. pair with vert. gutter (10)	—
V69PP	6 items (80)	—
	Horiz. pair with vert. gutter (10)	—
495PI	Pair (80)	—
	Horiz. pair with vert. gutter (20)	—
496PI	Pair (80)	—
	Horiz. pair with vert. gutter (20)	—
G154PI	Pair (80)	—
	Horiz. pair with vert. gutter (20)	—
G155PI	Pair (80)	—
	Horiz. pair with vert. gutter (20)	—
V68PI	Pair (80)	—
	Horiz. pair with vert. gutter (20)	—
V69PI	Pair (80)	—
	Horiz. pair with vert. gutter (20)	—

New York #497-498, Geneva #156-157, Vienna #70-71
Fight Drug Abuse

1987

498PDa	Card, #497PD-498PD, #G156PD-G157PD, #V70PD-V71PD with approval handstamp (5)	1,450.
497PP	8 items (50)	—
498PP	8 items (50)	—
G156PP	8 items (50)	—
G157PP	8 items (50)	—
V70PP	8 items (50)	—
V71PP	8 items (50)	—
497PI	Pair (100)	—
498PI	Pair (100)	—
G156PI	Pair (100)	—
G157PI	Pair (100)	—
V70PI	Pair (100)	—
V71PI	Pair (100)	—

Six "not approved" cards contain essays of the six stamps, each lacking the white line separating the halves of the vignette.

Vienna #72-73
Definitives

1987

V73PDa	Card, #V72PD-V73PD (5)	575.
V72PP	8 items (50)	—
V73PP	7 items (50)	—
V72PI	Pair (100)	—
V73PI	Pair (100)	—

New York #499-514
Flags

1987

511PDa	Card, #500PD, 501PD, 503PD, 507PD, 509PD, 511PD (1)	—
514PDa	Card, #499PD-514PD (5)	3,750.
514PDb	Card, #499PD, 500PD, 502PD, 504PD-506PD, 508PD, 510PD, 512PD-514PD (1)	—
499-514PP	Set of 24 sheets (1)	—
499-502PI	Sheet (2)	—
503-506PI	Sheet (2)	—

On Nos. 499-514PP, there are six progressive proof sheets per issued sheet.

New York #515-516, Geneva #158-159, Vienna #74-75
United Nations Day

1987

515PDa	Card, #515PD, #V74PD, essay of #G158 (1)	—
516PDa	Card, #516PD, #G159PD, #V75PD (1)	—
516PDb	Card, #515PD-516PD, #G159PD, #V74PD-V75PD, essay of #G158 (4)	1,250.
515PP	8 items (36)	—
	Cross gutter block (3)	—
	Horiz. pair with vert. gutter (6)	—
	Vert. pair with horiz. gutter (18)	—
516PP	8 items (36)	—
	Cross gutter block (3)	—
	Horiz. pair with vert. gutter (6)	—
	Vert. pair with horiz. gutter (18)	—
G158PP	8 items (36)	—
	Cross gutter block (3)	—
	Horiz. pair with vert. gutter (6)	—
	Vert. pair with horiz. gutter (18)	—
G159PP	8 items (36)	—
	Cross gutter block (3)	—
	Horiz. pair with vert. gutter (6)	—
	Vert. pair with horiz. gutter (18)	—
V74PP	8 items (36)	—
	Cross gutter block (3)	—
	Horiz. pair with vert. gutter (6)	—
	Vert. pair with horiz. gutter (18)	—
V75PP	8 items (36)	—
	Cross gutter block (3)	—
	Horiz. pair with vert. gutter (6)	—
	Vert. pair with horiz. gutter (18)	—
515PI	Pair (12)	—
516PI	Pair (12)	—
G158PI	Pair (28)	—
	Cross gutter block (3)	—
	Horiz. pair with vert. gutter (6)	—
	Vert. pair with horiz. gutter (18)	—
G159PI	Pair (28)	—
	Cross gutter block (3)	—
	Horiz. pair with vert. gutter (6)	—
	Vert. pair with horiz. gutter (18)	—
V74PI	Pair (28)	—
	Cross gutter block (3)	—
	Horiz. pair with vert. gutter (6)	—
	Vert. pair with horiz. gutter (18)	—
V75PI	Pair (28)	—
	Cross gutter block (3)	—
	Horiz. pair with vert. gutter (6)	—
	Vert. pair with horiz. gutter (18)	—

Essay of No. G158 lacks accent in "Journée."

New York #517-518, Geneva #160-161, Vienna #76-77, Souvenir Card #32
Immunize Every Child

1987

518PDa	Card, #517PD-518PD, #G161PD, #V76PD-V77PD, 35c essay of #G160 (11)	1,500.
SC32PD	(11)	—
517PP	11 items (50)	—
518PP	11 items (50)	—
G160PP	11 items (50)	—
G161PP	12 items (50)	—
V76PP	12 items (50)	—
V77PP	9 items (50)	—
5178PI	Pair (50)	—
518PI	Pair (50)	—
G160PI	Pair (75)	—
G161PI	Pair (75)	—
V76PI	Pair (75)	—
V77PI	Pair (75)	—

All examples of No. SC32PD have the essay of No. G160. There is no appreciable difference between approved and not approved examples of Nos. 518PDa or SC32PD.

New York #519-520, Geneva #162-163, Vienna #78-79
International Fund for Agricultural Development

1988

520PDa	Card, #519PD-520PD, #G162PD-G163PD, #V78PD-V79PD (4)	1,550.
519PP	8 items (50)	—
520PP	8 items (50)	—
G162PP	9 items (50)	—
G163PP	9 items (50)	—
V78PP	9 items (50)	—
V79PP	9 items (50)	—
519PI	Pair (50)	—
520PI	Pair (50)	—
G162PI	Pair (50)	—
G163PI	Pair (50)	—
V78PI	Pair (50)	—
V79PI	Pair (50)	—

New York #521, Geneva #164
Definitives

1988

521PD	(4)	575.
G164PD	(6)	300.
521PP	6 items (50)	—
G164PP	11 items (50)	—
521PI	Pair (50)	—
G164PI	Pair (50)	—

New York #523a, Geneva #166a, Vienna #81a
Survival of the Forests

1988

523aPDa	Card, imperforate pane of 6 pairs with approval handstamp (6)	2,750.
523aPDb	Card, perforated pane of 6 pairs with approval handstamp (1)	—
G166aPDa	Card, imperforate pane of 6 pairs with approval handstamp (7)	2,400.
V81aPDa	Card, imperforate pane of 6 pairs with approval handstamp (7)	2,400.
523aPP	8 items (6 pairs)	—
G166aPP	8 items (6 pairs)	—
V81aPP	8 items (6 pairs)	—
523aPI	Pair (12)	—
G166aPI	Pair (24)	—
V81aPI	Pair (24)	—

Panes on Nos. 523aPDa, 523aPDb, G166aPDa, V81aPDa are not affixed to cards but are between stamp mounts.

New York #524-525, Geneva #167-168, Vienna #82-83, Souvenir Card #33
Intl. Volunteer Day

1988

524PDa	Card, #524PD, #G167PD-G168PD, #V82PD-V83PD with approval handstamp (4)	1,400.
525PDa	Card, #525PD, #G168PD, #V83PD, essays of #524, #G167, #V82 with "not approved" handstamp (4)	875.
SC33PD	(4)	—
SC33TC	light blue signature (4)	—
524PP	6 items (40)	—
525PP	6 items (40)	—
525PPa	Horiz. se-tenant pair with vert. gutter, #524PP-525PP (10)	—
G167PP	6 items (40)	—
G168PP	6 items (40)	—
G168PPa	Horiz. se-tenant pair with vert. gutter, #G167PP-G168PP (10)	—
V82PP	6 items (40)	—
V83PP	6 items (40)	—
V83PPa	Horiz. se-tenant pair with vert. gutter, #V82PP-V83PP (10)	—
524PI	Pair (70)	—
525PI	Pair (70)	—
G167PI	Pair (70)	—
G168PI	Pair (70)	—
V82PI	Pair (70)	—
V83PI	Pair (70)	—

Essays have incomplete dates at bottom.

New York #526-527, Geneva #169-170, Vienna #84-85, Souvenir Card #34
Health in Sports

1988

526PD	With approval handstamp(2)	250.
526PDa	Card, #526PD, #527TC (1)	—
526PDb	Card, imperforate pane of 50 #526PD (1)	—
527PD	(6)	150.
527PDa	Card, 2 #527PD (1)	—
527PDb	Card, imperforate pane of 50 #527PD (2)	—
G169PD	(6)	350.
G169PDa	Card, 2 #G169PD (1)	—
G169PDb	Card, imperforate pane of 50 #G169PD (2)	—
G170PD	With approval handstamp (2)	350.
G170PDa	Card, #G170PD, #G170TC (1)	—
G170PDb	Card, imperforate pane of 50 #G170PD (1)	—
V84PD	With approval handstamp (2)	450.
V84PDa	Card, #V84PD, #V84TC (1)	—
V84PDb	Card, imperforate pane of 50 #V84PD (1)	—
V85PD	(6)	450.
V85PDa	Card, 2 #V85PD (1)	—
V85PDb	Card, imperforate pane of 50 #V85PD (2)	—
SC34PD	With approval handstamp (5)	—
526TC	Card, darker brown in LL part of vignette (not approved) (4)	325.
526TCa	Card, imperforate pane of 50 #526TC (1)	—
G170TC	Card, black "F.S." (not approved) (4)	—
G170TCa	Card, imperforate pane of 50 #G170TC (1)	—
V84TC	Card, red splotches in UL of vignette (not approved) (4)	325.
V84TCa	Card, imperforate pane of 50 #V84TC (109)	—
SC34TC	With #526TC (not approved) (4)	—
526PP	4 items (50)	—
527PP	4 items (50)	—
G169PP	4 items (50)	—
G170PP	4 items (50)	—
V84PP	5 items (50)	—
V85PP	4 items (50)	—
526PI	Pair (50)	—
527PI	Pair (50)	—
G169PI	Pair (50)	—
G170PI	Pair (45)	—
V84PI	Pair (50)	—
V85PI	Pair (50)	—

There is no appreciable difference between approved and not approved examples of Nos. 527PD, G169PD and V85PD.

New York #528-543
Flags

1988

543PDa	Card, #540PD, 543PD (2)	425.
543PDb	Card, #540PD, 543PD, 22c essays of #528-539, 541-542 (2)	—
528-543PP	Set of 24 sheets (1)	—
528-543PI	Set of 4 sheets (2)	3,000.

Nine cards each containing 22c essays of Nos. 528-543 exist. Value $2,900 each. On Nos. 528-543PP, there are six progressive proof sheets per issued sheet.

New York #544-545, Geneva #171-172, Vienna #86-87
Universal Declaration of Human Rights, 40th Anniv.

1988

545PDa	Card, #544PD-545PD, #G171PD-G172PD, #V86PD-V87PD (5)	2,900.
G172PDa	Card, #172PD, 90c essay of #G172 (6)	775.
544PP	6 items (50)	—
545PP	6 items (1)	—
G171PP	6 items (50)	—
G172PP	6 items (1)	—
V86PP	6 items (50)	—
V87PP	6 items (1)	
544PI	Pair (50)	—
545PI	souvenir sheets (2)	650.
G171PI	Pair (50)	—
G172PI	souvenir sheets (2)	975.
V86PI	Pair (50)	625.
V87PI	souvenir sheets (2)	—

New York #546-547, Geneva #173-174, Vienna #88-89, Souvenir Card #35
World Bank

1989

547PDa	Card, #546PD-547PD, #G173PD-G174PD, #V88PD-V89PD with approval handstamp (4)	1,250.
547PDb	Card, #547PD in slightly lighter colors, #V88PD, #G173TC, essays of #546, #G174, #V89 (5)	1,150.
SC35PD	With "29 Aug. 1988" handstamp on back (4)	—
546PP	6 items (40)	—
547PP	6 items (40)	—
547PPa	Vert. se-tenant pair with horiz. gutter, #546PP-547PP (10)	—
G173PP	6 items (40)	—
G174PP	6 items (40)	—
G174PPa	Vert. se-tenant pair with horiz. gutter, #G173PP-G174PP (10)	—
V88PP	6 items (40)	—
V89PP	6 items (40)	—
V89PPa	Vert. se-tenant pair with horiz. gutter, #V88PP-V89PP (10)	—
546PI	Pair (40)	—
547PI	Pair (40)	—
G173PI	Pair (70)	—
G174PI	Pair (70)	—
G174PIa	Vert. se-tenant pair with horiz. gutter, #G173PI-G174PI (10)	—
V88PI	Pair (50)	—
V89PI	Pair (50)	—

No. G173TC has lighter orange background. Essays of Nos. 546, G174, and V89 have incomplete years at bottom.

New York #548, Geneva #175, Vienna #90
UN Peace-keeping Force

1989

548PD	Imperforate pane of 50 with "not approved" handstamp (1)	—
548PDa	Card, #548PD, #G175PD, #V90PD (5)	—
G175PD	Imperforate pane of 50 with "not approved" handstamp (1)	—
V90PD	Imperforate pane of 50 with "not approved" handstamp (1)	—
548PP	6 items (90)	—
	Horiz. pair with vert. gutter (5)	—
G175PP	6 items (90)	—
	Horiz. pair with vert. gutter (5)	—
V90PP	6 items (90)	—
	Horiz. pair with vert. gutter (5)	—
548PI	Pair (70)	—
G175PI	Pair (138)	—
	Horiz. pair with vert. gutter (10)	—
V90PI	Pair (138)	—
	Horiz. pair with vert. gutter (10)	—

There is no appreciable difference between approved and not approved examples of No. 548PDa.

New York #549
Definitive

1989

549PD	(9)	—
549PP	6 items (64)	—
	Cross gutter block (1)	—
	Horiz. pair with vert. gutter (8)	—
	Vert. pair with horiz. gutter (8)	—
549PI	Pair (24)	—

There is no appreciable difference between approved and not approved examples of No. 549PD.

New York #550-551, Geneva #176-177, Vienna #91-92, Souvenir Card #36
World Weather Watch

1989

551PDa	Card, #550PD-551PD, #G176PD-G177PD, #V91PD-V92PD (9)	—
SC36PD	(4)	—
550PP	6 items (40)	—
551PP	6 items (40)	—
551PPa	Vert. se-tenant pair with horiz. gutter, #550PP-551PP (10)	—
G176PP	6 items (40)	—
G177PP	6 items (40)	—
G177PPa	Vert. se-tenant pair with horiz. gutter, #G176PP-G177PP (10)	—
V91PP	6 items (40)	—
V92PP	6 items (40)	—
V92PPa	Vert. se-tenant pair with horiz. gutter, #V91PP-V92PP (10)	—
550PI	(50 pairs)	—
551PI	(50 pairs)	—
G176PI	(70 pairs)	—
G177PI	(70 pairs)	—
G177PIa	Vert. se-tenant pair with horiz. gutter, #G176PI-G177PI (10)	—
V91PI	(50 pairs)	—
V92PI	(50 pairs)	—

There is no appreciable difference between approved and not approved examples of No. 551PDa.

New York #552-553, Geneva #178-179, Vienna #93-94
Offices in Vienna, 10th Anniv.

1989

552PD	With approval handstamp (4)	—
553PD	(4)	—
G178PD	(4)	—
G179PDa	Card, #G179PD, #G179TC orange background, #G179TC dull green background (4)	—
V93PD	(4)	—
V94PD	(9)	—
552PP	10 items (25)	—
553PP	12 items (25)	—
G178PP	10 items (25)	—
G179PP	10 items (25)	—
V93PP	10 items (25)	—
V94PP	10 items (25)	—
552PI	(24 pairs)	—
553PI	(24 pairs)	—
G178PI	(24 pairs)	—
G179PI	(24 pairs)	—
V93PI	(24 pairs)	—
V94PI	(24 pairs)	—

Five not approved essays of #552 have clearly defined cross-hatching in background. There is no appreciable difference between approved and not approved examples of No. V94PD. One item from No. G179PP and V93PP is blank as it is from progressive proof sheet showing only black sheet margins.

New York #554-569
Flags

1989

568PDa	Card, #558PD-561PD, 563PD, 564PD, 566PD-568PD (6)	—
569PDa	Card, #554PD-569PD (5)	—
554-569PP	Set of 24 sheets (1)	—
554-569PI	Set of 4 sheets (2)	—

On Nos. 554-569PP, there are six progressive proof sheets per issued sheet.

New York #570-571, Geneva #180-181, Vienna #95-96
Human Rights

1989

570PD	Strip of 3 + 3 labels (4)	—
571PD	Strip of 3 + 3 labels (4)	—
571PDa	Card, #570PD-571PD, #G180PD-G181PD, #V95PD-V96PD (5)	—
G180PD	3 singles or strip of 3 + 3 labels (4)	—
G181PD	Strip of 3 + 3 labels (4)	—
V95PD	Strip of 3 + 3 labels (4)	—
V96PD	3 singles or strip of 3 + 3 labels (4)	—
570PP	6 items (20)	—
	Cross gutter block (1)	—
	Horiz. pair with vert. gutter (2)	—
	Vert. pair with horiz. gutter (10)	—
571PP	6 items (20)	—
	Cross gutter block (1)	—
	Horiz. pair with vert. gutter (2)	—
	Vert. pair with horiz. gutter (10)	—
G180PP	6 items (20)	—
	Cross gutter block (1)	—
	Horiz. pair with vert. gutter (2)	—
	Vert. pair with horiz. gutter (10)	—
G181PP	6 items (20)	—
	Cross gutter block (1)	—
	Horiz. pair with vert. gutter (2)	—
	Vert. pair with horiz. gutter (10)	—
V95PP	6 items (48)	—
	Cross gutter block (1)	—
	Horiz. pair with vert. gutter (2)	—
	Vert. pair with horiz. gutter (10)	—
V96PP	6 items (48)	—
	Cross gutter block (1)	—
	Horiz. pair with vert. gutter (2)	—
	Vert. pair with horiz. gutter (10)	—
570PI	(12 pairs)	—
	Cross gutter block (1)	—
	Horiz. pair with vert. gutter (2)	—
	Vert. pair with horiz. gutter (10)	—
571PI	(12 pairs)	—
	Cross gutter block (1)	—
	Horiz. pair with vert. gutter (2)	—
	Vert. pair with horiz. gutter (10)	—
G180PI	(20 pairs)	—
	Cross gutter block (1)	—
	Horiz. pair with vert. gutter (2)	—
	Vert. pair with horiz. gutter (10)	—
G181PI	(20 pairs)	—
	Cross gutter block (1)	—
	Horiz. pair with vert. gutter (2)	—
	Vert. pair with horiz. gutter (10)	—
V95PI	(20 pairs)	—
	Cross gutter block (1)	—
	Horiz. pair with vert. gutter (2)	—
	Vert. pair with horiz. gutter (10)	—
V96PI	(20 pairs)	—
	Cross gutter block (1)	—
	Horiz. pair with vert. gutter (2)	—
	Vert. pair with horiz. gutter (10)	—

New York #572, Geneva #182, Vienna #97
International Trade Center

1990

572PDa	Card, #572PD, #G182PD, #V97PD with approval handstamp (5)	—
572TCa	Card, #572TC blue green ship, #G182TC red orange ship, #V97TC light pink building, with "not approved" handstamp (6)	—
572PP	9 items (50)	—

G182PP	7 items (50)	—
V97PP	8 items (50)	—
572PI	(50 pairs)	—
G182PI	(75 pairs)	—
V97PI	(50 pairs)	—

Geneva #183, Vienna #98 Definitives

1990

G183PD	(6)	—
V98PD	Proof on large sheet with approval or "not approved" handstamp, and set of 7 progressive proofs on large sheets (9)	—
G183PP	9 items (1)	—
V98PP	7 items (50)	—
G183PI	(50 pairs)	—
V98PI	(50 pairs)	—

The not approved proofs of No. V98PD are slightly lighter in color than the approved proofs.

New York #573-574, Geneva #184-185, Vienna #99-100, Souvenir Card #37 Fight AIDS Worldwide

1990

573PDa	Card, #573PD, #G184PD, #V99PD (4)	—
574PDa	Card, #574PD, #G185PD, #573TC white background, #G184TC white background, #V99TC white background, 10s essay of #V100 (4)	—
SC37PD	(4)	—
573PP	7 items (50)	—
574PP	6 items (50)	—
G184PP	7 items (50)	—
G185PP	7 items (50)	—
V99PP	7 items (50)	—
V100PP	6 items (50)	—
573PI	(50 pairs)	—
574PI	(50 pairs)	—
G184PI	(75 pairs)	—
G185PI	(75 pairs)	—
V99PI	(75 pairs)	—
V100PI	(75 pairs)	—

New York #575-576, Geneva #186-187, Vienna #101-102 Medicinal Plants

1990

576PDa	Card, #575PD-576PD, #G186PD-G187PD, #V101PD-V102PD (4)	—
G187PD	(4)	—
G186PP	6 items (50)	—
G187PP	6 items (50)	—
V101PP	6 items (50)	—
V102PP	6 items (50)	—
575PI	(50 pairs)	—
576PI	(50 pairs)	—
G186PI	(50 pairs)	—
G187PI	(50 pairs)	—
V101PI	(50 pairs)	—
V102PI	(50 pairs)	—

New York #577-579, Geneva #188-190, Vienna #103-105 United Nations, 45th Anniv.

1990

578PDa	Card, #577PD-578PD, #G188PD-G189PD, 6s essay of #V103, 8s essay of #V104 (4)	—
579PDa	Card, #579PD, #G190PD, #V105PD (4)	—
577PP	8 items (320)	—
	Horiz. pair with vert. gutter (40)	—
578PP	8 items (320)	—
	Horiz. pair with vert. gutter (40)	—
579PP	8 items (100)	—
G188PP	10 items (160)	—
	Horiz. pair with vert. gutter (20)	—
G189PP	8 items (320)	—
	Horiz. pair with vert. gutter (40)	—
G190PP	9 items (100)	—
V103PP	8 items (320)	—
	Horiz. pair with vert. gutter (40)	—
V104PP	8 items (320)	—
	Horiz. pair with vert. gutter (40)	—
V105PP	8 items (100)	—
577PI	(80 pairs)	—
	Horiz. pair with vert. gutter (10)	—
578PI	(80 pairs)	—
	Horiz. pair with vert. gutter (10)	—
579PI	(100 souvenir sheets)	—
G188PI	(260 pairs)	—
	Horiz. pair with vert. gutter (40)	—
G189PI	(260 pairs)	—
	Horiz. pair with vert. gutter (40)	—
G190PI	(100 souvenir sheets)	—
V103PI	(260 pairs)	—
	Horiz. pair with vert. gutter (40)	—
V104PI	(260 pairs)	—
	Horiz. pair with vert. gutter (40)	—
V105PI	(100 souvenir sheets)	—

New York #580-581, Geneva #191-192, Vienna #106-107, Souvenir Card #38 Crime Prevention

1990

581PDa	Card, #580PD-581PD, #G191PD-G192PD, #V106PD-V107PD, #SC38PD (5)	—
580PP	8 items (50)	—
581PP	8 items (50)	—
G191PP	8 items (50)	—
G192PP	8 items (50)	—
V106PP	8 items (100)	—
V107PP	8 items (100)	—
580PI	(50 pairs)	—
581PI	(50 pairs)	—
G191PI	(75 pairs)	—
G192PI	(75 pairs)	—
V106PI	(75 pairs)	—
V107PI	(75 pairs)	—

New York #582-583, Geneva #193-194, Vienna #108-109, Human Rights

1990

582PDa	Strip of 3 + 3 labels (9)	—
583PDa	Strip of 3 + 3 labels with approval handstamp (4)	—
G193PDa	Strip of 3 + 3 labels (9)	—
G194PDa	Strip of 3 + 3 labels (9)	—
V108PDa	Strip of 3 + 3 labels (9)	—
V109PDa	Strip of 3 + 3 labels (9)	—
583TCa	Strip of 3 + 3 labels (chocolate panels) with "not approved" handstamp (5)	—
582PP	6 items (20)	—
	Cross gutter block (1)	—
	Horiz. pair with vert. gutter (2)	—
	Vert. pair with horiz. gutter (10)	—
583PP	6 items (20)	—
	Cross gutter block (1)	—
	Horiz. pair with vert. gutter (2)	—
	Vert. pair with horiz. gutter (10)	—
G193PP	6 items (20)	—
	Cross gutter block (1)	—
	Horiz. pair with vert. gutter (2)	—
	Vert. pair with horiz. gutter (10)	—
G194PP	8 items (20)	—
	Cross gutter block (1)	—
	Horiz. pair with vert. gutter (2)	—
	Vert. pair with horiz. gutter (10)	—
V108PP	6 items (20)	—
	Cross gutter block (1)	—
	Horiz. pair with vert. gutter (2)	—
	Vert. pair with horiz. gutter (10)	—
V109PP	6 items (20)	—
	Cross gutter block (1)	—
	Horiz. pair with vert. gutter (2)	—
	Vert. pair with horiz. gutter (10)	—
582PI	(20 pairs)	—
	Cross gutter block (1)	—
	Horiz. pair with vert. gutter (2)	—
	Vert. pair with horiz. gutter (10)	—
583PI	(20 pairs)	—
	Cross gutter block (1)	—
	Horiz. pair with vert. gutter (2)	—
	Vert. pair with horiz. gutter (10)	—
G193PI	(20 pairs)	—
	Cross gutter block (1)	—
	Horiz. pair with vert. gutter (2)	—
	Vert. pair with horiz. gutter (10)	—
G194PI	(20 pairs)	—
	Cross gutter block (1)	—
	Horiz. pair with vert. gutter (2)	—
	Vert. pair with horiz. gutter (10)	—
V108PI	(20 pairs)	—
	Cross gutter block (1)	—
	Horiz. pair with vert. gutter (2)	—
	Vert. pair with horiz. gutter (10)	—

V109PI	(20 pairs)	—
	Cross gutter block (1)	—
	Horiz. pair with vert. gutter (2)	—
	Vert. pair with horiz. gutter (10)	—

There is no appreciable difference between approved and not approved examples of Nos. 582PD, G193PD, G194PD, V108PD and V109PD.

New York #587a, Geneva #198a, Vienna #113a, Souvenir Card #39
Economic Council for Europe

1991

587aPDa	Card, #587aPD, #G198aPD, #V113aPD with printed perforations (2)	—
587aPDb	Card, #587aPDa, SC39PD (1)	—
SC39PD	(1)	—
587aPP	13 items (20 blocks)	—
G198aPP	13 items (20 blocks)	—
V113aPP	13 items (20 blocks)	—
587aPI	(40 blocks)	—
G198aPI	(40 blocks)	—
V113aPI	(40 blocks)	—

Second sets of blocks of Nos. 587aPP and G198aPP with 10 items, and No. V113aPP with 11 items (some items differing from the 13 item set) exist.

New York #588-589, Geneva #199-200, Vienna #114-115
Namibian Independence

1991

588PDa	Card, #588PD, #G199PD-G200PD, #V114PD-V115PD, 36c essay of #589 (8)	—
589PDa	Card, #588PD-589PD, #G199PD-G200PD, #V114PD-V115PD (1)	—
588PP	7 items (50)	—
589PP	7 items (50)	—
G199PP	8 items (50)	—
G200PP	8 items (50)	—
V114PP	6 items (50)	—
V115PP	6 items (50)	—
588PI	(100 pairs)	—
589PI	(100 pairs)	—
G199PI	(75 pairs)	—
G200PI	(75 pairs)	—
V114PI	(75 pairs)	—
V115PI	(75 pairs)	—

New York #590-592, Geneva #201-202, Vienna #116
Definitives

1991

590PD	With approval handstamp (4)	—
592PD	(4)	—
592PDa	Card, imperforate pane of 50 (1)	—
G201PD	(5)	—
G202PDa	Card, #G201PD-G202PD, #G213PD, #V116PD (4)	—
590TC	deep blue background (not approved) (5)	—
592TC	black (1)	—
590PP	8 items (80)	—
	Horiz. pair with vert. gutter (10)	—
591PP	4 items (150)	—
G201PP	8 items (50)	—
G202PP	7 items (50)	—
V116PP	7 items (50)	—
590PI	(90 pairs)	—
	Horiz. pair with vert. gutter (10)	—
591PI	(175 pairs)	—
592PI	(50 pairs)	—
G201PI	(75 pairs)	—
G202PI	(100 pairs)	—
V116PI	(75 pairs)	—

An essay of No. 592 with emblem in solid color exists.

New York #593-594, Geneva #203-204, Vienna #117-118, Souvenir Card #40
Rights of the Child

1991

593PDa	Card, #593PD, #G203PD-G204PD, #V117PD-V118PD, 90c essay of #594 (6)	—
594PDa	Card, #593PD-594PD, #G203PD-G204PD, #V117PD-V118PD (4)	—
594PDb	Card, #593PD-594PD (4)	—
SC40PD	(4)	—
593PP	9 items (50)	—
594PP	9 items (50)	—
G203PP	8 items (50)	—
G204PP	7 items (50)	—
V117PP	7 items (50)	—
V118PP	7 items (50)	—
SC40PP	15 items (1)	—
593PI	(75 pairs)	—
594PI	(75 pairs)	—
G203PI	(75 pairs)	—
G204PI	(75 pairs)	—
V117PI	(75 pairs)	—
V118PI	(75 pairs)	—

No. SC40PP may not be a complete set of progressive proofs. Five essays of No. SC40PD with the 90c essay of No. 594 exist; one is attached to No. 593PDa.

New York #595-596, Geneva #205-206, Vienna #119-120,
Banning of Chemical Weapons

1991

596PDa	Card, #595PD-596PD, #G205PD-G206PD, #V119PD-V120PD with approval handstamp (5)	—
596PDb	Card, #596PD, #G206PD, #V120PD, essays of #595, #G205, #V119 (each with gray panels taller than numerals) with "not approved" handstamp (4)	—
595PP	9 items (50)	—
596PP	9 items (50)	—
G205PP	9 items (100)	—
G206PP	9 items (100)	—
V119PP	8 items (50)	—
V120PP	8 items (50)	—
595PI	(125 pairs)	—
596PI	(125 pairs)	—
G205PI	(125 pairs)	—
G206PI	(125 pairs)	—
V119PI	(125 pairs)	—
V120PI	(125 pairs)	—

Second sets of six items of Nos. 595PP-596PP, G205PP-G206PP, and V119PP-V120PP exist. Some items differ from those found in the listed sets.

New York #597-598, Geneva #207-208, Vienna #121-122
UN Postal Administration, 40th Anniv.

1991

598PDa	Card, #597PD-598PD, #G207PD-G208PD, #V121PD-V122PD (4)	—
597TCa	Card, #597TC, #G207TC-G208TCD, #V121TC-V122TC (each with white background), 36c essay of #598 (6)	—
597PP	2 items (64)	—
	Cross gutter block (1)	—
	Horiz. pair with vert. gutter (8)	—
	Vert. pair with horiz. gutter (8)	—
598PP	2 items (64)	—
	Cross gutter block (1)	—
	Horiz. pair with vert. gutter (8)	—
	Vert. pair with horiz. gutter (8)	—
G207PP	2 items (64)	—
	Cross gutter block (1)	—
	Horiz. pair with vert. gutter (8)	—
	Vert. pair with horiz. gutter (8)	—
G208PP	2 items (64)	—
	Cross gutter block (1)	—
	Horiz. pair with vert. gutter (8)	—
	Vert. pair with horiz. gutter (8)	—
V121PP	2 items (64)	—
	Cross gutter block (1)	—
	Horiz. pair with vert. gutter (8)	—
	Vert. pair with horiz. gutter (8)	—
V122PP	2 items (64)	—
	Cross gutter block (1)	—
	Horiz. pair with vert. gutter (8)	—
	Vert. pair with horiz. gutter (8)	—
597PI	(120 pairs)	—
	Cross gutter block (3)	—
	Horiz. pair with vert. gutter (24)	—
	Vert. pair with horiz. gutter (24)	—
598PI	(120 pairs)	—
	Cross gutter block (3)	—
	Horiz. pair with vert. gutter (24)	—
	Vert. pair with horiz. gutter (24)	—
G207PI	(120 pairs)	—
	Cross gutter block (3)	—
	Horiz. pair with vert. gutter (24)	—
	Vert. pair with horiz. gutter (24)	—

G208PI (120 pairs) —
Cross gutter block (3) —
Horiz. pair with vert. gutter (24) —
Vert. pair with horiz. gutter (24) —
V121PI (120 pairs) —
Cross gutter block (3) —
Horiz. pair with vert. gutter (24) —
Vert. pair with horiz. gutter (24) —
V122PI (120 pairs) —
Cross gutter block (3) —
Horiz. pair with vert. gutter (24) —
Vert. pair with horiz. gutter (24) —

Four cross gutter blocks, 32 horizontal pairs with vertical gutters and 32 vertical pairs with horizontal gutters can be cut from four perforated sheets of Nos. 597PI-598PI, G207PI-G208PI, V119PI-V120PI. No. 598PI is difficult to distinguish from one item from No. 598PP.

New York #599-600, Geneva #209-210, Vienna #123-124, Human Rights

1991

599PDa Strip of 3 + 3 labels with approval handstamp (4) —
600PDa Strip of 3 + 3 labels with approval handstamp (4) —
G209PDa Strip of 3 + 3 labels with approval handstamp (4) —
G210PDa Strip of 3 + 3 labels with approval handstamp (4) —
V123PDa Strip of 3 + 3 labels with approval handstamp (4) —
V124PDa Strip of 3 + 3 labels with approval handstamp (4) —
599TC Strip of 3 (dark gray background) + 3 labels with "not approved" handstamp (5) —
600TC Strip of 3 (dark green background) + 3 labels with "not approved" handstamp (5) —
G209TC Strip of 3 (light brown in painting) + 3 labels with "not approved" handstamp (5) —
G210TC Strip of 3 (dark green background) + 3 labels with "not approved" handstamp (5) —
V124TC Strip of 3 (black background) + 3 labels with "not approved" handstamp (5) —
599PP 6 items (20) —
Cross gutter block (1) —
Horiz. pair with vert. gutter (2) —
Vert. pair with horiz. gutter (10) —
600PP 6 items (20) —
Cross gutter block (1) —
Horiz. pair with vert. gutter (2) —
Vert. pair with horiz. gutter (10) —
G209PP 6 items (20) —
Cross gutter block (1) —
Horiz. pair with vert. gutter (2) —
Vert. pair with horiz. gutter (10) —
G210PP 6 items (20) —
Cross gutter block (1) —
Horiz. pair with vert. gutter (2) —
Vert. pair with horiz. gutter (10) —
V123PP 6 items (20) —
Cross gutter block (1) —
Horiz. pair with vert. gutter (2) —
Vert. pair with horiz. gutter (10) —
V124PP 6 items (20) —
Cross gutter block (1) —
Horiz. pair with vert. gutter (2) —
Vert. pair with horiz. gutter (10) —
599PI (56 pairs) —
Cross gutter block (1) —
Horiz. pair with vert. gutter (2) —
Vert. pair with horiz. gutter (10) —
600PI (56 pairs) —
Cross gutter block (1) —
Horiz. pair with vert. gutter (2) —
Vert. pair with horiz. gutter (10) —
G209PI (56 pairs) —
Cross gutter block (1) —
Horiz. pair with vert. gutter (2) —
Vert. pair with horiz. gutter (10) —
G210PI (56 pairs) —
Cross gutter block (1) —
Horiz. pair with vert. gutter (2) —
Vert. pair with horiz. gutter (10) —
V123PI (56 pairs) —
Cross gutter block (1) —
Horiz. pair with vert. gutter (2) —
Vert. pair with horiz. gutter (10) —
V124PI (56 pairs) —
Cross gutter block (1) —
Horiz. pair with vert. gutter (2) —
Vert. pair with horiz. gutter (10) —

New York #601-602, Geneva #211-212, Vienna #125-126 World Heritage

1992

602PDa Card, #601PD-602PD (5) —
G212PDa Card, #G211PD-G212PD (5) —
V126PDa Card, #V125PD-V126PD (5) —
601PP 6 items (50) —
602PP 6 items (50) —
G211PP 6 items (50) —
G212PP 6 items (50) —
V125PP 6 items (50) —
V126PP 6 items (50) —
601PI (50 pairs) —
602PI (50 pairs) —
G211PI (50 pairs) —
G212PI (50 pairs) —
V125PI (50 pairs) —
V126PI (50 pairs) —

Geneva #213 Definitive

1992

G213PP 6 items (50) —
G213PI (75 pairs) —

See No. G202PDa.

New York #604a, Geneva #215a, Vienna #128a Clean Oceans

1992

604aPDa Card, imperforate pane of 6 #604aPD (2) —
604aPDb Card, as "a," with one pair removed (1) —
G215aPDa Card, imperforate pane of 6 #G215aPD (2) —
G215aPDb (Card, as "a," with one pair removed (1) —
V128aPDa Card, imperforate pane of 6 #V128aPD (2) —
V128aPDb Card, as "a," with one pair removed (1) —
604aPP 8 items, vert. pair of pairs with narrow horiz. gutter (20) —
Cross gutter block (1) —
Horiz. pair of pairs with vert. gutter (4) —
Vert. pair of pairs with wide horiz. gutter (10) —
G215aPP 8 items, vert. pair of pairs with narrow horiz. gutter (20) —
Cross gutter block (1) —
Horiz. pair of pairs with vert. gutter (4) —
Vert. pair of pairs with wide horiz. gutter (10) —
V128aPP 8 items, vert. pair of pairs with narrow horiz. gutter (20) —
Cross gutter block (1) —
Horiz. pair of pairs with vert. gutter (4) —
Vert. pair of pairs with wide horiz. gutter (10) —
604aPI Vert. pair of pairs with narrow horiz. gutter (20) —
Cross gutter block (1) —
Horiz. pair of pairs with vert. gutter (4) —
Vert. pair of pairs with wide horiz. gutter (10) —
G215aPI Vert. pair of pairs with narrow horiz. gutter (20) —
Cross gutter block (1) —
Horiz. pair of pairs with vert. gutter (4) —
Vert. pair of pairs with wide horiz. gutter (10) —
V128aPI Vert. pair of pairs with narrow horiz. gutter (20) —
Cross gutter block (1) —
Horiz. pair of pairs with vert. gutter (4) —
Vert. pair of pairs with wide horiz. gutter (10) —

New York #608a, Geneva #219a, Vienna #132a Earth Summit

1992

608aPDa Card, #608aPD, #G219aPD, #V132aPD (5) —
608aPP 4 items (10) —

G219aPP	4 items (10)	—
V132aPP	4 items (10)	—
608aPl	(20 blocks)	—
G219aPl	(20 blocks)	—
V132aPl	(20 blocks)	—

New York #609-610, Geneva #220-221, Vienna #133-134
Mission to Planet Earth

1992

610PDa	Card, #610aPD, G221aPD, #V134aPD (3)	—
SC41PD	(3)	—
610aPP	6 items (5)	—
G221aPP	6 items (5)	—
V134aPP	6 items (5)	—
610aPl	(10 pairs)	—
G221aPl	(10 pairs)	—
V134aPl	(10 pairs)	—

One item in No. G221aPP is a blank from a sheet showing marginal inscriptions only.

New York #611-612, Geneva #222-223, Vienna #135-136, Souvenir Card #42
Science and Technology for Development

1992

611PDa	Card, 2 #611PD, 2 #V136PD (4)	—
612PDa	Card, #611PD-612PD, #G222PD-G223PD, #V135PD-V136PD (4)	—
SC42PD	(18)	—
611PP	6 items (50)	—
612PP	6 items (50)	—
G222PP	6 items (50)	—
G223PP	6 items (50)	—
V135PP	6 items (50)	—
V136PP	6 items (50)	—
611Pl	(100 pairs)	—
612Pl	(100 pairs)	—
G222Pl	(100 pairs)	—
G223Pl	(100 pairs)	—
V135Pl	(100 pairs)	—
V136Pl	(100 pairs)	—

There is no appreciable difference between approved and not approved die proofs.

New York #613-615, Vienna #137-138
Definitives

1992

614PDa	Card, #614PD, #V137PD-V138PD (4)	—
615PDa	Card, #613PD, #615PD (3)	—
613PP	6 items (50)	—
614PP	6 items (50)	—
615PP	6 items (50)	—
V137PP	6 items (50)	—
V138PP	6 items (50)	—
613Pl	(50 pairs)	—
614Pl	(269 pairs)	—
	Cross gutter block (2)	—
	Horiz. pair with vert. gutter (36)	—
	Vert. pair with horiz. gutter (16)	—
615Pl	(50 pairs)	—
V137Pl	(269 pairs)	—
	Cross gutter block (2)	—
	Horiz. pair with vert. gutter (16)	—
	Vert. pair with horiz. gutter (36)	—
V138Pl	(269 pairs)	—
	Cross gutter block (2)	—
	Horiz. pair with vert. gutter (36)	—
	Vert. pair with horiz. gutter (16)	—

Three "not approved" cards containing essays of Nos. 613 and 615 lacking year date and designer inscriptions exist.

New York #616-617, Geneva #224-225, Vienna #139-140
Human Rights

1992

616PDa	Strip of 3 + 3 labels (4)	—
617PDa	Strip of 3 + 3 labels (4)	—
G224PDa	Strip of 3 + 3 labels (4)	—
G225PDa	Strip of 3 + 3 labels (4)	—
V139PDa	Strip of 3 + 3 labels (4)	—
V140PDa	Strip of 3 + 3 labels (4)	—
G225TCa	Strip of 3 (dark brown background under chair) + 3 labels (not approved) (5)	—
616PP	6 items (20)	—
	Cross gutter block (1)	—
	Horiz. pair with vert. gutter (2)	—
	Vert. pair with horiz. gutter (10)	—
617PP	6 items (20)	—
	Cross gutter block (1)	—
	Horiz. pair with vert. gutter (2)	—
	Vert. pair with horiz. gutter (10)	—
G224PP	6 items (20)	—
	Cross gutter block (1)	—
	Horiz. pair with vert. gutter (2)	—
	Vert. pair with horiz. gutter (10)	—
G225PP	6 items (20)	—
	Cross gutter block (1)	—
	Horiz. pair with vert. gutter (2)	—
	Vert. pair with horiz. gutter (10)	—
V139PP	6 items (20)	—
	Cross gutter block (1)	—
	Horiz. pair with vert. gutter (2)	—
	Vert. pair with horiz. gutter (10)	—
V140PP	6 items (20)	—
	Cross gutter block (1)	—
	Horiz. pair with vert. gutter (2)	—
	Vert. pair with horiz. gutter (10)	—
616Pl	(32 pairs)	—
	Cross gutter block (4)	—
	Horiz. pair with vert. gutter (8)	—
	Vert. pair with horiz. gutter (40)	—
617Pl	(32 pairs)	—
	Cross gutter block (4)	—
	Horiz. pair with vert. gutter (8)	—
	Vert. pair with horiz. gutter (40)	—
G224Pl	(32 pairs)	—
	Cross gutter block (4)	—
	Horiz. pair with vert. gutter (8)	—
	Vert. pair with horiz. gutter (40)	—
G225Pl	(32 pairs)	—
	Cross gutter block (4)	—
	Horiz. pair with vert. gutter (8)	—
	Vert. pair with horiz. gutter (40)	—
V139Pl	(32 pairs)	—
	Cross gutter block (4)	—
	Horiz. pair with vert. gutter (8)	—
	Vert. pair with horiz. gutter (40)	—
V140Pl	(32 pairs)	—
	Cross gutter block (4)	—
	Horiz. pair with vert. gutter (8)	—
	Vert. pair with horiz. gutter (40)	—

Five "not approved" cards contain 4.50s essays of No. V139, and five "not approved" cards contain 9.50s essays of No. V140.

New York #618-619, Geneva #226-227, Vienna #141-142
Aging With Dignity

1993

618PDa	Card, #618PD, #G226PD-G227PD, #V141PD-V142PD, #619TC yellow flowers (not approved) (5)	—
619PDa	Card, #618PD-619PD, #V141PD-V142PD, #G226TC pink denomination, #G227TC yellow denomination, with approval handstamp (4)	—
619TCb	Card, #618TC-619TC, #G226TC-G227TC, #V141TC-V142TC, each with white denominations (5)	—
618PP	7 items (50)	—
619PP	7 items (50)	—
G226PP	7 items (50)	—
G227PP	7 items (50)	—
V141PP	7 items (50)	—
V142PP	7 items (50)	—
618Pl	(50 pairs)	—
619Pl	(50 pairs)	—
G226Pl	(50 pairs)	—
G227Pl	(50 pairs)	—
V141Pl	(50 pairs)	—
V142Pl	(50 pairs)	—

New York #623a, Geneva #231a, Vienna #146a
Endangered Species

1993

623aPDa	Card, imperforate pane of 4 blocks of #623aPD (3)	—
G231aPDa	Card, imperforate pane of 4 blocks of #G231aPD (4)	—
V146aPDa	Card, imperforate pane of 4 blocks of #V146aPD (3)	—
G231aTCa	Card, imperforate pane of 4 blocks of #G231aTC black (1)	—
G231aPP	6 items (4 blocks)	—
	Cross gutter block (1)	—
	Horiz. pair with vert. gutter (2)	—
	Vert. pair with horiz. gutter (4)	—

V146aPP 6 items (4 blocks) —
Cross gutter block (1) —
Horiz. pair with vert. gutter (2) —
Vert. pair with horiz. gutter (4) —
623aPI (20 blocks) —
Cross gutter block (8) —
Horiz. pair with vert. gutter (8) —
Vert. pair with horiz. gutter (16) —
G231aPI (44 blocks) —
Cross gutter block (10) —
Horiz. pair with vert. gutter (10) —
Vert. pair with horiz. gutter (20) —
V146aPI (20 blocks) —
Cross gutter block (8) —
Horiz. pair with vert. gutter (8) —
Vert. pair with horiz. gutter (16) —

New York #624-625, Geneva #232-233, Vienna #147-148, Souvenir Card #43
Healthy Environment

1993
625PDa Card, #624PD-625PD, #V147PD-V148PD, 90c essay of #G232, 1.10fr essay of #G233 (4) —
SC43PD (4) —
624PP 6 items (50) —
625PP 6 items (50) —
G232PP 6 items (50) —
G233PP 6 items (50) —
V147PP 6 items (50) —
V148PP 6 items (50) —
624PI (50 pairs) —
625PI (50 pairs) —
G232PI (50 pairs) —
G233PI (50 pairs) —
V147PI (50 pairs) —
V148PI (50 pairs) —

New York #626, Vienna #149
Definitives

1993
626PD (5) —
V149PD (5) —
626PP 8 items (144) —
Cross gutter block (1) —
Horiz. pair with vert. gutter (18) —
Vert. pair with horiz. gutter (8) —
V149PP 5 items (50) —
626PI (194 pairs) —
Cross gutter block (2) —
Horiz. pair with vert. gutter (36) —
Vert. pair with horiz. gutter (16) —
V149PI (50 pairs) —

New York #627-628, Geneva #234-235, Vienna #150-151
Human Rights

1993
627PDa Strip of 3 + 3 labels (4) —
628PDa Strip of 3 + 3 labels (4) —
G234PDa Strip of 3 + 3 labels (4)
G235PDa Strip of 3 + 3 labels (4) —
V150PDa Strip of 3 + 3 labels (3) —
V151PDa Strip of 3 + 3 labels (4) —
627PP 6 items (20) —
Cross gutter block (1) —
Horiz. pair with vert. gutter (2) —
Vert. pair with horiz. gutter (10) —
628PP 6 items (20) —
Cross gutter block (1) —
Horiz. pair with vert. gutter (2) —
Vert. pair with horiz. gutter (10) —
G234PP 6 items (20) —
Cross gutter block (1) —
Horiz. pair with vert. gutter (2) —
Vert. pair with horiz. gutter (10) —
G235PP 6 items (20) —
Cross gutter block (1) —
Horiz. pair with vert. gutter (2) —
Vert. pair with horiz. gutter (10) —
627PI (20 pairs) —
Cross gutter block (1) —
Horiz. pair with vert. gutter (2) —
Vert. pair with horiz. gutter (10) —
628PI (20 pairs) —
Cross gutter block (1) —
Horiz. pair with vert. gutter (2) —
Vert. pair with horiz. gutter (10) —
G234PI (20 pairs) —
Cross gutter block (1) —
Horiz. pair with vert. gutter (2) —
Vert. pair with horiz. gutter (10) —
G235PI (20 pairs) —
Cross gutter block (1) —
Horiz. pair with vert. gutter (2) —
Vert. pair with horiz. gutter (10) —
V150PI (6 pairs) —
V151PI (6 pairs) —

New York #632a, Geneva #239a, Vienna #155a, Souvenir Card #44
International Peace Day

1993
632aPD (4) —
G239aPD (4) —
V155aPD (4) —
SC44PD (4) —
632aPP 7 items (10 blocks) —
G239aPP 7 items (10 blocks) —
V155aPP 7 items (10 blocks) —
632aPI (40 blocks) —
G239aPI (40 blocks) —
V155aPI (40 blocks) —

New York #636a, Geneva #243a, Vienna #159a
Environment & Climate

1993
636aPDa Card, #636aPD, #V159aPD (4) —
G243aPD (4) —
636aPP 8 items (6 strips) —
Horiz. pair of strips with vert. gutter (6) —
G243aPP 8 items (6 strips) —
Horiz. pair of strips with vert. gutter (6) —
V155aPP 8 items (6 strips) —
Horiz. pair of strips with vert. gutter (6) —
636aPI (18 strips) —
Horiz. pair of strips with vert. gutter (18) —
G243aPI (18 strips) —
Horiz. pair of strips with vert. gutter (18) —
V159aPI (18 strips) —
Horiz. pair of strips with vert. gutter (18) —

New York #637-638, Geneva #244-245, Vienna #160-161, Souvenir Card #45
International Year of the Family

1994
638PDa Card, #637PD-638PD, #G244PD-G245PD, #V160PD-V161PD (4) —
SC45PD (4) —
637PP 11 items (50) —
638PP 11 items (50) —
G244PP 10 items (50) —
G245PP 10 items (50) —
V160PP 11 items (50) —
V161PP 11 items (50) —
637PI (100 pairs) —
638PI (100 pairs) —
G244PI (100 pairs) —
G245PI (100 pairs) —
V160PI (100 pairs) —
V161PI (100 pairs) —

New York #642a, Geneva #249a, Vienna #165a
Endangered Species

1994
642aPDa Card, imperforate pane of 4 #642aPD (9) —
G249aPDa Card, imperforate pane of 4 #G249aPD (4) —
V165aPDa Card, imperforate pane of 4 #V165aPD (4) —
642aPP 6 items (4 blocks) —
Cross gutter block (2) —
Horiz. pair with vert. gutter (2) —
Vert. pair with horiz. gutter (4) —
G249aPP 6 items (4 blocks) —
Cross gutter block (2) —
Horiz. pair with vert. gutter (2) —
Vert. pair with horiz. gutter (4) —
V165aPP 6 items (4 blocks) —
Cross gutter block (2) —
Horiz. pair with vert. gutter (2) —
Vert. pair with horiz. gutter (4) —
642aPI (16 blocks) —
Cross gutter block (8) —
Horiz. pair with vert. gutter (8) —
Vert. pair with horiz. gutter (16) —
G249aPI (16 blocks) —
Cross gutter block (8) —
Horiz. pair with vert. gutter (8) —
Vert. pair with horiz. gutter (16) —

V165aPI	(16 blocks)	—
	Cross gutter block (8)	—
	Horiz. pair with vert. gutter (8)	—
	Vert. pair with horiz. gutter (16)	—

There is no appreciable difference between appoved and not approved examples of No. 642aPD. Five cards with imperforate panes of 40c essays of No. G249a and five cards with imperforate panes of 5s essays of No. V165a exist.

New York #643, Geneva #250, Vienna #166
Protection for Refugees

1994

643PDa	Card, #643PD, #G250PD, #V166PD (4)	—
643PP	8 items (50)	—
G250PP	8 items (50)	—
V166PP	6 items (50)	—
643PI	(69 pairs)	—
	Horiz. pair with vert. gutter (8)	—
G250PI	(69 pairs)	—
	Horiz. pair with vert. gutter (8)	—
V166PI	(69 pairs)	—
	Horiz. pair with vert. gutter (8)	—

New York #644-646, Vienna #167-169
Definitives

1994

645PDa	Card, #644PD-645PD, #V167PD-V169PD (5)	—
646PD	(1)	—
644PP	6 items (50)	—
645PP	6 items (50)	—
V167PP	12 items (50)	—
V168PP	11 items (50)	—
V169PP	11 items (50)	—
644PI	(100 pairs)	—
645PI	(100 pairs)	—
646PI	(50 pairs)	—
V167PI	(100 pairs)	—
V168PI	(100 pairs)	—
V169PI	(100 pairs)	—

There is no appreciable difference between approved and not approved examples of No. 645PDa.

New York #650a, Geneva #254a, Vienna #173a
International Decade for Natural Disaster Reduction

1994

650aPDa	Card, #650aPD, #G254aPD, #V173aPD (5)	—
650aPP	6 items (16 blocks)	—
	Cross gutter block (1)	—
	Horiz. pair with vert. gutter (8)	—
	Vert. pair with horiz. gutter (2)	—
G254aPP	6 items (16 blocks)	—
	Cross gutter block (1)	—
	Horiz. pair with vert. gutter (8)	—
	Vert. pair with horiz. gutter (2)	—
V173aPP	6 items (16 blocks)	—
	Cross gutter block (1)	—
	Horiz. pair with vert. gutter (8)	—
	Vert. pair with horiz. gutter (2)	—
650aPI	(48 blocks)	—
	Cross gutter block (3)	—
	Horiz. pair with vert. gutter (24)	—
	Vert. pair with horiz. gutter (6)	—
G254aPI	(48 blocks)	—
	Cross gutter block (3)	—
	Horiz. pair with vert. gutter (24)	—
	Vert. pair with horiz. gutter (6)	—
V173aPI	(48 blocks)	—
	Cross gutter block (3)	—
	Horiz. pair with vert. gutter (24)	—
	Vert. pair with horiz. gutter (6)	—

Geneva #255-257
Definitives

1994

G257PDa	Card, #G255PD-G257PD (5)	—
G255PP	10 items (144)	—
	Cross gutter block (1)	—
	Horiz. pair with vert. gutter (18)	—
	Vert. pair with horiz. gutter (8)	—
G256PP	10 items (144)	—
	Cross gutter block (1)	—
	Horiz. pair with vert. gutter (18)	—
	Vert. pair with horiz. gutter (8)	—
G257PP	11 items (144)	—
	Cross gutter block (1)	—
	Horiz. pair with vert. gutter (18)	—
	Vert. pair with horiz. gutter (8)	—
G255PI	(288 pairs)	—
	Cross gutter block (4)	—
	Horiz. pair with vert. gutter (72)	—
	Vert. pair with horiz. gutter (32)	—
G256PI	(288 pairs)	—
	Cross gutter block (4)	—
	Horiz. pair with vert. gutter (72)	—
	Vert. pair with horiz. gutter (32)	—
G257PI	(288 pairs)	—
	Cross gutter block (4)	—
	Horiz. pair with vert. gutter (72)	—
	Vert. pair with horiz. gutter (32)	—

New York #651-652, Geneva #258-259, Vienna #174-175, Souvenir Card #46
Population and Development

1994

652PDa	Card, #651PD-652PD, #G258PD-G259PD, #V174PD-V175PD (4)	—
SC46PD	(4)	—
G258PP	6 items (40)	—
G259PP	6 items (40)	—
G259PPa	Horiz. se-tenant pair with vert. gutter, #G258PP-G259PP (10)	—
V174PP	6 items (40)	—
V175PP	6 items (40)	—
V175PPa	Horiz. se-tenant pair with vert. gutter, #V174PP-V175PP (10)	—
651PI	(50 pairs)	—
652PI	(50 pairs)	—
G258PI	(70 pairs)	—
G259PI	(70 pairs)	—
G259PIa	Horiz. se-tenant pair with vert. gutter, #G258PI-G259PI (10)	—
V174PI	(70 pairs)	—
V175PI	(70 pairs)	—
V175PIa	Horiz. se-tenant pair with vert. gutter, #V174PI-V175PI (10)	—

New York #653-654, Geneva #260-261, Vienna #176-177
UNCTAD, 30th Anniv.

1994

653PP	15 items (40)	—
654PP	15 items (40)	—
654PPa	Horiz. se-tenant pair with vert. gutter, #653PP-654PP (10)	—
G260PP	16 items (40)	—
G261PP	16 items (40)	—
G261PPa	Horiz. se-tenant pair with vert. gutter, #G260PP-G261PP (10)	—
V176PP	14 items (40)	—
V177PP	14 items (40)	—
V177PPa	Horiz. se-tenant pair with vert. gutter, #V176PP-V177PP (10)	—
653PI	(60 pairs)	—
654PI	(60 pairs)	—
654PIa	Horiz. se-tenant pair with vert. gutter, #653PI-654PI (30)	—
G260PI	(60 pairs)	—
G261PI	(60 pairs)	—
G261PIa	Horiz. se-tenant pair with vert. gutter, #G260PI-G261PI (30)	—
V176PI	(60 pairs)	—
V177PI	(60 pairs)	—
V177PIa	Horiz. se-tenant pair with vert. gutter, #V176PI-V177PI (30)	—

Two items from No. G260PP and one from No. V176PP are blank due to color arrangement on progressive proof sheet.

New York # 655, Geneva #262, Vienna #178
United Nations, 50th Anniv.

1995

655PD	(3)	—
G262PD	(3)	—
V178PD	(3)	—
655PP	8 items (50)	—
G262PP	8 items (50)	—
V178PP	8 items (50)	—
655PI	(100 pairs)	—
G262PI	(200 pairs)	—
V178PI	(200 pairs)	—

New York #656, Geneva #263, Vienna #179, Souvenir Card #47
World Summit for Social Development, Copenhagen

1995

656PDa	Card, #656PD, #G263PD, #V179PD (3)	—
SC47PD	Card, 4 #SC47PD (1)	—

656PP	12 items (25)	—
G263PP	8 items (25)	—
V179PP	8 items (25)	—
656PI	(24 pairs)	—
G263PI	(24 pairs)	—
V179PI	(24 pairs)	—

New York #660a, Geneva #267a, Vienna #183a Endangered Species

1995

660aPDa	Card, imperforate pane of 4 blocks, #660aPD (5)	—
660aPDb	Card, broken imperforate pane of 4 blocks, #660aPD (1)	—
660aPDc	Card, 2 imperforate panes of 4 blocks, #660aPD (1)	—
G267aPDa	Card, imperforate pane of 4 blocks, #G267aPD (6)	—
G267aPDb	Card, 2 imperforate panes of 4 blocks, #G267aPD (1)	—
V183aPDa	Card, imperforate pane of 4 blocks, #V183aPD with "14. Okt. 1994" handstamp (approved) (3)	—
V183aTCa	Card, imperforate pane of 4 blocks, #V183aTC (violet blue sky on #181TC), not approved (3)	—
V183aTCb	Card, 2 imperforate pane of 4 blocks, #V183aTC, not approved (1)	—
660aPP	6 items (9 blocks)	—
	Cross gutter block (3)	—
	Horiz. pair with vert. gutter (4)	—
	Vert. pair with horiz. gutter (7)	—
G267aPP	6 items (12 blocks)	—
	Cross gutter block (3)	—
	Horiz. pair with vert. gutter (4)	—
	Vert. pair with horiz. gutter (6)	—
V183aPP	6 items (12 blocks)	—
	Cross gutter block (3)	—
	Horiz. pair with vert. gutter (4)	—
	Vert. pair with horiz. gutter (7)	—
660aPI	(11 blocks)	—
	Cross gutter block (3)	—
	Horiz. pair with vert. gutter (4)	—
	Vert. pair with horiz. gutter (7)	—
G267aPI	(16 blocks)	—
	Cross gutter block (3)	—
	Horiz. pair with vert. gutter (4)	—
	Vert. pair with horiz. gutter (6)	—
V183aPI	(11 blocks)	—
	Cross gutter block (3)	—
	Horiz. pair with vert. gutter (4)	—
	Vert. pair with horiz. gutter (7)	—

Three cross gutter blocks, four horizontal pairs with vertical gutters, seven vertical pairs with horizontal gutters and nine blocks with untrimmed margins can be cut from perforated sheets of Nos. V180PI-V183PI.

New York #661-662, Geneva #268-269, Vienna #184-185, Souvenir Card #48 International Youth Year

1995

662PDa	Card, #661PD-662PD, #G268PD-G269PD, #V184PD-V185PD (6)	—
SC48PD	(6)	—
661PP	5 items (160)	—
	Cross gutter block (5)	—
	Horiz. pair with vert. gutter (25)	—
	Vert. pair with horiz. gutter (44)	—
662PP	8 items (160)	—
	Cross gutter block (5)	—
	Horiz. pair with vert. gutter (25)	—
	Vert. pair with horiz. gutter (44)	—
G268PP	6 items (208)	—
	Cross gutter block (5)	—
	Horiz. pair with vert. gutter (25)	—
	Vert. pair with horiz. gutter (44)	—
G269PP	5 items (208)	—
	Cross gutter block (5)	—
	Horiz. pair with vert. gutter (25)	—
	Vert. pair with horiz. gutter (44)	—
V184PP	7 items (101)	—
	Cross gutter block (2)	—
	Horiz. pair with vert. gutter (11)	—
	Vert. pair with horiz. gutter (12)	—
V185PP	6 items (197)	—
	Cross gutter block (5)	—
	Horiz. pair with vert. gutter (25)	—
	Vert. pair with horiz. gutter (44)	—
661PI	(128 pairs)	—
	Cross gutter block (5)	—
	Horiz. pair with vert. gutter (25)	—
	Vert. pair with horiz. gutter (44)	—
662PI	(128 pairs)	—
	Cross gutter block (5)	—
	Horiz. pair with vert. gutter (25)	—
	Vert. pair with horiz. gutter (44)	—
G268PI	(128 pairs)	—
	Cross gutter block (5)	—
	Horiz. pair with vert. gutter (25)	—
	Vert. pair with horiz. gutter (44)	—
G269PI	(128 pairs)	—
	Cross gutter block (5)	—
	Horiz. pair with vert. gutter (25)	—
	Vert. pair with horiz. gutter (44)	—
V184PI	(128 pairs)	—
	Cross gutter block (5)	—
	Horiz. pair with vert. gutter (25)	—
	Vert. pair with horiz. gutter (44)	—
V185PI	(128 pairs)	—
	Cross gutter block (5)	—
	Horiz. pair with vert. gutter (25)	—
	Vert. pair with horiz. gutter (44)	—

New York #663-665, Geneva #270-272, Vienna #186-188 United Nations, 50th Anniv.

1995

664PDa	Card, # 664PD, #663TC maroon, #663TC dark blue, #663TC green, #664TC dark blue, #664TC green (3)	—
663PI	(80 pairs)	—
664PI	(80 pairs)	—
664PIa	Horiz. se-tenant pair with vert. gutter, #663PI-664PI (40)	—
665PI	(8 pairs of souvenir sheets)	—
G270PI	(80 pairs)	—
G271PI	(80 pairs)	—
G271PIa	Horiz. se-tenant pair with vert. gutter, #G270PI-G271PI (40)	—
G272PI	(8 pairs of souvenir sheets)	—
V186PI	(80 pairs)	—
V187PI	(80 pairs)	—
V187PIa	Horiz. se-tenant pair with vert. gutter, #V186PI-V187PI (40)	—
V188PI	(8 pairs of souvenir sheets)	—

Three cards with non-engraved essays of No. 665 in red violet exist.

New York #666-667, Geneva #273-274, Vienna #189-190 Fourth World Conference on Women

1995

666PP	10 items, perforated (275)	—
667PP	10 items, perforated (250)	—
G273PP	10 items, perforated (100)	—
G274PP	10 items, perforated (250)	—
V189PP	9 items, perforated (275)	—
V190PP	9 items, perforated (275)	—
666PI	(144 pairs)	—
667PI	(144 pairs)	—
G273PI	(108 pairs)	—
G274PI	(144 pairs)	—
V189PI	(132 pairs)	—
V190PI	(144 pairs)	—

On No. V189PP and V190PP, 125 sets have a red and multicolored item while the remaining 150 sets have a blue and multicolored item.

New York #668 UN Headquarters

1995

668PD	(5)	—
668PP	6 items (162)	—
	Horiz. pair with vert. gutter (9)	—
	Vert. pair with horiz. gutter (5)	—
668PI	(85 pairs)	—
	Horiz. pair with vert. gutter (9)	—
	Vert. pair with horiz. gutter (5)	—

New York #669-670, Geneva #275-276, Vienna #191-192 United Nations, 50th Anniversary

1995

669PD	(4)	—
G275PD	(4)	—
V191PD	(4)	—
669PP	6 items (6)	—
G275PP	8 items (6)	—
V191PP	7 items (6)	—
669PI	(2 full panes)	—
669PIa	(3 pairs of full panes)	—

670PI	(3 booklets)	—
G275PI	(2 full panes)	—
G275PIa	(3 pairs of full panes)	—
G276PI	(3 booklets)	—
V191PI	(2 full panes)	—
V191PIa	(4 pairs of full panes)	—
V192PI	(3 booklets)	—

New York #671, Geneva #277, Vienna #193, Souvenir Card #49
World Federation of United Nations Associations, 50th Anniv.

1996

671PDa	Card, #671PD, #G277PD, #V193PD (3)	—
SC49PD	(4)	—
671PP	6 items (150)	—
	Horiz. pair with vert. gutter (25)	—
G277PP	6 items (150)	—
	Horiz. pair with vert. gutter (25)	—
V193PP	6 items (305)	—
	Cross gutter block (5)	—
	Horiz. pair with vert. gutter (40)	—
	Vert. pair with horiz. gutter (30)	—
671PI	(155 pairs)	—
	Horiz. pair with vert. gutter (55)	—
G277PI	(155 pairs)	—
	Horiz. pair with vert. gutter (55)	—
V193PI	(264 pairs)	—
	Cross gutter block (11)	—
	Horiz. pair with vert. gutter (88)	—
	Vert. pair with horiz. gutter (63)	—

New York #672-673, Geneva #278-279, Vienna #194-195
Definitives

1996

673PDa	Card, #672PD-673PD, #G278PD-G279PD, #V194PD-V195PD with approval handstamp (4)	—
673PDb	Card, #673PD, #672TC gray in vignette, #G278TC-G279TC tan background in panel, essays of #V194PD-V195PD (larger frames) (not approved) (4)	—
673PDc	#673PDa and 673PDb stapled together (1)	—
672PP	8 items (144)	—
	Cross gutter block (1)	—
	Horiz. pair with vert. gutter (18)	—
	Vert. pair with horiz. gutter (8)	—
673PP	8 items (144)	—
	Cross gutter block (1)	—
	Horiz. pair with vert. gutter (18)	—
	Vert. pair with horiz. gutter (8)	—
G278PP	8 items (144)	—
	Cross gutter block (1)	—
	Horiz. pair with vert. gutter (18)	—
	Vert. pair with horiz. gutter (8)	—
G279PP	8 items (144)	—
	Cross gutter block (1)	—
	Horiz. pair with vert. gutter (18)	—
	Vert. pair with horiz. gutter (8)	—
V194PP	8 items (144)	—
	Cross gutter block (1)	—
	Horiz. pair with vert. gutter (18)	—
	Vert. pair with horiz. gutter (8)	—
V195PP	8 items (144)	—
	Cross gutter block (1)	—
	Horiz. pair with vert. gutter (18)	—
	Vert. pair with horiz. gutter (8)	—
672PI	(216 pairs)	—
	Cross gutter block (3)	—
	Horiz. pair with vert. gutter (54)	—
	Vert. pair with horiz. gutter (16)	—
673PI	(144 pairs)	—
	Cross gutter block (3)	—
	Horiz. pair with vert. gutter (54)	—
	Vert. pair with horiz. gutter (16)	—
G278PI	(216 pairs)	—
	Cross gutter block (3)	—
	Horiz. pair with vert. gutter (54)	—
	Vert. pair with horiz. gutter (24)	—
G279PI	(216 pairs)	—
	Cross gutter block (3)	—
	Horiz. pair with vert. gutter (54)	—
	Vert. pair with horiz. gutter (24)	—
V194PI	(216 pairs)	—
	Cross gutter block (3)	—
	Horiz. pair with vert. gutter (24)	—
	Vert. pair with horiz. gutter (36)	—
V195PI	(216 pairs)	—
	Cross gutter block (3)	—
	Horiz. pair with vert. gutter (24)	—
	Vert. pair with horiz. gutter (36)	—

New York #677a, Geneva #283a, Vienna #199a
Endangered Species

1996

677aPDa	Card, imperforate pane of 4 blocks, #677aPD (3)	—
677aPDb	Card, broken imperforate pane of 4 blocks, #677aPD (1)	—
G283aPDa	Card, imperforate pane of 4 blocks, #G283aPD (3)	—
G283aPDb	Card, broken imperforate pane of 4 blocks, #G283aPD (1)	—
V199aPDa	Card, imperforate pane of 4 blocks, #V199aPD (3)	—
V199aPDb	Card, broken imperforate pane of 4 blocks, #V199aPD (1)	—
677aPP	6 items (14 blocks)	—
	Cross gutter block (5)	—
	Horiz. pair with vert. gutter (6)	—
	Vert. pair with horiz. gutter (11)	—
G283aPP	6 items (14 blocks)	—
	Cross gutter block (5)	—
	Horiz. pair with vert. gutter (6)	—
	Vert. pair with horiz. gutter (11)	—
V199aPP	6 items (14 blocks)	—
	Cross gutter block (5)	—
	Horiz. pair with vert. gutter (6)	—
	Vert. pair with horiz. gutter (11)	—
677aPI	(25 blocks)	—
	Cross gutter block (11)	—
	Horiz. pair with vert. gutter (12)	—
	Vert. pair with horiz. gutter (23)	—
G283aPI	(25 blocks)	—
	Cross gutter block (11)	—
	Horiz. pair with vert. gutter (12)	—
	Vert. pair with horiz. gutter (23)	—
V199aPI	(25 blocks)	—
	Cross gutter block (11)	—
	Horiz. pair with vert. gutter (12)	—
	Vert. pair with horiz. gutter (23)	—

New York #682a, Geneva #288a, Vienna #204a
City Summit

1996

682aPDa	Card, imperforate pane of 5 strips, #682aPD (4)	—
G288aPDa	Card, imperforate pane of 5 strips, #G288aPD (4)	—
V204aPDa	Card, imperforate pane of 5 strips, #V204aPD (4)	—
682aPP	10 items (15 horiz. pairs of strips with vert. gutter)	—
G288aPP	10 items (24 horiz. pairs of strips with vert. gutter)	—
	Cross gutter block of strips (3)	—
V204aPP	10 items (15 horiz. pairs of strips with vert. gutter)	—
682aPI	(35 horiz. pairs of strips with vert. gutter)	—
G288aPI	(56 horiz. pairs of strips with vert. gutter)	—
	Cross gutter block of strips (7)	—
V204aPI	(35 horiz. pairs of strips with vert. gutter)	—

New York #683-685, Geneva #289-291, Vienna #205-207
Sport and the Environment

1996

684PDa	Card, #683PD-684PD (10)	—
685PD	(10)	—
G290PDa	Card, #G289PD-G290PD (10)	—
G291PD	(10)	—
V206PDa	Card, #V205PD-V206PD (10)	—
V207PD	(10)	—
683PP	8 items (88)	—
	Cross gutter block (2)	—
	Horiz. pair with vert. gutter (16)	—
	Vert. pair with horiz. gutter (11)	—
684PP	8 items (88)	—
	Cross gutter block (2)	—
	Horiz. pair with vert. gutter (11)	—
	Vert. pair with horiz. gutter (16)	—
685PP	12 items (25 souvenir sheets)	—
G289PP	8 items (88)	—
	Cross gutter block (2)	—
	Horiz. pair with vert. gutter (16)	—
	Vert. pair with horiz. gutter (11)	—

G290PP	8 items (88)	—
	Cross gutter block (2)	—
	Horiz. pair with vert. gutter (11)	—
	Vert. pair with horiz. gutter (16)	—
G291PP	10 items (25 souvenir sheets)	—
V205PP	8 items (88)	—
	Cross gutter block (2)	—
	Horiz. pair with vert. gutter (16)	—
	Vert. pair with horiz. gutter (11)	—
V206PP	8 items (88)	—
	Cross gutter block (2)	—
	Horiz. pair with vert. gutter (11)	—
	Vert. pair with horiz. gutter (16)	—
V207PP	11 items (25 souvenir sheets)	—
683PI	(44 pairs)	—
	Cross gutter block (2)	—
	Horiz. pair with vert. gutter (16)	—
	Vert. pair with horiz. gutter (11)	—
684PI	(44 pairs)	—
	Cross gutter block (2)	—
	Horiz. pair with vert. gutter (11)	—
	Vert. pair with horiz. gutter (16)	—
685PI	(75 souvenir sheets)	—
G289PI	(88 pairs)	—
	Cross gutter block (4)	—
	Horiz. pair with vert. gutter (32)	—
	Vert. pair with horiz. gutter (22)	—
G290PI	(88 pairs)	—
	Cross gutter block (4)	—
	Horiz. pair with vert. gutter (22)	—
	Vert. pair with horiz. gutter (32)	—
G291PI	(75 souvenir sheets)	—
V205PI	(132 pairs)	—
	Cross gutter block (6)	—
	Horiz. pair with vert. gutter (48)	—
	Vert. pair with horiz. gutter (33)	—
V206PI	(132 pairs)	—
	Cross gutter block (6)	—
	Horiz. pair with vert. gutter (33)	—
	Vert. pair with horiz. gutter (48)	—
V207PI	(75 souvenir sheets)	—

New York #686-687, Geneva #292-293, Vienna #208-209
Plea for Peace

1996

687PDa	Card, #686PD-687PD, #G292PD-G293PD, #V208PD-V209PD (4)	—
686PP	10 items (112)	—
	Cross gutter block (3)	—
	Horiz. pair with vert. gutter (14)	—
	Vert. pair with horiz. gutter (24)	—
687PP	10 items (112)	—
	Cross gutter block (3)	—
	Horiz. pair with vert. gutter (14)	—
	Vert. pair with horiz. gutter (24)	—
G292PP	10 items (112)	—
	Cross gutter block (3)	—
	Horiz. pair with vert. gutter (24)	—
	Vert. pair with horiz. gutter (14)	—
G293PP	10 items (112)	—
	Cross gutter block (2)	—
	Horiz. pair with vert. gutter (24)	—
	Vert. pair with horiz. gutter (14)	—
V208PP	10 items (112)	—
	Cross gutter block (3)	—
	Horiz. pair with vert. gutter (14)	—
	Vert. pair with horiz. gutter (24)	—
V209PP	10 items (112)	—
	Cross gutter block (3)	—
	Horiz. pair with vert. gutter (14)	—
	Vert. pair with horiz. gutter (24)	—
686PI	(104 pairs)	—
	Cross gutter block (3)	—
	Horiz. pair with vert. gutter (14)	—
	Vert. pair with horiz. gutter (24)	—
687PI	(104 pairs)	—
	Cross gutter block (3)	—
	Horiz. pair with vert. gutter (14)	—
	Vert. pair with horiz. gutter (24)	—
G292PI	(80 pairs)	—
	Cross gutter block (3)	—
	Horiz. pair with vert. gutter (24)	—
	Vert. pair with horiz. gutter (14)	—
G293PI	(80 pairs)	—
	Cross gutter block (3)	—
	Horiz. pair with vert. gutter (24)	—
	Vert. pair with horiz. gutter (14)	—
V208PI	(80 pairs)	—
	Cross gutter block (3)	—
	Horiz. pair with vert. gutter (14)	—
	Vert. pair with horiz. gutter (24)	—
V209PI	(80 pairs)	—
	Cross gutter block (3)	—
	Horiz. pair with vert. gutter (14)	—
	Vert. pair with horiz. gutter (24)	—

New York #688-689, Geneva #294-295, Vienna #210-211, Souvenir Card #50
UNICEF, 50th Anniv.

1996

689PDa	Imperforate pane, #689PD (4)	—
G294PDa	Imperforate pane, #G294PD (4)	—
G295PDa	Imperforate pane, #G295PD (6)	—
V210PDa	Imperforate pane, #V210PD (on photographic paper) (2)	—
V211PDa	Imperforate pane, #V211PD (4)	—
SC50PD	(1)	—
688PP	10 items (18)	—
	Cross gutter block (6)	—
	Horiz. pair with vert. gutter (12)	—
	Vert. pair with horiz. gutter (15)	—
689PP	11 items (18)	—
	Cross gutter block (6)	—
	Horiz. pair with vert. gutter (12)	—
	Vert. pair with horiz. gutter (15)	—
G294PP	9 items (18)	—
	Cross gutter block (6)	—
	Horiz. pair with vert. gutter (12)	—
	Vert. pair with horiz. gutter (15)	—
G295PP	9 items (18)	—
	Cross gutter block (6)	—
	Horiz. pair with vert. gutter (12)	—
	Vert. pair with horiz. gutter (15)	—
V210PP	9 items (18)	—
	Cross gutter block (6)	—
	Horiz. pair with vert. gutter (18)	—
	Vert. pair with horiz. gutter (14)	—
V211PP	9 items (18)	—
	Cross gutter block (6)	—
	Horiz. pair with vert. gutter (18)	—
	Vert. pair with horiz. gutter (14)	—
688PI	(12 pairs)	—
	Cross gutter block (18)	—
	Horiz. pair with vert. gutter (36)	—
	Vert. pair with horiz. gutter (45)	—
689PI	(12 pairs)	—
	Cross gutter block (18)	—
	Horiz. pair with vert. gutter (36)	—
	Vert. pair with horiz. gutter (45)	—
G294PI	(12 pairs)	—
	Cross gutter block (18)	—
	Horiz. pair with vert. gutter (36)	—
	Vert. pair with horiz. gutter (45)	—
G295PI	(12 pairs)	—
	Cross gutter block (18)	—
	Horiz. pair with vert. gutter (36)	—
	Vert. pair with horiz. gutter (45)	—
V210PI	(12 pairs)	—
	Cross gutter block (18)	—
	Horiz. pair with vert. gutter (36)	—
	Vert. pair with horiz. gutter (45)	—
V211PI	(12 pairs)	—
	Cross gutter block (18)	—
	Horiz. pair with vert. gutter (36)	—
	Vert. pair with horiz. gutter (45)	—

Two of the No. G295PDa items are on photographic paper. Four cards with imperforate panes of 32c Hansel & Gretel essays exist. Four cards with imperforate panes of 5.50s Yeh-Shen essays exist. Four essays of No. SC50 showing these two essay items exist.

New York #690-697
Flags

1997

690-697PP	Set of 20 sheets (1)	—
690-697PI	Set of 2 sheets (3)	—

On Nos. 690-697PP, there are ten progressive proof sheets per issued sheet.

New York #698-699, Geneva #296-297, Vienna #212-213
Definitives

1997

698PDa	Card, #698PD, #G296PD-G297PD, #V212PD-V213PD (1)	—
699PDa	Card, #698PD-699PD, #G296PD-G297PD, #V212PD-V213PD (4)	—
698PP	8 items (84)	—
	Cross gutter block (3)	—
	Horiz. pair with vert. gutter (18)	—
	Vert. pair with horiz. gutter (14)	—

699PP	8 items (84)	—
	Cross gutter block (3)	—
	Horiz. pair with vert. gutter (14)	—
	Vert. pair with horiz. gutter (18)	—
G296PP	8 items (84)	—
	Cross gutter block (3)	—
	Horiz. pair with vert. gutter (14)	—
	Vert. pair with horiz. gutter (18)	—
G297PP	8 items (84)	—
	Cross gutter block (3)	—
	Horiz. pair with vert. gutter (14)	—
	Vert. pair with horiz. gutter (18)	—
V212PP	10 items (84)	—
	Cross gutter block (3)	—
	Horiz. pair with vert. gutter (18)	—
	Vert. pair with horiz. gutter (14)	—
V213PP	10 items (84)	—
	Cross gutter block (3)	—
	Horiz. pair with vert. gutter (18)	—
	Vert. pair with horiz. gutter (14)	—
698PI	(60 pairs)	—
	Cross gutter block (3)	—
	Horiz. pair with vert. gutter (18)	—
	Vert. pair with horiz. gutter (14)	—
699PI	(60 pairs)	—
	Cross gutter block (3)	—
	Horiz. pair with vert. gutter (14)	—
	Vert. pair with horiz. gutter (18)	—
G296PI	(60 pairs)	—
	Cross gutter block (3)	—
	Horiz. pair with vert. gutter (14)	—
	Vert. pair with horiz. gutter (18)	—
G297PI	(60 pairs)	—
	Cross gutter block (3)	—
	Horiz. pair with vert. gutter (14)	—
	Vert. pair with horiz. gutter (18)	—
V212PI	(60 pairs)	—
	Cross gutter block (3)	—
	Horiz. pair with vert. gutter (18)	—
	Vert. pair with horiz. gutter (14)	—
V213PI	(60 pairs)	—
	Cross gutter block (3)	—
	Horiz. pair with vert. gutter (18)	—
	Vert. pair with horiz. gutter (14)	—

New York #703a, Geneva #301a, Vienna #217a Endangered Species

1997

703aPDa	Card, imperforate pane of 4 blocks #703aPD, imperforate pane of 4 blocks #G301aPD (4)	—
V217aPDa	Card, imperforate pane of 4 blocks #V217aPD (4)	—
703aPP	6 items (4 blocks)	—
	Cross gutter block (2)	—
	Horiz. pair with vert. gutter (2)	—
	Vert. pair with horiz. gutter (4)	—
G301aPP	6 items (4 blocks)	—
	Cross gutter block (2)	—
	Horiz. pair with vert. gutter (2)	—
	Vert. pair with horiz. gutter (4)	—
V217aPP	6 items (4 blocks)	—
	Cross gutter block (2)	—
	Horiz. pair with vert. gutter (2)	—
	Vert. pair with horiz. gutter (4)	—
703aPI	(12 blocks)	—
	Cross gutter block (6)	—
	Horiz. pair with vert. gutter (6)	—
	Vert. pair with horiz. gutter (12)	—
G301aPI	(12 blocks)	—
	Cross gutter block (6)	—
	Horiz. pair with vert. gutter (6)	—
	Vert. pair with horiz. gutter (12)	—
V217aPI	(12 blocks)	—
	Cross gutter block (6)	—
	Horiz. pair with vert. gutter (6)	—
	Vert. pair with horiz. gutter (12)	—

New York #707a, 708, Geneva #305a, 306, Vienna #221a, 222 Earth Summit

1997

707aPP	6 items (6 blocks)	—
708PP	6 items (1 souvenir sheet)	—
708aPP	6 items (1 souvenir sheet)	—
G305aPP	6 items (6 blocks)	—
V221aPP	6 items (6 blocks)	—
707aPI	(15 blocks)	—
708PI	(6 souvenir sheets)	—
708aPI	(6 souvenir sheets)	—
G305aPI	(15 blocks)	—
G306PI	(6 souvenir sheets)	—
V221aPI	(15 blocks)	—
V222PI	(6 souvenir sheets)	—

New York #713a, Geneva #311a, Vienna #227a Transportation

1997

713aPDa	Imperforate pane, #713aPD (9)	—
G311aPDa	Imperforate pane, #G311aPD (9)	—
V227aPDa	Imperforate pane, #V227aPD (9)	—
713aPP	9 items (6 strips)	—
	Cross gutter block of strips (1)	—
	Horiz. pair of strips with vert. gutter (6)	—
	Vert. pair of strips with horiz. gutter (1)	—
G311aPP	10 items (6 strips)	—
	Cross gutter block of strips (1)	—
	Horiz. pair of strips with vert. gutter (6)	—
	Vert. pair of strips with horiz. gutter (1)	—
V227aPP	9 items (6 strips)	—
	Cross gutter block of strips (1)	—
	Horiz. pair of strips with vert. gutter (6)	—
	Vert. pair of strips with horiz. gutter (1)	—
713aPI	(14 strips)	—
	Cross gutter block of strips (1)	—
	Horiz. pair of strips with vert. gutter (6)	—
	Vert. pair of strips with horiz. gutter (1)	—
G311aPI	(14 strips)	—
	Cross gutter block of strips (1)	—
	Horiz. pair of strips with vert. gutter (6)	—
	Vert. pair of strips with horiz. gutter (1)	—
V227aPI	(14 strips)	—
	Cross gutter block of strips (1)	—
	Horiz. pair of strips with vert. gutter (6)	—
	Vert. pair of strips with horiz. gutter (1)	—

New York #714-715, Geneva #312-313, Vienna #228-229, Souvenir Card #51 Philately

1997

715TCa	Card, #714TC-715TC, #G312TC-G313TC, #V228TC-V229TC, all with white denominations (4)	—
715TCb	Card, #714TC-715TC, #G312TC-G313TC, #V228TC-V229TC, all with light blue green backgrounds (1)	—
SC51PD	(4)	—
714PP	11 items (33)	—
	Horiz. pair with vert. gutter (6)	—
715PP	11 items (33)	—
	Horiz. pair with vert. gutter (6)	—
715PPa	Cross gutter block, 2 each #714PP-715PP (2)	—
715PPb	Vert. pair with horiz. gutter, #714PP-715PP (11)	—
G312PP	11 items (33)	—
	Horiz. pair with vert. gutter (6)	—
G313PP	11 items (33)	—
	Horiz. pair with vert. gutter (6)	—
G313PPa	Cross gutter block, 2 each #G312PP-G313PP (2)	—
G313PPb	Vert. pair with horiz. gutter, #G312PP-G313PP (11)	—
V228PP	10 items (33)	—
	Horiz. pair with vert. gutter (6)	—
V229PP	10 items (33)	—
	Horiz. pair with vert. gutter (6)	—
V229PPa	Cross gutter block, 2 each #V228PP-V229PP (2)	—
V229PPb	Vert. pair with horiz. gutter, #V228PP-V229PP (11)	—
714PI	(48 pairs)	—
	Horiz. pair with vert. gutter (18)	—
715PI	(48 pairs)	—
	Horiz. pair with vert. gutter (18)	—
715PIa	Cross gutter block, 2 each #714PI-715PI (6)	—
715PIb	Vert. pair with horiz. gutter, #714PI-715PI (33)	—
G312PI	(48 pairs)	—
	Horiz. pair with vert. gutter (18)	—
G313PI	(48 pairs)	—
	Horiz. pair with vert. gutter (18)	—
G313PIa	Cross gutter block, 2 each #G312PI-G313PI (6)	—
G313PIb	Vert. pair with horiz. gutter, #G312PI-G313PI (33)	—
V228PI	(48 pairs)	—
	Horiz. pair with vert. gutter (18)	—
V229PI	(48 pairs)	—
	Horiz. pair with vert. gutter (18)	—
V229PIa	Cross gutter block, 2 each #V228PI-V229PI (6)	—
V229PIb	Vert. pair with horiz. gutter, #V228PI-V229PI (33)	—

On Nos. 714PP-715PP, G312PP-G313PP and V228PP-V229PP some progressive proof items are blank due to color arrangements on sheets.

New York #716-717, Geneva #314-315, Vienna #230-231
World Heritage

1997

717PDa	Stapled set of 6 layout sheets with #716PD-717PD, #G314PD-G315PD, #V230PD-V231PD affixed (3)	—
716PP	10 items (20)	—
717PP	10 items (20)	—
G314PP	10 items (20)	—
G315PP	10 items (20)	—
V230PP	10 items (20)	—
V231PP	10 items (20)	—
716PI	(30 pairs)	—
717PI	(30 pairs)	—
G314PI	(30 pairs)	—
G315PI	(30 pairs)	—
V230PI	(30 pairs)	—
V231PI	(30 pairs)	—

New York #719-726
Flags

1998

719-726PP	Set of 20 sheets (1)	—
719-726PI	Set of 2 sheets (3)	—

On Nos. 719-726PP, there are ten progressive proof sheets per issued sheet.

New York #727-729, Geneva #317, Vienna #233-234
Definitives

1998

727PDa	Card, #727PD, #G317TC black (1)	—
729PDa	Card, #727PD-729PD, #G317PD, #V233PD-V234PD (4)	—
727PP	10 items (84)	—
	Cross gutter block (3)	—
	Horiz. pair with vert. gutter (14)	—
	Vert. pair with horiz. gutter (18)	—
728PP	8 items (84)	—
	Cross gutter block (3)	—
	Horiz. pair with vert. gutter (14)	—
	Vert. pair with horiz. gutter (18)	—
729PP	9 items (84)	—
	Cross gutter block (3)	—
	Horiz. pair with vert. gutter (18)	—
	Vert. pair with horiz. gutter (14)	—
G317PP	10 items (84)	—
	Cross gutter block (3)	—
	Horiz. pair with vert. gutter (14)	—
	Vert. pair with horiz. gutter (18)	—
V233PP	8 items (84)	—
	Cross gutter block (3)	—
	Horiz. pair with vert. gutter (18)	—
	Vert. pair with horiz. gutter (14)	—
V234PP	10 items (84)	—
	Cross gutter block (3)	—
	Horiz. pair with vert. gutter (18)	—
	Vert. pair with horiz. gutter (14)	—
727PI	(60 pairs)	—
	Cross gutter block (3)	—
	Horiz. pair with vert. gutter (14)	—
	Vert. pair with horiz. gutter (18)	—
728PI	(60 pairs)	—
	Cross gutter block (3)	—
	Horiz. pair with vert. gutter (14)	—
	Vert. pair with horiz. gutter (18)	—
729PI	(60 pairs)	—
	Cross gutter block (3)	—
	Horiz. pair with vert. gutter (18)	—
	Vert. pair with horiz. gutter (14)	—
G317PI	(60 pairs)	—
	Cross gutter block (3)	—
	Horiz. pair with vert. gutter (14)	—
	Vert. pair with horiz. gutter (18)	—
V233PI	(60 pairs)	—
	Cross gutter block (3)	—
	Horiz. pair with vert. gutter (18)	—
	Vert. pair with horiz. gutter (14)	—
V234PI	(60 pairs)	—
	Cross gutter block (3)	—
	Horiz. pair with vert. gutter (18)	—
	Vert. pair with horiz. gutter (14)	—

New York #733a, Geneva #321a, Vienna #238a
Endangered Species

1998

733PDa	Card, imperforate pane of 4 blocks, #733aPD (1)	—
733PDb	Card, broken imperforate pane of 4 blocks, #733aPD (1)	—
G321PDa	Card, imperforate pane of 4 blocks, #G321aPD (1)	—
G321PDb	Card, broken imperforate pane of 4 blocks, #G321aPD (1)	—
V238PDa	Card, imperforate pane of 4 blocks, #V238aPD (1)	—
V238PDb	Card, broken imperforate pane of 4 blocks, #V238aPD (1)	—
733aPP	6 items (4 blocks)	—
	Cross gutter block (2)	—
	Horiz. pair with vert. gutter (2)	—
	Vert. pair with horiz. gutter (4)	—
G321aPP	4 items (4 blocks)	—
	Cross gutter block (2)	—
	Horiz. pair with vert. gutter (2)	—
	Vert. pair with horiz. gutter (4)	—
V238aPP	6 items (4 blocks)	—
	Cross gutter block (2)	—
	Horiz. pair with vert. gutter (2)	—
	Vert. pair with horiz. gutter (4)	—
733aPI	(12 blocks)	—
	Cross gutter block (2)	—
	Horiz. pair with vert. gutter (2)	—
	Vert. pair with horiz. gutter (4)	—
G321aPI	(12 blocks)	—
	Cross gutter block (2)	—
	Horiz. pair with vert. gutter (2)	—
	Vert. pair with horiz. gutter (4)	—
V238aPI	(12 blocks)	—
	Cross gutter block (2)	—
	Horiz. pair with vert. gutter (2)	—
	Vert. pair with horiz. gutter (4)	—

No. G321aPP is not a complete set, as there are no black only and cyan only items.

New York #734, Geneva #322, Vienna #239
International Year of the Ocean

1998

734PD	(not approved) (4)	—
G322PD	(4)	—
V239PD	(4)	—
734PP	6 items (6 panes)	—
G322PP	6 items (6 panes)	—
V239PP	6 items (6 panes)	—
734PI	(18 panes)	—
G322PI	(18 panes)	—
V239PI	(18 panes)	—

New York #735-736, Geneva #323-324, Vienna #240-241
Rain Forests

1998

735PDa	Card, imperforate pane of 20 #735PD (8)	—
736PDa	Card, #736PD, #G324PD, #V241PD (8)	—
G323PDa	Card, imperforate pane of 20 #G323PD (8)	—
V240PDa	Card, imperforate pane of 20 #V240PD (8)	—
735PP	6 items (see note)	—
G323PP	6 items (see note)	—
V240PP	6 items (see note)	—
735PI	(see note)	—
G323PI	(see note)	—
V240PI	(see note)	—

There are two types of Nos. 735PP and V240PP, one with cats lacking spots on the red item, the other with the cat with spots on the magenta item. There are 20 of each type.

There are two types of No. G323PP, one with orangutan with small dots in eyes on the cyan item, the other with large dots in eyes.

Similarly, there are two types of Nos. 735PI, G323PI and V240PI, one with a lighter background, the other with a bolder background. There are 20 pairs of each type.

New York #737-738, Geneva #325-326, Vienna #242-243, Souvenir Card #52
UN Peacekeeping Forces, 50th Anniv.

1998

737TC	Dark blue panel (on Cromalin paper) (5)	—
738TC	Dark blue panel (on Cromalin paper) (5)	—
G325TC	Dark blue panel (on Cromalin paper) (5)	—
G326TC	Dark blue panel (on Cromalin paper) (5)	—
V242TC	Dark blue panel (on Cromalin paper) (5)	—

V243TC	Dark blue panel (on Cromalin paper) (5)	—
SC52PD	(4)	—
737PP	10 items (20)	—
738PP	10 items (20)	—
G325PP	10 items (20)	—
G326PP	10 items (20)	—
V242PP	10 items (20)	—
V243PP	10 items (20)	—
737PI	(20 pairs)	—
738PI	(20 pairs)	—
G325PI	(20 pairs)	—
G326PI	(20 pairs)	—
V242PI	(20 pairs)	—
V243PI	(20 pairs)	—

New York #739-740, Geneva #327-328, Vienna #244-245, Souvenir Card #53
Universal Declaration of Human Rights, 50th Anniv.

1998

740PDa	Card, #739PD-740PD, #G327PD-G328PD, #V244PD-V245PD (4)	—
SC53PD	(4)	—
739PP	8 items (64)	—
	Cross gutter block (2)	—
	Horiz. pair with vert. gutter (8)	—
	Vert. pair with horiz. gutter (16)	—
740PP	8 items (64)	—
	Cross gutter block (2)	—
	Horiz. pair with vert. gutter (8)	—
	Vert. pair with horiz. gutter (16)	—
G327PP	8 items (64)	—
	Cross gutter block (2)	—
	Horiz. pair with vert. gutter (8)	—
	Vert. pair with horiz. gutter (16)	—
G328PP	8 items (64)	—
	Cross gutter block (2)	—
	Horiz. pair with vert. gutter (8)	—
	Vert. pair with horiz. gutter (16)	—
V244PP	8 items (64)	—
	Cross gutter block (2)	—
	Horiz. pair with vert. gutter (8)	—
	Vert. pair with horiz. gutter (16)	—
V245PP	8 items (64)	—
	Cross gutter block (2)	—
	Horiz. pair with vert. gutter (8)	—
	Vert. pair with horiz. gutter (16)	—
739PI	(52 pairs)	—
	Cross gutter block (2)	—
	Horiz. pair with vert. gutter (8)	—
	Vert. pair with horiz. gutter (16)	—
740PI	(52 pairs)	—
	Cross gutter block (2)	—
	Horiz. pair with vert. gutter (8)	—
	Vert. pair with horiz. gutter (16)	—
G327PI	(52 pairs)	—
	Cross gutter block (2)	—
	Horiz. pair with vert. gutter (8)	—
	Vert. pair with horiz. gutter (16)	—
G328PI	(52 pairs)	—
	Cross gutter block (2)	—
	Horiz. pair with vert. gutter (8)	—
	Vert. pair with horiz. gutter (16)	—
V244PI	(52 pairs)	—
	Cross gutter block (2)	—
	Horiz. pair with vert. gutter (8)	—
	Vert. pair with horiz. gutter (16)	—
V245PI	(52 pairs)	—
	Cross gutter block (2)	—
	Horiz. pair with vert. gutter (8)	—
	Vert. pair with horiz. gutter (16)	—

New York #741-743, Geneva #329-331, Vienna #246-248
Schönbrunn Palace

1998

742PDa	Card, blocks of 4, #741PD-742PD (3)	—
742PDb	Card, cut apart blocks of 4, #741PD-742PD (1)	—
G330PDa	Card, blocks of 4, #G329PD-G330PD (3)	—
G330PDb	Card, cut apart blocks of 4, #G329PD-G330PD (1)	—
V247PDa	Card, blocks of 4, #V246PD-V247PD (3)	—
V247PDb	Card, cut apart blocks of 4, #V246PD-V247PD (1)	—
742TCa	Card, block of 4 #742TC dark blue denomination (on photographic paper) (1)	—
743TCa	Card, strips of 3, #743aTC-743cTC bright red violet denomination (on photographic paper) (1)	—
743TCb	Card, blocks of 4, #743dTC-743fTC bright red violet denomination (on photographic paper) (1)	—
743TCc	Entire booklet (black & white, on photographic paper) (1)	—
G330TCa	Card, blocks of 4, #G329TC-G330TC bright red violet denominations (on photographic paper) (1)	—
G331TCa	Card, blocks of 4, #G331aTC-G331cTC bright red violet denomination (on photographic paper) (1)	—
G331TCb	Card, strips of 3, #G331dTC-G331fTC bright red violet denomination (on photographic paper) (1)	—
G331TCc	Entire booklet (black & white, on photographic paper) (1)	—
V247TCa	Card, block of 4 #V247TC bright green denomination (on photographic paper) (1)	—
V248TCa	Card, strips of 3, #V248aTC-V248cTC bright red violet denomination (on photographic paper) (1)	—
V248TCb	Card, blocks of 4, #V248dTC-V248fTC bright red violet denomination (on photographic paper) (1)	—
V248TCc	Entire booklet (black & white, on photographic paper) (1)	—
741PP	10 items (24)	—
	Vert. pair with horiz. gutter (3)	—
742PP	10 items (24)	—
	Horiz. pair with vert. gutter (3)	—
742PPa	Cross gutter block, 2 #741PP-742PP (1)	—
742PPb	Vert. pair with horiz. gutter, #741PP-742PP (8)	—
G329PP	10 items (24)	—
	Vert. pair with horiz. gutter (3)	—
G330PP	10 items (24)	—
	Horiz. pair with vert. gutter (3)	—
G330PPa	Cross gutter block, 2 #G329PP-G330PP (1)	—
G330PPb	Vert. pair with horiz. gutter, #G329PP-G330PP (8)	—
V246PP	10 items (24)	—
	Vert. pair with horiz. gutter (3)	—
V247PP	10 items (24)	—
	Horiz. pair with vert. gutter (3)	—
V247PPa	Cross gutter block, 2 #V246PP-V247PP (1)	—
V247PPb	Vert. pair with horiz. gutter, #V246PP-V247PP (8)	—
741PI	(32 pairs)	—
	Vert. pair with horiz. gutter (3)	—
742PI	(32 pairs)	—
	Horiz. pair with vert. gutter (3)	—
742PIa	Cross gutter block, 2 #741PI-742PI (1)	—
742PIb	Vert. pair with horiz. gutter, #741PI-742PI (8)	—
G329PI	(32 pairs)	—
	Vert. pair with horiz. gutter (3)	—
G330PI	(32 pairs)	—
	Horiz. pair with vert. gutter (3)	—
G330PIa	Cross gutter block, 2 #G329PI-G330PI (1)	—
G330PIb	Vert. pair with horiz. gutter, #G329PI-G330PI (8)	—
V246PI	(32 pairs)	—
	Vert. pair with horiz. gutter (3)	—
V247PI	(32 pairs)	—
	Horiz. pair with vert. gutter (3)	—
V247PIa	Cross gutter block, 2 #V246PI-V247PI (1)	—
V247PIb	Vert. pair with horiz. gutter, #V246PI-V247PI (8)	—

Five cards with blocks of four essays with gold frames over vignette exist for each of the New York, Geneva and Vienna pairings.

New York #744-751
Flags

1999

744-751PP	Set of 20 sheets (1)	—
744-751PI	Set of 2 sheets (4)	—

On Nos. 744-751PP, there are ten progressive proof sheets per issued sheet.

New York #752-753, Geneva #332, Vienna #249
Definitives

1999

752PDa	Card, #752PD, #V249PD (3)	—
752PDb	Card, #752PD, #V249PD, #753TC lacking gray in pink frame boxes (1)	—

753PDa	Card, block of 4, #753PD (2)	—
753TC	Lacking gray in pink frame boxes (3)	—
G332TC	red (4)	—
G332TC	brown (4)	—
752PP	9 items (48)	—
	Cross gutter block (1)	—
	Horiz. pair with vert. gutter (6)	—
	Vert. pair with horiz. gutter (8)	—
753PP	10 items (20)	—
V249PP	9 items (48)	—
	Cross gutter block (1)	—
	Horiz. pair with vert. gutter (6)	—
	Vert. pair with horiz. gutter (8)	—
752PI	(24 pairs)	—
	Cross gutter block (3)	—
	Horiz. pair with vert. gutter (18)	—
	Vert. pair with horiz. gutter (24)	—
753PI	(20 pairs)	—
G332PI	(20 pairs)	—
V249PI	(72 pairs)	—
	Cross gutter block (3)	—
	Horiz. pair with vert. gutter (18)	—
	Vert. pair with horiz. gutter (24)	—

New York #754-756, Geneva #333-335, Vienna #250-252
World Heritage

1999

755PDa	Card, pairs of #754PD-755PD, #G333PD-G334PD, #V250PD-V251PD (1)	—
756PDa	Card, pairs of #756aPD-756fPD (1)	—
756PDb	Sheet, pairs of #754PD-755PD, #756aPD-756fPD, #G333PD-G334PD, #G335aPD-G335fPD, #V250PD-V251PD, #V252aPD-V252fPD (2)	—
756PDc	Cut-up section of #756PDb with pairs of stamps issued in sheets (2)	—
756PDd	Cut-up section of #756PDb with pairs of stamps issued in booklets (2)	—
754TC	Black and white image on layout sheet of photographic paper (2)	—
755TC	Black and white image on layout sheet of photographic paper (2)	—
G333TC	Black and white image on layout sheet of photographic paper (2)	—
G334TC	Black and white image on layout sheet of photographic paper (2)	—
V250TCa	Black and white image on layout sheet of photographic paper (2)	—
V250TCb	2 pairs of black and white images on layout sheet of photographic paper, affixed to card (1)	—
V251TCa	Black and white image on layout sheet of photographic paper (2)	—
V251TCb	2 pairs of black and white images on layout sheet of photographic paper, affixed to card (1)	—
754PP	6 items (32)	—
	Horiz. pair with vert. gutter (8)	—
755PP	6 items (32)	—
	Horiz. pair with vert. gutter (8)	—
755PPa	Cross gutter block, 2 #754PP-755PP (2)	—
755PPb	Vert. pair with horiz. gutter, #754PP-755PP (8)	—
G333PP	6 items (32)	—
	Horiz. pair with vert. gutter (8)	—
G334PP	6 items (32)	—
	Horiz. pair with vert. gutter (8)	—
G334PPa	Cross gutter block, 2 #G333PP-G334PP (2)	—
G334PPb	Vert. pair with horiz. gutter, #G333PP-G334PP (8)	—
V250PP	6 items (32)	—
	Horiz. pair with vert. gutter (8)	—
V251PP	6 items (32)	—
	Horiz. pair with vert. gutter (8)	—
V251PPa	Cross gutter block, 2 #V250PP-V251PP (2)	—
V251PPb	Vert. pair with horiz. gutter, #V250PP-V251PP (8)	—
754PI	(52 pairs)	—
	Horiz. pair with vert. gutter (16)	—
755PI	(52 pairs)	—
	Horiz. pair with vert. gutter (16)	—
755PIa	Cross gutter block, 2 #754PI-755PI (4)	—
755PIb	Vert. pair with horiz. gutter, #754PI-755PI (16)	—
G333PI	(36 pairs)	—
	Horiz. pair with vert. gutter (8)	—
G334PI	(36 pairs)	—
	Horiz. pair with vert. gutter (8)	—
G334PIa	Cross gutter block, 2 #G333PI-G334PI (2)	—
G334PIb	Vert. pair with horiz. gutter, #G333PI-G334PI (8)	—
V250PI	(36 pairs)	—
	Horiz. pair with vert. gutter (8)	—
V251PI	(36 pairs)	—
	Horiz. pair with vert. gutter (8)	—
V251PIa	Cross gutter block, 2 #V250PI-V251PI (2)	—
V251PIb	Vert. pair with horiz. gutter, #V250PI-V251PI (8)	—

New York #760a, Geneva #339a, Vienna #256a
Endangered Species

1999

760aPDa	Card, imperf pane of 4 blocks, #760aPD (2)	—
760aPDb	Card, 2 each #757PD-760PD (1)	—
G339aPDa	Card, 2 each #G336PD-G339PD (on Cromalin paper), broken pane of 80c essays of #G336-G339 (1)	—
V256aPDa	Card, imperf pane of 4 blocks, #V256aPD (3)	—
V256aPDb	Card, 2 each #V253PD-V256PD (1)	—
760aPP	6 items (4 blocks)	—
	Cross gutter block (2)	—
	Horiz. pair with vert. gutter (2)	—
	Vert. pair with horiz. gutter (4)	—
G339aPP	6 items (4 blocks)	—
	Cross gutter block (2)	—
	Horiz. pair with vert. gutter (2)	—
	Vert. pair with horiz. gutter (4)	—
V256aPP	6 items (4 blocks)	—
	Cross gutter block (2)	—
	Horiz. pair with vert. gutter (2)	—
	Vert. pair with horiz. gutter (4)	—
760aPI	(12 blocks)	—
	Cross gutter block (2)	—
	Horiz. pair with vert. gutter (2)	—
	Vert. pair with horiz. gutter (4)	—
G339aPI	(12 blocks)	—
	Cross gutter block (2)	—
	Horiz. pair with vert. gutter (2)	—
	Vert. pair with horiz. gutter (4)	—
V256aPI	(12 blocks)	—
	Cross gutter block (2)	—
	Horiz. pair with vert. gutter (2)	—
	Vert. pair with horiz. gutter (4)	—

Three cards exist containing imperforate panes of four blocks of the 80c essays.

New York #762a, 763, Geneva #341a, 342, Vienna #258a, 259
UNISPACE III

1999

762aPDa	Card, imperforate pane of 5 pairs, #762aPD (3)	—
763PD	With printed perforations on overlay (3)	—
763aPD	With printed perforations on overlay (2)	—
G341aPDa	Card, imperforate pane of 5 pairs, #G341aPD (4)	—
G342PD	With printed perforations on overlay (2)	—
G342aPD	With printed perforations on overlay (2)	—
V258aPDa	Card, imperforate pane of 5 pairs, #V258aPD (4)	—
V259PD	With printed perforations on overlay (2)	—
762PP	8 items (5 pairs)	—
762aPP	8 items (1 souvenir sheet)	—
763PP	9 items (1 pair)	—
763aPP	10 items (1 souvenir sheet)	—
762aPI	(10 pairs)	—
763PI	(3 souvenir sheets)	—
763aPI	(4 souvenir sheets)	—
G341aPI	(10 pairs)	—
G342PI	(3 souvenir sheets)	—
V258aPI	(10 pairs)	—
V259PI	(3 souvenir sheets)	—

New York #767a, Geneva #346a, Vienna #263a, Souvenir Card #54
Universal Postal Union, 125th Anniv.

1999

767aPDa	Card, #767aPD, #G346aPD, #V263aPD with approval handstamp (4)	—

767aTCa Card, #767aTC, #G346aTCD, #V263aTC (dark blue denominations, not approved (4) —
SC54PD (4) —
767aPP 8 items (6 blocks) —
G346aPP 8 items (6 blocks) —
V263aPP 8 items (6 blocks) —
767aPI (12 blocks) —
G346aPI (12 blocks) —
V263aPI (12 blocks) —

New York #768-769, Geneva #347-348, Vienna #264-265
In Memoriam

1999
769PDa Card, #768PD-769PD (4) —
G348PDa Card, #G347PD-G348PD (4) —
V265PDa Card, #V264PD-V265PD (4) —
768PP 10 items (66) —
Cross gutter block (2) —
Horiz. pair with vert. gutter (12) —
Vert. pair with horiz. gutter (11) —
769PP 10 items (24 souvenir sheets) —
G347PP 10 items (66) —
Cross gutter block (2) —
Horiz. pair with vert. gutter (12) —
Vert. pair with horiz. gutter (11) —
G348PP 10 items (24 souvenir sheets) —
V264PP 10 items (66) —
Cross gutter block (2) —
Horiz. pair with vert. gutter (12) —
Vert. pair with horiz. gutter (11) —
V265PP 10 items (24 souvenir sheets) —
768PI (52 pairs) —
Cross gutter block (2) —
Horiz. pair with vert. gutter (12) —
Vert. pair with horiz. gutter (11) —
769PI (24 souvenir sheets) —
G347PI (52 pairs) —
Cross gutter block (2) —
Horiz. pair with vert. gutter (12) —
Vert. pair with horiz. gutter (11) —
G348PI (24 souvenir sheets) —
V264PI (52 pairs) —
Cross gutter block (2) —
Horiz. pair with vert. gutter (12) —
Vert. pair with horiz. gutter (11) —
V265PI (24 souvenir sheets) —

New York #770-771, Geneva #349-350, Vienna #266-267
Education

1999
771PDa Card, #770PD-771PD, #G349PD-G350PD, #V266PD-V267PD with approval handstamp (4) —
771PDb Card, #770PD, #G350PD, #V266PD-V267PD, #771TC red denomination, #G349TC red violet denomination with "approved with corrections" handstamp (4) —
770PP 9 items (20) —
771PP 8 items (20) —
G349PP 7 items (20) —
G350PP 7 items (20) —
V266PP 7 items (20) —
V267PP 8 items (20) —
770PI (20 pairs) —
771PI (20 pairs) —
G349PI (30 pairs) —
G350PI (30 pairs) —
V266PI (30 pairs) —
V267PI (30 pairs) —

New York #772, Geneva #351, Vienna #268
International Year of Thanksgiving

2000
772PDa Card, #772PD, #G351PD, #V268PD (4) —
772TCa Card, #772TC, #G351TC, #V268TC, all with black background (4) —
772PP 12 items (32) —
Horiz. pair with vert. gutter (4) —
G351PP 12 items (32) —
Horiz. pair with vert. gutter (4) —
V268PP 12 items (32) —
Horiz. pair with vert. gutter (4) —
772PI (36 pairs) —
Horiz. pair with vert. gutter (4) —
G351PI (36 pairs) —
Horiz. pair with vert. gutter (4) —
V268PI (36 pairs) —
Horiz. pair with vert. gutter (4) —

New York #776a, Geneva #355a, Vienna #272a
Endangered Species

2000
776aPDa Card, imperforate pane of 4 blocks, #776aPD (3) —
776aPDb Card, 3 each #773PD-776PD (1) —
G355aPDa Card, imperforate pane of 4 blocks, #G355aPD, imperforate pane of 4 blocks, #V272aPD (3) —
G355aPDb Card, 3 each #G352PD-G355PD, #V269PD-V272PD (1) —
776aPP 6 items (4 blocks) —
Cross gutter block (2) —
Horiz. pair with vert. gutter (2) —
Vert. pair with horiz. gutter (4) —
G355aPP 6 items (4 blocks) —
Cross gutter block (2) —
Horiz. pair with vert. gutter (2) —
Vert. pair with horiz. gutter (4) —
V272aPP 6 items (4 blocks) —
Cross gutter block (2) —
Horiz. pair with vert. gutter (2) —
Vert. pair with horiz. gutter (4) —
776aPI (12 blocks) —
Cross gutter block (2) —
Horiz. pair with vert. gutter (2) —
Vert. pair with horiz. gutter (4) —
G355aPI (12 blocks) —
Cross gutter block (2) —
Horiz. pair with vert. gutter (2) —
Vert. pair with horiz. gutter (4) —
V272aPI (12 blocks) —
Cross gutter block (2) —
Horiz. pair with vert. gutter (2) —
Vert. pair with horiz. gutter (4) —

New York #777-778, Geneva #356-357, Vienna #273-274
Our World 2000

2000
778PDa Card, #777PD-778PD, #G356PD-G357PD, #V273PD-V274PD (4) —
778PDb Card, #777PD-778PD, #G356PD-G357PD, #V274PD, #V273TC black denomination, with "not approved" handstamp (2) —
777PP 8 items (64) —
Cross gutter block (2) —
Horiz. pair with vert. gutter (16) —
Vert. pair with horiz. gutter (8) —
778PP 8 items (64) —
Cross gutter block (2) —
Horiz. pair with vert. gutter (8) —
Vert. pair with horiz. gutter (16) —
G356PP 8 items (64) —
Cross gutter block (2) —
Horiz. pair with vert. gutter (8) —
Vert. pair with horiz. gutter (16) —
G357PP 8 items (64) —
Cross gutter block (2) —
Horiz. pair with vert. gutter (16) —
Vert. pair with horiz. gutter (8) —
V273PP 8 items (64) —
Cross gutter block (2) —
Horiz. pair with vert. gutter (16) —
Vert. pair with horiz. gutter (8) —
V274PP 8 items (64) —
Cross gutter block (2) —
Horiz. pair with vert. gutter (8) —
Vert. pair with horiz. gutter (16) —
777PI (52 pairs) —
Cross gutter block (2) —
Horiz. pair with vert. gutter (16) —
Vert. pair with horiz. gutter (8) —
778PI (52 pairs) —
Cross gutter block (2) —
Horiz. pair with vert. gutter (8) —
Vert. pair with horiz. gutter (16) —
G356PI (52 pairs) —
Cross gutter block (2) —
Horiz. pair with vert. gutter (16) —
Vert. pair with horiz. gutter (8) —
G357PI (52 pairs) —
Cross gutter block (2) —
Horiz. pair with vert. gutter (8) —
Vert. pair with horiz. gutter (16) —
V273PI (52 pairs) —
Cross gutter block (2) —
Horiz. pair with vert. gutter (16) —
Vert. pair with horiz. gutter (8) —
V274PI (52 pairs) —
Cross gutter block (2) —
Horiz. pair with vert. gutter (8) —
Vert. pair with horiz. gutter (16) —

New York #779-781, Geneva #358-360, Vienna #275-277
United Nations, 55th Anniv.

2000

No.	Description	Value
780TCa	Card, #779TC-780TC, #G358TC-G359TC, #V275TC-V276TC (all with white denominations with colored outlines (4)	—
781TCa	Card, #781TC, #G360TC, #V277TC (all with white denominations with colored outlines (4)	—
781TCb	Card, #779TC-781TC ultramarine & silver (2)	—
781TCc	Card, #779TC-781TC blue & silver (2)	—
781TCd	Card, #781TC, #G360TC silver backgrounds, white denominations with colored outlines (5)	—
G359TCa	Card, #G358TC-G359TC brown red & silver (2)	—
G360TCa	Card, #G358TC-G360TC carmine & silver (2)	—
G360TCb	Card, #G358TC-G360TC cerise & silver (2)	—
V277TCa	Card, #V275TC-V277TC green & silver (2)	—
V277TCb	Card, #V275TC-V277TC dark green & silver (2)	—
V277TCc	Silver background, white denominations with green outlines (5)	—
779PP	7 items (128)	—
	Cross gutter block (4)	—
	Horiz. pair with vert. gutter (16)	—
	Vert. pair with horiz. gutter (32)	—
780PP	7 items (128)	—
	Cross gutter block (4)	—
	Horiz. pair with vert. gutter (16)	—
	Vert. pair with horiz. gutter (32)	—
781PP	6 items (60 souvenir sheets)	—
G358PP	9 items (128)	—
	Cross gutter block (4)	—
	Horiz. pair with vert. gutter (16)	—
	Vert. pair with horiz. gutter (32)	—
G359PP	9 items (128)	—
	Cross gutter block (4)	—
	Horiz. pair with vert. gutter (16)	—
	Vert. pair with horiz. gutter (32)	—
G360PP	9 items (60 souvenir sheets)	—
V275PP	10 items (128)	—
	Cross gutter block (4)	—
	Horiz. pair with vert. gutter (16)	—
	Vert. pair with horiz. gutter (32)	—
V276PP	10 items (128)	—
	Cross gutter block (4)	—
	Horiz. pair with vert. gutter (16)	—
	Vert. pair with horiz. gutter (32)	—
V277PP	10 items (60 souvenir sheets)	—
779PI	(84 pairs)	—
	Cross gutter block (4)	—
	Horiz. pair with vert. gutter (16)	—
	Vert. pair with horiz. gutter (32)	—
780PI	(84 pairs)	—
	Cross gutter block (4)	—
	Horiz. pair with vert. gutter (16)	—
	Vert. pair with horiz. gutter (32)	—
781PI	(60 souvenir sheets)	—
G358PI	(84 pairs)	—
	Cross gutter block (4)	—
	Horiz. pair with vert. gutter (16)	—
	Vert. pair with horiz. gutter (32)	—
G359PI	(84 pairs)	—
	Cross gutter block (4)	—
	Horiz. pair with vert. gutter (16)	—
	Vert. pair with horiz. gutter (32)	—
V275PI	(84 pairs)	—
	Cross gutter block (4)	—
	Horiz. pair with vert. gutter (16)	—
	Vert. pair with horiz. gutter (32)	—
V276PI	(84 pairs)	—
	Cross gutter block (4)	—
	Horiz. pair with vert. gutter (16)	—
	Vert. pair with horiz. gutter (32)	—
781PI	(60 souvenir sheets)	—

One item in Nos. G358PP and G359PP is blank, coming from sheet with marginal inscriptions only.

New York #782
International Flag of Peace

2000

No.	Description	Value
782PD	With approval handstamp (4)	—
782TC	Black and white photocopy of layout of pane of 20, with approval handstamp and signature (1)	—
782PP	9 items (96)	—
	Cross gutter block (2)	—
	Horiz. pair with vert. gutter (16)	—
	Vert. pair with horiz. gutter (8)	—
782PI	(96 pairs)	—
	Cross gutter block (6)	—
	Horiz. pair with vert. gutter (48)	—
	Vert. pair with horiz. gutter (24)	—

An essay with "age 12" after artist's name exists in five cards and a black and white layout of the pane of 20 on photographic paper.

New York #783, Geneva #361, Vienna #278
UN in the 21st Century

2000

No.	Description	Value
783PDa	Card, #783PD, #G361PD, #V278PD with approval handstamp (4)	—
783TCa	Card, #783TC, #G361TC, #V278TC all with washed-out colors, with "not approved" handstamp (5)	—
783PP	8 items (1)	—
G361PP	8 items (1)	—
V278PP	8 items (1)	—
783PI	(2 sheets)	—
G361PI	(2 sheets)	—
V278PI	(2 sheets)	—

New York #784-786, Geneva #362-364, Vienna #279-281
World Heritage

2000

No.	Description	Value
785PDa	Card, #784PD-785PD, #G362PD-G364PD, #V279PD-V280PD (4)	—
784TC	Black and white image of pane of 20 on layout sheet on photographic paper (1)	—
785TC	Black and white image of pane of 20 on layout sheet on photographic paper (1)	—
G362TC	Black and white image of pane of 20 on layout sheet on photographic paper (1)	—
G363TC	Black and white image of pane of 20 on layout sheet on photographic paper (1)	—
V279TC	Black and white image of pane of 20 on layout sheet on photographic paper (1)	—
V280TC	Black and white image of pane of 20 on layout sheet on photographic paper (1)	—
784PP	9 items (24)	—
	Vert. pair with horiz. gutter (3)	—
785PP	9 items (24)	—
	Vert. pair with horiz. gutter (3)	—
785PPa	Cross gutter block, 2 #784PP-785PP (1)	—
785PPb	Horiz. pair with vert. gutter, #784PP-785PP (8)	—
786lPPa	9 items, Strip of #786gPP-786iPP, with vert. gutters between (4)	—
G362PP	9 items (24)	—
	Vert. pair with horiz. gutter (3)	—
G363PP	9 items (24)	—
	Vert. pair with horiz. gutter (3)	—
G363PPa	Cross gutter block, 2 #G362PP-G363PP (1)	—
G363PPb	Horiz. pair with vert. gutter, #G362PP-G363PP (8)	—
V279PP	7 items (24)	—
	Vert. pair with horiz. gutter (3)	—
V280PP	7 items (24)	—
	Vert. pair with horiz. gutter (3)	—
V280PPa	Cross gutter block, 2 #V279PP-V280PP (1)	—
V280PPb	Horiz. pair with vert. gutter, #V279PP-V280PP (8)	—
784PI	(32 pairs)	—
	Vert. pair with horiz. gutter (3)	—
785PI	(32 pairs)	—
	Vert. pair with horiz. gutter (3)	—
785PIa	Cross gutter block, 2 #784PI-785PI (1)	—
785PIb	Horiz. pair with vert. gutter, #784PI-785PI (8)	—
786gPI	(5 booklet panes)	—
786hPI	(5 booklet panes)	—
786iPI	(5 booklet panes)	—
786iPIa	Strip of #786gPI-786iPI, with vert. gutters between (4)	—
786jPI	(5 booklet panes)	—
786kPI	(5 booklet panes)	—
786lPI	(5 booklet panes)	—
G362PI	(32 pairs)	—
	Vert. pair with horiz. gutter (3)	—

G363PI (32 pairs) —
Vert. pair with horiz. gutter (3) —
G363PIa Cross gutter block, 2 #G362PI-G363PI (1) —
G363PIb Horiz. pair with vert. gutter, #G362PI-G363PI (8) —
G364gPI (5 booklet panes) —
G364hPI (5 booklet panes) —
G364iPI (5 booklet panes) —
G364jPI (5 booklet panes) —
G364kPI (5 booklet panes) —
G364lPI (5 booklet panes) —
V279PI (82 pairs) —
Vert. pair with horiz. gutter (3) —
V280PI (32 pairs) —
Vert. pair with horiz. gutter (3) —
V280PIa Cross gutter block, 2 #V279PI-V280PI (1) —
V280PIb Horiz. pair with vert. gutter, #V279PI-V280PI (8) —
V281gPI (5 booklet panes) —
V281hPI (5 booklet panes) —
V281iPI (5 booklet panes) —
V281jPI (5 booklet panes) —
V281kPI (5 booklet panes) —
V281lPI (5 booklet panes) —

Some pairs of No. V279PI are defaced with blue marker.

New York #787-788, Geneva #365-366, Vienna #282-283, Souvenir Card #55
Respect for Refugees

2000
787PDa Card, #787PD, #G365PD, #V282PD (4) —
788PDa Card, #788PD, #G366PD, #V283PD (4) —
SC55PD (4) —
787PP 6 items (32) —
Horiz. pair with vert. gutter (4) —
788PP 6 items (20 souvenir sheets) —
G365PP 6 items (32) —
Cross gutter block (1) —
Horiz. pair with vert. gutter (6) —
Vert. pair with horiz. gutter (8) —
G366PP 6 items (20 souvenir sheets) —
V282PP 6 items (32) —
Horiz. pair with vert. gutter (4) —
V283PP 6 items (20 souvenir sheets) —
787PI (36 pairs) —
Horiz. pair with vert. gutter (4) —
788PI (20 souvenir sheets) —
G365PI (44 pairs) —
Cross gutter block (1) —
Horiz. pair with vert. gutter (6) —
Vert. pair with horiz. gutter (8) —
G366PI (20 souvenir sheets) —
V282PI (36 pairs) —
Horiz. pair with vert. gutter (4) —
V283PI (20 souvenir sheets) —

AIR POST STAMPS
New York #C1-C4
Plane and Gull, Swallows and UN Emblem

1951
C1PD (1) —
C2PD (1) —
C3PD (1) —
C4PD (1) —
C1PI (25 pairs) —
C2PI (25 pairs) —
C3PI (25 pairs) —
C4PI (25 pairs) —

New York #C5
Airplane Wing and Globe

1957
C5PD (4) —
C5TC brown (not approved) (5) —
C5TC indigo (5) —
C5PI (40 pairs) —
Vert. pair with horiz. gutter (10) —

New York #C6-C7
Airplane Wing and Globe; UN Flag and Plane

1959
C6PD (1) —
C6PDa Card, #C6PD, 2 #C6TC in slightly different shades (2) —
C6PDb Card, 2 #C6PD, 2 #C7TC Prussian blue (1) —
C7PD (1) —
C7PDa Card, #C7PD, #C7TC Prussian blue, #C7TC dark blue (2) —
C6TC black (1) —
C7TC black (1) —
C6PI (115 pairs) —
Vert. pair with horiz. gutter (10) —
C7PI (90 pairs) —
Horiz. pair with vert. gutter (10) —

New York #C8-C10
Definitives

1963
C10PDa Card, #C8PD-C10PD (3) —
C10PDb Card, #C8PD, #C10PD, 3 #C9PD (3) —
C8PP 3 items (80) —
Horiz. pair with vert. gutter (10) —
C9PP 4 items (80) —
Vert. pair with horiz. gutter (10) —
C10PP 4 items (80) —
Horiz. pair with vert. gutter (10) —
C8PI (80 pairs) —
Horiz. pair with vert. gutter (20) —
C9PI (80 pairs) —
Vert. pair with horiz. gutter (20) —
C10PI (80 pairs) —
Horiz. pair with vert. gutter (20) —

New York #C11-C12
Definitives

1964
C11PDa Card, #C11PD, #C12TC peach and brown background (disapproved) (2) —
C12PD (2) —
C12PDa Card, #C11PD-C12PD (4) —
C11PI (25 pairs) —
C12PI (25 pairs) —

New York #C13
Jet and UN Emblem

1968
C13PD (3) —
C13PDa Card, #C13PD, 2 #C13TC with slightly different shades (2) —
C13PP 9 items, perforated, mounted on card (1) —

New York #C14
Wings, Envelopes and UN Emblem

1969
C14PD (4) —
C14PP 6 items, perforated (50) —

New York #C15-C18
Definitives

1972
C15PD (2) —
C16PD With approval handstamp (2) —
C17PD (2) —
C18PD (2) —
C16TC dark blue emblem (dated 16. Oct. 1971) (2) —
C15PP 4 items (100) —
C16PP 10 items (100) —
C17PP 4 items (100) —
C18PP 10 items (160) —
Horiz. pair with vert. gutter (20) —
C16PI (50 pairs) —
C17PI (50 pairs) —

New York #C19-C21
Definitives

1974
C19PD (3) —
C20PD (3) —
C21PD (3) —
C19PP 8 items (50) —
C21PP 5 items (50) —
C19PI (50 pairs) —
C20PI (50 pairs) —
C21PI (50 pairs) —

Five cards with essays of No. C21 with incorrect Russian inscription exist.

New York #C22-C23
Definitives

1977
C22PD With approval handstamp (4) —
C22TC Gray wings and envelope, with "not approved" handstamp (2) —

C23PD	(1)	—
C23PDa	Card, #C23PD, #C22TC gray wings and envelope (3)	—
C22PP	6 items (50)	—
C22PI	(50 pairs)	—
C23PI	(50 pairs)	—

ENVELOPES

New York #U1 UN Emblem

1952

U1PD	(1)	—
U1TC	black (1)	—

New York #U2 UN Emblem

1958

U2PD	with manuscript approval (2)	—
U2TC	black, on card, with manuscript approval (1)	—

New York #U3 Stylized Globe and Weather Vane

1963

U3PD	(2)	—
U3PI	Indicia only on small piece of paper (1)	—

See No. UC6PI.

New York #U5 UN Headquarters

1973

U5PD	(41)	—
U5PP	6 items (5)	—
U5PI	Unfolded and uncut (2)	—

New York #U6 UN Headquarters

1975

U6PD	With approval handstamp (5)	—
U6PDa	Die cut and unfolded, without approval handstamp (4)	—

New York #U7 Bouquet of Ribbons

1985

U7PD	Indicia only, in folder (9)	—

Vienna #U1-U2 Donaupark

1995

VU1PD	On Cromalin paper (approved) (6)	—
VU1PDa	On AGFA paper (not approved) (5)	—
VU2PD	On Cromalin paper (approved) (6)	—
VU2PDa	On AGFA paper (not approved) (5)	—

New York #U10-U11 Cripticandina

1997

U10PD	On Cromalin paper (4)	—
U11PD	On Cromalin paper (4)	—

Vienna #U3 Landscape

1998

VU3PD	On Cromalin paper (4)	—

AIR POST ENVELOPES & AIR LETTER SHEETS New York #UC1 Swallows and UN Emblem

1952

UC1PI	(32)	—
UC1PIa	On white paper (22)	—

New York #UC3 UN Flag and Plane Envelope

1959

UC3PD	(1)	—

New York #UC4 UN Flag and Plane Letter Sheet

1960

UC4PD	(1)	—

Two "not approved" essays exist with diagonal lines rather than bars around envelope.

New York #UC5 Plane and Gull

1961

UC5PD	With approval handstamp (1)	—
UC5aPD	With approval handstamp (3)	—

New York #UC6 UN Emblem

1963

UC6PDa	Sheet, #UC6PD, #U3PD, with approval handstamp (2)	—
UC6PI	(1)	—
UC6PIa	Sheet, #UC6PD (2 sizes), #U3PD (2 sizes) (6)	—
UC6PIb	As #UC6PIa with one #U3PI removed (1)	—

New York #UC7 UN Emblem and Stylized Plane

1968

UC7PD	With specimen perfin and approval handstamp (7)	—

New York #UC8 UN Emblem

1969

UC8PD	With specimen perfin at left (4)	—

Geneva #UC1 UN Emblem and Stylized Plane

1969

GUC1PD	With specimen perfin and approval handstamp (1)	—
GUC1TC	light blue (2)	—
GUC1TC	ultramarine (3)	—

New York #UC9 UN Emblem, "UN," Globe and Plane

1972

UC9PD	With approval handstamp (2)	—

New York #UC10 Birds in Flight

1973

UC10PDa	Small envelope, die cut and folded, with approval handstamp (1)	—
UC10PDb	Large envelope, partially folded, with approval handstamp (2)	—
UC10PPa	Uncut and unfolded, large and small envelopes (6 items)	—

Three sets of essays exist with blue UN inscriptions close.

New York #UC11 Globe and Jet

1975

UC11PD	With approval handstamp (5)	—
UC11PDa	Die cut and unfolded, without approval handstamp (1)	—

New York #UC12 UN Headquarters

1975

UC12PD	With approval handstamp (1)	—

New York #UC13 UN Emblem and Birds

1977

UC13PD	With approval handstamp (2)	—

Five "not approved" essays have design flaw at end of orange line.

New York #UC14, Vienna #UC1
Paper Airplane, Dove

1982

UC14PD	With approval handstamp (3)	—
UC14PDa	On thin card stock (1)	—
VUC1PD	With approval handstamp (3)	—
VUC1PDa	On thin card stock (1)	—

Vienna #UC3
Birds in Flight and UN Emblem

1987

VUC3PD	On plastic, with approval handstamp (4)	—

New York #UC16
UN Headquarters

1989

UC16PD	With approval handstamp (approved) (3)	—
UC16PDa	With approval handstamp (not approved) (10)	—

Vienna #UC5
Donaupark

1992

VUC5PD	On Cromalin paper (3)	—

New York #UC19
Winged Hand With Envelopes Surcharge

1995

UC19PD	On Cromalin paper (1)	—

New York #UC20
Cherry Blossoms

1997

UC20PD	(5)	—

POSTAL CARDS
New York #UX1
UN Headquarters

1952

UX1TC	olive brown, on white paper (1)	—
UX1PI	(4 pairs)	—

New York #UX2
UN Headquarters

1958

UX2PD	With approval handstamp (2)	—

New York #UX3
World Map

1963

UX3PD	(2)	—

New York #UX4
UN Emblem and Post Horn

1969

UX4PD	With approval handstamp on reverse (1)	—

Geneva #UX1-UX2
UN Emblem and Post Horn, Stylized Space View

1969

GUX1PD	With approval handstamp (3)	—
GUX1PI	(53 pairs)	—
GUX2PI	(52 pairs)	—

New York #UX5
"UN"

1973

UX5PD	(1)	—

Five "not approved" essays similar to #UX5 exist. Ten 7c essays exist, three with approval handstamp, the others lacking any handstamp.

New York #UX6
"UN"

1975

UX6PD	With specimen perfin and approval handstamp (4)	—

Five "not approved" essays have incorrect Russian inscription.

New York #UX7, Geneva #UX3-UX4
UN Emblem, UN Emblem in Rectangles, UN Emblem and Ribbons

1977

UX7PD	With specimen perfin at left (4)	—
GUX3PD	With specimen perfin (5)	—
GUX4PD	With specimen perfin at left (4)	—

New York #UX8, Vienna #UX1-UX2
"United Nations," Olive Branch, Bird Carrying Olive Branch

1982

UX8PD	(2)	—
VUX1PD	With approval handstamp on reverse (4)	—
VUX2PD	With approval handstamp on reverse (16)	—

Geneva #UX5-UX6, Vienna #UX3
Peace Dove, UN Emblem

1985

GUX5PD	(3)	—
GUX6PD	With approval handstamp on reverse (3)	—
VUX3PD	(3)	—

One example of No. GUX5PD has inked lines at left of card. One example of No. GUX6PD has inked lines around address lines.

New York #UX9-UX18
Views of UN Headquarters

1989

UX9PD	Message side (4)	—
UX9PDa	Picture side (4)	—
UX10PD	Message side (4)	—
UX10PDa	Picture side (4)	—
UX11PD	Message side (4)	—
UX11PDa	Picture side (4)	—
UX12PD	Message side (4)	—
UX12PDa	Picture side (4)	—
UX13PD	Message side (4)	—
UX13PDa	Picture side (4)	—
UX14PD	Message side (4)	—
UX14PDa	Picture side (4)	—
UX15PD	Message side (4)	—
UX15PDa	Picture side (4)	—
UX16PD	Message side (4)	—
UX16PDa	Picture side (4)	—
UX17PD	Message side (4)	—
UX17PDa	Picture side (4)	—
UX18PD	Message side (4)	—
UX18PDa	Picture side (4)	—

New York #UX19, Geneva #UX8, Vienna #UX5
UN Headquarters, Palais des Nations, Regschek Painting

1992

UX19PD	On Cromalin paper (4)	—
GUX8PD	On Cromalin paper (4)	—
VUX5PD	On Cromalin paper (4)	—
VUX5PDa	Sheet, #GUX8PD, #VUX5PD on Cromalin paper (1)	—
UX19TC	ultramarine (1)	—

Geneva #UX10, Vienna #UX6-UX7
Palais des Nations, Peoples of the World United, Donaupark

1993

GUX10PD	On Cromalin paper (4)	—
VUX6PD	On Cromalin paper (4)	—
VUX7PD	On Cromalin paper (4)	—

Vienna #UX12
The Gloriette

1999

VUX12TCa	Light blue text (4)	—

AIR POST POSTAL CARDS
New York #UXC1
UN Flag and Plane

1957

UXC1PD	With printer and approval handstamps (6)	—
UXC1PI	(30 pairs)	—

New York #UXC3
Airplane Wing and Globe

1959

UXC3PD	With approval handstamp (3)	—

Six essays of No. UXC3 lacking outlined letters on "Airmail" and "Poste Aerienne" exist.

New York #UXC4
Outer Space

1963

UXC4PD	(2)	—

New York #UXC6
Outer Space

1968

UXC6PD	With "Canceled" perfin (2)	—
UXC6PDa	Strip of 3 cards with 2 "Canceled" perfins (2)	—

New York #UXC7
UN Emblem and Stylized Planes

1969

UXC7PD	(1)	—
UXC7TC	black (2)	—

New York #UXC8
UN Emblem and Stylized Wing

1972

UXC8PDa	Folder with mounted #UXC8PD with approval handstamp, and #UXC8 (2)	—

New York #UXC9
UN Emblem and Stylized Planes

1972

UXC9PD	Folder with mounted #UXC9, with approval handstamp (2)	—

New York #UXC10-UXC11
Clouds; Pathways

1975

UXC10PD	With specimen perfin and approval handstamp (4)	—
UXC11PD	With specimen perfin and approval handstamp (4)	—
UXC10TC	With manuscript "Lighter as on sample," and approval handstamp (not approved) (5)	—

New York #UXC12
Flying Mailman

1982

UXC12PD	With approval handstamp on reverse (5)	—

U.N. TEMPORARY EXECUTIVE AUTHORITY, WEST NEW GUINEA

Located in the western half of New Guinea, southwest Pacific Ocean, the former Netherlands New Guinea became a territory under the administration of the United Nations Temporary Executive Authority on Oct. 1, 1962. The size was 151,789 sq. mi. and the population was estimated at 730,000 in 1958. The capital was Hollandia.

The territory came under Indonesian administration on May 1, 1963. For stamps issued by Indonesia see listings following Indonesia in Volume 3.

100 Cents = 1 Gulden

Catalogue values for all unused stamps in this country are for Never Hinged items.

First Printing (Hollandia)

Netherlands New Guinea Stamps of 1950-60 Overprinted

Overprint size: 17x3½mm. Top of "N" is slightly lower than the "U," and the base of the "T" is straight, or nearly so.

Photo.; Litho. (#4, 6, 8)

1962, Oct. 1 Unwmk. *Perf. 12½x12, 12½x13½*

No.	Type	Value	Description	Unused	Used
1	A4	1c	**vermilion & yellow,** *Oct. 1*	.25	.25
2	A1	2c	**deep orange,** *Oct. 1*	.25	.25
3	A4	5c	**chocolate & yellow,** *Oct. 1*	.25	.25
4	A5	7c	**org red, bl & brn vio,** *Nov. 1*	.25	.35
5	A4	10c	**aqua & red brown,** *Oct. 1*	.25	.35
6	A5	12c	**green, bl & brn vio,** *Nov. 1*	.25	.35
7	A4	15c	**deep yel & red brn,** *Nov. 1*	.45	.45
8	A5	17c	**brown violet & blue,** *Oct. 1*	.55	.70
9	A4	20c	**lt bl grn & red brn,** *Nov. 1*	.60	.75
10	A6	25c	**red,** *Oct. 1*	.40	.55
11	A6	30c	**deep blue,** *Oct. 1*	.75	.75
12	A6	40c	**deep orange,** *Oct. 1*	.75	.75
13	A6	45c	**dark olive,** *Nov. 1*	1.25	1.50
14	A6	55c	**slate blue,** *Nov. 1*	29.00	2.25
15	A6	80c	**dull gray violet,** *Nov. 1*	6.00	6.00
16	A6	85c	**dark violet brown,** *Nov. 1*	3.00	3.00
17	A6	1g	**plum,** *Oct. 1*	9.25	3.00

Engr.

No.	Type	Value	Description	Unused	Used
18	A3	2g	**reddish brown,** *Oct. 1*	12.50	30.00
19	A3	5g	**green,** *Oct. 1*	9.00	8.00
			Nos. 1-19 (19)	75.00	59.50

Overprinted locally and sold in West New Guinea. Stamps of the second printing were used to complete sets sold to collectors.

Second Printing (Haarlen, Netherlands)

Overprint size: 17x3½mm. Top of the "N" is slightly higher than the "U," and the base of the "T" is concave.

Photo.; Litho. (#4a, 6a, 8a)

1962 Unwmk. *Perf. 12½x12, 12½x13½*

No.	Type	Value	Description	Unused	Used
1a	A4	1c	**vermilion & yellow**	.25	.25
2a	A1	2c	**deep orange**	.25	.25
3a	A4	5c	**chocolate & yellow**	.25	.25
4a	A5	7c	**org red, bl & brn vio**	.25	.25
5a	A4	10c	**aqua & red brown**	.25	.25
6a	A5	12c	**green, bl & brn vio**	.25	.25
7a	A4	15c	**deep yel & red brn**	.50	.25
8a	A5	17c	**brown violet & blue**	.60	.40
9a	A4	20c	**lt blue grn & red brn**	.60	.40
10a	A6	25c	**red**	.35	.35
11a	A6	30c	**deep blue**	.90	.40
12a	A6	40c	**deep orange**	.90	.40
13a	A6	45c	**dark olive**	1.75	.75
14a	A6	55c	**slate blue**	5.00	1.00
15a	A6	80c	**dull gray violet**	7.00	9.00
16a	A6	85c	**dark violet brown**	3.75	4.75
17a	A6	1g	**plum**	4.25	2.00

Engr.

No.	Type	Value	Description	Unused	Used
18a	A3	2g	**reddish brown**	16.00	27.50
19a	A3	5g	**green**	8.00	6.50
			Nos. 1a-19a (19)	51.10	55.20

Overprinted in the Netherlands and sold by the UN in New York.

Third Printing

Overprint 14mm long.

Photo.; Litho. (#4b, 6b, 8b)

1963, Mar. Photo. Unwmk. *Perf. 12½x12*

No.	Type	Value	Description	Unused	Used
1b	A4	1c	**vermilion & yellow**	5.00	3.00
3b	A4	5c	**chocolate & yellow**	6.00	4.00
4b	A5	7c	**org red, bl & brn vio**	20.00	20.00
5b	A4	10c	**aqua & red brown**	6.00	4.00
6b	A5	12c	**green, bl & brn vio**	35.00	35.00
7b	A4	15c	**deep yel & red brn**	130.00	130.00
8b	A5	17c	**brown violet & blue**	15.00	12.00
9b	A4	20c	**lt blue grn & red brn**	7.50	5.00
			Nos. 1b-9b (8)	224.50	213.00

The third printing was applied in West New Guinea and it is doubtful whether it was regularly issued. Used values are for canceled to order stamps.

Fourth Printing

Overprint 19mm long.

Photogravure

1963, Mar. Unwmk. *Perf. 12½x12*

No.	Type	Value	Description	Unused	Used
1c	A4	1c	**vermilion & yellow**	50.00	50.00
5c	A4	10c	**aqua & red brown**	150.00	150.00

The fourth printing was applied in West New Guinea and it is doubtful whether it was regularly issued. Used values are for canceled to order stamps.

U.N. TRANSITIONAL AUTHORITY IN EAST TIMOR

A30

2000, Apr. 29 **Litho.** ***Perf. 12x11¾***

350 A30 Dom. red & multi		*35.00*	*102.50*
351 A30 Int. blue & multi		*47.50*	*112.50*
First day cover, #350, 351			*80.00*

No. 350 sold for 10c and No. 351 sold for 50c on day of issue.

U.N. INTERIM ADMINISTRATION, KOSOVO

These stamps were issued by the United Nations Interim Administration Mission in Kosovo and the Post & Telecommunications of Kosovo. Service was local for the first two months, with international use starting in mid-May 2000.

Starting with No. 6, stamps were not made available to collectors through the United Nations Postal Administration.

100 pfennigs = 1 mark
100 cents = €1 (2002)

Catalogue values for all unused stamps in this country are for Never Hinged items.

Stamps Issued for Kosovo by the United Nations Interim Administration

Peace in Kosovo — A1

Printed by La Poste, France. Panes of 40. Designed by Shyqri Nimani, Kosovo.

Designs: 20pf, Mosaic depicting Orpheus, c. 5th-6th cent., Podujeve. 30pf, Dardinian idol, Museum of Kosovo. 50pf, Silver coin of Damastion from 4th cent. B.C. 1m, Statue of Mother Teresa, Prizren. 2m, Map of Kosovo.

Perf. 13½x13, 13½x13¼ (30pf)

2000, Mar. 14	**Litho.**		**Unwmk.**
1 A1 20pf **multicolored**		.65	.65
First day cover			1.50
2 A1 30pf **multicolored**		1.25	1.25
First day cover			1.50
3 A1 50pf **multicolored**		1.60	1.60
First day cover			2.25
4 A1 1m **multicolored**		2.00	1.80
First day cover			4.50
5 A1 2m **multicolored**		3.75	3.50
First day cover			9.00
First day cover, #1-5			12.00
Nos. 1-5 (5)		9.25	8.80

Nos. 1-5 were demonetized July 1, 2002.

Peace in Kosovo — A2

Designs: 20pf, Bird. 30pf, Street musician. 50pf, Butterfly and pear. 1m, Children and stars. 2m, Globe and handprints.

2001, Nov. 12	**Litho.**		***Perf. 14***
6 A2 20pf **multicolored**		1.00	1.00
7 A2 30pf **multicolored**		1.25	1.25
8 A2 50pf **multicolored**		2.00	2.00
9 A2 1m **multicolored**		4.00	4.00
10 A2 2m **multicolored**		7.50	7.50
First day cover, #6-10			22.00
Nos. 6-10 (5)		15.75	15.75

100 Cents = 1 Euro (€)

Peace in Kosovo Type of 2001 With Denominations in Euros Only

2002, May 2	**Litho.**		***Perf. 14***
11 A2 10c Like #6		.75	.75
12 A2 15c Like #7		1.00	1.00
13 A2 26c Like #8		1.50	1.50
14 A2 51c Like #9		4.50	4.50
15 A2 €1.02 Like #10		8.00	8.00
First day cover, #11-15			20.00
Nos. 11-15 (5)		15.75	15.75

Christmas — A3

Designs: 50c, Candles and garland. €1, Stylized men.

2003, Dec. 20	**Litho.**		***Perf. 14***
16 A3 50c **multicolored** *(30,000)*		*7.50*	*7.50*
17 A3 €1 **multicolored** *(30,000)*		*14.50*	*14.50*
First day cover, #16-17			*20.00*

Return of Refugees — A4

Five Years of Peace — A5

2004, June 29 **Litho.** ***Perf. 13¼x13***

18 A4 €1 **multicolored** *(40,000)* *7.00 7.00*
19 A5 €2 **multicolored** *(40,000)* *16.00 16.00*
First day cover, #18-19 *25.00*

Musical Instruments — A6

2004, Aug. 31 **Litho.** ***Perf. 13¼x13***

20 A6 20c Flute *(30,000)* *5.00 5.00*
21 A6 30c Ocarina *(30,000)* *10.00 10.00*
First day cover, #20-21 *12.00*

Aprons — A7

Vests — A8

Designs: 20c, Apron from Prizren. 30c, Apron from Rugova. 50c, Three vests. €1, Two vests.

2004, Oct. 28 **Litho.** ***Perf. 13x13¼***

22 A7 20c **multicolored** *(30,000)* *5.50 5.50*
23 A7 30c **multicolored** *(30,000)* *8.50 8.50*
24 A8 50c **multicolored** *(30,000)* *12.00 12.00*
25 A8 €1 **multicolored** *(30,000)* *26.00 26.00*
First day cover, #22-25 *30.00*
Nos. 22-25 (4) *52.00 52.00*

Mirusha Waterfall — A9

2004, Nov. 26 **Litho.** ***Perf. 13x13¼***

26 A9 €2 **multicolored** *(40,000)* *7.50 7.50*
First day cover *7.50*

House — A10

2004, Dec. 14 **Litho.** ***Perf. 13x13¼***

27 A10 50c **multicolored** *(40,000)* *4.50 4.50*
First day cover *8.00*

Flowers — A11

2005, June 29 **Litho.** ***Perf. 13½***

28 A11 15c Peony *(50,000)* *2.25 2.25*
29 A11 20c Poppies *(50,000)* *3.25 3.25*
30 A11 30c Gentian *(50,000)* *5.00 5.00*
First day cover, #28-30 *17.00*
Nos. 28-30 (3) *10.50 10.50*

A12

Handicrafts — A13

2005, July 20 ***Perf. 13¼x13***

31	A12	20c shown *(40,000)*	*2.50*	*2.50*
32	A12	30c Cradle *(40,000)*	*3.00*	*3.00*
33	A13	50c shown *(40,000)*	*3.25*	*3.25*
34	A12	€1 Necklace *(40,000)*	*4.25*	*4.25*
		First day cover, #31-34		*17.00*
		Nos. 31-34 (4)	*13.00*	*13.00*

Village — A14

Town — A15

City — A16

2005, Sept. 15 ***Perf. 13x13½***

35	A14	20c **multicolored** *(50,000)*	*2.00*	*2.00*
36	A15	50c **multicolored** *(110,000)*	*3.00*	*3.00*
37	A16	€1 **multicolored** *(110,000)*	*6.00*	*6.00*
		First day cover, #35-37		*17.00*
		Nos. 35-37 (3)	*11.00*	*11.00*

Archaeological Artifacts — A17

2005, Nov. 2 ***Perf. 13½x13***

38	A17	20c shown *(25,000)*	*1.25*	*1.25*
39	A17	30c Statue *(25,000)*	*1.75*	*1.75*
40	A17	50c Sculpture *(25,000)*	*2.50*	*2.50*
41	A17	€1 Helmet *(25,000)*	*7.50*	*7.50*
		First day cover, #38-41		*17.00*
		Nos. 38-41 (4)	*13.00*	*13.00*

Minerals — A18

2005, Dec. 10 ***Perf. 13x13½***

42	A18	€2 **multicolored** *(45,000)*	*10.00*	*10.00*
		First day cover		*10.00*

A19

Europa — A20

2006, July 20 ***Perf. 13¼x13***

43	A19	50c **multicolored** *(60,000)*	*2.25*	*2.25*
44	A20	€1 **multicolored** *(60,000)*	*4.25*	*4.25*
		First day cover, #43-44		*10.00*

Exists Imperf. Value set of two, $75.

Fauna — A21

2006, May 23 **Litho.** ***Perf. 13***

45	A21	15c Wolf *(190,000)*	*1.00*	*1.00*
46	A21	20c Cow *(190,000)*	*1.25*	*1.25*
47	A21	30c Pigeon *(190,000)*	*1.40*	*1.40*
48	A21	50c Swan *(190,000)*	*1.60*	*1.60*
49	A21	€1 Dog *(190,000)*	*2.75*	*2.75*
a.		Souvenir sheet, #45-49, + label *(15,000)*	*8.75*	*8.75*
		First day cover, #45-49		*22.00*
		First day cover, #49a		*15.00*
		Nos. 45-49 (5)	*8.00*	*8.00*

Nos. 45-49 are inscribed CPU. Stamps with "Leoprint" imprint are from No. 63a.

No. 49a exists in two shades of green selvage.

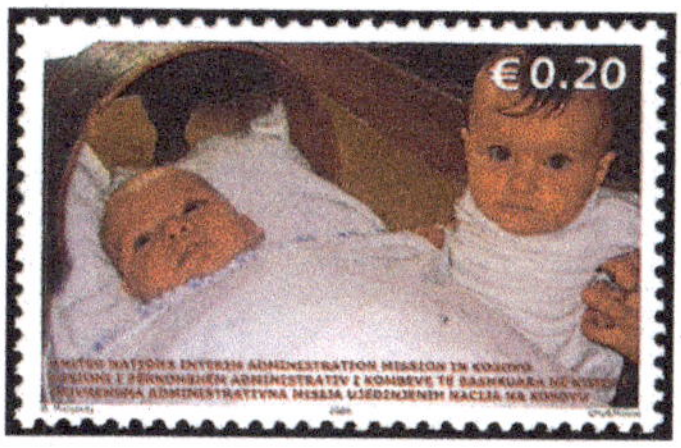

Children — A22

Designs: 20c, Children in cradle. 30c, Children reading. 50c, Girls dancing. €1, Child in water.

2006, June 30 **Litho.** ***Perf. 13***

50	A22	20c **multicolored** *(40,000)*	*1.00*	*1.00*
51	A22	30c **multicolored** *(40,000)*	*1.25*	*1.25*
52	A22	50c **multicolored** *(40,000)*	*1.75*	*1.75*
53	A22	€1 **multicolored** *(40,000)*	*3.50*	*3.50*
a.		Souvenir sheet, #50-53 *(12,500)*	*7.75*	*7.75*
		First day cover, #50-53		*20.00*
		First day cover, #53a		*22.00*
		Nos. 50-53 (4)	*7.50*	*7.50*

Nos. 50-53 were printed by CPU & Moare. No. 53a was printed by two printers: 7,500 inscribed "CPU&Moare," and 5,000 inscribed "Leoprint."

Nos. 50-53 from CPO & Moare exists imperforate. Value, set, $75.

No. 53a by CPU & Moare exists imperforate. Value $75.

A23

A24

A25

Tourist Attractions A26

2006, Sept. 1 **Litho.** ***Perf. 13***

54	A23	20c **multicolored** *(40,000)*	*1.00*	*1.00*
55	A24	30c **multicolored** *(40,000)*	*1.25*	*1.25*
56	A25	50c **multicolored** *(40,000)*	*1.75*	*1.75*
57	A26	€1 **multicolored** *(40,000)*	*3.25*	*3.25*
a.		Souvenir sheet, #54-57 *(12,500)*	*9.50*	*9.50*
		First day cover, #54-57		*20.00*
		First day cover, #57a		*22.00*
		Nos. 54-57 (4)	*7.25*	*7.25*

Nos. 54-57 were printed by CPU & Moare. No. 57a was printed by two printers: 7,500 inscribed "CPU&Moare," and 5,000 inscribed "Leoprint."

Intl. Peace Day — A27

2006, Sept. 21 **Litho.** ***Perf. 13***

58	A27	€2 **multicolored** *(40,000)*	*7.00*	*7.00*
		Min. sheet of 4	*55.00*	
		First day cover		*12.50*
		First day cover, min. sheet of 4		*30.00*

No. 58 was printed by CPU.

Ancient Coins — A28

Various coins.

2006, Nov. 1 **Litho.** ***Perf. 13***

59	A28	20c **multicolored** *(30,000)*	*1.00*	*1.00*
60	A28	30c **multicolored** *(30,000)*	*1.50*	*1.50*
61	A28	50c **multicolored** *(30,000)*	*1.75*	*1.75*
62	A28	€1 **multicolored** *(30,000)*	*3.25*	*3.25*
a.		Souvenir sheet, #59-62 *(15,000)*	*9.50*	*9.50*
		First day cover, #59-62		*20.00*
		First day cover, #62a		*22.00*
		Nos. 59-62 (4)	*7.50*	*7.50*

Nos. 59-62 are inscribed CPU. Stamps with "Leoprint" imprint are from No. 63a.

No. 62a exists imperforate. Value, $75.

Sculpture — A29

2006, Dec. 1 **Litho.** ***Perf. 13***

63 A29 €2 **multicolored** *(45,000)* *8.00 8.00*
a. Miniature sheet, #45-57, 59-63, + 2 labels *(5,000)* *80.00 80.00*
First day cover *10.00*
First day cover, #63a *90.00*

Issue dates: No. 63, Dec. 1. No. 63a, Dec. 15.

No. 63 is inscribed "CPU&Moare." No. 63a stamps are inscribed "CPU" or "CPU&Moare" throughout the sheet as they were inscribed when originally printed. No. 63a also exists with stamps inscribed "Leoprint."

Convention on the Rights of Persons With Disabilities — A30

Emblems of handicaps and: 20c, Children and butterfly. 50c, Handicapped women. 70c, Map of Kosovo. €1, Stylized flower.

2007, Apr. 23 **Litho.** ***Perf. 14x14¼***

64 A30 20c **multicolored** *(15,000)* *1.25 1.25*
65 A30 50c **multicolored** *(15,000)* *2.50 2.50*
66 A30 70c **multicolored** *(15,000)* *3.00 3.00*
67 A30 €1 **multicolored** *(15,000)* *3.75 3.75*
a. Souvenir sheet, #64-67 *(20,000)* *12.50 12.50*
First day cover, #64-67 *12.50*
First day cover, #67a *12.50*
Nos. 64-67 (4) *10.50 10.50*

Color shades vary widely. Printer's waste of this issue exists in the marketplace, including partial prints, missing design elements, and missing colors.

Two varieties of No. 67a, exist differing in text surrounding the stamps. It has not been established if both varieties were officially issued.

Scouting, Cent. — A31

Europa — A32

2007, May 12 **Litho.** ***Perf. 13¼***

68 A31 70c **multicolored** *(35,000)* *4.25 4.25*
69 A32 €1 **multicolored** *(35,000)* *6.25 6.25*
a. Souvenir sheet, #68-69 *(15,000)* *90.00 90.00*
First day cover, #68-69 *12.50*
First day cover, #69a *45.00*

Nos. 68-69 exist imperf. Value, set, $40.

No. 69a exists imperf. Value, $250.

No. 69a exists with perforations inverted (leaving the stamps imperforate). Value, $250.

A33

A34

A35

International Children's Day — A36

2007, June 1 **Litho.** ***Perf. 13¼***

70 A33 20c **multicolored** *(38,000)* *1.25 1.25*
71 A34 30c **multicolored** *(38,000)* *1.50 1.50*
72 A35 70c **multicolored** *(38,000)* *2.50 2.50*

73 A36 €1 **multicolored** *(38,000)* *4.00 4.00*
First day cover, #70-73 *15.00*
Nos. 70-73 (4) *9.25 9.25*

Nos. 70-73 exist imperf. Value, set $45

Native Costumes — A37

Designs: 20c, Serbian woman. 30c, Prizren Region woman. 50c, Sword dancer. 70c, Drenica Region woman. €1, Shepherd, Rugova.

2007, July 6 **Litho.** ***Perf. 13½x13¼***

74 A37 20c **multicolored** *(35,000)* *1.25 1.25*
75 A37 30c **multicolored** *(35,000)* *1.75 1.75*
76 A37 50c **multicolored** *(35,000)* *2.00 2.00*
77 A37 70c **multicolored** *(35,000)* *2.50 2.50*
78 A37 €1 **multicolored** *(35,000)* *3.25 3.25*
a. Souvenir sheet, #74-78, + label *(15,000)* *12.50 12.50*
First day cover, #74-78 *17.50*
First day cover, #78a *17.50*
Nos. 74-78 (5) *10.75 10.75*

Masks — A38

Various masks.

2007, Sept. 11 **Litho.** ***Perf. 13½x13¼***

79 A38 15c **multicolored** *(38,000)* *.75 .75*
80 A38 30c **multicolored** *(38,000)* *1.00 1.00*
81 A38 50c **multicolored** *(38,000)* *2.00 2.00*
82 A38 €1 **multicolored** *(38,000)* *3.00 3.00*
First day cover, #79-82 *15.00*
Nos. 79-82 (4) *6.75 6.75*

Sports — A39

Designs: 20c, Soccer ball, basketball, two people standing, person in wheelchair. 50c, Wrestlers. €1, Symbols of 24 sports.

2007, Oct. 2 **Litho.** ***Perf. 13¼x13½***

83 A39 20c **multicolored** *(38,000)* *1.00 1.00*
84 A39 50c **multicolored** *(38,000)* *2.25 2.25*
85 A39 €1 **multicolored** *(38,000)* *4.00 4.00*
First day cover, #83-85 *15.00*
Nos. 83-85 (3) *7.25 7.25*

Nos. 83-85 exist imperf. Value, set $65.

Architecture — A40

Designs: 30c, Stone bridge, Vushtrri. 50c, Hamam, Prizren. 70c, Tower. €1, Tower, diff.

2007, Nov. 6 **Litho.** ***Perf. 13¼***

86 A40 30c **multicolored** *(38,000)* *1.50 1.50*
87 A40 50c **multicolored** *(38,000)* *2.00 2.00*
88 A40 70c **multicolored** *(38,000)* *2.50 2.50*
89 A40 €1 **multicolored** *(38,000)* *3.50 3.50*
First day cover, #86-89 *17.50*
Nos. 86-89 (4) *9.50 9.50*

Nos. 86-89 exist imperf. Value, set $85.

Locomotives — A41

Designs: €1, Diesel locomotive. €2, Steam locomotive

2007, Dec. 7 **Litho.** ***Perf. 13¼***

90 A41 €1 **multicolored** *(50,000)* *4.00 4.00*
91 A41 €2 **multicolored** *(50,000)* *8.00 8.00*
First day cover, #90-91 *22.50*

Nos. 90-91 exist imperf. Value, set $125.

Skanderbeg (1405-68), Albanian National Hero — A42

2008, Jan. 17 **Litho.** ***Perf. 13¼***

92 A42 €2 **multicolored** *(140,000)* *7.50 7.50*
First day cover *10.00*

No. 92 exists imperf. Value, $35.

Kosovo declared its independence from Serbia on Feb. 17, 2008, ending the United Nations Interim Administration. Stamps issued after Feb. 17, 2008, by the Republic of Kosovo will be listed under Kosovo in the *Scott Standard Postage Stamp Catalogue*.